Andy Gilbrook

An Ordinary Guy
#secretlyjustlikeyou

Copyright © Andrew Gilbrook 2023
All rights reserved. This book or any portion thereof
may not be reproduced or used in any manner whatsoever
without the express written permission of the publisher
except for the use of brief quotations in a book review.

The End	9
Early Days	11
Interview	22
Spy School	30
Starting at MI6	39
Xerox	43
Morocco	48
In Love	50
A History of the Philippines	58
Inheriting the Philippines	63
Agent 1, Rosa	71
Agent 2, Trisha	80
Agent 3, Si	95
Agent 4, Fidel Ramos	106
Agent 5, Juan Enrile	152
The End of President Marcos	158
Closing Operations	180
Secrets and Lies	199
The Alleged End to Adolf Hitler	214
Operation Paperclip and Overcast	219
The Honeys and the trap	222
Clean Up	243
The Spanish Incident	248
Don Ángel Alcázar de Velasco	249
The Spanish Incident continued.	251
The Don Ángel Alcázar de Velasco Story	296
CIA Riddles	324
Chile	338

Inalco House	354
Operation Saponify	360
Let There Be War	383
In another Love	388
Love And Marriage	391
Chris Curwen And Oleg Gordievsky	393
The Falklands War	395
Invitation To Angola	399
Comandante Anselmo Gil	405
Moving To Angola	408
Moxico, Not A Holiday Destination	411
Mr Filipe Lomba	417
Taken Prisoner	421
On The Run	437
My First Solo Flight	442
Landing My First Solo Flight	450
Safe	458
My Dad	465
Four Days Later	470
Aftermath	477
My Brain Is Broken	485
A New Life In Devon	489
Business Is Good, Until...	492
Event 1. Deep Depression	496
Event 2 and 3. Goodbye John and Dad	506
End Note	517
Photo Sources.	520

To Karen, beautiful, intelligent and the reason for this book. Lost to cancer, the world is worse off without you.

To Diwa, an intelligent, pretty and smart, brave lady. Sadly lost. I miss you.

For security reasons, names have been changed and some situations described in these pages have been altered to protect those in it. This book is based on fact. All events happened, but some dates and times may slightly differ from true, as most of this book is based on my memories. But that should not detract from the incredible story that it is. Nothing was written down, I have little to refer to. Pictures, if not mine, are credited at the back of this book.

The End

I squint against the morning sunlight as I stagger out into the fresh air after days in the dark interrogation room, my hands bound behind me, my legs struggling to support me. One of the three black men guarding me shoves me in the back to keep me moving. He shouts something in Chokwe, the local language in the province of Moxico, the eastern extremity of Angola. Another shove forces me to the right. After days of brutal beatings, I am covered with bruises, but their blows no longer hurt. I'm in a bad way.

I had identified the head interrogator as a Russian foreign operation and intelligence professional, probably SVR or GRU, but he hadn't cracked me. I had stuck to my story as being a member of the United Nations Angola Verification Mission (UNAVEM) team, which, while technically true, served only as a cover to my real mission. Somehow though, he knew my real identity as an officer of the UK's Intelligence Service, MI6. But how did he know? I'm not going to find out – in a few minutes I will be .

I'm being marched into the woods nearby, far enough in so that the smell of my rotting body won't offend the occupants of this camp. I am to be shot and left for the animals to squabble over for breakfast. These human animals won't bother digging a grave, this country is too uncivilised for that. They are laughing, still drunk and high after a night of drinking Cuca beer and chewing khat. I keep walking toward my death.

Four hundred yards from the camp, we reach a small clearing. A hand grabs my filthy bloodstained shirt collar and yanks me to a halt. One of the men shoves me around to face them and pushes me backwards, against a tree. I stand, looking at them enjoying their cigarettes, I hope they can shoot straight and make my end quick. I settle back against the tree as my thirty-three years on this earth flash before my eyes.

I don't want to die here. My daughter is only a year old. I want to see her grow up. I want to see my wife Julie again.

I lean into the tree, my bound wrists press against the rough bark. Almost immediately, a stinging ant bites the base of my thumb. Fuck it! Is there anything in this country that doesn't cause pain and discomfort? Even though I'm about to die, I shake my hands to rid myself of this biting nuisance.

Cigarettes finished, the three begin to prepare their weapons, pulling back the bolts of their AK47s.

This is it. I'm going to die in just a few seconds, no rescue, no help.

Go on. Do it! Do it NOW!

Early Days

My childhood was quite normal I think. I was born in London 23rd October 1955. My first real memories are of the day my parents and brother Steven, two years older than myself, moved home in 1959. We got lost on the way to Maple Cross near Rickmansworth, Hertfordshire. I couldn't believe my dad didn't remember where our new house was. Once we did find our street and house our furniture and belongings didn't arrive until the next day. A neighbour was kind enough to lend us some blankets and we all slept on the floor in our new home, a three-bedroom semi-detached house, with a nice large 100 feet long garden. Maple Cross was built to accommodate an overflow population from London, most people either commuted or found new jobs when they moved there. Now it is just inside the M25 circular road around London.

I loved living in the countryside, I spent most of my days playing in the fields and woods, and in those days, there was little traffic so the kids of the village could quite safely play in the streets. With my friends we would build tree houses, come autumn we'd make castles in the fields from the straw bales, light fires and make camps in the woods nearby. One friend and I used to spend hours, if not days teaching ourselves how to follow animal tracks, working out how to move silently through the trees so as not to scare the birds and animals away. All good stuff that would pay dividends later, once I became an intelligence officer, where being the invisible man was often an essential skill.

My parents didn't ever have a lot of money to spare. My father at that time worked for the Royal Insurance Group in Acton, and my mother was a housewife, but soon my dad would start his own business when the Royal Insurance moved to Liverpool, my dad didn't want us to live in a big city.

By the time I left school, I'd never been to a restaurant or knew how to write a cheque and pay bills. Most times I was shipped off to my grandparents when Mum and Dad went away on holidays, so I never travelled. All my friends seemed to have the latest toys, I rarely did. In the summer my friends would go on day trips to the coast in a big neighbourhood group, we never joined them. On those occasions I'd just take myself off to the woods alone, moving quietly, to get close to the multitude of birds and animals one could never normally get near. I remember one time I managed to get within 30 feet of a large stag deer before it saw me. It stood staring at me for a bit before walking away without alarm or panic. I'd learn how to snare birds, prepare and cook them on a small fire rather than walk all the way home for lunch. I spent many hours teaching myself how to shoot air-rifles, fixing and zeroing the telephoto sight. I think I became quite expert, I could hit an ice lolly stick at 60 feet with a .22 rifle.

Many weekends and school holidays were spent finding and cutting off pram wheels and making what we called trolleys, charging down our street with bows and arrows that we had made ourselves, firing at each other playing Cowboys and Indians. I wouldn't say we were feral kids, but we did do a little vandalism, for no real reason other than we could, and always get away with it. In those days many sheds and garages had roofs of asbestos corrugated sheeting. We discovered if you threw pieces onto a bonfire in a short while it would explode. I'm sure that would be a practice well and truly frowned upon these days.

I learnt the difference between rich and poor, as just a few miles away was the stockbroker belt of Chorleywood and private estates such as Loudwater and Heronsgate. The big houses and posh new cars in those areas taught me there was always people much better off than our family and that those types rarely mixed with the likes of us living in the council estates at Maple Cross. In my street though, the houses were mostly owned and mortgaged properties with a few at the bottom of the street privately rented.

I did complete my childhood without breaking any bones falling out of trees or drowning in the gravel pits that stretch for miles from Rickmansworth to Denham. In those days before they all became private fishing lakes, we could witness Pike taking ducklings, grass snakes, and catch sticklebacks or nine eyes in the streams that fed the watercress beds in West Hyde.

I started my education at West Hyde School but when it closed, we moved into the newly built Maple Cross JMI at the end of my street. I didn't like it much, I hated being stuck indoors. I did occasionally become spelling king or won gold stars in the weekly maths tests. My best times though were when I was in Miss Willox's class. She was a large, formidable woman, and very strict. When she sat at her desk at the front of the class, she always sat legs open and one could see her knee-length bloomers - not a pretty sight. I realise now, that despite her slaps and "chivvies" as she called them, she was a very good teacher. She was a keen ornithologist too. There were a few of us that were invited to her home in Heronsgate at weekends, to watch and learn about all the birds in her garden. Around Maple Cross, we could see some quite rare birds, Treecreepers, Bee-Eaters, even a Ring Ouzel to name just a few.

The Headmaster Mr Naylor or "Naggy" Naylor, as we called him, was also a good man and teacher. He wrote plays for school productions. I can still remember the words and storylines of a few even now.

One year I invented a new Christmas decoration made by bending two coloured paper straws into triangles, tying them together with cotton so that they formed a six-pointed star, He was so impressed he got the entire school to make one each and hang them on the school Christmas tree. I think I was always more practically minded than academic, although I didn't really struggle with maths or English. We weren't taught languages at junior school, something I found to be a disadvantage later in secondary school. In sport, I was the only boy that could stand on his head. Parent's days were often entertained by my gymnastic demonstration. One year I stood on my head with my legs apart, while other kids dived between my open legs, landing with a somersault on the mat behind. Something my mother later said caused her to break into a sweat watching. At the time I didn't understand why, I think I do now.

One year we had an exchange teacher from New Zealand, Mr Gundy. He knew nothing about maths, we spent the entire year learning everything New Zealand. He was a great guy and made a lasting impression on me, I think I can still sing "Pokarekare Ana" or "Now is the Hour" in Māori some fifty-five years later.

Because of my birth date, I and a few others had to stay in the top class for two years, as the cut-off date for moving up to secondary school was September. This meant we became more like school prefects and having to learn things twice meant we did well in exams to grade us for next school. In the end, I was offered the option of taking the eleven plus exam, I passed, and I was told my next school would be Rickmansworth Grammar School. I didn't want to go there at all. I knew I wouldn't do well there, plus all my best friends were going to William Penn Secondary School, Mill End. I wanted to be with my friends. A few other kids were also going to "Ricky" Grammar, but I hardly knew them.

September 1967, I started my life as a "Grammar Grub." My parents couldn't afford the school uniform. In a second-hand shop, mum found a green blazer for me. It was a lighter green to the correct uniform, so I stood out as different right from the start. I certainly felt different.

By now I had a reputation for being a bit of a fighter, word had got around to the other kids, so no one ever tried to bully me for being different. Realistically, I didn't fight anyone just for the sake of it. I hated bullies, still do, and would never take any nonsense from them. In fact, my reputation grew while at Junior School, anyone being bullied seemed to come to me, point out the bully and I would sort them out street style. Once the bully knew I was looking out for the poor kid being harassed by them they tended to leave them alone. I certainly knew I couldn't win every fight, but I would make sure the bully would feel some pain before I'd get whooped myself. I just never showed fear and they knew I'd get stuck into them. I had a big fight one day with the toughest kid in school. I couldn't beat him, but he couldn't get me to surrender either. Despite getting hurt myself, I had hurt him enough to admit to others I was a tough cookie. From then on, they gave me respect and my word alone was enough to stop any other kids getting bullied if they asked for my help.

I remember one rainy day our P.E. lesson had to be in the gym. Our teacher Mr Barret, a short man, as wide as he was tall and muscles everywhere, decided we would have a wrestling competition. Two boys would enter a circle of mats, the first to get pushed or thrown out of the circle lost the match. Each boy was partnered with another about the same size and weight - except me. I was partnered with the tallest and fittest boy in our year, Ralph Carpenter. Apparently, my fighting reputation had reached even the staff at this school. Mr Barret was obviously expecting big things of me. On the whistle, I ran straight at Ralph, who grabbed me by my rugby shirt collar, spun me around a couple of times, let go and I flew out of the ring. Mr Barret looked less disappointed when I stood up laughing after my flight and crash landing. I think my reputation dropped a couple of points but I survived.

I enjoyed P.E., but I seemed to have stopped growing, which put me at a disadvantage in rugby. We weren't permitted to play football as Mr Barret thought the game was for wimps, which may be true. So, I alternated between rugby and hockey playing in either team at away games just to make up numbers it seemed to me. Even though

I played in most home and away games, I was never awarded a cap. The cap system was never explained to me and to this day I don't know what I had to do to be awarded one. Lads that I had played alongside in the same team all filed up to the stage in assembly to be applauded and awarded a cap, yet I was always left out. I don't understand why, what didn't I do?

We never won any inter-school sports, simply because for some reason we always played the year above us, so in the second year, we played another school's third year. None of us could understand why, and we became quite despondent about it. So instead of trying to win, as a team, we would pick out someone from the opposing team that we didn't like the look of, and, each of us did our best to have a go at ripping the shirt off the lads back. Some of our victims ended the game with almost no shirt left. It was the only way we could get any pleasure from our losses with scores such as 84-12, quite humiliating.

Sports days in the summer, I was quite good at athletics, I seemed to be good at sprints and long-distance running. One year I even won the triple jump by one centimetre from the favourite boy. I was also pretty good at javelin but gave it up after a practice session, when I did my usual run-up, as I concentrated on hitting the mark for the throw, I lost control of the javelin which had turned ninety degrees and as I put all effort into the launch throw, it hit me with a huge whack on the back of my head, pretty much knocking me unconscious, I executed a perfect face-plant into the ground and the spear landed point down, still in my hand about half an inch from my ear. I never threw another one ever again.

As for cricket, forget it.

In my second year at "Ricky" School, we were placed in Maths forms according to our grade after the end of year exams. I was in the bottom grade, yet because the teacher was so good and I liked her, I did quite well. Unlike other maths teachers, she took time to help individuals that struggled with certain aspects of the subject. My favourite subject was Physics because it is mostly practical logical stuff. In chemistry, I just couldn't grasp chemical formulae at all, I didn't get it and no one bothered to help. Biology was ok, the teacher was hateful, but she was quite young and always wore very short skirts. In languages, it was compulsory to learn French. I didn't like French, mainly because I never saw the point and the teacher was quite hateful. He could clearly see I was not trying, so his tactic seemed to be to do anything to humiliate me and make me feel useless. He didn't have to try hard. I was, however, keen to learn German. I had an uncle, an ex-para that I liked, he lived in Germany, and while stationed there he had met and married a German girl. Quite something in those days, so many people still had strong memories of the second world war, his parents, my grandparents were firmly against it. Anyhow, I liked Uncle Peter and his wife at the time Ziggy. I always thought one day I would like to visit them in Bünde, so I wanted to make some effort to learn the language. I asked the school language department head if I could give up French and learn German instead. The answer I got was, "As I was rubbish at French, I would be rubbish at German too and they didn't want to waste time with me." Always encouraging my teachers! So I bought some books of my own and taught myself. I did get to visit Peter and Ziggy in Germany. I travelled over with Peter by car and came back all the way from Bielefeld by bus alone, at 14 years old and never having travelled abroad before. I was put on the bus with no food or water for a 24-hour journey, to be met in London by Mum and Dad starving hungry and dehydrated, my parents showed little concern for my plight. But the German language I picked up in those two weeks have stuck with me, and I was quite capable of helping my two daughters when they were at school with their German homework.

The third year at secondary school is always the year kids get naughty and a little cocky, the year most pupils either get caned or expelled. I think only one pupil in my year was expelled, after being caned. I recall that he was caught smoking, with quite possibly not 100% tobacco in his cigarette, he was that type. A nice guy, a bit rough around the edges, but popular, and I remember several girls crying after hearing the news. This year was also the year I started to play up too. I realised I stood no chance of ever getting good grades in any exams. My parents had the attitude that university was a waste of time and that everyone should get to work to earn money. So, I felt I had nothing to aim for.

Because of the distance I lived from school, I had to catch a bus at about 6 am, as the next one would arrive with about ten minutes to spare before the start of classes. If the bus was late, so would I be, and the detention for that was never appreciated, as I felt it wasn't my fault. Jo Franek and I came up with a plan. A classmate and very good friend, who lived in Chorleywood in a huge house had the same problem. He had to catch a train first to Rickmansworth with all the commuters on the Metropolitan line, then catch a bus to the school. So, we decided to arrive early to avoid these problems. This meant we got to school about 7 am, a little uncomfortable on cold wet days. So, before we left school the day before, we would leave a window in our ground floor classroom slightly ajar. We could then climb in and sit in the warm doing our homework. We never did anything wrong or bad, we just wanted shelter and spent the time productively. Jo was way better than me at schoolwork. So, he did his work, and I would copy. After a while, the prefects patrolling inside the school would catch us in our classroom, which was a big no-no before 9 am. We would get caught and thrown out into the cold and rain. So, we took to hiding in the classroom cupboard. This was quite large, there was even a desk and chair in there so that during the day sixth formers could sit and do extra studies. Our classroom was in the French department, so I assume these sixth formers were studying French. Eventually, the school caught on that we were leaving the window ajar, and the janitor would come after we left at the end of the day and close the window. We thought we could outwit him by leaving a window open on the first floor, in the geography department. We'd climb a drainpipe to a flat roof above some cloakrooms, then another drainpipe up to the window. Here we'd have to do a leap of faith from the drainpipe and grab the window frame. Once we had a good grip let go with one hand, with the other open the window fully and climb in. From here after closing the window, creep downstairs and into our classroom and into the cupboard. Because the downstairs window was being locked, the janitor had no idea of our new route in. Until, one day, Jo, after doing the leap of faith, hauled himself too enthusiastically up into the not quite so open window, and cracked his head on the window frame, causing him to fall. He had a severe cut on his head, with no one around yet, there wasn't anyone I could call for help. In those days mobile phones hadn't been invented yet so Jo lay on the cold floor a long time bleeding before help did arrive. Later that day, I was interrogated by my form teacher as to what we were doing. He didn't seem to understand we were just cold, wet, did no damage or harm and simply got on with some work each morning. We didn't get into trouble for it though. It was deemed Jo had suffered enough, but it had to stop.

    April Fool's Day that year was hilarious. All five classes in my year got up to such funny tricks, all harmless and well planned. I think the teachers got it, and some even managed to laugh along. I remember the class next to mine, the boys removed all the screws from the door hinges, so they fell in when the teacher opened them. In my class, most of the kids were more of the nerdy type and weren't quite so bothered. But I didn't let the class down. I asked one of my classmates a few days earlier to help. He was particularly good at chemistry. On the day, he produced, as requested, an amount of 2,4 dinitrophenylhydrazine or 2,4-DNPH a yellowy red chemical. This is a chemical often used in school A-level practical's, some schools stocked it. It's used to identify organic carbon-based compounds called aldehydes and ketones. Dry 2,4-DNPH is friction and shock sensitive. For this reason, it's supplied damp or 'wetted' when a school purchases it from a chemical supplier. It's important that it's kept wet, so the storage advice is to keep it in a sealed container, which is itself kept in an outer container filled with a small amount of liquid. If the chemical is allowed to dry out, there is a risk of a small fire or explosion. Johnathon brought it to school in a jar inside a jar. The jar inside suspended by elastic bands so that it wouldn't bump, and the inner jar was filled with a fluid to keep the chemical wet. I thought it was a very clever homemade design. Johnathon gave me the jars and wanted nothing more to do with the caper. Just before our English lesson and before the others entered, I got into the classroom opened the jars and spread the chemical around the classroom, some on the windowsills and quite a bit around the teacher's desk and floor. Mr Daykin our English teacher began the class. As the grains dried, the windowsill first as it was in the sunlight, started to explode. In small amounts, it sounded like cap guns going off with a crack. I could see Mr Daykin becoming more and more annoyed and agitated by the noises. Eventually, he shouted,

"All right, who's got the cap gun." Everyone looked around at each other as only I knew what it was. Crack! Another went off. Everyone was puzzled. "Alright Gilbrook." he said to me, "Outside." I had to go stand outside the classroom. Of course, the cracks didn't stop so he couldn't be sure it was me. I felt a little indignant that he chose me as the culprit, correctly of course, but with no evidence. The little explosions were going off all day, in fact, a few still the next day. I never owned up to it, but I learnt a huge lesson. Never stand out from the crowd. While everyone in the room was looking mystified as to what was going on, I was the only person laughing, that's why I was singled out, even with no proof of guilt.

Standing outside the classroom was a dangerous place to be. The Headmaster, Mr Morrill, would often patrol the corridors. Anyone found stood outside, must have been naughty, resulting in some kind of punishment. I saw him coming further down the corridor. By the time he reached me, he found me staring into my locker opposite the classroom looking most forlorn. Asking what I was doing outside the classroom, I proclaimed the contents of my locker had been stolen and my books and equipment had gone. I had simply emptied it into another, as in those days the lockers were wooden with no locks. It was a major crime, to steal from a locker. Anyhow, seeing how I was so upset (great acting on my part), he took me back into the classroom and instructed Mr Daykin to find me new books and everything I needed to resume class. My teacher was red-faced fuming at being reprimanded. From that day forward it was a hate-hate relationship. He never really bothered to teach me anything more and would only speak to me if he thought it was a question or something I didn't know, in an attempt to humiliate me. I didn't care, the other kids in the class took sympathy on me, always showing concern that this teacher would always pick on me, for some reason, I happily took the sympathy.

Outside school, at the age of fifteen, Jo, from school, and I taught ourselves to drive. Jo did a lot of car maintenance for his family, one of his sisters had bought a Fiat 500. After working together doing whatever repairs we had to do, of course, the car would need to be road tested. Jo would normally drive, but one time, on a road that crossed Chorleywood Common he offered to let me have a go. It wasn't so difficult, except that model of car didn't have synchromesh gears. To anyone that doesn't know, in a normal car these days, when using gears, cars have a gearbox that can move up and down gears without any crunching. Simply stated, a synchronous transmission matches engine speeds to the rpm's of the gearbox so that as the clutch moves the throw-out bearing the two engaging gears will mate smoothly without grinding. In the Fiat 500, the gears have to match for speed before you can slip into the lower gear, a method called double de-clutching. It took a little practice but I got it quite quickly. Neither of us had a license or insurance.

After school, a few days per week, I would go work for a few hours with my father at his new business, a printing company. Eventually, this gave me enough money to buy a motorbike. A Honda 50. With no clutch, it was easy to drive. The school wouldn't allow me to ride to school, so I rode from home and left it at the back of a shop just opposite school, where the owner, Michael Thame a friend of my father, permitted me to park.

As I approached the age where I could leave school, I decided I would quit at the earliest opportunity. My mock 'O' level exams had gone badly, and it was clear to me I could never pass anything, and I was wasting time at a Grammar School. It seemed to me that if you were a highflyer and destined for university, you got all the help you needed. For someone like me, not stupid, but practically minded, there was only humiliation and the total lack of any care by the faculty. There were a few teachers I did like, but to continue was pointless in my mind. My mock 'O' results were a joke. In French, my friend Jo managed to pass his paper to me to copy. I copied the lot. He got a result of 84%, I got 2%. Apparently, I'd written each answer one line down, so got all the right answers in the wrong place. 2% was for getting my name correct I think.

I told Mum and Dad I wanted to leave school. They, for some reason, were against it. I didn't understand this as it was clear they were against further education and wanted me to work to bring money into the house. I was flummoxed by this attitude. I think it was the shame of me failing while all the other kids around were aiming high. They refused to write a letter for me to the school to say I was leaving. It was left to me to do it myself. I decided to speak to the teachers personally. I went to my form teacher Mr Drew first. I told him I was going to leave the day I was legally permitted at 16. He told me that this was the best thing I'd done since I got here. Next, I went to my Physics teacher who I did like. He tried to persuade me to stay, but I explained it was pointless coming for just one lesson, it wouldn't get me anywhere. He was sad to see me go. My Maths teacher, a lady I liked a lot, did have the patience to get some of the harder subjects into my head. I did appreciate her efforts. She cried when I told her I was leaving. All the rest could hardly speak to me and gave me no encouragement to stay. Finally, I went to the headmaster to tell him I'd spoken to all the teachers that needed to be told, and it seemed fairly unanimous that it was better I left, to allow the others that wanted to learn to get on with it, without mini-explosions going on around them. He asked me what I was going to do. I told him that I had little idea what I was capable of doing, but that I was probably going to help my dad, who was just starting up a printing business. It wasn't planned, but I had to say something. He asked me if I had ever thought of working for my country. I had no idea what he was on about, so replied that, as I was going to have to pay taxes, I would probably be working for them all my life. I added that if he had any idea himself what he thought would suit me I'd appreciate the advice. He said he thought he had a good career in mind for me and that he would check a few things and would write to me shortly.

As it turned out, a letter arrived at home for me quite soon after, inviting me to an interview in London. Not saying much more than that, as the letter seemed quite official it did intrigue me.

So, I went.

Interview

On November 23rd, 1971, I travelled from Rickmansworth Station to Lambeth North Station, London, a journey of about an hour with one change at Baker Street Station to the Bakerloo Line. My destination was Century House, 100 Westminster Bridge Road, the then home of the Secret Intelligence Service (SIS), commonly known as MI6.

The letter I received, following the school resignation chat with my Headmaster, gave me brief instructions on how I should keep my business with SIS secret, but that I may tell my closest family or spouse what I was doing. I chose not to tell anyone, as I felt sure there was no way, I would pass the interview, thus save some face and not disappoint my parents again. The dress code was "grey man" smart. I didn't know what this meant, I had no grey clothes at all, nothing other than jeans, as I never went anywhere 'posh'. I decided the best option was school trousers, school shirt, grey tie, and shoes, with a kind of black cotton/denim jacket for warmth against the November cold. In those days November was cold, there was often a frost lasting most of the day, we don't get cold weather like that these days in England.

I found the entrance quite easily, but as I had allowed far too much time to travel to London as I hate being late, I decided to wander around outside for a while until a more suitable time for my appointment to enter the building. About 400 yards away, opposite the station, down Kensington Road, is the Imperial War Museum. I walked there in just a few minutes, I didn't go in, outside the front gate was an ice-cream van, I bought an ice cream cone to stop the beginnings of hunger pangs. I ate while looking at the two big guns in the garden facing out from the entrance of the building before returning to Century House. Little did I know this ice-cream van would become part of a major spy scandal that I discovered in a few years' time.

A modern looking twenty-two story building, I entered not knowing what to expect. Immediately approached by two security guys, set up on two ordinary tables either side of the doorway, it seemed to be a temporary arrangement, surprisingly. It was the first time I'd ever been frisked, bringing home to me that perhaps this place might be something special. After checking I was on the visitor's list they directed me to a waiting area, I sat for just a few moments before a lady arrived. She stayed behind the revolving bomb-proof doors, completely made of clear Perspex glass or something stronger, she called my name and waved me through the revolving door to where she stood. I thought I should start taking mental notes of my surroundings, quite rightly, I had a feeling

Century House, London MI6 Headquarters

somehow it would come up later.

The interview was surprisingly easy. After completing yet another form, more sections requiring my personal details again, which I'm sure they knew anyway, there was a very simple informal chat in a small room with another woman, presumably from HR. I talked about my interests, which at that time were few, and what I knew about the service, which was nothing. It was stressed several times that it was imperative that I always answered questions honestly, they preferred the truth, even if it was something that might normally be considered bad, such as, had I ever taken drugs, which I haven't, ever. It was thought that passing through the university system it was unlikely that one could get through without experiencing drugs at some point, it wasn't frowned upon at all, and wouldn't necessarily result in a fail today if I admitted I had tried them. I moved on to another room where there was what looked like an exam room at school. Desks in a row with papers prepared and laid on each desk, I thought, maybe others were expected, but none arrived. I was invited to sit at a desk and complete what seemed a psychological profile test of some kind. There were about 100 simple scenario questions, which, toward the end, I started to lose concentration and interest in. The problem for me was, it seemed to be all scenarios I had never faced, such as, how did I cope with someone collapsing in the street, what did I do in that situation? I hadn't experienced anything like that yet. So, I made up answers how I thought I might act because I didn't want to appear stupid, probably that was a mistake. Toward the end, I started to think maybe I should be honest, and simply answer "I have not experienced this." I completed the paper with most answers completed this way. The time given to finish the test was quite tight, so I rushed through the questions. I think this would have usually resulted in a fail, but maybe because they had already decided they wanted me, I passed anyhow. I don't know how these psychological things work.

Back to a third person for another easy informal chat. The guy here wanted to test my powers of observation. He asked me to describe the man that brought me from reception to this department. I started by saying, first of all, it wasn't a man but a woman, which he seemed surprised at. I described her from top to bottom easily as I had made mental notes expecting something like this. He said he then knew who I was describing but couldn't understand why she had fetched me and not the guy that was assigned. Not my problem. He asked if I had any questions myself. I had a million. I asked if I could have a look round to see what went on here. I wasn't permitted. I asked what role they thought they had in mind for me. He claimed he didn't know, I'm pretty sure he did. But he did describe what facilities were available for staff, such as canteen, gym and gun range. I asked about pay. He did give me examples according to role, rank, length of service and so on. It seemed pretty poor compared to how well paid I thought it should be. None the more for that, it was better than anything I could expect anywhere else. It was suggested that I should continue to work in my current job until I heard more. The whole thing had taken about two hours. I was then informed that if my application was to continue there would be background checks, including immediate family and any significant others, and only then would I hear if I was going to be a successful applicant. I was a little surprised because I had thought it was them that wanted me. But then I suppose I could fail if they found something they didn't like about my family. I had to be a British National, I didn't know anyone in my family that wasn't. I left quite exhausted. I travelled home thinking I had no choice but to go to work with my dad in his business.

My Dad's business was very small, renting a garage at the back of a parade of shops in Mill End, Hertfordshire. My father said he needed me to help, I'm sure my wages put a strain on his finances. I started working for him immediately. He taught me the basics of letterpress, typesetting, and finishing. I operated a Heidelberg Platen Press and a small electric guillotine. Everything was hands-on and incredibly boring. I was paid £6.50 per week, a wage well below the normal basic rate. When I complained about the poor wages, it was explained to me that one day the company would be mine and working for next to nothing was an investment in my future, let alone help the company grow with less of a financial strain upon it. I wasn't entirely sure printing was my future as it was so boring, but I did almost enjoy the practical aspect of it, especially later, as the company grew, and we began to print using the lithography method, and more chemicals and processing was involved.

It took six weeks for the checks and processing to be completed at MI6, a letter dropped on my parent's doormat addressed to me. I had been successful! I was invited, should I wish to proceed, to a second interview. I continued to hold back from telling anyone, as it seemed to me there was still a possibility I could fail.

After what seemed a lifetime waiting with excitement, I was on the train again, travelling back to Century House. This time I was interviewed more intensely by, as it turned out, my mentor to be, John. Dressed quite casually John was easy to get on with and I liked him, later in life, we continued to stay in touch and often, with our wives, had dinners together. After a break for coffee, a whole mass of paperwork had to be completed, some seemed so irrelevant, and why did I need to fill my name and date of birth and National Insurance number so many times? The formalities took ages. The mess hall was well equipped and a very busy place, but it seemed to me, was mostly secretaries and admin staff here, with no sign of any spies.

After a good lunch, which John paid for us both, he asked if I'd like to have a look around the building. I couldn't help feeling excited now, surely this meant I have been accepted. There were rooms equipped with computers of all kinds. Computers, were as yet not a household item, seeing these quite advanced systems was of huge interest to me. I had no idea of their capabilities. In those days rows of Winchester drives with the large 24-inch- and 14-inch-diameter media were typically mounted in standalone boxes resembling washing machines. Newer, smaller diameter media drives using 8-inch media and 5.25-inch media were also evident, I later found out that at that time data was being transferred from the large disks to these smaller, faster and higher capacity machines. I could tell I was going to love working with such advanced computers systems, for a person like me there would be little chance to be able to work with such technology anywhere else. Of course, I had very little idea what these machines were being used to store.

Upper floors, were corridors of offices, decorated in business-like colour schemes, not dull, but efficient magnolia or white walls and oak wood door frames. I could see secretaries busy at typewriters, some looking up to give an acknowledging smile, others were concentrating and taking notes on their telephones. It was obvious to me that this was a place where serious work was done. John led me down the corridors, often stopping to chat with people, introducing me as a prospective officer, everyone seemed quite happy and friendly. Working our way up the floors, missing some floors out to avoid repetition as several were much the same, we finally arrived at the top floor, where the offices were more hushed and better appointed, I was taken into one office and introduced to 'C'.

I learnt the term 'C' originates from the initial used by Captain Sir Mansfield Smith-Cumming, RN, when he would sign a letter "C" in green ink. Since then, all chiefs have been known as 'C'.

Sir John Ogilvy Rennie, KCMG, was the 6th Director of the SIS (MI6) from 1968 to 1973. When appointed, his brief was to reform the organisation. I learnt later that it was his association with my Headmaster Mr Morrill, and, because of my practical abilities, skills at cheating, lying, apparent nerve, yet obviously not as dumb as I made out, placed me as a good candidate for his purpose.

Post World War 2, there were mumblings that MI6 recruited only those in the old boy networks, Oxford and Cambridge Universities in particular. MI6 was presented as an ever-present and incestuous web of prep schools, old-school-tie bureaucracies, and smoke-filled Soho clubs. It was said Kim Philby, Britain's most notorious Cold War traitor, was able to pass secrets to Moscow because British Intelligence was 'staffed by ill-disciplined and inept upper-class twits' - twits who were prepared to turn a blind eye to the misdemeanours of one of their own.

The Cambridge 5 Spy Ring is a very good example of how those traitors' passed information to the Soviet Union during World War 2 and were active at least into the early 1950s. Yet none were ever prosecuted for spying. The term "Cambridge" refers to the recruitment of the group during their education at Cambridge University in the 1930s. This particular topic is covered extensively in other good well-researched books and is not a subject I want to cover here but could be considered the reason as to why I believe I had been selected, from a most unusual background. I believe initially I was more an experiment, and my expected failure could be used to prove the mumblers wrong.

It became a major worry, to the USA especially, that British Secret Services could no longer be trusted. Something had to be done within the Security Services to, in my words "lower the tone" of the establishment. My innocence in such things at the time probably helped me survive. I had no idea how these places worked or operated, I had never read a book on any Intelligence Service, in fact, I don't recall reading any books at all. The Beano was my limit. My naiveté was a particular attribute that was being sought, after all, from the moment I would be recruited everything I learnt, would be what they wanted me to learn. My entire knowledge of SIS was James Bond movies. A total misconception, far from pistols, unarmed combat or irresistible sexual magnetism, a normal SIS officer's primary tools for motivating foreigners to do what he wants are bribery, bullshit and in certain circumstances blackmail. The only Bond-like quality a normal SIS officer will be required to show is the ability to drink heavily and remain functional, as any diplomat must on the embassy cocktail circuit. I guess my ability to think quickly, especially when I need to save my skin, to have no qualms about telling the odd lie, were skills perfect for the role. The downside to my appointment into the service was that I had absolutely none of the people networking that all the "upper class" types had.

In order to prove the old system of recruiting for MI6 should be favoured and maintained, I formed an opinion shortly after beginning work for SIS, that I was being set up to fail.

To some extent, I have to agree with the old system despite my position. In the SIS world, there can be nothing more valuable than networking, to always know someone in the right place, or even to know someone that knows someone. The public school and Oxbridge Universities must be the best places to form your network base, after inherited networks. To this day, I have no idea what was expected to be the outcome of my employment in SIS. To my mind, and I found this out very quickly, I was merely an experiment, a joke that many of the "toffs" quite openly sneered or laughed at. Once I realised this, it simply served to make me want to prove them all wrong, my background with dealing with bullies would pay off. I wasn't defending just myself, but in my opinion, all of my social class. I believe and can find no evidence to the contrary that I was, and still remain, the only recruit never to pass through any university or private school system. Whether that means I failed later in my career. As my story unfolds, it remains to be seen.

After my second interview, I returned home to continue work at Peter Gilbrook Printers, to await further instructions. It was now that I broached the subject to my father. I told him that I had been offered a good job. It was always a good idea to have some employment somewhere as a cover should the need arise, so I explained the nature of the job and that I needed to continue working with him, but also needed a lot of time out. Never one to express emotion to me my father hardly reacted at all. I wasn't sure he believed me. I told him I would continue to work with him until I received further instructions, and then, we could decide from there how we could work the two jobs together. I told him that my employment at SIS would need to remain a secret and that I would leave it up to him whether he told mum. My mother was a difficult problem, she could never be relied upon to keep such a secret, and it was of some concern to me how to deal with her knowing. I asked Dad how he thought it best to approach her. He decided there and then to not tell her, if we couldn't keep my employment with MI6 from her it would be all over Maple Cross, and Hertfordshire by tea-time. That is how my MI6 career remained all his life, he never revealed what I did to a single soul. He assured me that he could manage some kind of cover for me. It absolutely worked so well and for so long.

After a week or two, I received instructions to report again to Century House, where I signed in, with John, now appointed my mentor, signed all the papers necessary, including the Official Secrets Act, I was given papers to study which set out the offences related to spying, sabotage and related crimes. I wanted John to know that he would be working with a blank canvas as far as I was concerned, I knew nothing of what was expected of me. He kindly reassured me that I had been selected for precisely those reasons and that having studied my reports he was confident I would do well, so long as I paid attention and realised this was a serious business. His character was such that I always felt at ease in his company, and, often despite his serious warning, we had many a good laugh together.

We went together to visit "C" in his office. I was surprised and impressed how much Sir John knew about me, I didn't have to explain anything to him, and he seemed to know everything, even what I had eaten for breakfast that day. I told him that I was feeling like a fish out of water here, I had no idea where to start or how. He informed me that I would be attending "Spy School" to learn the trade and after I completed the courses, he had something in mind for me to do.

I left more nervous than before. I was most probably so scared by the time I disembarked the train at Rickmansworth Station, I felt I had already a few grey hairs on my head. Being frightened is no bad thing, it makes one sharper, less likely to make errors, and as long as one can control any fear, learn to use it in a positive way.

Instructions arrived shortly after telling me when and where to report for training.

Spy School

I'm not giving any secrets away in this book, and it is public knowledge, to anyone interested in these matters, 296-302 Borough High Street, London was a 'spy school' for SIS Officers. The Ministry of Defence has now moved out, but the building remains. Until the 1990s, the establishment stood opposite Southwark police station in a MOD building, a quite unremarkable building, one could easily walk past it not caring what went on inside. Called a 'non-field training headquarters' rather than a spy school, it would teach spies the techniques that they would use in their work. Another establishment building was Fort Monckton, the secret service training base on the seafront just outside Gosport, Hampshire. Here, new recruits to Britain's Secret Intelligence Service are taught their art-form of the more physical kind, including my favourite, pistol shooting, by a retired sergeant-major. I won several contests, while my air gun exploits as a young boy were useful, most public schoolboys had already experienced and fired real guns, but I think my natural ability came to the fore.

The chances are, however, is that spies will never get to use this skill because the world of spying is almost nothing like its popular portrayal. Real-life James Bonds, for instance, don't get to run around like mavericks these days, running riot around cities in car chases, or getting into gunfights. Nor do many intelligence officers get to have sex with their sources of intelligence. "It isn't normal to sleep with a target. If you have to, it means you are not in control." said one former British operative. Someone once summed up the role of the building: "Essentially, James Bond would have been trained to kill in Fort Monckton, Hampshire and then would have been taught what documents to complete, when he had killed someone, at Borough." I did attend some other specialist schools, these places will remain secret.

The London school, while interesting was not so much fun for me as the practical lessons that I enjoyed so much in Gosport. It wasn't easy by any means, especially for me, compared to the other "students" who had been recruited from normal university routes. Initially, I did find myself sitting alone as someone not worthy of the company of those from private school backgrounds. Some individuals were working class, in fact, there was quite a good cross-section of society in the classes, but I was the only person so young at seventeen and so uneducated. I was age disadvantaged by a good three years, if not more.

Many of the lessons were of the initiative type. It has been written about in several other books notably Peter Wright's "Spycatcher." I believe his book was the first to reveal Fort Monckton as to what its purpose really was. He wrote about one of the skill tests given at Gosport in which the student had to obtain an unknown person's name, address, and passport number. He accomplished this using great initiative when a couple of girls in a bar were asked if they would like to accompany him to France on his yacht. As Gosport is close to many marinas filled with yachts it wasn't that unusual for skippers to be looking for crew. The girls were told their passport details were required for customs in France. Easy!

In my class, people were given various tasks. The one given to me sounded simple, but then once I thought about it, I realised how difficult it could be. I was told that by the following week, I had to plant something blue on one of my classmates, it would be my choice to which person would be my victim. Easy I thought. But then it dawned on me, that as everyone knew each other's task, they would all be looking out for me, not wanting to be the 'victim', and for me to fail the test.

The following week, on the day we all had to produce the fruits of our labours for the test, everyone was carefully avoiding me. It was obvious I could only plant something blue onto one of my classmates on the actual day. No-one wanted to sit next to me or pass closely to me. On that day I became the subject of a number of jokes sitting alone, working alone, to be avoided at all costs, I couldn't get near anyone. At the morning coffee break we trouped off to the canteen, which was a simple room, self-service, one made their own coffee and helped themselves to biscuits, or make some toast etc. Not one person would come near me. I said,

"ok guys I get it that no one wants to come near me. You all sit over there, I'll make the teas and coffees." They were giggling like children that I would not be able to plant something on any of them while they were watching me like a hawk. I stood alone in the kitchen area preparing teas, coffees and biscuits for them all, looking quite forlorn. After the break we wandered back to the classroom, my so-called colleagues hanging back letting me walk in front of them, so I would not make a last-minute attempt to plant any kind of blue item on any of them. I love being the butt of jokes!

In class everyone produced the results of their particular task, some were quite ingenious. Explaining how they achieved the aim of each task. My turn came.

"OK, Andy, can you reveal who, if anyone, you have planted a blue item onto, and how did you complete the task, please." my lecturer asked. Everyone in the room was checking pockets, shoes, even hair in some cases. Happy that I was going to fail my task, there was a lot of giggling among them all.

"Actually." I said "I have planted something blue on Peter." Peter looked horrified I had beaten him, "and Mark." pointing at Mark, equally mortified. "Oh, and Mike, in fact, everyone here in this room, including you." I said pointing at my lecturer. They all looked mystified, how had I done it? What was it? None of them could find anything in their pockets. The lecturer asked me "What have you planted?"

"Well." I replied, "During tea-break, I put a few grains of Methylene Blue Powder onto your biscuits, in your teas and coffees. In a few hours, you will all be pissing bright blue." Methylene Blue has several medical uses. It is a safe drug when used in small doses. Before using it on my fellow students, a few days earlier I tested it on myself, I took about 30 grains of the powder in water. The dose was a little strong. On the day I guessed about ten grains would suffice. I also found there was a slight narcotic effect that made me a little hyperactive and I spent the afternoon after taking the powder telling non-stop jokes. The effect at toilet time was amazing and hysterically funny. My pee was bright sky blue. It is also a great April fool's joke as my wife can testify, I recommend it. Some of the guys got the joke, others thought I was taking a risk with their health. I didn't care, after the treatment they gave me that day, they deserved everything they got. Next day, classmates were reporting good results, some said they found it hilarious having such bright blue pee, a few didn't get the joke at all. My lecturer reported I had received full marks. No previous students had ever been quite so imaginative with that particular task, or for that matter, had ever managed to plant something blue onto (or into) every student including himself. After that day I felt a little more accepted among my peers, a couple even congratulated me.

Had I been the lecturer on that day, I would have given me a fail. The point of both the tests mentioned in this chapter was that the student should learn the ability to persuade. In the passport test, the only solution was to trick someone into believing that by giving the information required, something good will happen, i.e. a nice sail to France. The proper solution to my test, I believe, would be to plant something blue on a comrade by persuading someone to come onto my side, and help me to pass. In my case, I had no real friend in class. They kept themselves away. I should have selected a person that I could have persuaded to come onto my side, knowingly take a blue item from me and place it upon their person for me. My solution, while hilarious, could have led, in a real situation, to the chemical being detected, identified, and potentially cause an international incident, place the UK as a nation prepared to injure, or worse. Of course, I know that now after years of experience, but my solution does demonstrate to some extent the danger of out casting a person, a company or nation. Backed into a corner they will bite. I think today we have seen examples of that and the international reaction to real events such as the attack on Sergei Skripal, and his daughter Yulia, in Salisbury, which left them hospitalised for weeks. Georgi Markov, September 1978, the Bulgarian dissident who was poisoned by a specially adapted umbrella on Waterloo Bridge. As he waited for a bus, Markov felt a sharp prick in his leg. The opposition activist, who was an irritant to the authoritarian communist government of Bulgaria, died three days later. A deadly 1.7mm-wide pellet containing the poison ricin was found in his skin. Alexander Litvinenko, November 2006, victim of the fatal poisoning of the former officer with the Russian spy agency FSB sparked a major international incident. Litvinenko fell ill after drinking a cup of tea laced with radioactive polonium. The United Kingdom does not want to be seen to be involved in such dirty business in public.

As generous as my lecturer was, maybe because I did actually achieve the aim of the test in an original and complete way, he felt I should earn a pass. Maybe he saw I had little chance of persuasion in the situation I was in with the other students, and that the solution to the problem was a subtle underhand blunt stick approach. Maybe I had to pass because I was destined to be the fall guy in the establishment, who knows. At the end of the day, in my opinion, I hadn't achieved the point of the lesson, I should have failed that test. At best, I had proven that I was prepared to poison anyone I had to.

A skill we had to learn to a high level was the ability to track and follow a subject, both on foot and in vehicles. Having spent so many of my childhood days tracking and stalking animals I found it quite easy to adapt my methods. My character is such that I can quite often enter a party or something similar, walk through a room full of people and be completely unnoticed. I don't know what it is about me that makes me invisible to people, it can be a useful skill, as well as upsetting when people can't remember me. We were taught how to work in teams and alone. We had to learn to be the subject being followed too. Being the subject, there are methods to detect and avoid being followed. We were taught when playing the target, to walk, for instance, down a high street and to have a theme. You walk looking into shop windows that sell a certain type of product, so you become a man looking for a shirt or shoes. I never thought these tactics were of much use when one is a known target, in that case, evasive tactics might serve one better. I was always of the opinion that one shouldn't become a target in the first place, it means you've lost your anonymity already and can easily be picked up again later if you evade your followers. Once we became proficient at this skill, there was, unknown to us, one final test where we would follow a target alone. The target would duck down an alleyway in an attempt to lose the identified stalker. What the stalker doesn't know is, this is a trap. There would be some guys in the alley waiting for the stalker. They would grab him, bundle him into a vehicle and give him a good roughing up, in a quite realistic manner, I have to say. The kidnapping is then followed by imprisonment and interrogation - all very realistic and quite uncomfortable. The guys kidnapping the stalker would be Special Forces and have no qualms about throwing very realistic punches. It's all intended for the student to experience real capture, including sleep deprivation and being placed in very uncomfortable stress positions. It was, of course, to evaluate how the student copes with such treatment. None of the trainees had any idea that the tracking of the subject was about to lead to a few days capture, interrogation and pain. Quite a few failed at this point in the course.

One by one, about an hour apart, each of us was told to go wait by the Portsmouth to Gosport Ferry terminal in Gosport. We had been given a description of the subject to follow who was going to arrive by ferry from Portsmouth. We were to identify him, follow him and produce a full report on where he went in town and who he met, if anyone, without being spotted. None of us suspected at all what was about to happen. I arrived at the ferry terminal, maybe I should have gone to the ticket office to look at the timetable. I thought it a bit obvious, anyone trying to spot me would pick me up easily. Instead, I sat on a low wall at the back of the new bus station next door among some trees, I could easily see the ferry depart on the other side of the estuary. I hadn't been given a time of arrival for the ferry that the subject would be on. At that time of day, the ferry ran every 15 minutes. I saw the ferry pull away from the landing on the other side, it took about four minutes to cross the water to the Gosport side. People disembarked, although a little distance from the ramp, I could make out each person, I didn't want to risk moving closer, in case anyone was looking out for me. I couldn't see anyone fitting the description. No panic, I carried on waiting, trying to look like one of the many locals and tourists around the place. I didn't want to move my location, so I waited for the next ferry. About 15 minutes later the next ferry arrived, passengers disembarked, still no subject. The ramp cleared of people, and the next line of waiting passengers started to walk down the ramp onto the ferry to cross to Portsmouth. There, as the passengers started to board a lone figure fitting the description walked up the ramp. He continued to walk straight, momentary moving behind the bus station out of sight from where I was sitting. I started to walk around the far side of the bus station from where he was, bringing him back into view as he neared the roundabout at the end of the High Street. I walked along the bus platform between the buses and the waiting rooms where there was plenty of cover, looking around for any other characters that were trying to pick me up and follow me too. At that time in 1972, Gosport High Street was still open to traffic, it has since been pedestrianised in 1991 but there were the beginnings of the works to convert it providing good cover for me to use. The whole area was being renovated after so much war damage, many of the ruined buildings were under reconstruction still. He entered the High Street which runs west from the ferry, four shops up, he paused, and entered the Woolworth's store. I moved north from the bus station, around the north side of the roundabout, so that I would end up on the opposite side of the High Street from Woolworth's. On the roundabout was the Ark Royal pub, I entered a door to move out of sight, from here at the top end of the bar I could clearly see Woolworth's doors. I ordered a drink while I stood watching the shop opposite and took my jacket off, a quite natural action in the bar, but realistically it was to change my look, now I was wearing a jumper. I hung my jacket on a hook under the bar so that the barmaid would not see I had left it behind. I would come back later to collect my lost property. This also gave me a chance to see if anyone looked as though they may be following me. No sign of anything odd so far. If the subject decided to try to duck out the back of the shop, it was better to give up, as it may mean I had already been compromised. But a minute or two later and only a few sips into my drink he reappeared in the doorway. Pausing slightly to take a look round, he turned left and continued west up the High Street. As he was about to disappear from my view from the pub, I placed my drink on the bar and left by the door into the High Street to follow. He stayed on the same side of the road, pausing occasionally to look into shop windows. I was sure he had not seen me leave the pub. Making sure never to pause or waver whenever he stopped, I continued walking at the same slow pace using window reflections to watch him rather than look directly at him. He also entered a bank halfway up the road, but it was easy for me to fake a stop at a shop and again use the reflection to watch out for him to reappear. Taking about 15 minutes to walk almost to the far end of the street. We were at a junction with Clarence Road. I believed I had still not been identified following him. On the southwest corner of High Street and Walpole Road is a social club (currently Gosport Conservative Club), along the west edge of the building, there is a narrow alleyway leading to staff car parks and then on to South Street behind. Here he quite slowly and deliberately turned left and walked down this alley. I was sure he did this to make sure that I followed, even though I was still convinced he hadn't seen me. I didn't like the look of this at all. Something wasn't right. He could have walked down the road just before the social club building. I wasn't going to follow him it would expose me for sure. I could easily have walked toward South Street from where I was, but that would have meant a sudden change in direction and slightly doubling back on myself. I chose to continue on to the end of the High Street at a much faster pace and hope to pick him up again in Creek Road or South Street. It was a risky strategy, but I did indeed spot him much further away on South Street walking east. This meant he had effectively doubled back on himself. It didn't make any sense and I felt very uneasy that maybe he had spotted me. He turned left into Thorngate Way, a road that doglegged north then east behind the police station (now closed). Again, I was some distance away and I felt sure he had not seen me. I crossed the road and walked briskly east down South Street, ducked behind the flats opposite South Cross Street because by now he should be appearing from Thorngate Way into this street. Edging around the buildings using the few trees as cover, there was no sign of him, he was still in Thorngate Way. I walked further down South Street about an extra 200 yards and dodged left into Coats Road, another road that doglegs north then west. This put me in a road that heads toward where he should be and I should be able to see him somewhere at the rear of the police station. Using the car park the east end of Coats Road I could peer around the corner to try to spot him. Indeed, there he was, at the rear gate of the police station that led into the car park for police cars. He was talking to four other rough-looking men. They seemed confused and looking around for me but in the wrong direction. They hadn't expected me to get on the east side of them. One guy was flapping his arms as if to say, "where is he?" I had no idea that the trap was meant for me to be captured and bundled into their van parked in the police station car park out of public view in this quiet road. I waited a few minutes to see what they did next. In the end, they all got into the van and drove away. I had successfully followed the target from the ferry to a point where it was impossible to follow any further. I had no backup to call so I couldn't follow in a car. A strange exercise I thought, far too easy. I had no clue that in fact they had failed to kidnap me for the interrogation phase. I returned to Fort Monckton unaware I wasn't supposed to be free. I found my instructor who wasn't amused. I thought I would be debriefed, giving a full account of the afternoon's work. Instead, I got a roasting, I don't know why as I had evaded the target, I evaded the other men that were meant to grab me as I walked past the gate of the police station and bundled me into their van. It was explained to me what was meant to happen. So what should I do now? Go give myself up? I was told to wait, while he went to find the interrogation team. No, the surprise had gone, I now knew what the afternoon should have led to. I was given a partial pass for evading everyone involved. Did I think it an unfair result, surely, I had been successful? As a result of my success, I never did endure what everyone else had to. I spent the next few days, reflecting on my luck, while my fellow trainee spies were being subjected to abuse. When the other guys returned from days of imprisonment and interrogation, they looked a right mess. They had been stripped of all clothes, put into stress positions, deprived of sleep, quite realistically beaten until they cracked and gave the information their torturers wanted - while I sat in comfort enjoying hot meals, tea and biscuits and spending time in my favourite place, the shooting range. If anything could serve to restore the class divide that did. My response to my critics "fuck off and learn to tail someone properly."

I attended various other courses around the country before I was given a pass with credit, not the best in class, but I was happy with that, despite missing out on a beating. I returned home to begin my work as a fully qualified spy.

Starting at MI6

Late 1973 saw me arrive at Century House SIS Headquarters in London with the rank of Officer. I am not entirely sure what they liked about me, but I have always had a good memory for small details. I can forget people's names two minutes after being introduced to them, but I retain a lot of seemingly unimportant information which can be important when dealing with a mass of paperwork on your desk or when you are out in the field trying to remember what your brief was. I arrived at the security check-in where I was on the visitor list, but this time directed to an office to the right from the security tables. In this room sat a lady who, on checking my ID, gave me my staff pass, and instructed me to always wear or carry it while in the building. John was called on the internal phone network, and five minutes later met me in the lobby waiting area. With a big smile, he welcomed and congratulated me and led me upstairs. He took me to my own office, a simple room, on the fourth floor. There was a desk with a computer terminal linked to the SIS network, a few cabinets, a small safe and a couch with a low coffee table. There was a through-door to an office where I was introduced to Karen my secretary. With that John announced he would leave us to get acquainted and that was it.

I was only just eighteen, had my own office and secretary, and, no idea what-so-ever what I was supposed to do next. Karen was without a doubt the most professional person I have ever met. Unfortunately for me, she was also stunningly beautiful to distraction. Blond shoulder-length hair tied back in a ponytail. Immaculate makeup. Dressed in a white shirt, dark navy jacket and matching knee-length pencil skirt. While I couldn't believe my luck that I would be awarded such a vision, I knew her looks would be a distraction. Her sense of humour matched mine perfectly. I don't know if the secretarial pool matched staff so that they would work together well or not, if this was a dating game, it would have been a perfect match. Except she was about seven years my senior. I must have stared too long, with a smile she said "I should close my mouth now" after John left the room. She held out a perfectly soft hand to shake. Shy as I am with girls, our handshake was a little on the brief side. She had the kindest eyes and smile. After the brief introductions, I shrugged and said:

"I have no idea where to start, what do I do? I've been given no brief."

Karen replied,

"Not to worry today, I will take you around the building and introduce you to the people you should know. I'll show you how to use the computer network to the best advantage, ignore everything you've been taught on that, there are better ways. I will make an appointment for you to meet "C" sometime today, hopefully, he will give you a brief. Do as he asks, do it professionally and you will be ok here. Would you like coffee or tea?"

"Tea, white with two sugars please" I stumbled my reply, now shaking with nerves. It had dawned on me I was way out of my depth, and I told her so.

"It's your first day, no one would expect you to be an ace, take time to settle. Let's go to the canteen and meet a few people." With that she placed her notepad and pen onto her desk, we walked through to my office, locked the interconnecting door, I wondered why. Were there thieves or spies about!

We took the elevator down to level one where the canteen was. I looked at her, she smiled back. I informed her that I had been to the canteen before and that there seemed to be so few Officers. Karen told me that the building was mostly admin staff. It seemed reasonable, why would Officers expose themselves to the risk of being identified entering Century House. It made sense to me.

At the canteen we collected tea and coffee, I was too nervous to eat. We sat at a table where two of her colleagues were sat.

"May I introduce Andy, his first day" she added in a whisper. "Andy this is Elaine and Penny, they have offices on our floor too." I shook hands with them both, nice young girls but nowhere near as attractive as Karen, unsure what to say, better I say nothing and just smiled.

Penny broke the ice, "Andy, what do you think of Karen, isn't she attractive?"

Elaine added, "Yes, all the men here fancy her" they both giggled.

Karen stopped the line of conversation, "Not very professional ladies. Come on Andy let's get back to work." Well, that was a short break. Back in our office, Karen proceeded to show me the computer network system and how to get the best from it. I had never seen such an information source. Computers in those days were still in their infancy. This system was something else. Of course, I had had lessons on how to use it in Spy School, but it didn't show me half of what was being demonstrated to me now. There was so much to learn here. It was nice to sit close to Karen and she didn't move away if any part of our bodies touched. We spent some time going through protocols and procedures, by lunchtime my head was overloaded with information. As I was about to suggest some lunch, her phone buzzed, it was "C's" secretary confirming an appointment at 14:30 that afternoon. I asked if I could eat at my desk and asked her if she could fetch what she thought was good to eat, before leaving she made me a cup of tea in her room and brought it to my desk. While she was away, I set my safe code, then stood to stare out the window for a few minutes in quiet reflection. What was expected of me? Am I really capable of doing this job in a manner equal to others that have gone before and those that are here now? I watched the outside world go about their business until Karen returned with lunch.

After my food, Karen's phone buzzed, John Rennie "C" was ready to see me. I took the elevator up to the top-floor, where I was shown into his office straight away. He held out his hand to welcome me to my new job and motioned for me to sit on one of the two sofas, arranged so that they faced each other with a low coffee table between. I declined another tea. He talked a while, telling me what was expected, that his door was always open should I need advice. I should get at least six aliases and continue to perfect my languages. I asked if I had a brief so that I could begin work proper, a little unsure that I was ready to get into real work right away. My only concern was that I had never travelled overseas, my one trip to Germany as a fourteen-year-old was my entire experience. He told me that he would arrange a trip for me. He could see that I was still shy and nervous and told me that I should take time to get acclimatised to my new surroundings and that he did have something in mind for me, but not just yet. We sat talking, he seemed unhurried and willing to give me all the time I needed. I'm sure he was using this time to assess me, to figure out how I thought and worked. We ended the meeting by agreeing to meet again, at a time when he thought I would be ready for my first brief.

I headed back down to my office, spoke to Karen, I told her I was heading home and not to expect to see me for a few days. I had no idea how she occupied her day, but she always seemed busy. I had rented a small top floor flat in Linden Lea, Leavesden near Watford, quite close to what at that time was Leavesden airport owned by Rolls Royce, now Warner Bros. studios. A friend's mother worked for a rental agency and had found me this nice little bedsit flat, one room, a separate kitchen, and quite a large bathroom, it also included a garage. If anyone had done their maths properly, they would see I couldn't afford to live there on wages from my printing job, where I was now earning £7.50 a week! The flat cost £45 per week plus bills. I also purchased my second car after my first car an Austin Mini finally died. My pride and joy was now a white Triumph Dolomite. To rent the flat I was merely asked if I thought I could afford it, no checks, nothing!

Next day I went to work at Peter Gilbrook Printers again. By now it had grown, and Dad had acquired the garage next to his and knocked a door through. He had a huge contract to print two hundred and fifty thousand sponges for Johnnie Walker Whiskey Company. The job would last months, and he had taken on a part-time worker to help too. The sponges were dehydrated and like a rough, thick piece of card. We'd print a red Johnnie Walker logo on them on a semi-automatic letterpress machine. The sponges had to be fed into the machine by hand as they were irregular in shape. A laborious job, it gave me a chance to think about how I should begin my secret career and demonstrate I was capable, while I was working at the printing company. I began to form a plan while I stood shoving sponges on and off the press.

Xerox

I had a friend that worked at Xerox photocopy machines in Uxbridge, a large office block a few miles from where I lived and worked. I had heard somewhere that photocopy machines had a hard drive or ROM chip that kept an image of each copy that was made, but that this image was not deleted by the machine after the item being copied was printed. Copiers scan your documents to create replicas and then they store that information on an internal hard drive. That means a drive you can't easily access and may not know about, could be holding some of the most sensitive company data that you've got. Estimates say that a multi-function copier can hold as many as 25,000 documents in its memory, maybe more. I didn't know if this was true. I made a date with Janice, a girl I had liked back in Maple Cross Junior School, but were separated when I went to Grammar, and she went to Comprehensive School. She agreed to meet me, after a catch-up, I broached the question about the copiers. At first reluctant, she did, after a short time, give me the information I needed, and yes it was true. I explained that if the information got out it could have dire consequences for her company, which she could understand. I asked her if it would be possible to get hold of a copy of the design of a machine, so that I could develop a way to delete the drives, thus saving her company a red face if it were ever found out they had this huge flaw. This device could be used to provide the company engineers with a method to delete the hard drives at each service, thus Xerox will not need to admit to all their customers the fault in design, and I would get rich by manufacturing the hard drive deleting devices. Of course, this is only what I told her in order to get blueprints of the machines. Surprisingly she agreed, as she had easy access to everything I required, so long as I never admitted where I got the information from. A week later I had copies of the designs of every machine they made! A brilliant piece of espionage by Janice, if ever there was one. It can be said she was my first agent recruit. With this, I approached another friend Steve from Grammar School days, who worked for a computer design company in Watford, he saw the potential of what I was doing. He agreed to design and build a simple device that could plug into the machine's drive. Apparently, many of the models used the same drive. He built one device for me with a few different plugs connected to a battery-powered mobile drive that could first copy all the data, and then delete the drive in the Xerox machine. I now had the capability to copy hundreds of thousands of images of photocopies (and a few office party backsides!). We tested the device at Steve's place of work in a photocopy machine. We downloaded about fifteen thousand images. These could now be transferred to a computer by simply plugging the device into the back of almost any computer at that time.

I wanted to test my device for real. One of the companies Gilbrook Printers did printing work for, was Rolls Royce in Leavesden, where they manufactured small engines for helicopters, from memory it was the Gemini engine. Next time I delivered some printed stationery to Rolls Royce, it was easy to get through security at the gate. I delivered the packages of printed stationery, left the stores and entered a random office where through the glass windows in the corridor, I could see there was a photocopier. I announced to the guy in the room I was there to service the photocopy machine. He pointed to the machine against the wall, without hardly lifting his head from the drawing board where he was working. I opened the machine, plugged in my device and downloaded over ten thousand images. I closed everything up, stood up after a few minutes pretending to service the machine and announced all was well and good for another six months. Spying was going to be this easy.

In those days modems were incredibly slow, I couldn't send the information to Karen at Century House London, so the results of my theft had to remain with me for a few days. Next time I visited Century House, I plugged it into my computer and uploaded the images. I told Karen what I had done, but I wanted to keep it secret from my colleagues in MI6. Karen and I agreed we should create a database and work out a method of filing to aid retrieval in an organised manner. Karen was happy to work out a system for me on an independent, firewalled computer system, to keep it all to ourselves.

Although I didn't go to Century House very often, I did maintain communication with Karen by phone for more or less daily updates, we always knew what the other was doing. We gradually built a relationship that was more than just professional. She knew I didn't have a girlfriend, I was very shy when it came to girls. I knew she didn't have a boyfriend, it seemed to me that she wasn't really looking for one, concentrating on her career more than her personal life, my secretary was always available, day or night 24/7.

I needed to expand my enterprise. I contacted Janice at Xerox again. I told her I had come up with a method to delete the stored images during servicing. I made up a story to get her to supply me with all the documents needed to make me look like a Xerox Service Engineer. She was completely on board with me, not realising I could see all the copied documents after I uploaded them. A few days later I could pose as a legitimate copy machine engineer with ID and all the papers necessary to appear I was contract servicing the machines.

The next few weeks saw me a couple of days a week visiting companies in south-east England and downloading the contents of their photocopying machine drives. I visited Marconi North London, British Aerospace, London and Farnborough, Lockheed Martin, London, Martin-Baker near Uxbridge, Private Banks in London, High Street Banks and Building Societies, Investment Companies in London, Share dealing companies, and many, many more. I couldn't count how many images I had stolen. Probably several million! Poor Karen had trouble indexing so much data, but she was happy to be kept busy and always greeted me with a smile. Eventually some years later, as technology advanced, I would send the images by Internet from home, rather than visit Century House, but for now, I would take my drive device to my office for Karen to upload.

I had an appointment with "C" a few months after I started work, on one of my rare visits to SIS London, he asked me what I had learnt and had I found a way to be productive. I said "Yes I had very much found a way to keep myself busy." he asked me what I had been doing. Not wanting to reveal my crime, I gave him the answer "Doing my job, spying." He questioned whether he would see results of whatever it was I was busy doing. "Of course." I replied, I told him when the information I am gathering is as complete as I can get it, he would be given a full briefing. Lying through my teeth, I wasn't going to tell anyone, even him. Walking back to my office to retrieve my device after Karen had finished the latest upload, passing an open office door, I overheard a conversation between two men I didn't know, and they were talking about one of the companies I had raided. I popped my head through the door, I said I could help with the information they required. Looking down their noses as I had come to expect, one of them asked what I knew. I said I can get information on almost anything they want, a bit of a brag on my part, I had no idea if I could or not. They asked me if I would give them anything I knew. "Sure, we work on the same team don't we?" I asked what it was they wanted and to give me a few days. I saw them sneer as I turned to leave. What is it with these people? My face clearly didn't fit, and it was time I proved to them I could do my job. I arrived back at my office, asked my secretary "Karen, we have a problem. I've promised two guys down the corridor information about a company, how much do we have, and how do we sort out the rubbish from the good stuff?" She looked at her screen, we had thirty thousand images of copied material regarding the company.

"If you could print out, let's say, three thousand of the most useful stuff for them and throw in a few backside images if we have any." It's amazing how many people photocopy their private parts, for whatever reason. I guess sexting hadn't been invented yet.

"No problem" she replied, confident her data system would work on its first test. It was done in no time, but we waited a few days to make it look like we had to work for the information. After an appropriate wait, I wasn't in the building but Karen delivered several boxes, about three thousand pages of information to their office.

"Courtesy of Andy." she said, as she dumped the last box down on his desk. She left before he had a chance to say anything. A few days later, I got a phone call from one of the two guys.

"Andy this stuff is everything we need, how did you do this work, and so quickly? It's good stuff thank you." Finally, I had made my mark. So many times after that, people started coming to me asking if I had any information useful for whatever they were working on. So many times Karen and I could help. They started to question Karen to give up our secret, how did we have so much information and so quickly. She never did, nor did I. It was so simple, thinking always outside the established boxes, I developed different ways to achieve goals, in more efficient and less dangerous ways. Always with Karen right there for me, she was an incredible lady.

A few weeks later I had a call from "C."

"I hear you are being very useful, well done. Meet me soon I have your first brief." I'd done it, I was becoming trusted and people began to talk to me, not as someone from the wrong side of the tracks. I was happy.

If you are in some doubt to the point of all the information gleaned from these photocopies it is this. Ask yourself what is the role of an MI6 Officer? The Secret Intelligence Service is the foreign intelligence service of the government of the United Kingdom, tasked mainly with the covert overseas collection and analysis of human intelligence (HUMINT) in support of the UK's national security. Agents are at the heart of what MI6 does. Usually foreign nationals, voluntarily work with us to provide secret intelligence that helps to keep the UK - and often the rest of the world – safe and secure. Our intelligence officers' major role is identifying, recruiting, and running these agents. Those copies of copies from so many companies, nearly all of whom export their business, provided invaluable information at base level, almost every photocopy gave us a name, address, and telephone numbers of people, of a potential that may be turned to help the UK. The stated priority roles of SIS are counterterrorism, counter-proliferation, and supporting stability overseas to disrupt terrorism and other criminal activities.

Around 2010 the photocopy machine hard drive problem was recognised by the machine manufacturers as a security risk. All manufacturers changed the method the images were stored. Nowadays these machines no longer store the images. Did that confine the SIS's capability to harvest such basic information? GCHQ centres around the country have grown, to more than replace my very simplistic method of the 70's. The technology is here now to do incredible things.

Morocco

One disadvantage I had as a new recruit was my absolute lack of experience abroad. By now there was a new "C" at MI6, Maurice Oldfield. A northerner, I liked him a lot. He had a much warmer character and treated me very fairly. He was identified in 1968 to the Russians as a prominent member of MI6 by the double agent Kim Philby. Oldfield was the main participant in restoring American confidence in the British intelligence service. He was knighted in 1975, and he retired in 1979, but he was called out of retirement by Prime Minister Margaret Thatcher to act as security coordinator in Northern Ireland. He stayed in that role from October 1979 to March 1980, when rumours of his hidden homosexuality forced his resignation. Already stricken with cancer, he died a year later.

Maurice offered me the opportunity to experience my first trip to foreign lands. I was given a brief for a small task in Morocco. Nothing heavy or too difficult, actually as it turned out it was more of a holiday. I arrived at Heathrow Airport and after checking in with Air Maroc to Tangier, I had no idea what to do next! I sat down on a seat watching everyone else. They seemed to go toward the back of the terminal for some reason, so I thought I'd better do the same. In those days security was almost nil, maybe a quick frisk down if you were unlucky. I cottoned on that I needed to find my flight on the screen and at the appropriate time, head to the gate. I arrived in Tangier a few hours later, the smells of spices and different scents immediately noticeable, and I loved it. I found my contact waiting in arrivals, who took me south to a small town called Asilah on the coast, about 45 minutes' drive away. I stayed at a place right by the sandy beach that stretched about 30 miles. I had a day to relax, I did some surfing and ate well in restaurants in town. Next day we took a drive further south to Rabat to the Royal Palace where King Hassan II had faced an attempted coup in 1972. The palace was a beautiful low complex, with gardens and opulence I'd never seen before. My job was to liaise with several people, one being a CIA agent, who was present to negotiate terms for secret US bases, and to pay rent directly to the King. The rent to be somewhere in the region of six hundred million US dollars. I had to set up a line of communication for shared intelligence with several agencies. There was some considerable corruption to clinch the deal. I passed information to the King about several corrupt officials, who were later sacked. Job done, I returned to Asilah hung around a few days enjoying new foods and the sun. My biggest mistake was not realising how strong the sun was this far south. Surfing and sunbathing I ended up with the most severe sunstroke. Shaking and vomiting most of two days it was a terrible experience I'd never repeat. As soon as I could move again, I returned to Tangier and my flight home. Lessons learnt: how an airport works, how to eat couscous with one hand correctly, foreign sun can be dangerous.

In Love

After the successful Morocco trip, just before Christmas, Karen called me by telephone.

"Hi Andy, are you coming to the company Christmas party?"

"I hadn't thought about it" I replied. I enjoyed parties, and indeed in those days I went to many among my group of friends. I wasn't good at dancing, and I rarely did, but they were always good fun.

"Come to the party please, it's always a good laugh, and it will be good to see my boss before Christmas."

"Well, I don't know anyone, but yes, it will be good to see you in an informal atmosphere for a change."

"Great, see you there, meet you at the bar, I drink gin and tonic if you're buying." She said cheekily.

"Of course, I wouldn't have it any other way." Call me old fashion, but I'd never let a girl buy her own drinks. It's how it was in those days.

On the evening of the party, I took a small overnight bag intending to sleep on one of the cots. There were rooms with single beds for staff to sleep on for those working late-night moments, which was quite often as officers and staff work with so many people in other countries. I left my bag in my office.

I wandered down to the common room where the party was warming up. No sign of Karen, so I sat alone at the bar and ordered myself a gin and tonic which I sipped slowly, I didn't want to get drunk too quickly.

About twenty minutes later Karen arrived, looking absolutely stunning, a few heads turned as she walked toward me at the bar. It was the first time I'd seen her out of secretarial dress code. She had an amazing dress sense that complimented a perfect figure. The nearest I could describe her would be a shorter Holly Willoughby, with a bit of Kelly Brook thrown in, both well know TV personalities in the UK. She was wearing a little black dress and matching heels, cut low enough at the front to reveal a very sexy cleavage. Oh my, she had boobs and legs to match. For the first time, I saw her with her hair down. I was very pleased that she chose to sit next to me at the bar, I bought her gin and tonic as requested. We sat and made small talk trying to avoid business matters. We chatted for about three drinks, occasionally interrupted by the odd guy coming up to ask her to dance, she refused them all. A few girls came to chat too, I didn't know any of them, but they inferred that I was becoming famous within SIS for the work I was doing. I didn't want to talk about any of it, so just smiled politely. One or two of them asked me to dance, I declined, because my dance technique was definitely "no dad" in style.

After our three drinks, I could see that Karen was getting into the party mood, and she said she would like to dance. I just don't do dancing, although I can manage a slow waltz or last dance. I told Karen to go enjoy herself, and I would look after our drinks. I'm a proper wallflower. She went to the dancefloor and danced with a few of the girls, she could move well too. A few of the guys tried to join her but she turned away each time, slowly making her way toward me. It seemed she was dancing for my benefit and pleasure, looking at me most of the time. She did have the kindest eyes and best smile. After about three songs she came back to the bar where I was still sat, complaining she was thirsty. I bought more drinks for us both. She asked if I ever danced, I told her I may try the slow dances when the DJ gets to the slow section. I was loosening up enough to start telling jokes and funny stories, to anyone that came to join us. It was a great evening, people let their hair down after the year of hard work. A slow song came on, and I finally plucked up the courage to ask Karen to dance with me, to my surprise she said yes! We held each other like old friends, I whispered a few corny words to her such as how beautiful she looked, and that I was the luckiest boss to have the best secretary in the whole building, to which she replied,

"What? Not the whole of London?" and then whispered, "I'm glad you came tonight, and I've dressed for you." This took me back a bit. Was this the drink talking? She was certainly the most attractive girl in the room, and a few guys were looking at me jealously for sure.

"Well, thank you, you have dressed perfectly" not quite sure what to say next. I really am useless when it comes to girls. We danced close together until the song ended. We walked back to the bar holding hands. At the bar, Karen started,

"Sorry Andy that wasn't very professional of me"

I replied, "It's fine, it is the first time I've enjoyed a dance, and I expect it was just the drink talking."

To which she replied looking into my eyes,

"No it's not." we looked at each other for a second or two. She then perked up, "Another drink? The evening hasn't finished yet" killing the moment completely.

We sat at the bar, had more drinks, had many laughs, she was very easy to get on with, if she wasn't my secretary, I could have fallen in love with her, I probably had.

The last dance came, and we held hands back to the dance floor, Karen rejecting requests from other guys on the way and holding my hand tighter, we had a very slow dance together. The evening ended and people were talking in groups and slowly drifting off. Karen asked me if I was travelling back to Leavesden, I said no I was planning on crashing on a cot. She suggested it may be more comfortable if I crashed at her flat, she would feel safer in my company on the train home that late at night. She lived one stop away on the London Underground at Elephant and Castle. It seemed a good idea, I wasn't going to argue.

Karen had a beautiful modern flat, bought for her by her father, a London Banker of some sort working for one of the banks I had stolen photocopy images from, but I didn't know that at the time. It was about 2 am by the time we arrived there. Not only did she have a perfect dress sense, but she also knew how to furnish a flat, it was a lovely place, painted in soft relaxing colours, the furnishings match well, and it was easy to make myself at home, as she asked me to do. There were two bedrooms, to keep running costs down she rented the second bedroom to a colleague, one of the admin staff. We had no idea if she was home or not but we didn't keep particularly quiet other than the normal low voice one naturally uses late at night. I stood looking at the sofa, wondering how I was going to fold myself to sleep on it, as it was only a two-seater, while she made two cups of filtered coffee. Karen came into the lounge from the kitchen, placed the coffees on a low table next to the sofa and put some music on her record player. Sly & The Family Stone, Fresh album. The songs seemed quite mellow after the loud party music. I should have listened to the words, all the clues were in her music choice. We sat and chatted while drinking our coffees. When the music finished, she took the cups to the kitchen, came back into the lounge and declared she was going to bed. I asked if she had a blanket.

"Andy, don't be silly, come with me." With that, she took my hand and led me into her bedroom. I was so slow with girls, I honestly didn't read the situation at all, I genuinely thought she was offering her sofa for the night.

In the morning, we woke at about eight, I opened my eyes to see her smiling at me. She gave me a morning kiss, got out of bed naked and went to the kitchen to make coffee. I wasn't quite sure what had happened, she was seven years older than me, yet, at work my subordinate. She came back to bed with a coffee each. It was an awkward moment for me. Did this mean we were together now? Karen broke the silence.

"You know we can't be together. Fraternising at work is severely frowned upon." My heart sank, I knew I had fallen in love with her. "I'm sorry it wasn't very professional of me to lead you on." She added.

"So, I'm a one-night stand? Is that what you are saying?" I questioned,

"Not at all, I've loved you from the first day I met you, it was love at first sight."

"Me too" I replied, I could not understand why she fell in love with me, the boy from nowhere.

"I will be transferred to another department if they find out. I don't want that. I love working for you."

"Why?" I asked, "Why am I so different from any of the others?"

"Because you treat me like an equal, you never ask me to do anything you are not prepared to do yourself, you are polite and kind. Unlike some of those private school idiots. They treat women like a lesser being, something to show off and abuse. Plus, I have to admit, you are very handsome too. But I need to remain professional, I love my job, I do not want to lose it." I blushed, no one had ever said such nice words to me, I'd not had any girlfriends at school or since until now if that is the label I should give her. I could see her point though, tough as it was, there were security implications prohibiting staff from getting so close. I was prepared to quit my job today if it meant we could be together. I left for home around midday after a delightful morning together.

Not being able to be with Karen was difficult for me to cope with. I had fallen in love with her, I knew she liked me too, yet, we could not be together openly. To compensate, I spent the next few years enjoying all kinds of sports. I started windsurfing, a guy at Rickmansworth Aquadrome was giving lessons and I took to it straight away. I'd done some dinghy sailing with my father which made the principles of windsurfing easier. My Dad and I sailed an

Enterprise dinghy at a club at Henley-on-Thames. Later he bought a kit, a self-build Mirror dinghy. I helped to build the boat with him which was fun. The windsurfing took off well, my instructor, I and a few others formed the windsurfing section at Rickmansworth Sailing Club, Troy Lake, West Hyde.

I'm not sure if the windsurfing section still exists today. I also bought a Plancraft Stingray speedboat and learnt to water ski. I often went with friends to Swanage, Poole or Willen Lake near Milton Keynes for weekends water-skiing. I also had a go at parachuting at Sibson Airfield near Peterborough. In those days, we were trained to jump a solo static-line jump, I don't think tandem jumping had been invented yet. I spent a day learning how to do Parachute Landing Falls, or PLF's, which meant a lot of running and jumping off various heights forward, sideways, and backwards. The beginner group progressed by the end of a weekend to jumping out of a mock aircraft door on a short zip-line to practice every kind of PLF. Finally, we had to jump from just below the roof of the hanger on a fan-line, which was just a line wound around a winch on a fan. The fan provided resistance to slow your fall slightly. Some of the group dropped out at this point, they couldn't jump from so high. I completed the weekend course but the weather was too bad to try an actual jump from the club's Pilatus Porter aircraft. I went back a few weeks later and did my first static line jump, I did find the landing harder than I had been trained for, but it was not too painful. I was the only person in my jump group that landed on target, a circle of gravel in the field. Work and other matters prevented me from continuing with parachuting. I had plenty of other sports I preferred. However, I also had a love for flying, I'd had a go at trial flights in gliders and small aircraft, so I decided to try for my Private Pilot's Licence (PPL). In those days learning to fly was far easier and cheaper than today. I joined a Flying Club for Servicemen and women and affiliated civilians. I started flying a Cessna 172 from RAF Halton near Aylesbury, Buckinghamshire. Unfortunately, after starting the course, my instructor fell ill and died, my lessons were cancelled, my workload increased, one thing led to another and I never completed the course or achieved my PPL.

I also pushed loads of weights in the gym and attended men's keep-fit classes. All of this was my way to distract myself in my

The author water-skiing at Willen Lake, Milton Keynes.

spare time from thinking about girls, especially Karen, as well as to keep me very fit.

As computer systems became the norm and communicating on networks developed. It occurred to me this should be a quicker and simpler method for Karen and me to utilise. By now I had a computer at home and seldom went to London. My meetings were mostly outside the building in randomly selected venues, safer and more secure for private conversations. Many private clubs in the city became known meeting places, London seemed to be the spy centre of the world. As this list shows just a few well-known locations, anyone wanting to avoid being suspected a spy avoided Century House, as I did.

Tin and Stone Bridge, St James's Park. Between Buckingham Palace and the ministries of Whitehall, this location was used by British Intelligence (and may still be) as a meeting point with all manner of people. New recruits were often met here, the location instilling a sense of pride and importance in those about to embark upon a career in the Service.

In and Out Club, Piccadilly. A recruiting venue for MI5 and MI6, this address was also used in correspondence found on a dead British officer who was deliberately dropped into the sea off Spain by MI6 during the Second World War. Named Operation Mincemeat, this deception operation tricked the Nazis into believing the Normandy invasion force would land elsewhere. It is still a private members' club.

Boodle's, 28 St James's Street. This London club played host to many famous MI6 officers. It was an ideal location for events and recruiting. Ian Fleming, the creator of James Bond and an MI6 man, was a frequent visitor during his days in the city.

White's, 37-38 St James's Street. Another popular meeting point and recruitment venue, this members' club was used for decades by MI5 and MI6.

St Ermin's Hotel, Caxton Street. Used by MI6 as a Second World War operational centre. Parts of the building were also occupied by operatives from Britain's wartime Special Operations Executive (SOE).

The Tophams Hotel, 26 Ebury Court. A venue used extensively in the Second World War by officers from MI6 and the SOE. The SOE expanded greatly during the war, and this location hosted many foreign nationals who signed up to become agents.

Leconfield House, Mayfair. This building became MI5's headquarters in early 1945. Its original structure had specially designed windows to support machine guns, just in case the Germans ever reached London. Also, inside was an MI5 bar called the "Pig and Eye." Many famous names from the Service drank here, including Peter Wright, author of one of the world's most famous espionage books, Spycatcher.

18 Carlyle Square, Chelsea. This address was once home to one of Britain's most infamous spy figures, Kim Philby. Philby was an MI6 officer who became a top KGB spy, betraying many secrets to Moscow in the 1950s.

Brompton Oratory, Knightsbridge. At the beginning of the Cold War, the KGB planted dozens of agents in London. One of the most famous locations for exchanging information was this building. Packages were secreted behind pillars and collected by agents.

Holy Trinity Church, Knightsbridge. Just behind Brompton Oratory. It too was used by KGB agents as a "dead letter drop" – a form of spy tradecraft that involves the deposit and collection of secret materials. In this case, packages were tucked behind the statue.

Cafe Daquise, near South Kensington Tube. The cafe, which has been modernised, is a short walk from Brompton Oratory and was used by the KGB and other spy agencies for years. Perhaps two of its most famous clients were Christine Keeler, a London socialite in the Sixties, and John Profumo, Britain's Secretary of State for War. Unbeknown to Profumo, Keeler's other lover happened to be a top Soviet diplomat – Eugene Ivanov. The 1963 liaison became known as "The Profumo Affair" – a scandal that almost brought down the British Government.

Millennium Hotel, Knightsbridge. In 2006 this hotel unknowingly played host to a small party of Russians, at least one with a deadly agenda. Among the group, former KGB man and exile Alexander Litvinenko ordered a cup of green tea. Within days he fell critically ill, suffering from the effects of deadly Polonium-210, a particle of which had been slipped into his tea.

The list goes on! For me London was not the place to be, in my opinion, why would I want to be seen meeting and hanging around in these places. Business could be done outside the city, and that is how I operated. Despite how it seems, working for SIS is not a very dangerous job. Normally what happens in the services is that the risks are run by the agents – the people I and the other Officers recruit. For example, if I wanted to find out about a country's nuclear production tomorrow, I couldn't wander into a facility in that country, no matter how good my cover was. But I can recruit a scientist who is already there. Of course, if the operation goes tits up, the person who is usually going to suffer is the agent, not me.

A History of the Philippines

To understand this book's relevance and my role in the Philippines and President Ferdinand Marcos's covert surveillance. I will provide a short and concise history of the Philippines under President Marcos in order that you understand the reason why the British took such interest in the strategic geography of that country and the trade potential for Britain.

Known for running a corrupt, undemocratic regime, Ferdinand Marcos was the Philippines' President from 1965 to 1986, when, with the aid of the United States, he and his family fled to Hawaii.

Ferdinand Marcos.

Marcos was born on 11th September 1917 in the municipality of Sarrat; part of the Ilocos Norte province. He went to school in Manila and went on to law school at the University of the Philippines. His father, Mariano Marcos, was a Filipino politician. On 20th September 1935, after Julio Nalundasan defeated Mariano for a seat in the National Assembly for the second time, Nalundasan was shot and killed in his home. Ferdinand, Mariano and other family members were eventually tried for the assassination, and Ferdinand was found guilty of murder.

Appealing the verdict, Ferdinand argued on his own behalf to his country's supreme court and won an acquittal in 1940. Remarkably, while Marcos was preparing his case in jail, he was studying for the bar exam and became a trial lawyer in Manila after the acquittal. It has been reported that Judge Ferdinand Chua, who was also believed by some to be Marcos's actual biological father, awarded Marcos's freedom.

During World War II, Ferdinand Marcos served as an officer in his country's armed forces. Later claiming that he was also a top figure in the Filipino guerrilla resistance movement. United States government records eventually revealed this to be false. At the end of the war, when the American government granted the Philippines independence on 4th July 1946, the Philippine Congress was created. After working as a corporate attorney, Marcos campaigned and was twice elected as representative to his district, serving from 1949 to 1959.

Marcos married singer and beauty queen Imelda Romualdez in 1954 after an 11-day courtship. The couple went on to have three children: Maria Imelda "Imee" born 1955, Ferdinand "Bongbong" Marcos Jr., born 1957 and Irene, born 1960. The Marcoses later adopted a fourth child, Aimee.

In 1959, Marcos took a seat in the Senate, a position he would hold until he ran for and won the presidency in 1965 for the Nationalist Party. Marcos was inaugurated on 30th December 1965. His first presidential term was notable for sending troops into the Vietnam War, a move he had previously opposed as a Liberal Party senator. He also focused on construction projects and bolstering the country's rice production.

Marcos was re-elected in 1969, the first Filipino President to win a second term. Violence and fraud were associated with his campaign, which was believed to be funded with millions from the national treasury. What arose from the campaign unrest became known as the First Quarter Storm. Leftists took to the streets to demonstrate against both American involvement in Philippine affairs and the increasingly dictatorial style of Ferdinand Marcos. During his second term, he declared martial law in 1972, establishing with his wife Imelda an autocratic regime based on widespread favouritism that eventually led to economic stagnation and recurring reports of human rights violations. Imelda eventually becoming an official who often appointed her relatives to lucrative governmental and industrial positions.

Imelda would later be known for accumulating upward of 1,000 pairs of shoes and Manhattan luxury real estate. These acts were part of Marcos's state-imposed "crony capitalism." Private businesses were seized by the government and handed over to friends and relatives of regime members. This would later lead to much economic instability, though making domestic headway over time with infrastructure projects. Marcos's administration bolstered the military by huge numbers, curtailed public discourse, took over the media, and imprisoned political opponents, students and denouncers at will.

Marcos also oversaw a 1973 national referendum that allowed him to hold power indefinitely. Preceding a visit by Pope John Paul II, martial law ended in January 1981. Marcos, serving as both President and Prime Minister by this point, resigned from the latter post. He still retained the power to implement laws at his command and imprison dissenters without due process. In June 1981, he would win presidency for another six years, with his political opponents boycotting the vote.

On 21st August 1983, the previously jailed Benigno Aquino Jr. returned from his long exile to offer the Philippine people new hope. Aquino was shot and killed as he stepped off the plane in Manila. Countrywide demonstrations followed in the wake of the killing. Marcos launched a civilian-based independent commission whose findings implicated military personnel in Aquino's assassination. However, it has since been suggested that Marcos or his wife had ordered the murder.

With the country's economy plummeting and Aquino's murder becoming part of the national consciousness, the urban wealthy and middle class, often core supporters of Marcos, began to push for an end to his power. Also contributing to Marcos's downfall was a far-reaching Communist insurgency and the resolution signed in 1985 by 56 assemblymen. They called for his impeachment for enriching his personal coffers via crony capitalism, monopolies, and overseas investments that violated the law. To quiet the opposition and reassert his power, Marcos called for special presidential elections to be held in 1986, just over a year before the end of his current six-year term. The popular Corazon Aquino, the widow of assassinated Benigno, became the presidential candidate of the opposition.

Marcos managed to defeat Aquino and retained the presidency, but his victory was deemed by many to be fraudulent. As word spread of the rigged election, a tense standoff ensued between supporters of Marcos and those of Aquino, with thousands upon thousands of citizens taking to the streets to support a non-violent military rebellion.

With his health failing and support for his regime fading fast, on 25th February 1986, Ferdinand Marcos and much of his family were airlifted from the Manila presidential palace, going into exile in Hawaii. Evidence was later uncovered, showing that Marcos and his associates had stolen billions from the Philippine economy.

Focusing on racketeering charges, a federal grand jury then indicted both Ferdinand and Imelda Marcos. But Ferdinand died in Honolulu in 1989 from cardiac arrest after suffering from an array of ailments. Imelda was acquitted of all charges and returned to the Philippines the following year. However, she went on to face other legal challenges. She would later run unsuccessfully for President but win congressional elections, with two of her three children, Imee and Ferdinand Jr., also serving as governmental officials.

When the Marcos's went into exile, they took with them a reported $15 million. However, the government of the Philippines was aware Marcos had collected a far more considerable fortune. The country's supreme court estimated he had amassed $10 billion while in office.

Since 1993 Marcos's corpse had been embalmed in a glass casket in his home province of Ilocos Norte. In 2016, President Rodrigo Duterte ordered Marcos's body to be buried at the National Heroes' Cemetery in Manila, with protests erupting in opposition to such a move considering Marcos's human rights abuses. Nonetheless, in November, Marcos's remains were interred at the new site in a hero's burial.

Marcos is renowned for controversial actions, bombings, killing innocent civilians, murders of the opposition and activists and lying about his own history. The most significant controversy arising from Marcos's service during World War II was his claims during the 1962 Senatorial Campaign of being "the most decorated war hero of the Philippines." He claimed to have been the recipient of thirty-three war medals and decorations, including the Distinguished Service Cross and the Medal of Honour. Still, researchers later found that stories about Marcos's wartime exploits were mostly propaganda, being inaccurate or untrue. Only two of the supposed thirty-three awards - the Gold Cross and the Distinguished Service Star - were given during the war. Both had been contested by Marcos's superiors.

I do not want to bore you with more of Marcos history that you may or may not know. Still, I should provide you with a reason why the British were so interested in Marcos, and the reason is, in its simplest form, the USA. Money, of course, big money, lots of money. With a strategic location, the proximity to China, Asia and

East Russia. America has military bases in the Philippines. They have to protect their investment. Americans being Americans, will protect their assets by whatever means, even if they are cruel and murderous. Americans, or at least the American Government and its agencies, have no moral standard. They are prepared to allow other regimes to do their dirty work through departments such as the CIA. Possibly the dirtiest agency in the world, in my opinion. Of course, what you are permitted to see and know through the mainstream media is carefully controlled in America's favour. Another view is that Britain and USA had an agreement to share information. If we knew something we were obliged to pass it on. Though in my opinion we only ever passed what we wanted them to know and I always felt it was a pretty one way street.

Under intense pressure from the administration of Lyndon B. Johnson, Marcos reversed his pre-presidency position of not sending Philippine forces to the Vietnam War. He consented to a limited involvement, asking Congress to approve sending a combat engineer unit. Despite opposition to the new plan, the Marcos government gained Congressional approval. Philippine troops were sent in the middle of 1966 as the Philippines Civic Action Group (PHILCAG). PHILCAG reached a strength of some 1,600 soldiers in 1968. Between 1966 and 1970, over 10,000 Filipino soldiers served in South Vietnam, mainly involved in civilian infrastructure projects.

My role was one of not only watching Marcos's behaviour closely, but also monitoring communications between Marcos and the USA too. Most importantly, it should be done covertly to not upset the UK/USA relationship, which was supposed to be friendly, an image created purely for the public eye. In my opinion and from observation, the reality was very different.

Inheriting the Philippines

A new opportunity was presented to me in April 1975. I was offered the job to control intelligence gathering in the Philippines. The Intelligence Officer that ran that station was due to retire. For reasons unknown, I was presented with an offer to take over. I was invited to a meeting at the Millennium Hotel, London.

Maurice Oldfield, head of MI6 at that time, often went to the Millennium. I suspected that as there were rumours he was gay he used this place often to meet young men. My suspicion was simply that, I had no evidence to support it. I had no evidence nor looked for any. This meeting took place in one of the event rooms, a room with a table and chairs for twelve people. Maurice sat at the head of the table. Two others were seated to his right. The room, typical of the hotel group was business-like yet warm and comfortable. There was no echo like some other venues of this nature. It was also soundproof, and no doubt regularly swept for listening bugs by a British Intelligence specialist team. I knew this room was used often for Intelligence meetings.

I had been given some idea of the nature of the meeting. I was a little nervous. As always, I never liked meeting my peers in the Service as I knew they always treated me as an outsider, not being from the same background as them. I was an experiment, proof that accepting Officers from outside the usually closed ranks of the upper class, connected and ruling classes would be detrimental to the Service. I had so far proven them wrong. It was they who were coming to me for information, information from my personal database.

Maurice remained seated as I was ushered into the room by an overt MI6 security guard in the corridor outside. I was expected, and the guard required no ID. The two men next to Maurice stood to shake hands with me as I approached. I held out a hand to Maurice, he was my boss, but I felt that didn't give him the right to ignore a polite greeting. He was trying to create an air of formality, but it didn't work with me. We had met many times before, and his behaviour that day was out of character. Maybe it was because we had never met in the company of others before, and he wanted to demonstrate his status. When we had met previously, we were alone.

The first man to the left of Maurice was Francis, his handshake weak and limp. I had met him before, head of HUMINT or human intelligence. He headed the team that received and collated all human-sourced information from Officers like me that, in turn, gleaned information from agents on the ground around the world.

Francis welcomed me in a friendly enough way, after all, we had the same rank, but I did get the feeling he was expecting me to not produce the anticipated results in this job. But that was just my own neurotic mind. He looked quite weaselly, clean, yet he had that greasy hair look and round rimless glasses like a stereo-typical German SS officer from WWII. I always felt I could trust him to grass me up if I ever messed up. He was the kind that was probably bullied at school for good reason. He said he looked forward to working with me and that he heard good things about my work. Yeh, of course he did, he was one of those that had come to me for information and was weaselly enough not to thank me in front of Maurice just in case I got some credit. I turned my eyes away from him and looked at the other guy present.

Christopher was in his sixties, retirement age. Even at this age, he had a voice to die for, dry with a slow drawl. He should have been an actor in cowboy films if he could put on an American accent. His voice would be like Bradly Cooper from the movie "A Star is Born" with Lady Gaga. Christopher's voice was a little faster. I liked him instantly. He wasn't good-looking or anything beyond the service requirement to be grey man in appearance, a look necessary for a spy that can remain invisible in a crowd. But that voice! His handshake was that of a man at least, unlike Francis. I like a good handshake from a man. He spoke, "Good to meet you Andy, are you up to this? The Philippines is a tough country."

"Well, I've survived the critics in Century House, so it should be a doddle." I replied. Century House was then the headquarters of MI6 in London. My comment brought a polite laugh to all the men present, "I expect it to be a challenge, of course, but I'll take a fresh look at things, and I'm confident I can produce good work."

In front of Christopher, there was a pile of files on the table. I noticed his name on the cover of the top folder. Christopher Mass, seriously!

"Do you prefer your name shortened to Chris? Shall I call you Chris?" It sounded as though I was trying to be less formal, but in fact, it was an awful attempt at a joke.

"No, I much prefer my name in full." Christopher replied in an aloof tone hoping to stop my following comment in its tracks.

"I like Chris, it's easier, I'm going to call you Chris." I stated, "Chris Mass."

I shouldn't have been so rude so early in the handover. But, with these Oxbridge types, I preferred to let them know early on I wasn't going to take any of the usual crap from them. Luckily, Maurice interrupted before any more was said.

"Chris." Maurice's intentional slip let me know he got the joke. I don't know if anyone had realised before Christopher's name was quite silly, but that was my poor sense of humour at work. His Derbyshire farmer's background had a sense of humour too. "I have recommended Andy for this position for a good reason. I trust him fully, and I have no doubt he can continue your good work professionally and thoroughly. If you have any doubts about his ability, then talk to me, but my choice isn't going to be questioned right now."

"I wasn't questioning his ability." Chris said, "but his inexperience abroad doesn't equal the importance of the post."

Maurice and I had always got on well. I appreciated his confidence in me, but I could hold my own with these people. I didn't need his help, but I decided to stay quiet and listen.

Francis jumped in now, full of his own importance. He began as though he was running this section when, in fact, he was the collector and collator of the material that others would pass him. Not that it isn't important, but it's a zero-risk job and one that he tried to raise in profile. Some people can talk the talk, while others walk the walk, Francis was a talker.

Francis went through the files, all three men speaking when there was a point to be made to me on any particular subject. It was interesting work, and I listened to every word. I had a lot to learn, and the content of the files was good. I knew what I had to do, but my interest was what the content contained. I hadn't realised the country's significance. President Marcos was dangerous, and I did need to be particularly careful how I ran agents in Manila or elsewhere, for their safety. The CIA had influence in the area of course.

After a couple of hours, Maurice called a break, and he went off to make calls. Teas and coffees were ordered for us, the time-out was welcome. It is arduous work studying such matters. Christopher questioned me while we sipped our drinks.

"Have you established any agents before?" he asked.

"Yes, I have several, they are working well and providing good intel." I replied, "I recruited them and turned them with no problem." I didn't want him to think I was a total amateur newbie. By now, I had a few years' experience. I had, of course, agents under my control, but the Philippines was a long way away, and I had no experience in Asia. As I talked to the two men, it was clear that they thought I was lower, less important, than them. They didn't speak to me as an equal. As Maurice himself had said, my reputation was exemplary, so why this attitude toward me. I was used to being talked down to by others. It was a class thing that they probably would never let go, but I certainly wasn't going to let them bully me. I don't give in to bullies, never had and never will. I felt I would need to put them in their place quite quickly.

After a quarter of an hour, Maurice returned. He sat down at the table and the two men sat next to him as before, ready to resume the briefing. I spoke first.

"Maurice, I've had a few hours looking at Christopher's work. While it's good, it's not good enough. There is not one agent close to President Marcos, no one in his office. There's little FININT, not one agent capable of direct access to his banks. The only FININT we have is American money. These files contain good stuff, but they must improve, if you want me to take over this post, I will get better intel than this. I want a fresh approach. I hope your recommendation is that I run this area and I have carte blanche. The agents are going stale. I think it's time to refresh the lot of them."

I saw Christopher flush with anger that I was putting down his life's work. Francis's jaw dropped at my overconfidence. Maurice answered, "Andy, I've seen your work. You are precisely the reason I'm handing you the Philippines. I believe and trust in you, and you do a great job, but don't get overconfident and cocky. don't let your personal class war cloud your vision."

"I won't let you down, Maurice. Just let me do things my way. I'll update you as often as you require. One thing is for certain, I can do better work than this." I said, pointing at the pile of files on the table.

Christopher interjected, feeling the need to justify his work, "Maurice! Andy's claim is preposterous. You can't let him just junk my agents. It's taken me years, the intel coming in is good, my..."

Maurice held his hand up to stop him, "Christopher, I'm handing this over to Andy. The Philippines will be his now. While different to everyone else's, his methods always get us the results we need, don't question his ability. I'm bringing this meeting to an end. Your work is done. It's Andy's now. Enjoy your retirement."

With that, he stood, shook Francis and Christopher by the hand, thanking them for their time today. He turned to me and shook my hand too, the handshake was longer and more sincere, I had his full confidence. I was honoured and smiled in thanks. I gathered the pile of folders containing Christopher's life work and followed Maurice out of the room. I felt good, confident, not overconfident, but serious about the task just handed to me. Most of all, Maurice had told these guys my lack of education or class wasn't going to be my downfall. All I had to do now was live up to his expectation. I didn't look back at the two men leaving the meeting room behind us. No smirking was necessary. It was the last time I saw Christopher. I required no further meetings with him.

I took a taxi to Century House. Karen, my secretary, of course, was at her desk, working hard, I kept her busy, and she loved the work and me. As I entered her office, she greeted me with a beautiful smile, I gave her a kiss as she sat at her desk. Her kisses were always soft, her perfume beautiful and expensive. I told her about the meeting as I walked through to my adjoining office. She got up from her desk, made coffee and sat next to me on the sofa to hear the news I had.

I explained that I intended to find new agents. "The current people in the Philippines were not producing high-quality intel, in my opinion."

"Are you crazy?" she exclaimed, "you can't get rid of all his agents just like that! It will take ages to get new people that you can trust."

"It makes sense to me. I'm sure the current agents won't trust me. It's easier and better to find my own." I said a little overconfidently.

"Are you going to move to Manila?" Karen asked.

"No, I can't. I will do everything from here."

"Impossible!" she declared.

"Well, we will see." My claim was more in hope than anything else.

I didn't want to live in Manila or anywhere in the Philippines. For one thing, I knew I couldn't stand the heat, and secondly, I just thought I could manage everything from London. My family and friends had no idea what I did. As far as anyone knew, I worked for my father in his printing company. My father was the only person outside the Service that had any idea what I did. He often covered for me when I needed to go away. We never told my mother or anyone else. My work was a total secret. I liked it that way. I had to lie a lot about what I was doing. I found it easy to lie, SIS calls it acting.

"How long have you got to set things up?" Karen asked.

"A few months, Christopher will retire as soon as I say I am ready."

"Well, good luck with that time scale." Karen said as she returned to her desk. She turned in the doorway through to her office, "dinner tonight? Stay over if you like." She asked. Karen was seven years older than me, beautiful and perfect in every way. She was extremely good-looking, intelligent and from a banking family, she was well off financially.

"Persuade me." I said, jokingly enticing her to behave badly right here in the office. It was always a risk, but most times, the threat of losing our jobs we judged as minimal.

Karen walked back into my office like a model, one foot crossing over the other as she stepped forward. Her face seductive and intent on fulfilling my request. She unbuttoned the top two buttons of her white shirt and a sexy cleavage burst into view as she reached where I was sitting. She leaned on the arm of the sofa, swinging her chest side to side, her back arched, her curvy bum looking irresistible in the pencil skirt she filled perfectly. She spoke in a sexy tone,

"Andy, if you don't stay tonight, you will miss this." She ran a finger down her cleavage, pulling her shirt lower. She grabbed my head and pulled it close to her chest. Her perfume was divine, the view no man could resist.

"If you go home." she spoke as she backed away to her room, "you won't get your hands on these" she cupped her bosoms tantalisingly in her hands and shook them at me as she left my room. Karen was good at sex. She had taught me everything, she was older and more experienced in bedroom matters.

"Ok, you've convinced me." I exclaimed, "you know how to send out an invite." I smiled. "We can go home together when I've finished going through these files. I need to learn this lot." I opened my Samsonite briefcase and dumped the files onto my desk. Karen rebuttoned her shirt and sat at her desk to continue her work and no doubt planned another night of pleasure for me. It's an excellent way to work with this sexy woman, always full of fun and laughter.

Working with me, she was rarely negative or low, always professional, and my best friend.

I worked through the folders of files, some of which were profiles of the agents Christopher ran. These were the files I was most interested in now. By the time I had memorised them, I had a clear idea that I definitely should, at the very least, find more agents closer to President Marcos as he *was* the Philippines. Nothing happened there without Marcos saying so.

The President wasn't all bad. He had done some good in his early days. Before his inauguration on 30th December 1965, there was no electricity or mains water. He continued to work on the infrastructure, having just signed a deal on 28th August 1974 with the Asian Development Bank for a $51.3 million US dollar loan to develop the metro manila water supply system. It was the bank's most significant and largest loan ever at the time. That was on top of a loan from Kuwait on 24th June for $17 million. But now, it all began to go downhill for the population. The Philippines had been under Martial Law since September 1972.

Government forces shut down media outlets, including broadsheets the Manila Times, Daily Mirror, Manila Chronicle, Manila Daily Bulletin, Philippine Daily Express, Philippines Herald and Philippine Free Press. National Media outlets owned by Marcos's crony Roberto Benedicto were exempted, namely the newspaper Daily Express and television and radio stations of the Kanlaon Broadcasting System.

In the hours following Marcos's martial law announcement, hundreds of media practitioners and opposition figures were arrested, including Senators Francisco Soc Rodrigo, Jose Diokno, and Ramon Mitra Jr., joining Senator Benigno Aquino, who had been arrested the day before the formal declaration. As well as the media, demonstrations were banned.

The Marcos family began to plunder the wealthy and take land for projects that enhanced his own, or his family's vanity or personal wealth. All in the eyes of the Americans and often seemingly with their blessing. The American concern was purely for maintaining their military bases considered to be of such strategic high value. Marcos was definitely anti-communist. The Americans would see to it that Marcos would be supported, unconcerned about the atrocities Marcos and his family would orchestrate.

I was taking over from Christopher at a most challenging time. Martial law would mean I could be intensely scrutinised on entry to the country. Luckily for me, the "Thriller in Manila" Heavyweight World Championship boxing match between Muhammad Ali and Joe Frazier was to be held on 2nd October at the Araneta Coliseum Cubao, Quezon City. I would use this to invisibly enter the country among the crowds from across the world and set up my new spy ring.

I now had a clearer idea of how my plan could work, it relied a lot on luck, but luck, it seems, can be controlled to some extent.

Agent 1, Rosa

At the end of September 1975, I took two weeks' leave from my father's printing company. I had tickets to Manila, a long flight on my own, including two changes of flights. It was over thirty hours, and with the seven-hour time difference, I arrived tired and jet-lagged. Tickets hadn't been easy to get. It seemed like the entire world wanted to see the boxing match. I wasn't interested in that. I was going on business. Karen had arranged for a driver to collect me from Manila Airport. It was busy and crowded with people arriving for the big fight. President Marcos sought to hold the bout in Metro Manila. He sponsored it to bring attention to the Philippines as a 'great' nation, having declared martial law three years earlier.

I found my driver easily at the exit. A privately arranged car and driver, I didn't want any association with the British Embassy at all. The embassy staff knew of my existence, of course, but I didn't keep them informed of my movements at all. Jonny, my driver, was a lovely happy chap despite the conditions in Manila for ordinary folk. Karen had arranged the car for me using an alias company name. I had many alias companies for such occasions. Officially, or as far as the Philippine authorities knew, I was here on business on procurement, seeking wood carvings and other artefacts for export. That would give me a cover story to interview anyone to set up a new office in the city. I had so much to do, and I had to do it on an impossible time scale. I had two weeks to find and rent a small office, set up trusted staff, find agents, establish secret drop points, set up communication methods and leave without any suspicion of the real nature of my work here. The time scale was a real worry. What I was trying to achieve would typically take months or years. But I didn't want to remain for longer, as this would arouse suspicion back at home among friends and family. I'd face questions on my return. It had to look like a holiday trip. Of course, when no one is looking for suspicious activity, it's easier to hide it.

My driver Jonny was my first stroke of luck. He was amenable to anything I wanted, and he was prepared to work 24/7. It was mid-morning as we left the airport, a little early to check into the hotel, so I asked him to take me on a quick tour of the city to get my bearings a little. I asked him to drive past a few significant landmarks, including the presidential palace, Malacañang Palace.

At that time, surprisingly, there wasn't much in the way of places to see, but we drove around the city, a city full of traffic and travel was slow. At least not as bad as today, where the traffic is so heavy most main streets are at a standstill and depending on your car registration, you can only drive on certain days of the week. What struck me was the contrast between the rich and the poor. The poor lived in shanty houses, wooden, crammed into tiny spaces, run down and made of scraps of anything. The owner could build with a tin sheet here, a pallet there and wood that is not suitable for building at all. Little children could be seen, some with few clothes, some naked and almost none had shoes. It was the first time I saw such poverty in such a large city. There were, of course, more affluent houses and gated estates, all within feet of the slum areas.

We drove past the palace. There wasn't much to see from Jose Laurel Street, the palace was low and set back from the road. I counted seven gates. It was unclear to me, as we drove past, which would be the main entrance, each gate had a plaque with a name on it, and there were seven on this road. Jonny told me the palace backed directly onto the Pasig River, and there was a river entrance for the occupants. Half a mile further after the palace, we took a left turn over the Ayala Bridge. A mile further on was my hotel, The Manila Hotel.

Karen's choice of hotel couldn't have been better. Outside security seemed higher than at any usual hotel. Imelda Marcos was known to frequently visit this hotel. There was no red carpet out today, so I assumed she was not expected. Jonny dropped me outside the reception, and the concierge ordered bellboys to take my bags inside. I asked Jonny to make himself available later in the afternoon and expect to be out late. He was such a happy chap, always smiling and always ready to do anything for me.

The reception was vast and grand, chandeliers hung from wooden ceilings and a sense of luxury prevailed. Most importantly, the air conditioning made the place cool from the oppressive heat outside. In the few seconds I spent walking from the car to the entrance, my shirt was instantly wet with my sweat. I would always struggle with the heat and humidity of the Philippines. I was glad I had decided not to move here more permanently. I checked in and was shown to my room. It was a sunset suite, a two-room suite with window views to the west, which, I assumed, would provide a great view of the sunset in the evening. The room was beautiful and well-furnished, classical yet bright. One room was my bedroom with a sliding double door to isolate it from the lounge area. In the lounge there was a sofa, two armchairs and a desk in front of the window.

I needed to start work right away. I was on a tight time schedule. I called reception and asked if the manager would come to my room as soon as possible. Just as I finished unpacking my cases, he arrived with another staff member presumably to deal with whatever problem I had.

He appeared apologetic, expecting me to have a complaint or a problem with my room. I told him the room was excellent and perfect for my needs. Which cheered him up, yet he had a worried look on his face as he didn't understand why I had summoned him when I was happy with my room. I told him I was here on business, that I was looking to do big business while in Manila, which would be good for his country. I was looking to employ staff to open an office in the city. I asked him if he could provide me with a staff member to assist if he would be so kind. I needed to interview people for various jobs, and I needed help ushering interviewees to my room and to do other work for me personally. Of course, I expected to pay for the service.

It was an unusual request, but the manager assured me he could help, and he would find someone and send them to my room shortly. The hotel was big enough to have spare staff around, even with the extra influx of tourists coming to Manila for the boxing match.

Before I left for Manila, Karen had placed adverts in various publications for an office manager to run an office that I intended to rent. Interviews would begin the next day. Today, I would scan the papers for a property, and I found several that looked good. I sat at the desk in my room, working my way through the shortlist I made, calling various agencies with the intention to view some the next day. I was very jetlagged, but time was so short I had to push through the tiredness. Early evening, I took a much-needed break and went for dinner in the hotel restaurant.

As I walked through the lobby to find the restaurant, the manager stopped me to introduce me to the staff member who would assist me the following morning. An attractive young girl in the hotel's uniform. I asked her to join me at my table to have a chat. We were directed to a table in a secluded corner of the restaurant. She was shy and pretty, I found the dark shiny hair of the Asian girls here quite attractive. I told her that I needed her in the morning to usher anyone coming for their interview to my room. I asked her to get them to wait on arranged chairs in the corridor outside my room.

My advert had invited prospective interviewees to come to the hotel from 9 a.m. She was to take names and addresses, and basic information before they would be invited into my room for the interview. That way, I could read their qualifications and experience as they came in. The girl, aptly named Angel, assured me she could manage that job and seemed pretty capable. She told me her regular job was team-leader for housekeeping, which meant she had some brains too. I asked her to be available from 8:30 a.m. the next day and she seemed happy with that. She left me to my excellent dinner, declining the offer to join me to eat. By the time I finished my meal and a few glasses of wine had kicked in, the jetlag won the battle for sleep. I returned early to my room and collapsed onto my bed, asleep before I hit the sheets.

The morning arrived by surprise, I was woken by a knocking on my door, and I looked at my watch. Because of jetlag and the time difference, my body was totally out of sync with Manila time. It was already 8:30a.m.! My body was somewhere between 01:30 English time and the time here. I had overslept, the curtains doing an excellent job of blocking out the morning sunlight. I leapt out of bed and threw on a hotel dressing gown to open the door. Angel was there, surprised I was not ready. I apologised and invited her in. She looked a little reluctant at first, but she entered the room after a quick glance around.

I can understand her need to be professional, but I was late and now had to get ready in double-quick time. This was not a great start to our working relationship. I asked her to order breakfast and coffee to consume in my room. She stood at the desk in the lounge to phone through my order as I dashed into my bedroom and went through my wardrobe to find fresh clothes. Angel finished the breakfast order and had the initiative to come through and make my bed for me. She worked in the hotel housekeeping department so it took no time at all. I asked her if she had any embarrassing stories about people taking liberties in their room with such a pretty girl. She giggled a reply as I found my clothes. Apparently, many men try to take advantage of the housekeeping girls. I apologised again, I don't know why. She seemed to understand my situation and told me to throw out my nightwear, and she folded them for me and placed them under my pillow. I liked this girl's initiative. I shaved and showered in double-quick time and emerged from the bathroom, almost ready for work.

I asked her if anyone had arrived for the interview. She again giggled and said many people were waiting. Angel asked me to take a look outside my room. I opened the room door and leant out, the queue was all the way down the corridor! Mostly young girls, a few males, some of dubious gender. Angel told me there were also many in the lobby, and other staff were controlling the numbers at the front door. I hadn't considered how desperate the people were for work here. I couldn't interview all these people, I would be here for days. I told Angel I needed a quick solution to reduce the number of people waiting. I asked her to work her way down the line of people and tell anyone under twenty-five years old to leave. Anyone with less than five years' experience as a manager should go. Anyone else she just didn't like the look of should also leave. I would trust her judgment. Angel left the room to get on with the work I had just given her as my breakfast arrived. It was ageist and unfair, but I had to do something. I was very conscious of drawing way too much attention to myself and my activities, and I needed the afternoon free to go look at properties.

I gobbled a little breakfast and slurped a coffee down, went to the door, and looked out. Angel was there with a clipboard taking notes from people and quite bravely turning people away. As the queue reduced, she got on her walkie-talkie and called someone downstairs to send more people up. I asked the first person in the now bewildered-looking queue to come into my room, and I sat at my desk. I motioned the lady to sit at a chair opposite and began a long line of questioning. I am quite good at first impressions, I knew within moments if I liked someone or not.

Most of the interviewees were just desperate to get work and quite nervous. None seemed to be what I was looking for. After an hour or so of relatively quick unsuccessful interviewing, each person taking five minutes to interview, a lady sat in front of me. She handed me her resumé. She introduced herself as Rosa Malabanan, aged thirty-nine, married, with ten years' experience managing a busy Estate Agency. I thought to myself, not quite the right profession, but I was looking for an office manager, and she fitted the bill. She told me the Estate Agency had closed down a few months previous. She had a kind smile, a very quiet and professional demeanour, and was actually quite attractive, not that it mattered for the job, and she didn't appear nervous or desperate.

I took to her instantly, there was something about her. As it turned out, she would be my first stroke of luck in this mammoth task. After about two minutes of interviewing her, I knew she would be right. I told her there and then that I would shortlist her, and she could expect a second interview very soon. I told her a little about the job. I expected her to run a small office space, which I had not acquired yet. I told her the business was procurement for a variety of goods and she would have to handle the export papers and so on. Because time was so tight, I didn't waste much time chatting too much, but I instinctively knew she would be suitable for the job. Then quite a surprising thing happened. Rosa asked me if I was going to work with the Philippine government or the President. I said no, I was not looking for government contracts, but of course, I might have to get an export licence. She told me that her son had gone missing, he was a student, a bit of an activist, and he had disappeared one night. He had been taken by plain-clothed police, according to witnesses. She continued to explain that she had no idea whether he was dead or in prison. She hated the Marcos regime for doing this to her son. This was a very brave thing to say aloud to a stranger in this country, but a mother suffering from the loss of a son was an animal cornered. I could not believe how my visit to Manila was going. This was perfect. I could probably get her onside quite easily if she had this hatred for her President stewing inside her.

I decided right there and then, I told her she had the job, and I would ask the others to leave. She couldn't have looked happier. I stood to shake her hand to congratulate her success. She was most surprised I made such a quick decision. I told her that I know a good person when I see one and look forward to a great working relationship. I realised I hadn't mentioned money in my excitement. I sat back down at my desk and motioned for her to do the same. I offered her coffee. I asked Rosa how much she thought the job was worth. This is always a difficult question for an interviewee. If the candidate asks too much, they might price themselves out of the job. If too low, it may devalue their worth. Rosa didn't hesitate. She wanted the equivalent of £5 ($6.50) per week. That was quite good pay for a Filipina in 1975. Rosa was smart and knew my eagerness to employ her meant she could pitch high. I liked her more for her intelligence and forwardness. I leaned back in my chair and eyed her deliberately for a moment. Her expression didn't falter, she held her stance.

"Ok." I said, "here's my proposal. For the first 3 months, you will work for 350 Philippine pesos (Php) per week, about £5 or about $6.50 US Dollars. If you prove yourself worthy after that, you will receive 475 Php per week. How does that sound?" Her face changed to a beautiful broad smile, a slight glint of a tear in her eye.

"Sir, I don't know what to say. I promise I will be worthy. I will prove to you I am good at my work. I won't let you down."

"I am sure you won't let me down." I knew the hatred she had for the President and his population's oppression would be useful. I couldn't let this stroke of luck and opportunity pass.

"Sir, may I ask when you would like me to start? I am available for you right away."

"Right away Rosa?"

"Yes sir."

"Today?" I asked, expecting her to falter.

"May I fetch you another coffee, sir?" she said. In her mind, right away meant right away. I liked her gutsy attitude. We were going to get on really well, I could tell.

"I tell you what, Rosa, I have appointments to see some properties this afternoon. Would you join me and I would be happy to get your opinion on them? After all, it is you that will be working there, and as an ex-estate agent, you should know the business."

"Yes sir." she replied without hesitation. I stood up to walk to the door. Rosa followed me. As I walked, I asked her,

"Would you like to go home and come back after lunch?"

"I live too far away sir, I can wait in the lobby for you." I hadn't learnt all the city zones yet and I hadn't any idea where she lived. I opened the door, stepped into the corridor and asked Angel to tell everyone waiting to leave as the position was filled. I offered my apologies to those within earshot. I turned back to Rosa,

"Well then, join me for lunch, please. Lesson one, Rosa, I am your boss, but you are to treat me as a friend, and if at all possible, please stop calling me sir! My name is Andy."

"Yes sir." she replied. We looked at each other, and I laughed. This was the beginning of a very long relationship. Rosa became an excellent member of my staff and a lifelong friend. I could not believe how lucky I had been to find her, it was a very quick decision and the right one, it was that easy. Even after I closed down my Manila office and our friendship continued, Rosa still called me sir.

I realised it was only 10:20 a.m., too early for lunch, but there was too much to do to sit around and wait. Rosa and I got to work immediately. We sat opposite each other at my desk, and I showed her the details of the properties we were going to view that afternoon. Rosa was immediately invaluable. Her local knowledge was so useful. She was able to sift out properties in the wrong areas or properties she knew were in poorly managed buildings. Her knowledge as an estate agent came in very useful indeed. I was impressed by her efficiency and capability right away. I patted myself on the back for making a great choice with her and hoped in all hope the remainder of my time here would be this easy.

Angel knocked on my door to ask if I had any further work for her. I invited her in to meet the successful candidate. I thanked her for her excellent work controlling and managing the queues of people. I shook hands and slipped her 200Php, more than half a week's pay. She looked at it.

"No sir." I looked at Rosa, and we smiled at the joke. Angel didn't get it, she wasn't in on this one, and it was too complicated to explain.

"The hotel will bill you for my time." Angel told me.

"No, that is for your good work Angel, it's for you."

"Sir thank you, may I ask you a question." she looked sheepish being so forward, I beckoned to her to ask, "are you looking for any other staff?"

"Why? Are you not happy working here? You do a good job as far as I have seen."

"No sir, my cousin is looking for work. She currently works in Malacañang Palace. She is unhappy and isn't treated particularly well. She asked me to keep a lookout for other work for her. She was in the queue outside, but I had to turn her away as she was too young."

I liked Angel for her bravery for asking and her loyalty to her cousin. To say out loud someone in the palace is unhappy could cause you to end up in prison, or worse, that was the nature of Marcos. I could not believe my luck! This was unbelievable.

"Can you fetch her? Has she gone already?"

"She is still in the lobby sir, just in case I could ask you."

"Tell her to come up right away."

Angel left to fetch her cousin. I shouted after her, "Angel, can you keep yourself available in case I have more work for you to do?"

"Yes sir, of course."

I wasn't sure if I needed her now, but I wanted to keep my options open. A few minutes later, Angel knocked on the door again. Rosa answered it for me as I was sitting at my desk on the wrong side to get to the door quickly. Angel entered with a very pretty, shy young girl following behind. The girl's shiny black hair catching the light.

"Sir, may I introduce my cousin, Trisha."

"Come in Trisha, please sit." I motioned to the chair opposite my desk. Angel left the room, and Rosa went to leave too, but I asked her to stay. I would take a considerable risk letting her see my game so early in our relationship, but I had to take a few chances as time wasn't on my side. Even though I liked her, Rosa was a total stranger, but she had a way about her that made me trust her right away. I wanted to test her loyalty to me already. Rosa sat on the sofa to my right to listen. She had no clue why she should be here or what role I had in mind for Trisha.

Agent 2, Trisha

My plan, all be it made up spontaneously, was to get Rosa to know the actual role she would be taking on if she went along with the treasonable work I was expecting of her. I introduced myself to Trisha by name only, not what I did. I asked,

"What kind of work do you think you can do for me in an export business?" The question surprised her as she had come for an interview as an office manager. She was very shy and clearly not qualified for admin work.

"Well, sir." she thought a second or two before saying, "I can clean, make food and drink and answer the phone."

"Ok, Rosa has been taken on for the role of manager. I'm not sure that she needs that kind of help. The office just won't be that busy." I told her. Her face dropped as she realised there was nothing for her. I continued,

"So how would you like to double the money you make at the moment?" She had no clue what I was going to suggest. Poor Trisha had a puzzled look on her face. But a very slight smile, a look of excitement let me know the promise of money was going to work.

"Doing what job? I'm not sure what you mean, sir?" she replied. Maybe she had a fear that I was about to propose something inappropriate.

"I'm told you are unhappy in your current work. Which is what?" I asked.

"I work in Malacañang Palace. I am a servant for Madam Marcos. I help her dress and look after her wardrobe."

"I hear she has an extensive wardrobe. That must be a big job?" I asked.

"It is busy. When Madam Marcos is away, I still have to make sure her clothes and shoes are clean and all in the right place. She is not a nice woman. She bullies all her staff. She is rude and quite spiteful when we make mistakes."

"Do you make many mistakes?"

"It is easy to do things wrong. We are expected to know what madam needs. When we don't read her mind properly, she gets cross and is rude to us."

"When she is away, do you go with her?"

"No, she takes the Ladies Maid and one other, not me. The President takes his valet and staff."

"And you don't like your job? It must be quite interesting meeting the President and the First Lady?"

"I like the job, but not the people. The First Lady is difficult for me to get on with. I do my best, but most times, my best isn't good enough for her." She stopped talking, realising she just told me she wasn't very good at her job.

"Ok. I understand. May I ask, how long have you worked for Madam Marcos?"

"I have been there for two years." Trisha replied.

"That is a long time to put up with a job that you don't like!" I stated.

"Yes, but what is my alternative? I have no other skills."

I put Trisha out of her misery.

"If I ask you to stay in the job you have, and you agree, I will pay you extra. Is that something that would make your work easier?"

"I don't understand?" I glanced at Rosa too. She was looking equally puzzled.

"For my business, I want someone inside the palace. Perhaps you will hear something that may give me a head start over others in the same line of work. You let me know about anything you hear, and then I get a lead over my competitors. I make more money, and you benefit too."

"I don't hear much business talk, I work in the bedrooms." She complained.

"It doesn't matter to me. I want to hear everything you hear. Maybe, you don't realise the relevance of what is being said. For instance, Mrs Marcos may talk about new jewellery. I could go to the shop where she buys from, and I could offer that shop a new range to sell to her. Getting a head start will help my business grow." I glanced at Rosa. She could see I was bullshitting. I would handle her shortly. Trisha wasn't smart enough to know what I was doing, Rosa probably was.

"Is it legal?" Trisha asked.

"Many things in business probably cross a grey line of legality. But a head start is for winners. I would say it's a grey area."

"And you would pay me when I give you information?" Trisha was taking the money bait.

"I will pay you a regular fee each month." Trisha thought for a moment. I allowed it to sink in to see if she realised what I was asking. Trisha didn't indicate she knew what I was saying or what she would be doing for me. She was too innocent and immature.

"That is what you mean by double my pay? I get paid by the palace and by you?"

"Yes, if you agree."

"250 pesos per week?" Trisha asked.

"If that is what you would like to earn, yes."

"What if I can't give you anything of use?"

"Tell me everything you hear. Let me judge if it is of use. Don't take too long to decide it's a limited-time offer. I have more people to see." I bluffed her into making a snap decision.

"It seems a good offer, but I'm worried I may get into trouble." she said, and I understood why.

"Just keep this between you and me, and you won't get into any trouble. Don't take any risks, just report to Rosa or me." I glanced at Rosa, her eyebrows raised a little.

I asked Trisha for her details, asked her to return for a training meeting, and told her strictly not to talk to anyone about her new job. I made her promise it would remain secret. She went off looking happy but in a slightly worried way. I felt happy she would be onside and provide some excellent intelligence. I was a little unhappy with myself for taking such a huge risk and trusting these strangers with such things that were obviously illegal or at worst, treasonable.

I looked at Rosa now. She was looking quite bewildered and appeared a little worried. Was I moving too fast? Yes, undoubtedly, ridiculously fast. It would typically take weeks or months to groom an agent. As always, I was rushing my job. This could so easily go seriously wrong. It was quite unprofessional the speed I was moving. I was expecting to have to make several trips to the Philippines to get this far.

So now I had to work on Rosa. I needed to see what she was thinking. So far, she appeared to be on my side. I needed a little insurance.

I turned to Rosa. Before she had a chance to speak, I spoke first.

"If you are wanting to spend the day with me, I think we should also get your employment formalised." I paused to give her the chance to decide that this job was not what she thought and make her excuses. If she did, I would need to leave the hotel pretty much instantly. The security implications were too high. I was playing a high-risk game. I took a pre-written contract from my case. Karen had prepared some before I left England. It was a pretty open-worded document, with spaces I could fill in by hand. Rosa didn't back out as I half expected. In fact, quite the opposite. This woman was smarter than I thought.

"That was a piece of luck getting someone inside the presidential palace. I hope Trisha can somehow find information on my son." Rosa said. I was so surprised, and I tried not to show it on my face.

"Rosa, if you still want to spend time with me this afternoon. I will be delighted for you to stay if you are able." This would keep her in sight for now. I would know where and what she is doing until I knew she could be trusted as much as I would trust anyone.

"We will get an early lunch, and my driver will take us out to view a few offices. I want to pay you in advance for your time today if I may. Just to show you good faith." I continued.

"There's no need, sir."

"No, I insist this is so unusual to take you on instantly. I want you to know your job is secure and above board."

Above board! I took money from my locked Samsonite case, counted out 200Php, the same amount as I had given Angel and added an extra 50Php. I took a sheet of paper and quickly wrote a receipt to make this somehow appear official. I passed the money and the receipt and then handed her a pen and the contract for Rosa to fill in and sign. I requested that she sign for her first pay also.

I did this deliberately because if she were to query my actions or intentions and threatened to run to the authorities, I would tell her it was too late. She was now on the payroll she has been paid and signed, therefore implicating herself in whatever she thought this was. It would be a mild form of blackmail if needed.

As it happened, I didn't need the insurance. This mother with a missing son was hoping so much that I could help find him. Trisha was inside the palace, which was a glimmer of hope for Rosa. She had received no help from anyone until now. The authorities would always turn her away with no information. This was her way in, it worked for me and Rosa.

After lunch, Rosa and I went out to view some offices to rent. Having her with me was not only useful, but she was also fun and good company. Rosa's local knowledge of the property market proved to be excellent. Who would have thought this is how my recruitment campaign would go. I never expected it to be this easy.

With Jonny driving, our first visit that day was to a Roxas Boulevard property. A long dual carriageway on the coast of Manila Bay.

Roxas Boulevard, 1975

Passing the United States Embassy at the north end of the boulevard we found the office block about halfway down the road. We met the estate agent outside the property. After an introduction to the building itself, he took us up to the office space. It was small, but exactly the size I was looking for and a little cheaper than other properties in the building because it was on the building's side and not directly overlooking the beachfront. There was a slight sea view if you looked to the left out the window, but Rosa said she wasn't going to be there looking out of the window while working. Off from the office space was a tiny room, more a corridor than a room, where there was a sink and a door to a toilet. Rosa didn't seem happy with it. I couldn't see the problem. I asked her opinion, and she told me it was way overpriced because of the sea view. I asked the estate agent if the price was negotiable, and he told me it was not as there was great demand for this property. I told him to leave us for a moment while Rosa and I discussed it. Rosa told me to walk away. She thought he was bluffing. The property had a layer of dust that told her it had been empty for a while. The agent was probably trying to take advantage of a foreigner and his money. It was the right size and had a nice view, but she thought it was not suitable. So, I thanked the estate agent said no to this office and we left for the next viewing.

We looked at three other properties that afternoon. It was very tiring indeed for me. I was suffering from the oppressive heat whenever we stepped out of air-conditioned buildings or the car. Rosa was worth more than I was paying her. She was so valuable, I couldn't have done the job without her, and I told her so many times that day.

Finally, almost exhausted and beginning to think this was an impossible task, we visited a property on Chino Roces Avenue, Makati, on the outskirts of the now famous Legazpi Village. We found an ideal office space, with incredibly low rent for the area. Rosa knew the agent that was showing us around the building. It was a large building with security in the reception, small office spaces were rented with communal facilities such as conference rooms and toilets or comfort rooms, CR as the Filipinos say.

On a busy street, the area was regenerating and space clearing after the war, which I took to mean slum clearing. It was becoming a major industrial area. The first office buildings of this regeneration were built in what is now the Makati Central Business District. Since the late 1960s, Makati was transformed into the financial and commercial capital of the country. Two years later, in late July 1977, the area would be the setting of what is believed to be one of the single biggest disappearances during martial law, the "Southern Tagalog 10." Ten activists from the nearby Southern Tagalog region, mostly in their twenties, were abducted at the Makati Medical Centre. The district had also become an area for protests against Marcos, led by employees of major corporations in the area. This was good from my perspective. It might be easy to speak to anti-government activists. We looked around the property. I was a little worried about the security of the office. I didn't want people wandering in from other businesses on the same floor, as the design was not quite open plan, but everyone shared spaces such as the kitchen and toilets. But we had a choice of rooms. I chose one set back down a corridor where there was no need for nosey office workers to pass as it was at the end of a kind of cul-de-sac corridor. Rosa talked to the estate agent and negotiated a brilliant deal for me. I really was impressed by this lady, I'd known her literally five hours, and yet already it felt as though she was an old friend. I was promised the papers would be ready the next day and would be brought to the hotel for signing. I paid a deposit in cash. I was already way ahead of the schedule I had for myself. I couldn't believe my luck that day.

We left the office block. Jonny was waiting by his car, enjoying a cigarette. I asked him to take Rosa home wherever that was. Rosa spoke to him in Tagalog.

The Makati area 1975

I realised it was the first time I had heard the language spoken. Here more English is used than the native languages. I wanted to go with them in order to see the kind of place she lived. It took a good forty-five minutes to reach her home by car. Even in those days, the traffic was heavy on many streets. Rosa assured me travelling to and from work by bus or train would be easy for her each day. I don't know if she was just being polite, but it seemed a long way to me. I watched her climb out of the car, and she disappeared into her modest home, looking so happy to be in work again.

The next day Rosa joined me at the hotel before breakfast, which we took together in the restaurant. I felt it necessary that she knew only certain operatives for security reasons. It would also help the agents I'm looking to recruit feel more secure if no one in my Philippine business knew anything about them. Rosa already knew Trisha, so she could be in on Trisha's training. I was exposed now. Rosa possibly knew what I was and what I was doing. Trisha might have had some idea, but she seemed ok with keeping it to herself.

Trisha returned as instructed to the hotel shortly after breakfast. She came to my room to join Rosa and me. On her own initiative, Rosa offered a drink and a snack to Trisha from the small bar stock. What a great choice I made appointing her. Trisha wasn't so shy now, more confident around me. That was ok, I like people around me not to feel nervous, I find they are more open with me this way.

I spent the next two hours teaching and instructing Trisha on what information I wanted, how to stay safe and how to pass the information on. It was useful to me that Rosa also heard this. It would end any last doubt she had. I used a couple of tricks to get both ladies to reveal to me how they were thinking at this point and they seemed happy. Rosa was too wise to not know what was happening. I could tell she saw me as a way to find her son and I promised I would do anything and everything I could to help her. A promise I would keep.

I had not established a method for Trisha to pass information over to me. I knew what I was going to do for that, I told her to expect instructions very soon. I didn't plan for it to be a dead drop. I never liked the lack of security or control in leaving notes in a secret place to be picked up later, sometimes after a sign was left when a message was waiting. The signal might be a mark on a wall or something. I preferred a different method. For security reasons, Trisha did not need to know the location of our office. She would never know any more than I told her at this briefing. Of course, she had seen Rosa, but she had no knowledge of her surname, address, or anything else and later I instructed Rosa never to reveal the office location.

I was reasonably satisfied that Trisha was onside by the end of our meeting. I wasn't wrong. Trisha proved to be a source of high-quality information from the palace over the years. She would somehow find access to Imelda Marcos's diary almost every day and because of this, I very often knew what the First Lady was going to be doing before Imelda herself did. Of course, my money was an incentive, but mistreating people will always come back on you. I made it clear to Trisha that if she felt she had been compromised or was uncomfortable doing what she did for me, then I would look after her, always and forever. These were not just words, over the next few months, I made sure Trisha knew there was a safe house and how she would get there if she felt she needed to get away quickly. I did the same for Rosa. Loyalty produces loyalty, it has to be earnt. This promise was put to the test as you will read later in the story.

Later that day, I asked Jonny to drive me around the city and to pass by some of the government buildings and Malacañang Palace again. I was keen, not only to get my bearings but also as we drove past the palace, I wanted to look for the staff entrances. Of course, Jonny had no clue what I was doing. To him, I was a businessman/tourist. The palace was difficult to access. There were so many entrances, all guarded, of course. As we drove down Jose Laurel Street with the palace on our left, I asked Jonny to take the first road to the left that he could. He turned onto a small, short road, and just at the end of this road, there was a guarded gate on the left. We were forced to take a right because the river was now in front of us. This gate looked like the staff entrance. I told Jonny to take me back to the hotel. Now I knew how I would get messages from Trisha.

I wanted people, not only in the palace but in other places too. HUMINT is helpful for so many purposes. Christopher had several people he used for low-level intelligence. I could have used them if they trusted me. But I knew I wanted to find my own people, I felt much safer that way.

Rosa and I got access to and moved into the office we found on Chino Roces Avenue two days after viewing it. I was amazed at how quickly things happened here compared to the time it takes in the UK. It came ready furnished, but we needed more filing cabinets. Rosa noticed some in another of the empty offices. We spoke to the building manager, but he was a little reluctant to let us have them. We took them anyway. Rosa found it funny that more and more, I was proving to do nothing conventionally. We spent a few hours getting the office ready. It was small and had minimal furniture. While I moved the furniture around and set up phone lines, I sent Jonny and Rosa out to organise the stationery that Rosa needed. A radio fax machine arrived by private courier from the British consulate. When Rosa returned from the shopping trip, I gave her instructions on how to use the machine.

By now, I was quite sure she had guessed this was no export office. So, once the office space was reasonably usable, I sat her down to chat over a coffee.

"Rosa, it's time to fill you in on your role here. You've not worked in an export office before, obviously." I began.

"Sir." I smiled at her inability to call me Andy, and she smiled back, knowing she couldn't either. "What I do know about this office is you are not exporting products of any kind. I want to make it clear to you that I like you and whatever it is you are really doing is fine with me. My number one ambition here is to find my missing son."

"What did your son do?" I asked.

"Donato." she replied, "was taken from the University of the Philippines (UP) here in Manila last year."

Students of UP are known for their activism. The university has plenty of student groups focused on political change. It also has various partisan groups ranging from liberal to conservative and several third-party organisations.

"By taken, you mean arrested?" I asked.

"As I understand it, there was a raid by Marcos police, but they were not in uniform. They grabbed several students."

Rosa went on to tell me about her son's political views. They didn't appear to be extreme enough to warrant prison, or worse.

"Leave it to me. I will see if there is anything I can do to help but understand I cannot promise anything other than I will try. Ok?" I had so little time to spare while on this trip, I picked up the phone and dialled the British Embassy in Manila. I ask to speak to an attaché and got through to him after a short delay. I was put through to Tony. We had not met before, but both of us had been briefed on the existence of each other. I didn't really want much to do with Embassy personnel, but I had little choice. I arranged with Tony to meet the next day at a bar in the city centre. Rosa had heard the entire call. She would be in no doubt now who and what I was. She didn't bat an eye, but I saw some hope on her face, and that was good. After the call was over, I spoke to Rosa again.

"I can't just give the name of your son alone. It may put him under some special scrutiny or danger by his jailers if indeed he is alive somewhere. They will wonder why there is special attention being paid to him by the British. Can you find a list of names of missing people, let's say thirty names, by tomorrow."

"Sir, I can give you that now. I know the names of many mother's sons and daughters that have disappeared." Rosa sat at her new typewriter. She produced a list of about forty names right out of her head. Her memory was astonishing. She handed me the list. She was smart too, as she had not put her son's name at the top of the list but further down so as not to appear special. I knew then that

Rosa was going to be an incredible asset to my office in Manila and to the SIS. I took the piece of paper with the list, folded it, and put it into my briefcase. I made a mental note that the names on this list all of whom had mothers and fathers. All of them would probably be useful to me if needed, by means of a trade of information on their sons and daughters. I told Rosa it would be passed on to my Embassy. A meeting would be arranged where information be requested from Philippine authorities. The British Embassy and Ambassador James Turpin had good relations with the Philippine Government, namely Marcos. I was sure some information could be obtained in the form of a trade if necessary. As it turned out, a few long months later, we were given Donato's location and confirmation that he was alive. It was no coincidence that the provider of the information was also, at that time, an agent passing us information. I would later make him my own contact.

I needed to set up the means of communication for Trisha and others that may be recruited later. This wasn't difficult at all. I asked Rosa, and of course, she knew a nephew that needed work. Everyone in this country needed work. Makisig, or Mak as I would call him, came in for an interview the next day. Although he was twenty years old, he wasn't a hot head or into any vices such as drugs or alcohol. Mak did smoke, but that was fine with me. He would not need to know the real reason he would do what I would ask of him. That was ok, the people here will do anything for a wage, and as Trisha's family member, he would remain loyal. He came to meet me at the Manila Hotel, as he didn't need to know the location of the office and I did not tell him what our office did. Rosa had told me he was clean as far as police records went, and I trusted her completely by now. If she said he was a good lad, I knew he was.

I chatted with him, I liked him, he had a sense of humour but a coolness that I liked. After twenty minutes, I offered him the job.

How he would work was simple. I provided him with a second-hand scooter, not new, as people might wonder where he got money from. We went out later in Jonny's car to a motorbike dealer in a cheaper part of town. Scooters are very common in the Philippines. It's quite possibly the most popular means of transport. Whole families would cram onto one, shopping and all. I'd even seen some with a plank across the bike like a wing with people sitting on it. I let Mak choose one he liked, and with minimal checks or paperwork, I paid in cash, and we left the shop an hour or so later with a smiling Mak on a gleaming Honda. It was his first bike and he was over the moon with delight. I warned him not to show off or to attract attention to it, he didn't quite understand our relationship, maybe he thought Rosa and I were having an affair. He was a good lad and kept his side of the bargain as far as I knew. I told him I would give him further instructions later regarding picking up Trisha, taking her notes, delivering her near to her home and then taking the notes from Trisha to the office block. The note would be put in an envelope and addressed to a fake name by Mak. I asked the reception security to keep an unmarked spare letterbox for me for personal mail, with a tip that guaranteed compliance. Luckily the communal letter boxes were out of sight around a corner from the security desk under the staircase, they would never see who emptied the box as long as Rosa made sure no one was around when she emptied it. It sounds more complicated than it was. It worked for years, even when the security guards changed over time.

I asked Rosa to call Trisha to come in for a chat again at the hotel. I told her how Mak would pick her up on his motorcycle. Rosa was present which helped with the question of trust, she was a quick learner and I was happy she was smart enough not to get caught. Mostly her role would be observation and listening. Listening to palace conversations, making a short report and passing the note to Mak at the end of her working day. I asked her if she could safely take a look at any diaries or schedules to report on those too. She went along with it all. The doubling of her pay played a part, but I'm convinced over the years Rosa gave her a better idea of my real interest in the Marcos's. Trisha proved to be my undisputed best agent. She was never suspected by any other palace staff or compromised taking a sneak peek at the easily accessed Imelda Marcos diary. By the time she passed her notes to Mak, who placed the notes daily into the office letterbox, Rosa encrypted them soon after and sent them to me in England, via fax, and destroy the original note once it had been sent. I very often knew what the Marcos's would be doing the next day before they did.

Every day that Trisha was working, Mak would pull up by the staff entrance to the palace and have a cigarette while waiting for her to exit, just like a boyfriend might. She jumped on the back of the bike, and together they would ride away. Mak would take her close to her home and she would walk the last few yards, although I later found out they had become an item and he dropped her at home, a little unwise. While riding along, she would slip a piece of paper with her notes into his jacket pocket. As I understood it, security at the gate may have checked for larger items being stolen, but there was little risk of a piece of folded paper that Trisha placed down her bra being found. Searches would never be that personal, only bags or pockets were searched as staff exited the palace. No one would see and no one would care. They looked like a normal couple riding together. I understand they became good friends and would often stop for a beer or something on their way. Why not, Trisha was very pretty, and Mak was a good lad. After dropping Trisha off, if Mak had not been asked to do another pick-up somewhere else, he would ride to the office building not far away and drop the notepaper into the letterbox, a locked mailbox in the foyer and fortunately out of sight of the main road, should anyone be watching. It all worked very well, and they did this for years. But he never knew if the note was headed for one of the offices or elsewhere. Mak would also ride around town, picking up notes from other drop sites when asked. He was busy every day. The amount of information arriving at the office was astounding. A lot low-grade, but as I said before, all information is good and can add up to build a full story of the goings-on in and around Marcos and Manila. I don't think any other Controller of agents collected as much intelligence as I did. Add that to my photocopy machine downloads, and I believe I was the most prolific source of information in MI6, probably including Russian controllers. Karen would receive encrypted messages via the radio fax machine and log them all into the central MI6 database for Head of HUMINT Francis to collate. Mak was a handy guy to have working for us. He would do anything Rosa or I asked of him. On his scooter, he could whizz around the city on all manner of jobs.

    That was the end of the easy period for me in Manila. Luck had played a significant part, if not all, in my success so far. Now, it would get more challenging. My second week in Manila would rely more on my skills rather than luck. The basic system and methods were set up, and I had the office up and running in only five days. Rosa was an amazing lady, trustworthy and honest. In thirteen years of working for me, she never let me down. Trisha started providing information slowly at first. She was unsure what information she needed to supply me with. But after a while, notes were being passed via Mak every day. I didn't consider any of the information trivial. Knowing the everyday movements and actions of the

Marcos couple was always valuable. Knowing what they spoke about and how their mood was at certain times built a clear picture of what was going on in the palace and beyond.

One unexpected side effect of Trisha working for me was that she became more careful at the palace, for obvious reasons. Imelda Marcos and Trisha's higher-ranking colleagues scolded her for doing something wrong less and less. I think that helped Trisha a lot.

Now I needed to expand my agents. I'd get another in the Presidential Palace soon.

As the purpose of my intelligence gathering was to know what the Americans were up to as well, I should have contacts in that circle also. I also needed people inside any viable opposition parties. Only then I would have a clear picture of all the political goings-on. I would never trust the Americans. They would drop a bomb on their own countrymen if they thought it would serve a purpose. Maybe they did in 9/11, 2001.

I guessed, and it wasn't an intelligent guess, that the Marcos reign of power would not be tolerated for long. The people would not tolerate a dictator who undertook killings, jailing's without trial, curfews and plunder of treasure. I was wrong there. His reign of power and plunder lasted another eleven years.

I needed to know who was going to be behind any opposition or insurrection attempts. I needed insiders in the opposition parties, if any could survive in this country. I had a week left of my visit. I did not want to keep trekking back and forth from London to Manila. It was difficult and dangerous for me, and the jetlag was murder.

Once she discovered what the job was really about, Rosa became the most valuable asset in Manila for British Intelligence and for me. She would soon know what she was doing for me was extremely dangerous for her. Her role became more and more involved, and Rosa proved herself many times to be very loyal to Britain, even though, she loved her own country. She kept her real job as an outpost agent manager totally secret of course. With some help from the British Embassy, we did find out what had happened to her son. He was released from prison in August 1977, when Marcos had an amnesty for people found guilty of subversion. Although I doubt there was much of a real trial. I wasn't sure Rosa's son was a subversive, just opinionated. He was a student activist, but Marcos would invent crimes for those he wanted to eliminate.

Donato was fortunate indeed not to be shot by firing squad, or a similar fate, as many others were.

Agent 3, Si

The Americans were concerned that communists would be the main opposition to Marcos, and the reality was the USA would keep Marcos in power for as long as they thought communists would have any chance to take over the Philippines. Their leased military bases had to be protected. That was the most important thing for them, no president would stand in their way, but for now, Marcos, however he operated, would be their man.

I thought differently.

In 1972 shortly after the imposition of martial law, Marcos imprisoned Benigno Aquino on trumped-up charges. Aquino, together with Gerardo Roxas and Jovito Salonga, had helped form the leadership of an opposition against President Ferdinand Marcos.

Marcos declared martial law through Proclamation No. 1081 and went on air to broadcast his declaration at midnight September 23rd. Aquino and Senator Diokno were some of the first to be arrested and imprisoned on trumped-up charges of murder, illegal possession of firearms and subversion. Aquino was tried before a Military Commission and sentenced to seven years imprisonment. He had been arrested along with other members of the New People's Army (NPA), a communist armed insurgency group.

The Plaza Miranda bombing on 21st August 1971 Marcos and Aquino's direct confrontation emerged. At 9:15 p.m., at the kick-off rally of the Liberal Party, the candidates formed a line on a makeshift platform. They were raising their hands as the crowd applauded. The band played and a firework display drew all eyes. Suddenly, there were two loud explosions. In an instant, the stage became a scene of carnage. The police later discovered two fragmentation grenades had been thrown at the stage by persons unknown. Eight people died, and 120 others were wounded. As Aquino was the only Liberal Party senatorial candidate not present at the incident, many assumed that Aquino's NPA friends tipped him off in advance. Years later, some former communists claimed responsibility and accused Aquino of being involved. The party leadership dismissed this as absurd. No one has ever been prosecuted for the attack. Many historians continue to suspect Marcos, as he was known to have used false flag attacks as a pretext for his declaration of martial law at that time.

At the time of my arrival in Manila in 1975, Aquino had started a hunger strike to protest his military trial's injustices. Ten days into his hunger strike, he instructed his lawyers to withdraw all the motions he had submitted to the Supreme Court. As weeks went by, Aquino subsisted solely on salt tablets, sodium bicarbonate, amino acids and two glasses of water a day. Even as he grew weaker, suffering from chills and cramps, soldiers forcibly dragged him to the military tribunal's session. His family and hundreds of friends and supporters heard Mass nightly at the Santuario de San Jose in Greenhills, San Juan, praying for his survival. Near the end, Aquino's weight dropped from 54 to 36 kilograms. Aquino nonetheless was able to walk throughout his ordeal. On 13th May 1975, on the 40th day, his family, several priests and friends, begged him to end his fast, pointing out that even Christ fasted only for 40 days. He acquiesced, confident that he had made a symbolic gesture. However, he remained in prison, and the trial continued, drawn out for several years.

It was not until 25th November 1977, that the Military Commission found Aquino, along with NPA leaders Bernabe Buscayno and Lieutenant Victor Corpuz, guilty of all charges and sentenced them to death by firing squad. Marcos, however, spared them from execution.

So, it seemed sensible to me, that in order to gain good overall multi-partisan intelligence, I should find agents inside each of the parties, Liberals and communist NPA.

I didn't think it would be too difficult, opposition parties need help, financially or with publicity. The British will not support political parties abroad, financially, at least, not in the Philippines. We definitely would not be known for assistance with political promotion openly. Although, gentle manipulation, was not unknown but in a very subversive way. Selective and edited news reports were not too difficult to arrange. So, it seemed to me the CIA should be a good source of information. They, after all, would know who they were helping Marcos to suppress.

From the former MI6 controller Christopher's files, I knew the CIA's man in Manila was a guy called Mike. A man I would never trust. Anyone who supported a tyrant such as Marcos in order to maintain the ability to lease military bases in the Philippines was not a friend of mine.

I have to add this is not the official British line. I just have a deep mistrust of Americans, period, full stop. USA President Reagan was quite openly chummy with Marcos. I knew Clarke Air Base on Manila Island had a lease until 1992, probably also, I guessed, American Navy Station Subic Bay. A good guess at the time, as both bases closed and pulled out of the Philippines in 1992. The Americans did not want to lose their strategic military position for now. They certainly would, if the NPA gain control of the Philippines.

STRATEGIC LOCATION

The strategic position of the Philippines

I phoned Mike from my hotel room. I didn't want to risk him tracing my office number or where I operated from. That would heighten a burglary risk. Even though we would meet a few times, it would be only in bars. I didn't need to keep myself a secret from him. The British, after all, are supposed to work with the Americans. I found them to be bullies, so I'd never worked with them as I was supposed to.

I introduced myself and arranged to meet. Of course, the location Mike wanted to get together was a strip club. Americans abroad, they can't help themselves! Mind you, it was a fun place. I arrived mid-evening, a little early for these places, but it meant it wasn't too busy. Inside the club, I quickly noticed a guy sitting at a bar where topless girls were dancing. It wasn't too difficult to know this was Mike, a loose Hawaiian shirt, smoking a cigar and placing dollar bills in the G-strings of any girl that danced in front of him. I had seen a photograph of Mike in Christopher's file back in London. I sat next to him. The room was smoky and a little noisy with the dance music. I struggled to understand how we could talk privately without shouting and being overheard. Mike pretended not to look at me as I sat down. I thought, this was very Hollywood spy film stuff. I realised that films weren't too wrong in the portrayal of meeting spies. The bartender leaned over the bar in order to hear me shout my order. I pointed to Mike's drink and ordered whatever he was drinking with one for him too. I have never liked whiskey, but a man's got to do what a man's got to do. I guessed Mike was in his late thirties and looked as though he could be straight out of a Hollywood film, with average looks that were nothing special. He did look as though he could handle himself. His hands were large and strong.

"Good to meet you, thanks for the drink." Mike shouted without turning toward me, keeping his eyes on the topless girl dancing in front of him, posting another dollar bill down the front of her thong.

"Christ, are the British using children now?" He said as he took his first glance at me. I was only twenty. I did look young.

"We just like to be of similar age to the girls we take home." I replied, "I see weight comes with age in Fairfax." Fairfax County is the home of the CIA in America. This let him know I knew who he was, but he probably recognised my voice from the phone call anyway. He probably hadn't talked on the phone to many English people that day. Mike wasn't fat, a little overweight maybe, he had offended me, so I had a dig back at him. I was a skinny eight-and-a-half stone (54kg) in those days. I did not want or need to be his best friend.

The dancing girls were a little distracting for me. I suggested to Mike that we move somewhere quieter.

"These girls *have* to do this, they have no choice. There's no other work for them." he told me as he slowly placed another bill into the side of a girl's not much more than a piece of string clothing. He seemed to be proud that he was keeping the girl fed that day. I didn't like Mike already. I beckoned to the girl, whispered in her ear, and slipped her a 200 Philippine peso note. She jumped down off the bar, took Mike by the hand and led him away from the other dancers. I followed. The dancer walked us across the room to a private booth, pushed Mike into a plush curved bench seat and sat next to him with her hand between his thighs, kissing his ear. I sat at the end of the bench and placed our drinks onto the table.

"I just need to contact the NPA and the Liberal party. You know these people. It's all I need from you." I told him. He put his arm around the girl as she was unzipping his trousers and reaching inside. Before he became embarrassed by me sitting there watching the impending sex act, he beckoned to a passing waitress and asked for a pencil and paper. She handed him a sheet from her order pad. Mike scribbled a name and number on it and threw it to me across the table. With the note now in my jacket pocket, I stood up, tapped the girl on her shoulder, with her hand on his now exposed penis, and motioned to her to leave.

"No, she doesn't *have* to do *this*." I said sarcastically, and we left him sitting there alone, zipping himself up. I passed the girl another 200php, thanked her and joked that she should go wash her hands. I left Mike looking very lonely and annoyed. I'd see him again, we didn't like each other and as far as I was concerned, we didn't have to. It was only our jobs that occasionally had us working together.

The contact Mike handed me was really good in fact, though I didn't know it yet. The name on the paper, Si with no surname. Next morning, I dialled the number. I had no idea who it was before I spoke. Mike gave no clues whether the contact was NPA or anything.

I called and someone answered, a female. I found out later it was a housemaid. This family wasn't hard-up for money.

"Hello, may I speak to Si please." I began.

"May I ask who is calling" came the reply.

"Si doesn't know me. I have been given her number by a mutual friend, an American called Mike." I dropped in Mike's name. If she knew who Mike was, she may guess what the call was concerning, which might encourage her to talk to me.

"Please hold, sir." the voice instructed. I had to wait only a few seconds.

"Hello, this is Si. Who's calling?" she inquired. Her voice young and cute.

"Hello, you may know an American called Mike. He gave me your number. I am Andy, I have similar interests to Mike, but I'm British. I am making enquiries into political party activity in Manila. I believe you may be the person that can be of help."

"Where are you from?" She asked.

"I am English." I didn't use the term British again, I thought it would sound too formal.

"Are you press?" she asked.

"Would it concern you if I were?" I replied with a question.

"My uncle is the proprietor of a newspaper in Manila, and my best friend works for an American newspaper also. So no, it doesn't concern me." I got the feeling she would talk. The tone in her voice became less enquiring.

"I'd like to ask you if we could meet, you say where, somewhere you feel safe. Don't worry, I am on your side. You have nothing to fear from me. Come with a friend if you wish." I didn't yet know what her side was. I was only trying to make her feel at ease in order to meet her.

"Why would I want to meet you? I don't know you." She asked a little rudely.

"Mike gave me your number. You know who Mike is, who he works for. I know people that work in similar circles. The British have asked me to talk to you. They are interested in promoting a sustainable opposition party. Mike looks after his own interests. I doubt the Americans would help the communist party. The British like to take a more pragmatic approach."

"Why me, why am I so important?" she asked.

"Mike gave me your number, that's all. He must think you are worth talking to. I don't know anyone else in this city. I have to start somewhere. Maybe you can help me contact someone that is interested in party support." I wasn't going to support anyone, but I had to dangle something in order to hook her.

"At least talk to me. I won't keep you long. I want to discuss with you in private, how you or your party can be given the support you surely need."

"Today?" she asked.

"Yes, that would be ideal. I am only here for a few days." I replied. There was a pause of a few seconds while Si thought about it.

"Do you know the Little Tokyo area just off Amorsolo Street? I'll let you buy me lunch." she giggled, a little embarrassed at her forward suggestion.

"I don't know it offhand, but I am sure I can find it. I am a relative newcomer here and it would be my pleasure to buy you lunch. It will be nice to dine with some company for a change."

"Ok, 2 p.m., you pass through the Little Tokyo archway, the restaurant Kazuwa." She instructed. This girl was capable of making a decision fast. I liked that.

"Great, see you at 2 p.m. Thank you very much. I'm sure our meeting will be of mutual benefit."

"See you later Andy." And she hung up her phone. I was impressed she had caught my name and remembered it.

I immediately called Jonny to ask if he could drive me there.

"Where are you?" he asked.

"At my hotel." I replied.

"Ok, I'll pick you up at 1:30. It's about twenty-five minutes' drive from your hotel. You know it's just around the corner from your office." Jonny told me. It could only be pure coincidence. Given it was close to the Makati business district, I suppose it wasn't a surprise. Later I found out Si was an associate lawyer for a firm in the district, so it was probably convenient for her to meet near her work.

When Jonny dropped me off, I knew where I was, I could walk to my office from here in a few minutes. Passing under the archway with a sign announcing the Little Tokyo area, I walked to the restaurant down a little alley, narrow but bright because the buildings here were ground floor height only. The tables were outside under a covered area on both sides of the street. It was busy and I entered. I was a couple of minutes early. I couldn't see any young women sitting alone, so I guessed I was here before Si. A Japanese-looking lady greeted me. I asked for a table for two and told her I would be joined by a friend shortly. As I spoke, I recognised a young girl's voice from behind me, the voice from the phone call just a short while ago.

"Andy?" she enquired.

"Si." I said and held out a hand to shake as I turned to face her. She was an extremely pretty young girl, I guessed in her twenties. She looked adorable in a quality flower-patterned dress that didn't look cheap. She was clearly not struggling for money. Her makeup was perfect, her dark hair styled in an American bob. I doubted she was a communist. I guessed she must be a Liberal.

The Maître d' led us to a table, luckily at a quiet spot next to a wall, so we were not surrounded by people. I waited until Si was seated by the waiter before I sat, but I managed to get to a seat on the side of the table with a view of the street. I always do. It makes me feel more comfortable. Habit or training, I just always do.

"Thank you for meeting me, erm, miss?" I started.

"Tadad, Simone Tadad, please call me Si." She replied.

"Good choice of restaurant Si, do you eat here often?"

"I work for a law firm nearby. I am an associate lawyer." I wondered why Mike had given me her name. She didn't sound like someone that would be working in opposition to Marcos. A waiter came to take our order. I wasn't particularly hungry. The heat stopped me from wanting to eat so much. I didn't want a starter course.

There was a lot of chit chat about nothing special, just small talk, until, well into our main course I asked, "So, why do you think Mike has put me on to you? How do you even know Mike?" I inquired of her.

"My brother and I are orphans. Our parents were killed. We suspect they were murdered by Marcos's henchmen. We live with my uncle Melchor Tadad here in Manila now. My uncle is the proprietor of the newspaper Manila Dispatches. Have you read his paper? Mike speaks to my uncle occasionally. The paper remains one of the few that are not under the control of President Marcos. Uncle Melchor is very brave. How long he can keep printing his paper, who knows. One thing is true, his circulation grows daily."

"So, that's your uncle. What about you?" I asked.

"My brother is more radical. He associates with the NPA. He is a bit of a hothead. We do argue a lot. I disagree with the violent side of his beliefs. I agree with strong opposition, but I waver between loyalty to my brother and a less radical party."

"So that's why Mike has passed your name to me. You really know everyone, don't you."

"You mentioned before that your boyfriend was also working for a newspaper, is that with your uncle?" I asked.

"Did I say boyfriend? I think I said best friend. Tony O'Neil works for the New York Times. He is one of the top reporters with them." These were all useful people to get to know. I'd make a point to try to meet them all before I left in a few days. I really wished I had given myself more time.

Our lunch lasted well over an hour. I found Si to be very open, intelligent and happy to talk. But sadly eventually she had to go, she was already late back to work. We had chatted non-stop and there were no awkward silences. I liked her. I knew already she was definitely a good contact. More importantly, she was in contact with almost every political party I needed to know. In the short time we had talked I grew to like Si, and she seemed to like me too. She smiled a lot as we talked. We were at least about the same age. She agreed to meet again. I had not promised her anything from the

British. I had steered her away from asking. But I knew I could now meet with someone inside the NPA, the Liberals, and through Si, I hoped to hear more from inside the Marcos camp via her law firm as Si had mentioned in our chat that they did work for the Marcos's. I was sure this was a breach of confidentiality, but I equally thought Si knew what she was doing by telling me, a British spy.

I paid the bill, and we walked to the door to exit back into the hot and humid air of the narrow street. We walked together to the end of the road under the archway. Si needed to go right from here back to her place of work. She had told me the name of the company she worked for. I didn't need to follow her to find out where she worked. We agreed that we should meet again, why not, she was my age, attractive, very easy to talk to and I hoped that she would be willing to give me information about political parties in the Philippines, she definitely had her finger on the pulse here and I believed she could be a very good contact. We parted with a polite handshake. I made it my ambition that next time it would be a friendly hug. We walked away from each other in opposite directions, and I found my way back to my office and some air-conditioned cool.

As it turned out Si became a source of very good information, and we were in contact for many years.

Entering my office, Rosa was at her desk.

I was feeling most confident in Rosa now, she was capable in her job, she knew what she was doing and because I felt that there was a need, I had also arranged that she could sign cheques on behalf of the office business from the business account that was set up prior to my arrival in Manila. This was so that she could run the office completely independently with no need to consult me to settle invoices that the day-to-day running of the office would need. I had told her what her budget was, and she was perfectly capable of running the office on that. I would rarely ask to see accounts in Manila, but I could see the spending from budgeting in London.

"Sir." she said as I entered the room. I smiled back at Rosa, she was still unable to shake the habit of not calling me by my name. "I wasn't expecting you in today."

"No, I had a meeting nearby. I thought I'd pop in to see how you are doing."

"I have news for you." Rosa said excitedly, always keen to help me, "one of the missing child mothers has told me she knows a man inside the Security Defence Ministry. She will arrange a meeting for you.

"Rosa! Please be careful who you speak to about this office and why I am here." This was so worrying knowing Rosa was talking about me to other people.

"No, I never mention your name. I told the mum I know a man, that's all. This man she knows is searching for help. The man is asking the Americans for arms. It's the beginning of opposition inside the Marcos government." Rosa replied.

"Just be careful Rosa, please." I was open to Rosa. She knew full well who I was. She wasn't stupid, but I just never said it directly to her. Anyway, if what she said about this man was true, this was exciting news, and I couldn't turn down an offer to meet him. Rosa was smart and actually the best contact I could ever have in the Philippines, which was incredible considering she was just an ordinary mother and wife. It was me that needed to learn to trust her, not the other way round. Rosa wanted me to find her son. I needed her to help me find, well, just about everyone.

"So, Rosa." I said after a short pause to think about what she was offering. I realised this would be a fantastic contact if it were true, "who is this man? Can I trust him? Can I trust the mum?"

"Yes, the mum is like me. We need to find our children. I trust her, and I have known her for years. She is not my best friend, but I trust her. She wants the same as me, her child to be home."

"Okay, how do we do this?"

"There is a meeting tonight, a secret meeting. My friend can get you in."

"How is that possible? They won't let anyone just walk into a secret meeting!"

"Just trust me, sir." Both our eyes rolled up as Rosa once again let habit use the 'S' word. "I can call her and arrange it." Rosa's hand was on her phone, ready to call.

"Woah! You call her from here?" I exclaimed, not wanting my office to become known for what it was.

"She is a missing child's mum. She knows nothing of this office. I tell her I work for a foreigner, that's all. Please, sir."

I interrupted Rosa, "Ok, Rosa, I trust you. How do I do this?"

"Let me call her." Rosa lifted the phone and called her friend. Rosa spoke in Tagalog. I didn't understand most of what she said. But the Philippine habit of dropping lines of English into a sentence gave me clues. After the sweltering heat of my walk to the office, I drank a cup of water as she talked, waiting to hear what I was to do. This would be risky, and I didn't like it, but I had to take some real risks to get anywhere during my short stay in this country.

    Rosa hung up, smiling, pleased to be of such great importance to me. She immediately made another call and summoned Jonny to come to pick me up and take me back to my hotel to freshen up before my evening meeting. Who was in charge of my business, I wondered? Ok, I did need a fresh shirt. This one was soaking wet after the heat of my walk. Rosa told me to be ready to go out at 7pm.

Agent 4, Fidel Ramos

His Excellency Fidel V. Ramos 12th President of the Philippines.
CCLH GCS GCMG KGE CYC D.M.N. DK BD

Former Secretary of National Defence Fidel V. Ramos taking his oath of office as the 12th president of the Philippines on June 30, 1992.

In 1974 Ramos, as a General, was Chief of the Philippine Constabulary, in office from 1972 to 1986 a major service branch of the Armed Forces of the Philippines. In 1975, all civic and municipal police forces in the country were integrated by a Marcos decree, and it became known as the Integrated National Police (INP), which was under the control and supervision of the Philippine Constabulary (PC). As head of the PC, Ramos was the INP's first Director-General. In 1975 I didn't know, of course, that

Ramos would have such an important future and become President of the Philippines, also known as the Ramos administration, which spanned six years from 30th June, 1992, to 30th June, 1998. Ramos was the first Protestant president of the country, and the first Christian Democrat to be elected, being the founder of Lakas-CMD (Christian-Muslim Democrats Party) in 1991. He was included as one of the most influential leaders and the unofficial spokesman of liberal democracy in Asia.

I left my hotel room just before 7pm and took the lift down to the reception area. As I walked to a chair to wait for Jonny, the manager bid me a good evening. As I sat, Angel passed through with an arm of fresh towels for a guest, she smiled at me, nodded and mouthed a good evening to me as she was out of speaking range. I was beginning to love this friendly place. Despite having one of the worst leaders and oppressive governments in the world, the people were happy as they went about their work. As I sat, more staff arrived with trolleys loaded with rolls of red carpets and went outside to the front of the hotel to sweep the pavements to lay the red carpets. Jonny pulled up outside. I stood to walk to the car. As I passed the manager, I jokingly asked was the red carpet for me. He informed me Madam First Lady was arriving in the morning. I'm not sure he should have told me this for security reasons, but it did show the level of trust the staff had for me now. I was always polite and courteous toward them, I got back what I gave.

I jumped into the car next to Jonny, greeted him again, and he sped away from the busy hotel. I had no clue where I was being taken. I felt uneasy now. Nervous that I had no idea who or what I was about to walk into. Would the people at the meeting treat me with hostility? How would I get them to trust me and become informers for me? All I knew was that this was a new dissident group that was growing inside the Marcos government. That's all.

I was going to be in on the very start of Marcos's downfall in 1975, but I didn't know it yet.

We pulled up outside a bungalow in the wealthier suburbs of Muntinlupa. The streets were clean, quiet and wide. The houses were large and owned by people with money and contacts. The street was dimly lit, but the lights in the house were on. There was no sign of anyone moving inside, no shadows cast on the closed curtains and no sign of anyone outside keeping a look out. I sat looking and wondering what I was walking into. Was this a trap?

Jonny jumped out of the car and ran around the front to open my door.

"I will come with you to introduce you." Jonny said quite calmly. Did he know these people too? We walked together up the front path where two steps led up onto a front porch. There was no one here on watch or keeping lookout. This didn't feel right to me at all. I was about to turn and walk away when, without us knocking, the door opened. Someone inside had been watching us approach. A man in a police uniform opened the door ajar only a couple of inches to peer out. His foot was behind the door to block it, as if he was expecting me to barge in. I saw the uniform was different to those you see on the streets, it seemed cleaner, smarter and higher ranking. I spoke first.

"Good evening. I am Andy, Rosa asked me to attend tonight."

"Rosa? Rosa, who?" the police officer replied. I had studied army uniforms and I knew the ranks of the armed forces. I had not looked at police uniforms, I wasn't expecting to see anyone above the rank of those on the streets. Of course, it wasn't Rosa, it was her friend that arranged this meeting, and I had no idea what her name was.

"Mr Ramos agreed to meet me. I am Andy, an English businessman" The man opened the door wider, more confident now.

"I'll leave you gentlemen now." Jonny spoke, "I'll wait in the car, sir." He walked away having taken no part in my introduction. I think he got scared and decided to have no part in this, I don't blame him, this situation was scary and I was stupid for being here. But you know what they say, nothing ventured, nothing gained.

As Jonny left, the man in the doorway spoke to him.

"Park further down the road. I don't want crowds outside the house."

"Certainly, sir." Jonny replied with a semi-salute. He had done military service and he still had old habits. I had no clue who this man was, I should have, it was my job to know.

The door swung wide open, and the man stepped aside to let me pass into a lounge area. There was no one else here that I could see. From behind, the officer patted me down roughly, I voluntarily put my hands up to show I meant no harm, and he was welcome to check. As he worked over me, he came round to my front to finish the pat-down. He was quite handsome, fit-looking, not overweight, with short dark hair but longer than a regulation haircut, I guessed in his mid-forties. His rank afforded him some freedom of hairstyle. He had a pistol in a holster on his hip.

"I am General Fidel Ramos." he spoke without offering a hand to shake. He didn't trust me enough to greet me in a more friendly manner. "Who exactly are you, Mr Andy?" he asked.

"I have friends that represent the British government." I began, "I've been asked to find those that are looking for support."

"Support for what?" Ramos asked.

"Well, that's what I'm here to find out. If I report back to my friends that you are a credible...." I stuttered, not able to think what I should call them. I didn't want to insult him by calling him a dissident or a terrorist group. I chose my word, "opposition."

"Hmmm, and if we are credible. What can your people offer us?" he asked.

"Openly nothing, covertly, whatever you need." My words were extremely high risk and a little foolish. I made the promise in order to get inside this group, if this was not a setup. If this was a setup high ranking police don't usually do the dirty work. So, I had to think fast and on my feet. The British don't usually act as arms suppliers. Well, of course, they do, but through untraceable contacts and arms dealers, who would be totally deniable if discovered.

"Why should I trust you?" he asked.

"Firstly, I'm British." The British do have a reputation for being trustworthy. A reputation not entirely true, but right now in this house, I think it stood good stead. "Secondly, I believe we may have a mutual friend, an American called Mike. We have spoken, and he says I should help you." This was total bullshit, a guess. I wanted to get inside, and I had to use some tricks to do that. In the days since meeting Mike, I had done some background work on him. The intelligence coming back to me was that the Americans were not likely to be helping any opposition with arms, despite any promises. If the police had asked Mike for firearms, the Americans were not going to help. It was good to be one step ahead with this information.

"I did meet with Mike. He doesn't seem to think he wants to help us. So, you think you can?" Ramos asked me. We had not moved from the front door.

"Not think. I know we can." I bullshitted again.

"I hope you can." He indicated I should move forward. I followed him through an arch into the kitchen where other straight-faced uniformed men stood in silence. One man was in civilian clothes. I wasn't introduced to any of them. I could understand why.

"Gentlemen, this is Andy. He is British. He thinks he can assist us." That was my introduction. I wondered how Rosa's friend knew of this meeting. Six men in total, it wasn't a big meeting of followers. It was clearly the early days of the formation of this secret opposition group. I later found out the civilian man was none other than Juan Ponce Enrile, then Minister of National Defence. As Defence Minister, he was the highest commissioned officer of the nation's armed forces.

I never found out who the others in the room were. I never met them again. But the group of men I was standing with were to become the driving force that led to the People Power Revolution in 1986. The downfall of Marcos that led to his exile. We will come to that story later, but right now, I didn't know it yet, but I was in the company of some of the country's soon-to-be most famous men.

As I stood in that kitchen, I tried hard not to show how nervous I was. I was visibly shaking. I'm a foreign spy, surrounded by police and army men, some of whom were clearly high-ranking. This was no setup, but I was feeling way out of my depth here. I had zero experience at that time dealing with people of such power. Had I taken too many risks? I needed to take more, and quickly, thinking on my feet. I spoke.

"Gentlemen, I have good reason to believe the Americans are not going to support you with arms or money. The British tell me I can come here today to propose their support to any party that can credibly oppose Marcos."

If I was talking to the wrong people, I was dead for sure now, or worse, tortured and interrogated. I was a spy, and they would love to try to find out anything I knew. Luckily for the British, I was young and knew little yet and could tell little under interrogation. Ramos stepped toward me a little, I tried my hardest not to flinch. I hoped I didn't look as scared as I felt.

"Andy, thank you for your offer. You may tell your British friends we are working to form a party to oppose Marcos. We are persuading Benigno Aquino to lead a party in legal elections. He does need funding to register his Lakas ng Bayan party. Prove your words and help him, then we can work together to rid our country of this tyrant Marcos." Ramos was dropping Aquino right in it. He was naming him as the person to depose Marcos in future elections.

I would have to do something to prove my word, then I could get these men onside as truly high-ranking informers.

"Well then, you should arrange a meeting for me with Aquino, can you do this?" I asked, "And, how do I meet you again?" Ramos pulled from his pocket a card and handed it to me. It had only a phone number on it. The area code was Manila.

"Thank you, gentlemen, for your time today" My nerves were preventing me from thinking of any reason why I should continue speaking at this meeting. I wanted to retreat, think and get back to them more on my terms. I made to move toward the archway out of the kitchen to leave. One of the men ran and grabbed me violently. His grip hurt, he was strong. Another man joined him, and I was pinned to the wall. Shit! They didn't trust me. There was a lot of shouting from all the men, and I was dragged out of the kitchen into a bedroom off the lounge. They threw me onto the bed. One of the uniformed men pulled a pair of handcuffs from his belt, and as they turned me onto my front, I felt the handcuffs tighten on my wrists. I was surely dead.

Ramos and Enrile entered the room as I was dragged into a sitting position. My shoulders hurt and the handcuffs dug into my wrists. I heard other men leaving through the front door. Ramos spoke.

"I'm sorry Andy, we can't let you leave yet. We are meeting here. You may go and then inform on us while we are here. We will let you go when our meeting is over." He spoke with a half-smile to try to reassure me of the reason for my detainment. I sat there, hands behind my back, helpless. But despite my discomfort, I had to agree with their position. It made sense to me. A moment later, Jonny was also dragged into the room, protesting his innocence. He was also handcuffed and dumped onto the bed with me.

"Jonny, it's ok. They can't let us go yet, don't worry, everything will be fine in a while." I spoke not only to Jonny but also so that the men could see I believed their intent. Everything I did now, I wanted them to see their actions were right. I wanted them to trust me, and I wanted to show them that was what I wanted most. I had no choice. Jonny was clearly not happy and sweating profusely. Who would be happy in this situation? The men left the room, and the door to the bedroom closed. I could hear them talking in the kitchen but couldn't make out their words. We sat there for maybe 2 hours, and it was very uncomfortable and my wrists were very painful. Jonny and I talked quietly a little, I wanted to show him that we were okay.

As the men ended their meeting, they came back to the bedroom. Apologised for the inconvenience, uncuffed us, offered us a drink, which we refused, and they told us we were free to leave. As I left, I told Ramos that I would be in touch soon and that it wasn't the most pleasant meeting I had attended, but I understood the point of our detention. He told me he hoped that the British would keep their promise of help. My problem was now, how would I achieve that promise.

Sometime later, I discovered the bungalow property where the meeting was held was that of Rosa's friend. The men didn't, at this point, use their own properties for such meetings. I never knew how the group had chosen her house or how she was affiliated.

Jonny seemed to understand the reason we were held in handcuffs, which showed his level of trust in me also. He drove me back to my hotel, where I walked up the red carpet into reception and went to the bar for a stiff drink to calm my nerves and think.

I had very little time before I was due to return to the UK. I wished I had more time here. I now had so much to do. These were particularly good, if not excellent, contacts I was making and very little time to complete my work.

Early the following day I called Jonny. He claimed he was over his ordeal, but if he felt the same as me, I'm sure inside, he was still shaking.

After breakfast, I waited in the hotel lobby for Jonny to arrive with the car to take me to my office. Suddenly there was a great commotion. The reception area seemed instantly filled with security men. I was asked to stand back from my chair and wait further back in the large room. A line of cars swooped up the hotel drive and one car stopped next to the red carpet. A security man opened the door and out stepped Imelda Marcos. Apparently, she used this hotel regularly. Imelda would come to view jewellery and clothing and partake in makeup and beauty treatments here. She was an ex-actress herself and definitely had the presence of a celebrity. A considerable entourage followed her up the carpet and into the hotel reception. I was now at the back of the huge room, so I wasn't that close. But I had seen the reason, or at least one of the reasons I was here. I have to say it was an impressive sight. The security men and women were very professional. It would be exceedingly difficult for anyone to try to infiltrate through their lines. Imelda herself was beautiful, very confident and full of her own importance as she entered and walked to a room somewhere in the hotel. She had clearly forgotten her roots, she was an actress when Marcos met her. Her head held high and proud, barely giving those around her a glance. She was too important, in her mind, to share a moment with ordinary people working for her at this hotel. I could see why there was hate and jealousy in this impoverished country.

Once the parade of Marcos cars pulled away from the front of the hotel, the hotel lobby slowly turned into a more exciting buzz. Outside normal traffic could resume for now. Jonny's car pulled up and I jumped in beside him. He seemed ok about everything that happened to us the previous evening. I felt I owed him an explanation. After working for me for just a few days he was getting a clue things weren't what they seemed, but unlike Rosa, I didn't feel he needed to know everything. I asked him if he was ok. He laughingly told me that he enjoyed working for me, he never knew what the day would bring and that he would miss me when I left and hoped that I would call him whenever I returned.

"As you see Jonny, I'm a businessman that works in different ways. I do anything to get what I want. Last night was a deal to work with Aquino. I have contacts in the mainstream media across the world that will promote him when the next election begins. But it was a secret deal. Obviously, it would be seen as cheating if it were known the media was being manipulated in favour of Aquino. They simply didn't want us to leave the meeting early as they thought we may have reported the meeting to Marcos. It was a trust thing. They don't know who I am, but I will prove to them I can be trusted. So, Jonny I am sorry you were involved and I sincerely hope you were not hurt or scared too much." I explained to my driver.

"Ah, Sir, you have powerful contacts. I hope you achieve the election of Aquino, we need honest politicians. Don't worry, what happened last night did scare me when I saw the uniforms, but now I understand, I am fine." I could see Jonny was still a little bemused, but that was fine, he didn't need to know everything. Of course, I wasn't going to tell him what I was really going to be up to. For now, what I explained to him was enough to stop him from wondering what it was all about. I asked him not to say anything to anyone about what had happened and he promised he would not. Maybe he had already spoken to his wife or someone, but there wasn't much I could do about that. Anyway, it seemed he kept his promise as nothing ever came to light that the Marcos regime knew who I was or what I was up to in Manila. I was so incredibly lucky to have found such loyal staff.

We chatted as normal, as Jonny pushed our car through the busy Manila traffic and we arrived at my office. I liked Jonny, he was always happy, worked hard, and was always on time and available 24/7. His wife and kids must have been very understanding. But that's life in Manila for a loyal driver.

I entered my office, where Rosa was in the process of sending the previous day's notes from Trisha, the system was working well. It was a little risky, if Trisha was ever compromised, Mak would likely tell where he dropped the notes in the post box, possibly compromising my office. But I felt it was a better system than dead drops, I never like them. I feel it is too easy to spot someone leaving a note, especially if they are being followed. While the note is waiting to be picked up it can be read by the wrong people. With my system here, the notes never leave the hands of trusted people, then it waits to be picked up in a locked post box inside a building.

I greeted Rosa, who responded as always with a smile and a cup of coffee, whether I wanted it or not. Actually, it became a kind of secret signal that all was well. No coffee, things were not good.

After some chit-chat, I asked Rosa,

"I want to buy a property, somewhere away from metro Manila in the country, or perhaps another island that has good transport, ferry connections or an airport. I also needed someone to maintain it. It won't get used too much, more like a holiday home. This is your area of expertise, give me some ideas."

"How often would the house be used, once or twice a year?" she asked.

"Hopefully never." I wanted a safe house, somewhere should the situation arise, my people in Manila could run and hide. I was promising them safety and that I would always care for them if they got into trouble or compromised. I needed to prove it, maybe not openly but Rosa would know and I knew she would make sure others knew there was relative safety somewhere for them to run to, should they ever need it. I had read in Christopher's notes he did the same, I wasn't going to use anything of his. Perhaps it was wasteful, but I needed my own setup in the knowledge no one back in leaky MI6 London could interfere.

"Well, I think if it won't be used a lot, you don't want to commit a huge investment. You want somewhere with fairly easy access, yet away from Manila, maybe away from this island. Your best location might be Mindanao Island. It's the biggest island, easy access by plane or ferry and property prices are very inexpensive. You can get a wooden house for under 135,000php (£2000) or brick for 200,000php (£3000). You can fly to Butuan. The island does have mixed religions and Muslims cause some problems, but it tends to be specific areas, the mid-west is the most dangerous place. Stay away from those places and you are fine. Your biggest problem will be that foreigners cannot own land. You can own property but not land."

"Hmmm, sounds good Rosa. Is the land ownership a problem can I own a house on someone else's land?"

"Oh, it's easily overcome. You have a local on the deeds, so the deed will read something like, 'the property is owned by so and so who is the wife or business partner of Andrew Gilbrook.' It's a backdoor way to get your name on the papers."

"I don't have much time to sort this out, can I get there quickly to have a look around? It may be better if you come with me, I would need a local to show me the ropes so this gets done fast."

"Leave it with me." Rosa in her usual unflappable way knew what to do, what an amazing find this woman was. She got on the phone right away to make arrangements for me.

I sat down and went through some of the messages that Trisha had already passed from the palace. There was some interesting stuff, but nothing eyebrow-raising. Maybe that was because nothing much was going on at this time. I really needed someone in Marcos's office to get the really juicy stuff. I did smirk a little, there was a note from two days earlier. In it, Trisha informed us that Imelda Marcos would be visiting the Manila Hotel to view a collection of shoes and jewellery. So, we knew, probably before the First Lady did, that she would be at the hotel this morning. This was great stuff, this was going to work well, and Trisha was going to be the great asset I thought she would be.

Once I finished reviewing what was going on in the Marcos Palace, Rosa was busy arranging my property search trip, so I decided to take a walk around the building. Other small businesses were on our floor, it would be nice to see what they were doing. I wandered off down the corridor and checked out some of the doors of the other offices. Some were open and I could see the occupants at work. One office that caught my eye was a company dealing in computers, WWMB Computernet was the name. The door was open and four guys were working on computers, two of them were busy around a system plugging wires and checking boxes. I had never seen such small computers. There was a keyboard, a green screen, about twelve inches in diameter and wires to boxes with lights flashing. Every now and then they typed something and there was a horrible screeching noise, weeee, weeow, dang and the thing would make sounds as though it was connecting somewhere and failing.

I knocked on the open door and the men, more like students all looked up at me.

"Hi." I smiled, "Andy from down the corridor, just being nosey, what is all this, it looks fascinating."

"Hi, I'm Amado, this is Sinag, Joriz and Josh, my associates. Nice to meet you. Come in. You are English? We heard someone foreign had moved in. How are you finding it here?"

"Oh, we are settling in, getting things going. Looking for things to buy and sell, you know." I answered.

"That's what you do?" Amado asked.

"Yes, it keeps us busy. What is all this? I've never seen such a setup. Looks and sounds interesting."

"Desktop computers. The internet is going to be the next big thing. We are trying to be first in the game." He told me.

"What is the internet?" I sounded dumb but I had never seen a system working in such a small environment. I was used to the huge computer system in Century House, back in London. Here the boxes and equipment seemed so small. Very innovative.

"The internet is a way to communicate, by email. We can write an email, send it to someone on the other side of the world with a similar setup and it gets there instantly."

"No, really? If it works, this would be great to have in my office. We need to send messages fast to my office in England. Do you need special cables all the way around the world, that surely has to be expensive?" I asked.

"No, it uses normal telephone lines, you just dial the number like using a telephone."

"So, it's a fax machine." I proclaimed trying to know more than I did about this stuff.

"Not really, it sends a message to the other computer, rather than a printout. That letter can then be edited or printed. It's going to be big in the very near future and we are going to be first in there."

Amado educated me, "come in, take a look." He beckoned me into the room.

There followed a full demonstration of how this all worked. I was astonished but worried that the phone lines using this system could be tapped, but Amado and his team reassured me it was all secure. Well, they would wouldn't they! They had in the office a working Apple 1 computer and a Hayes modem. Very innovative technology for the day. There was another more homemade computer, which apparently ran using the latest Z80 microprocessor at an astonishing 8MHz. I was amused by the dreadful noises the modem made as it sent a one-line message. It took about ten minutes to send a short message to the second computer, which could be anywhere in the world. But I was impressed. The boys in the office seemed pleased their demonstration went well, and a little surprised it went without a hitch. This was very new stuff. I could see the potential, but I decided to wait for the technology to become more reliable before thinking about a purchase, the whole system would cost about £500 to install, a lot of money in those days. The British Intelligence Service had its own methods to communicate across the world. We did buy a system from these boys eventually, they had to wait a few years when things had moved on quite a lot and the system was more reliable. But the demonstration did tell me that exciting times were coming in the home computer world, and I should be in on it.

Returning to my office, Rosa was still busy, she finished a phone call, from what I heard, I gathered this call was to an airline, she was booking an internal flight from Manila to Butuan, Mindanao Island for later today. This untrained woman was incredible. What a fantastic asset she was to my little setup, for British Intelligence and to the United Kingdom. She was completely onside, hard-working and I trusted her.

"There, all done sir. You are off to Mindanao, in three hours, Jonny will take us to pack a bag." She proclaimed looking pleased with herself that her arrangements had gone smoothly. I didn't smirk at the continued use of the word 'sir' for once.

"Us?" I said surprised,

"I will come to your hotel, help you pack an overnight bag and we will pick up my niece on the way. I have arranged that you will go with Diwa. She will help you with everything and she will be the person on the deeds with you."

"My God Rosa! I should call this the Malabanan family company." I was getting concerned that too many people were becoming involved in my business here. Rosa was taking over. None the more for that, I was very impressed with how fast this lady worked, and always did the right thing, amazing!

"She will be staying in Mindanao. You need someone to manage your house when you find it. Diwa will take care of everything." Rosa continued to run my business for me. At that moment, I realised that, actually, this was perfect. With Rosa in charge, I didn't need to be here. She can run everything. I could return to London knowing everything was being run by an efficient loyal lady. The whole setup was running now and what's more incredibly inexpensively. All I had to do was to recruit people as agents and they would become part of an independent outstation. This was far better than travelling back and forth like Chris Mass had to. Far less tiring and stressful. Yes, it was right then that I knew this would all work, with the trusted Rosa running things for me. I couldn't have asked for more. Of course, there was the added benefit that not having to travel often to the Philippines there would be less chance of getting noticed. Less chance of my family and friends noticing I was away a lot. Best of all, less chance of compromise or danger for me personally. I couldn't have planned this, it had all fallen into place by pure luck and the biggest piece of luck was Rosa coming for an interview on that first day in Manila.

"I assume." I questioned Rosa, "Diwa, being your family can be trusted. She is discreet and will do what she is told?"

"Diwa is my closest niece, not my first but we are very close. She hasn't had the best of luck in life. Her first husband died in an accident. To survive she had to turn to escort work. I am the only family member that she has confided in because we are so close. She wants so badly to get out of the shameful things she has to do. This is her opportunity to start fresh and begin a new life."

"Rosa, I can't have my house associated with running a brothel!"

"No, no, she will make a new life don't worry, she badly wants to get out of that business, she will sure as anything bring shame to our family if she doesn't end that bad business."

"Doing what exactly? Am I expected to finance her, can I trust her not to turn any house I find into a place of ill repute?" I couldn't understand how someone could leave a big city like Manila, where surely there are plenty of job opportunities, to go to live in a more remote town and make a go of it.

"I don't expect you to give her anything other than a chance, sir. She has a little money and she will look after herself and your house as you wish it to be. You will have no worries, your house will be taken care of and I promise that I will oversee it."

"You know what this house is for right?" I asked her.

"Yes, of course. Sir, I know what you do, why you are here. You trust me I hope, and I trust that you will find my son and that you will always be loyal to me in return. I know you need some kind of bolt hole, and this house will be it." Perhaps I had been too open with Rosa, I hadn't hidden anything from her. She knew the score, she hadn't walked out, called the police or anything. She was 100% involved and took an equal if not greater risk than me. I had and would never openly say what I was, but she knew. She would be handling Trisha's messages it was quite clear to her what the office was.

"Rosa, I will go to Mindanao, find a house, and if ever you feel you need to get out, it's yours to use, to get away from Manila and I will make sure, always, for the rest of my life to look after you." I said calmly and quietly.

"I know sir, I trust you and appreciate everything you do for me." Rosa smiled knowing I meant it.

With Jonny driving, Rosa and I sat in the car together, Rosa instructed Jonny where to go to pick up Diwa. His knowledge of the city was amazing.

Shortly we pulled up at a slightly above slum-looking building, almost entirely made of wood. It was in the midst of what I could only call a shantytown to the west of the city. Jonny and Rosa went inside a door and disappeared into the dark space inside, while I waited by the car looking around, taking in this dreadful part of the city. Children, not at school, the parents probably not able to afford the fees, play in the dirty slum street, all barefooted. Dogs lay in the shade panting and one or two adults were standing in doorways looking at me, probably wondering who this well-dressed man could be and why was I here.

In no time at all Rosa reappeared, with Jonny carrying two large heavy suitcases, he staggered down the few steps from the door. The cases must have been loaded with Diwa's entire life. I helped Jonny lift them into the car's boot. Rosa and Diwa slid into the back seat, I sat in the front.

"Diwa, this is my boss, Andy." Rosa introduced us.

"Pleased to meet you Diwa." I replied.

"Hello sir." Diwa replied in a quiet very shy voice. She was unable to look at me, keeping her eyes on her lap as she spoke.

"Diwa don't be nervous." I tried to reassure her, "I don't bite. Are you worried about your new venture? It sounds exciting. Have you been to Mindanao before?"

"Oh, yes sir, I used to live there, I know it well" Diwa replied a little less timid.

"Good, and how do you think you will live if you stay there, what will you do for work?" I asked, not wanting to be expected to finance her life, even though I needed her to maintain the house I would buy.

"Well, I hope I can make a little business, I want to bake cakes and sell them." She explained.

"And you know how to do that, you know how to run a small kitchen bakery?" I didn't want to sound negative to her, after all, I think she was doing me the favour by going there.

"Yes, I tried here, but I couldn't make it work, there's a lot of competition." She went on.

"Everyone here tries to make ends meet by selling on street corners."

"Yes, I've noticed." I commented.

Rosa then chipped in too.

"Andy, I hope you will find a suitable property, I've arranged a few viewings of furnished properties for you. You see how fast things work here, you'll get the paperwork done in no time and you can call me if you need advice. Diwa can move in and that's all you need to do. I am confident Diwa will keep the place in order, the Manila office I assume will look after the bills?" Rosa seemed more in charge than me now. I didn't feel like my nose was being put out of joint, this was what I wanted. The more autonomy I could have, the better it would be for me.

"Well, I hope so" I didn't make much more conversation as we drew up at my hotel. Rosa and I stepped out into the heat, even though it was under the shade of the reception canopy.

Time was short before my flight, Rosa and I walked quickly to the elevator and took it up to my room. Both of us grabbed a few bits and pieces, enough clothes and wash stuff for a few days and threw them into a hand luggage-sized bag. I put in extra shirts as I knew I instantly get wet with sweat in the heat of the Philippines. We did a final check and took the elevator back down to ground level and jumped back into the car with Jonny and Diwa.

I assumed Jonny and Diwa had been chatting, Jonny must have reassured Diwa that I can be trusted, so she seemed much more relaxed now. I asked Rosa if I could sit next to Diwa, a chance to get to know the girl I would be spending the next few days with. Diwa had a half smile when I sat down in the car next to her.

Now I had the chance to study her properly. It's always difficult to judge how old Asians are. They always look young until they reach their late fifties. Then suddenly their young girl looks seem to change into something more resembling their age. Diwa could be sixteen or thirty, I had no clue. She had the long shiny black hair that the people here have. A nice figure, not under-fed as one would expect of someone whose life hasn't gone well. She had a pretty smile, straight white teeth and the biggest brown eyes ever. I soon noticed that she knew exactly when to use them to attract attention. Her clothes were of course cheap, modest, but figure-hugging. I tend to like short girls with curves, but Asians tend not to have huge boobs, but somehow Diwa's figure, from what I could see in the back seat of the car was nicely put together. I hoped her personality would match her looks, cute, sexy and brave. As an escort, she would need to know how to make polite conversation with her clients to be successful, her life wasn't going too well, so maybe there was a mismatch, rather, more hope that she could make things work in that line of business. I hadn't yet found any Philippine people that weren't happy and smiling by nature. Everyone I met, no matter their situation, always seemed happy, polite and of pleasant disposition.

I half turned in my seat to face Diwa to talk to her.

"So, Diwa, are you happy to come with me on this trip?" I began,

"Yes sir, tita (aunt) has said I should trust you and that you will help me" Diwa replied in a cute heavy Philippine accent. There always seems to be a North American twang to their accent.

"Well, Diwa, that's all I ask, that you trust me. Never lie to me and we will get on." I replied sincerely.

I paused a moment to see if she would ask why we were going to buy a house and if I would support her. She just sat with a blank expression, maybe she was nervous at the thought of travelling with me, a stranger. No, an escort travels with many strangers. That wasn't it.

"So, do you have any concerns about this adventure?" I asked her.

"No, tita Rosa has said you are a very nice man, you will make me a new life in Mindanao. I trust her judgement and so I trust you if she says I should." She said somewhat matter-of-factly.

"Ok, and what do you know of Mindanao, I've never been there, I'll be lost without you, so, it's you that is taking care of me. I don't speak Tagalog, and I don't yet know the way things work here. Your aunty has made my life amazingly easy for me so far. If you are anything like Rosa we will do very well in the next few days."

"I don't think I can live up to tita, but I hope I can be of service to you." I am sure she was being modest, the next few days would confirm my thoughts.

We chatted as Jonny pushed and beeped the car through the heavy traffic to Manila airport, by the time we arrived at the drop-off zone, I had got to quite like Diwa.

As the car drew to a halt, we all stepped into the heat and instantly as always, my shirt turned into a sticky wet clog of cotton. We all took a bag and moved toward the security point outside the entrance to the departure terminal. In the Philippines expect a security check at just about every point in an airport. By the time we got to check in, we had passed through two check points already. Jonny left the bag he was carrying to get back to the car before it would be towed, he left with a short salute, somewhat embarrassing me, as I hate people thinking I am in any way superior to them. We are a team.

Rosa handed me our tickets, my return journey, alone, would be in three days.

"Rosa, if three days isn't long enough, will it be easy to swap my return for another day?" I asked after studying the tickets.

"Yes, sir." she paused as she realised she had said it again, I did a half giggle "just call me I'll make arrangements if needed."

"Rosa, you are an absolute star" and I gave her a best-friend hug, as I did so she put her arms around me and patted me on my back like a mother. I loved this lady, she was a real talent and I was so happy to have her on the team.

Diwa and I joined the queue to check in and Rosa left us and walked briskly back to Jonny waiting in the car before he was moved on for parking too long at the drop off.

After check-in, Diwa and I went through security yet again and made our way through to airside and found our flight was already boarding. We made our way to the gate and boarded the domestic flight to Butuan, Mindanao.

On board, I sat by the window and hoped to see some amazing views of the volcano Taal as we fly past Tagaytay or Mayon if we fly close enough. I'd never seen a real volcano.

As we waited for push back, Diwa told me she was nervous about flying, apparently, she hadn't flown before, as she couldn't afford it. Instead, she had taken the ferry previously, as it was much cheaper if a lot slower. I said it was ok to hold my hand if it helped, as she did so I could feel her hand clammy and shaking. I looked at her and gave her a kind smile to try to help her confidence. I don't think in those situations it helps much, but what else could I do. I did ask if she preferred to sit by the window, but she said it would make her worse and I noticed throughout the flight she didn't even glance out the window. It didn't help her at all when later in the flight we hit some very bad turbulence, the like of which I had never felt myself. She asked if it was always this bumpy, I said it was very often like that and not to worry as planes are built to withstand such treatment, just as a particularly big bump hit the plane, people screamed, attendants braced themselves and I saw one even sit on the lap of a passenger for safety. I'd never seen that before. I noticed the pilot was navigating around the big cumulonimbus clouds rather than flying in a straight line through them. I dread to think what it would have been like if we went through one of those massive white monsters. I think by then my own hand had got clammy as well. It was a bumpy flight never to be repeated until 2014. When, I was flying again into Manila, the first flight at the tail end of a typhoon storm had cancelled all other flights into the city, I'm sure the plane was pummelled to its limits on that flight, not a comfortable feeling at all.

Finally, we descended onto Mindanao Island and landed at the tiny single runway airport of Butuan City. There was a sigh of relief from many passengers as we landed safely at last. The plane braked very harshly, as the runway is very short at this airport.

Butuan airport in those days had a very amusing system for baggage collection. You passed through passport control and then stood outside in the car park by a gate. At the gate was an excited group of men, who, once the baggage truck with our flight's baggage drew up and the gate opened, the men rushed to grab a bag from the trailer and then returned with it to find the owner. On claiming your bag, the man with your luggage would carry it for you to his favourite taxi driver, no doubt on commission, and try to load your bag into the taxi and expect a fee for carrying your bag.

Rosa had arranged a driver for me, who I could see was standing back from the milling crowd with my name on a card. I ripped my bag off the baggage claim man and went to my driver and car. I did pay the disgruntled man for his service, but he seemed disappointed he hadn't earnt his taxi commission too. I wasn't going to add to his tip for the lost commission, it was a daft system and ended in 2021 when a new terminal was opened. I hope all the baggage men got jobs in the airport, it was crazy but sad if they lost their jobs due to progress.

Our driver was a cheerful and happy chap, quite shy, but very good at negotiating the busy, confusing mass of tuk-tuks, taxis, jeepneys and all other vehicles pushing for space on the roads. I asked Diwa if she would translate for me, as our driver's English wasn't the best. She chatted away with him like they knew each other already, but she assured me it was the first time she met him. I was out of my comfort zone and she was in her hometown.

After twenty minutes of passing through confusing streets busy with traffic, we pulled off the street into a peaceful haven, the grounds of the Balanghai Hotel. The hotel, whilst in beautiful gardens, away from the noise of the streets seemed to me to be quite old, not run down, but definitely in need of renovation. But anyway, we would only be here for two nights, hopefully. I respected Rosa's choice of hotels for me at such short notice and I appreciated her effort in trying to impress me. Of course, no one could ever do the job as well as Karen back home in London.

Once again, we stepped out of the car and into the energy-sapping Philippine heat. Miki, the driver helped place our bags onto a trolley the bell boys had produced. I asked Miki if he was available in the morning to drive for us all day, he assured me he had been booked for three days and he would see us in the morning, he said goodbye and left, so Diwa and I walked into the cooler foyer to check in.

I realised I hadn't asked Rosa what rooms she had booked for us. I had no idea, and when the clerk announced we had a twin room, I was quite shocked. Apparently, in an effort to keep costs low, Rosa had booked me a twin room with her niece. What an open-minded family! I asked Diwa if the twin room was ok with her and she nodded yes. This could be a problem, not only would I need to be careful with any communications back to London, but in those days, things weren't as liberal as today. I could cause eyebrows to raise, especially in this attempt at a high-class hotel. The clerk asked what the name of my wife was, I answered Diwa, and that was it. No ID check or anything for her, her name was entered as Mrs Diwa Gilbrook. Of course, I had to have my passport photocopied, but nothing was required of Diwa.

We followed the bellboy to our room on the ground floor. The hotel is also a convention centre, but there didn't appear to be any events on that day and only a few people were milling around. Once we were in our room and the bellboy tipped and gone, I looked at Diwa and asked her if she knew this was the room setup. She did and it was ok, and she trusted me because her tita Rosa had told her to. Well, that's a mistake I thought. I'm in my twenties and in a room alone with a pretty girl for a few days, I hoped I could maintain some sense of decorum. The room had a double bed and a single, like a family room. It was an unremarkable room otherwise, with simple furniture, a heavy old-style box TV on a stand in the corner next to a French-window out to a patio with 2 chairs and a small table. A bit odd I thought, a family room would surely require more chairs.

It was now early evening, and I was starving. I asked Diwa if she'd like to go out for a meal or to eat in. I had looked at the list of properties that Rosa had organised for me, and all the appointments were tomorrow, so our evening was free. We could visit her family if she would like. She explained they lived further north in the Surigao area, it was hours away and there was no time to visit. But anyway, if she was going to live here again, she would have plenty of time to visit family. So, we settled for dinner in the hotel and drinks in the bar spending the evening chatting. I guessed Rosa had briefed her not to ask questions about me, because she didn't ask me anything about myself at all. Nonetheless, the evening was fun, not difficult to make small talk and I got to know Diwa a little. I came to the conclusion she was a nice girl, she'd had an unfortunate life and I believed I could trust her. A belief confirmed in the years to come.

Time eventually came to retire to our room. It was a little embarrassing and I was wondering how to deal with this situation. I put the old heavy TV on and casually took my night clothes and wash stuff from my bag and went into the bathroom to change, while Diwa sat watching TV. She had told me she didn't have a TV before, so this was a novelty for her. She had explained to me her escorting work had been, just having drinks with men in a bar, and she earned commission from the bar for the drinks she persuaded the men to have. I wasn't sure if she was telling the truth about this, as most men drinking with a girl like that would pay a bar fine and take her back to a hotel. But I gave her the benefit of the doubt, why would she lie to me about that, family shame perhaps. Rosa was the only family member that knew what she did. I didn't care, nothing to do with me. Diwa had explained her plans to make a little business here making cakes, she knew a few people, and wasn't a stranger and she had contacts that would hopefully buy from her. I had decided if there was time, that I would help her by buying all the equipment she needed to get started on her venture. It seemed fair, as she was moving here for me.

After, a shower and changing into my night clothes I exited the bathroom and told her the bathroom was free if she needed it. After a few minutes with her eyes fixed on the TV, she gathered her night things before disappearing into the bathroom. A moment later she called me from the bathroom,

"Andy"

"Yes, what's up?" I shouted from the patio door where I stood looking out into the gardens.

"Can you help me?" she yelled back.

"Of course, what's the problem" I turned to move to the bathroom door, where Diwa appeared wrapped in the hotel bath towel looking very sheepish and embarrassed.

"Can you show me how to turn on the shower, please? I've never used one."

This was the moment I truly realise the poverty some of the Philippine people live in. She had only ever washed from a single cold tap and a bucket. My heart genuinely felt sorry for Diwa and all the others like her. Never having a shower or proper bath. As I travelled around the Philippines, I saw shanty lean-to type houses. But it never occurred to me that these homes didn't have proper facilities as we do, a toilet may also be a bucket, flushed by filling from the same single tap. When you are on those roads, you see the hap-hazard way power cables are slung in untidy knots along the poles, probably stealing the electricity until the power company takes them down, only to be replaced the next day.

I went into the bathroom with Diwa and explained how to operate the shower, how to adjust the temperature and asked her if she was happy with how the mixer taps on the sink worked, and the hairdryer just needed to be taken from its rack on the wall. She told me she had never used a hairdryer. My heart just melted for these people. I told her to give me a shout any time she was not sure about anything and that I would help. I smiled, in a way to show her I was not laughing at her and left her to get on with washing.

She didn't shower for long, not used to the fact that it was not at any cost to use, she wanted to show she was frugal.

Diwa reappeared ten minutes later, her beautiful long black hair still wet, wearing a pyjama top and shorts. Her nipples were hard against the cloth of her top, looking sexy as hell. She had a beautiful figure and beautiful olive skin. Her legs were a little chunky on her thighs but quite appealing to this young man, always happy in the company of a sexy young girl. I was sure now that she was telling the truth about her escort work, surely she would have had many showers if she was in the business of going with men back to their hotels.

"Did you manage ok, you sussed out the shower?" I asked as she placed her day clothes neatly over a chair by a small table next to the TV.

"Yes, thank you Andy, it was magical, can I have another tomorrow?" Oh my goodness! This poor girl didn't have a clue how the hotel system worked.

"You can have 10 a day, it's free, everything in this room is free" I didn't get it that there are people in this world that don't know what a hotel room means. I ignored the fact the mini bar would be added to the bill, but I didn't want to complicate it for her.

"Really, that's ok?" she stared at me, her big brown eyes wide with the prospect of more showers, her innocence was very appealing.

"You can watch TV, take a shower, have a drink from the fridge, sit outside, sit inside, you are free to do as you please. In the morning, we will go for breakfast, it's included in the price, eat as much as you want." I didn't want to patronise her, but I thought I needed to explain.

She smiled a big smile and sat on the single bed watching TV. I offered her a beer from the fridge, which she took. I sat outside on the patio, the evening still hot and humid, looking out into the gardens wondering if this lovely innocent girl could cope with running my house, if I found one. I had to trust she was capable of learning.

I read the appointment list tomorrow and I guessed I would have to rush through each viewing, I prayed that luck would continue to be favourable to me on this ridiculous time schedule, for the whole trip, not just house viewings.

Diwa appeared with another beer for each of us and sat in the other chair, we chinked bottles,

"Tagay" she toasted as our bottles connected.

"Cheers." I said, "let's hope tomorrow brings success." We both took a swig from our beer bottles and I looked up at the clear sky, the stars bright and in their millions above the dark garden.

We chatted about life into the night, I think neither of us knew how to say we were going to bed, it was all a bit awkward. But after ordering more beers to our room and four beers each I was getting very drowsy, so I decided to make the first move.

"I'm tired and ready for bed, which one would you like?" I said as I stood up.

"Me too." she replied and stood with me.

We moved into the room locking the door behind us.

"I'll take this one" she offered as she pressed down on the single bed. She had already been sitting on it to watch TV and to dry her hair with a towel, so it kind of made sense that she had already chosen that one. Maybe she wanted to feel safe that I couldn't make a move on her in the night in the small bed.

"If you are sure" I replied and sat on the double bed. It didn't feel too comfortable, but it was what it was. After a moment I went into the bathroom to brush my teeth. When I came out, she was already in her bed half sitting half laying to continue watching TV. I got into my bed and asked her to turn off the TV when she had finished.

I slept to one side of my bed, the side furthest away from her, I don't know why. We continued to chat in the dark, about nothing much. I'm sure she was feeling as awkward as I was.

It took me a long time to fall asleep, the noise of the air conditioning unit didn't help, why do they always make them so noisy? My head was full of thoughts of how I was going to develop contacts inside the opposition parties and whether I needed more time to complete this mission. Had I made an error of judgement in starting from fresh. My brain swirled a thousand thoughts, until finally after hours of thinking, I drifted off into a light sleep. No alarm was set for the morning, I didn't have one.

Sometime later, it was still very dark, I felt my bed move slightly and my heart began to pound, did we not close the doors properly? Part of me froze as I was not sure if I was dreaming. The bed moved again, there was no sound but the quiet rustle of my bed sheets. I turned my whole body quickly to face my intruder, in the dimness of the room I was ready to leap into a defensive move, but a scent, a softness of movement told me it was a woman, Diwa!

"Diwa! What are you doing?" I spoke, not shouting or with any anger in my voice.

"I'm sorry sir, I can't sleep, can you cuddle me?" she asked softly.

"Do you think it's appropriate? Your aunty Rosa is trusting me with you."

"She won't know if you don't tell her. I'm worried about my future here, I can't sleep" she said shyly.

"I won't leave you here unless we've found a place we both like. I will make sure you are set up for your business before I leave. You have family here. You will be fine, trust me." I rolled back turning away from her, I didn't want to appear eager to take advantage of her.

She lay still for a moment, then slowly she slipped her arms around me and moved to spoon me. I could feel her nipples pressing into my back and she really smelt sweet and cute. It was the hardest thing to resist her.

She whispered, "Thank you" and I fell back to sleep comfortable in myself that I had behaved.

During the night, it was difficult to move around, at some point I half woke to find we had switched around and I was now facing the other way spooning her, with my arms around her. She was holding my hand in her sleep. Her hair smelt good, the skin on her body tight on her nicely shaped skeleton frame, her cute round bum in my lap. I was comfortable and I didn't move until I drifted back to sleep.

As the sun rose and began to shine through the cracks in our curtains, in a semi-light I woke. We were now facing each other, arms around each other. Close up, she was beautiful, her face as pretty as any and her breath gentle and soft. Whether she felt me move, or it was a coincidence she woke at the same moment, I don't know, but her eyes opened slowly and she smiled a sweet smile at me. She moved to give me a gentle kiss on my cheek.

"Thank you." she said again.

"What for?" I asked.

"For being a perfect gentleman, you are rare."

"Well, I'm struggling to resist, it's not easy, you are very beautiful, do you know that?" She moved her hand into my crotch "Not resisting too much I feel." she said invitingly.

I sat up, wondering how to make a run to the bathroom with an embarrassing bump in my shorts. I decided to go for it, I got out of bed and made my way to the bathroom with my back to Diwa. Once in the bathroom, I brushed my teeth and took a pee which relaxed the tension in me. I moved back into the bedroom and apologised.

"Diwa, I promised Rosa I would take care of you and today you will see that I will. Shall we dress and go for breakfast? We have a lot to do today."

Were her advances sexual or purely for comfort? I will never know. It would have been so easy to take advantage of this pretty girl. How would I get through the next few days and not give in to my own desires?

We reversed the process of the night before, each taking turns to use the bathroom to wash and dress. This time, Diwa didn't need to ask how to use any of the bathroom facilities. Within thirty minutes we left our room and made our way to breakfast. As we passed through reception heading to the restaurant, I saw Miki sitting on a seat waiting for us. We hadn't set a time to meet, my mistake.

"Sorry, Miki." I apologised, "are we late?"

"No sir, I thought I would get here early just in case you needed me." He replied enthusiastically seemingly keen to get on with his day.

"Would you like to join us for breakfast?" I asked. For some reason, he glanced at Diwa before replying.

"No, I am fine sir, take your time, I can wait."

"Miki, could you please call me Andy, I don't like sir."

"Yes sir, Andy" he replied, here we go again!

"Just Andy, please"

"Yes Andy, sir" Filipinos really can't help it. It is so ingrained into their DNA they can't stop using the title. I noticed that Diwa hadn't called me anything, my name or sir.

"Ok, we won't be long, see you shortly Miki." I took Diwa gently by the arm and we walked to breakfast like a married couple for the benefit of the reception staff. I think Diwa appreciated the gesture, as she took to holding my arm as a couple would. I looked at her as we walked together, she was pretty, how on earth I had resisted any temptation last night, I do not know. She had made the moves on me.

At the restaurant, we were shown to a table and the waitress explained it was a self-service buffet and took our orders for tea or coffee. Diwa ordered coffee and I ordered my favourite English breakfast tea. I'm not sure if the waiter understood it was a flavour of tea or, they tried to fool me, because the tea I got was horrid. I made a note, to have coffee from now on.

Diwa looked at me, unsure what she should do, she clearly had never stayed at a hotel before and now I did believe her when she said she was only a bar girl and never went with men outside the bar. I explained the process of helping herself and that she could return and eat as much as she liked. Her face lit up as she surveyed the rows of food available. She followed me to the counters and I loaded my plate English breakfast style. Diwa took a fried egg and a mountain of bacon. On returning to our table, I asked her, "Do you like bacon?"

"I can't afford it, I rarely have it."

"Well, have as much as you like, now's your chance." I lost count of how many times she returned to the bacon and filled her plate, as she sat each time giggling with excitement and tucking into the mound of crispy bacon on her plate.

"Would you like to make a sandwich and take it with us?" I asked.

"Can I?" she looked greedily around for the bread.

"Well, I don't think you are supposed to, but I'm sure if you are discreet, you'll get away with it." I wondered where this little lady was putting all this meat. She actually emptied the bowl on the counter.

We made small talk for the rest of breakfast, before she returned to the bacon one last time with two slices of bread and filled a sandwich, wrapped it in a serviette and placed it into her handbag for later.

We joined Miki in the foyer and as we approached, he stood with a smile to greet us.

"Miki, they have bacon, eat as much as you like here, I've made a sandwich, would you like it?" Diwa exclaimed.

"Bacon really?" I think he regretted not joining us for breakfast now. Diwa took the wrapped bacon sandwich from her bag and handed it to him.

"Oh, thank you." He said with a smile. "I'll enjoy that later." he said, and we made our way to the exit. Miki asked us to wait, he would bring the car to us. Diwa and I waited a few minutes and when Miki pulled up, we both sat in the back of his car. I handed Miki the list of viewings with the times of appointments. I asked him to try to keep us on time as he knew how long each would take to drive to. It was a list of five properties. With that Miki pulled out of the beautiful hotel grounds and headed to our first appointment.

"There's no hurry." he said, "the first isn't far away, so if you wish I will drive you around the city for a little while. I hope you like it here."

"Well, I'm not staying here, the house we are looking for is for Diwa."

"Oh, I see sir." He replied, looking in the mirror briefly at Diwa. I don't know what he thought was going on here, maybe he thought I was her sugar daddy.

"Diwa is the niece of my secretary in Manila, we are helping her make a fresh start here after some difficult times."

"I see sir." he said as he swerved to avoid a tuk-tuk that shot straight out of a side road. The first of many near misses, tuk-tuk drivers are a law unto themselves.

The city wasn't that impressive, there were no what I would call tourist attractions, such as statues or buildings of any beauty. It was a bustling city, people getting on with their day, quite crowded, most travelling by tuk-tuk, jeepney or bus and the never-ending lines of mopeds, some with entire families packed onto it, shopping and all! Some of the loads these motorbikes carried were astonishing, a few you couldn't even see the driver sat under a pile of hay, boxes, pipes, you name it.

Finally, we headed out of the city and further into the suburbs. I was a little disorientated by the driving round and round killing time for the appointment, but I was sure we were to the north of the city on a road parallel and west of the Agusan River maybe two and a half miles from the hotel. From my point of view, it was a good location, quieter, more secluded than the city centre, but here I thought people might get nosey. In the city you can lose yourself in the crowds. We pulled off the road and Miki parked the car on a bumpy patch of dirt next to the house. Diwa and I exited and walked to the front door. There was no sign of the agent and no one was in the house. The garden, I use the term loosely, as it was just rough grass and trees, was overgrown, clearly no one had lived here for a while. I was surprised no squatters were living here. We wandered around outside the house, a single-story wooden building on three feet high stilts. Diwa explained that the river sometimes floods, and raising the house was necessary. I noticed a single plastic water pipe laid on top of the ground, no attempt to bury it, it rose up into the property at the back, where a small three feet by three feet extension overhung the rest of the house. Diwa explained this would probably be the CR (comfort room) and there was indeed another pipe down, this time into the ground which I assumed to be a waste pipe.

"What do you think? Is this too far from town for you?" I asked Diwa,

"A little, but it's not a problem, there are shops along the street here and there's always passing tuk-tuks." Diwa didn't seem put off by the location.

A car pulled up and a man stepped out and walked towards us, introducing himself as the estate agent, he shook both our hands. He was driving a Toyota Corona, I don't think we had them in Europe, but it showed me there was money in selling houses in Mindanao, not many people could afford a car.

Greetings over, the agent unlocked the only door into the house and invited us in. The door led into a large room, about twenty by twenty feet, obviously a lounge as there was a single sofa to one side. The floor was a worn vinyl, brown and white in colour. Halfway down the room, there was a step up. I have no idea why. Maybe an attempt to separate a dining area, but there was no other furniture here. To the left was a doorless doorway, through to what was described as a kitchen. The room was the length of the lounge with a long bench-type table on which was a two-burner butane gas cooker. A porcelain sink had been cut into the bench with a single cold tap. I tried the tap and water did run from it, but I was told it wasn't drinking water, of course, that was obvious by the colour of it. Maybe, it would clear after some runoff. There were shelves to one end of the room with bits and pieces on, nothing much of any use. A bucket or two under the bench. That was basically it. Back out into the lounge at the back of the room was two curtained doors. One led to a toilet or CR. Two buckets and a tap. A rough tiled floor with a drain in the middle. I was told this was the wash area, you use one bucket for a toilet and one to fill and tip over yourself to wash. There was no way I could ever use such a facility, but I was assured later by Diwa that it was normal here.

Next to the CR was the other curtained entrance to a single bedroom which was two-thirds the width of the house. No cupboards or wardrobe, just two double mattresses on the floor and a floor-standing fan. Again, I was told it was quite normal, with no beds or anything.

We moved back into the lounge where I asked the price. Where I was told it would be the equivalent of just over £800! The house was solid, it didn't creek as you moved around and had a good roof of various materials, predominately corrugated tin, which I imagined would be horrendously noisy when it rained, which is often in these tropical climes.

We couldn't deliberate long, we had another to see. I asked the agent how long it would take to complete the formalities. He informed me about a month after I paid a deposit. I said I would need it done in four days. He promised to do his best on that. We left promising I'd get back to him once we had seen more as this was our first viewing.

We left him to lock up and we set off for the next.

Heading south for two miles over the Agusan River bridge to the east and turning north heading back up to almost opposite where we just came from except on the other side of the river, I could almost see the house we just left.

We found the house and the agent waiting outside. The property was quite similar in layout to the first, but not in such good exterior repair. I felt it was too difficult to reach in an emergency and crossing the bridge could be a pinch point if anyone was being chased. I wasn't so impressed if that is the right word for such properties, despite its price of about the equivalent of £400. The visit took no longer than five minutes and we left telling the agent it wasn't for us.

We drove to the next viewing, back across the bridge and into the city, I guessed slightly to the south of the centre. The area seemed a rundown tightly crammed part of town. Miki parked up in a narrow street blocking the road to other vehicles, only people on foot and motorbikes could pass, but this didn't worry Miki. The agent was waiting in the street. After greeting us, led us down a very narrow alley street only just wide enough for a person and a bike to squeeze passed, hooting to warn us as they approached. A door led up wooden stairs that creaked and seemed to make the whole building wobble as the three of us climbed the stairs. A hallway led us to a door into a large space, sparsely furnished again as the first property was. Windows on two sides attempted to light the dark room, it had a similar kitchen, an attempt at a bathroom, but this time including a shower, and two bedrooms though the total space of these was probably the same as the first property. At £400 it seemed overpriced for what it was, by now I was getting used to the value of property in Butuan, but I was told this was because it was in the city centre. After looking around the property, I looked at Diwa she nodded a discrete negative, she didn't like it. When we were back in the car she told me it was too noisy for her in such a space close to other families, kids playing and shouting.

"We have three more to see." I said to her, "Of those we've seen so far which do you like most?"

"I like the first place, quiet, enough distance from other properties not to hear other people talking. A nice area." She told me.

"I think I agree with you. Miki, do you have an idea what the other properties might be like?" I asked our driver.

"Looking at this list sir, I think they are going to be flats in the city, similar to the one you've seen, and one looks like it's far into the countryside. I'd guess it's bigger or more land." He replied.

"Shall we skip the flats and look at the one in the country?" I suggested to both of them.

"No, I don't want to be out in the country, I don't need land." Diwa replied.

"Ok, then, let's not waste time looking anymore. Miki, please head to the estate agent's office." Miki took a look at the piece of paper with the list of properties and headed away as instructed.

We stopped on a busy main street in the city. I saw the agent's office close to us. Diwa and I got out of the car and entered the office. The agent we met wasn't there. I spoke to a woman at a desk that acknowledged us as we walked in.

"Hello, I am Mr Gilbrook, we viewed this property this morning" I showed the list on my sheet of paper pointing to the address.

"Ah, Mr Gilbrook, Jack isn't here, he is at another viewing. You are very quick, we didn't expect to see you today." The woman said.

"Well, I am on a very tight time schedule. I explained to Jack this morning I need to complete the contract in four days."

"Goodness, that's a bit quick, I'm not sure we can." She replied.

"There's a bonus for you if you can make it happen." I offered.

"Ok, let's get some details. I will try my best for you." She continued, opened a drawer in her desk and took out a form.

"Please sit down, would you like coffee? What would you want to offer on the property?" she asked as Diwa and I sat on the two chairs opposite her desk.

"Yes please, coffee white and sugar. Full asking price if we can complete quickly, four days." I offered. She looked at me in surprise.

"The same for me" Diwa chipped in. I was glad her confidence was growing by the minute. I liked this. The agent asked an assistant to make coffee for all of us.

"Andrew Gilbrook, and this is Diwa" I said before being asked.

"What nationality are you?" I was asked.

"British."

"You know you can't own land as a foreigner in the Philippines" she stated.

"What can I do then?" I asked.

"I can put your wife on the deeds and word it like this: Diwa Gilbrook wife of Andrew Gilbrook. It's a grey area but it does get your name on the deeds."

"Diwa isn't my wife. I'm not living here, but it will be my house." I replied.

"That doesn't matter, I can put her name, Diwa....?"

"Malabanan." Diwa chipped in. Her surname was the same as Rosa back in Manila I hadn't thought about it, and yet I had slept with her I felt a little guilty about that.

"Ok, so Diwa Malabanan, fiancé of Andrew Gilbrook." the agent wrote without batting an eyelid.

She took the rest of our details. Until finally, she asked,

"How would you like to pay and what deposit can you pay, do you have finance arranged?"

"I will pay cash in full on completion this week. Only if you can complete this week." I insisted again.

"I will put all my effort into helping you, I can assure you of this." she said.

We drank our coffees, completed all formalities and paid a 10% deposit, the equivalent of £80, to show good faith. There was time for some small talk as the urgency to view houses was over. Everyone was happy. With the completion of business, Diwa and I left the office and returned to Miki waiting in the car. It was that easy!

How should I best spend my time now, maybe I should try to get an early flight back to Manila? I asked myself. I needed to have time to talk to Diwa, to explain to her how I wanted the house to be run. I instructed Miki to return to our hotel and to wait there.

"Now we have time before I have to return to Manila for some leisure time." I said to them both. "Firstly, Diwa, would you like to stay at the hotel or go stay with relatives?"

"My relatives are far. It's too far away."

"Ok, perfect. I need to talk to you about the house." I didn't want Miki to know what was going on here, so I change the subject to chit-chat for the rest of the ride.

"What shall we do for dinner tonight?" I asked her.

"It would be nice if you experience some local food, some street food. Why don't we walk into the city." Diwa's confidence was growing by the minute, I really liked this, it made me feel more confident she would be able to live here looking after "our house."

"Ok, let's return to the hotel, have some lunch, I would like a swim, then go out in the evening. It will do us good to relax." My plan was more for my benefit, the heat of this country was draining and I needed to cool down and get my wet sweaty shirt off.

"I don't have a bathing costume, so you can swim, I am ok watching you." Diwa looked disappointed.

"No, Miki please stop somewhere we can buy Diwa a bikini or something."

"Bikini! Women can't wear bikinis in Mindanao. We have to cover up." Diwa exclaimed.

"Ok, whatever you would like. You can swim at least I take it?"

"No, I've never learnt, but I am happy to paddle my feet."

"Oh really! Can I teach you?" I asked her. "It's easy."

"You can try." she said less confidently.

"Can you hold your breath and go underwater?" I asked her.

"I think so."

"If you can do that, you can swim, and I can get you doing some kind of swim stroke in ten minutes." I said a little over confidently.

"Ok, we can try." She replied with a big smile.

I instructed Miki to pull up somewhere near a shop with swimwear. It wasn't easy to find one, it was rare for women to swim here in costumes. I assumed men and boys just go in shorts. For women, it seemed more unusual to get into the water and non-exposure laws made it even more difficult. I found it a little odd, as many millions wash in a bucket in the garden in this country as they have no bath or shower in their homes. We did find a shop in the more exclusive part of the city. We went in and Diwa found a costume that she was happy with quite quickly.

We arrived back at the hotel, and I instructed Miki to return the next morning when the shops were opening and I thanked him for the day.

Back in our room, we took turns changing into swimwear, wrap in a towel and went out to the pool. We found a couple of sunbeds and settled for the day. I ordered some snack food and drinks to take away any hunger pangs and the cool drinks were very welcome.

Diwa's outfit was a loose baggy but colourful pair of shorts and a swimsuit with short sleeves. No stomach was permitted to show and her legs were covered as much as possible by her shorts. Strangely, her top had no padded bra, so her nipples were clearly visible through the tight material, which, considering the strict laws seemed a very odd style.

We sat and enjoyed the day. As promised, I showed Diwa how to swim. First by getting her to hold the side of the pool, and then to take a breath and duck underwater, her hand on the side of the pool to keep her balance. Of course, her beautiful long black hair covered her face when she came back up out of the water, which made her panic slightly on the first attempt, but she soon got used to sweeping it away from her face. This progressed to taking a breath three steps from the side of the pool and pushing to float to the side. This progressed to a few kicks to get to the side of the pool from further back. Before she realised it she was kicking and taking strokes while holding her breath across the pool. In order to breathe she felt she preferred to swim on her back, floating easily and kicking with some natural arm strokes. After a few minutes she could float on her back and make a width of the pool. She was so happy she could swim to some degree. Throughout our time by the pool she put a lot of effort into perfecting her moves to swim. She couldn't believe her ability.

One incident spoiled the day for us. The pool lifeguard kept staring at her, I noticed there were few women wearing swimwear, only the men and kids.

"Is that lifeguard making you feel uncomfortable?" I asked her.

"It's ok, don't worry" she replied sheepishly.

"It's not their job to stare at girls." I said.

"It's my costume. I suppose it's too revealing" she said.

Now I'm not one for disrespecting different country's laws and customs, but when it makes a person feel bad, as in this case, something has to be done. I went over to the guard on the other side of the pool, as I got closer, I guessed he sensed I was coming to speak to him, so he climbed up the high seat where the guards can view the whole pool, this pool had no more than three people in it.

"Have you got a problem with my wife?" I asked making sure respectability was maintained regarding our marriage status.

"Her outfit is too revealing." he said "she must cover up more."

"My wife just bought that outfit from a top fashion shop here in Butuan. I am her husband, I tell her what she should wear and what she can't." I said in a tone that told him I meant business if he wanted to argue.

"If I see you staring at my wife one more time. You will have me to deal with. Am I clear on that?" He didn't answer, he had his own point of view and he was in charge of this pool. That was a challenge to me and I was up for it.

"I said, is that clear? Do you want to come down here and talk face to face or are you going to stay up there?" With that he blew his whistle, a manager on the other side of the pool near the food counter looked across and the lifeguard waved him over. Before the guard could speak to him, I walked toward the manager.

"Your lifeguard keeps staring at my wife, do you find that appropriate behaviour in this hotel?"

Without any further fuss, the manager asked the lifeguard to switch positions and a lifeguard that had been working in the pump room took over by the pool.

"The problem is sir." the manager explained "the outfit your wife is wearing, is too revealing. She should cover up in this country."

"The problem is, we just bought this outfit from a top fashion shop here in Butuan. Your issue should be with them for selling it to us. I think you and your staff should adhere to your own beliefs, and I can quote you, *'Tell the believing men to restrain their looks, and to guard their privates. That is purer for them. God is aware of what they do.'* Quran 24.30. There is nothing wrong with a quick glance to talk, but staring as he has been doing? Now, shall we take this further or is the matter settled." I stared at the man in a way to tell him I was serious.

"I see you know the Quran very well, sir. I shall for the time being keep my subordinate away. Tomorrow, I hope you can find the time to dress your wife more according to the rules."

"Tomorrow, I leave your city, so there won't be a problem again. I thank you for showing respect to me and my wife." That was the end of the matter, I returned to my sunbed and there was no further incident.

It was pure luck that the only preparation I had made for visiting a part Muslim country was to read the etiquette of talking to others, more particularly women, as I didn't want to get into any problems in the Philippines. Sleeping with an unmarried girl, in the strictest sense, I was probably open to arrest, or worse. I found it difficult to understand this country, it was probably the most prostitute ridden, including child sex and abuse, in the world, yet was supposedly a mix of many religions, predominantly Roman Catholic, Muslim being only 5% of the population, yet Muslims seemed to dominate when it came to rules and laws. I guess 80% Catholic population explains the child abuse.

As we enjoyed the afternoon in the sun, I was feeling very much like I wasn't achieving much, my time was so limited, but I made a mental list of everything I needed to do for the rest of my stay here. It had been non-stop since I arrived in Manila, at least I could gather my thoughts and plan for the next few days.

It was only an hour and a half before the heat of the day was at its highest, and I felt I needed to escape the sun for a while. I suggested to Diwa we retired to our room. She didn't seem upset to go. I guessed she had been embarrassed by the lifeguard and Philippine girls don't actually like getting a tan. They are quite the opposite to Europeans, they want to be pale. I believe it's something to do with the appearance of not being a country peasant, working in the fields. More affluent people stay inside the house or office.

Back in our room, the air-con made the room feel cold compared to outside, but I sat on the chair at the table and Diwa stood wondering if she should dress.

"Diwa." I said before she disappeared into the bathroom to change. "I want to talk to you. I need to make sure you fully understand what I want the house for and your role in its upkeep. What did Rosa tell you about me and why I am here?"

"She simply said, you are an English businessman, that you wanted a house here and that I would take care of it ready for whenever you need it. I am not clear how often you will visit. The house you chose has only one bedroom, so should I leave when you come to stay? Do you have a family to bring with you?"

"No, I don't have family, I am single. I am committed to my work. That is not to say I am not looking, but as you must see I am away from home often and it's difficult for me to find a girlfriend, let alone a wife." I began.

"Well, there are plenty of girls here that would snap you up, you are ...."

"I'm sure there are, I'm pretty sure you would make a great wife for someone one day." I interrupted her before she embarrassed me by telling me I'm handsome or whatever she was about to add. "You see I may need the house very soon for emergency purposes. People I know in Manila may come here." I paused, I knew she would have questions now. I waited for her to ask the first and obvious one.

"Are you mixed up in anything dodgy? Tata Rosa didn't tell me you are in a gang or mixed up with crime." was the obvious question.

"No, I have people that work for me. It is all legitimate, some are in positions that if your President gets to find out about could be in danger from him. You know for instance Donato, Rosa's son, has already disappeared. I am helping Rosa find him. That's the kind of work I do."

"Like a detective." Diwa said.

"Yes, a similar thing to a detective. I have people in places that help me in my work. So, you live here, in my house, which is yours. It's your name on the deeds, isn't it? You keep it clean and available at short notice for anyone to come here and hide out until the heat on them blows over. So, there should be spare mattresses, blankets and things in the house, for guests. Hopefully, it will never happen. So, you must live a normal life here, get married if you wish. But you must never tell anyone what I have told you. Not a boyfriend, husband, neighbour, no one. The only people you can talk to about this are me and Rosa, no one else, EVER."

"Ok, I see." Diwa said a little bewildered. She must have been wondering what she had got into here.

"Don't worry. If people do their jobs properly, you will be safe. I will promise you one thing, and that is, I will always make sure you are safe and that you can live your life while keeping our house as I require. By always I mean for the rest of my, our, lives. I look after my people. As you see, I have bought this house for their safety and you are part of it now. Are you happy you can trust me, do you have any questions?"

"So, I live here, always, waiting for people that may never come?" Diwa asked, it was slightly annoying for me, it showed she wasn't quite getting it.

"You live a normal life. A key will be hidden somewhere in a safe place. You don't have to wait in the house. Just lead a life as you normally would. Tomorrow morning before my flight back to Manila, we will go out and buy for you everything you need to make a small business to improve the house and things you feel you will need to live here. You make a list tonight, and tomorrow we make it happen. I want you to be happy and safe. The house is the one you chose, you make it yours."

"Ok, tata Rosa told me to trust you and nothing but trust you. She told me you will look after me, I didn't realise you wouldn't be here, I thought perhaps this was her arranging some kind of marriage." She looked slightly disappointed.

"Is that why you got into bed with me last night? You thought I was going to be your husband? No, it doesn't work like that where I come from."

"No, I felt I needed to be close to you." She said, I wasn't sure what she meant, close can mean many things.

"That's ok, I don't mind, but for now I'm not looking for a wife."

"Ok, I get it."

"But that's not to say I won't have some girlfriends as I wait for the right time. I don't know how I resisted being a naughty boy last night. You are very cute, I like you and I am sure under normal circumstances we could have fun. You were very lucky to escape with just a cuddle, I don't get girls jumping into my bed." My own naivety with girls was always my problem, I could never be forward with them, and I had no chat-up lines.

"Shame you resisted, I like you a lot. I am sad you are leaving so soon. Tonight, is your last night with me." Diwa genuinely looked sad that I was leaving tomorrow.

"Well then, let's make our very limited time together the best we can. Come." I said to her as I stood and took her hand and led her into the bathroom, stripped her and myself naked. We took a very sexy shower and spent the rest of the afternoon in bed together. I did feel guilty about it, I was going tomorrow and she had no chance of looking to me for a relationship, I'm not really a one-night stand guy, but she knew now what she was doing the same as me. One thing I did know, now we had slept together under these circumstances, I was sure we had a kind of bond, there would be no mystery if I ever visited Butuan again.

In the evening we ate in town. Now we acted more like a couple, holding hands as we walked, smiling, joking, we had a great evening, Diwa was good company, she had lost her shyness, she kind of knew who I was and she seemed happy. After the evening out, we returned to the hotel and had a few drinks on the patio together, before retiring to bed together, sleep didn't seem to be on the agenda that night.

We got up early as the sun rose over the city. I packed my bags. Went to the hotel reception and booked Diwa the room to stay for another week, with an option to extend if the house wasn't completed and ready for her to move into by then. I paid in advance for Diwa. We had breakfast, which, for Diwa was another mountain of bacon. After I collected my bags from the room, we found Miki waiting by his car, he helped me load my bags in the boot. Diwa and I jumped in the back together and I asked Miki to take us to the shops.

Diwa had a plan to make a small business, she wanted to try the cake business idea. There was no formal business plan, but she had contacts here, it was her hometown after all. What she lacked was the equipment. So, we found catering shops and I bought her a professional mixing machine, baking trays, cake tins, and an extensive list of bits and pieces for her. The house didn't have a proper cooker, so we found her a suitable gas oven, the retailer would deliver it and connect it to a gas cylinder. I was worried the house wasn't designed to take such an electricity load, but Diwa assured me she would get that sorted. We bought mattresses and blankets and some new clothes for Diwa too. Anything she wanted she got, but she wasn't greedy, it was all things she needed. Everything was ordered and, in a few days, would be delivered to a garage storeroom of a friend of Diwa. When the house was ready, it would all be moved to the house. I would not be in Butuan at that time, but I was later told it all went in and worked fine.

When we were done it was time for me to leave, Miki took me straight to the airport for my return flight to Manila. I still had lots to do there and I was keen to get back now.

As we drove Miki asked me,

"Do you need a driver in Manila? I have a brother who also drives."

"No, sorry, I already have a driver." I replied.

"That's ok, I thought I'd ask." Miki came back.

"Does your brother get much work in Manila, it's a busy place?" I asked just to make conversation.

"Well, he is not really a private driver, he is a driver in the army. He drives the top brass around, it's a good job."

"I bet it is." I thought, was this another astonishing piece of luck.

"Maybe I should meet him. I might be able to find work among my colleagues. How can he drive civilians and army staff?" I asked Miki.

"He gets some weekends off, and he does a bit of moonlighting here and there. He would rather buy himself out of the army, he sees trouble coming, and there is a growing feeling of rebellion against Marcos. Please don't tell anyone I told you that." Miki told me, but he didn't go into whether his brother used military cars for his moonlighting.

"Oh, I already hear there is growing opposition. It may get dangerous if it takes off. Give me his contact details and I will call him in Manila."

Out of the corner of my eye I saw Diwa give me a look. Did she really know what I did, had Rosa told her more? I never knew, if she did, she never ever revealed it to me.

While driving with one hand Miki found a pen in his centre consul and scrawled a number on a scrap of paper and passed it back to me. I stuffed it in a pocket for later.

At the airport, Miki parked the car, took my bags from the car and carried them to the departure entrance for me, fighting off a couple of the baggage carriers, as there was no incoming plane needing unloading.

Miki and Diwa couldn't come into the airport terminal to wave goodbye, because there was a security check at the departure door and only ticket holders could pass. Diwa and I had a long kiss and a hug that went on for a little too long. Miki and Diwa waited by the bag collection gate, the only place that had a view of the apron area and runway where I would board the plane. I genuinely had a tear in my eye as I left this lovely girl behind, in any other circumstance, I could have fallen in love with that beautiful girl. A while later, as I walked to the steps of the aeroplane, she was still at the gate, gave me a little wave and I could see she was crying. I smiled back and blew a kiss, turned and climbed the steps into the plane. I knew Diwa couldn't see me on the plane. But she stood waving, wiping a tear until the plane took off.

On my return to Manila, Jonny and Rosa greeted me at the airport. Jonny drove us to the office. Rosa and I settled into the back of the car, I spoke to her.

"Thank you for organising everything Rosa, you are a star. I should find you a medal. We found a house and Diwa is waiting for completion before moving in. The estate agent claims they can get contracts sorted in a week. I hope they do, I need to get everything sorted before I leave."

"They should, it's not difficult in Butuan, paperwork is minimal. Is it in the name of Diwa?" Rosa asked.

"Diwa who is fiancé of me." I replied.

"Oh, that is a smart way to do it. Was that your idea?"

"No, the agent suggested it. But I knew it was ok to do it that way, because you also told me that's how it should be done."

"Very good. I will keep my eye on it and push them if necessary. We will get it completed I am sure there won't be a problem." Rosa promised.

"Listen, when we get to the office, I want you to set up a meeting with this guy." I didn't want to say more in the car, Jonny might think I'm about to sack him. I handed Rosa the piece of paper Miki had scrawled on in the car with the name and phone number of his brother. I nodded to Rosa, toward Jonny, she understood I couldn't speak in the car.

I should add here, that during my time in the Philippines, UK Intelligence checked Rosa out as much as they could. There wasn't a lot to go on, she was not on any radar, so I concluded she was genuinely on my side. I had received confirmation while in Butuan she had passed every check they could do in the time available. I was more confident in her now and I felt I should be more open with her about my work.

At the office, Jonny went off to fill up the car with petrol, Rosa and I sat and talked over a coffee. I pointed at the piece of paper I had given Rosa.

"This is the brother of Miki, he is a military driver here in Manila. I am told he drives some top brass. I need to chat with him. Call him and set up a meeting somewhere please. Just tell him he was recommended as a driver by Miki, I will meet him and do the rest."

Rosa got on the phone. I loved the way she worked and spoke to people, I learnt a lot from observing her at work. She was kind yet direct, a difficult mix sometimes and in many ways worked in a similar way to Karen back home in London. She arranged to meet Ken, Miki's brother in an hour. It would be a little late in the evening, but time was so short. I had so few days to get everything I wanted up and running. I was so close to achieving my aims and I needed to continue my run of good luck. But now I was getting close to dealing with some of the heavyweights in power. From now on it would get very dangerous for me.

Jonny returned from his petrol run and I instructed him to take me to the meeting with Ken. We drove to the Quezon City area of Manila, Jonny pulled up and parked in Masikap, a road at the back of the National Police Headquarters on East Avenue. I left the car giving Jonny instructions to wait. I was extremely nervous. It was very close to the police station, so I guessed there would be many police around here. I wouldn't know if a police officer in plain clothes was taking coffee and overhearing anything we talked about. For that reason, when I met Ken in a coffee shop as arranged by Rosa, I asked if we could chat in his car, on the pretence it was to see if his car was suitable enough for my work.

Ken was a happy chap, much like his brother in Mindanao Island. So, we sat in the front seats of his car.

I spoke first to break the ice, he knew I had employed his brother in Mindanao. "Your brother was a great driver, I liked him, very good, careful and efficient, we even had a joke or two."

"Yes, I spoke to him yesterday. He told me you were a good customer, and I should treat you well." He replied.

"How is it everyone has a Toyota here, are they particularly cheap?" I asked.

"Yes, there are always deals on them, they are good value and I get good mileage too." He answered. The small talk continued, but I didn't really have time, nor did I want to keep him, just in case he had to go drive for his boss.

"Listen, I have a very good driver, I don't really need a second one, especially as you can't work for me full time. I am a businessman and I'm always looking for new deals. civilian or military. Do the people you drive for have anything to do with procurement, in the army? Because that is what my business is. Can you put me in touch with anyone? I will reward you well." I risked jumping in at reckless speed.

"Mostly I drive for General Ramos, he is the police chief. He doesn't get involved in procurement directly." Ken replied.

"Ramos! I met him a few days ago!" I exclaimed.

"Ah, well then you know he doesn't buy things." Ken said, he must have been wondering now why I was wasting his time.

"Listen." I said "Please ask the general to contact me. We parted the other day and he didn't leave a contact number, but he said he would contact me. Tell him I have very important news. VERY import news. Tell him I have some news about the Americans." I said only because I needed to set up a meeting quickly and wanted to instil some sense of urgency into Ken.

"I can't, I don't converse with the general, it's above my station to talk to senior ranks." Ken sounded like he didn't want to get involved.

"It's a matter of security. You have to help your country. For this you'll be considered a hero for your country." I reached into my pocket and pulled out a wad of cash. "Tell him I will meet him anywhere he wants." And I passed the equivalent of £50 to Ken. Anyone that moonlights, needs money, he doesn't work for the love of it. He took it and now he was working for me.

"Ok, I can't guarantee anything."

"Good man. You won't regret it, and you have helped your country today." I told him boldly.

"How will he contact you, if he wishes to?" Ken asked.

I handed him a business card. The address and telephone number on it had already been set up by the Intelligence Service in the UK. It was a fake telephone line that seems as though it is a legitimate company. Whenever a number calls the receptionist knows who the number has been obtained from and will respond to the call as if the business was genuine. If anyone were to check, they would find a registered company and address that checks out. All a bit James Bond really.

"Ask him to call this number, tell him it is Andy the gentleman that came to the house the other night. Tell him it's important, please."

"I will try my best, if he responds badly, I could get into trouble." Ken worried.

"He seemed a very nice man when we met the other night in Muntinlupa. Had you driven him there?" I dropped the name so Ken knew I had really been there.

"What was the name of the street?" Ken tested me. Should I tell him? I might be risking the General and his group. I had to tell Ken, I had little choice, I wanted him to believe me.

"General Gregorio Del Pilar Street." I said boldly and somewhat rashly. Ken thought for a moment, he wasn't going to admit he took Ramos to an opposition meeting.

"Ok, I'll give him your card. I don't think he will get back to you, especially as tomorrow afternoon I take the General to the airport, he is away for a few days in Cebu." Ken finally offered.

Hell, the Generals driver was as leaky as my grandmother! This was a serious breach of security to tell me this. Maybe it was a setup, but I doubted it. I wouldn't be asking Ken for anything after this, he was too risky.

"Thank you so much." I handed him another £50, this was a lot of money in those days, more than a month's wages.

"Thank you for meeting me Ken and thank your brother for passing your name to me. You both have been very helpful today."

I returned to my car where Jonny was waiting and got in the front next to him.

"Another clandestine meeting sir?" Jonny asked and it was an impertinent question. I didn't answer him. He would know too much.

"Hotel Jonny, thank you" I replied.

The next morning, I woke, I felt alone. No naked girl next to me, no giggles as I watched her consume a mountain of bacon. Instead, I dressed and ate alone and I didn't like it. Jonny was waiting in the lobby of the hotel. I greeted him and he drove me through the busy Manila streets to my office on Chino Roces Avenue, Makati. Jonny waited in the car, Rosa hadn't arrived yet it was earlier than I would normally turn up to the office. I took the time to check some of the cyphers that were already being received from Trisha, one note from her a day, each with information from Imelda Marcos's diary and anything else that she had overheard, it was very good intelligence. This girl was doing fantastic work, and she was very brave to send it.

I coded and sent information on the meeting I had with Si, the secret house meeting, and everything else I had done here. I did not include the safe house with Diwa. That would remain a secret to me, Rosa and Karen only.

By the time I finished, Rosa had arrived, she made a coffee for us both and sat down at her desk to chat. The phone rang.

"Sir." she said, "it's General Ramos."

"I'll take it." trying hard to contain my excitement, we switched places. I didn't have my own phone, there was little point in the expense, I would never normally be here once I returned to the UK. The call had been routed through the London reception service. I was very excited that he thought I was important enough to call as soon as Ken gave him my message.

"Hello sir, thank you for calling so soon." I greeted Ramos. There was some small talk before we got down to business.

"I understand you want to talk again. You have something important to tell me." Ramos stated.

"I want to tell you not to trust the Americans." I began.

"Why? They are providing us money for our cause, they promise arms." He began.

"Really, you have received shipments already?" I asked.

"Not yet, they have said it will arrive nearer the time we need the items." He continued.

"The items will never arrive. This is what I need to tell you. I suggest you test them, test the Americans. Ask for something, maybe ten weapons, see if they deliver. I can promise you they will not. The Americans are full of promise and nothing more." I told Ramos.

"Why are you so certain of this?" Ramos asked.

"I know the Americans, I work with them all the time in my line of business."

"And, just what is your line of business?" Ramos sounded rattled.

"I tell you, the British won't promise you anything they can't deliver. That way you can trust every word I say."

"You promised us weapons before, is that the truth?" Ramos asked.

"The British can't get you weapons directly, but they will help you indirectly. I promise you this."

"You promise? A promise is a bold statement. So, what is in this for the British? You must want something?" he asked.

"Good relations, that's all. The British want good relations with their friends. To do good business between us, yes, ok, I'll say it, maybe sometimes they may not be able to offer the cheapest, but they provide the best. British reputation is the best in the world. We will offer you advice. We have the know-how, and world-leading technology, we can bring you prosperity, you name it and none of it will be false promises. Check my words, test the Americans." I told him.

We talked on the phone for well over an hour, in this book I have shortened the conversation for obvious reasons. I could tell gradually his tone was becoming more friendly and trusting. It was, like all my time in the Philippines, very high risk and time was the cause. I just had not allowed myself the time to develop people properly. In a way, the shortness of time forced me to be bolder and take a few risks, but I was, amazingly, getting the job done. As our conversation progressed and I sensed he began to trust what I was telling him, I decided to go all out and throw myself to the wolves.

"To prove how the British can be of use to you, I will tell you this, and perhaps you will then see, how useful I can be." I paused, I ran through in my head the ramifications of what I was about to tell Ramos. My next sentence was going to be the riskiest I had ever been, it would totally expose me, but I felt I needed to give Ramos something to prove what we could provide him.

"Tomorrow, Imelda Marcos will be visiting the Manila Hotel, she will be looking at and probably buying some shoes, there is a new brand of high fashion, high-end shoe, Monolo Blahnik, have you heard of the brand? This new shoe brand is looking to open a shop in Manila for the rich and famous. Have you heard of them?"

"No, what do I want with women's shoes?" Ramos replied.

"For your lady perhaps? Monolo Blahnik was on the cover of Vogue magazine this year. Of course, you can't go see for yourself at the hotel, you will be in Cebu, you leave this afternoon." I could almost hear Ramos's incredulous rage, it was anger because he now saw that I knew about Marcos's movements, and he was angrier that I knew his own movements too. Of course, it had just been obtained from Ken the day before, and at the end of the day, it was a tiny speck of intelligence, but it was still intelligence. If he had asked for more now, I had very little to give.

"So, you see, in your coming struggle, the revolution, the British can give you an advantage over your enemy, we can help your cause by supplying you with intelligence."

History tells us that it wouldn't be until 1986 that the EDSA (the road, Epifanio de los Santos Avenue) People Power Revolution would topple Marcos.

The files I had been given by Chris Mass back in London indicated that Ramos, while Chief of Police, was very unhappy at being told to arrest, torture and murder many people for Marcos all without trial. He confided in me years later, that he thought that it would be him that would face the consequences for such horrific actions. The beginnings of the revolt, and early dissent meetings were happening, I knew because I had been to one a few days earlier.

The phone call ended with a promise to meet again in a couple of days, but this never happened, there wasn't really a need and I felt it would be far too dangerous. Ramos now knew who I was, there would be no real need to hide my purpose in the Philippines from him and I thought it was good that he knew the British were there as well as the CIA who openly operated in Manila. I could operate in the same way, but I wasn't going to openly say where I was based. I had to protect my agents at all cost and I wanted them to know they were under my protection. Contact would be via the special number in London, diverted to me, wherever I was.

I never fully trusted Ramos, after all, what policeman can you trust! But I continued to supply any intelligence I thought suitable, not all, but only particular information necessary for my cause rather than his, but it was all made to look like I was helping him. In a few weeks, I would ask for a return of favour, just to test Ramos. I asked if he could give me any information regarding the disappearance of Rosa's son. Not only did Ramos find him, but he got him released. Whether this was just a simple ploy on his behalf to get me to provide more intelligence or a genuine act of kindness who knows.

Our relationship slowly developed over the years, later our connection would play a better part during the weeks leading up to Marcos's exile, and I will go into that later in this book in the chapter "End of President Marcos." In that chapter also Ramos found out, as I had said, that the Americans were not about to supply him arms either. It would be a few years later, but I did remind Ramos that I had told him so.

Agent 5, Juan Enrile

The night I went to Rosa's friend's house for the secret meeting, also present was Juan Valentin Furagganan Ponce Enrile Senior. Marcos appointed Enrile as his Secretary of National Defence on February 9, 1970, a position Enrile held until August 27, 1971, when he resigned to run unsuccessfully for the senate. He was reappointed Defence Secretary by Marcos on January 4, 1972, which was his position when I met him in 1975 at that house meeting. I realised, more than they did, that he and Ramos together formed a very powerful alliance and could form a very strong opposition to Marcos, if only they could get organised properly. Should I be the one to get involved in the politics of the Philippines? It was clear Marcos was headed for a downward slide with his imposition of martial law. The Americans were only interested in the strategic importance of the islands for themselves. They might protect Marcos if their own position was under threat. I saw the American position as wasteful, wouldn't it be cheaper to supply a few arms and support a coup and a new president with a new cheaper lease deal, in return of the favour?

I didn't have to work hard at all to bring Enrile into the fold. He and Ramos needed support from foreign sympathisers they were willing to risk sticking their necks out for support. I couldn't understand why they needed weapons as any coup attempt was bound to involve sections of the army, because Ramos in particular, was army. Both men were at the secret meeting I attended. They knew I was bringing British money and intelligence. I couldn't bring weapon supplies, the British weren't willing to get involved in such an open way. Guns were visible, people may ask about the origin. The British prefer to be more subtle in aid. Intelligence, while not so obvious, can be more powerful if used in the right way.

Enrile knew I was offering help, it would only be time before he would contact me, then, provided I offered the right kind of help, he would be onside, and I felt sure I could use him as an agent for British Intelligence. My goal in all this was to build relations, provide the foundation for better trade and have a good base of intelligence in the strategic location that the Philippines has.

One of Marcos's justifications for the declaration of martial law was terrorism. He cited the alleged ambush attack on Enrile's car on September 22, 1972, as a pretext for martial law. At the time, many people doubted that the attack actually took place.

Marcos, said "It was a good thing he was riding in his security car as a protective measure... This makes the martial law proclamation a necessity." Oscar Lopez, a resident of Wack-Wack, who lived along the street of the alleged ambush, stated that he had heard a lot of shooting on the night of the incident. When he went out to see what was happening, he saw only an empty car riddled with bullets. Lopez's driver, who had happened to witness the incident, stated that "there was a car that came and stopped beside a Meralco post (electricity pole). Some people exited the car, and another car came by to shoot at the car, to make it look like it was ambushed."

Juan Ponce Enrile 1987

Doubts surrounding the alleged ambush were further confirmed in a press conference on February 23, 1986 when then Lieutenant General Fidel Ramos and Enrile admitted that the attack was staged to justify the martial law declaration. Both radio and television media covered this, and millions of Filipinos witnessed the said confession. Furthermore, in several interviews, Enrile was reported as confirming that the attempted assassination was faked to justify the Martial Law declaration.

So, my work in Manila, I felt, was complete. I had achieved the basic establishment of an outstation. If there were a need to expand further, I could always return. It was time to return to London. I was feeling happy with myself. I had once again achieved the impossible. Of course, luck had played a significant role, but I took pleasure in my now proven ability to spot perfect character fits within moments. You may think it could be foolish, but it has never failed me. Certainly, how the Manila office ran over the next eleven years or so was the proof.

I had a day and a half of free time left. For my own safety I decided it would be a good idea that I checked out of the Manila Hotel. In the office, within earshot of Rosa, I pretended to book flights home, but I actually booked for two days' time. I also booked to spend a night at the Luneta Hotel. I wanted it to look like I was leaving later that day. There was a small gathering in the lounge in my room at the Manila Hotel, Rosa, Jonny my ever-faithful driver and Angel, the hotel assistant who helped me with the interviews in what now seemed years ago, so much had happened since. The gathering could not be larger than this, everyone else had to remain anonymous, Mak the scooter driver for instance, although known to Rosa and Ken, I could not let Angel see him, for each other's safety. We were joined for a short while by the hotel manager who had also done so much for me, especially allowing Angel to help me on my first day.

After the small goodbye party, Ken drove me and my bags to Manila airport which, in a few years, unknown to us all, would be part of the arguably most famous event in Philippine history. The assassination of Ninoy Aquino, which would be the event that would mark the beginning of the end of the Marcos reign.

At the airport, Ken left me with my bags at the departure lounge. After I was sure he had left, I jumped into a taxi and checked into the Luneta Hotel, Kalaw Avenue, near Rizal Park, Manila. Unknown to me, during the war, the hotel became a brothel for American soldiers who stayed in Manila. Just my luck, it was still showing signs that it was still used for that purpose. It definitely needed a makeover, it had seen better days, but I needed a place to stay for a night in order to secretly check that my office would run as I hoped in my absence. Reasonably close to the Makati area, in the evening I could secretly enter my office and take a look around make sure messages had been coded and sent correctly. How could I doubt Rosa, she was the most loyal employee, agent, friend I could have. None the less, I felt I needed to check all was well in my absence. It was all good, I need not have any doubts.

Later that evening as I returned to the hotel there were a few girls loitering outside the hotel, so I invited one of them to join me for dinner, I never really like eating alone.

After breakfast, she left, I checked out of the hotel and I took a taxi ride around the city taking a last look, for the moment, at the city, my office and places I had been over the previous couple of weeks. All looked normal and the bustle of Manila would carry on without me for a while.

The taxi dropped me at the airport, and I did feel genuine sorrow that I was leaving. The people here were so poor and yet so generous and kind. My stay was etched into my forever-memory. I took a deep breath to take in the last remnants of Manila air and checked in my bags for my flight home, a long thirty-two-hour journey.

Arriving home, I was feeling the worse jetlag ever, also the stress of the mission added to my tiredness, but after twelve hours sleep and feeling no better, I checked in with Karen by phone, I promised to see her later that day and travelled into London by train to meet 'C' Maurice Oldfield. The city seemed cold and grey and uninviting compared to Manila. The people here never seem to smile, or even say good morning. I wanted to be back in the Philippines, I missed it already. Our meeting was set for the Millennium Club. Not wanting to be seen entering Century House as usual, but I did feel after that I should go to visit Karen, just to report and to check messages were working well from Manila.

We were joined at the meeting by Francis, Head of HUMINT, who was equally as astonished I had achieved so much in a ridiculously short time. He commented it should have taken months if not years to put together such a group of agents. Maurice complimented me by telling Francis I was one of the better controllers and that many could learn from me, which I took as a massive compliment indeed.

The meeting with Maurice lasted a good two hours, as I briefed him and we discussed further the role my agents could play. He seemed incredulous that I had set up the whole thing so quickly and easily, at first, he doubted the loyalty of the agents. By the time our meeting finished, he seemed happy that everything was good. He did question a few of my expenses, in particular the cost of one night in the Luneta Hotel, apparently, I had eaten enough for two. But business is business and over all I left him very happy that good intelligence was already coming from my office. Especially as I was able to tell him Imelda Marcos's movements for the next day, as Trisha had seen Imelda's diary and had sent a coded note. Luckily, Fidel Ramos had also checked in with some information. Maurice left very happy that I had good contacts. Of course, for everyone's safety, he didn't know precisely who, what names, were acting for me, each person had been assigned a code name, and in this book all names have been changed apart from Enrile and Ramos.

After the meeting, I went to Karen's flat, let myself in and waited for her to return from work. I had told her I would be there, so that she wouldn't work until ten at night or some late hour.

She arrived with a huge, gorgeous smile for me, I stood up from the dining chair in the window where I was sat watching London. We kissed the most loving kiss.

She told me to go sit in the lounge and she would prepare a meal, I poured a couple of drinks for us both. I didn't sit in the lounge, instead I stood, and we talked in the kitchen as she got busy rustling up some food. We were so good together. It was fantastic to be in her company again, it made London a so much warmer place to be. As she served the food onto plates, I moved into the lounge put on soft music and sat on the sofa. Moments later Karen entered the room with our food, to find me fast asleep, I was so tired. Somehow, she moved me to her bed, I have no idea how. I woke late next morning, undressed. I have no clue whatsoever how I got there or how I was undressed, I was just totally exhausted. I hadn't realised how tiring and stressful the previous few weeks had been. As I sat up in bed and gathered my senses and figured out where I was, Karen came in to the bedroom naked, with cups of tea. It was normal for her to be naked in her own home. Her flat mate at the time Jenny, who features later in this story, was her best friend, they shared everything, was equally at ease with herself and I'd sometimes visit to find them both semi-clad or naked on warm days in the summer. It was natural and sweet to be that at ease with each other. I apologised to Karen for falling asleep last night, she giggled and told me I would never know what I had missed. She understood completely the reason for my exhaustion.

And so, began years of monitoring and controlling the Philippine agents. Mostly trivial stuff from Trisha and Si. Occasionally, some titbit from Rosa added to her coded messages. Ramos and Enrile sent me information, so long as in return or beforehand I would give something useful to them. Over the years nearer to 1986 that got quite intense. Of course, there were other sources, from worldwide contacts, the Americans, press, other media and volunteers. All-in-all, a more or less complete picture could be built on the state of the country from the main area of concern in Manila. All information was passed to the Head of HUMINT, Francis, who seemed happy with the kind of intelligence being sent from the new sources. At least he didn't say anything to me if he wasn't. But I found the British hierarchy above me did seem hypocritical as far as the Philippines went. I heard that millions of pounds were sent to the Marcos regime. Call it what you like, but to me it was to grease the wheels to assist the flow of trade deals, and it was certainly working. My set up was perfect should the powers that be decide that it was time to help the poor people of the Philippines rid themselves of the embezzling murdering tyrant known as President Ferdinand Emmanuel Edralin Marcos. Over the years opposition was growing. Of course, it would grow, people wouldn't stand for what was happening to them for long. Ramos and Enrile were two of the leaders, among others, who were forming a growing discontented voice. Several times I was asked by them or their associates for arms, the British would not help in that department and I had to keep reminding them of this. But I was able to help in other ways. I also knew the Americans via the CIA in Manila were promising arms, but the game they were playing was not the game I would join. I preferred to be honest with what the British would help with. Despite Ramos and Enrile showing me discontent with our help, in the end it was the right choice. When the revolution was in full flow the opposition groups showed real anger toward the Americans, whereas the British via me were treated as real friends, and I hadn't promised anything other than intel.

The End of President Marcos

In order to provide a clear picture of the years leading up to Marcos's downfall and exile and beyond, I have to exclude so many names and political groups, it is just too complicated to fill these pages with everything that was going on. I need to keep my story simple enough to keep it interesting. I apologise if you feel I leave out something you know happened, I just want to present my story with some clarity.

To present this section of my story, I will tell it in a timeline. If you feel the way I write this section of the history of the Philippines is too simplistic, then there are plenty of other publications where you can read the full picture.

What follows is a combination of popular press and media reports, with my own account (*in italics*) as witness to some of the events of the time.

1967, Benigno "Ninoy" Aquino was elected to the Philippine Senate and became very critical of Marcos. Aquino was imprisoned on trumped up charges shortly after Marcos's 1972 declaration of martial law.

1978, while still in prison, Aquino founded his political party, Lakas ng Bayan (LABAN meaning, People's Power), to run for office in the Interim Batasang Pambansa (the House of Representatives). All LABAN candidates lost, primarily to candidates of Marcos's party, amid allegations of election fraud.

1980, Aquino had a heart attack in prison and was allowed to leave the country two months later by Marcos's wife, Imelda. He spent the next three years in exile near Boston, USA, before deciding to return to the Philippines.

Ninoy was getting impatient in Boston, he felt isolated by the flow of events in the Philippines. In early 1983, Marcos was seriously ailing, the Philippine economy was just as rapidly declining, and insurgency was becoming a serious problem. Ninoy thought that by coming home he might be able to persuade Marcos to restore democracy and somehow revitalise the Liberal Party. However, Ninoy was completely aware of the danger that he was heading into.

1983, August 21, Former Congressman Rashid Lucman helped Aquino circumvent a Marcos order not to issue passports to the Aquino family, providing him with a passport under the alias "Marcial Bonifacio" – a reference to martial law as well as Aquino's detention at Fort Bonifacio.

Aquino flew a long and roundabout route from the United States to several Asian cities such as Singapore and Kuala Lumpur to meet Malaysian leaders, and then to Hong Kong, where he boarded a China Airlines plane in Taipei before landing in Manila.

Prior to his departure from Taipei, Aquino gave an interview from his room at the Grand Hotel in which he indicated that he would be wearing a bulletproof vest. He advised the journalists that would be accompanying him on the flight,
"You have to be ready with your hand cameras, because this action can become very fast. In a matter of three or four minutes it could be all over, and I may not be able to talk to you again after this."
His last few moments in the flight while being interviewed by the journalist Jim Laurie, and just prior to disembarking from the flight at Manila airport, were recorded on camera. Accompanied by his brother-in-law, ABC News correspondent Ken Kashiwahara, along with other members of the press, Aquino boarded China Airlines Flight 811, a Boeing 767-200 registered as B-1836, that departed Chiang Kai-shek International Airport. In Manila, a contingent of over 1,000 armed soldiers and police were assigned by the government to provide security for Aquino's arrival. Flight 811 arrived at Manila International Airport at gate number 8 (now 11) at 13:04.
When the airplane's arrived at the gate, soldiers boarded the airplane to fetch Aquino. The soldiers escorted him off the airplane and onto the jet bridge. However, instead of following the jet bridge to the terminal, they exited down the service staircase onto the apron, where a military vehicle was waiting. As Aquino disembarked the plane, one of the military personnel was heard saying "Pusila! Pusila! Op! Pusila! Pusila! Pusila!" (Pusila is the Visayan word for "shoot") before gunshots were heard. It was recorded on the news camera, but the actual shooting of Aquino was not caught on camera due to flashes of bright sunlight as the camera left the plane looking into the sun.

When the firing stopped, Aquino and a man later identified as Rolando Galman lay dead on the apron, both from gunshot wounds. Aquino's body was carried into an Aviation Security Command (AVSECOM) van by two AVSECOM SWAT soldiers, while another soldier at the bumper of the van continued to fire shots at Galman. The AVSECOM van sped away, leaving behind the bullet-riddled body of Galman.

Just a few hours after the shooting, the government alleged that Rolando Galman was the man who killed Aquino, accusing him of being a hitman acting on orders from Philippine Communist Party chair Rodolfo Salas. A government re-enactment that aired on television days after the shooting alleged that Galman hid under the service staircase while Aquino and his military escorts descended it, and as Aquino neared the van, Galman emerged from under the staircase and shot Aquino in the back of the head. Several members of the security detail in turn fired several shots at Galman, killing him.

There were numerous irregularities in this version of events, including the amount of time between Aquino leaving the plane to the sound of gunfire (eight seconds), whereas it has been calculated it would have taken at least 13 seconds to reach the bottom of the stairs as well as how an alleged lone gunman could have penetrated a security detail of over 1,000 people at the airport without assistance. Politicians and diplomats found evident contradictions between the claim as well as the photos and videotape footage that documented the time before and after the shooting. Years later, the official investigation into the assassination concluded that Galman was a scapegoat in a larger plot to kill Aquino.

In my opinion not just a scapegoat, but a plant, employed to assassinate Aquino, Galman unaware that Marcos's men, in order to hide the evidence, would shoot him too. How did Galman know Aquino would be taking the stairs? Surely the normal route would be across the bridge and into the terminal building.

1984, May 14, Elections for the Batasang Pambansa (House of Representatives) were held. The United Nationalist Democratic Organization (UNIDO) and the Partido Demokratiko Pilipino-Lakas ng Bayan (PDP-LABAN) coalition decided to take part. Aquino's widow, Corazón, threw her support behind the opposition candidates, who surprised Marcos by winning 56 seats out of the 183 amidst familiar allegations of fraud.

October 24, The Agrava Board, a fact-finding commission tasked with investigating the Aquino assassination, concluded that there was a military conspiracy behind the killing and implicated Armed Forces Chief of Staff, General Fabián Ver.

Ver becomes an important player in this story, keep his name in mind.

1985, February 22, General Ver, 24 soldiers, and one civilian stand trial before the Sandiganbayan for the Aquino murder. Ver takes a leave of absence as Armed Forces Chief of Staff. (*Sandiganbayan is a special court in the Philippines that has jurisdiction over criminal and civil cases, corrupt practices and other offenses committed by public officers and employees, including those in government-owned and controlled corporations*).

August 13, Opposition MPs filed a motion for impeachment against Marcos in the Batasang, citing culpable violation of the Constitution and "hidden wealth." The majority party denied the motion.

November 3, Marcos suddenly announced the holding of snap elections after alleged prodding from the United States.

In fact, the British presented evidence to the Americans from intelligence my people had sent from Manila, so, while the media might announce that it was prodding it was actually 'strong' advice and definitely not alleged.

December 2, General Ver and all his co-accused are acquitted by the Sandiganbayan. Marcos reinstated him as Chief of Staff amid widespread protest.

December 5, The Opposition made a formal announcement of the Aquino-Laurel alliance for the elections.

1986, February 7, attempts of fraud, vote-buying, intimidation, and violence were reported and election returns were tampered with. The Commission on Elections (COMELEC) tally board showed Marcos leading while the National Citizen's Movement for the Free Elections (NAMFREL) consistently showed Cory Aquino ahead by a comfortable margin.

February 9, thirty-five computer workers at the COMELEC tabulation centre in the Philippine International Convention

Centre walked out and sought refuge at the Baclaran Church, protesting the tampering of election results.

February 11, Oppositionist ex-Governor Evelio Javier of Antique was murdered in front of the provincial capitol where canvassing was being held. Primary suspects were the bodyguards of the local KBL leader.

February 13, The Catholic Bishops' Conference of the Philippines issued a statement condemning the elections as fraudulent.

February 15, President Ferdinand Marcos and his running mate Arturo Tolentino declared winners of the February 7 Elections.

February 16, around two million people gathered at the Quirino Grandstand in Luneta Park, Manila to protest the proclamation of Marcos and Tolentino as winners of the February 7 Snap Elections. Opposition leader and UNIDO presidential candidate Corazon Aquino called for nationwide civil disobedience and a boycott of all Marcos crony-owned companies in protest of the proclamation.

Things are moving so fast, you can imagine how busy my office was at that time. I was receiving so much intelligence from Ramos and Enrile. Their aim was to supply me so much information that when it came to a real push to supply them with arms, they would hope it would be hard for me to refuse. I had to figure a way to let them down on that score very gently or I would lose them. I knew from intelligence from Trisha in the palace that the next few days would be a good time for a coup attempt. One reason was because the Marcos's were just not getting it. They didn't understand how much unrest outside the palace there really was. If it was left too late, they might cotton on and batten down or start to slaughter opposition leaders and their followers. Also, I had to let Trisha know that if there was an invasion of the palace, she was to get out fast and to flee to the safe house in Butuan, Mindanao Island. Enrile clearly took my advice as the next few days proves.

February 22, 12:00 AM: Defence Minister Enrile and key aides finalised Enrile's speech in which he proclaimed himself head of a ruling junta after rebel troops led by the Reform the Armed Forces Movement (RAM) were to make an assault on Malacañang (Marcos's Palace). An assault was planned for February 23 at 2:00 am.

February 22, Final meeting of the RAM at Enrile's house in Dasmariñas Village before the assault on Malacañang Palace.

Quite expectedly an appeal for arms arrives at my office. I delay a reply while I go into conference with "C" now Chris Curwen. I knew what the answer would be realistically, but I need to update all heads of departments in London what is happening and about to go down. I cannot stress how dangerous life was in Manila for anyone outside the Marcos circle now. I delayed by asking what arms America would be supplying, knowing they would not be helping at all, they preferred to hedge their bets on Marcos coming out on top. They protected their army base lease at all costs to the population of the Philippines detriment. A bad choice in my view, and I told CIA contact Mike Heseltine in Manila as much. I really don't like Americans, self-serving as always.

2:00 AM, Chief of Staff Fabian Ver (now Marcos's right-hand man) called in additional units to defend Malacañang.

3:00 AM: The final meeting at the Defence Minister's home concluded. Lieutenant Colonel Honasan and Kapunan began their reconnaissance of Malacañang Palace. To their dismay, they discovered battle-hardened Marines stationed at their main point of attack. It looked like the Americans had tipped off Marcos that their may be an imminent attack on the palace.

6:30 AM: Major Avelino Razon briefs AFP Vice Chief of Staff General Ramos on the developments of RAM's plans.

9:00 AM: Ver sent Colonel Rolando Abadilla to Colonel Honasan to inform him that their plans had been made known already and that RAM should not make any rash decisions.

Cory Aquino leaves for Cebu to continue the Civil Disobedience Campaign.

United States Ambassador Stephen Bosworth along with Philip Habib, President Ronald Reagan's personal special envoy to Marcos, visited the Palace for a meeting with the President. They discussed the recent elections and the political situation. The U.S. envoys called on Marcos to retire Ver.

12:45 PM: While Marcos had his meeting with the U.S. envoys, Captain Ricardo Morales, one of Imelda Marcos's close security team and who was a mole of RAM in the PSG (*Morales mole* activities also reached me, but I have not mentioned him as an agent of mine as he didn't deal directly with me), reconnoitred the defences of the Palace grounds, and took the initiative to withdraw some firearms from the PSG armoury. He was arrested and was brought to the office of the Aide-de-camp for interrogation.

Trisha must surely be in the greatest of danger now. I try not to panic her but I get a message to her to go home and pack to leave. I tell Rosa to arrange transportation to Butuan and onward to the safe house. Unknown to me, Trisha and Mak, the scooter rider that delivered Trisha's messages had become lovers, not surprising really, as they were young and in contact almost every day. So, travel arrangements were made for both of them. This would leave me without much in the way of a direct intelligence source inside the palace, but there was enough coming from Enrile and Ramos for me to be kept fully informed. Trisha and Mak had done their bit for Britain.

1:45 PM: As the meeting came to a close, barely had Ambassador Bosworth left the room, General Ver stormed into the Presidential study to convey the recent arrest of four officers in the PSG who were found to be members of RAM.

American diplomat Philip Habib met Marcos and as he left Malacañang Palace confided to the press that, "Cory won the election and deserves our support. Marcos is finished, and we ought to offer him asylum in the United States."

This is the first public clue that the Americans see the end for Marcos.

2:00 PM: With their plans discovered, Enrile and the RAM officers, had to change their direction. They decided that they need to draw the public support if they are going to succeed.

2:15 PM: Cory in the rally in Cebu called for the boycott of Marcos crony-owned businesses.

3:00 PM: Honasan gives the signal to prepare his men for combat. He, Enrile and Kapunan fly to Aguinaldo in a helicopter.

3:30 PM: At Camp Aguinaldo, Enrile's guards brought out brand-new M-16s, Uzis and Galils. Enrile orders troop deployment around Camp Crame.

A Galil is an Israeli brand of gun. I have no idea how or when the Israelis began supporting Marcos, this was news to me. I had been asked yet again for help with arms supply. I had suggested as the British would not help in that department that I would help through personal contacts. It was a fake promise to keep intelligence flowing from Manila. I messaged Enrile that my weapon supply would not get delivered in time as things were moving too fast. I pretended that I had found a supply in Hong Kong to make it sound as though I was in full support. But it would take two weeks at least to arrange delivery. I hoped that this lie would get me off the hook.

3:45 PM: Thinking that he will not survive the day, Enrile got through to Cardinal Sin (*yes, that's his real name*) and sought his moral and active support.

4:30 PM: The first military region to go over to the rebel side was Regional Unified Command No. 8, which included troops in Mrs. Marcos's own province, Leyte, led by commander, Brigadier General Salvador Mison who was in Camp Aguinaldo.

5:00 PM: Unaware of unfolding events, Ver and Imelda Marcos attended the wedding of a general's son at Villamor Air Base. Ver was stunned when told. Marcos calls his three children to Malacañang. Enrile tells Sin: "I will be dead within one hour. I don't want to die … If it is possible, do something. I'd still like to live."

5:30 PM: President Marcos's first response to the mutiny was to call his family to Malacañang.

6:00 PM: General Ramos arrived at Camp Aguinaldo after a dialogue in his Alabang house with a group called the Cory Crusaders.

6:30 PM: Malacañang Palace received a "report" that Ramos and Enrile were "officially withdrawing their support" of the Marcos administration.

I suspected the informant was the American CIA Mike Heseltine, but I have no proof of this.

6:45 PM: Enrile and Ramos, surrounded by their staff and guards held a press conference at the Social Hall of the GHQAFP, and made the official announcement of their withdrawal of support of the Marcos administration.

Enrile stated, "We are going to die here fighting."

Ramos added, "There has become an elite Armed Forces of the Philippines that no longer represents the rank and officers' corps of the Armed Forces. The President of 1986 is not the President to whom we dedicated our service. It is clear that he no longer is the able and capable commander-in-chief that we count upon. He has put his personal family interest above the interest of the people. We do not consider President Marcos as now being a duly constituted authority."

Enrile adds, "I cannot in my conscience recognise the President as the commander-in-chief of the Armed Forces and I am appealing to the other members of the Cabinet to heed the will of the people expressed during the last elections. Because in my own region, I know that we cheated in the elections to the extent of 350,000 votes. No, I will not serve under Mrs. Aquino even if she is installed as a president. Our loyalty is to the Constitution and the Country. You are welcome to join us. We have no food..."

Ramos closes, "I am not even acting Chief of Staff of the Armed Forces. I think that when he made that announcement to you and to the whole world last Sunday, he was just fooling us, and he was fooling the entire world because he flip-flopped so many times already. I would like to appeal to the fair and to the dedicated and people-oriented members of the AFP and the INP to join us in this crusade for better government."

7:00 PM: Cory Aquino received the news of the withdrawal of support to Marcos by Enrile and Ramos. She called Manila to verify the report.

Marcos remained in the Palace study room with Fabian, Irwin Ver, and Information Minister Gregorio Cendaña.

8:15 PM: General Ver ordered Brigadier General Fidel Singson, Chief of the Intelligence Service of the Armed Forces of the Philippines (ISAFP) to "Destroy Radio Veritas!"

Unbeknown to Ver, Singson was already in the process of defecting to the rebel group. Singson sends his men to Radio Veritas, not to destroy, but only to reconnoitre the area.

I had been in touch with Singson over the years leading up to 1986, via the CIA's Mike Heseltine. Intelligence Services sometimes, when it can prove useful, do occasionally contact their counter parts, similar to how I knew of and contacted Mike in the CIA. I have not mention him before because I never considered him to be an agent of mine, but he did pass information to me, most likely to try to bring me, therefore the British onside. It was only once the Americans began to realise Marcos was close to falling that Singson indicated he would switch sides. This was purely to save his own skin. I didn't think much of his loyalty. However, he was a source of useful information when it suited him. I never met him personally.

8:30 PM: Cardinal Sin went on air and called the people, "Please, do not be alarmed, stay home."

8:45 PM: The rebel group were taken aback by the Cardinal's announcement and calls him to clarify their request. They asked him to send the people to the camps.

9:00 PM: Cardinal Sin went on air once more and said, "Leave your homes now ...I ask you to support Mr. Enrile and General Ramos, give them food if you like, they are our friends."

Enrile ended a phone conversation with Ver, with both adversaries agreeing not to attack that night. It was a revolution that started with a ceasefire.

9:30 PM: Butz Aquino, the younger brother of Ninoy Aquino, with the August Twenty-One Movement (ATOM) Executive Committee deliberated whether to support Enrile and Ramos. The Executive Committee wanted to wait on Cory Aquino for instructions. Aquino finally decided to head to Camp Aguinaldo to support the rebels.

Cory Aquino meanwhile is also deciding on what actions to take after receiving the call from ATOM. She requested to speak with Enrile first.

Colonel Antonio Sotelo, Commander of the 15th Strike Wing, received a call at his Villamor Air Base office from Colonel Hector Tarrazona, who was also a member of RAM, he asked the Commander whether he was with them. Colonel Sotelo confirms that he supports RAM and orders his Squadron Commanders to arm their attack helicopters.

10:00 PM: Radio Veritas continued with the blow-by-blow account of the rebellion.

Enrile calls Aquino who was secured in the Carmelite convent in Cebu City, they have a brief phone conversation. (Aquino had known of Enrile's coup plans. But she returned to Cebu with her vice-presidential running mate Doy Laurel to thank the Cebuanos for the 70,000 margin of victory given her "despite the goons of Marcos allies." Aquino also went to sell her seven-point program of non-violent protest, which was just a week old, to the second most populous city in the country.)

In Malacañang, Imelda tells reporters of a plot to kill her and Marcos at 12:30 AM.

10:20 PM: The August Twenty-One Movement's Butz Aquino, despite his group's decision to wait, threw his support behind the rebels and calls on volunteers to meet him at Isetann department store in Cubao to prepare to march to EDSA to support the so-called breakaway Marcos military.

10:30 PM: Marcos announced over government-owned Channel 4, that he is in total control of the situation and calls on Enrile and Ramos "to stop this stupidity and surrender so that we may negotiate." He reported the thwarting of an attempt on his life by one of Imelda's bodyguards in a conspiracy involving Enrile and Ramos and then proceeded to present the alleged assassin, Morales, who read a supposed confession.

Nuns and seminarians of Bandila, a moderate coalition, were the first to form a human barricade around Camp Crame.

Superstar Nora Aunor arrives at EDSA.

Food starts arriving in response to Enrile's appeal that while they are ready to die for their country, they have no food for the troops.

11:00 PM: Enrile told Marcos over Radio Veritas: "Enough is enough, Mr. President. Your time is up. Do not miscalculate our strength now."

11:15 PM: Ver orders power and water lines at Aguinaldo and Crame cut, but he was ignored.

The crowd at EDSA grows.

Others that withdrew support for Marcos: Lieutenant. Colonel Jerry Albano and his security and escort battalion of 200 officers and men.

February 23, 12:00 midnight: People began to grow by the thousands around the two camps along EDSA in response to the radio address of Cardinal Sin on Radio Veritas.

1:45 AM: Supreme Court Justice Nestor Alampay resigned.

3:00 AM: AFP Chief General Fabian Ver gathered his men in Fort Bonifacio and appointed Ramas (*not to be confused with Ramos*), his protégé, to lead the assault on Camps Aguinaldo and Crame. Enrile urged Cory Aquino to announce her government, with her as duly elected president.

Sin went on air on Radio Veritas to ask Marcos and Ver not to use force.

Cardinal Jaime Sin

4:00 AM: In Washington, US Secretary of State George Shultz assembled a small group, including former Ambassador to the Philippines Michael Armacost, to lay down a firm policy on the Philippines.

I guess they are now worried they chose the wrong strategy not to support the Marcos opposition through any group.

5:30 AM: Marcos's loyalist troops destroyed Radio Veritas' transmitter in Bulacan province, limiting its reach to Luzon.

Marine commander General Artemio Tadiar is stunned to learn that Ramas, who had little combat experience, had been assigned to lead the attack on rebels. Tadiar and his men are standing guard in Malacañang.

Cory Aquino, still in Cebu City, turned down Assemblyman Ramon Mitra's offer to bring her to Palawan province, and decided to return to Manila.

Outside, in EDSA, people continued to arrive, some on foot. Human barricades were further fortified.

6:00 AM: ATOM leadership and members proceeded to EDSA and the military camps after a brief meeting in Cubao district.

7:30 AM: Radio Veritas restarted broadcasts from a backup transmitter as government forces damaged the main one in Barangay. Plans are made to move operations in Manila.

8:00 AM: Marcos ordered Colonel Antonio Sotelo, commander of the Air Force's 15th Strike Wing based in Sangley Point, to disable the helicopters in Camp Crame. No one volunteered to carry out the attack, Sotelo discusses with his men a plan to fight alongside the Enrile/Ramos troops.

10:00 AM: Soldiers from the Philippine Army and the Philippine Marine Corps from Fort Bonifacio and other camps begin to be deployed in opposition to the rebel forces. Mounted on M35 carrier trucks, LVT-5s, M113s and AIFVs and V150s, they were stopped by the massive crowd, nuns and clergy at the front of the rebel's camp Aguinaldo.

11:00 AM: Cory Aquino held a brief press conference in Cebu, asking the people to support the military rebels and calling on Marcos to step down.

12:00 Noon: Marcos men present at the presidential table included Presidential Executive Assistant Juan C. Tuvera, Agrarian Reform Minister Conrado Estrella, Public Works Minister Jesus Hipolito, Food Administrator Jesus Tanchangco, Agriculture Minister Salvador Escudero III, Education Minister Jaime C. Laya, Member of Parliament Teodulo Natividad, Budget Minister Manuel Alba, MP Salvador Britanico, former Acting Foreign Minister Pacifico Castro, MIA Manager Luis Tabuena, Isabela Govenor Faustino Dy, Information Minister Gregorio Cendaña, Justice Minister Estelito Mendoza, Justice Buenaventura Guerrero, Assistant Press Secretary Amante Bigornia, MP Antonio Raquiza, Economic Planning Minister Vicente Valdepeñas and former Senator Rodolfo Ganzon. Standing behind them are military men, including General Ver, Rear Admiral Brillante Ochoco, Felix Brawner, Carlos Martel, Juanito Veridiano, Hamilton Dimaya, Eustaquio Purugganan, Telesforo Tayko, Serapio Martillano, Pompeyo Vasquez, Victorino Azada, Arsenio Silva, Evaristo Sanches, Emerson Tangan and Navy Captain Danilo Lazo.

Marcos joined his men at the table and then appeared again on television and presented two more arrested military officers, Lieutenant Colonel Jake Malajacan and Major Ricardo Brillantes who both read statements.

Marcos said other officers had been arrested and were being interrogated. He scoffed at Enrile and Ramos and demanded that they resign. He brushed aside claims that 300,000 to 400,000 people are gathered at EDSA, some carrying images of the Virgin Mary.

1:30 PM: Police forces led by Metropolitan Police Chief Alfredo Lim ignored orders to disperse the crowd at EDSA.

2:20 PM: Cory Aquino arrives in Manila and proceeded to her sister's house in Wack-Wack, Mandaluyong.

Enrile and Ramos decided to consolidate their forces at Camp Crame.

Linking arms, the people at EDSA created a protective wall for Enrile and RAM troops as they left Camp Aguinaldo and crossed the highway to get to Crame on the other side.

2:47 PM: A car with tinted windows carrying Cory Aquino cruised alongside a Marcos loyalist column of seven tanks and two Marine battalions led by Tadiar moving on EDSA.

3:00 PM: A PMC armoured contingent stopped in full view of the crowd along Ortigas Avenue. They would later pull back. Radio Veritas had earlier learned of their planned attack on the camps.

4:00 PM: Marcos called Enrile and offered him absolute pardon. He rejected Enrile's demand that the tanks be stopped.

6:30 PM: Radio Veritas signed off after the emergency transmitter breaks down. In a news conference, Enrile announced his men's rejection of Marcos's offer of pardon. Ramos talks about "New Armed Forces."

7:00 PM: Papal Nuncio Bruno Torpigliani handed Marcos a letter from Pope John Paul II asking for a peaceful resolution of the crisis.

The White House issued a statement questioning "credibility and legitimacy" of the Marcos government. (*Finally, the Americans realised they chose the wrong side and were making attempts to appear neutral for the moment*)

9:00 PM: General Ramos made a speech to the crowd, "What is happening here is not a Coup d'état, but a revolution of the people!"

11:30 PM: As Radio Veritas signed off, due to difficulties in electricity, June Keithley and station staff took over the DZRJ radio headquarters in Santa Mesa, Manila, along Ramon Magsaysay Boulevard, planning to restart transmissions at midnight.

February 24, 12:00 midnight: Radio Veritas broadcasted from its new, secret location as "Radyo Bandido" (Outlaw radio) from the DZRJ station building.

1:00 AM: Church bells rang and word spreads that President Marcos was planning an attack.

People again converged on EDSA; tyres were set ablaze, sandbags and rocks were piled up to block the roads to Camp Crame.

3:00 AM: Armed Forces Chief of Staff General Fabian Ver was still unable to locate DZRJ, which is very near Malacañang.

3:30 AM: At Camp Crame, Defence Minister Juan Ponce Enrile warned of two oncoming armoured personnel carriers (APCs).

Human barricades led by nuns and priests prepare to block the path of the APCs.

4:00 AM: In Washington, US President Ronald Reagan refused to personally tell Marcos to step down but agreed to give him asylum.

US Secretary of State George Shultz called Ambassador Stephen Bosworth in Manila with instructions to tell Marcos "His time is up."

5:00 AM: Marcos rejected the US stand. Speaking on radio, he vows: "We'll wipe them out. It is obvious they are committing rebellion." Ver and the Army commander, Major General Josephus Ramas, gave a go signal for an all-out attack on EDSA using tear gas, gunships, jet fighters and Marine artillery.

At Camp Crame, AFP Vice Chief of Staff Lieutenant General Fidel Ramos calls for civilian reinforcements amid reports that a large loyalist military force is being assembled.

Rebel soldiers tearfully prepare for battle and ask for absolution. They sing the Philippine Military Academy hymn and bid one another farewell.

5:15 AM: The first tear-gas attack on the people by personnel of the Philippine Marines along Santolan Road.

6:00 AM: Tension rose as helicopters approached Camp Crame. Seven Sikorski's armed with rockets and cannons land inside the camp. These were the helicopters coming from the 15th Strike Wing and together with several of their helicopter crews' defect to the people and the Enrile/Ramos side upon landing in the grounds of the camp, much to their delight. It would later turn out that Colonel Antonio Sotero is a RAM supporter.

Balbas trained awesome firepower on Camp Crame after hearing an exaggerated account of rebel strength from Rodolfo Estrellado of military intelligence. Unknown to Balbas, Estrellado defected to the Enrile/Ramos forces. *After a conversation with me, advising him that it would be wiser to do so. Estrellado definitely wanted his skin to stay in tact.*

Aboard a gunboat, Commodore Tagumpay Jardiniano announced to his 50 officers that he is supporting the Ramos/Enrile forces. Officers rejoiced after minutes of silence. The frigate soon dropped anchor in the Pasig River with guns trained on Malacañang.

6:30 AM: Keithley announced that Ver and Marcos and his family had fled the country.

7:30 AM: Triumphant, Enrile and Ramos addressed an ecstatic crowd outside Camp Crame.

Two fighter planes with orders to bomb the camp tilt their wings and head toward Clark Air Base in Pampanga province.

9:00 AM: To show that they had not fled, Marcos, his family and his generals appear on television. He announces the lifting of his "maximum tolerance" policy and declares a nationwide state of emergency.

Ramas issued a "kill" order to Balbas. In reply, Balbas said he and his men were looking for maps.

9:20 AM: Ramas again ordered Balbas to fire. Balbas answers: "Sir, I am still positioning the cannons."

9:50 AM: As President Marcos made another TV appearance, MBS Channel 4 was taken over by reformist soldiers of the AFP and then signed off as its studios and facilities at the ABS-CBN Broadcasting Centre were captured.

10:15 AM: Rebel soldiers inflicted slight damage on Malacañang to indicate their capacity to strike back.

12:00 Noon: Three rebel gunships destroyed helicopters at Villamor Air Base.

12:30 PM: Marines led by Balbas withdrew from Camp Aguinaldo.

1:25 PM: Channel 4 restarted transmissions under the interim name The New TV-4 (until it was officially rebranded as the People's Television Network in April of the same year) with ex-ABS-CBN technicians supervising, within minutes Radio Veritas moved into the complex restarting transmissions.

3:00 PM: With more and more people converging on EDSA and surrounding areas, Singaporean Ambassador Peter Sung offered to fly the Marcoses to his country. Marcos refused.

4:30 PM: Ver and Ramas decide to launch a final "suicide assault."

Cory Aquino showed up on a makeshift stage in front of the Philippine Overseas Employment Agency office on EDSA and Ortigas Avenue and delivered a brief speech to the crowd.

6:00 PM: In Washington, Reagan agreed to make a public call for Marcos's resignation.

Philippine Airlines chair Roman Cruz Jr. sent his resignation letter to Cory Aquino, making him the first public official to recognise her as the duly elected president.

7:30 PM: The United States endorsed Aquino's provisional government.

8:10 PM: Marcos and his entire family appeared on television. He appealed to loyalist civilians to go to Mendiola and called on people to obey only orders issued by him as the "duly constituted authority."

He declares a 6 PM to 6 AM curfew. No one observed his curfew.

Enrile called the people to ignore the curfew citing the country is the country of the free Filipino citizens.

9:00 PM: A meeting between Aquino and the Ramos/Enrile group ended with a decision that her inauguration as President would be held at Club Filipino in San Juan the following morning.

The rebels want the inauguration to be held at Camp Crame.

11:00 PM: In Malacañang, the Marcos children's dinner with Chief Justice Ramon Aquino and his son ended. Present are Imee and Irene and their husbands, Tommy Manotoc and Greggy Araneta, and Marcos Jr., who is dressed in fatigues.

Outside, people defy the curfew and continued to roam the streets of Manila.

February 25, 12:00 midnight: Marcos loyalist soldiers fired through barbed wire barricades on Nagtahan Street, injuring several people.

Some of Marcoses' belongings were taken out of Malacañang.

3:30 AM: Marines rejoice as orders to attack Camp Crame are cancelled.

3:45 AM: Airplanes carrying reinforcements ordered by Armed Forces Chief of Staff General Fabián Ver headed for Clark Air Base. The troops stayed there for the duration of the revolt.

5:00 AM: On the phone to Washington, President Marcos asked US Senator Paul Laxalt if he should resign. Laxalt's replied, "I think you should cut and cut cleanly. The time has come."

Marcos told Labour Minister Blas Ople, who is in Washington lobbying for the Marcos regime, that he is not stepping down because first lady Imelda Marcos does not want him to.

5:15 AM: Marcos gave the go-ahead signal for his family to prepare to leave.

6:00 AM: Rebel soldiers advanced towards the Broadcast City complex, hundreds of people with them, accompanied by a rebel S-76 helicopter

8:00 AM: People are called to guard Club Filipino in San Juan in case Marcos attempted to disrupt Aquino's inauguration as president.

10:00 AM: Aquino arrived at Club Filipino. Opposition lawyer Neptali Gonzales read a resolution proclaiming her and former

Senator Salvador Laurel as duly elected President and Vice President.

10:46 AM: Aquino was sworn in as President by Senior Associate Justice Claudio Teehankee, and Salvador Laurel as Vice-President by Justice Vicente Abad Santos, at Club Filipino in San Juan.

Aquino appoints Enrile as Defence Secretary and Ramos as AFP Chief of Staff.

11:45 AM: Marcos entered Malacañang's Ceremonial Hall for his own inauguration.

11:55 AM: Just as President Marcos addressed the crowds at Malacañang Palace, RPN-9, BBC Channel 2 and IBC-13 all sign-off as rebel soldiers captured the Broadcast City complex, transmitters and studios of the stations. The New TV-4 and GMA Network continued airing as usual. The President had just taken what would be his final inauguration oath of office.

3:45 PM: Loyalist soldiers tried to ram down barricades set up at Tomas Morato and Timog Avenue in Quezon City, but people power prevailed.

On Nagtahan, pro-Aquino groups and loyalists coming from Marcos's inauguration clash.

4:30 PM: Imee Marcos's husband, Tommy Manotoc, relayed the offer of US Brigadier General Ted Allen to use American helicopters or boats to move Marcos from the Palace.

5:00 PM: Marcos called Enrile again to coordinate his departure from Malacañang.

His aides start packing not only clothes and books but also boxes of money that had been stored in his bedroom since the start of the election campaign. Prime Minister Cesar Virata negotiated Marcos's departure with Aquino.

6:30 PM: Imee and Irene Marcos pleaded with their father to leave Malacañang after he told his remaining men that he has decided to die there.

7:00 PM: US Ambassador Stephen Bosworth asked Cory Aquino if Marcos can be allowed two days in Paoay, Ilocos Norte province, before heading abroad. To prevent possible regrouping of Marcos loyalists, Aquino refused.

In Malacañang, luggage was loaded on boats, which proceeded to Pangarap golf course across the Pasig River where US helicopters were to collect the Marcos family.

It is a this point that Trisha took an opportunity while carrying some luggage to the boats. She dropped the cases by the boat and on her way back slipped out the staff entrance in the grounds. Mak later collected her and took her home, then left a message at the post box in the office. Rosa had organised tickets for the Manila to Mindanao ferry for both Mak and Trisha. The ferry was a journey of some thirty-six hours. On arrival they were met and taken to the safe house in Butuan. I had lost a valuable source of information, but I was glad the two of them were safe, Trisha had done her bit passing messages for so many years undetected. Anyhow, the Marcos's were clearly going and it was obvious there would be nothing for her to do. I'd see to it she and Mak would be safe and well looked after for the rest of their lives.

7:30 PM: The families of Ver and Eduardo Cojuangco moved to Clark Air Base in Pampanga province.

8:40 PM: A convoy of heavily secured vehicles made an escape to the US Clark Air base.

8:45 PM: The Marcos family and other government officials boarded helicopters. Some of their possessions were loaded on the helicopters.

9:05 PM: President Marcos and his family left the Malacañang Palace and were now on Clark Air Base, Radio Veritas and The New TV-4 announced the departure. As news of their departure reached the people, the millions who gathered at EDSA rejoiced, since their departure signalled the conclusion of the revolution. Crowds were already positioned along Mendiola Street, Recto Avenue and Legarda Street, having arrived there late in the afternoon and awaited the departure of the First Family. They had already encountered the pro-Marcos crowd at Nagtahan earlier.

9:20 PM: Within minutes of the announcement of the departure of the Marcos family, President Aquino made her first ever live address to the nation as chief executive via Channel 4

EDSA Avenue. Huge crowds blocking the army, estimated to be 300,000 people.

9:30 PM: Remaining members of the presidential household and employees began to pack up and leave the palace complex while the pro-Aquino crowds began to walk to the gates. *Trisha had left an hour and half earlier.*

9:45 PM: Marcos landed in Clark Air Base and is met by Bosworth. People in the area welcome him with chants of "Cory! Cory!"

9:52 PM: DZRH announced, "The Marcos's have fled the country."

10:00 PM: US Air Force TV station FEN confirmed Marcos's departure.

11:30 PM: Pro-Aquino crowds forced the opening of the Malacañang Palace gates, as they opened, thousands of Aquino supporters and participants of the revolution stormed the palace complex with little resistance.

Nuns On EDSA blocking armed troops.

During the above timeline I received very few messages from Ramos and Enrile for obvious reasons. They were far too busy with what was happening on the ground, and they had huge concerns for their own safety. My concern now the Marcos family had gone was to make sure all my agents were safe and secure. I sent messages to my office in Manila to get updates on the whereabouts of everyone. With that knowledge I could arrange a meeting with Chris Curwen in London.

Closing Operations

I had to meet with "C" Chris Curwen, the question was, should I shut down my operation. Ramos and Enrile knew who I was, the other agents in the Philippines needed to be safe. Curwen was less concerned with their safety than I was. In his opinion, they knew what they were getting into. I thought differently, Trisha certainly didn't know what she was getting into, only Ramos and Enrile did. There was a need for continued monitoring of the Philippines of course, but not at the expense of my people there. I now had no inside informant at Malacañang Palace. Ramos and Enrile were too busy looking after themselves and not likely to be of any use now they gained power. They knew who I was, so stuff would dry up from them too. Essentially, with the Marcos's gone I had no agents of worth, other than Ramos and Enrile, and those sources were not likely to spy on their own side.

Curwen wanted me to continue relations with Manila, but I saw no point. Rosa was sat in an office with little to nothing to do. I suggested I retire from the Philippines, I had seen the office through the most difficult yet, exciting times, arguably in the history of the Philippines. Really, my time in control of the office was just for a tiny section of that turbulent history. Eleven years inside Manila was enough.

In the end, it was my choice, I can't be forced to run a pointless office. I informed Chris Curwen I'd return to Manila and shut things down safely, he understood why. I'd always be able to stay in contact with Ramos and Enrile by phone from London. So, I took the long journey back to Manila eleven years after I opened the office, with all the luck I had doing that. I wouldn't need luck now. But I needed some compassion, as I knew I was making Rosa and others redundant. Not something I'd enjoy.

In March 1986, I flew back to Manila, Jonny was no longer around, it had been years since he was needed by me. A new driver was arranged, I was met at the airport by Donato, Rosa's son, he was pleased to meet the man that had assisted in his release from prison years earlier. I found him to be as pleasant as Jonny to work with. Traffic in Manila was worse than ever, it seemed to take forever to get to the office, the car seemed to be standing still more than moving. We eventually pulled up outside the luxurious Peninsula Hotel in the district of Makati, not too far from my Manila office. On the corner of Ayala and Makati Avenues, there was a stunning waterfall that create a 90-degree corner, where two symmetrical blocks of rooms rose either side in each road. The interior of the highest quality and standard. Donato pulled up to the superbly grand entrance, where the concierge organised my bags to be taken from the car. I told Donato I would like him to pick me up in the morning about 7:30 to go to the office, even though my hotel was in the same district, it was a little too far to walk in the heat.

After checking in, I was led to my room, an executive suite. The room was a spacious living room with lush sofa, daybed and TV. A separate master bedroom included a large walk-in closet, a dressing area and marble bathroom. I had no idea what price Karen my secretary had paid for this room, but it felt very expensive.

With half a day to clear my head of jet lag, after the bell boy left my bag, I felt I needed to eat and take in some of my surroundings. After all, this could be my last visit to Manila.

I changed into lighter clothes and explored the hotel facilities. There were two swimming pools, one indoor and one outside. I chose to sit near the bar outside, ordered some late lunch and rested on a sun bed watching people enjoy the pool, before cooling off myself in the cooling water. If I wasn't careful, I could get used to this life!

I used my time to mentally prepare myself for the next day. I knew I would be closing down my operation in Manila, making Rosa redundant, I wasn't going to enjoy that part of my mission. Rosa had been perfect. She had been loyal, smart and did not deserve to be put out of work. I couldn't find the right words to rehearse how I would break the news to her. Trisha and Mak had left a few weeks ago for Mindanao, they were at the safe house. I intended to visit them to make sure they were ok and to ensure they were set up with some work for their future. I knew they had no jobs yet as the food bills I was receiving from them indicated they were not earning. This was going to be a tough trip for me. I hated the idea of putting these people out of work.

I spent an enjoyable afternoon despite my worries, it was nice to relax in the sun. I realised I hadn't rested for a very long time with everything that had been going on. I had a high work load back in London. The Philippines wasn't my only concern as a controller of agents. Life was busy and high in responsibility, but I loved the work. I lived in a world I would never experience in any other way of life that my school qualifications, or lack of, would bring me.

This hotel and this city being one of those extraordinary experiences.

Being such a high class hotel, I wasn't pestered by girls wanting to be my best friend, like other places in this city. Later, when I visited again in 2007, I actually hired a girl to be my escort, just to put off others that would annoy me continuously. It's not so flattering, they don't really think I'm handsome or would make a good husband. They simply see white men as an opportunity to take money and gifts. Despite saying they would love you for ever, as soon as you are out of sight, they are pestering another easily flattered European man. Even having an escort to defend me, didn't stop some of them trying. Their desperation to escape the poverty of the Philippines had no morals and were ready to enter a life of polygamy if you let them. At least those were the kind of offers I experienced. I suppose I can understand it, but please girls just don't be so annoying, no means no.

Having said that, I don't like being alone, some part of me wished I would find some company for dinner that evening. Eating alone, I find, is never a pleasant experience. In the end, I managed one evening alone, which was for the best, as jet lag kicked in around 6pm, so I went to bed, set an alarm for 6:30am and fell asleep almost instantly.

I woke slowly to the sound of my alarm, it took me a few moments to gather my senses and to work out where in the world I was. I rose, washed and dressed and went down to breakfast by 7am. Like all hotels of this calibre, the breakfast spread was amazing, I ate my full English breakfast while reliving the memories of Diwa stuffing her face with bacon, what a charming young lady she was. I hoped to see her the next day in Butuan, Mindanao Island. At 7:30 sharp, a concierge found me finishing my breakfast coffee to inform me my car was waiting outside. I'm not sure why, maybe they didn't like such a low-grade car in the front of reception. Donato's car being a simple Toyota. Maybe a Ferrari or Rolls Royce would be more welcome to stay longer, to show off the magnificence of the hotel. It didn't hurry me, I'd leave when I'm ready, which actually I was, but I didn't want to move just because the hotel wanted me to.

When I arrived fifteen minutes later at the porte-cochère, Donato was stood leaning on the side of his car smoking a cigarette looking equally as unflustered as the concierge was staring him down from the pavement dais. As I walked passed, I thanked the concierge for his helpfulness in a voice that told him I was going to be unhurried by him. I approached Donato and shook his hand, we both knew these snobs didn't want us lowering the tone of the place, so we stood and chatted for a short while and watched a couple of high-class cars pick up their owners. I had to sit in the car to hide my laughter when Donato walked across to a bellboy and asked him to take his cigarette butt as there didn't seem to be a bin for the stub. I could see why Marcos thought he was a dissident and arrested Donato, he wasn't, he just had a teenager attitude and I liked him for not succumbing to the bullish attitude of the staff at this hotel. While we had chatted, Donato asked me to call him Don and I said it was fine to call me Andy if he could get over the need to say "sir" in every sentence. The age-old habit of Filipino's saying sir still existed.

Don drove me to my office just a few blocks away, I was early, it was only 8am, Rosa had not arrived yet. That was fine, I wanted to take a look around the office anyway. It had changed over the years, it was more homely, functional, even though Rosa spent most of her time alone here. Flowers were on her desk and family photos made the room a nice place to be. There were four coffee cups but only one showed signs of years of use. Why do we humans always seem to prefer one cup over another as a favourite? This was a good sign, it meant Rosa hadn't had many guests to poke around and maybe see any messages from Trisha or others. I noticed nothing was left untidy and nothing left to view, even though she worked alone. Rosa was good at her job and today wasn't going to be fun for me.

Around 8:30am Rosa arrived with her husband, I stood in the middle of the room and gave her the biggest hug, it was good to see her again, and she told me she had missed me. I hadn't been here for eleven years, but I knew what she felt, I felt the same way. I had not met her husband before, and he was introduced as John Mark.

Rosa made coffees and we sat to talk. I had still not found the right words for my "letting you go" speech, I delayed the moment with small talk. I was dreading this day.

"Sir." Rosa began, "I am thinking there is not much for me to do now. Trisha and Makisig have gone, I have nothing to process from them now."

"Yes, I can appreciate that you must be feeling a little underused now" was my best effort at comforting her.

"My husband and I have plans. My employment with you has enabled us to save and my husband has opened a restaurant. It has been our dream for years and we think now is the time to live our dream."

"Really? I'm pleased for you, that sounds marvellous." I stumbled.

"I hate to leave you in the lurch, after all you have done for me, I can still make arrangements for you if you need anything done." She added trying to let me down gently.

"To be honest Rosa, the reason I came here is to let you know, I have to close this office, so you aren't letting me down, you are making my job easier." I said, "So, tell me all about your plans, where is the restaurant, how is it going? Are you going to work together?"

"Firstly, let me admit, the reason my husband came today is because I was not sure what your purpose was today. Being who you are, I felt unsafe, maybe you are going to kill me for security reasons."

"Rosa, I am so sad you feel that way! I am here to tell you face to face that the office has to close, because I'm sure you realise there is almost nothing for you to do now." I was genuinely saddened that she thought this way about me. "I am here to make sure you have a safe future, not to end it."

"Well, I am sorry, I don't know how your world works." Rosa said.

"It doesn't work like that, we don't go around killing people willy-nilly! You know I have made sure everyone can be safe, Trisha has already fled to the safe house. Really Rosa, you've disappointed me, that you don't trust me this way."

"I am so sorry, I had to be sure what you were here for, I do trust you, but you have to agree, because I know everything you have done, I know your contacts, your cypher methods, everything!" she was almost crying, Rosa knew she had misread how I work and had let herself down.

"No, maybe in my absence for the last few years, I have let you forget that you are my most trusted employee and I haven't told you as such enough. It's me that has let you down." I tried to calm Rosa.

"Ok, well, if you want to close this office, I'll send a letter to the building agent, there needs to be a month's notice." Rosa calmed a little.

"I will have to get someone to remove the radio fax machine, probably from the…." I stumbled my words, I didn't know what John Mark knew about the office, I didn't want him to know someone from the British Embassy would have to remove the machine.

"It's ok, John Mark doesn't speak English. He has no idea about this place and what I really do. I have kept it secret from even him all these years." Rosa told me.

"Ok, well, I will let you know the arrangement for the machine, if you can organise the disposal of the other bits and pieces, please" I said. "Rosa, I really don't want to part on this bad ending. We will stay in touch, I want to know your restaurant is going well and you are happy. After eleven years good service I owe you a lot."

"The restaurant is close to here, it's a busy area as you know, there is accommodation above, so we can move into the apartment above it. We still have a lot to do to make it how we want. It is our dream, we will make it work." Rosa began to smile again. "I do have a favour to ask of you, I am embarrassed to ask." Rosa added.

"Rosa, you don't have to be embarrassed, you know I will help you." I told her.

"We need a guarantor for a loan, would you do that for us please?"

"Of course I will, you surely know that. How much is the loan and what are the requirements?"

Rosa told me they needed to borrow the equivalent of £2500, which was a lot in those days in the Philippines, probably still is.

"Rosa, you don't need a loan to burden you. I will give you the money, call it severance pay, it's the least I can do for you. Also, you can keep the deposit on this place when it is returned."

Rosa jumped out of her chair with the biggest smile and gave me the biggest tightest hug and smothered me with kisses.

"Oh, sir, you have made me so happy" Rosa turned to her husband and explained in their language the offer. John Mark smiled too, looking a little unsure, but I think he understood.

"What did I do to find such a kind man?" Rosa now ecstatic, couldn't stop hugging me, I had clearly lifted a big burden from them.

"Ok, why don't we go and have a look at your restaurant?" I asked. "Let me see your new future. There's nothing to do here." Rosa explained to John Mark what we were going to do, and again he shook my hand and thanked me in his own language. It was unusual for a Filipino not to have a smattering of English, I felt he would need the language to run a restaurant and I asked Rosa as such.

"John Mark is chef, he will be back of house and I will be, together with Donato and his wife, front of house and also help the kitchen when it gets busy."

With that, we exited the office, locked it for the last time, at least for me. I hadn't been there enough to feel emotion for the place, Rosa would return to empty everything.

In the car, Rosa was obviously very excited and couldn't wait to show me their restaurant. I just sat there thinking how lucky I seemed to be whenever I came here. I didn't have to face giving Rosa her notice.

We pulled up in the street and had to walk a little way as there were no available parking spaces outside their place. They had already done the deal to rent the place and they had started doing business there. I found out when I walked in the reason for the loan. It badly needed updating, the tables, chairs and general décor really needed upgrading. It was functional, but not attractive. Walking into the eating area it was dark and gloomy, but I saw the potential. I was sure, if they could brighten the place up, the passing trade would flock in. In the kitchen the equipment was again a little dated but for Philippine standards, quite acceptable. I told the family I thought they had found a real gem, and I wished them every success. I was taken upstairs to the living space. Again it was quite adequate, with a little TLC the place would be quite comfortable. The sale of their current home would enable them to make the space as they wanted. Rosa told me they still had some mortgage to pay off from the sale, but the profit would be ploughed into the business. But I could see the money I was giving them would help greatly and I got the greatest pleasure knowing they would be prosperous and happy working as a family, as Philippine families do. On the way back downstairs in a small courtyard, were small cages of chickens, I joked they had their own egg supply, it turned out they were destined for the table, in this hot country the best way to keep meat fresh, is to keep it alive.

I was invited to sample the food, I sat down with Rosa while her husband and Donato disappeared into the kitchen to prepare lunch. Donato's wife was busying herself and came over to be introduced. It was a lovely little family unit, we joked that as the business grew she could produce children as new staff. I enjoyed the company of these people, with so little and such hard workers, always smiling I really felt at home. I began to get thoughts that maybe sometime I should make my home here too. It was cheap to live and I love the people.

When the food arrived it was a stunning spread, I hadn't chosen from the menu, they made what they knew was good. There was fresh grilled fish, chicken adobo, fries, pad-thai, lumpia, sisig (a popular Filipino dish. It is composed of minced pork, chopped onion, and chicken liver), which was nice but if I had known beforehand what it was, I would not have chosen to eat it. Of course, there was mountains of rice. Asians eat rice with every meal. Rice does get a little tiresome for me, but it's always steamed so beautifully. If they could produce meals like this, the business would definitely be a success. By the time we had finished eating, people had begun to drift in for take aways and sit in lunches. The business area of Makati was a good place to be.

I explained to Rosa I was travelling to Mindanao Island to visit Diwa early morning the next day. If there was anything she wanted me to take or pass on to Diwa, I would. Rosa thought I was going to close the safehouse down too and was worried for Diwa. I told her I was not going for that reason. Only to tell her that now the Marcos's were gone there was little danger anyone would be fleeing there. She could keep the house for herself if she wanted. The choice was hers. This pleased Rosa a lot, she couldn't stop telling me how kind I was. I didn't need compliments, it was just for the best. I wasn't in the business of putting people out of their homes. I promised that if any of Rosa's family ever needed help, I would always do my best to assist them and that was my promise for ever. That was my promise, and I have kept it to this day. There was no rush to leave, we sat talking for a few hours, I had nothing to do until the morning when I had an early flight to Butuan. Donato would take me to the airport in the car.

Late afternoon I return to my hotel and spent another evening alone cooling off in the pool, sipping a few beers, I wasn't hungry enough for another big meal, so I ate just a few snacks before taking early retirement to bed, ready for a 4:30am rise for my flight.

In the morning the flight was on time, and I recalled the bizarre luggage system at Butuan airport, maybe by now it had been modernised. On arrival at Butuan I could see, sadly the system was still operating. After passport control, I made my way outside the terminal building, as I exited the doors, Trisha and Mak were waving with big smiles for me. We hugged our greetings and stood in the steaming hot car park near the gate lined with men about to rush the trolleys as they arrived from the plane. As the gate opened the baggage handlers ran to the trolley and grabbed the bags and began to search for the owners. I saw my bag and man exiting the gate and made my way toward him. Of course, he was disappointed when he found we were not taking his preferred taxi driver, who would pay him the best commission to bring the passengers and bags to him. I did tip the man, but Trisha told me a more Philippine rate of tipping, the poor man didn't do too well from this tourist that day. Trisha and Mak had a tuktuk driver friend to take me to my hotel and onward to Trisha's house, my safehouse. Somehow, we all managed to fit in the back of the tuktuk with my bags. As I stepped inside the vehicle, the front wheel of the attached motorbike lifted off the ground, I had to sit on a front seat next to the driver to keep the wheel on the road. We did have a laugh about it, but the driver seemed a little put out and couldn't raise a smile with us.

Apparently, for some reason there was one road, Iligan Road, from the airport that tuktuk's aren't allowed to drive on, I'm not sure why, so we had to take a rather back street route to the hotel. We zig zagged across the road finding dirt roads in the fields and crossing the road a couple of times. No one seemed able to explain why this was, but as we weren't on a meter it didn't worry me that much, it was interesting to see some different views as we trundled around, the front wheel barely keeping traction on the dusty roads.

Eventually, we pulled up and piled out the little tuktuk, I was back at the Balanghai Hotel I stayed at before. Bellboys took my bags and we followed them inside to check in. I joked that I hoped the hotel had restocked the bacon, if Diwa was going to come for breakfast again. It was a joke that needed explaining to Mak and Trish.

Once settled in my room, I ordered some drinks and a little lunch for us all to eat, we sat outside on the small patio, finding another chair from the room for Mak. We small talked until lunch arrived. Sitting around the table I began, "I've come here to check on how you guys are, and to inform you that I need to shut down my office in Manila. There won't be any support coming from there in the very near future." Both Trisha and Mak looked horrified. "I need to get your thoughts on what you'd like to do. Would you like to stay here, find jobs or go back to Manila. I appreciate neither of you have work at the palace now, so I will help you set yourselves up in whatever you'd like to do. Could you both give it some thought and let me know."

Mak answered, "Do you mean stay here with Trisha and Diwa or in our own place?"

"Well, I need to ask Diwa what she would like to do, do you know if she is home right now?"

"Yes, she was preparing some food for you. She was expecting us to go straight there."

"Oh, I see. Shall we go there, or shall I send a taxi for her?" I asked.

"I'm sure she would love to come here, she is always telling us how much she enjoyed her stay here. She never mentioned bacon though." Mak joked.

"OK, I'll send a car for her. I hope she won't be offended not going to her place. I'd like to see it tomorrow though."

"If Diwa wants to stay in the house, and you decide you would like to as well, how awkward is that, living together?" I asked the couple.

"I think it's a little awkward, we fled here and have only ever thought of the house as temporary. I think we should go somewhere else." Trisha put her thoughts on the table. I guessed she was worried for her relationship, I'm sure Mak enjoyed living with two girls.

"Ok, let's get Diwa here to join us, I'm sure a taxi won't take long to get her here." I suggested. I called the hotel reception and asked them to arrange a taxi to bring Diwa from the house to the hotel, it wasn't far away, it would only take twenty minutes if the taxi was quick enough to get to her place.

We sat eating and chatting small talk waiting for Diwa, I knew they would need to think about their futures, to me it sounded like Trisha would prefer to move on to somewhere new or back to Manila.

Thirty minutes later, Diwa arrived, I opened the door and invited her in. I gave her the biggest hug and a kiss on the cheek. In the years since I saw her, she had matured into a very beautiful girl, well dressed and tonight I could tell she had put on some perfume, which was not really necessary for me.

I apologised for not going straight to her house, and I asked if maybe we could eat the food she had prepared tomorrow. I wanted them all here rather than the house so that they were on my turf, should I need to make decisions for them, it seemed the right way to do things. She said it was no problem, it would be nice to do that, and she presented me with a plastic box of her cupcakes she made for me. I realised it was tradition that visitors brought gifts whenever they visited and I hadn't got anything, my mind too busy on other things. I made up my mind I'd get something in the morning before visiting them at the house.

I ordered a little more food and drink to refresh everyone's plates and glasses and we all sat on the patio, I found a chair in the corridor so we could all sit down round the little circular table outside.

I repeated to Diwa the problem of the office closing and suggested that maybe tomorrow, after they had time to think about the situation, they could all tell me what they felt they wanted to do in the future. Although to me, it seemed Mak was the only person happy to live three in a house, well he would wouldn't he.

We sat and enjoyed the evening, even though they must have felt some stress knowing now that life as they knew it was about to change again for them.

As the evening drew to a close, I offered to pay for a car for them to get home and I phoned reception to order one. I told them I would join them late morning next day at their house. I asked whether they would be at home, Trisha and Mak said they would, Diwa explained she had some cakes to make first thing and she needed to deliver them to a nearby school and then she would be free.

After a few minutes the phone rang, it was the hotel reception telling me the car was waiting. We all stood and Trisha and Mak left from the patio across the garden to take a shortcut to the reception area. Diwa hung back, when the other two were out of sight, she moved to me and held my hands facing me.

"I appreciate everything you have done for me, for us. I am very happy with my life here, I want to stay." She said quietly.

"It's the least I can do to help you, it has been a pleasure seeing you again." I replied, "I'll see you tomorrow and we will decide what everyone wants to do now, don't rush, no hurry." I replied and kissed her on the cheek.

"No, I mean, I want to stay, here, now, tonight." She said, showing very little embarrassment at her forwardness.

I was shocked, it hadn't occurred to me that was her intent.

"Diwa, much as I like you, even love you, you are very pretty, attractive, and I'd love for you to stay, but I have to tell you." I held up my left hand to reveal a wedding ring. "I am now married, sorry." I was surprised she hadn't noticed, a wedding ring was usually the first thing a woman notices. We had been so busy talking about their three lives, I hadn't talked about mine, there just wasn't the chance and when working in my capacity as SIS controller I don't talk about my personal life. There's nothing wrong with that, I always thought it was better for security reasons.

Diwa's face dropped, maybe her escort background allowed her to say, "I don't mind if you don't, I have missed you all these years, dreaming of the day you would come back."

"Diwa, do you think it is appropriate? I've only been married two years."

"I hope that you will think I would make a better wife and I should prove it tonight."

"And if you don't stay, you'd miss the bacon for breakfast too." I replied.

I had met my wife to be in 1980. Shortly after we had lived together for four years before getting married. When we first met, as seemed to be my luck, my relations never seemed to last, so I never mentioned my secret work to any girlfriend outside the service. In this case, my relationship had lasted and then I realised if I told my secret, what were the chances I wouldn't be believed and probably accused of being a fantasist. I always felt I was in a no win situation. Imagine meeting someone and on being asked what I did, and I said I was a spy. Who in their right mind would believe me. The chances are the girl would never be seen again. So, I always told people I worked for my father in his printing business. I was never able to have a long-term girlfriend, until I met the girl I married. Then how do you break the news to them? With Karen we had a great friendship and were lovers secretly as the service would never allow us to be together as a couple, for security reasons. I missed out on what should have been my best teenage and young man years, relationship wise. I have become a little resentful of the service depriving me of that. On the other hand, I did lead a rather exciting life, and I wouldn't have missed it for anything.

Next morning the four of us were gathered at Diwa's house, she had made it nice, but obvious that she was unable to afford much in the way of furniture or the small comforts in life. There was still one tap in the curtained off toilet space, a bucket to fill and flush with. In the kitchen there was the minimum of cooking facilities, but this was how Filipino's live, it seemed sparse to me, to them it was normal. The professional mixer for her cake business had gone.

When I asked what had happened to it Diwa told me that it had lasted three years then broke, so she then had to mix with a hand whisk. I told her off for not telling me about it, I would have replaced it for her. I guessed she had some pride that stopped her from telling me.

There was no air-conditioning, only a fan moved the air in an attempt to cool the space down and it was hot. We moved outside to the veranda and sat talking. Diwa brought cold drinks and cakes, she did have a fridge, which I'm sure contributed to the heat in the kitchen. I have no clue how hot it must have been when she was baking. I didn't need to say much, Trisha and Mak told me they wanted to return to Manila if I thought it was safe. The excitement of the Marcos family exile had died down by now with Aquino seemingly in control of the country. I couldn't see any safety reasons why they shouldn't return home now, and, it was their call, I wasn't forcing anyone to do anything unsafe. The only reason Trisha had fled was because in the heat of the moment when the Marcos's fled from their own mistreated people there could have been problems from an excited crowd as they invaded and ransacked the presidential palace. I told them to arrange whatever they wanted to return, whether by ferry or plane, and I would help by paying, or at least the British tax payer would. They would find work and didn't seem to want to worry me with support in the meantime. They both had families to help. I learnt later Trisha went to work at the Manila Hotel with her cousin Angel, who had now been promoted to a housekeeping manager. Mak got a job with the water company in Manila. The world seems so small sometimes, as in 1997 the Metropolitan Waterworks and Sewerage System (MWSS) was privatised by a formal handover ceremony at the Malacañang Presidential Palace hosted by the now President Fidel Ramos. Ramos being president was a very good reason that I should not have any part of affairs in the Philippines. I don't think it a good idea for a President to know a former spy he traded information with still operated in Manila.

This meant Diwa would have her home for so many years to herself once again. She wanted to stay, she was surviving with her small business and happy. She had relatives on the island, so she wasn't completely alone. So, I promised that we would go into the city that afternoon and buy new equipment for her. I promised them all that I was always going to help them if ever they needed it. They had risked their lives doing what they did for me, and I would never forget it. I never needed to help Trisha and Mak, they never asked for help or even sent me any distress messages and our contact slowly faded over the years. But I would always think about them and wonder how they were doing, they had given me ten years of their lives. I hope one day I will find them again.

Diwa, being single, was different. We always stayed in contact, made even easier by the internet in later years. We would occasionally message each other and in 2007, when I felt my marriage to Julie was coming to an end, I have to admit, mainly due to me and my struggle with PTSD. I visited the Philippines again and caught up with a few old friends. My trip to Butuan, Mindanao Island was a visit that was almost cancelled. A week before my visit on October 26th an Airbus 320 overshot the runway and came to a halt in the trees at the end of the runway, narrowly missing an army camp. Fortunately, no one was killed, just a few minor injuries, but being such a small airport and quite remote, the authorities didn't have the facilities to remove the plane. The airport closed for a few days, but reopened just before I was due to arrive. The airplane was still there, the high tail fin a hazard to landing aircraft who had to fly past the obstruction, it was very unnerving to watch the fin whiz past the window just off the tip of the wing of the plane I was a passenger on. I had booked into the Almont Inland Resort hotel, I had a nice bungalow type room in the gardens just next to the pool. Diwa met me at Butuan airport and wanted me to go immediately to her home. I didn't realise she had arranged for many of her family to be there to meet me. But I insisted I booked into the hotel first, we checked in as husband and wife, the reception staff requiring my passport to be copied, but luckily no requirement was made of Diwa just as before. I was very tired after the journey, together with jetlag, it was a very good excuse to have a few hours in bed, though I didn't get any sleep, it was good to be back with Diwa and all thoughts of home in England and divorce disappeared.

We spent the week shopping together, visiting her relatives up on the north coast in Surigao City, a good two and a half hours by bus. Bus travel was exciting for me. It was a chance to see how the locals live for sure. People travelling with chickens, or a goat was common, as was hijackings. Diwa told me a story how once when she was on a bus it was hijacked. It was difficult to say who was doing the hijacking, there were rebel groups, ISIS, robbers and just bad people that needed money. They took the bus, with its passengers, robbed everyone and left fairly peacefully. It's best not to try to fight them, they are always armed and not afraid to use their guns. I found it funny at shops and banks, there is always an armed guard on the door, standing next to a sign to hand in your guns before entering. At the bus station there were armed guards hanging around with ancient AK47's. A few weeks after I left, I heard one guard had an unintentional discharge of his weapon, the bullet missed people standing around and went through the ticket window. You know you are in a bad place when there is an armed guard on the door of a McDonalds. But I do find the Mindanao Island people, friendly and on the whole seemingly happy. In my opinion, poverty is the cause of most of the unrest and bad behaviour.

As Diwa and I became closer, I began to have thoughts that Mindanao may be a good place to live. I was thinking when I retire, on my pension, I would live very well. So, we began looking at something for me to do. We found a little shop for sale, and on the spur of the moment I thought I would buy it. I probably should have thought a little harder about it, but that's what I did. With Diwa's name we also bought some land way out in the countryside, that we thought a good location to have a project to build our own house someday. Anyway, it seemed a good investment. My proposal to Diwa was that I would return to England, begin divorce proceedings, sell everything and return to Mindanao to live. It would be hard and a different life for me, but at that time it was what I felt I needed to do.

While at some point I was in the street outside Diwa's (my) house, the local mayor passed by to say hi. She offered me a way to get a permanent visa. It was definitely not legal, but not legal was often the best way to get things done, anywhere. A few thousand Pesos would get me what I wanted. I left it that I would see her when I returned, if I felt I needed to go that route. Diwa was so excited to make a better business for herself with the new shop. It would be set up to sell small amounts of most day-to-day things people needed. That is how people live over there. They would buy for instance one cigarette, because they couldn't afford a whole packet. Later the shop expanded so that there was a slot machine (unlicenced) and beer (unlicenced). Now people would come for a cigarette, play a game, have a beer and then need another cigarette. Spending more than they possibly should, but that was business. Cooked food was introduced soon after. But the shop sold almost anything and later, mobile phone top-ups.

The week went so quickly, I didn't want to return home, life felt so simple and relaxed, made easy by the attention of Diwa. But I knew I had to get everything in the UK sorted, so, I returned home to England.

Back home in England my wife began our divorce. She didn't want anything from me at all. So, it was very easy for me to get through it. I moved into a share home temporarily while everything would be sold and finalised. There was, however, something inside me that was yelling at me that this was wrong. Not the divorce, it was too late to stop that, and I didn't want it to stop, it had to be finished. But my idea of utopia in the Philippines now seemed a bad idea. Now I was in a quandary. If I didn't move to Mindanao, I would wonder for the rest of my life what had I missed, if I did move, there was no coming back. Everything would be sold, and I'd have nothing to return to if it all went wrong. Something deep inside me was yelling at me that my plan was wrong. At the share house, almost immediately myself and my next-door roommate got on very well. A Lithuanian lady seemed to attach herself to me and I did not resist. If I was honest with myself I should have just been a good neighbour. Every day she would make dinner for me or offer to do ironing, something I absolutely hate doing myself, so I was happy to let her do it for me. She knew my situation, she knew I had a girlfriend in the Philippines. Yet she wanted to include me in her everyday life, and for whatever reason I didn't resist. I needed a friend at that moment, and I guess she became my best friend. In the end I decided it would be far simpler to stay in England, cowardly as it sounds. My parents objected to me leaving the country too. So I had to let down Diwa. I wasn't proud of that moment, the two women had argued online over me, and I had to do something. To this day I regret letting down Diwa. I can never forgive myself. I have spoken to Diwa since, and I can hear the pain in her voice.

The voices in my head that were yelling at me, turned out to be right. Diwa lived happily in the house since I last saw her. She made it the best she could for herself, her little shop business kept her employed for years. I heard some years later that she and Miki became a couple, I was very happy about that. I wanted Diwa to be happy. Sadly, Miki died in a car crash, I knew it could not have been his fault, he was a very good careful driver. His happy smiling face etched into my memories of him for ever.

What amazes me so much and why I admire the ordinary people of the Philippines is, no matter what their circumstance, they are clean, clothes are washed, hair tidy, and always presentable, and many do this from a bucket of cold water. I was never near anyone that smells bad. Can you say that for your country? How many times have you been in a shop and there's someone that stinks? We have running water and baths and yet, for many, laziness makes them not wash or keep themselves tidy and presentable.

I have kept my promise to look after her for the rest of my life. Not that she has needed much, but a couple of hospital bills I paid helped her a little.

In 2013 typhoon Haiyan, known in the Philippines as Super Typhoon Yolanda hit the Philippines. It was one of the most powerful tropical cyclones ever recorded. Killing at least 6300 people in the Philippines alone. In 2014 bodies were still being found. Diwa's house, my house, was totally wrecked and lost in major flooding and destructive winds, it was close to the Agusan River which flooded other houses to roof height. Diwa was sadly lost and I somehow miss her, even though I didn't spend much time with her. Somehow the world doesn't feel the same knowing her smile isn't brightening this world somewhere.

Above: Flooded area around Diwa's house. An estimated 3500 people lost their lives during storm Yolanda.

Below: Diwa's home ruined and filled with mud. Diwa was sadly lost.

If that wasn't enough of a message telling me I had made the right choice, if, for the wrong reasons, I don't know what is, and just in case I still had any doubts, a year later I had a heart attack. Someone wanted to tell me I made the right choice, to ease my own pain of the guilt. If I had been in Mindanao I could have died too. If I survived that, then I would certainly have died from my heart attack. Mindanao medical facilities are too remote, I would not have made it to hospital in time. I would not have received the excellent attention that I did here in the UK. I do feel guilt Diwa may have died in great panic or stress, even pain. I can't think of her in that way.

The only good thing to end this tale with is, Diwa and Miki had a child, a daughter. I have always kept in touch with her. I have promised the same promise that I gave her mother and father, that I will always help if needed, and I have.

In 2022, we reunited. I wanted to meet her. So, my now new Lithuanian wife, who has to be one of the most understanding women on the planet, and I travelled to Koh Samui, Thailand. Diwa's daughter Hanna, came from the Philippines and we had the most fantastic time all together, even during the end of the covid pandemic. It wasn't easy, with flights and changes to laws and regulations post pandemic. But we made it. We all agreed that we should refer to her as my daughter.

I am sure this story has not ended.

Secrets and Lies

Timeline - February 1976

Most Officers in MI6 have a cover, usually a small business or something to provide the deception of normality while they do their darker business. I worked with my father, the only person in my family that knew what I did. He'd cover for me whenever I needed to go away somewhere, I could use a telephone at work, not secure but I worked that way for years.

Given the choice Karen and I would be together, but sadly it was never to be. There were security issues if we became a couple. One day I was at my father's business, a printing company near Rickmansworth, Hertfordshire. The phone rang. I took the phone call in the general office. I recognised the voice immediately as Karen's.

"Andy, could you come in please." that was all I needed to know it was a request to go to Century House, MI6. The line wasn't secure, I wouldn't ask any questions to clarify, I'd find out what this was about when I got to London.

"Tomorrow OK?" I replied.

"Yes, not urgent." was the brief reply and I hung up.

The next day was Saturday, so it was a little quieter on the Metropolitan trainline from Rickmansworth into London, 39 minutes and a change onto the Bakerloo Line, a few stops and a quick walk to the MI6 building.

It was very unusual for me to go to London, I never thought it a wise thing to do, but I guessed there must be a good reason to be asked. I wasn't worried about the request, there was no point in worrying, worry and stress isn't my thing.

Through security and up to my office, I found Karen busy at her desk, did she ever go home! As there was almost no one around on the floor where my office was, I kissed a greeting on her cheek,

"Good morning Karen, you are looking gorgeous as always." she smiled back happy to see me again.

"Morning Andy, good to see you too, your visits are too rare." Karen looked immaculate as always, she was a beautiful lady her blonde hair tied back in a ponytail, dressed less formally, I guessed as it was Saturday and fewer people were around, I never minded how she dressed, and my heart rate always went up when I was in her presence.

"So, what have we got?" I asked. Karen reached into her desk drawer and handed me a folder, there were easily a hundred pages inside. The front had the inscription "TOP SECRET" and someone had handwritten an unusual addition "ULTRA" to the left of it. I had never seen this category level of secrecy, it wasn't official, Top Secret being the highest level, I wondered if this was just graffiti.

"Go read, I'll bring some tea, and have a talk to you about this."

"Okaaay." I said intrigued by the mystery, staring at the folder of files.

I turned to check the office door to the corridor was closed and made my way through the adjoining door to my office and sat at my desk, so I could easily open and arrange the file contents on the top. My office was bright, light and a good place to work, it was business-like yet comfortable with a desk and a sofa where more informal talks could take place, though in my case that would rarely happen here, I'd prefer a hotel or one of the many private clubs that we had membership to.

The first thing I noticed was that the folder hadn't been signed out, or for that matter in. Inside the folder should be a Routing and Record Sheet, a form where anyone wanting to review the folder would have to sign for it, giving their name, department, a short reason for the review, and then signing back in. This is a permanent part of the folder, so it has a history as to who has seen it. I looked at the front again and noticed in small type at the bottom-right the address, Hanslope Park. This place, basically a secret storage building, was near Milton Keynes, Buckinghamshire and I believe it is run by the RAF to appear to look like a small base that few people would question if they even noticed it. I had heard of this place, "Q" division, I knew the place contained thousands, if not millions, of highly sensitive documents and files. I had never been there, but I heard that the place was huge and contained files that were supposed to *never* be released after the 30-year rule came up. The 30-year rule is the period before papers can be released on request under the Official Secrets Act. I had heard some documents could be 200 years old and their existence never to be admitted should anyone request any files on whatever subject they contained. Britain is very good, or very bad at hiding secrets from its people. So what was this file doing here? This was highly improper.

"So, where is this from and why have we got it?" I needed to raise my voice so Karen could hear in the adjoining room.

"It came from Jenny." Karen came back.

Jenny was Karen's flatmate and the two were best friends. To live with Karen, you had to share her wicked sense of humour. Karen owned a nice flat quite near to Century House, one underground stop away at Elephant and Castle. I had been there a few times, beautifully furnished a gift from her banker father. Jenny was a sweet girl about two years younger than Karen. She also worked at Century House in the secretarial department doing admin work. She was pleasant and very attractive.

I flicked through some of the papers in the file, they seemed to be mostly American CIA documents, some had been redacted, which means they had probably come from the public domain. Redaction is when papers requested by the public are censored by blacking out names or information that could be sensitive to release, what's left is a readable document, but all the best stuff is covered up.

I started to read some of the pages,

"JEEZ!" I exclaimed under my breath, this stuff was shocking. I'd seen some secrets before, created some secrets before, but this was shocking. If what I was reading was true, history books would have to be altered.

Karen came through with two teas and sat with me at the desk, her beauty was a distraction, I loved her so much and she loved me.

"So, come on fill me in, what's the story? This is shocking to read I have to say, have you read all this too?" I asked her.

"I've read some of it, not all." and she began to recount how the folder had found its way to my office.

"Jenny has been seconded to the digitalisation department for a while."

"What is dig-i-tal-isation?" I said the word in struggled syllables as it was a new word for me, although we used computers and today it's a commonly used word, this was the first time I'd heard it, I wasn't a technical person.

"There's a team converting secret paper files onto the new computer system. Files are delivered to her desk, they are photographed and entered into a database, it's huge, and the work will take years."

"Sounds quite boring work, unless she has time to read some of this stuff, I don't think I'd have the patience for that work." I said and added "Dig-i-tal-isation, is difficult and long-winded to say, I think I'll call the department Double D it's easier."

Karen smiled at my simple ignorance,

"So, this file passed over her desk, and it has concerned her." Karen informed me.

"She shouldn't let that happen, what the files contain is none of her business, I agree this file is highly controversial, but she must be seeing thousands of controversial files, why this one in particular? Also, by removing it from the department, she has committed a grave offence, she could be in big trouble if it's found missing. Why has this concerned her so much she was prepared to risk her job and everything?" I added.

"The simple answer is – she is Jewish." Karen answered the question.

"This is worrying, that she is letting her religion affect what she does here, is Jenny available to come and chat?" I asked.

"She is at home I'll call her, she is half expecting you to ask her in any way, it won't take her long to get here."

"OK, do that, while I study this stuff, this is incredible."

I continued to read the papers one at a time, I couldn't believe what I was seeing, I hadn't heard even the tiniest rumour about this, so I was shocked by what I was reading, and, if it were true it meant the world has been and is continuing to be lied to. One by one I read each document and turned them over to the left, as I'm left-handed, to keep it all in the same order.

What was unfolding on my desk was altering history as I knew it. I'm no historian, I never had much interest at school, because my history teacher was quite possibly the most boring teacher I had. He tried to get me to absorb into my brain names and dates about what seemed to me to be quite irrelevant things. Things from the past that can't be changed, they've happened, nothing can be done to change it, so why worry about it. Now I see how history is important and this file was changing it. We've all been lied to. What I knew then about the Second World War, I could write on a matchbox, but since school, and because I'm involved in creating history in my job of Intelligence Officer, I'd taken some interest. I'd watched a few documentaries on television, but I'd still not read much. I had a small idea of how the war had ended.

What I was reading now meant all history books on this subject had to be thrown in the bin. The files I was reading were some reports of sightings, some reports of witnesses, reports of interviews with witnesses, and a few pictures offering proof, nearly all of which were CIA, one or two were British pages also, which meant the British were for some reason involved.

According to these documents, Hitler was alive, alive and living in Argentina, but also having travelled via other countries such as Columbia and Chile. He had not died in Berlin by his own hand as we are told in history lessons, books and documentaries. Hitler and his wife Eva Braun were possibly using the surname Shüttelmayer.

By the time I read most of the stuff in front of me, Jenny had arrived. Karen brought her through into my office. She looked quite cute, dressed in a black tracksuit quite tight-fitting that showed her figure off well. About 5'3" tall, curvy in all the right places, obviously fit from working out, her body was tight and slightly muscular. She was attractive, with short inch long black hair, she had an enviable complexion with no moles or imperfections and a slight natural tan that indicated to me there was a Mediterranean heritage in her somewhere. I would be quite attracted to her if I weren't in love with Karen.

After greetings, I invited her to sit at my desk and Karen sat on the sofa to support Jenny.

"Am I going to be in trouble for this?" she asked nervously.

Karen jumped into the conversation before I could speak.

"Jenny, you can trust Andy."

"Jenny, you realise by removing this file you have committed a crime, you've effectively stolen the file even though it's still in the building. But I want you to know, if you have a concern, you can trust me, and if you are asking for my help, if I can, I will. I'll try to resolve whatever your problem is with this. Nothing said in this office ever leaves this office, ok?"

"Ok." Jenny wasn't completely at ease with my reassurance. We had met before of course, and we had chatted before, but the poor girl was concerned by her actions.

"Tea or coffee?" I asked her, I continued to try to reassure her that I was on her side, but I was simply trying to get her to tell all she knew and then I'd decide if she was right or wrong.

"No, thank you, I thought I would go down to the gym and have a workout while I'm here, so no." This explained her outfit.

"So, what's your problem, I have read the contents and I have to say I am shocked myself. What do you want me to do and what resolution are you looking for? How do you want this to end? You are in Double D, right?"

Jenny, "What?"

Me, "Double D"

Jenny, "What?"

Me, "Karen told me."
Jenny, "You've been discussing my boobs?"
Me, "No"
"Yes" Karen said at the same time.
Jenny "What?"
Karen was trying to prolong the comedy.
"He's finding it difficult to say, it's on the tip of his tongue."
Jenny, "What?"
Me, "Karen stop it!"
Karen, "Boobs, tip of the tongue"
Me, "What?"
Jenny, "You're playing with me."
Karen, "I'm sure he'd love to."
Me, "What?" Jenny at the same moment "What?"
Karen, "Play with you, I'm sure he'd love to play with you."
Me, "Stop it, Karen."
Karen to me, "Just ask, I'm sure Jenny will oblige."
Me, "No, stop, get out, go to your room, bad girl!" I pointed to Karen's room through the door indicating she should leave now.

Any other time I'd have gone along with the comedy sketch, but right now wasn't the right moment at all. Jenny obviously had a problem with this folder, and it should be taken seriously. Karen's sense of humour was one reason I loved her so much, but now wasn't the time. Two sexy women and discussing boobs has to be on the agenda for another day.

"Tell me first why this file hasn't been signed out?" I asked Jenny, we were now alone together as Karen did as she was told, walking away she sat at her desk with a dead straight back and pretending to type in the air with her hands like a good secretary, nose up in the air. Signalling she wasn't at all bothered by my demand for sensibility to return. Fun is always encouraged in my office!

Jenny began,

"The files arrive in the Digitalisation Department, or Double D room, as you put it, by trolley, there is a runner who fetches and returns the trollies loaded with boxes of the files. We take a box, do what we have to do to transfer to the computer, put everything back into the box exactly as it was, the box is returned to a pile for the runner to return a loaded trolley to the filing room. Nothing is signed in or out, other than a dated label that shows the box has been digitalised. It would be far too complicated and time consuming to sign everything in and out."

"I see, but this file has no record of ever being created or updated, yet the documents inside are from different locations and dates." I said.

Jenny continued, "Yes this folder is very different from any other I've seen, there is no coherence, and everything is a mishmash of origination."

I questioned,

"Do you think it's been put together deliberately for you to find?"

"I have no idea" Jenny replied.

"So, what do you want me to do, and what resolution are you looking for?" I asked.

"My family were persecuted by the Nazis, my grandfather was gassed with his brother, it means too much to me to ignore. I'd like to know the truth, for my family, I want the truth, I saw this file, read it and I want answers."

"But we can't reveal any of the secrets contained in this folder." I pointed out to her still not knowing what I could do for her.

"May I ask if you could try to find the truth, please? I think by looking into this you will find the resolution yourself. You will realise what needs to be done about this." Jenny asked slightly begging in her tone.

"Ok, here's what I will do, but of course I make no promises. If I find a truth that I think you should know, I will tell you. I can't do this full time, I will work on it as a side-line, and it may take some months. Can you be patient enough to wait however long this takes?"

"Yes, however long." she started to smile because I had agreed to help.

"No promises." I said.

"I believe you will discover the truth, I have faith in your abilities." Jenny flattered me.

"I have no expertise in detective work." I added.

"Karen, could you copy all this folder, we need to get it back to where it should be." I raised my voice toward the now professional secretary in the other room. I handed the folder to Jenny who took it to Karen.

"Jenny, when Karen is done with this file can you return it unnoticed to where it's supposed to be, as it should be"

"Sure" Jenny replied.

"Karen when you are done, I'll delete the photocopier hard drive, you never know, in this place someone may be making copies of our copies." I half-joked but I wanted to be sure to leave no trace.

"Thank you, Andy." Jenny seemed happier now, I couldn't imagine what this news meant to her and her family.

"I'll keep you updated, should I find anything, but promise me not to reveal anything to anyone until I say my work is complete, ok?"

"I promise." with that Jenny left my room and went to say goodbye to Karen next door. I sat back thinking about how to go about this. As soon as Jenny left the office, I asked Karen to come back.

"Karen, I need Jenny's personal file" I requested.

"I trust her, don't you? She has been fully background checked, she's worked here for years." Karen said accusingly, because I was doubting her best friend.

"Karen, what she is asking me to do is the work of Israel's Mossad or the Nazi Hunters or any other kind of anti-Nazi group. To seek the truth, and to find escaped Nazis and the biggest prize of all, to find Adolf Hitler and Eva Braun as according to these files he may be still alive. I must check her out, right now, I think she may be an infiltrator, think about it, you've seen the files, and, where has this file come from? I find it very odd indeed it has no routing attached to it."

Karen looked hurt that I didn't trust her best friend.

"I'll get her file, but you'll see she is legitimate, even you have to see this is really important incredible stuff, we are best friends and I think I know her well enough."

"I have to double-check her background Karen, I'm sorry." I tried to assure her, I had the best intentions for everyone, including discovering moles within MI6.

"Oh, and Karen"

"Yes?" Karen sounded hurt.

"I love you and never forget it."

"I love you too Andy."

Karen took the file and began copying the contents taking care to replace each file in the exact order they came from the folder. I sat pondering where to start and how to go about this project.

Karen came back, the copying finished, and the file locked away in her drawer again, she handed me an unmarked folder containing all the copies she just made. I stood up to place the folder in my safe.

"Andy, can you stay tonight? I'll make some dinner. I miss you."

"I can't Karen, I'm so sorry, I wish I could but I'm out tonight. Of course, I'd rather be with you"

"Anywhere nice?" She enquired in her hurt voice again.

"Sally Lunn's restaurant in St. Albans. There's a group of about ten of us going. I can't drop out now, I'll have to give them a reason. I wish there was a way that you could join me, but you know it would be awkward to explain who you are." I needed to keep my job a secret, I'd much prefer to be with Karen and I hated myself for turning her down.

With that Karen walked right up to me wrapped her arms around my neck, her face next to mine she whispered in my ear.

"Then do me now."

"What?" I replied surprised.

"Right here and now, do me" Damn this sexy woman, I couldn't resist her, I kissed her on the lips, her breasts pressing into my chest, I felt so good. Our lust grew, we kissed passionately, we were safe in the office on this Saturday morning. Very few people were around, and no one was likely to disturb us. As we kissed, clothes were removed and dropped onto the floor and we made a move for the sofa. In no time at all, we were both naked and enjoying our intertwined bodies together. Her legs wrapped around my waist encouraging me to enter her.

The love and passion we had for each other showed in the way we moved and the lovemaking went on for some time. As we turned again for a different sex position I felt Karen freeze,

"What happened, cramp?" No, stood inside the office, the door having silently opened and closed was Jenny, arms folded, her weight on her right leg while her left foot tapped the floor like a cross teacher. Now I froze too.

"I came back to ask Andy if he would like to work out with me, maybe spot some weights for me. I see though, you're already having a workout" she said trying to stifle a giggle and to look sternly at us both naked on the sofa, legs and bits dangling over the side, my manhood disappearing like a tortoise had been tapped on the nose.

"Ermm, another time perhaps?" Was all I could muster.

"Another time then." she spoke to me, then pointing at Karen, "and you madam, I'll talk to you later." She left as easily and unembarrassed as she had arrived muttering as she went, "That's what happens when you talk about my boobs, you get all horny and you can't help yourselves." she disappeared through the door closing it behind her.

Karen and I burst out laughing, giggling like school kids, caught and guilty.

"How long had she been there?" I asked Karen.

"I have no idea, goodness only knows what she's seen standing at the foot of the sofa."

"Most people would have opened the door, seen what was going on and left quietly closing the door behind them, but she, Jenny, just came in and stood there watching!" I exclaimed.

We were both laughing with embarrassment, we couldn't stop, laughing while we gathered our clothes together and got ourselves dressed.

"I think she is jealous, she hasn't had any sex for ages." Karen theorised.

"Really? I replied, "She is such an attractive girl, I can't believe she can't get any when she wants it, or even find a nice boyfriend."

Karen informed me,
"We share everything at home, we talk about everything, we are best friends in every sense, so close that even our periods have synchronised."

"Is that a thing?" I asked, having never heard of this phenomenon.

"Apparently so." Karen responded.

"Must be bad news for the Sheik and his harem." I tried to make light of my embarrassment. I added, "But you see that strengthens my worry that she may be Mossad or something, she has no boyfriend, no place of her own, her set up is quite temporary, how long has she lived with you?" I asked.

"Must be four years by now, that's not so temporary." Karen was sure her friend was legitimate.

"But don't you see, she arrives, and you take her as a lodger almost at the same time you become my secretary, give or take a few months. Doesn't that strike you as odd?"

Karen went back to work looking slightly miffed, our lovemaking was not finished, but the coitus interruptus by Jenny had ruined the moment. I sat at my desk and decided, as I had a few hours before I needed to get home to change and drive to St. Albans to join my friends on our evening out, that I would spend a little time setting about my new job as a detective. I retrieved the folder

I had just placed in the safe and sat again at my desk. Now I looked at the copies of the documents, I didn't have to be so careful to keep it all in order, but I did anyway to retain some kind of chronology, if there was one.

I got a few sheets of paper and started to create lists from the documents. A list of names, code names, places, countries and then dates. Once all the information was on paper in a simpler form it was easier to see if names and places repeated to try to visualise which were the stronger most often mentioned items. I then thought how all this could be verified from another source. Some names and places repeated, Bariloche, Argentina seemed to have several references and the names that were at those locations seemed to occur more than once too. I called Karen into my room.

"Want to go again Andy?" she asked cheekily.

"No, the moment has passed, but thank you for asking, another time soon I hope. I want you to check on the company database or any files, to see if we have anything on Bariloche, Argentina please."

"Of course." Karen returned to her desk and started to type on her computer. I knew she was way more efficient at looking for the data than me, sometimes I'd watch her work to try to learn something from her, computers were still very new to me.

My thoughts went to the files again. If what I was seeing was true, this was going to be incredible stuff. I had four lines of thought on this.

- Who compiled this folder and how did it get here?
- Is Hitler still alive? How did he escape Berlin if indeed this was all true?
- Who was complicit in allowing Hitler and other Nazis to live and continue to operate, and, did they have any great influence?
- I think the biggest question, why, was Hitler permitted to escape and continue to live, as these documents in front of me seemed to infer his survival was known by various agencies including the British.

I continued to look at the lists to try to find a chronology of events. Just from these few documents, the results were shocking but there was nothing solid of Hitler.

Here is a list of just a few of the Nazis and war criminals who escaped, according to these documents. They are in the chronological order I created from the files:

- Sándor Képíró, fled to Argentina date not stated.
- Dinko Sakic, fled to Argentina in 1947.
- Ante Pavelić, escaped to Argentina in 1948, died in Spain, in December 1959, of wounds sustained two years earlier in an assassination attempt.
- Eduard Roschmann, escaped to Argentina in 1948
- Hans-Ulrich Rudel, fled to Argentina in 1948, started the "Kameradenwerk." a relief organization for Nazi criminals that helped fugitives escape.
- Josef Mengele, fled to Argentina in 1949.
- Erich Priebke, fled to Argentina in 1949.
- Adolf Eichmann, fled to Argentina in 1950, captured in 1960 by Mossad, executed in Israel on the 1st June 1962.
- Joachim Peiper, also known as Jochen Peiper, did not flee to Argentina. Rather, he was apprehended on 22nd May 1945 by American troops, sent to trial and convicted of war crimes.

Note: I have included Jochen Peiper in this list for a very special reason which will become apparent further into this story. More on him in a bit.

Here was massive evidence of Nazis fleeing to Argentina. This was shocking to learn.

I kept Hitler out of this list, I made a separate one for him because I felt his escape, if he had escaped, was the only one in the list whose documentation appeared to be possibly fake. Therefore, I needed to verify by some other means the reports on him as true before I included him in this list.

I left for home a few hours later for my evening out with my friends, leaving Karen still working after kissing her goodbye and apologising again that I could not invite her to be with me. She understood and I always loved her for that.

A few days later Karen received the personal file on Jenny from the human resources department and called me back to London to look at it. It would have been so much easier if everything was computerised as things are today, it would have saved me so much travel. I read it briefly as there wasn't much I could do alone. I took it to a specialist department that could do an even more thorough job at checking her out. I requested under the strongest terms that their investigations came to me and only me first, which they agreed, with little explanation from me as to why I was asking. There could be multiple reasons for this, and it wasn't their job to ask, only to do the work I requested and give me the completed work. I didn't know why but I had a hunch, a huge hunch, that Jenny wasn't all that she appeared, lovely as she was. I went with Karen to the in-house library. This was more of a depository of knowledge and data rather than a reading library. Two people working together could find far more information than one and Karen knew her way around this place far better than me. I wanted all kinds of stuff, Argentinian census results, maps, anything demographic to try to figure if new villages or towns had sprung up in the period from 1943 to more recent times. I wanted anything on the Argentinian scientific development, I knew that some Germans had gone to live there by invitation to work on rocket development. We found documentation on Operation Paperclip and Operation Overcast. There was a Project Safehaven which seemed to be tied into what we were looking for. All in all, it became apparent there was plenty of reading for me to do and learn. None of this stuff was likely ever taught in Rickmansworth Grammar School lessons that I attended. After a few hours, we had a trolley loaded with documents, reports, papers, and books. All this would take a while to sift through and Karen kindly volunteered to help day and night.

I have to stress that I treated this project as a side-line and worked on this in whatever spare time I could find. I continued to work on my normal activities, and I did not allow this to interfere with the work I was doing at that time. But for the purposes of this book, my normal work is not of any relevance to this story, so I do not include it here.

Very soon it was clear to me many Nazis were running and hiding all over the world, I suppose that is a natural thing to do to escape trial or whatever they thought may happen if they stayed in Germany. Their escape was via what has been called "Ratlines."

"Ratlines" were a system of escape routes for Nazis and other fascists fleeing Europe in the aftermath of World War II. These escape routes mainly led toward havens in Southern America,

> 105-410
>
> was one of four men who met HITLER and his party when they landed from two submarines in Argentina approximately two and one-half weeks after the fall of Berlin. ▮▮▮ continued that the first sub came close to shore about 11:00 p.m. after it had been signaled that it was safe to land and a doctor and several men disembarked. Approximately two hours later the second sub came ashore and HITLER, two women, another doctor, and several more men, making the whole party arriving by submarines approximately 50, were aboard. By pre-arranged plan with six top Argentine officials, pack horses were waiting for the group and by daylight all supplies were loaded on the horses and an all-day trip inland toward the foothills of the southern Andes was started. At dusk the party arrived at the ranch where HITLER and his party, according to ▮▮▮, are now in hiding. ▮▮▮ most specifically explained that the subs landed along the tip of the Valdez Peninsula along the southern tip of Argentina in the gulf of San Matias. ▮▮▮ told ▮▮▮ that there are several tiny villages in this area where members of HITLER's party would eventually stay with German families. He named the towns as San Antonio, Videma, Neuquen, Muster, Carmena, and Rason.
>
> ▮▮▮ maintains that he can name the six Argentine officials and also the names of the three other men who helped HITLER inland to his hiding place. ▮▮▮ explained that he was given $15,000 for helping in the deal. ▮▮▮ explained to ▮▮▮ that he was hiding out in the United States now so that he could later tell how he got out of Argentina. He stated to ▮▮▮ that he would tell his story to the United States officials after HITLER's capture so that they might keep him from having to return to Argentina. He further explained to ▮▮▮ that the matter was weighing on his mind and that he did not wish to be mixed up in the business any further.
>
> According to ▮▮▮, HITLER is suffering from asthma and ulcers, has shaved off his mustache and has a long "but" on his upper lip.
>
> ▮▮▮ gave the following directions to ▮▮▮ "If you will go to a hotel in San Antonio, Argentina, I will arrange for a man to meet you there and locate the ranch where HITLER is. It is heavily guarded, of course, and you will be risking your life to go there. If you do go to Argentina, place an ad in the Examiner stating, ▮▮▮ call Hempstead 8458,' and I know that you are on the way to San Antonio."
>
> The above information was given to ▮▮▮, reporter on the Los Angeles Examiner on July 29, 1945.
>
> The writer contacted ▮▮▮ in an attempt to locate ▮▮▮ in order that he might be vigorously interviewed in detail concerning the above store. ▮▮▮ reiterated the information set out above, adding that the friend to whom ▮▮▮ was talking in front of the Melody Lane Restaurant was a friend of his by the name of "JACK," last name unknown, but that since the introduction he has had further conversation with "JACK" and "JACK" advised him that while he was eating his lunch at the Melody Lane Restaurant ▮▮▮ sat at his table
>
> -2-

A typical document I had to read and collate information from to form a coherent database.

particularly Argentina, Chile, Paraguay, Colombia, Brazil, Uruguay, Mexico, Guatemala, Ecuador, and Bolivia, as well as the United States and Switzerland.

There were two primary routes: the first went from Germany to Spain, then Argentina; the second from Germany to Rome to Genoa, then South America. The two routes developed independently but eventually came together. The ratlines were supported by clergy of the Catholic Church, and there are claims this was supported by the Vatican. Indeed, evidence would soon arrive to confirm this.

The important realisation to me was that we could find so many records regarding this topic in MI6 archives. To me, this meant whatever happened after the war British Intelligence knew full well of it. If there were any clues, I became more determined to find them and cross-check by other means, to confirm the truth rather than rely on what may be false news or information. At this point, I had no idea how I would make the cross-checks, but I was hoping to come across actual witnesses that may be in a position to talk, if not to me but through an agent I would set up if necessary.

Soon, I decided as we were finding so much information, we had to narrow the spectrum and refine the search to just Hitler, or our work would become endless because there was just too many escaped Nazis.

So, before I get too deep into my work to find Hitler, in case you are not aware of the official story I'll give you a short history lesson as we are taught in schools and history.

The Alleged End to Adolf Hitler

By early 1945, Germany was on the verge of total military collapse. Occupied Poland had fallen to the advancing Soviet Red Army, who had crossed the River Oder to capture Berlin. German forces had recently lost to the Allies in the Ardennes Offensive, with British and allied forces, mainly Canadian, crossing the Rhine into the German industrial heartland of the Ruhr. American forces in the south had captured Lorraine and were advancing northwards. German forces in Italy were withdrawing north, as they were pressed by American and Commonwealth forces to advance across the river Po and into the foothills of the Alps.

Hitler retreated to his Führerbunker in Berlin on 16th January 1945. It was clear to the Nazi leadership that the battle for Berlin would be the final battle of the war in Europe. Some 325,000 soldiers of Germany's Army were surrounded and captured on 18th April, leaving the path open for American forces to reach Berlin. By 11th April the Americans crossed the River Elbe, 62 miles to the west of the city. On 16th April, Soviet forces to the east crossed the River Oder and commenced the battle for Berlin on that side. By 19th April, the Germans were in full retreat, leaving no front line. Berlin was bombarded by Soviet artillery for the first time on 20th April, which was also Hitler's birthday. By the evening of 21st April, Red Army tanks reached the outskirts of the city.

At the afternoon situation conference on 22nd April, Hitler suffered a total nervous collapse when he was informed that the orders he had issued the previous day to counterattack had not been obeyed. Hitler launched a tirade against the treachery and incompetence of his commanders which culminated in a declaration that the war was lost. Hitler announced that he would stay in Berlin until the end and then shoot himself. Later that day, he asked his SS physician about the most reliable method of suicide. It was suggested the "pistol-and-poison method" of combining a dose of cyanide with a gunshot to the head. Luftwaffe chief Hermann Göring learned about this and sent a telegram to Hitler asking for permission to take over the leadership of the Reich following Hitler's 1941 decree naming him as his successor. Hitler's secretary Martin Bormann convinced Hitler that Göring was threatening a coup. In response, Hitler informed Göring that he would be executed unless he resigned all of his posts. Later that day, he sacked Göring from all of his offices and ordered his arrest.

By 27th April, Berlin was cut off from the rest of Germany. Secure radio communications with defending units had been lost; the command staff in the bunker had to depend on telephone lines for passing instructions and orders, and public radio for news and information. On 28th April, Hitler received a BBC report, the report stated that Heinrich Himmler had offered to surrender to the Western Allies. The offer was declined. Himmler had implied to the Allies that he had the authority to negotiate a surrender, and Hitler considered this treason. That afternoon, Hitler's anger and bitterness escalated into a rage against Himmler. Hitler ordered Himmler's arrest.

By this time, the Red Army had advanced to the Potsdamer Platz, and all indications were that they were preparing to storm the Chancellery. This report and Himmler's treachery prompted Hitler to make the last decisions of his life. Shortly after midnight on 29th April, he married Eva Braun in a small civil ceremony in a map room within the Führerbunker. Hitler then hosted a modest wedding breakfast with his new wife, after which he took Secretary Traudl Junge to another room and dictated his last will and testament.

On the afternoon of 29th April, Hitler learned that his ally, Mussolini, had been executed by Italian partisans. The bodies of Mussolini and his mistress had been strung up by their feet. The corpses were later cut down and thrown into the gutter, where they were mocked by Italian dissenters. These events may have strengthened Hitler's resolve not to allow himself or his wife to be made a spectacle, as he had earlier recorded in his testament. Doubting the efficacy of the cyanide capsules distributed by his SS physician, Hitler ordered a test on his dog Blondi, who died as a result. Hitler and Braun lived together as husband and wife in the bunker for less than 40 hours. By 01:00 on 30th April, it was reported that all of the forces on which Hitler had been depending to rescue Berlin had either been encircled or forced onto the defensive. At around 02:30, Hitler appeared in the corridor where about 20 people, mostly women, were assembled to give their farewells. He walked the line and shook hands with each of them before retiring to his quarters late in the morning, with the Soviets less than 500 metres from the bunker.

Hitler, two secretaries, and his cook then had lunch, after which Hitler and Braun said farewell to members of staff and fellow occupants, including Bormann, Goebbels and his family, the secretaries, and several military officers. At around 14:30 Adolf and Eva Hitler went into Hitler's study. Several witnesses later reported that they heard a loud gunshot at approximately 15:30. After waiting a few minutes, Hitler's valet, Heinz Linge, opened the study door with Bormann at his side. Linge later stated that he immediately noted a scent of burnt almonds, which is a common observation in the presence of cyanide.

Hitler's adjutant entered the study and found the two lifeless bodies on the sofa. Eva, with her legs drawn up, was to Hitler's left and slumped away from him. Hitler was bent over, with blood dripping out of his right temple. He had shot himself with his pistol. The gun lay at his feet and Hitler's head was lying on the table in front of him. Blood dripping from Hitler's right temple and chin had made a large stain on the right arm of the sofa and was pooling on the carpet. According to Linge, Eva's body had no visible physical wounds, she had died by cyanide.

Following Hitler's prior written and verbal instructions, the two bodies were carried up the stairs and through the bunker's emergency exit to the garden behind the Reich Chancellery, where they were to be burned with petrol.

The Soviets shelled the area in and around the Reich Chancellery on and off during the afternoon. SS guards brought over additional cans of petrol to further burn the corpses.

The first inkling to the outside world that Hitler was dead came from the Germans themselves. On 1st May, a Hamburg radio station interrupted their normal program to announce that Hitler had died that afternoon and introduced his successor, President Karl Dönitz. Dönitz called upon the German people to mourn their Führer, who he stated had died a hero defending the capital of the Reich. Hoping to save the army and the nation by negotiating a partial surrender to the British and Americans, Dönitz authorised a fighting withdrawal to the west. His tactic was somewhat successful, it enabled about 1.8 million German soldiers to avoid capture by the Soviets, but it came at a high cost in bloodshed, as troops continued to fight until 8th May.

On 4th May, the thoroughly burned remains of Hitler, Braun, and two dogs were discovered in a shell crater by SMERSH commander Ivan Klimenko. They were exhumed the next day and secretly delivered to the SMERSH Counter-Espionage Section of the 3rd Assault Army. Stalin was wary of believing Hitler was dead and restricted the release of information to the public. By 11th May, part of a lower jaw with dental work was identified as Hitler's. Details of the Soviet autopsy were made public in 1968 and used to confirm the remains as Hitler's in 1972.

In early June 1945, the bodies of Hitler, Braun, Joseph and Magda Goebbels, the six Goebbels children, Krebs, Blondi and another dog were moved from Buch to Finow, where the SS guard who buried Hitler re-identified his remains. The bodies were reburied in a forest in Brandenburg on 3rd June, and finally exhumed and moved to the SMERSH unit's new facility in Magdeburg, where they were buried in five wooden boxes on 21st February 1946. By 1970, the facility was under the control of the KGB but was scheduled to be returned to East Germany. Concerned that a known Hitler burial site might become a neo-Nazi shrine, KGB director Yuri Andropov authorised an operation to destroy the remains that were buried there in 1946. A KGB team was given detailed burial charts and on 4th April 1970 secretly exhumed the remains of 10 or 11 bodies. The remains were thoroughly burned and crushed, and the ashes were thrown into the Biederitz river, a tributary of the nearby Elbe.

For politically motivated reasons, the Soviet Union presented various versions of Hitler's fate. When asked in July 1945 how Hitler had died, Stalin said he was living "in Spain or Argentina." In November 1945, Dick White, the head of counterintelligence in the British sector of Berlin, had their agent Hugh Trevor-Roper investigate the matter to counter the Soviet claims. His report was published in 1947 as *The Last Days of Hitler*.

In the years immediately after the war, the Soviets maintained that Hitler was not dead, but had escaped and was being shielded by the former Western Allies.

On 30th May 1946, MVD (Ministry of Internal Affairs) agents recovered two fragments of a skull from the crater where Hitler was buried. The left parietal bone had gunshot damage. This piece remained uncatalogued until 1975 and was rediscovered in the Russian State Archives in 1993. In 2009, DNA and forensic tests were performed on a small piece detached from the skull fragment, which Soviet officials had long believed to be Hitler's. According to the American researchers, their tests revealed that it belonged to a woman and the examination of the skull sutures placed her at less than 40 years old.

Throughout the late 1940's and 1950's, the FBI and CIA documented many possible leads that Hitler might still be alive.

In 1968, Soviet journalist Lev Bezymenski published his book. The purported Soviet forensic examination led by Faust Shkaravsky concluded that Hitler had died by cyanide poisoning, while Bezymenski theorizes that Hitler requested a *coup de gras* to ensure his quick death. Bezymenski later admitted that his work included "deliberate lies." as to the manner of Hitler's death.

That is the official story. Now you make up your mind if you think that is the truth. To me, there are several contradictions. Read on . . . .

Operation Paperclip and Overcast

To understand *why* we have been and continue to be lied to, I thought it was necessary to figure who was in on this secret, the documents we were finding led me to believe the British were complicit, along with the USA, so why? Operation Paperclip and Operation Overcast contained what I thought was the answer.

... A deal ...

To prove my point, I needed to find the deal. It was an open secret of the Joint Intelligence Objectives Agency (JIOA), in which more than 1,600 German scientists, engineers, and technicians, such as Wernher von Braun and his V-2 rocket team, were taken from Germany to America for U.S. government employment, primarily between 1945 and 1959. Many were former members, and some were former leaders of the Nazi Party. This story has been well publicised in many books and other publications.

The primary purpose for Operation Paperclip was U.S. military advantage in the Soviet–American Cold War and the Space Race. The Soviet Union was more aggressive in forcibly recruiting more than 2,200 German specialists, a total of more than 6,000 people including family members, with Operation Osoaviakhim during one night on 22nd October 1946. This Soviet operation was to forcibly remove scientists to continue their work in Russia. Probably, this alone caused many of the German scientist to want to live in the USA.

The Joint Chiefs of Staff (JCS) established the first secret recruitment program, called Operation Overcast, on 20th July 1945, initially "to assist in shortening the Japanese war and to aid our post-war military research." The term "Overcast" was the name first given by the German scientists' family members for the housing camp where they were held in Bavaria. Operation Overcast was renamed Operation Paperclip by Ordnance Corps (United States Army) officers, who would attach a paperclip to the folders of those rocket experts whom they wished to employ in America.

In a secret directive circulated on 3rd September 1946, President Truman officially approved Operation Paperclip and expanded it to include one thousand German scientists under "temporary, limited military custody."

The Osenberg List.

In the later part of World War II, Nazi Germany found itself at a logistical disadvantage, having failed to conquer the USSR with Operation Barbarossa (June - December 1941), the Siege of Leningrad (September 1941 - January 1944), Operation Nordlicht ("Northern Light." August - October 1942), and the Battle of Stalingrad (July 1942 - February 1943). The failed conquest had depleted German resources, and its military-industrial complex was unprepared to defend the Großdeutsches Reich (Greater German Reich) against the Red Army's westward counterattack. By early 1943, the German government began recalling from combat many scientists, engineers, and technicians. They returned to work in research and development to bolster German defence. The recall from frontline combat included 4,000 rocketeers returned to Peenemünde, in northeast coastal Germany.

"Overnight, Ph.Ds. were liberated from KP duty, masters of science were recalled from orderly service, mathematicians were hauled out of bakeries, and precision mechanics ceased to be truck drivers."

- Dieter K. Huzel, Peenemünde to Canaveral

The Nazi government's recall of their now-useful intellectuals for scientific work first required identifying and locating the scientists, engineers, and technicians, then ascertaining their political and ideological reliability. Werner Osenberg, the engineer-scientist heading the *Wehrforschungsgemeinschaft* (Defence Research Association), recorded the names of the politically cleared men to the Osenberg List, to reinstate them to scientific work.

In March 1945, at Bonn University, a Polish laboratory technician found pieces of the Osenberg List stuffed in a toilet. The list subsequently reached MI6, who transmitted it to U.S. Intelligence. Then U.S. Army Major Robert B. Staver, Chief of the Jet Propulsion Section of the Research and Intelligence Branch of the U.S. Army Ordnance Corps, used the Osenberg List to compile his list of German scientists to be captured. Wernher von Braun, Germany's premier rocket scientist, headed Major Staver's list.

In Operation Overcast, Major Staver's original intent was only to interview the scientists, but what he learned changed the operation's purpose. On 22nd May 1945, he transmitted to the U.S. Pentagon headquarters Colonel Joel Holmes's telegram urging the evacuation of German scientists and their families, as most "important for the Pacific war" effort. Most of the Osenberg List engineers worked at the Baltic coast German Army Research Centre Peenemünde, developing the V-2 rocket. After capturing them, the Allies initially housed them and their families in Landshut, Bavaria, in southern Germany.

Beginning on 19th July 1945, the U.S. JCS managed the captured ARC rocketeers under Operation Overcast. However, when the "Camp Overcast" name of the scientists' quarters became locally known, the program was renamed Operation Paperclip in November 1945. Despite these attempts at secrecy, later that year the press interviewed several of the scientists.

For years the scientists were held or invited to work in scientific bases around the USA under contract. In 1959, 94 Operation Paperclip men went to the United States.

Overall, through its operations to 1990, Operation Paperclip imported 1,600 men, as part of the *intellectual reparations* owed to the US and the UK, valued at $10 billion in patents and industrial processes.

So how does this mean that a deal had been struck with Hitler? Surely this was the USA and Russia helping themselves to their war reparations.

It was known Hitler had a double, it would be too easy to replace Hitler in the bunker with one of his doubles, kill him and burn the evidence, as has been written earlier. Is there proof that Hitler escaped?

My evidence is witness. Of course, a witness would need to be proved to be reliable, but think, why would a witness lie in the case of Hitler's escape from Berlin? Hitler's end, as described in the history books is enough, the end of a mad vicious dictator. Why lie that he has escaped? There is no reason to lie. That would be my logic. So now I needed to find any witnesses that categorically state they had some part in or saw Hitler anywhere other than a burnt grave in Berlin beyond 4th May 1945.

So began a trawl of any document I could find relating to the subject. There were thousands, and Karen was brilliant at sifting through the mass and only passing on to me to scrutinise the useful parts. We made a brilliant team, with access to the most secret of documents and reports that any other reporter or writer would certainly not have access.

The Honeys and the trap

Timeline - June 1976

During this time, one thing that continued to worry me was Jenny, and who she said she was. There was something about finding the folder that started all this that just didn't seem right. It was time to find out. In February I had passed Jenny's personnel file to a specialist team to deep investigate. Unknown to Jenny and Karen, they had re-checked her background, followed her every move, in and out of Century House, tapped phone lines, intercepted letters, read and returned them looking perfectly normal at the post office. The result of all this work, nothing. Nothing could be found that she was anything but a hard-working secretary, working honestly and diligently, apart from the one folder she had removed to my possession, but now returned to its correct place, hidden from requests under the 30 years Act back at Hanslope Park. I hadn't told the investigation team about the folder. I had checked that it had dropped on her desk as it should have done and not spirited away as suspiciously as it had arrived.

I have no idea why, but I couldn't take the result of the deep check team as I should have. It was just something about the folder, its contents and lack of any routing record. Something in my mind wasn't right with that part of her story. So I decided there should be a test, a test for Jenny. A bait was needed to draw her out if she was anything but what she appeared.

Early June, now almost five months into this project, I phoned to ask Karen to arrange for me to see Jenny.

"Come over to my home for dinner Friday evening, we'll make a night of it." Karen suggested. This was perfect, I would have the chance to "loosen Jenny up" with drinks and some fun. Best of all I'd stay the night and be with the love of my life. Karen wanted me to stay, but she had no idea I was going to set up Jenny with a bait trap.

"Karen, do you trust me?" I asked on the phone to her.

"Of course I do, I couldn't work with you if I didn't. I trust you completely." she replied.

"Whatever happens I need you to trust me and that there is a reason for everything I do. I may flirt a bit with Jenny." I told Karen.

"Oh, you still don't trust her." Karen got it right away, there was no pulling the wool over her eyes. It was almost that she could read my mind.

"OK, do what you have to do, flirt all you like, but trust me, she is my best friend, I know her better than anyone, you'll see."

"I ask nothing but your trust, I love you, but I have to do something to allay my feelings that she is more than she seems, these are strong feelings, you know me, when I get this feeling there's always a reason." We weren't arguing, we never did. Karen was just torn between loyalty to her best friend and me. I understood that and couldn't get cross with her for standing up for her friend.

The following Friday evening, I arrived at Karen's flat loaded with bottles of wine, chocolates and flowers for both girls. Jenny answered the door intercom and buzzed me in, I went by the lift to the fourth floor and Jenny was already waiting at the open door to Karen's flat. She looked very attractive, really cute in a black tight-fitting top and mini skirt, she had the sexiest tanned legs, shapely and fit looking. I kissed a greeting on Jenny's cheek, she smelt very nice too, she was wearing an expensive perfume her whole image was sexy and irresistible. As I kissed her, I said how nice she looked and passed her the flowers and some chocolates. June 1976 was a hot and dry summer, swelteringly hot, entering the flat it felt nice and cool as there was air conditioning, it was comfortable after the heat of the London streets outside. Karen's flat always had a comfortable feel, the colour scheme was relaxing, she knew what she was doing when she decorated the place and I learnt a lot from her about how colours can set your mood.

Karen was in the kitchen, if Jenny looked sexy this girl outshone her ten times over. Everything about her was perfect, her hair was down today, which I didn't get to see very often, shiny and healthy, her makeup couldn't be faulted and her face as pretty as any Hollywood star. Her figure was just pure sex, she wore a white loose shirt like a men's shirt, with almost too many buttons undone, so that a little too much boob could be seen, but what the hell it's her home, she can dress as she likes. She also wore a short dark purple mini skirt, and her legs as sexy as any, tanned and perfect in every way. She was barefooted and looking busy but not stressed as she cooked, in control as always. I moved into the kitchen stood behind her and kissed her on the neck, she tilted her head to the side to allow me to kiss longer than just a greeting, I could see her smile, her perfect white teeth the kind only celebrities have and her perfume was working its charm on me. Karen greeted me.

"Hi Andy, good to see you, perfect timing, food is almost ready, five minutes and I'll join you. Want to pour some wine? There's cold white in the fridge or red in the rack in the lounge. We both have glasses already." I knew to make myself at home, Karen liked me to feel at ease and treat the place like it was mine. I wished so much I could be a permanent part of her life. Jenny was stood smiling at the kitchen door and walked with me through to the lounge, where she handed me her glass for a top-up of red wine. We chatted about nothing special as I, with my back to her, poured three red wines but into Jenny's, I added half a tot of vodka, I hoped she wouldn't taste it too much. Jenny moved the conversation onto Nazis.

"Have you found anything yet Andy?" she sat down on the sofa, folding her suntanned legs under her, revealing very sexy thighs and her short skirt high up on her legs revealing a hint of a white panty beneath.

"Well, yes but the information isn't complete enough to give to you. I have to confirm what I have." I said.

"Oh, who is it, Hitler?" she enquired.

"No, I do have information on Hitler, that is still a bit sketchy at the moment. I have another Nazi, but you are only interested in Hitler I thought?" I knew what I was telling her, I wanted to draw her into my trap.

"Well if you have found any Nazi's then I'm interested of course." she continued.

"No, I'll tell you when I am sure and have the address confirmed." I teased.

"You have an address, oh come on you have to tell me."

I had every intention of telling Jenny the address, but I wanted to see how far she would go to get the information. For now, I'd pretend to be investigating even though my investigations were complete on this particular Nazi.

"Andy." she said in one of those female 'promise of something more if you give me what I want' voices.

"Don't be such a tease, who is it?"

At that Karen entered the room with perfect timing though she had no idea how perfect.

"If you two would like to come to the table dinner is served." she said putting several dishes onto the laid table in the corner of the lounge room. The room was plenty big enough for the 4 seat round dining table in one corner under an overhead light.

I got up and moved to the table to end the line of talk leaving Jenny looking forgotten, but I was certain she had plans to get the information from me, and I wanted to see how she would do that, how desperate she would be to get anything I had on Nazis.

Karen announced the menu,

"Osso buco veal shanks braised with vegetables, white wine and broth, with risotto alla Milanese." wow, Karen could cook too, there was no end to her talents, what an incredible lady. We sat at the table to one side so we all had a view outside through the full-length floor to ceiling window. Me between the two ladies, I was a lucky man today. During the meal, Jenny tried hard to find out how my project to find Hitler was proceeding. I wasn't going to tell her anything, so she changed tack and tried to work on Karen.

"How hard has Andy been working on this, it sounds like he's done so much?"

"He hasn't allowed it to interrupt his normal work, but I think the progress is good." I knew she had done more than I on this project, I think it intrigued her more than me, or maybe she just wanted to help her friend, I don't know.

The main course was followed by lemon meringue pie, my favourite, and Karen knew it. I loved this woman.

I kept the wine coming, each time I topped up the glasses, I secretly dropped half a tot of vodka into Jenny's drink and it was beginning to take effect.

After the meal, we all helped to clear the table and tidy the kitchen, it didn't take long as Karen had cleared up as she cooked, so it was just the serving dishes and plates to sort out. The talk was becoming more amusing and Jenny was asking more questions about Germans but also being quite amusing in her manner, definitely becoming more flirtier with me. I don't know how Karen was feeling but I was a little uncomfortable with it, but during a moment while Jenny went off to the bathroom I spoke with Karen about it.

"Are you ok if I return some of the flirting, I need to try to prise out of her who she maybe?" I asked her quietly.

"Do what you have to do, I know what you need to do, I get it." Karen wasn't cross or angry, this was me at work now, but also having fun.

"I want you to know, whatever happens, I love you, only you." I told Karen.

"Likewise." and Karen kissed me on the lips to confirm her love just as Jenny returned.

"Oh, you two what are you like, as soon as I leave the room you are at it. I hope you haven't been discussing my boobs again, you know what happened last time."

"Well, your boobs are a big subject, takes a lot of talking about." I said jokingly.

Karen joined in the thread, "Andy, between us two who has the best boobs, in your opinion?"

"That's a tough question, one I'm sitting next to the girl I love and two I've only ever seen your boobs." I replied a little shocked.

"Come on Jenny show Andy your tits." Karen laughing now.

"Nooo." I cried, "Don't, I'll be embarrassed. I have a better idea, let's play 'Did you ever'." I thought I needed to get Jenny relaxed and talking freely.

Everyone agreed it would be fun to play and now we were on our third bottle of wine and Jenny with about three tots of vodka extra. So we played and as always with games like this the 'Did you ever' questions got dirtier and ruder.

Karen and Jenny were so funny, I couldn't begin to describe to you, you had to be there with more than a bottle of wine inside you. We laughed so much Jenny's questions were always the dirtiest and I noticed Jenny placed the occasional hand on my leg as I sat with Karen laying on my shoulder, Jenny's touches were becoming more brazen and Karen didn't flinch at all, she must have noticed too. After an hour or so playing the game, I think we knew just about everything about each other, especially our sex lives. Mine was simple, I'd only ever been with Karen. Karen, on the other hand, had surprised me with her answers. I now knew she had seen both her parents naked, had never kissed a girl before, had sex once in a public place, had a wee in a public place, had watched porn and masturbated while doing so. As for Jenny, I found out she had seen her mum naked but not her dad, she had kissed a girl and at university had sex with her female roommate more than once, to this answer Karen had asked Jenny if she had any thoughts about having sex with her, and Jenny had replied

"Yes of course, why not, you are so perfect, so sexy." to which Karen replied,

"I had no idea you thought like that." in the '70s being openly gay was still frowned upon and ridiculed and men were still being imprisoned for "unnatural offences." but women were less prone to prosecution. Jenny continued to explain.

"I'm not lesbian, I enjoy both, I'd call myself bi-sexual." I'd not heard this term before I hadn't even thought about it. I was 21 and still very green on the subject of sex. Karen had been my only partner and sex teacher.

I got up from the sofa to get yet more drinks, I didn't spike Jenny's now, she'd had enough and I didn't want her to collapse or something, I still needed her to be capable of knowing what she was talking about. There was dance music on Karen's Bang & Olufsen music system and as I walked to the drinks cabinet, I kind of danced to the music across the room. I don't normally dance at all, but I was relaxed, a little drunk and this evening I was in fantastic company. As I poured the drinks, prompted by my display, the girls got up and started to dance themselves. They danced in a kind of arms up style with plenty of loud whooping and noise, they were having so much fun. I returned with the drinks, trying hard not to spill them shuffling around the dancing girls, placed them on the table and made an attempt at my no-dad style of dance with them. 1976 was a very hot year and even with the air conditioning, it was feeling quite warm now. The two girls decided it was time to take off their tops. They danced as they stripped to their bras and miniskirts, it was a very sexy sight I have to say. As one song ended they embraced each other laughing and Karen reached around and removed Jenny's bra, hugging each other so her boobs were not visible. Jenny repeated the action on Karen and in a moment they were both topless, dancing close in each other's arms. I stood for a moment to take in the scene, and what a sexy scene it was. Karen reached out for me to join the huddle, slow dancing in the middle of the room the three of us slowly circling laughing and enjoying the dance. When the song ended our little group broke up to take a sip of drinks, Jenny asked the question,

"OK, Andy, now you see me, who has the best tits?"

"Wow that's a difficult question, how can I answer that? You are asking me to judge the love of my life, but Jenny, I love you too." I studied the boobs of the two girls who were dancing slowly in a kind of slow stripper style rolling their hips around.

"Hmmm, I'm going to have to announce the winner is . . . drum roll . . . for the reason that Jenny's boobs are firm and completely defying gravity . . . yet Karen's are in my opinion slightly larger and the perfect shape, with the best perfect nipples and areola . . . oh this is so difficult."

"Come on Andy, don't be shy, I won't take offence if you pick Jenny, she is so beautiful and cute and look at those double D's." Karen was trying to help me, she knew I was playing Jenny this evening.

I took hold of the two girl's hands like a boxing referee announcing the result.

"I have to announce, the winner is . . . a draw." and I raised both girl's arms as winners.

"Ohhhh." both girls cried out together, "Coward" and other remarks aimed at my cowardice.

"No, really both of you are fantastic, a man couldn't ask for better." I tried badly to disguise my cowardly competition result. Everyone laughed and the music machine continued to play dance music, so we danced, with the girls remaining topless.

We had a great evening with Jenny non-stop pestering me to give her the information I had on the German. She had found out by now that I had a piece of paper in my back pocket with the details of the Nazi. But I wouldn't let her grab hold of it. Why was she so desperate to get it I wondered? I thought she wanted to know about Hitler.

We had so many laughs that evening, eventually, at about 1am, as Jenny went to the bathroom, Karen took me by the hand and led me to her bedroom. It didn't take us long to get undressed and lay on the bed. As I undressed, I removed the notepaper from my back pocket and hid it in Karen's knicker drawer. We kissed naked and Karen whispered,

"Did you get what you wanted from Jenny?"

"Not yet." I replied, "I'm still playing her, I have to push her hard to expose her if there is something to expose." We laughed at the irony of my statement. Given the girl's state of undress most of the evening.

With that Jenny burst into the bedroom pouting,

"Hey, you two, you left me, Andy hasn't given me the name yet, and now I'm just a lonely gooseberry." she was still topless and her slight anger didn't fit the way she was dressed. It looked slightly comical. Karen and I didn't flinch in our nakedness, Jenny had seen us like this before in the office anyway, drink and at ease with each other as friends it was just natural to remain where we were on the bed uncovered.

"Oh come on Jenny." Karen spoke sympathetically, "sorry, to leave you unannounced, come and give us a kiss goodnight." Jenny knelt on the bed leaned down to kiss me, I turned to accept the kiss which caused the kiss to hit my lips rather than the left cheek that she was aiming for, she was a nice kisser. Karen put her hand on Jenny's back and Jenny moved across to her to kiss her too. My goodness her boobs looked sexy, as she crawled over me they hung down and dragged over my body. Their kiss became a little extended, became less of a kiss goodnight, more a kiss of passion, of lust. Karen naked and Jenny topless, it was such a sexy scene, the kiss became a full-on snog, to use a term of the time. I lay on the bed taking in the two girls becoming more and more passionate in their kisses and embrace, hands beginning to wander over each other's bodies. After a while, it was my turn to exclaim,

"Hey, now I'm the gooseberry here!" now the girls, hot in their lust for sex, turned to me and the three of us became one mass of bodies, arms and legs. Jenny somehow in the writhing became naked with us, and over the next few hours we took part in the most sex-filled, no holds barred threesome one could ever imagine. No one was jealous, no one was shy about their sex, we all enjoyed the night to the full.

In the morning I woke, still naked, next to me Karen was starting to stir too, Jenny was gone. I kissed Karen good morning and we both smiled at the memory of the night.

"Hmmm." I said.

"What?" Karen asked.

"Your lips taste of Jenny's vagina."

"Oh you disgust me." Karen laughed as she slapped me on the upper arm "get out and go make coffee, anyway I don't think I can walk after all that sex." I got up forgetting I was still naked and wandered out of the room, as I went Karen called after me,

"Don't go kissing Jenny good morning."

"Why? Are you jealous?" I enquired.

"No, her lips will taste of your cum." she retorted giggling loudly.

"Ohhh, now who's being disgusting." as I left the room into the corridor and the kitchen a few paces away.

I found Jenny in the kitchen also naked.

"Oh, good morning Andy, you're awake then. I've made coffee help yourself." she moved to kiss me a greeting. For some reason, I backed away.

"Are you ok? She enquired "no regrets? Thank you for a lovely night." she talked as I poured three coffees,

"Yes, thank you for an evening I'm never going to forget, I'll take these to the bedroom are you coming back?"

"Shortly. Andy, can I ask you to stop messing with me, can you give me that name please."

"Why are you not being patient? You said you'd be patient until I had all the information checked." the truth was I had the information on the notepaper in Karen's knicker draw, it was double-checked and confirmed, I was always going to give it to Jenny, but I needed to see how desperate she wanted it . . . so to speak.

We walked back to Karen in the bedroom together. I placed the coffee cups beside the bed and climbed in next to Karen. As I turned to face the room, Jenny was looking in my back pocket for the note.

"Jesus Jenny!" I moaned at her "You can't wait can you." now Jenny was showing signs of impatience, I had pushed her enough. "It's in that drawer..." pointing toward where the paper was hidden. Jenny now moving fast still naked to take the paper out of the drawer, read the contents regarding the Nazi Joachim Peiper, I'm not sure if she knew who he was but it didn't matter. She shouted a thank you and left the room.

"Wow." Karen said, "She was desperate for that." I should have replied, "What the sex or the piece of paper?" but I didn't.

We slowly drank our coffee and wondered why Jenny needed that information so badly.

"So did you accomplish what you needed to with Jenny?" Karen asked.

"Now we wait." I said.

"Wait for what?" Karen, still not sure what I was up to.

"Well, it's simple, I'm either right or wrong about Jenny, if I'm right then I expect something will happen, and if I'm wrong, well, I suspect life will go on as normal."

"What do you think will happen?" Karen was unsure what game I was playing now.

"We wait that's all we do, say nothing to her out of the ordinary and wait."

"How long do we wait?" asked Karen.

"Well, could be a while but my hunch says soon."

"I don't know how you are so sure about my best friend, so we will see, and if you are wrong there will be a penance to pay." she giggled.

"And what will the penance be?" I enquired. With that, she pushed my head below the sheets down passed her breasts, over her belly to the sweet spot between her legs. After at least four hours of sex during the night, it wasn't a pleasant place to be, but I managed to satisfy the imposed penance. After Karen finished, it was announced to me that it would be my job to make brunch with more coffee.

Jenny in the meantime had showered dressed and shouted goodbye as she left the apartment. She didn't say where she was going but I had an idea. Ideally, I should have had her followed, but this was an unofficial job, and it was all just a hunch for now anyway.

Karen and I spent the rest of Saturday and Sunday together, it was the only time in all my years working at MI6 we spent a weekend as lovers do, I wished it could be more often. Sunday afternoon I went home ready to go back to work Monday morning.

The following Wednesday, Karen was at Century House and I was at my Dad's business, I received a call from Karen again.

"Andy, you've been summoned to a meeting, you are to talk to HR (Human Resources) and it sounds like trouble."

"What kind of trouble?" I enquired.

"I have no idea, they wouldn't tell me. Tomorrow at 11am at the In and Out Club, Piccadilly." This was an ironic location, a private members club properly named the Naval and Military Club. The club came to be known as the "In and Out." from the prominent traffic-directing signs on its entrance and exit gates. Members included T. E. Lawrence and Ian Fleming. Not only was it a recruiting venue for MI5 and MI6, but this address was also used in correspondence found on a dead British officer who was deliberately dropped into seas off Spain by MI6 during the Second World War. This deception operation, Operation Mincemeat, tricked the Nazis into believing the Normandy invasion force would land elsewhere. I wondered for a moment if someone knew what I was working on in my spare time.

The next day I arrived in Piccadilly and found the club on the eastern side of Saint James's Square. At the front door, feeling a little out of place, as this club was mostly for the military. I was redirected to the rear entrance in Babmaes Street, just off Jermyn Street. It is less formal on this side of the building and is the entrance to the business centre. On entering I was ushered to a private room where I found a lady sitting at a table looking very stern indeed. A note-taker was to one side of the table, this was going to be some kind of disciplinary meeting I realised. As I entered she stood and introduced herself as Barbara Busch-Rash, head of HR. I barely stifled my laughter, poor woman. She only introduced the other lady as the note-taker, which I thought a bit rude. I asked if she was ok to sit, it seemed this was a sense of humour deficit area, and a cold wind was blowing from the north, it may have been better blowing south, it may have eased her discomfort. She didn't get the joke, I struggled to see how I was going to take this as seriously as her face and her name suggested I should. I guessed she was in her sixties and if she wasn't in this job she would have to be a headmistress from an old fifties film, dowdily dressed, with rimless glasses clinging to the end of her nose she peered over the top whenever she looked at me.

She had my file and under it, I assume Karen's too. She began,

"It has come to our attention that a rule is being broken, you are aware that relationships are not permitted between staff within the service." I guessed right away what this was going to be about, but my sense of humour refused to take this seriously.

"Well, that's why I'm not dating you." I replied, I was no longer a schoolchild and took umbrage at being talked at as if I was. I was supposed to be an adult.

"No need to be flippant, this is serious." she tried to take charge, but I was having none of it.

"As serious as the rash?" I tested flippancy to the max.

"What rash?" she asked as she rubbed a hand over her arm as if to search for one. Where did this woman come from for goodness sake?

"Strange." I replied.

"What is?" she questioned.

"Your name, Barbara means strange, it's Greek for strange." I knew this fact as my mother's given name is Barbara and suits her well too.

"Could you not say anything for a moment while I explain why we are here today." she continued to headmistress me. I drew a zip across my mouth signifying I would now remain quiet. She explained the procedure of the disciplinary and began,

"It has come to our attention that you and your secretary Miss Middleton have been having, well . . . relations. Do you not understand the security implications?" and she just droned on for what seemed ages about policy, security and morals. I finally got a chance to speak when she asked if I had anything to say.

"I am well aware of the security aspect of everything I do, and if I had the slightest inkling that Miss Middleton was anything but trustworthy, I'd refuse to work with her. I take your accusation seriously Miss Nappy-Rash."

"Busch-Rash." she corrected me still not showing any sign of a sense of humour.

"Miss Busch-Fire, I have a very good working relationship with my secretary, the work she does for me is exemplary and professional, and is, quite possibly, the most hard-working person in the building."

"None the more for that." she continued "you are being formally warned in a written letter to cease your, your" she stumbled her words trying to think of the correct phrase to apply to my relationship with Karen, "your perverse sexual desires."

"Perverse? What are you on about? Have you lost your hydrocortisone?"

"Hydrocortisone?" she came back totally lost in the joke that was endless in its possibilities. She continued,

"We are aware that you, Miss Middleton and Miss Avraham spent a night together last weekend."

Now it dawned on me, oh shit, I exclaimed to myself, I'd ordered a deep check on Jenny, and they have bugged Karen's apartment. They must have installed secret cameras too!

"Research!" I grabbed the first word that came into my head.

"What?" the strange woman replied.

"We were working on Miss Avraham, it's official business and in this business, we use all means to find out what we need. I suggest you don't interfere and remove whatever you have bugged Miss Middleton's apartment with and allow us to do our important work." I guessed the word important wasn't going to go down too well in this room but it was out now, "plus I demand a list of all those that have viewed or listened to any conversations between the three of us. There are higher-level security implications in what we are doing and I'm not having you and your friends rub your BV at my expense."

"BV?" she queried, now well and truly lost in my stream of Busch-Rash jokes.

"You will have to look that one up yourself I'm not here to complete your education." I continued to rant. I don't know why I continued to try to get out of the admonishment, but I was angry at myself for being so stupid and this woman was ripe for targeting my anger at.

"Well, I think we can wrap this meeting up then." I think she had had enough of me by now, I can wind up the best of them.

"Your written instruction is here, and if you can sign the notes of the meeting on each page, please." she had clearly had enough of me.

"I'm not signing anything."

"You have to sign the foot of each page to say you agree that it's a correct record of our conversation today."

"You'll get a swift foot to your gash-mash before I sign anything you have." I'd be in further trouble now for the rudeness and insubordination, but I stopped caring now, I was embarrassed I forgot the place would be bugged, I was sick of being talked to like a child by Miss double-barrelled Haughty-Taughty. I forgot the poor note-taker was sat to one side, I looked at her and saw she was stifling a smile herself at my barrage of abuse, clearly, she didn't like Miss Burning-Britches either. It spurred me on to continue the abuse.

"This meeting is over Miss Red-Rash-Rump." with that, I stormed out of the room and the building, angry at myself for being so stupid in so many ways. But I did get the second irony, that I had been scolded for my sex life and the meeting was held in the In and Out Club. MI6 does have a sense of humour after all. But I hated the fact that I had been treated like a school kid, talked down to. I am an adult doing a job with high risk and responsibilities, I wasn't going to be talked at in that way and let anyone get away with it. None the more for that I did understand the issue, and I felt a little embarrassed at my behaviour toward Busch-Rash.

The In and Out Club, London.

The morning of Saturday 19th June 1976, I remember the day well. I was at my home, Karen phoned in distress.

"Andy, its Jenny, she is leaving."

"How do you mean leaving?" I enquired.

"She's quit her job, she's paid me a month's rent and now she is packing her stuff and going." Karen spoke, clearly crying. Her best friend was going, so suddenly.

"Christ, where is she going?" I asked.

"She says home, I was trying to talk to her to ask why, but I saw a ticket in her passport as she was packing."

"Did you manage to catch where she is going from her ticket?"

"No, Andy, what's happening, she won't tell me why, or anything, she will be gone within the hour." Karen spoke through her sobs

"OK, I won't have time to get to you, this is what we were waiting for, it's happening." I said.

"What's happening?"

"Jenny, she is an agent for an organisation, I don't know which yet. I'll jump in my car and start driving, in twenty minutes I'll stop and give you a call." Mobile phones in 1976 were not a thing that everyone had, how we managed without I don't know.

"Find out what flight she is on, for now, I'll assume it's Heathrow. When I call if it's any different, I'll divert. Once you find out the airport call the Border Agency at that airport and have her picked up and to hold her in an interview room and tell them I'm on my way. No way are they to let her fly. Can you do that without her knowing?" I gave my instructions grabbing my car keys.

"I will have to go into the office I don't have those phone numbers here." Karen replied.

"Ok, don't give her any idea what you are doing, is she still at your place?"

"Well, she is now waiting for a taxi. I'll take my car to the office, I will be a couple of minutes." Karen now switching into her efficient work mode.

"Say goodbye to her as you would normally, make some excuse like you can't bear to watch her leave or something, I'll call you in twenty minutes." With that, I flew out of my flat in Leavesden and jumped in my car. I had a white Triumph Dolomite 1850, it was the car of the day, it was the car the boy racers wanted. It would take me forty minutes to get to Heathrow if I was lucky, I'd have to stop and make sure Jenny was going to Heathrow by calling Karen for the information shortly. I broke every speed limit, if the police stopped me for speeding, I'd possibly miss Jenny, maybe I'd ask them to escort me or even take me to the airport, but I didn't want to give away my identity to anyone. Luckily, that didn't happen. I guessed Jenny was leaving from Heathrow because any other airport is further and would be very expensive by taxi. I was sure she'd take some other means of transport to get there if she were leaving from any other airport. I was good at these hunches, and I trusted my intuition. After 20 minutes, I stopped by a phone box, luckily it was working. The call to Karen at the office confirmed Heathrow was indeed the airport and that Jenny on her way to France would be nabbed by border police after clearing check-in and security.

I arrived at the airport, Karen had already warned them I was coming, and I needed no introduction, I was led to an interview room with Jenny inside waiting with a female Border Agent.

"What time is her flight?" I asked the staff as I arrived outside the room.

"You have forty minutes if you want her on the flight." An officer informed me.

"I do." I told him as I entered alone. A female Border Control Officer remained in the room, female prisoner protocol I assume, but that was ok by me.

When Jenny saw me enter her face changed from worried to a half-smile. She knew my friendly face meant things should be easier for her. I sat opposite her with the door and the Border Control Officer guarding the door behind me.

"So, Jenny, you are disappearing rather quickly, what's happened? You know you are breaking Karen's heart leaving her." I began trying to make her believe this was personal rather than official.

"Am I under arrest, what are you doing with me? What's the charge?" she asked quite coldly.

"I could have you arrested for spying, I don't want to do that, so, it depends on the next few minutes, you decide your fate. It's a stupid move leaving, you've exposed yourself as being a spy, for what organisation, Israeli?" I asked her.

"No, not Israeli, I have no choice but to leave. I've been four years in MI6, I've given them almost nothing of any use. I asked you to find Hitler, but you gave me Peiper instead." She spoke looking down at the table, I was a little surprised she talked so much, our friendship must have made some difference.

"Who's *them*? You are exactly, right, and if you had waited, as I asked you to, you would have been given information on Hitler, a doubly stupid move to leave, but to leave after getting Peiper's information, that's so stupid, such a small player in the Nazi world." I said

"They don't think so, they say he's a big player in HIAG." Jenny continued. HIAG (German: Hilfsgemeinschaft auf Gegenseitigkeit der Angehörigen der ehemaligen Waffen-SS, literally 'Mutual aid association of former Waffen-SS members' a far-right neo-Nazi group).

"I had no choice, they were going to pull me out as I had gotten so little from MI6, four years was enough for them. Now, I am to go because of Peiper." Jenny realised she had said too much and stopped short of telling me more.

"What's going to happen to Peiper, something unhealthy I assume?" I asked her.

"I can't say. Are you going to try to stop them?" she asked me

"No, I'm not in the business of interfering in the business of other people's business." I said, a weak attempt to relax her with a half-joke line.

"Do you have something on Hitler? You know where he is?" she asked me, I knew a little about him, I was on a track that was proving to be interesting, but I wanted her to believe I had more.

"You will never know what I know about Hitler. So tell me, that folder you originally gave me, did you create that?"

"No, the folder was genuine, it crossed my desk as I said." This answer left me with a further quandary, who had compiled it and why? Was there another spy inside MI6?

"How did you pass the information out? Give me something I can use to take the heat off you." I asked her further.

"Ok, I'll give you this, the ice-cream van at the Imperial War Museum is a conduit." She knew she had to give me something.

"Good God, I've bought ice-cream from that van." I remembered my first interview at Century House in 1971, I had arrived early and walked down to the museum to pass some time away. I had bought an ice-cream while looking at the two huge guns in the front garden of the museum. It was just a short walk from Century House.

"So why this?" she said looking around the room with her eyes

"Personal, you are breaking Karen's heart. Personal, you used me." I knew all along Jenny was using me for something, I gave her the information, if I had her arrested, it would implicate me. I wasn't sure if Jenny realised this. But I had discovered that the fortress walls of the Intelligence Service had yet again been breached and somehow I'd have to report this without implicating Karen or myself. I reached across the table and held Jenny's hand with both of my hands to try to convey friendship and to some extent the love there might be between us.

"If I let you get on your plane today, can you promise me that you stay in touch with Karen, she is crying her eyes out at home. She loves you, you are, were, her best friend, you don't have to leave her behind. Please promise."

"I can't it was all an act, I'm working for a dangerous organisation." She said looking down again.

"We had sex, I saw how you were such close friends, how you acted, and that wasn't an act." I said to her. Jenny's eyes looked toward the female security guard by the door, she must have reacted to my statement about sex. Jenny didn't reply.

"Keep in touch, it doesn't matter that you are in whatever organisation, you are a lovely girl, you have a heart I know. Don't break Karen's heart."

"Ok." Jenny spoke the one word half-heartedly, I wasn't sure if she meant it. There wasn't much I could do right now, but I'd end this on a happy note.

"Both of us will miss you, we will both miss your sex, that threesome was the best thing that has happened to us." I said deliberately, nodding my head back and rolling my eyes toward the woman behind me at the door, I heard the guard choke slightly on hearing my words. Jenny realised what I was doing, trying to embarrass the poor woman. She was smart enough to go along with the joke being played on the poor girl.

"Yeh, I supposed our sex was good, I won't forget the taste of both of you too quickly." We both half-smiled at the joke and the discomfort of the female guard.

There was little I could do here, I could have Jenny followed but it would mean exposing myself and Karen to all kinds of scrutiny, maybe we'd even lose our jobs if I wasn't careful. I had to let this spy go. I didn't feel any guilt. None of the Cambridge five or others had been prosecuted for being double agents in the Intelligence Service. Why should this small pawn get arrested, and she hadn't taken any British Secrets, only information on a Nazi that I had given her. Still holding Jenny's hand I stood up.

"Ok, let's, get you on your plane." I asked the female guard, now flushed red, to lead us to the flight gate. I walked with Jenny, I was sad she was going to leave, I hate losing friends because I find it so hard to make them. She couldn't help having a heritage that needed her to find Nazi's that had been the cause of her family deaths. I understood her motive. We reached the flight gate without saying much, the three of us sat and waited for boarding onto the plane to begin. I watched her onto the plane and stood at the window and watched the flight take off to make sure she'd left the country.

I found Karen still in the office, waiting.

"Has she gone?" she asked me.

"I'm afraid so." Karen cried at losing her best friend of four years.

"She said she will stay in touch, I understand now why she has to go."

"She was a spy?" asked Karen.

"Yes, amazing how she beat the whole system." I answered. Karen had also received a reprimand for getting too close to me.

"But, how did they know we were seeing each other, how did they know we had sex together, the three of us?" Damn this was going to be awkward to explain to this lovely lady.

"I think that may have been my fault." I said.

"Why, how, what?" she asked.

"Well," I had no choice but to be honest with Karen "I had Jenny deep checked, a deep investigation," I saw the anger rise in Karen, we had never argued before and this was going to be the first time.

"You had my home bugged!" she screamed.

"No, not me the team do that." I said in a vain attempt to lessen the accusation, it wouldn't help me.

"You arsehole, you knew and you did that with me, sex, you knew there would be cameras hidden and you let me have sex with you, and, and, and Jenny. I tell you now, find those tapes and destroy them or we will fall out big time." All I could do was apologise to Karen, it did no good, she shouted and screamed at me, I couldn't stop her and I deserved it. I took my punishment. I hated seeing her angry with me. I promised I would do everything I could to find the tapes, it was all I could do to defend my actions. The fact is that the Intelligence Service is bigger than us, that Jenny needed to be rooted out didn't stand much stead at this moment. I left with my tail between my legs, heartbroken that I had upset Karen so much.

From that day onward Karen and I became more, I'll use the term professional, less intimate. We still spoke and talked professionally, but we no longer met outside of work. I'm sure HR and Miss Busch-Rash were happy about that. I couldn't stand the idea of being alone, I hated never being cuddled or loved, so it was the next year that I met Janine. Karen was ok with that, she wanted me to be happy. She never met anyone, always stayed single, devoting her life to her work until her cancer and death in 2014.

As for Jenny, we never heard from her again. I never found her or knew what she was doing. She infiltrated MI6 for four years, passed on almost no information, I believe she was only looking for Nazi's.

The morning of 14th July, a month later Joachim Peiper was murdered.

Joachim Peiper (30th January 1915 – 14th July 1976), also known as Jochen Peiper, was a member of the German SS and a war criminal who was responsible for the 1944 Malmedy massacre against American prisoners of war. During World War II in Europe, he served as personal adjutant to Heinrich Himmler, the head of the SS, between September 1939 and September/October 1941, and thereafter as a Waffen-SS commander.

During his career with Himmler, Peiper became witness to the SS policies of ethnic cleansing and genocide in Eastern Europe. Peiper persistently denied this fact following the war. Transferred to a combat role, Peiper served in the SS Division Leibstandarte on both the Eastern Front and the Western Front, commanding a battalion and then a regiment. He fought in the Third Battle of Kharkov and the Battle of the Bulge. Peiper's command became known for atrocities against civilians and prisoners of war. Peiper was convicted in the Malmedy massacre trial and sentenced to death. The sentence was commuted, with Peiper serving 12 years in prison. He was accused of committing the Boves massacre in Italy. The investigation was closed due to insufficient evidence that the order to kill civilians was issued directly by Peiper.

After his release from prison, Peiper worked for both Porsche and Volkswagen, before moving to France, where he worked as a freelance translator.

Throughout, Peiper maintained frequent, albeit discreet, contact with his SS network, including HIAG, a Waffen-SS lobby group. Peiper was murdered in France, after his identity as an SS man and war criminal had been handed over to Jenny including his address and whereabouts.

Joachim Peiper (30th January 1915 – 14th July 1976) Assassinated by the "Avengers"

Peiper was the easiest Nazi to find using my access to secret files in MI6 in London and Hanslope Park and there are plenty of records on file. He had continued to live and work under his real name.

During the early morning hours, Peiper's home was attacked and set on fire. In the ruins, Peiper's charred corpse was found together with a rifle and a pistol. Investigators determined that he died of smoke inhalation, apparently while trying to salvage documents, papers, and his wife's clothing. A group calling itself "The Avengers" claimed responsibility.

Clean Up

Timeline - late June 1976, 2 weeks before Joachim Peiper's murder.

1976 was a very hot year, one of the hottest, and I was working very early mornings at my dad's business because the chemicals used in the printing processes would overheat and not work correctly, so afternoons I was free to work my other secret job a lot more proactively. I had to figure a way to pass what I knew onto MI6 without getting Karen or myself into more trouble. My priority was to deal with the ice-cream salesman. Some questions needed to be answered by this guy of course. I contacted the Metropolitan Police and explained to them that there was a suspected spy ring using the ice-cream van as a letter drop. I wanted the guy picked up without much fuss and that there was no need to watch the guy before doing so for evidence. If he was there collecting information from Jenny, it meant there was a huge number of man-hours invested in her. She had only had the minimum to pass on, so I suspected there must be more people than Jenny in the group.

The police, as usual, overreacted, to say the least. The very next day a huge show of armed police turned up at the street outside the museum, they blocked the road off. I was there, I protested at the overkill by the police, but they had guns and they wanted to play with them on the pretext that a spy would be armed and the police could take no chances with him, nor did they want a car chasing gunfight in London. I'm sure the police do a good job sometimes, but the show was unnecessary and indiscrete, they did the opposite to how I asked the arrest should be made. The guy looked shocked as he was dragged heavy-handed from his van and taken into custody and his van taken away and ripped apart. They found nothing and got nothing from him. By the time I was permitted to talk to him, there were a few bruises on his face too. I went along as the good guy. His name I was told was Jean Avraham. I walked into the interview room and was left alone as I had requested. Jean was handsome dark-haired typically French-looking, medium height, with a slight tan that told me he was from the Mediterranean area originally. Dressed in a T-shirt that now had a few bloodstains on it, a pair of shorts, and a pair of Nike trainers. I began,

"Hello Jean, I am Andy, do you know who I am?" I was sure he would know me if he was part of the ring.

"No, I have never seen you before." he replied.

"Well for a start, I have bought an ice-cream from you, but it was in 1971 so I doubt you'd remember." I told him the date to imply he was being watched for a long time, if he was active at passing messages to more people than just Jenny, it may worry him into thinking we'd seen several people at his van passing information to him. I watched his eyes very carefully as I said it, he didn't react at all to this. Either he was clever and trained or he was stupid enough not to understand my point. He silently shrugged his shoulders to indicate he did not recognise me.

"Well, I know all about Jenny and she has passed messages to you, messages that I had given her. Now, do you understand who I am?" Jean sat back in his chair, his eyes squinted in vague recognition that I was with an intelligence service.

"I want you to know Jean that I am on your side, I understand your cause and what you do. I gave Jenny the information on Peiper knowing it would be passed to your organisation. The fact that you are here puts you in grave danger now. Your organisation will know you have been compromised. They may try to eliminate you to protect themselves. I can help you. I'm sorry you have been mistreated by the police. I can assure you that was not of my doing, quite the opposite. I am here to help you get out and to safety, away from both the Intelligence Service and your own group. Do you understand what I am saying, am I wrong?" I didn't give him the name of the organisation, I needed to get that from him. As yet, I didn't know the name of the group he and Jenny worked for. The information would come once I had befriended him.

"I understand what you say, but I am not part of the organisation." he replied, this was a good start, I'd got him talking.

"But you are Jewish, surely you are obligated by your faith to pass any information to Nazi hunters?" I questioned guessing his faith.

"Yes, but I came to England to live and work, Jenny asked me to take messages from her and to hand them over to another woman, I don't know her name, she would come and buy ice-cream and with the change I gave her, I would pass the note. Nothing more. I am living here as an ice-cream salesman that's all." I saw this as a classic reply from a trained operative. He would appear to talk, but claim innocence in all this and tell me little. His reply did not surprise me.

"Why would you do this for Jenny if you are not part of the organisation, it's risky as you have now found out?" I asked.

"You don't know who I am, and you think I belong to an organisation that my sister belongs to." he stated. Sister! I tried not to let my face show my surprise. Damn it! I had completely missed his surname, I was so stupid, Avraham was his surname, the same as Jenny's, I hadn't clicked the connection at all. I never used Jenny's surname and only heard it for the first time in the interview with Miss Busch-Rash. I needed to sharpen my act.

"So, you just do this as a favour for your sister, you risk your life and freedom and that's it?" I asked.

"Yes, that's it." Jean Avraham replied. Either he was covering his tail or telling the truth.

"And now you are in danger, you've been arrested on a charge of spying, and no doubt the organisation you passed information to wants to silence you to protect themselves. I can help you if you let me, but you have to tell me everything you know. Who is the lady that picks up the messages and how often? If you are not part of the organisation, you do not need to protect her, you need to protect yourself. Do you have a girlfriend? Kids? They will need protection too." I think I was starting to get through to him as he gave me more information.

"I have a girlfriend, we started to live together a month ago. Do you think she is in danger too?" he asked of me.

"Maybe, is she part of the organisation?"

"We are not part of it, I just did this for Jenny that's all. How will you help us?" the enormity of his situation was dawning on him and I was beginning to believe his story, he just seemed genuine.

"You need to tell me every smallest detail of what you know, give me a description of the girl, how did she know to come collect any messages?"

"I have a poster in the van if I put it in the window she comes. I saw her twice, both times with messages from Jenny, I didn't read the messages. She was a French girl, I don't know her name, medium height, shoulder-length brown hair, just normal looking I can't tell you more." He blurted, now the first signs of panic in his face.

"I don't believe you, I know you have been here for more than four years, you have only passed two messages in four years? There must be others, you need to tell me or I can't protect you. Don't you realise that what you do is illegal and that you will inevitably get caught and into trouble and here you are today in this police station?" I started to get tough with him. I had given Jenny the name and address of a Nazi in France, and she had passed it on, it wasn't a big British secret that would endanger my country or people.

"No that's it. I did this for my sister, she never really spoke about what she was doing. I don't know how she got the information, but she said there was little for me to do and in four years there have only been two notes passed to me. For that, you say I will be assassinated what kind of merde is she involved with." he continued to spill what he knew, which was nothing.

By now I knew this was his training he was bullshitting me about what he said he was, an ice-cream salesman, doing his sister a favour.

"Well, you have told me nothing, I can't help you unless you tell me everything. Do you want me to walk out of here and leave you to the thug police? Give me a reason to help you, at the moment I have nothing." I didn't want to waste my time on him any longer. We were beginning to go around in circles, if he was playing me, I would leave him to his fate and I told him so.

"I can't tell you what I don't know, what should I tell you?"

"OK, you have nothing for me, then it's ditto, I have nothing for you either. I told you I am your friend here to help you but you are not helping me at all, I don't understand why you want to put yourself in the danger you are in. Goodbye Jean Avraham, if that's your name, good luck." I was bluffing, hoping my departure would make him plead with me to help. I got up to leave, turned my back and walked to the door ready for him to speak. He didn't. I got to the door with him sat in silence, I didn't look back and left the room. I gave him back to the police who would have to figure for themselves what to do with him and I didn't care. The police are very good at fabricating lies to prosecute someone. I'd leave it to them. I knew his sister, as he claimed Jenny was, would never grass up her brother, it was as simple as that. Whoever this guy was, I guessed he was hoping I would let him go in the same way I let Jenny walk away. I heard nothing more and I didn't enquire. Although, I thought I might enquire if I heard from Jenny again as a bribe to get her to tell me more about her organisation. But I never heard from her or the organisation again, until I heard that "The Avengers" had murdered Peiper 2 weeks later.

So now what? I decided that my intrigue in the subject of the possibility that Hitler may still be alive was too great, in theory, he could, he would be 87, he was born in 1889. I was worried about where the folder that Jenny gave me had been compiled, by someone inside the service, someone else knew the answer, but who? I knew this was a secret truth kept hidden from the public, and I was unhappy with that. I knew a deal had been done with the Germans, one that in addition to the exchange of the scientists in Operation Paperclip and other operations, a payment of some kind would have been made. Was the payment for Hitler's freedom? Who instigated the negotiations? My interest wanted to know the answers, if I ever found the truth, I would have to decide for myself what to do with it.

The Spanish Incident

Timeline – September 1976

The work on discovering the truth behind the escaped Nazis, possibly including Hitler and Eva Braun continued as a side-line to my normal work in the Intelligence Service.

By September 1976, Karen and I had amassed mountains of documents and sifting through them was an endless task. It occurred to me that reading these documents wasn't enough. They could be false, they could be part of a Second World War conspiracy to confuse or detract, I didn't know. So, I decided it was time to try to talk to some of the personalities in those documents. It would provide evidence of the truth or prove the falsity. Though given the sheer quantity of the stuff we had found in the archives, I now doubted all this documentation was a fictional story.

One name that kept cropping up and a person I decided would be the perfect witness to try to talk to was an interesting character named Don Ángel Alcázar de Velasco. A Spaniard born 1909 with an extremely colourful life as a spy. One that when you read his life story becomes one of myth. He was involved in the ratlines and assisting of escaping Nazis.

Don Ángel Alcázar de Velasco

Born in 1909 in Guadalajara, central Spain Velasco earned a degree in Philosophy from the University of Salamanca in 1932. Don Angel was an apprentice bullfighter, journalist and spy. He was a Falangist, (a member of the Spanish fascist political party governing Spain after the civil war of 1936–39) and was awarded the *Palma de Plata* by José Antonio Primo de Rivera in 1934. During those years, he was a journalist in the Falangist press and the newspaper La Nación. He travelled as a correspondent to places like Ethiopia (during the Second Italo-Abyssinian War), where he met the German Wilhelm Oberbeil. Oberbeil was the one who introduced him to the Abwehr, a German military intelligence (information gathering) organization, in Berlin in 1935. They suggested he went to London as a spy for the German intelligence service, where his sources were mostly MI5 agents.

Don Angel Alcázar de Velasco

Don Angel Alcázar de Velasco created a spy network in Spain. His main objective in this task was to inform about the traffic of British ships, to gain information from the staff of British embassies and, eventually, to come up with a plan to blow up the Rock of Gibraltar.

Angel became involved in Operation Willi, in which his group tried to kidnap the Duke of Windsor in Portugal.

In 1944, he stayed in Berlin until the end of World War II. He narrates in his memoirs that he stayed at the Chancellery bunker until 24th April 1945. After that, he was able to escape to Switzerland and was repatriated to Spain.

After he arrived in Spain, he kept working for the Third Reich helping them escape from Germany. Most were national socialist leaders the most famous one being Martin Bormann. In his memoirs, he admits he did not abandon espionage until 1958.

Angelo himself was always monitored by MI5 and MI6, although there was no need for much effort to monitor his behavior. That gave me access to his personal information and enabled me to find his address quite easily.

Don Angel Alcázar de Velasco died in May 2001 at the age of 92 years in Galapagar, Spain.

The Spanish Incident continued.

Timeline - Late September 1977

I wrote to Don Angel to ask him to meet me. I was quite excited to meet a player that had achieved so much in his life, and he agreed to meet me in Spain where he was living at the time. He suggested a very strange location, I wouldn't know how strange until I arrived.

I hadn't had any vacation for a while, so I decided to take some time off to visit Spain, part holiday, part business with Don Angel. Karen booked me a room in the Parador de Tortosa situated in the spectacular Zuda Castle, overlooking the city. Before I arranged to visit, I called the local police station, explained who I was and requested to be accompanied by a police officer who could bring some officialdom to the meeting with Don Angel and they understood and agreed to assist me. There was a second reason I wanted to be assisted by the police, I had done some research into the location Don Angel had suggested to meet. It appeared to be a strange village, Los Puertos was high behind the mountain of Mont Caro overlooking Tortosa. It was very remote, a few scattered houses and a few restaurants. We were to meet in one of them, the Restaurant Pous de Neu. Being this remote, I felt anything could happen to me, an officer in British Intelligence, I had one of those feelings that made me believe I needed some backup should I need it. I wasn't wrong. The police were cooperating with the British much more closely now Franco had died and the country was beginning to open up to tourism, there was little difficulty in agreeing to cooperate in Nazi investigations.

(Note: *Los Puertos does not appear as a named village on Google Earth but can be found in Michelin maps and others. Interestingly there are no street-level pictures of the village on Google earth either. I've also noticed that many addresses I know to be of German ex-Nazis, are also blurred out in Google Earth. They quite clearly have some influence in high places.)*

I flew to Barcelona, hired a car and drove the two hours to Tortosa and checked into my hotel. Once I had freshened up, I went to find the Policia Nacional station. A small brown building on the banks of the river Ebro. I introduced myself to them. The officer on the reception desk was aware I was due to visit, thanks to some organisation by Karen, and took me to a back office to meet the officer that would accompany me, a Miss Manoli Gonzalez. As we entered an office a very attractive young lady about 27 or 28 years old, 6 years older than me, stood and held out a hand to shake and welcome me. She spoke excellent English to my relief. Dressed in the navy-blue uniform of the National Police which hugged a sexy figure, typically Spanish looking, she had black hair tied up neatly in a military-style ponytail. With a bright happy face a huge smile with slightly too many teeth, a curvy body and fit-looking, a bum that filled the seat of her police trousers, her gun belt exaggerated her curvy hips. I figured she was about 5 feet 8 inches tall. If she looked like any celebrity, I would say she mostly resembled Ana Ortiz from the TV series Whiskey Cavalier and Ugly Betty. She talked fast like most Spanish women, and I decided there and then her heavy Spanish accent was the sexiest.

I have to admit, I was surprised I was assigned a uniformed officer, I was expecting a plain-clothed officer, which was the norm.

If she was going to accompany me for my business with Don Angel this was going to be a great trip. The front desk officer left us alone in the office to chat and discuss the job in hand. Miss Gonzalez seemed quite excited to be working on something away from her usual mundane day to day stuff. She expressed surprise that I was so young and that she was expecting some stuffy old man. I appreciated the compliment. I told her I wanted her to be at my side, to translate if I needed help with the language. I was certain Don Angel would be quite capable of speaking English as he had worked in London. I requested we use informal first names, why not? Manoli agreed.

The meet was set for the next day, Manoli said she would meet me at the Parador in a police car. She asked if I was going to be dining alone to which I answered, I was. So, she kindly suggested we eat together later so I had some company, I was not going to decline, and she said she would join me at the hotel for dinner at 9:30 pm. I returned to the hotel and spent the afternoon getting a suntan, taking dips by the pool and sipping cold drinks. When the sun started to lower in the sky, I took a walk around the hotel, Karen had made an excellent choice, the place was beautiful with lovely views. Across the river I could see Mont Caro dominating the skyline, there were two communication aerials on top of its peak that I knew from a map I had studied to be 1,400 metres (4,500 feet) high.

In the evening, I dressed in fawn cotton trousers and a light blue shirt and at 9:30pm, I went to the restaurant to wait for Manoli to join me. I had my first lesson in Spanish timekeeping that evening. The Spanish always eat late, and she arrived at 10 pm, by then I was thinking she was not going to show and I was starving, but she eventually arrived looking gorgeous. In a white shirt and a white floral knee-length skirt, her legs a gorgeous suntanned brown, fit, and slightly muscly, her hair now down, typically Spanish looking in style, a little longer than shoulder length, heads did turn as she walked to our table. We had drinks, laughs and got to know each other, she was very easy to get on with, there were no awkward silences that I normally suffer because of my shyness with women. Dinner was superb. After, she taught me the tradition of drinking a Sol y Sombre, an anise and brandy drink, drunk by the locals after meals, the two ingredients stayed separate until drunk. The sol, the light colour of the anise and the sombre, dark colour of the brandy cognac, was a drink I would continue to drink after meals when in Spain to this day. Late in the evening, I walked her to the reception of the hotel where I paid for a taxi to take her home, we parted with a kiss and arranged to meet next morning at 10am when she would pick me up in a police car, assuming her Spanish time was in line with the rest of the world.

I woke up in the morning to a bright sunny day, the window to my room had stunning views across the town, it was a lovely place to wake up. I was feeling a little nervous as I knew Don Angel was a highly experienced spy, along with all the other work he had done, leaving me thinking I need to be very careful he does not try to recruit me as an informant within MI6. Maybe that is why he agreed to meet, who knows! I rehearsed in my head some of the questions I wanted to ask him. I wondered why he had decided this place was a good place to meet, one never knew what these people get up to and how their minds work!

Manoli arrived almost on time, her timekeeping had improved by a few minutes overnight. Back in her uniform, she looked sexy again and she was wearing more makeup than yesterday when I met her in the police station. She pulled up in front of the reception where I was waiting. I asked if she would like a coffee before we set off, even though we didn't have time. Luckily, she declined, so, we went to her police car, I jumped in the front passenger seat and we set off. As we drove down the narrowing roads across flat farmland toward the imposing Mont Caro, I asked what she knew of the village we were headed toward. Her reply surprised me. She told me that she had never been there. She had been born and grew up in the area but she had never ventured to the village. She said there were two reasons, firstly that it was a very difficult and dangerous road, but also that the village had a reputation for being very "spooky." I asked her in what way was it spooky, and she informed me that those that had gone there had not been made to feel very welcome, but more, the area was very odd and strange, she couldn't explain why as she hadn't been there. I joked that if a village had that reputation in England, that would be a good reason to go there especially for the youths to go get themselves scared by ghosts.

The road eventually started to steepen as we got to the base of the mountain. To me it looked as though the flat road would shoot straight up into the sky like a child's hot-wheels track, but the road became twisty and bendy and narrowed further. In some places it was down to one lane wide, meeting a car coming the other way would be a tricky moment. I asked how she was feeling as the road became very high with steep drops to the side and much more like a zig-zagging mountain road. She claimed she was ok with the driving and was doing her best to remain professional, but I could see from her pretty face she was beginning to feel some kind of nervousness, I tried not to let it affect me, but there was an odd feeling building inside me, I put it down to my nerves. We were getting higher and higher, I wondered how or why people would want to live in such a remote place. The whole journey was going to take about 40 minutes, and once we had begun to climb after the flat farmland of the valley below, we never saw or passed any cars, we were the only vehicle on this road, but I could understand why as it wasn't a pleasant drive.

I don't know how or why, but we missed a right turn toward the village. I think it was because there were no road signs to direct us to the village. We carried straight on up the mountain and soon the road turned into a gravelly track mostly one car wide. It kept getting steeper, twistier, higher and quite dangerous as most of the hairpin bends had no barriers and the drop was quite scary now. On some of the tight very steep bends, the car's wheels would skid on the gravel as the car dragged itself round yet another hairpin. We realised we must have missed the turn and decided we should turn around and head back. After a few more twists and turns and sliding gravel bends looking for a place to make a U-turn, we suddenly found ourselves at the top of the mountain. The two communication towers howling very loudly in the cold high wind. We did stop and get out of the car to admire the view. The wind must have been blowing 60mph or more. The noise of the towers screaming and making the place most inhospitable. We laughed nervously as we lent into the wind trying not to get blown off the mountain.

We realised then that we had to somehow turn around and head back down, now getting a little late for our meeting with Don Angel. I saw Manoli look at the road and make a face that told me she didn't fancy turning in such a narrow road with such a huge drop. We could see Tortosa across the river Ebro far below. I said that she should get out of the car and guide me to turn the car. I drove a Spanish police car for the first time, and it wasn't the most ideal place to learn a new car.

The widest place in the road to turn was at a closed gate in the fence surrounding the buildings and towers, I carefully reversed up to the fence, then inched forward until Manoli held up her hands and yelled whoa! I stopped the car, to me it looked as though the front bumper was hanging over the edge of the road, all I could see was the sky and out of the side window a very long drop. I carefully reversed back to the fence on the opposite lock, then back towards the edge, I could still not make the turn and again Manoli yelled against the wind for me to stop. This time, I was sure the right wheel of the car was on the edge of the road, there was no wall or barrier here to stop me from going over if I took it too far. Back in reverse again to the fence and this time to my relief I completed the U-turn. I stopped and waited for Manoli to jump into the passenger seat this time. I drove back down the gravel road. In some ways, the journey down was scarier. As we approached a bend and I braked, the car

Above: Mont Caro. The beginning of the climb was easy.

Below: The top of Mont Caro. The noise of the wind blowing through the towers was deafening.

would slide on the gravel and a few times refused to turn until a front wheel dug into the groove created by rain over many years at the edge of the road and this pulled the car into the turn. Nerves were jangling now. At last, the junction appeared on our left just as the road returned to a tarmac surface. I took the turn, there were no road signs or anything to indicate the village was this way, but a few yards on there was a small sign on a tree indicating the restaurant Pous de la Nou, that we were looking for, was one kilometre further.

As we drove to where the meeting was to take place, we noticed on gates, trees and rocks were symbols of witchcraft, I don't know what they were meant to mean, but they didn't look friendly. This created a very spooky atmosphere indeed. I don't believe in voodoo or that kind of mumbo-jumbo, but it did affect me for sure. It was quite a relief when we turned into the gravel car park of the restaurant. I parked the car facing out of the car park, I always do that, proper training I guess, the car is ready to make a quick exit if we needed. We didn't know it yet but it was a good choice to make, good training does pay off.

There was one other car in the car park near the back of the building, the sort of place only staff would park. I figured at least the place would be open, we needed a drink to calm our nerves. I turned off the engine and we both sighed with relief that the drive was over. There was no one about, no other cars, no people walking, nothing. The one car in the car park was the only sign of life here. We got out of the police car, the back of my shirt wet with nervous sweat from driving and probably a little from the nerves of the impending meeting with such a big character in the spy world. Around us, the buildings we could see all seemed to have a Bavarian feel to them, something you might find in the Alps, small villages in Germany or Austria. This was very odd for a village in Spain, which have a typical style about them. These were more like hunting lodges and chalets in ski resorts. The only sound was the now calmer wind in the lee of the mountain blowing through the fir trees. On the door of the restaurant was yet another unwelcoming witchcraft symbol with a witch's head on the sidewall, everything was dark and unwelcoming. We opened the door and entered, I gave back Manoli her car keys, she looked at me as if to say, "you think I'm driving back down this mountain?"

There was no one inside, except a lady behind the bar, I wondered who she might be expecting in this remote and uncongenial place. Despite everything, the lady greeted us with a smile beckoned us to sit and followed us to a table. I chose to sit at a table by a window as the room was so dark, I wanted some light just to be able to read the menu. I ordered a café con leche for myself and a café negro for Manoli, who was looking around very nervously. I added a few pastries to our order and the waitress left us alone while she disappeared into the kitchen to prepare our order. She then came out and went behind the bar to make our coffees using the large Bezzera machine at the back of the bar.

I was expecting Velasco to be sitting waiting for us after Manoli's timekeeping and the trip to the top of the mountain. I hoped he hadn't got fed up with waiting and left. Manoli was thinking the same thing and asked in Spanish if an elderly man had been here. The lady answered no, no one has been there yet, we were the first visitors of the day. So Manoli and I sat and drunk our coffees and ate the pastries, we chatted for a few minutes about nothing special, but we both commented on how the village was weird and spooky. For some reason the residents did not want visitors, I began to understand why. Quite soon after we finished our food and drink a car pulled up outside, it did not park as I had, facing the road. An elderly gentleman got out. He looked around a little and entered the restaurant. I stood up and walked over to him and enquired.

"Don Angel?" and held out my hand to shake a greeting.

"Si, y tu eres Andy?" I replied in English in the hope he would return the conversation in my language, but it didn't happen. That was a surprise, I was convinced he would be fluent in English. Manoli immediately sprung to my aid and began to translate for me. I had already told her my Spanish was only simple and not fully conversational. She would get the chance to talk after all. Manoli explained to me that he was sorry for being late and that his English was minimal, so it was a good job there was an interpreter here. I asked him to join us at the table and invited him to take coffee and pastries with us. I reordered with the waitress for three.

Don Angel expressed his concern about why the police were here, was this some kind of trap. I reassured him that it was purely a cheap way to get a guide and an interpreter for free. At which he laughed and made the joke asking if I was Jewish. The joke, if you call it that, broke the ice and the conversation began with chit-chat about why he chose this area to meet. I might find it interesting, but I continued to joke that, yes, we had found it interesting and had already ventured to the top of the mountain and that it had scared us as the road was so dangerous. Don Angel seemed very human and I studied his facial expressions closely and came to the conclusion he may seem to be a nice man, but that I need to be very careful he doesn't try to recruit me. I knew from files MI6 had on him that he claimed he finished espionage in 1958, one could never be too careful around spies. I asked him if he minded if I recorded our conversation, he had no objection, I took a Dictaphone from my pocket and placed it on the table and pressed record. I asked him first why he thought this location may be interesting for the meeting, which I was very honoured and grateful that he had agreed to. His reason was that he thought, given the nature of the meeting that I would find the area a very interesting place. He continued to explain that the village was one of the ratline transfer posts. Germans came here after the war hid in the village before moving on. He was not specific about where they moved on to, but for me, this was great news. I now had someone involved in the ratlines telling me first hand it actually happened. It was an end to the theories and speculation. I had proof of all those files and papers.

This was exciting stuff after months of pouring over boring reports and speculations, I was now with someone telling me verbally he had first-hand knowledge of the escape of so many Germans. I put it to him that if the village was part of the ratline's system the logistics meant that maybe people were still living here that were involved too. I speculated to Don Angel the reason for putting off visitors in such a bizarre way, that those logistical operators may have remained here unable to leave themselves waiting for years for the remnants of the Nazi regime to leave for friendlier countries. To which he replied,

"Of course." with a shrug of his shoulders. This made sense. At this point, Don Angel was talking freely and seemed to have nothing to hide. Maybe time was a healer or maybe he was being open in order to get something from me, who knows how spies think!

Don Angel pointed out that although he was involved in the ratlines he did not come to this area during the immediate post-war era. I asked where he had operated, and would he name any of the more well-known Germans that he assisted out of the country, given my lack of historical knowledge, I didn't hope for much. I was so grateful to Manoli who was doing a fantastic job as my interpreter, she seemed as fascinated as I by Don Angel's stories he was telling us.

"Well, one famous name you may have heard of would be, Martin Bormann, I took Bormann by submarine from Spain to Argentina."

"You're kidding me!" I exclaimed. "You took Bormann to Argentina?"

"I said so didn't I?" Don Angel seemed slightly cross I had questioned his claim.

"No no." I retorted "I wasn't questioning your statement I was exclaiming my utter surprise that's all." so quickly this man was providing me with exactly what I wanted from him. It was as if he knew just what I was thinking.

"I didn't know you were involved so high up." I stated.

"Yes, I spent a while in the Führerbunker, Hitler's headquarters beneath the Reich Chancellery. Hitler also presented me with the Iron Cross, maybe the first and only presented to a Spaniard." if I wasn't nervous before, I was becoming more so now. This man was more important than I expected. Manoli continued to translate perfectly for me.

We spent some time, it seemed minutes but I'm sure it was at least an hour talking about Don Angel's adventures and how he boarded a submarine with Bormann from Denia, Costa Blanca, Spain. This was a surprise too, as I was expecting the submarines to depart from Vigo in the North of Spain just north of the Portuguese border where there was a submarine base, or, Cartegena Naval Base south of Alicante. But he explained they took a fishing boat out to sea then transferred to the submarine a few kilometres out. Don Angel told me his whole story, eventually claiming he had entered a room in a house in Argentina where there was a gathering of Germans. One elderly man had a resemblance to Hitler. I pressed him that as he had spent so much time with Hitler in the bunker in Berlin, why did he claim that the man only had a resemblance. Surely, he would know him well and recognise him right away. He explained that the man he thought was Hitler had changed his appearance and that with his illness he was very different in looks. He had shaved off his moustache and some other features had changed. Maybe some surgery had been done on him, but he wasn't sure. I had my doubts, so I asked Don Angel to tell me where he had seen the man resembling Hitler.

"I can do better than that, if you are seeking to find Hitler, as I'm sure that is your aim. I can tell you where Hitler lived."

"Go on then, tell me." I dared him.

"You can find the remains of his house, Inalco House, near Bariloche." he told me. I could hardly contain my excitement. I had done it, I had found Hitler! Don Angel went on.

"But don't get excited, he died, I can't be sure, but I understand he died in Buenos Aires. I do know, however, for sure he died 13th February 1962. If I remember correctly, it was 3 pm. Age 73." I couldn't believe this man knew so much and in such detail. Should I doubt what he was telling me?

"How can you be so sure of the date" I asked him.

"Well, you have to trust me on that Andy, I've told you everything you want to know, why would I be making this up, what do I have to lose or gain from lies?"

Now Manoli cut in. She pointed out that while I was so engrossed in my conversation with Don Angel, several men, six in all, had entered the restaurant and were sitting staring at us. Don Angel noticed too, and he became agitated and nervous. He immediately stopped the flow of conversation. His demeanour changed completely. I had been so intensely occupied with Don Angel I hadn't noticed anything else around me. I nodded my head at Manoli indicating to her to deal with the very unfriendly looking men sat at tables staring at us. I asked Don Angel

"Do you know these men?"

"No," he replied nervously lowering his chin onto his chest as if he was trying badly to hide his identity, "but they look unfriendly."

One of the men spoke,

"Old man, why are you speaking to these police?" He spoke with a German accent, he thought I was police, but it didn't matter to me, the fact he was acting aggressively towards us was unnerving Don Angel. The man called again.

"Are you a traitor, what are you saying to them." It could have only been the woman behind the bar that had called them as she heard what we were talking about, and these local men didn't want Don Angel to talk to us. The situation was tense, and Don Angel wasn't going to say anything more in front of them. I had questioned why Don Angel had chosen this location, what was here that he wanted us to see? And this was it, aggressive action by the residents. Manoli rose from the table, walked toward the men and spoke to them out loud in Spanish.

"We are conducting a police investigation, if you men are not ordering anything here, I ask you to leave us, please. Come back shortly when we are done here." The men didn't move, they remained sitting at the tables defiant. Manoli tried again, raising her voice.

"Did you hear me, I asked you all to leave, NOW." None of them moved. The closest guy to us turned slightly to the table and placed his hands on the table-top with a grin on his face as if to say I'm not moving, I'm staying. Manoli came back to our table.

"They are not moving, what shall we do?" She looked a little frightened by the situation. I told her to tell Don Angel to leave. She did that and I stood and thanked him for his time and that I hoped we could continue some other time, Manoli continued to translate. I stopped the Dictaphone and put it back into my pocket. Don Angel remained in his seat, I think he was figuring if the men would follow him or stay with me, he looked very worried by the situation, he probably felt too old at 67 to start anything physical with these men. While he hesitated, I asked Manoli for her gun.

"No, you can't have it, I can't."

"Give it to me now." I whispered in her ear in such an assertive way she immediately unclipped her gun and stood close to me so that the men would not see her pass it to me. I hadn't held this type of weapon, a Star BM, before and I had to quickly look down to find the safety lever, which I clicked off with my right hand, I am left-handed, so I find it awkward, which is why I use Glock handguns, they have no safety as such. I noticed the waitress lady was also frozen with fear behind the bar, maybe she knew these men. I took the gun and walked swiftly over to the man that had placed his hands defiantly on the table. I spoke calmly but assertively to him.

"The officer has asked you to leave, now leave." I held the gun in a non-aggressive position, hanging loosely, my arm by my side. The man made the faintest of smiles in defiance of my order. I made the slightest movement with my arm to raise the gun and shot him in the leg, careful to avoid his femur thighbone, giving him a serious flesh wound. He screamed in pain, in less than a second I back-kicked the legs from under the chair of the guy next to him on the right, the chair went flying and he fell on the floor. I stood with my full weight on his throat, so hard he could not breathe and was gagging and gurgling unable to take a breath. The man to the left was still sat facing me, I pointed the gun between his legs and said in Spanish,

"Cojones o no cojones?" This was a difficult question to answer, balls or no balls, it can also mean bravery in slang Spanish. If he answered balls, it could mean he was going to be brave and try something. If he answered no balls, meant I could shoot him in his balls. While he thought about it for a quarter of a second, I fired the gun between his legs. The bullet passed between his legs and through the chair. It didn't harm him but his reflex reaction made him fall backwards off his chair as the seat splintered dangerously close to his sensitive parts. Another man made a move with his arm as if he was going for a gun in his jacket pocket, before his hand got inside the jacket, I shot his hand, a finger fell onto the table and rolled onto the floor. The room turned into bedlam with the screams of the shot men, the guy I was stood on was turning blue trying to get my foot off his throat. I turned my head to Manoli and Don Angel and shouted at them to get out. I stood my ground and with the gun now held up in both hands to defy anyone to move. As Manoli and Don Angel left the room, I backed off and the guy under my leg gasped his first breath. I held the gun at the group, the men I had just shot continued to scream in pain. I backed out the door covering them, they had seen I wasn't afraid to shoot if they made a move, so they all remained frozen until I left the room out the front door. Don Angel, getting into his car, started it and skidded in the rush to turn it around. Manoli was jumping into the driver's seat of the police car, I jumped into the passenger seat just a second after her, as she started the engine. We were the first car to leave the car park as we were facing outward and both cars sped off down the road, no sign yet of the men leaving the restaurant. We raced down the road toward Tortosa, with Don Angel following. After half a mile I saw a large rock on our right further down the road. I ordered Manoli,

"Pull in behind that rock and let Don Angel pass." I instructed Manoli, her knuckles white with the grip she had on the steering wheel. She swung the car behind the rock and Don Angel sped past.

"Turn it around face the road." I didn't shout but when this excited it's hard not to raise your voice. She reversed into the road did a quick J turn and reversed back behind the rock.

"What are we waiting for? Let's get out of here!" she cried.

"I want to see if they are following us, we don't want to lead them back to town. Here, reload your gun." I handed her the gun and she sat nervously shaking, while reloading it. I opened my window so I could hear if any cars were coming, but the road was silent. I gave it a few minutes before I told Manoli I thought we were safe. The relief changed her,

"Hijo de puta, Coño, hostia puta." a stream of swear words came out of her, I sat and looked at her quite calmly with a slight smile waiting for the cussing to finish.

"Andy, you just took on six men, you shot them, you are crazy!"

"Yes, I shot them, but not dead." I replied smiling.

"You are a maniac, how am I going to explain this?" she worried.

"You won't have to explain anything, it won't get into town, don't worry yourself."

"Fuck, un putero de fuck." she continued to swear.

"I thought you were a lady, your language!"

"No, you don't know what you have done to me, *puta madre*." with that last expletive she leant across the car toward me, I flinched expecting a slap or something, but I was wrong.

"Fuck me, fuck me now, you've turned me on so much." she began tugging at my trousers with one hand while unbuttoning her shirt with the other. In her frenzy, Manoli revealed a black bra and a very nice cleavage, I pulled away and gently pushed her back to her seat.

"No, no I'm not going to fuck you." I said.

"Why not, don't you like me?" she said in a hurt way.

"Yes, I do, very much and that is why I'm not going to fuck you here in this car all dirty and sweaty. I like you and I respect you, you don't deserve to be fucked in a car. I want to make love nicely, romantically, after a dinner, soft music playing and everything." She sat back in surprise and calmed down.

"Ok, well then, ok, erm, let's do that then." she stuttered calmly now. "I've never been treated so respectfully." she said thoughtfully as if talking to herself.

"I'm not surprised when you act like that. Now button your shirt and take us home." and she drove calmly and quietly back to Tortosa, without hardly a word spoken. I think I made a bit of an impression on her.

Only when we arrived back at the hotel did we begin to talk about what had just happened. Manoli pulled up in the car park and we sat there, thinking about what had happened. I began,

"I'm sorry if I scared you back there."

"You just started shooting them with no warning." she came back at me.

"Well, in my world its best, the best form of defence, I find, is attack. You said yourself there was six of them, if they came at us we wouldn't have stood much chance. The surprise and speed caught them all out and we got away safely enough." I explained calmly. "Have you ever seen any of those men before?" I questioned her.

"No, I've never been to that village before, why do you think they behaved like that?" Manoli asked. With its engine off the car quickly began to get very hot, so I suggested we moved into the cool inside the hotel. We chatted as we entered the hotel and found a table in a quiet corner in the bar, where I ordered two cool drinks for us.

"We know the village is one of those Nazi escape ratline places, those men were remnants from the end of the war, maybe sons of Nazis, who knows. I'm guessing that the actual Nazis were around somewhere in that village, but they must be old by now. I've heard of these towns and villages, I'm sure there are others. They don't like visitors and they discourage people from going there. I have no idea what they would have done, but who wants to wait to find out, I didn't. Are you going to be ok explaining the gun firing and the loss of your ammunition?"

"Yes, that's not a problem we often go into the fields and shoot at rabbits, it's not a problem to replace the bullets. It's sort of encouraged to keep our gun skills up, it's instead of going to the range to practice. Don't worry about that I'll protect you if there's any come back on this." Manoli was relaxed now but I think the event scared her big time.

"Don't get yourself into any trouble, if there are any complaints or problems I'll deal with it. I don't think there will be, they don't want people in their village, raising a complaint will cause them problems, I'm sure of that. But maybe keep an eye on your hospital and doctors, if anyone turns up with gunshot wounds, we should go investigate." I said.

"Andy, I never saw anyone move so fast as you did, do you do that kind of thing often? You shot three times and floored that guy in under four seconds." Manoli replied.

"No, it doesn't happen like that, but I practice for my fitness and pleasure, it's the first time I've had to react like that." We chatted for ten minutes or so about what happened. Manoli seemed ok about it all, I didn't think there would be any repercussions and she wouldn't say anything because she would be in trouble for passing her gun to me. I didn't bring up the strange sexual reaction she had as we hid behind the rock, I didn't think it appropriate, I didn't want to remind her and embarrass her.

"So, Andy, how long are you staying in Tortosa?" she asked.

"I will check out of the hotel tomorrow, I have a few days' vacation left, I was thinking that I would visit Barcelona. I have no flight booked yet as I didn't know what Don Angel would tell me, maybe it would lead to something else. But now I think travelling alone isn't much fun so I'll try to get a flight home as soon as possible." I told her.

"Why don't I show you around, there are so many places to see, don't rush home if you don't need to. I'll go back to the station now, check-in, and then see you later if you would like to spend some time with me."

"That would be nice, thank you, I hate being alone it's no fun. If you don't mind spending your time with me that would be lovely, thank you." I was happy to have her company. I got on well with her and it would be better than eating dinner alone, that's never much fun.

"Ok, I'll be back shortly, I'll find you here, yes?"

"Yes, see you later, thank you for being such an excellent help today, you were marvellous, it would have been difficult without you." With that, she left. I went to have a refreshing shower and change into my poolside clothing to spend the rest of the day relaxing by the pool and bar and getting a tan started.

An hour and a half later, I was sat enjoying the sun at a table on one of the beautiful patios by one of the bars, enjoying the view over the city eating a little tapas. This was an excellent choice of hotel, I was thinking to myself. The hotel is inside a castle on a hill overlooking Tortosa, superbly furnished with dark wood, yet it was bright and comfortable, perfectly in keeping with the classic style of the ancient building, yet modern and comfortable. I thought I should congratulate Karen when I return for finding such a stunning place for me to stay on this trip. I missed her, but now our relationship was not so close after the warning from Ms Battle Britches. Karen took her job seriously and nothing would come before it, even me. I decided while sitting in the sun, on my return to England we should have a sit-down chat and decide where we stand. I needed company, and now Karen, it was clear, wasn't able to move our partnership forward in a way that I wanted. We should talk about our future, I would give up my career for her if she gave me the option. I would make a good living working with my father in his printing business.

As I was quietly contemplating my future with Karen in the sun and in such a beautiful location, I noticed inside the bar a woman, I could only see her back, it was quite dark inside in contrast to the bright sunlight in the garden, I could only just make out shapes. I couldn't hear what she was saying. The woman was talking to the barman, who kept looking my way. The woman had her back to me, but I couldn't help but admire her figure, I could make out she was wearing a loose white shirt, quite suitable for staying cool in the Spanish sun. Why do white shirts always attract my attention I thought to myself, I must have a thing about them when worn by a lady. She was wearing tight slacks that stopped short of her ankles. Her legs were shapely, perfectly shapely, fit looking. From behind her dark hair flowed down to between her shoulder blades not straight but not curly, but sexily wavy, and I thought to myself, yeh I'm easily distracted by a pretty woman. She passed the barman a holdall bag and turned to walk toward the door to the patio where I was sitting near a wall with the best view over the city. The lady came out of the darkness of the room and into the sun and continued in my direction.

"Wow! Manoli, I wasn't expecting you so soon, I thought you were coming for dinner tonight." I exclaimed.

Manoli replied in her sexy Spanish accent. I had spent two days with her already but now she somehow looked different, more relaxed, a big smile, her mouth that had slightly too many teeth.

"Well, I thought we agreed I would spend some time showing you the sights, here I am." Her white teeth behind lips that only Spanish girls have, plump and kissable, someone once told me if a girl says the name Gina Lollobrigida it makes a girl's mouth look sexy, I thought I will have to ask her to try later.

"So, what's the deal?" I asked puzzled by her early arrival.

"I had a word with my boss, I am due some time off, so here I am, and I'm going to show you my country, places you wouldn't find if you were alone. Are you not happy with that idea?" I knew Spanish hospitality was good, but not this good!

"Ok, well then Miss Gonzalez." I stood to pull a chair next to mine, "Take a seat and tell me where we are going, what's the plan?" I thought to myself how shallow I was, one-minute sitting thinking of Karen the next a beautiful girl joins me and my loyalty changes. Did I crave company this much? How could I resist a pretty girl, I was 21 and lonely. I did not make friends easily, I was shy and could never approach a girl first, and here was a gorgeous girl, wanting to be with me!

One thing about Spanish women and I am generalising, they can talk, they can talk the hind off a donkey, maybe this was the reason I felt I got on so well with Manoli, she did all the talking. Maybe she was sometimes a little late, but late was a Spanish thing too.

"I think today we stay here, enjoy the view, relax, swim in the pool and dinner tonight. Tomorrow we will take a ride up the river and have a picnic somewhere, then check out from this hotel and I'll take you to a lovely place down the coast called Peñíscola, have you been there before? If you have then we will go somewhere else, it doesn't matter." Her talk rate was at an all-time fast, even for her, clearly, she was excited by the thought of showing me around.

"Ok, sounds good." I managed to butt in somehow, "Don't tell me everything keep it a surprise." I hoped this would slow her talk rate down a little. "I saw you pass something to the barman, what was that?" I asked.

"Well, I know the barman and a few staff here, it's my town, I have lived here all my life, I've sorted everything, don't worry." I had no idea what she was talking about, but I guessed it would be prudent not to pursue it, I was sure I would find out sooner or later.

We spent the afternoon talking, or at least Manoli talked, and I listened, it was ok, she was fun and I liked her, liked her a lot, despite the rapid-fire talking. It made it easy for me to listen and I didn't want to talk or explain my job to her. I preferred it that way. I don't like questions and I would avoid answering anything MI6 related.

The afternoon sun was hot and it was time for me to jump in the pool to cool down. I had a hotel pool towel on the back of my chair. I cut into Manoli still talking and said I was hot in the sun, we should move to the pool area for a swim and sit under a parasol.

"Maybe we should go to the hotel shop and see if they have a swimming costume for you." I said, hoping I would see her wearing a little less.

"It's ok I have." Now I found out what the bag was, she had brought with her an overnight bag. She didn't want to be presumptuous and assume she could stay with me, but anyhow she had arranged with the hotel staff to stay overnight in my room and have breakfast too. She had passed it to her friend behind the bar so I didn't see it, bless her. For sure I was not brave or forward enough to ask her to stay. That's how I am, and I'm sure now in retrospect I missed out on so many teenage and young man activities because of my shyness in this respect, I was very happy for her to be with me as much as she wanted.

I led Manoli to my room for her to change, I stood on the balcony outside enjoying views across the city while she changed into her bikini in the bathroom and expertly tied a sarong around her sexy body to walk back to the pool. I didn't want to leave her alone in my room because, well, I'm a spy and people shouldn't be alone in my room. She reappeared from the bathroom looking stunning in a tiny bright, almost dayglow green bikini, one of those that must chafe in certain places, her buttocks firm and round, even under the sarong I could see her suntan was an enviable Mediterranean brown. It was a little awkward containing my pleasure in my swimming shorts, I don't know if she noticed, but she was discreet enough not to say anything if she had.

Back at the pool, the cool water put an end to my discomfort, the water was a perfect temperature in the sun and we had fun showing off our water skills to each other. It was a great way to spend the afternoon. Sitting in the sun, having a few cool drinks, occasionally jumping in the pool to cool off and letting Manoli talk. In my mind, she won a gold medal for talking, but on the whole, I enjoyed her company, and she was certainly great eye candy.

By late afternoon as the sun lowered in the huge Spanish sky behind Mont Caro, we moved back to my room to change ready for our evening meal. I was always led to believe Spanish girls are good catholic girls and play hard to get, or can't get at all. Manoli seemed very comfortable in my company and me being me and shy with girls I waited on the balcony watching the sunset while she showered and changed into her evening clothes. Once she was dressed, as she put on her makeup, she told me that it was ok to come back into the room and that the bathroom was free for me to shower and dress. Manoli had a natural prettiness, I didn't think she needed any makeup especially after an afternoon in the sun, but she was busy applying eye makeup, what did I know about women, very little. I grabbed my clothes and went into the bathroom to do my bit. While I was showering through the screen I saw her come into the bathroom and take some more tissues from the shelf. She behaved as if it were a completely natural thing to do, in a situation like that I had no idea what to do. Was I supposed to make a play for her? I wished I had more experience in these matters. I just carried on with my shower and got dressed before leaving the bathroom. I had no idea what to say or do, so I carried on as normal, as she finished up the final touches to her gorgeous face. She didn't say anything, which I was hoping she would, so I was left feeling a little ashamed of my awkwardness with girls, I realised I don't have any chat-up lines. I did wonder about our age difference, she was about six years older than me, would she think that we weren't a good match in that respect? Anyhow, I was left with the feeling that if she was ok entering the bathroom while I shower things may proceed naturally later in the evening, and we left the room with hope in my head.

We sat outside on one of the garden patios watching the last rays of sun disappear and listened to the cicadas begin their evening calling. Manoli continued to talk about anything and everything while I made the right noises at the right time. I'm sure to many this would have been annoying, but I found her very easy for me to get on with. I didn't have to think of anything to say myself. I had to give her one thing, she never asked about my work in MI6. I assumed that was her professionalism, knowing I would tell her if I wanted.

At a reasonable time for a Spanish girl to think about dinner, about 9:30, we moved into the restaurant and had an excellent meal. I was worrying more and more what to do later when we sleep, I mean I had no idea how to ask her anything or suggest anything, I'd only been with Karen (and Jenny if you count that) and with Karen, everything was so easy and natural. After dinner Manoli asked me if I'd like to go into town where we'd have some fun, I was tired by now but this was a unique opportunity not to be missed. It's not often a local that knows all the best places would offer to show me the sights, so why not, I'd find some energy somewhere, I was young after all. We walked into town, her holding my arm as a good friend would. I felt nice and relaxed, I'd had an afternoon of relaxation and a few drinks, this was going to be a fun night out. Not far from the hotel, we entered a bar, it was very busy and there was music from a live band. A few people came up to Manoli to say hi, and I was introduced as her new friend. Manoli was smart enough not to mention anything about the Intelligence Service. People didn't seem to ask where I was from, the fact that I was with Manoli, and she had said I was a nice person was enough for them. In Spain, there is little to no class separation, very little snobbery, and people that consider themselves to be middle or upper-class had no problem mixing with working-class farmers and so on. I like this attitude and it is one of the factors why I love Spain so much. People chatted with me, some in Spanish, and some attempted to talk to me in English. I liked these people, everyone was friendly and had a great attitude to life. We had a great evening, and everyone danced to the music. I attempted to dance too once I'd summoned up the nerve after a few more drinks. At the end of a fantastic evening, the music ended at 3 am. People stood around in groups and the discussion moved onto what we were doing tomorrow. Manoli told her friends we were going for a picnic by the river, then move on to Peñíscola, then who knows what. Everyone asked us to join them at Arnes instead, a little village a short drive away, where there was the annual "Fiesta de la Miel" which is a fiesta all about honey that the village produces. We agreed we would go and that we would meet everyone there. Peñíscola will be postponed for a day. It felt so great to be away from the stresses of work, I knew this was going to be a fun vacation, and with such a great crowd.

Manoli and I walked back to the hotel and now I started to get nervous, how was I supposed to deal with this situation, should a younger man ask an older woman to sleep with him, and how? Manoli was still chatting away and I was making the right noises still when we found ourselves outside my room door again. What do I do? I need not have worried, whether Manoli noticed me hesitate or something I don't know, but as soon as the door opened she grabbed me by the hand and led me in.

"Andy, it's ok don't worry, I like you a lot, I want to be with you." I have no idea what she saw in me, I think my character is the silent boring type. I know jokes and so on and can hold a conversation with anyone when the other person starts one. What I find most difficult is starting a conversation myself. She took my hand and led me into my, now *our* room. As soon as the door closed behind us she kissed me on the lips. I found it a little awkward at first as her sexy mouth had slightly too many teeth and our front teeth clashed a little too hard, I thought I had cut my top lip. I pulled back and apologised, but she said there was nothing to apologise for, and so began my first night with another woman other than Karen. I thought I might feel a little guilty about cheating on Karen, but we had gone a little cold on the sex front, so, I enjoyed a night of lustful sex with a beautiful woman. I have no idea what time we finally fell asleep, but the sun was definitely on the rise, and we slept until there was a knock at the door. I got up dragged on a hotel dressing gown from the wardrobe and opened the door with my foot behind it so it did not open more than six inches. In the corridor was a couple from the evening before.

"Come on." they said excitedly, "we are all leaving for Arnes now, we will give you a lift in our car." I had such a headache and hangover, I hadn't realised how much I had drunk.

"Can you come back in an hour?" I asked. Manoli appeared, and there was a moment of realisation on the couple's faces and they both gave a knowing smile.

"You guys go ahead, we will come in Andy's car shortly, we'll see you in a bit guys." Manoli mumbled in a heavy hangover and an "I've been up all night with this sex-stud." voice, or, that's what I'd like to think it was. The two left slightly disappointed that we weren't ready, but said they'd see us in Arnes.

After a good morning kiss, we showered and dressed. Of course, her makeup took time, I made a coffee for us both using the room kettle. We had missed breakfast as we were up too late. Then, back at our room we packed our stuff, and checked out of the hotel and chucked our bags into my rented car. I managed to drive to Arnes while Manoli gave me directions to the village somehow half asleep. At Arnes the fiesta was getting underway, it didn't take long to find the friends that had knocked on our door earlier. The way things worked here was that you had to purchase tickets, at each stall if there was a product you want to sample you pay with tickets rather than cash, so we bought a hand full of the tickets. I said I was too hungover for this, at which the friend, Tomás told me to follow him and he led me to a stall where a guy had a still to convert honey wine into honey alcohol, pure alcohol. He asked the guy to give me a glass of the stuff and then told me to get it down me. I looked at it and I thought all this will do for me would be to induce instant vomiting. None the more for that, with Tomás's goading I downed the glass in one. It wasn't half bad, and as I stood waiting for the uprising to begin, I actually felt better. Within seconds the hangover had passed, and I was back to normal, and I asked for another. It was miracle stuff and rather nice. I did wonder how the guy could sit and use this still in the open, I wasn't sure how legal it was. Manoli on seeing my instant recovery took a glass of the drink and within moments, she seemed completely recovered too. We spent the morning wandering the streets of Arnes trying and tasting the honey-based food and drinks, the paying with the tickets system didn't last very long, soon everyone forgot to take tickets for anything. It was a fascinating experience. There was a small group of wandering minstrels from the Catalonia College of Music who were adding to the atmosphere. Manoli and her friends knew these people and we were invited to join them at a restaurant for lunch. We went along and the group of friends, fourteen in all, put the tables together to make one large table that we all sat around. Each person selected and ordered a dish of food, which was served in dishes for all to help themselves and try every dish. It was a great social way to eat. I was asked to try the local snails, I had a little trepidation about it. It is a different snail to the French type, quite small and cooked in a very nice garlic sauce. I can report I ate more than one, they were delicious. After the food, the minstrels began playing their traditional style Spanish music and everyone started to get up and dance, in a sort of country dance style. I didn't know any of the moves, but Manoli joined in and I enjoyed watching her have so much fun. We were the only people in the restaurant, we made as much noise as we wanted and it was a fantastic time experiencing the way of life of these happy kind people, all of whom made me feel welcome and part of the group of friends. The day continued with more merriment at the fiesta. Tomás taught me how to drink wine from a *porrón*. A *porrón* is a traditional glass *wine* pitcher, which holds 0.75 litres, typical of Spain, originating in Catalonia. It is a vase or pitcher that has a spout that ends in a point. The idea is to hold it at arm's length, pouring the wine directly into your mouth. I was a beginner and could only hold it successfully about an inch from my mouth, any further and it would go all over my face. Tomás, however, was an expert and could hold it at full arm's length and not spill a drop. Surprisingly, Manoli was only as good as me. There was traditional dancing by women and children, good food and drink. It was a great day out, one I will never forget.

As people began to drift away, we said our goodbyes to everyone, and I thanked them all for making me feel so welcome and shown such a great time. We made our way back to the car and decided to continue our drive to Peñíscola about an hour and a half away.

Peñíscola is a beautiful town, almost like an island in the sea with just a narrow stretch of land attaching it to the mainland. On top of the hill is a floodlit castle and in the half-light it looked stunningly romantic. We parked the car in the car park below the castle, we grabbed our bags and walked through a gateway in the wall of the town below the castle to find a hotel. I would never have found this town on my own, even though it is a very popular tourist town. There were plenty of hotels to try and we chose one built into the walls of the castle with nice views of the sea. We took a double room, which was nice, very old but furnished in solid wood furniture that gave it a very cosy authentic feel. The views from the window were of the Mediterranean Sea, which we would appreciate more in the daylight the next morning. We were very tired by now, but we managed to stagger out into the street and find a table at a restaurant nearby below the castle walls towering above us, the views stunningly beautiful. In such a romantic setting, it was hard not to feel something for Manoli, and I thanked her for the best day in my life. She had such a big smile and she put out her hand for me to hold. We sat looking at the sea and the stars in the warm Spanish air, drinking local wine and at last Manoli began to talk at a slower than normal speed. I sat saying romantic things to her, which she appeared to enjoy as I flattered her with words of romance. I finally found my way with words that I could not find last night. I felt at ease and comfortable with Manoli. Work and Nazis a million miles away. I was pretty close to heaven that evening.

After a good meal, we were so tired, we retired to our room, our last hour awake was spent expressing love rather than the lust of the previous night, at the right moments during our lovemaking, Manoli was whispering to me that she was in love with me. I didn't sleep much, I lay awake for hours wondering how I could make our relationship last if Manoli wanted it to be that way.

When I woke the next morning, it was early, I quietly made a coffee and sat in the window just reflecting and looking at the view. My journey to Spain had mostly been a success, I hadn't expected to start shooting people and I felt a little bad about that. Had I started the fight too soon, were the men innocent? What were they hoping to achieve? They had stopped Don Angel from talking, so he must have known that what he was telling me was going to be unwelcome to those men, he knew he shouldn't be telling me the things he did. How did the men know we were there? I guessed that the barwoman called them because she could hear what we were talking about, so she was part of whatever goes on in that village. I no longer felt guilty for backing out of the door of the restaurant without paying the bill at least. That village needed investigating by some authority, but the authorities must have known who lived in that place. Someone must have known Nazis had moved in, the place was built with buildings resembling Bohemian style chalets, definitely German. Should I worry about anything that was happening there, it had a reputation that the locals knew to stay away from. What had happened there to make the people around Tortosa stay away. I doubted simple icons of witches would keep them away, something more must have gone on. But, at the end of the day, Don Angel had told me Hitler had escaped Berlin. He had not died by his own hand as the history books tell us. Then the thought occurred to me, he had told me Hitler had died, but what of his wife Eva Braun? Don Angel hadn't said they both had died. I tried to remember when she was born, but at that moment in Spain I had too much going on in my head to recall her birthday, Braun had not been the main subject of my research. So I noted to myself to look into her history when I returned to England. It was the first real moment I had sat and thought about the events of the meeting at Los Puertos properly. Manoli had been a distraction.

Manoli began to wake, she looked beautiful, naked and very sexy, why was this gorgeous woman still single? Why did she want to be with a shy, clumsy around women young man? What did she see in me? I was too young, but I wanted to be with her.

"Coffee?" I asked her.

"Yes please, but first come back to bed, you look so handsome sitting by the window, you make me feel horny again." Well, that's one question answered already. I placed my coffee cup next to the bed and was happy at that moment to give this girl what she wanted, again.

After breakfast, we checked out of the hotel, put our bags in the car and spent a couple of hours wandering around the castle. We had a quick coffee and drove away from this romantic place. Barcelona, I was informed, was our next port of call, about two and a half hours drive away.

We arrived in the city and Manoli directed me to a hotel in the Calle Nou de la Rambla, right in the centre of everything. This was one of the few hotels in the city centre with its own car park underground below the hotel, so it was easy for us to park and enter the hotel. The Gaudi hotel was opposite the newly opened Palau Güell building, an amazing building built by Gaudí the famous architect. Manoli asked for a room on the fourth floor or higher so that we could see onto the roof of the museum opposite, where there were some samples of his amazing work. A great choice again by this amazing lady and another example of local knowledge. We were lucky to get a room, it was busy in June, but that seemed to be the way of this trip, I was lucky with everything. We went up to our room, dumped our bags and went out immediately for lunch. Only a hundred yards from the Ramblas, this was my first time in Barcelona, and I loved the city right away. I'd return here many times later in life.

The Rambla or more correctly, La Rambla, is a street a kilometre long. Stretching from the Plaça de Catalunya a large square with several statues, down to the Mirador de Colom, which is a roundabout with a tall monument column to Columbus near the port area. A few years after this visit, all this area would be regenerated in preparation for the Olympics.

In Barcelona you can't help but feel romantic, it's that kind of city. We lunched in an outdoor restaurant on the Rambla. People watching was the main activity, certainly more restful than the past few days. In those days there were none of the street human statues but the atmosphere was still buzzing.

We took in the sights and later had dinner in a lovely restaurant down a backstreet that only locals would have found. By late evening we were back at the hotel and in the bar for late drinks. I thought it was time I found out what she was thinking. I asked Manoli what our relationship meant to her. She seemed to like me

La Rambla, Barcelona, 1977.

a lot and was enjoying my company, but I couldn't get her to commit to much more than that. Maybe it was too soon to ask her for more. Spanish girls play hard to get after all. That night our sex was far more passionate and lustier than the previous nights, I wasn't sure why, but she was like a tiger that night and taught me a few things I hadn't done before. There are some benefits to going with a more experienced woman.

After breakfast we checked out of Barcelona and made our way back toward Tortosa, stopping briefly to view and walk over the Roman Aqueduct at Tarragona.

We continued on our journey back to Tortosa. I didn't want my time with Manoli to end. I suggested that we should book back into the Parador, but Manoli said we would stay at her home. I was happy to go along with that idea, to me it meant she must be feeling something for me, more than a casual relationship.

To get to her house she directed me through a maze of little narrow streets. The houses seemed quite old, and, typical of Spain, the front being directly on the street with no pathway, making the streets seem very narrow. She instructed me to stop in a little square, the junction of four roads where there was room to park. We took our bags and walked twenty-five yards to her house. A tall five-story building, the entrance next to a wider door that was a garage or storeroom entrance. The door was made of beautiful solid wood, wider and taller than the type of front door we have in England. As the building was five stories high, I was expecting it to be flats or apartments, but she told me her family owned the whole building. Each generation lived on one floor. Her grandmother lived on the first floor, her parents the second, Manoli the third and her sister would live on the top floor when she married in a few months. There were building materials on the ground floor as the top floor was being renovated ready for her sister and new husband to move in. I thought it was such a sociable way to live, and envied the fact that no one needed a mortgage, the property was already there. Each member of the family could redesign and furnish their floor to how they like. The whole family remain as a unit, and everyone is available to look after kids or the elderly. The more I was shown of Spain, particularly rural Catalan Spain, the more I grew to love it. I made a vow to myself that one day I would have a house in Spain too. The stairs to the right of the building were wide and seemed to be constructed of light bright marble. We went up, passing another wide door of solid wood that was her grandmothers' front door. I was told that her grandfather had passed away a few years earlier. We proceeded to climb the wide stairs to her parent's floor where Manoli knocked on the door but entered without waiting. I felt a little embarrassed being a stranger carrying my bag intending to stay. Inside, there was a huge lounge room, from the outside it didn't look possible the rooms would be so big. The room furnished with dark solid wood units and large sofas of the era when her parents would have married. Furniture must last well in Spain it didn't look as though any of it had ever been replaced. Manoli instructed me to put my bag down and I placed it behind one of the sofas in the centre of the room, hiding my embarrassment with it. We went into the kitchen where we found Manoli's mother cooking.

I was introduced as Andy an English police officer here on official police work. I thought, well done Manoli for not saying who I really was, this girl was smart. Her mother must have been good looking in her youth, still slim and attractive for her age, although her hair was dyed a dark burgundy, I had noticed many older Spanish women seem to dye their hair this colour, it must work well on black hair. I was immediately made to feel welcome and we stood in the kitchen chatting, with me struggling in my limited Spanish. I told her how I had been very well looked after by her daughter, the detail of which was kept to a minimum. I didn't understand a word Manoli was talking about to her mother, as she spoke so fast, as Spanish women do, I could not keep up with the two women. I was informed Manoli's father was out in town with his friends in a bar somewhere. It's what the men do in Spain. Neither of the women told me he was the ex-mayor of the town, I found that out later.

After a while, I was ushered, into the lounge where I sat on one of the sofas and was offered a drink of my choice, I chose coffee. I sat drinking while the two women wandered around the place going into cupboards, Manoli had asked her mother for some extra towels for me, as I would be staying. Her mother didn't bat an eyelid at the plan, I remember thinking how modern the family must be, catholic and all. Manoli announced we would go put our bags in her apartment and come back down for dinner later. Her mum went back to the kitchen to continue her cooking with a big smile, happy she had company later. I loved these people. I hoped her father would be as likeable as the two women.

After the long journey, I was quite exhausted, but the excitement of the situation kept my energy up. We went up the flight of stairs to Manoli's floor. Her place was more modern in décor, very comfortable and for such a large space quite cosy the way the furniture was arranged. I was shown around and as we got to Manoli's bedroom told to put my bag in there with hers. There was a second bedroom with another double bed, but I was to be with Manoli that night. A thought that excited me a lot.

In the lounge, there was a front-facing window and when it was opened the heat and the noise of the town came rushing in. To the right, a river view and the imposing grey of Mont Caro in the distance. Also, to the right was the little square where I had parked the hire car. The sound of kids playing and shouting, and the noise of traffic was lost once the window was closed again. Manoli poured two beers for us and we sat on the sofa and chatted. One question I had to ask Manoli was how come her sister hadn't moved into her floor yet while Manoli had. It was then Manoli told me that she was married. But her husband also a policeman, at the time of their marriage, had had an affair and left or more correctly kicked out. For the life of me, I could not think of any reason why a man would leave this gorgeous, sexy, intelligent girl for another. What on earth is wrong with men! I expressed my sorrow for her. Once she had explained that, I understood why she wasn't going to commit to anything so soon in our relationship. I also understood how she was so experienced in the bedroom. Manoli told me it had happened two years ago, she hasn't seen him since and that I was the first man she had brought home. While I felt privileged, I also now felt some pressure to behave with the best intentions. I asked how her parents would be feeling about me. She told me she was very close to her mother, they had had many heart-to-heart chats, and that they trusted her to make her own decisions as an adult. If only all parents could be so understanding. They had obviously helped Manoli through a very difficult time in a catholic society where divorce was very difficult indeed.

After an hour or so it was almost time to go down for dinner at her parent's apartment, we showered together in a huge modern rain shower, easily big enough for two or three people. There was a little horseplay of course, who wouldn't? The main thing was, Manoli was smiling and seemed happy with me.

At her parents, I was introduced to her father, her mother acting as if she had known me for years. Her father was a very handsome man, very typically Spanish in looks, dark hair, a physique I was jealous of in perfect proportions, he spoke no English and with a deep voice of someone of authority, which he must have had as he was once the city mayor. But he never told me he was, he didn't use his status to try to impress me, I admired his modesty greatly. The more I saw of Spain and its people the more I loved it. His handshake was strong like a farmer's and damn near broke my hand, mine must have felt so limp to him. I determined then to try to improve my handshake to be as manly as his. I was made to feel very welcome at their home, I never felt I was intruding, and the conversation was easy, they spoke slowly so I could understand everything, anything I didn't understand Manoli would offer a translation. Dinner was good wholesome food, nothing fancy or unusual like snails. We didn't stay long after dinner and retired to Manoli's apartment early as after a few days hard vacationing we were both tired. I think I was asleep before my head hit the pillow, but after an hour resting, I awoke to see the beautiful Manoli next to me. She looked gorgeous, my stare must have been intense, as shortly after she stirred too and we both lay smiling at each other and it wasn't long before just looking wasn't enough. In the morning we had coffee in bed and lay talking about nothing much, Manoli never once asked me any questions about my job. I admired her for that, she hadn't seen me operate at my best, I wasn't proud that I had shot two people, for no real reason other than to avoid any trouble when we were outnumbered. She must have had hundreds of questions, but I didn't offer any answers. I never have. We rose and Manoli suggested we take a picnic on a boat up the river as she had planned a couple of days ago. We dressed and went to a local shop to get some food for the picnic, packed it in a basket and drove a little way upriver to where there was a fishing boat rental business. As we only wanted a couple of hour's rental, the guy let us have the boat for only the cost of fuel, I don't know if he knew Manoli, but it was a great deal. The boat was a 14ft Dory type, a flat-bottomed boat stable for fishing from. It was a bit dirty and smelt of fish, but it was good as it was free. I drove and headed upriver through the canyons where when we slowed to look there were eagles nesting and circling high above us. We followed the river as far as the hydroelectric dam. Here we had no choice but to turn around and head back downstream. We carried on until we found a flat area of the riverbank with orange groves beyond. We tied the boat to a tree and found a nice grassy spot in the shade of the tree. Another romantic setting, I was beginning to think Manoli had some motive with all the places she took me. We sat and enjoyed the view of the river, before enjoying the food we'd bought. It was hot and I was wearing only my shorts, as no one was around Manoli had stripped

The Author navigating the River Ebro.

off to just her panties and was laying on her back sunbathing. She asked me to put some sun cream on her, I'm sure she could have done it herself as she was laying on her back. But who am I to say no? I dutifully did as she asked and soon my touches became more erotic, it wasn't very long before we were making love in the sun in that field. My first experience of sex outdoors.

Late afternoon still with plenty of light we navigated our way back to Tortosa and returned the boat. The boat hire place had already closed so we just tied it up with the other boats and left.

Back at Manoli's home, she said she felt like making something herself for dinner. I sat in her kitchen chatting with her while she busied around preparing the food. I liked talking to her, she was the easiest person to be with, the conversation just flowed, and she always had something to say. I began to think I would quite like to see her more, but how do I achieve a long-distance relationship? As we chatted away that evening, my useless ability with girls was beginning to annoy me. How do I ask her if she would like to see me more? Manoli finished preparing our meal and we sat at the table to eat. The table was by the window, there was a view of the street and the river, and it was all quite charming and romantic. Go on, I kept urging myself, but my confidence was low I didn't want to be rejected. Why would she reject me, it was her that came to me and organised my vacation with her, surely, she wouldn't say no? How would I combine my secret life, that she knows about, with her career and mine, would there be a clash? I was getting more and more nervous trying to pluck up the courage to ask her.

The meal of course was delicious, a kind of tapas of plates of tomatoes, hams, cheeses, a salad and some sardines. Light yet combined with the local wine, tasty and simple food. By the time we finished the eating, Manoli was chatting away at me. I decided to go for it. I'd start by asking how many more days would she like me to stay. I didn't want to overstay my welcome, but she seemed to be enjoying my company, this couldn't go wrong. I couldn't be rejected, our relationship was going too well surely.

Just as I opened my mouth to interrupt her and put the question, the bloody phone rang.

"Excuse me, I'll just get this." Manoli rose to answer the phone, "Si, Buenos tardes, Con quien hablo?" the person on the other end of the phone said something, "Si, he is here." Manoli turned to me and announced the call was for me! Who knows I'm here, no one! I took the phone.

"Hello, who is speaking?" I asked,

"Hello Andy." I recognised the voice immediately, it was Karen, which was slightly embarrassing.

"How on earth did you find me here?" I should know Karen is smart.

"I called the police station to ask them if they knew your whereabouts and they gave me this number. I didn't think it would be so easy to find you." in those days data protection wasn't a thing, people passed on phone numbers without thinking, it was normal.

"Are you enjoying your holiday?" Karen asked with a slightly sarcastic tone to her voice.

"Yes, Miss Gonzalez has been showing me some sights." I replied not sure how to deal with this, my training never seemed to extend to personal matters such as your girlfriend finding you at your other girlfriend's house.

"I bet she has." There was a pause while I tried to think of a reply, but failed, "The reason I'm calling is to bring you in, the shit is hitting the fan in Manila and there's another Nazi murder, I'm not sure if it's anything to do with Jenny."

"Yeh, not a secure line Karen, Ok, I'll get back, can you get me an early flight tomorrow?" I asked of her. Karen had dropped security measures for a moment, my being at Manoli's home was clearly affecting her, this was out of character for her.

"I've already checked the timetable, I'll get you on the first flight from Barcelona tomorrow." Karen, always unnervingly efficient as always.

"Ok, I'll be on it." I replied.

"How was your meeting, that is the reason you are there right?" Karen sounded a little upset, I thought our relationship was at a professional level after our warning, she must have thought we are still more than that. This could be complicated. Given the choice, I'd choose Karen every time, there is no competition.

"The meeting was going very well until we were interrupted, there was a situation and we had to leave in a hurry. But I have first-hand evidence now, and he gave me the top man's address." I half explained.

"No way! Wow, that's a eureka moment if ever there was one." Karen sounded genuinely pleased.

"I'll tell you all about it when I get back, but I need more, Don Angel has so much to tell, I need to meet him again. It's a shame we were interrupted. Anyway, I'll see you tomorrow and tell you everything." with that I hung up.

I turned to Manoli, who was busy clearing the table, I joined in helping her.

"That was my secretary, Karen. I have to return to England tomorrow. I was just about to ask you how long you think I should stay here in Spain, hopefully, with you, but now the situation has changed. I'm sorry." I spoke as I carried plates and cutlery to the kitchen. In the kitchen, I held Manoli by the hips and looked her in the eyes.

"I want to be with you if that is possible. How are your feelings toward me? Would you want me to stay longer?" I finally found some words. Manoli's answer was a surprise.

"You know what, we have had so much fun together, I have grown to like you a lot. My problem is you."

"Me?"

Manoli's voice was rising in volume and pitch, she was upset, her Spanish accent sexy as hell.

"All this time together, I have told you everything about me, you met my parents, we had great fun and so on, but you don't tell me anything, nothing at all. You know what? I don't even know where you live, I welcome you into my home and I don't know who you are or where you are from. I know you are a Secret Intelligence Serviceman and I appreciate you can't tell me anything, but your personal life, you should be able to. You haven't said anything, for all I know that could have been your wife on the phone! How do you think that makes me feel? You have to learn to separate work from home life. When you keep everything secret it's too much for me, I couldn't be in a relationship like that. I've waited for you to tell me something about yourself, but nothing, nothing at all, nada."

Her rant wasn't going to stop unless I stopped it, she was right of course, I do keep so many secrets and I let it cross over into my personal life too. It was my safe way, and for some reason I expected others to accept that.

"Manoli, you are right, I'm sorry, I haven't realised I am like that. I live in a world where I don't tell anyone anything. You are my first girlfriend if I can call you that, outside of the Intelligence community. I want to tell you things but I don't know how. You are such a beautiful girl, pretty, intelligent, funny, you would be the perfect girl for me. I want to be more in your life. You have to teach me how to talk to you. I could fall in love with you if you let me. I can return as soon as I have sorted out stuff going on at work. Can we do that?"

"Where do you live?" Manoli asked as a start.

"I live." I paused this was more of a difficult question than it seemed, "Actually, I have two homes, England and Manila."

"Oh, córcholis! You cant tell me! You are going to break my heart Andy." Manoli exclaimed.

"Be patient with me, I need to figure myself out." I replied sheepishly.

"Madre mía, you need time to work out where you live?"

It dawned on me now. It was always going to be like this. My work was always going to be a barrier. I'd always need to lie to my girlfriend just as I have to lie to my friends and family already. There can never be any trust.

"It seems to me that I can never have a girlfriend, I have found the most perfect girl for me, I love how you look, your sexy eyes, dark hair, big smile, your body and legs. I love your Mediterranean suntan, the way you talk, your sexy accent, your personality is the best I have ever known. I thought you liked me too, and all our time together you made me feel at ease."

"I do." Manoli interrupted me, "I could love you if you were, …. well, normal. Sorry, I don't mean it the way it sounds, you are a lovely man, so thoughtful and caring, clearly, you want to find love, but you are never going to find it the way you are now." I knew what she meant I didn't take offence.

"My job is all I know, I have been taught the way I am, how can I un-teach myself? Can you help me learn a better way?" I asked.

"You need to find your own way." she said.

"So, this is the end?" sadness was in my voice.

"Go home tomorrow, you have to be at your work."

"Can I return when I've sorted business, can we continue what we have, I can make a home here with you."

"I need to think where we are at, can I love you? Give me time por favour." she said with some sympathy in her voice at least.

"I need to sleep, I have to be awake at 4 am to get to the airport, it's midnight already."

"Who says you are going to sleep?" Manoli questioned.

"What? You are throwing me out in the middle of the night?"

"No, silly, you are taking me to bed and we are going to make love all night."

"All night?"

"Is my Englishman not up to it?"

"Your Englishman certainly is, I can't let my country down." With that, I took her hand kissed her lips and led her to the bedroom.

I did England proud, I kept my part of the bargain. Four hours of lovemaking made sure this particular gorgeous Spanish girl was going to be left in no uncertain terms that England was a strong nation and that the rumours of our poor lovemaking were totally untrue.

At 4 am, I rose for a shower, late for the journey to the airport already, I looked back at the bed as I stood over the crumpled sheets and saw one exhausted Spanish girl.

"I'll come with you to the airport." she spoke softly.

"You can get back home from there?"

"Yes, its an easy train ride. No problem with that, but first help me up I can't walk, you English do good work in the bedroom, all the rumours are untrue." I pulled Manoli up from the bed, steadied her while she got her legs to function again and helped her to the bathroom to shower together giggling as she staggered her way. The pain she had between her legs was good pain.

I packed my bag in a rush, loaded everything in the car and pulled away from the street as quietly as possible as the sun began to throw it's warmth over the land again. Manoli sat beside me with her hand on my leg as I drove to Barcelona airport. I drove a little fast as we were late, early morning traffic already filling the roads that ran along the coast towards the city. I was confused, last night Manoli told me in no uncertain terms that I needed to be more open and tell her stuff about myself, now she sat looking at me with her big brown eyes, her hand resting on my leg as though she was in love with me. I hadn't told her anything more than I already had, I wanted to tell her stuff, but I found it difficult. She knew what I was, she had witnessed me shoot my way out of the restaurant, but other than that, Manoli knew very little, but she knew I liked her a lot. I felt obliged as she talked about nothing in particular as she does to give her something about me.

"I tell you what." I said, "I'll go back and sort out all the shit that's gone on while I've been here enjoying myself with you. Then, can we have a long chat and I'll try to fill in some of the mysteries that you want to know. I'd like you to know everything so that you can be at ease with me and hopefully understand who I am."

"You can try." she replied, "but I have my doubts you can open up to anyone, especially to someone like me." She was probably right, I was a secretive person and talking about myself was a difficult subject. More and more I realised I can only be in a relationship so long as I could lie. This was something I'd not come across before until now, I had always been with Karen and she knew everything, often she knew stuff about me before I knew it. My career in the Secret Intelligence it seemed, was always going to be in the way of my love life. This wasn't something taught in Spy School, we had learnt the trade and how to hide it from everyone.

Saying nothing to anyone was how I knew life. Even my father, who was the only person in my family that knew what I did, never knew what I really did, he didn't ask, but he did help me cover up the times I needed to be away from home. After 6 years in the MI6, this was the first time I had any kind of relationship outside the service, and I had no idea how to cope. Running agents I can do, collecting information and using it, I can do, planning operations or actions I do quite naturally, living a life with no need to explain myself to anyone was all I knew. Now here was a girl I could fall in love with, and, combined with my real shyness toward women, I had little idea how to deal with the situation now she demanded to know all about me. I saw her demand was fair, how could you live with someone and not know who they are. The further complication was that she was foreign, not a British National, so there would be a concern to National Security. My work, I decided, was always going to prevent me from living a life in a way any normal young man could. It was a dawning that I didn't like. Life with Karen was always easier. As my secretary, she knew everything already, and I didn't need to explain myself.

"I can come back in a week or two, or if you'd rather we can have a long talk on the phone. Personally, I'd prefer to come back to Spain. How do you feel about that?"

"And you can tell me everything I want to know about you?" she asked in a hurt voice.

"Right now, I don't know what I can tell you, you are my first love outside of my work. I have to figure things out." I still didn't get it that she wanted me to be free to tell her enough so that she could always trust me. I felt it was a little unfair of her to ask. She replied,

"I can't live with a liar, I need honesty, not lies, even if they are the lies of spies."

It would be so much easier if the person I fell in love with didn't know a thing about me. I could be a printer working with my father, but Manoli knows I'm not. I needed to learn the ability to 'love them and leave them' as someone once put it. I not that kind of bloke. I'm not a one-night stand man, I like to think I'm more honourable than that. Some days I hated who I had become, taught by the State in the way the State wants me to be. I was capable of doing dark stuff without batting an eye, but when it comes to normal stuff I was out of my comfort zone. I wondered if the State wanted it this way.

Manoli was kind enough to change the subject, I got the feeling she too wanted us to work, somehow, in a way she could be happy with. But where was that place? We continued the journey with her doing the talking, as usual, with me adding a sentence here and there.

At the airport, I returned the hire car to the rental company and we walked into the terminal. Manoli stood with me while I collected my ticket and checked in my bag. She cried as I said goodbye, we kissed a long loving kiss, our arms wrapped around each other in a tight close hug, I had every hope it wasn't to be our last. As I disappeared through security and passport control she held a hand over her mouth to try to stifle her sobbing. We didn't know it yet, but that was to be our last kiss.

In London I went directly home, I arrived by mid-afternoon and immediately attended to the problems in Manila. This was my priority as the Argentina, Nazi, Hitler research was still a side-line. It took a few weeks to rectify the situation before I could even think about what had occurred in Spain. As I have said before my normal work at this point has nothing to do with Hitler and Nazis, but in this book, I need to indicate the passing of time somehow, which is important at this point in the story.

I wanted to write to Don Angel again and thank him for his time and to apologise for the rapid exit and the mess that was. I started to compose a long letter to say I thought what he knew was fantastically interesting and that I hoped he could continue to enlighten me with his knowledge. It took me a few days to get the letter as I wanted and suggested another meeting in a place of my choosing this time, as I thought his choice of location a little intimidating. Perhaps that is what he wanted to show me, that the Nazis are active and discouraging investigation. I passed my composition to Karen to type it up perfectly and then to post using official headed paper to let him know this was official – even though it wasn't.

The murdered Nazi that Karen had told me about in her phone call to me in Spain, was Hanns Martin Schleyer. There was a concern, of course, that this could be another activity by the group Jenny belonged to. I had not passed any information to her about this particular man. There was a second thought that maybe there is yet another mole inside MI6, now that would be of great concern. But a quick piece of research in the collection of data I had on escaped Nazis revealed to me that I had nothing on Schleyer at all. He hadn't really escaped. He had spent time in prison and released and was working in Germany quite openly. However, his kidnapping was particularly aggressive and interesting.

Hanns Martin Schleyer was a German member of the SS, business executive, and employer and industry representative, who served as President of two powerful commercial organizations, the *Confederation of German Employers' Associations* (Bundesvereinigung der Deutschen Arbeitgeberverbände, BDA) and the *Federation of German Industries* (Bundesverband der Deutschen Industrie, BDI). Schleyer's role in those business organisations, his positions in the labour disputes and aggressive appearances on television, his conservative anti-communist views and position as a prominent member of the *Christian Democratic Union*, and his past as an enthusiastic member of the *Nazi* student movement made him a target for radical elements of the *German student movement* in the 1970's.

The abduction and murder are commonly seen as the climax of the Red Army Faction (RAF) campaign in 1977, known as the *German Autumn*. After his death Schleyer has been extensively honoured in Germany; the Hanns Martin Schleyer Prize, the *Hanns Martin Schleyer Foundation* and the *Hanns-Martin-Schleyer-Halle* are named in his honour. In 2017 German President *Frank-Walter Steinmeier* and the German government marked the 40th anniversary of the kidnapping.

His uncompromising acts during industrial protests in the 1960's such as industrial lockouts, his history with the Nazi party, and his aggressive appearance, especially on TV (The New York Times described him as a "caricature of an ugly capitalist"), made Schleyer the ideal enemy for the 1968 student movement.

On 5th September 1977, an RAF "commando unit" attacked the chauffeured car carrying Hanns Martin Schleyer, then president of the German employers' association, in Cologne. Just after the car had turned right from Friedrich Schmidt Strasse into Vincenz-Statz Strasse. His driver was forced to brake when a baby carriage suddenly appeared in the street in front of them. The police escort vehicle behind them was unable to stop in time and crashed into

Schleyer's car. Four (or possibly five) masked RAF members then jumped out and sprayed bullets into the two vehicles, killing four members of the convoy. Schleyer was then pulled out of the car and forced into the RAF assailants' own getaway van.

The RAF demanded that the German government release captured members of their organization. After this demand was declined, the RAF members were all eventually found dead in their jail cells. After Schleyer's kidnappers received the news of the death of their imprisoned comrades, Schleyer was taken from Brussels and shot dead en route to Mulhouse, France, where his body was left in the boot of a green Audi 100 on the rue Charles Péguy.

I have included this murder as it demonstrates very well the active and aggressive way Nazi hunter groups will go to, and there are a few of these groups still active today in 2023, I doubt those that remain will ever give up identifying and dealing with Nazis. It also shows that even post-war many Nazis are given top jobs. Is that because they are great and intelligent industrialists or because there is still an embedded brotherhood alive and well in those circles of society, particularly in Germany and Europe. Something must be holding that brotherhood together, there must be a leadership, a secret society based on Nazi principles. Should we allow that to continue or should we seek out the leaders. Leaders, it seems, that may still be active in countries around the world. After the meeting with Don Angel, I now knew, with some uncertainty, that there *could* be, until 1963, only 15 years earlier, arguably the most despicable hated leader of all, Adolf Hitler.

I was feeling very guilty that I hadn't seen Karen since my return from Spain. I was so bad at dealing with my friends and lovers in those days. I had no idea what to say or do, again. We couldn't be together because the Service won't allow us to be. Neither of us at this point wanted to leave the Service, it was a great job and nothing could fulfil the freedom and excitement of the work. I could go back to Spain and try with Manoli, but she had made her demands and I couldn't think how to deal with those either. My career was in charge of my love life, and as a young man, that wasn't a good feeling. There was only one way to deal with it and that was to go talk with Karen.

The next time we spoke I asked that we meet, she suggested her home one evening. I reassured her that there were no longer any listening or camera devices they had been removed long ago so we were both ok with that. To me, it did indicate she still had feelings for me, if not, then I'm sure we would have met at a restaurant or somewhere, but not her home. I was more than happy to see her again, yet once the meeting was arranged, I had huge pangs of guilt because I'd been with Manoli and enjoyed it. Worse still, I wanted to be with her too. This was screwing with my head for sure.

I didn't take any flowers or chocolates to her home, I thought it too corny. Instead, I took as a gift a beautiful, framed picture of Karen. We had very few pictures of each other, in fact, I don't think there were any of me, but this one was one of those pictures that was accidentally great.

I'm not an artistic photographer by any means, but this was one of those lucky accidents. Of course, in those days there were no digital cameras, everything was still on film. The picture was of Karen standing in the window of her apartment. Just as I took the picture, she swept her blonde hair back with her hand, the light from the window with her arms up gave her the most provocative sexy look, a skilled photographer couldn't have done better. I didn't have the skill to plan such a pose. The picture from her waist up and wearing only a bra was one of those you'd put in your bedroom for private enjoyment. Anyway, I thought it would make an ideal and personal gift that showed my feelings perfectly. On arrival at her door, I was nervous, I don't know why. The manner in which she opened the door indicated to me she was too. I think she thought I was coming to end our relationship, which would have meant I would have to transfer her away to another department too. Karen opened the door to just eight inches and peeped around as if a stranger was at her doorstep. I think she was assessing how I looked and why I was there. Once I held up my wrapped present with a smile, she knew I was there on friendly terms. She opened the door fully and stepped back to enable me to enter. I stepped forward and gave her the biggest kiss and she responded, happy to be in my arms again. She quickly closed the door ever aware that we were not supposed to be together, ever aware that someone may be watching, she was right to do so, you never know in the business we were in. I gave her the photo and when she unwrapped it, her face lit up.

"Oh, it's beautiful, I can't believe that's me, I forgot you took this, thank you, Andy. I've missed you so much I hate us being apart."

"Me too." I replied, unsure how to apologise for being with Manoli, I shouldn't mention her, I decided not to until Karen brought up the subject, I didn't know if I was being cowardly or prudent.

"Come in pour some wine, I have to attend to the cooking." and with that, it was like days past, she smiling her gorgeous smile in the kitchen and me watching her cook. The only difference was, I was full to the brim with guilt, and I had no clue how to explain myself. Love was never taught in Spy School or anywhere else. I told Karen the full story of my meeting with Don Angel, what he had said, and how we had to leave in a hurry. I was sure he had so much more to tell. In fact, I was in awe of him, his demeanour and manner was something I had to learn from, but he seemed to freeze when the men in the restaurant became aggressive in their behaviour, that was a let-down, I had expectations he would be quick-thinking and maintain control of the situation. I had written to him hoping he would find the time or want to reply with more.

We ate and we were like our usual selves, we sat on her sofa talking, Karen with her head on my shoulder just like a normal couple, it felt good, warm and cosy, I loved this life. After a few wines, Karen became more inquisitive about my time in Spain. I knew what was coming.

"How much time did you spend with Miss Gonzalez?" she asked finally, here it was, and how do I deal with this? I went for honesty as that was the whole problem, wasn't it? Live with the lies or have the ability to talk openly and honestly with the one I love.

"Well, she was an excellent translator, I couldn't have managed the meeting without her, I was very lucky." I began.

"But you were at her home at midnight, I called to ask if she knew your whereabouts and lo and behold there you are late at night."

"After the meeting, I decided to have my first real holiday in six years, a few days away, she offered to accompany me and show me some places. It would have been boring on my own, and she was quite nice, easy to talk to and so on."

"And so on?" Of course, she had to ask. I described the places we had been, places I would have never found on my own, or enjoyed quite so much.

"And what were the sleeping arrangements while you did your little tour of Spain?"

"Comfortable, we found some very nice hotels." I was trying hard to skirt the details, but women are women and men are full of guilt, well, I was right at that moment.

"Andy, I don't mind if you slept together, I understand our situation and that you want to find love. You are still young and I'm seven years older than you."

"Find love? I have love, you are my love and age has nothing to do with it. And don't be so complacent, be angry at me if I stray from you."

"But you know they won't allow us to be together." Karen said in a resigned tone.

"Fuck them! What are they going to do, fire me?" I said as much to that HR woman.

"They don't fire Officers, but they will me and probably see me off with the worst reference or something, I'd never get work anywhere. You know what they are like." Karen said and I knew she loved her work and never wanted to leave MI6.

"This is all we can ever be, like we are this evening, one evening in a hundred apart. You can't go through your life like this, I know you want more and more is elsewhere. I will always be behind you and support you." Karen spoke, resigned to her life alone devoted to her job.

"It's not what I want, I would marry you if there was a way, I'd quit this job for you."

"They won't let you quit. You are a valuable asset to SIS. No one can do what you are doing, there is no one that can replace you in Manila. Your control over agents there is outstanding, I don't think anyone could do better. Our data collection is used continuously, your office has become *the* place to call for information on just about anything."

"No, you are just flattering me I'm not that valuable" I replied.

"Many people have commented, it's not my opinion. In such a short time and for someone so young you have achieved everything they have asked of you." Karen continued to flatter.

"Actually, it's you that has done that, I just get on with my work, you are my backbone. The way you organise my mess, there is no way I could achieve any of what I've done without you." I returned some of the flattery wafting around the room.

"It's called teamwork, we make a great team." Karen gave herself a little pat on the back.

"It's because we are so close, you know what I'm thinking always, sometimes I don't have to ask, you are right there already. Don't you see we have to be together" I said.

"We have a chemistry that can't be denied for sure, but out of work you need love and I'm not it if you want to be closer." Karen was always pragmatic on this subject. I have no idea how a woman like her could control her feelings so efficiently. She went on, "So we have to agree to the status quo in our relationship, it can never be anything more than it is. If you want more, go ahead, get it from somewhere else and you have my support, no jealousy or tantrums." These were impossible words from a woman, I'd never heard such words and never will. As Karen lay with her head on my shoulder, I couldn't see her expression, I hoped it was full of honest pain, she surely didn't mean what she said.

The rest of the evening was not our normal happy event, it was quite solemn in tone, both of us in deep thought about what was being said. I loved this beautiful woman and I'd die for her and very wisely and honestly, she was telling me her truth.

I did spend the night with her. Our lovemaking was always good but, on this occasion, it seemed more as though she was using me, or maybe, she knew I'd been with another woman and the thought was leaving her cold.

In the morning as we lay in bed naked with coffees happy to be together, I asked if she had ever been with another man since we had been together. She had not and was not interested. I believed her, the Intelligence Service makes some very unusual characters of people.

Once I arrived home, I called Manoli, she seemed happy to hear from me. I would have preferred to talk to her face to face and I asked if she wanted me to come and see her. But I was told to only go there if I could be open about everything, be honest and no lies, it wasn't a position she would compromise on. I understood that and sadly I said I could never talk openly about what I do, that was the way I had to be. I live a secret life and it has to stay secret. My job would always prevent me from being honest, if there is anything I do very well, even to those closest to me, and that is to lie, that is the nature of being a spy.

I would never see Manoli again, I did miss her and her endless talking and her habit of always being late. The episode did make me wonder if I could ever find a partner and live happily while doing the work I did. Would I leave the job if I thought I needed to be in a loving relationship? It is a complicated answer. I would find the answer in only a few weeks when Janine came into my life.

We met at a party and were engaged after a few years together. Janine had no idea whatsoever that I was not the person she thought I was. I kept it from her with lies. She thought I worked with my father at his printing business, which in a way was true, it was my cover for all the years I worked within the Service. She only found out in 2019. Who and what I was when I asked her permission to tell our story, which bravely she gave. Our time together and how we ended didn't paint her in the best colours, but my colours are stained by the sheer volume of lies I had to produce in order to be with her, that is the nature of the job, unfortunately. I thank Janine for permitting me to include her in my story.

The Don Ángel Alcázar de Velasco Story

Don Angel wrote back to me, I was astonished by the reply he sent me. In it, were many typewritten pages containing a full account of his time working for the Germans during and after the Second World War. How he helped Nazis escape using the ratlines developed by the Germans, how he accompanied one particular very famous Nazi to Argentina and, according to his letter, who he claimed to have met sometime after. The pages were written in Spanish, I had to have the text translated, which the language department in London assisted me with. What follows is an incredible account more or less as he told it. It answers all the questions I had wanted to put to him. I have edited it slightly and maybe some of the translation has caused some differences from his original letter.

Dear Andrew,

Well, that was an interesting end to our meeting. I have to congratulate you on your quick action in order for us to escape that situation safely, who knows how that may have ended otherwise. I am sad that in these days of my life I am not able to summon such speed and agility. Anyhow, ignoring the event that ended our meeting, it was a pleasure to meet you.

You may be wondering why I chose that village for our meeting. I wanted to demonstrate to you how the residents of that place far up in the mountains are capable of some aggression in defending the secrecy and privacy that they live under. The village was found after WWII to be one of the ratline routes out of Germany through Spain and away to wherever the escapees were to go. Routes from that place could go via boat to Northern Spain or to rendezvous with a submarine some way off the coast to cross the Atlantic, usually to South America. We had a perfect demonstration of how they defend that privacy they desire. I want to tell you the rest of my story now. I do not apologise for the many pages to this letter. I think you will agree that my story and the one you are enquiring after is one that can change the history of post-WWII. Do with this information what you will.

January 1945, as Germany was falling to the allies, I was summoned to the German capital to serve with Hitler's staff, I was the only non-German to work within Hitler's personal headquarters in the bunker. We lived in the shadow of a deranged genius out of which many conflicting stories are telling of the fate of Hitler and the elite of the Nazi Party. I was there I can tell you the truth of those last days. I know the truth about the suspected suicide of Hitler and Eva Braun.

I will tell you how I left Berlin under fire from the Russians and my escape from Germany. After my return to Spain, I assisted Adolf Eichman to escape Europe. I can reveal the fate of Martin Borman who was Hitler's top Lieutenant.

I was chosen by the party to escort Hitler's top deputy as he made his escape across the Atlantic by U-boat in May 1946.

I know the power of these people and their organization, I have seen their determination to plot their return to power, and I have helped form secret action groups on two continents. They are well organised, the High Command still exists and meets every year in Germany where they have much support. This then is my story:

I had been head of the Nazi espionage ring in Spain throughout the War and as such was one of their most trusted agents. In January 1945 when the Allies, British, America and Russia were fighting their way across the borders of the Fatherland, that I was called to the Führer's side. I had been working in SS Intelligence Headquarters near to the old Reichstag. I had been in Germany for seven months, directing activities of certain foreign agents abroad. I was informed by SS Commander Willie Oberbeil, my immediate superior, that we had been ordered to Hitler's bunker. We made our way to the Reich Chancellery our passes inspected by the guards at several doors down into the deep underground bunker. The doors were watertight and blast-proof which sealed off the fifty-foot-deep shelter. The final door where our passes were inspected again was so narrow, we had to pass through sideways.

Once inside near to Hitler's personal quarters, we were met by a Colonel Wagner, who was in charge of SS Intelligence in the bunker where Oberbeil and I were informed we were to be his staff. We were led to our own office, which was tiny, created by a floor to ceiling wooden partition at the far end of the typist's room. We had a radio transmitter and receiver and a decoding machine. It was very small with hardly any room to move between the desks and filing cabinets and chairs. Next to this tiny room was the noisy generator used to provide light and air. We shared a dormitory with sixteen others. Each day at noon, a guard would come to our office snap to attention and announce, "Today is the 23rd of February." or whatever the date was.

The bunker resembled a giant ant nest with messengers coming and going officials, officers and their staff made it difficult to move.

During my stay, I met with Hitler several times, he was prone to vile tantrums screaming at his staff many of whom were very frightened to be summoned to his room. I saw grown men cry after meeting him.

On April 15th, 1945, we received a very interesting visitor. Eva Braun.

Eva arrived from Bavaria, she came with no luggage, only carrying a fur coat. She disappeared into Hitler's personal quarters, and I only saw her once more after that.

On April 16th Oberbeil and myself were ordered to remove all the office records. We carried them into an adjoining room where they were burned in a boiler. Any further reports that arrived during the following days were destroyed as soon as they had been read by Hitler.

On April 21st we were ordered to evacuate the bunker. An hour before we were told this I saw Martin Bormann arrive. Looking very stern, his uniform torn and mud-spattered. He entered Hitler's quarters. While he was in with Hitler, Oberbeil and myself were told that this would be our last day in the bunker.

My concern was how I would get out of Berlin as we were surrounded by then. I saw Bormann leave the bunker. Two hours later I saw Eva Braun leave the Führer's quarters with her fur coat and a small bag. Behind her came two small girls and an elderly woman followed by three SS officers carrying cases. Eva looked terrible, hair unkempt and she looked like she had not slept for days. She walked slowly murmuring a 'Goodbye' to some of the staff. She could hardly walk and as she reached the foot of the stairs up, a young Colonel took her arm to help her.

As she disappeared Hitler himself appeared followed by a group of Generals. The Führer shuffled down the corridor shaking hands with all those of us assembled there. I know that many people *remaining in the bunker after I left have given their own explanation of what took place there, this is not my attempt to discredit them. But on evidence as I know it, this is my reconstruction for you Andy.*

A few minutes after Hitler had disappeared up the steps leading out of the Führerbunker I saw for myself a man who bore a startling resemblance to Hitler in stature and facial features being escorted by three SS officers into the Führer's private apartment. It was commonly known that there was on the Führer's staff a man who was said to be his double.

In conversations with Bormann who was insistent that Hitler had been removed from the bunker under the influence of drugs on 21st April. As creator of the Hitler suicide myth, he had seen to it that all participants had been carefully briefed.

I believe that it was Hitler's double who, nine days after I left played the most important role in the history of Nazism. It was the double who was shot through the mouth and whose body, dressed in Hitler's uniform was buried alongside Eva Braun in the Chancellery garden that same afternoon.

I cannot swear to the truth of this story, I was not there. But seven years later I was to witness a scene which would reinforce my view that Adolf Hitler did not die in Berlin in April 1945.

Three hours after shaking hands with Adolf Hitler I left the bunker staggering up to ground level into a scene of the most appalling confusion and noise. Russian artillery was pounding Berlin to ruins. I lay close to a wall waiting for a lull in the heavy shellfire from the Russians half a mile away. In a momentary lull, a voice yelled in my ear "Come on run!" I was jerked to my feet, I recognised the voice as Colonel SS Wagner, Chief of Intelligence in Hitler's underground headquarters. With him was Commander SS Willi Oberbeil, together the three of us ran out of the Chancellery garden. I might have been running for three minutes or three hours, I was so frightened. The streets were full of dead and dying men and women, rubble and dirt. I do not know how far I ran or where I was going. Suddenly the figure ahead of me stopped and friendly hands were guiding me into the back of a black Mercedes glad to be alive.

I felt Oberbeil fall into the seat beside me, followed by Wagner and a fourth man unknown to me. The great exodus from Berlin had begun, although the capital was lost, the brains of the Nazi party remained intact. I had no idea where we were going. The Russians had almost surrounded the city. Only the southwestern sector was still in the hands of the Germans. Several platoons of our troops backed by Hitler Youth battalions were holding off the enemy long enough for us to make our escape.

Once in the suburbs, the driver stopped the car and told us it would be safer to wait for the others and after ten minutes, we were a convoy of about eighteen cars headed for Munich. We drove all night nearly all the key people who had staffed the bunker were here. The nucleus of the Nazi High Command was moving to the last stronghold of the Thousand Year Reich. During a moment when we had to dive from our cars as a British fighter patrol attacked our convoy, a SS Colonel, I believe his name was Lachner called us together.

"The Führer wanted nothing more than to be left to die with his people." he yelled. "But Bormann wanted him out alive. Bormann had left orders that the Führer was to be drugged, by force if necessary and taken out of Berlin. That's what happened."

Lachner explained to us that Hitler was determined to stay and die defending the capital. But Bormann had assumed command and gave orders that Hitler and Eva Bruan were to be evacuated from the bunker with a fatal result for Eva Braun. This I learnt later was not true, as there is evidence that she was living. She was born in 1912 so in 1977 she would be 65.

I had to wait almost a year to hear from Bormann himself the true reason for this piece of treachery. Our escape lasted twenty hours during which Lachner told us more and more and insisted Hitler's worst errors were due to advice by a group of astrologers whom he regularly consulted.

Some years after the war, I discovered how the British Secret Service had managed to bribe the astrologers and gave them information to pass on to the Führer in their predictions. An English Secret Service agent told me that without their advice, Hitler would never have attacked Russia. If this were true, and I had no reason to doubt it, then this must be the biggest single triumph in the history of espionage.

In the evening of April 22nd, our convoy arrived at Rottach am Egern in the Bavarian mountains. It was here that the Nazis planned to make their last stand against the Allies. Here we were assigned an office for what was to be the new headquarters for Nazi Germany's espionage work. In the week that followed, we received and transmitted orders for the escape from Germany of dozens of top officials in the Nazi party. It was obvious to me this mass escape had been planned for some time.

After a week, I was called into Wagner's private office. Here he told me:

"I have good news for you. You have been ordered back to Madrid. There you are to contact members of your old organisation and prepare to receive a very special visitor."

"Who is he?" I asked.

"That I cannot tell you. What I can tell you is that if the Nazi party is to survive then this person must get safely out of the Reich and out of Europe. The job has been assigned to you. You will receive instructions in due course. They will be signed by the code name ZAPATO."

On the April 29th, 1945, I left the complex to München. SS intelligence had supplied me with false papers, identifying me as a Spanish chef. After a troubled journey, I reached Switzerland and after some interrogation, I was in Geneva. We had heard Germany had surrendered unconditionally. Many strings were pulled with the Inter-Allied Commission for the repatriation of Refugees. We made it to a hotel in Geneva under police supervision. From here it was easy to arrange passage to Barcelona. I had cabled my wife when I was arriving, and she waited for me in a car when we docked late in July.

By the time I reached home, the allies were celebrating the crushing of Nazi Germany. But I knew that their victory had not been complete. As they celebrated, thousands of men capable of keeping Nazism alive were being assisted to safety. I was one of those who assisted in these escapes.

The first stands convicted for the murder of millions. I met him in June 1946 a monk from a Swiss order called at my home in Madrid and asked me to give assistance to a German refugee. This refugee had sought sanctuary from the brotherhood. He said the man's name was Climents. I was told he was:

"A good man who wishes to start a new life in Argentina."

I travelled to the college of his order a few miles from Freiberge in Switzerland. I did not recognise the man but he told me:

"I am an officer of the SS and I am being hunted by the allies. Will you help me?"

I agreed.

Climents returned with me to Madrid on a special passport issued to him by the Vatican. These passports were issued to many refugees after the war but were only valid for travel inside Europe. I noticed the passport was in the name of Didier. I obtained an Argentine passport for him in the name of Climents. On 3rd July 1947, I drove him to Madrid airport to catch a plane to Buenos Aires. As we waited in the departure lounge, I asked if he could tell me his real name.

"My name is Eichmann." he replied. Meaning nothing to me then, now all these years later all the world knows what the name Eichmann means.

In December 1945 I received a visit from Felipe, a German who had worked with my organization in Spain. It had been some time since I last saw him, I was not surprised when he told me he was still working for the Nazis. I knew that large sums of money had been deposited with different agents in various parts of the world, all men dedicated to the Nazi cause. These men, and Felipe was one of them, had been chosen to keep Nazism strong in the event of Germany losing the war. They were all fanatics. Felipe was a key position in the escape route that had been reserved for top Nazis. Felipe handed to me a sealed envelope with a secret message. My instructions were in Spanish.

EXPECT SPECIAL VISITOR IN MADRID BETWEEN 1ST AND 15TH. THIS PERSON, WHOM YOU WILL RECOGNIZE WILL BE BROUGHT TO YOU BY THE BEARER OF THIS LETTER.
ZAPATO

Zapato! This was the code Wagner had made me memorize before leaving Rottach am Egern.

Felipe came to my house on 3rd January 1946. This time he was not alone. His companion I did not recognize at first. He was wearing a dark overcoat over a grey suit and wore a bottle-green trilby hat pulled down low over his eyes.

I knew I had seen this man before, Felipe introduced us.

"Angel, I would like to present you to Herr Fleischmann."

I shook his hand and I recognized the man as Martin Bormann. I last saw him in the bunker, now I noticed he had lost weight and he was now partially bald, though I discovered later this was artificially brought about from plastic surgery, which also had taken care of his prominent Greek nose.

Bormann handed me a white envelope, inside were further instructions, signed ZAPATO.

I was told to take Bormann down to a castle on the Mediterranean coast of Spain at Denia. I was told also that Macario, a German who had been living in Spain for thirty years and had been working for the Nazis since before the war would be expecting us. He had a large house and a small cottage built into the wall of the castle.

I assumed that was my part, but Bormann warned me,

"Get plenty of exercise. You must be fit to make a long journey very soon."

Bormann stayed with me in Madrid until 6th January. On that morning we left in my car for the eight-hour drive to the Castle in Denia. The castle had been used during the war as an espionage centre and the men living in the cottages had worked for the Nazi regime at some stage during the war. The castle was built to command a perfect view of the plains and the sea and was therefore an ideal hideout for a fugitive like Bormann. One room in the west tower had been roughly furnished and the glassless windows boarded up in preparation for Bormann's visit. I saw Bormann settle into his new basic but safe room before I set out on the return trip to Madrid.

I thought my part had ended, then three months later on 1st May, Felipe turned up again at my house. Once again, he brought a message, brief and to the point. Herr Fleischman would embark from Villagarcia, a fishing town on the north-west coast of Spain on the 7th May and that I would be accompanying him. But to where? There was no hint as to our final destination. I only knew I would be getting further instructions from our agent in Villagarcia.

On the 3rd May, I drove to Denia to find Bormann again, when we met I had to continue to use his pseudonym. He had spent his time in Denia learning Spanish which now was almost perfect, he looked a lot fitter too. Using his other name I greeted him "Herr Fleischmann, it is good to see you again. I trust your stay at the Castle has not been difficult."

Bormann grimaced. "I would not say difficult, Señor Gomez. But nevertheless, I am not unhappy at the thought of leaving."

Bormann had not spoken to anyone. He had not left the castle grounds, but at least his surroundings were beautiful. Acres of rose gardens and lawns lay inside the castle walls. He was in such good spirits that he sent Macario for a bottle of wine and insisted we toast. Bormann served the wine to each of us pulled himself to attention. He raised his glass.

"Gentlemen, we drink to the National Socialist Party and to its leader, Heil Hitler."

"Heil Hitler." we echoed. Could it be then that the Führer really was alive?

Macario and I left Bormann standing alone in his cell-like chamber and went to Macario's cottage where I slept well.

I was awoken at dawn to find Bormann dressed and waiting. We ate a good breakfast while Macario prepared for us a satchel of food and a bottle of cognac to take with us. We said our goodbyes and climbed into my car. It was an eight hundred mile journey and Bormann was unspeaking as we travelled along the coast road and then inland toward Granada and Seville. We stopped only to replenish our fuel tank, I deliberately chose small roadside filling stations where there was no risk of Bormann being recognised. We ate as I drove.

I had chosen a round-about route deliberately so as to avoid the bigger cities. Our first overnight stop was in the small market town of Merida, near the Portuguese border. We did not travel on passports and at the quiet hotel I picked out, I registered in my own name Angel de Velasco, showing my identity card and registering Bormann as Herr Fleischman. I was paying the bill and the concierge did not bother Bormann for his papers. Our second night was spent in Ponferrada, barely a hundred and twenty-five miles from our destination, Villagarcia. Those last miles took us the whole of the following day to cover. The road, an ill-made up potholed track, zig-zagged wildly across a chain of mountains and I arrived at Villagarcia exhausted. I drove to the house of one of my agents, a man named Martinez, who made us welcome. He was a genuine fisherman. Inside his house was poor but clean and Martinez had prepared supper.

Bormann and I ate ravenously and while we were still eating, Martinez brought in his son, who he said would be going with us in their fishing boat the following morning. Martinez had another envelope for me, but he said:

"I have been given strict orders not to hand this envelope to you before you are embarked."

Bormann and I smoked a last cigarette before climbing the stairs to a room where two single beds had been prepared for us. I was asleep before my head hit the pillow.

It was still dark when Martinez shook my shoulder roughly. "Señor, it is time to go." he whispered, and I heard Bormann grunt sleepily. We dressed and carrying a suitcase each, the former Nazi Party Chancellor and I followed the old fisherman out of the house and down to the harbour.

In the darkness of a moonless night, I could make out a dilapidated old fishing boat rocking unsteadily at its moorings. A stiff wind had risen and I could hear the crash of heavy breakers against the shore. Bormann was horrified.

"Mein Gott!" he exclaimed. "Don't tell me we have to make our journey in this thing. It will sink before it leaves the harbour."

The old fisherman told him not to worry and helped us board. I took a last look around before following Bormann aboard. I had made arrangements for my car to be driven back to Madrid and had given the driver a brief message for my wife, telling her I might be away longer than I had first believed.

We moved out into the open sea and when we had come about two miles from the coast Martinez slowed the engine and gave the order for the anchor to be dropped. It was then that Martinez produced the package from the pocket of his coat.

"This is the package you have been waiting for, Señor."

He handed me the packet, I wanted to open it there and then but Bormann told me.

"No, wait until we get on board our next craft."

We had both known that there must be another boat waiting for us. Outside a seaman shouted something and Martinez stood up and said, "Alright. It is time you were going."

On deck, I could see no sign of another ship, but two seamen were waiting to assist us over the side. I went to the rail and what I saw took my breath away. Bumping gently against the fishing boat's side was a rubber dinghy manned by two sailors wearing Kriegsmarine uniforms!

They gave a military salute as we lowered ourselves into the dinghy and Bormann returned their salute. We shouted farewell to Martinez and the two sailors cast us loose and began paddling away from the boat. As the sailors paddled away Bormann and I had our eyes fixed for some sign of an awaiting vessel. But there was nothing.

Then with incredible suddenness, the sea immediately in front of us began to boil and from the foaming waves rose the unmistakable shape of a submarine lifting itself from the depths. The sea cascaded from its decks and had it not been for the seamanship of the two sailors, we should have capsized. Even so, we were forced to bail frantically.

Moments later we were scrambling over the wet curved steel deck and hauling ourselves up the metal ladder to the top of the conning tower. Bormann and I paused a moment on the narrow gangway circling the open hatch. We caught a glimpse of the fishing boat heading back towards Spain.

Bormann gazed thoughtfully towards the coast and spoke softly as if voicing his thoughts to himself. "Europe will see me again leading a new and more powerful Germany."

He turned abruptly and lowered himself into the U-boat. I followed him down the narrow ladder and the two seamen, having stowed the dinghy came after me, closing the clips of the watertight hatch behind them. Bormann faced the U-boat Commander and together they saluted.

Then the Commander in full uniform with an Iron Cross on his tunic breast held out his arms and greeted Bormann in a firm embrace. He turned to me, extending his hand and clicking his heels, "Captain Karl Jui" he announced and gave a slight bow. He was no older than thirty-five although still a handsome man, his hair was prematurely white.

Authors Note: I cannot find any captain by this name. SO it's not clear if this name was changed.

The steward led Bormann and myself along a steel gangway towards the front of the boat's bow. As I stepped forward through a watertight door, I felt the boat surge and the deck ahead tilted downwards. We were going under, and I was embarking on the most fascinating voyage of my life. I glanced at my watch. It was 5:10am on the morning of 7th May 1946. Exactly a year to the day after Germany surrendered unconditionally to the Allies.

Now under war-time conditions, we were on a three-thousand-mile journey beneath the Atlantic. The crewman led Bormann and me to a small cabin in the bows of the U-boat. In this cramped steel box, we were to share eighteen long days together. Here Bormann laid before me his plans, plans he had prepared in the last months of the war, to ensure the continuance of the Nazi creed.

Captain Jui appeared at the door. Bormann went to the door and talked for a minute or two in German. I could not catch what they said, but as Jui shut the door and left us alone, Bormann remarked,

"From now on Angel, we consider ourselves to be Argentine subjects."

Then Bormann referred to the package of papers which had been handed to me by Martinez as we left Spain.

"I think now is the time to open the envelope. If I am not mistaken, it will contain certain instructions for our Captain."

I took the packet from my coat and laid it on the table. It was a plain envelope, not the usual kind used by the Nazi Intelligence Service. I slit it open. First, I withdrew a single sheet of paper. On it were instructions typed in Spanish referring to Martin Fleischmann, the name Bormann used during his escape. I was to instruct him in the way of life, the political situations and the language of those South American countries known personally to me. I was to pay particular attention to life in Argentina. From the envelope, I also took two Argentine passports. One was for Bormann in the name of Luis Oleaga, the other in the name of Adian Espana was for me.

Although the passports seemed genuine enough, they were issued by the Argentine Consul in San Sebastian, there was another note attached to the inside page of mine saying that these passports were intended for use only in an emergency and that people who would meet us in Argentina would supply us with more authentic papers when we arrived. The message was signed 'ZAPATO'. I knew then it had come from Colonel SS Wagner, former Chief of SS Intelligence in the Berlin Führerbunker.

The last item in the packet was another sheet of paper containing a lengthy message written in numbered code. I could not decipher it. I handed it to Bormann and he simply said, "Give it to the Captain."

The message was, in fact, Jui's sailing instructions.

We had been in the cabin for about two hours when I sensed the U-boat tilting it's nose upwards. Captain Jui knocked on our door and entered.

"Gentlemen, we have surfaced. We are just off the coast of Portugal. We shall be here for less than an hour to take on essential supplies."

I followed the Captain back to the operations deck and stood watching while two sailors opened the conning tower hatch and disappeared above us. A third man secured the hatch behind them, and the submarine sunk to three fathoms. We had to wait and from time-to-time Captain Jui glanced through the periscope. About an hour after the two men had left, Jui gave the order to surface. I felt the fresh air as the tower hatch was opened and the two men returned down the ladder each carrying a small box about the size of a cigar box. They looked extremely heavy as the men had difficulty carrying them down. The boxes were stacked on the deck and they returned for another load. Altogether, nineteen of these boxes were brought down. I suspected they contained gold. If Bormann knew, he was not saying, and my suspicion was never confirmed. After these boxes, two larger boxes were lowered, and I was told these contained food.

Fifteen minutes later, we were submerged again and life on board settled down for our eighteen-day non-stop run across the Atlantic. For most of the time, Bormann and I were together in our cabin, occasionally speaking with a member of the crew, but generally conversing between ourselves.

In accordance with my instructions, I began to coach Bormann in the ways of fluent Spanish. I tried to teach him the Argentine way, which has a different pronunciation to Spain. I had been to the Argentine several times. During the war I had passed several months there, engaged in espionage work for the Nazis. I arranged a spy network with Japanese Intelligence to relay information on the British-bound food convoys to our U-boat packs in the North Atlantic.

During our long hours together, he had told me something of his plans for keeping Nazism alive.

I asked him, "How is it possible for the National Socialist Party to continue after the battering it has suffered?"

He answered, "Neither I nor many of the others understood until it was too late what were our possibilities for the future. But now I am fully aware of those possibilities and will soon be in a position to take advantage of them."

At this stage, he was unwilling to reveal his plans in more detail. But he expressed his belief that Hitler's Germany could win a second war of conquest, within the next six years.

"Hitler's Germany?" I asked, "How can you talk of Hitler's Germany if the Führer is dead?"

He regarded me seriously before answering.

"You yourself saw the Führer leave the bunker. And if you saw him leave, then he could not have died there."

"Yes, I saw him leave." I agreed, "but I have no idea what happened to him after that. He could have returned, for all I know."

Bormann said nothing for a full minute.

"Do you not know where Adolf Hitler is today?"

"I am more concerned to know if he is alive." I answered. "As to where he is, it is not important."

"You are right. It is as important for our followers to know that he is alive as for the Allies to believe him dead."

Then he told me the incredible story of Hitler's fate. He said.

"Listen to me carefully and remember what I say. It is true. When Adolf Hitler left the Führenbunker, he was barely conscious of what was happening. After months of fighting the enemy on the battlefield and the treachery in his camp, he was both mentally and physically exhausted. Time and again he expressed to me his resolution to die with German soldiers around him. This I could not allow to happen. Hitler was the embodiment of the National Socialist Party cause. One could not survive without the other. At least not then.

By the 21st of April (1945), it was obvious that the war was lost. It became necessary to countermand the Führer's wishes and remove him physically from the bunker. I arranged to have him driven secretly from Berlin to Rottach am Ergen, escorted by officers from my personal staff. Only a handful of people besides myself knew that the Führer was there, and these were people whom I knew could be trusted to keep the secret of his escape for as long as it was necessary.

From Rottach he was driven across Germany and smuggled by ship to Norway. Two of my agents kept him in a place many miles from the nearest village until arrangements were completed for him to leave Europe."

I asked, "What of Eva Braun and the suicide?"

"Eva Braun never arrived in Norway. Unfortunately, she was given an overdose of drugs from which she later died. As for the suicide, I was the author of the story that Hitler and Eva Braun *committed suicide and their bodies burned with petrol. Those witnesses who afterwards testified to this end had been carefully briefed on my instructions."*

Authors Note: There is very strong proof that Eva Braun (Hitler) did not die and was indeed in Argentina.

Bormann leaned across the table;
"That Hitler did not die I know. I also know that he is still alive but more than that I am not prepared at the moment to tell you."
With that, I had to be content.
Yet later I was shown near conclusive evidence that what he had said was true. But as Bormann told me what he knows I gradually began to accept the incredible fact, Hitler was still alive.
Bormann told me he believed the news of Hitler's death was a source of satisfaction and pleasure to the Allies. He believed that with Hitler dead, the Allies would accept that Nazism could not be rebuilt. Bormann also wanted to perpetuate his own the myth of his own death for the same reason. On a number of occasions during our U-boat journey, he asked me what I would do if his name cropped up in conversation. During one such conversation, I assured him:
"Martin, from me everyone will believe you are dead."
This pleased Bormann. "That is what I wanted to hear."
But he added,
"Not that I died here. Tell them I died on the battlefield fighting the Bolsheviks."
Then I suggested to Bormann that he had given me so much information, and since I was the only person in the world who could tell the world that he was still alive, he might never allow me to return from this journey.
"I am more or less your prisoner." I told him.
Bormann reached out and clasped my hand in his.
"There is no question of your remaining my prisoner. You have proved yourself a good friend and a loyal member of the Party. There are, of course, certain things I cannot tell you. It is simply not convenient that you know everything, but that does not mean that I do not trust you. I am more than confident that you will not reveal the secret of my escape when you return to Spain."
It was the closest that Martin Bormann and I came to intimate friendship.

After politics, Bormann's favourite topic of conversation was his family. I was surprised to learn he was married and had a daughter, then aged fifteen. He said he hoped to arrange her passage to the Argentine as soon as he himself had settled. Years later, I learned that the girl had managed to join him and she now lives in Buenos Aires and is married with children of her own.

All in all, the voyage was quite uneventful, boredom mostly. There were a few events such as a minor breakdown when a large crack appeared on one of the accumulators (batteries).

Finally, our spirits were given a boost when we neared the river Platte estuary. It meant we were only a day or two from landfall. Bormann became excited and pulled out a large-scale map of South America. He drew a large cross over our point of disembarkation, the tiny port of Puerto Coig in the Argentine district of Patagonia.

One day I was in the captain's cabin sharing a bottle of French wine, while we were there Bormann joined us and almost immediately a rating appeared with a message. It read:

"Everything is prepared and we await you."

It was signed 'Rodriguez'. This message, our first direct contact with our agents ashore, brought a whoop of relief from us all,

Bormann asked me if I knew Rodriguez personally, and I told him I did not.

"This is strange." he said,

"I have been told that he is a priest and that you will know him."

"I have only known one priest who worked for us in the Argentine." I replied, "and his name certainly was not Rodriguez."

Bormann smiled, "Your name is not Adian, is it Angel? And mine is not Luis. So why should this priest's name not be Rodriguez?"

This message was not in code, I noticed and a second signal a few hours later made us certain at last that we had reached safety.

It said;

"You may proceed in perfect safety. We are in complete command. Heil Hitler!"

We had less than twenty-four hours to go before disembarking and the tension was tremendous. But Bormann and I spent the night restlessly tossing and turning in our bunks and were unable to sleep. Willy, the doctor gave us both a sedative and even suggested that I might like an injection to put me out for those last agonizing hours of suspense, but I would not agree. Even now I could not forget my espionage training and my cardinal rule; never trust anyone. I was *the only witness to Martin Bormann's escape. I was taking no chances.*

On the morning of 25th May, Captain Jui gave the order to surface. Bormann and I raced for the bridge in time to see Jui returning from a brief reconnaissance. Around his neck was a pair of powerful binoculars,
"You have a reception committee waiting for you." he told Bormann.
"How many?" asked Bormann
"I have counted eight men and two cars." Jui replied.
I could wait no longer. I scrambled up the steel ladder to the observation platform on the conning tower. It was my first sight of land in eighteen nerve-racking days. Through the mist, I could see the beach quite close and a number of figures waving at us.
Once ashore, I watched Martin Bormann walk up the beach near the tiny town of Puerto Coig with a feeling of intense satisfaction. My most important job as an espionage agent of the Nazi cause had been accomplished. Bormann, the most wanted war criminal in the world, had been safely smuggled out of Europe and was now safe on the friendly shores of the Argentine.
The crew gave the outstretched salute to us ashore and Bormann turned and stretched his arm toward the distant U-boat. Once the crew were below, the boat disappeared in the mist. The last mission complete, the boat was heading for Buenos Aires, surrender and asylum.

Authors Note: The boat did not reach Buenos Aires. It is believed it was scuttled in the Caleta de los Loros by her crew, revealed to me in a later letter from Don Angel.

We had been met on the beach by the Nazi agent Rodriguez, a priest whom I had recognised as a man who had worked with me some years before in that country under the name of Father Vogamiz. Rodriguez, wearing Roman Catholic garb, greeted Bormann enthusiastically. I doubt whether the good priest or anyone else there realised that they were the Welcoming Committee for the new Nazi Führer.

Now I jump to 1952. I had left Spain with my wife and family to live in Mexico three years earlier in Cuidad Juarez, close to the United States border.

I was working for a newspaper group, but as always my real work was with the Nazis, helping establish for the expanding Party in Central and South America a communications system for their intelligence service. It was a routine job with little travel and no risk. I began to think my usefulness to the Nazi cause had passed its peak.

In July 1952, I received a routine message ordering me to report to an isolated region on the southern tip of South America where I would be taken to see a 'most important person'. I assumed this might be my old friend, Martin Bormann. But I was wrong. I believe now after so many years in writing this to you Andy, I have the conclusion that the man I met was no less a person than the Führer himself, Adolf Hitler.

Once again, I was called to serve my Nazi masters. I wondered what mission they had in line for me. After several changes of aircraft and many hours of frustrating delay, finally arrived at the airfield named in my instructions. The airstrip was in wild forbidding country in the southernmost tip of the Argentine. I had been expected and when I entered the only building, a rough wooden shack in one corner of the field, I was greeted by a blond Aryan type who turned out to be a former Luftwaffe pilot.

Our transport, a twin-engine freight plane, was parked and already fuelled at the far end of the runway. The pilot told me to follow him and we boarded the aircraft. Within an hour, we were crossing the coast five thousand feet below. The only clue to our ultimate destination was that the aircraft was fitted with skis as well as wheels. We came to land on a smooth track of snow, we taxied towards the main hanger and a cluster of buildings a hundred yards further on. A party of three men left the shelter of the hanger and walked towards us. They greeted my pilot as an old friend and welcomed me in polite German. We hurried to the nearest house a hundred paces away.

Once inside the house, a wooden single-story affair, I was handed a steaming hot drink and shown my quarters. There appeared to be only myself and the three men who met me and a white-jacketed servant who cooked and served our food. Dinner that night found me no nearer the solution to the mystery of this desolate settlement. No one had volunteered why I, or anyone else for that matter, was here. Where was I going? Why was I here? Who was I to meet? And what were the connections between this place and photos of two children I had been instructed to bring with me?

I took the photos from my briefcase and studied them again. I knew these children well. In the past six months, I had received repeated instructions to check on their well-being. Several times I had visited their hometown of Las Cruces, New Mexico. I understood they had been brought over from Lisbon, Portugal in 1951. Often I had watched them from a discreet distance and taken photographs of them on their way to and from school. In what way were they linked with this mystery that I had flown three thousand miles for?

It was nearly mid-day 10th August when one of the men I had met, came to my room and announced,

"Señor Gomez, today you are going to meet the Führer." He mentioned the title so matter-of-factly that at first I did not grasp what he meant.

"The Führer?" I asked. "Who do you mean when you say the Führer?"

The man stared at me as if I was mad.

"There is only one." he replied "Adolf Hitler."

He motioned me to follow him, I let him lead me out of the house and across the snow to another, larger building. Just inside he stopped and knocked on the door of a room leading off from the hallway. A muffled voice answered his knock. He threw open the door and ushered me in. There were four men in the room. Three of them were standing. But these I scarcely noticed. My attention was riveted on the fourth man, who was seated behind a large wooden desk facing the door. I knew instantly that this must be the man I had heard referred to as the Führer.

If this was Hitler, he was barely recognisable as the man whom I had seen leaving the Berlin bunker in April 1945. To recognise in this person the Hitler who had dominated Germany for twelve years, it was necessary to have a willing imagination.

This man had no moustache. He was completely bald and the skin on his cheeks and temples had been stretched out of shape and left taught across the cheekbones. Yet his forehead and chin were heavily wrinkled and lined and an inch-long scar showed white on his left temple. This sinister face was framed against a huge scarlet and black Nazi banner, which hung on the wall at his back.

One of the three men standing to my left led me forward and introduced me to the figure behind the desk. I came to attention and gave the Nazi salute. The man behind the desk smiled and acknowledged me with a slight wave of the right hand.

Hitler, if it was Hitler, received me sitting down and later I learned that he had difficulty standing. I could see that his left arm was semi-paralysed and useless. His face was grey and every few moments he had to wipe a trickle of saliva from his sagging chin. When he did this, I noticed that his thin, wrinkled hand trembled violently. He looked like a man from whom most of the life had been wrung and his eyes were dull and almost devoid of spark. He wore a dark blue double-breasted suit with a Nazi Party emblem in the lapel. The suit fit badly and hung limply from his narrow shoulders.

The man ushered me to the desk now bade me sit down and produced a file of papers which he set in front of the old man before me. After a brief glance at the papers, he began to ask me questions in a thin, hesitant voice; questions about South America and the political and economic states of various countries of that continent. But he spoke as if not really interested and I had to lean forward in order to catch his words properly. I was gripped with such a strong feeling of dream-like unreality that I had to concentrate hard to answer intelligently.

He asked questions about the strength of the Nazi movement in South America and about my work for the cause of National Socialism. Only once did he show any signs of life and real interest, when with a sudden clench-fisted movement of his right arm, he asked me:

"Have you the pictures of the two children?"

I produced a pack of some fifty or sixty photographs of the children. I told the Führer that they seemed well and happy. As I spoke, he pored over the pictures and when I had finished, the questioning ceased. Without further sign from the old man behind the desk, the interview was over. One of the others in the room stepped up and tapped me on the shoulder, motioning me silently to leave. I rose and bowed slightly to the man at the desk and left the room. The following day, I was flown back to Argentina.

I never again saw the man they called the Führer.

In early 1957, I decided to quit working for my Nazi masters. I yearned to return to my native Spain and settle there once more with my wife and children and spend the rest of my life making up to them the time I had spent on the Nazis. But my plans were delayed.

On 6th June 1957, my radio receiver brought me news which was to send me chasing through South America for yet another meeting with Martin Bormann. At first, I baulked at the uninformative order to proceed to Panama City and await further contact with another Nazi agent. Instead of following my orders as I had done for so long, I decided to take the bold step of flying direct to Germany to make contact with the men at the heart of the Nazi cause.

Here I hoped to get more definite instructions. If I did not, I resolved to quit the organisation altogether and move back to a quiet life in Madrid.

To cover my trip, I proposed to my newspaper boss that I fly to Europe for a series of interviews. I managed to arrange one with General Franco and this was sufficient to justify my journey and I duly left. Immediately after my audience with Franco, I set out across Europe to the German town of Köln. The city had replaced München as the new shrine of Nazism and it was here, I knew, that men such as Bormann came from all over the world for top-level talks on the Nazi situation at least once a year.

The way I made contact with the Nazi underground movement was to insert a specially worded advertisement in a Köln newspaper, giving my whereabouts. The day the ad appeared, I took a telephone call at my hotel and was instructed to attend a rendezvous at a certain café in the city.

There I was met by a man I had known during the war, a former SS officer, who is now among the group of highly important men who control the Nazi party in Germany. This man took me to his home on Wagner Straße where I stayed for two days. I explained my feelings to him and asked him to be more explicit about the trip I was supposed to make from Panama City, but he refused to be drawn. He simply said that the High Command had requested me to attend one of their meetings somewhere in South America. He only added that when I got there, I would appreciate the reason why I had been sent for.

This news reversed my decision not to go. I resolved that I would make one more journey into South America, for I guessed that a request from the High Command could only lead to a meeting with Martin Bormann, the Nazi fugitive I had not seen since the day we stepped from a 'pirate' U-boat off the coast of Argentina ten years before.

I returned immediately to Mexico and laid plans for my last journey at the bidding of Nazi Intelligence. First, I packed my wife back to Spain and told her I would join her quite soon. Then, with my eldest son Angel, I moved to Chihuahua.

The next step was to shake off the American counter-espionage agent of the C.I.A. who had me under observation. This was not difficult since I had passed on considerable information about the activities of a communist cell in Mexico to the U.S. military attaché in Mexico City. The CIA agents who kept tabs on me did not seem unduly interested when I let it be known that I was to embark on a tour of Latin American countries with a bullfighting circus. I had been a pretty good bullfighter myself in arenas of Spain in the early 1930's and I looked forward to the trip as a pleasant holiday.

I also recruited a young woman who was trying to make a name for herself in the somewhat crude bullfights of Latin America. It would be useful to have her along. Having her in the show gave it an attraction and made my travels appear to be a serious business venture. I bought all the equipment we needed in Mexico City. We set out for Panama, travelling via El Salvador, Nicaragua and Costa Rica. All the way down my little show and the woman bullfighter proved a big attraction.

Just outside Panama City, in a little town called Davis, I met my contact agent. He was a German named Karl who had taken up cattle breeding. He had apparently been in the business since about 1947. I guessed his story. He informed me that I was to travel to Ecuador and he gave me the location of a farm in the state of Cuenta, where he said, the High Command meeting was due to take place.

It was a journey of some difficulty to find the farm, but I arrived by mule as the truck was unable to go the whole way. Worn out, I reached the farm. As I walked towards the house, I was approached by the apparent owner, an Ecuadorian and a posse of about fifty Indians. I explained I had come for the meeting.

"Meeting?" he said without emotion, "there is no meeting here."

Mystified and more than a little annoyed, I turned to go. The man called me back and said that since I had obviously come a long way, he would be pleased if I would join him in a drink. He led me into his house and poured me a glass of the local spirit. We talked in Spanish about nothing very much for a minute or two at the end of which, I drank up and made my farewell. I was just about to leave the house when a sunburned but obviously European man appeared in the doorway.

"Are you Don Angel Alcázar de Velasco?" he asked in German.

"Yes." I replied.

"Then come this way." he led me through a door and up a flight of narrow wooden stairs. At the top of the stairs, he hesitated a moment, then threw open the door and bade me to enter.

I walked into a very large room where seven men were seated around a long cloth-covered table and there, smiling a welcome from the top of the table was Martin Bormann. I recognised him instantly, but ten years had left their mark on his features. He was now almost completely bald and had deep pouches on his cheeks, but in his eyes and smiles, there was no mistaking the man I had brought out of Europe.

I made the Nazi salute as I entered the room and the group responded immediately by rising and answering, "Heil Hitler!"

Martin was first to speak, "Man, you've grown old, Angel."

"And the years have made a difference to you too Martin."

Bormann invited me to sit down at the table and join himself and the others for coffee. He made no attempt to introduce me to these men, mostly Germans and I recognised none of them.

As Bormann presented my coffee, he remarked,

"I have been keeping track of you ever since we parted Angel. I have seen plenty of reports about your good work for us, plus a few reports which you have made out yourself. I wanted to tell you personally how pleased I am with the work you have done for the Party."

I sipped my coffee, thanked him and went on,

"I myself have thought often about you and of the trip we made together."

Bormann insisted then that I should go downstairs and wash the dust from my body and rest before joining him at dinner. As I left the room, I nodded to the other men at the table, each of whom had a pile of papers in front of him, as if each had been given an agenda for an important meeting.

Later I returned upstairs where Bormann and his friends were sat at a table to dine, a place for me had been laid on Bormann's right-hand side. During dinner Bormann talked to me, questioning me, he wanted to know everything I had learned about Central and South America in the years I had lived there since we last met.

Further, he wanted to know who I knew in South American politics and what the situation was, as I saw it, with the organisation of underground Nazi agents in the continent. He listened intently while I outlined the social, political and economic affairs of those agents I knew personally. Then he pressed me for my views about certain Latin states and their ripeness for revolutionary take-over. On this subject, the other men began interjecting with their own questions about armaments, finance and the structure of various governments until, at the end of an hour, I felt like a well-squeezed lemon.

I did not mention I had recently been to Europe and they did not mention that part of the world.

Bormann did not tell me too much about himself and his life in South America, but I gathered that he had been well employed and dug his fingers into many political pies, but he did mention that he had been successful in setting up a number of youth movements along the same lines as the old Hitler Youth.

There was one thing above all that I wanted to tell Bormann and one question above all, that I wanted to ask.

First, I informed Bormann that I had decided to end my work for the Nazi cause and return to Madrid and my family. He did not seem surprised but asked me to think again.

"This is not the time to think about leaving us." he said fiercely.

"After all we have fought for over the years, now we can see the chance of realising our ambitions. Our party is now the strongest in South America and the revival of Nazi Germany is only a matter of a short time, a few years at the most. It has taken longer than planned I know, but soon we shall be in a position to put Germany back on the road to triumphs such as the Führer dreamed of in 1939."

He paused after his speech.

"It seems silly of you to leave us." he concluded, "when everything you have been working for is about to take on some meaning."

But I would not be persuaded.

"I'm glad that things are turning your way, Martin." I answered. "but I have lost much of my energies. I do not feel up to taking on further work. In a word, I am tired."

Bormann accepted my decision without further comment and changed the subject. I waited for my opportunity during the meal before asking my million-dollar question.

"What of the Führer?"

The question brought dead silence from all around the table. Bormann answered slowly.

"I don't follow. What about him?"

"Is he still waiting?" I asked.

"I planned to bring the Führer back into Germany at the correct psychological moment." said Bormann.

"That plan has now been abandoned."

"Does that mean Hitler is now dead?" I asked.

Bormann shrugged. He refused to answer me but turned the subject quickly. Bormann's last question during that strange meal was to ask me an out of character inquiry for this once publicity hating man. He wanted to know if people in Europe still talked about him.

"The people, yes. They are still talking about you. But you are rarely named in the press these days." I told him.

"That is good, that is good." came his reply.

I left the next morning. We parted solemnly, both expressing the wish and hope that we would meet again some time, some place and in more happy circumstances. The last words he ever spoke to me were these.

"I promised you once that I would return to Germany and that is still my promise. The destiny of the Fatherland lies with the National Socialist Party and its Führer. Heil Hitler!"

I began my journey home without looking back on the group of men standing near the farmhouse at the foot of the Andes, I returned to Cuenta. As soon as I could arrange a booking, I returned to Madrid. I had finished serving my Nazi masters. I had given them two decades of my life, two decades in which I had risked my life and made myself prematurely old with worry.

I do not work for them now, but thousands of others are helping to keep the Nazi cause alive and I am sure of that. However hard the democratic powers try to delay it, the re-emergence of the Nazi creed in Europe is bound to occur.

I know. I have seen the men who are working for that end. They have power. They have influence. They have the financial determination to put Germany back on top of the heap. They also have Martin Bormann. While men like him live, Nazism will never die.

Use my story as you wish and use it wisely. There is always a great resistance to change and my words here change things don't they!

Sincerely
(signed)
Don Ángel Alcázar de Velasco

That is the end of the letter sent to me just a few weeks after I returned from Spain. It is a lengthy letter and certainly not expected. I had hoped for another meeting, but for whatever reason Don Angel decided to present me with a written version of his belief that Hitler and others were alive in South America.

I replied by letter shortly after to thank him for such an effort to help me, and he sent a further letter, but not such a full account. In it, he made some additions to his story. The most significant being that he now thought Eva Braun did not die from an overdose administered to her in the bunker in Berlin. He provided a name and address where he believed Eva to be living at that time in Buenos Aires.

I had to think, I had almost completed my work finding Hitler. I felt I needed to actually see this property in Bariloche to complete my proof. But what most intrigued me was, why were the British so complicit? Why did they never do the work I had done? It hadn't been too difficult considering the access to documents. What was the deal? The scientists in Operation Paperclip would have wanted to work in the USA rather than be forced to work for the Russians. No deal for them would have been necessary, there was something else, something bigger, something the British and Americans wanted more than the scientists. That would, if I could find the answer to this question, be part of the proof of Hitler's escape and life in relative peace.

The project was still more of a hobby than a justified mission. I now thought it may be time to escalate it up, but would the British Intelligence permit me. It was time to put it to the test. The head of MI6 was now Maurice Oldfield, I liked Maurice and I hoped he liked me, he had been given the task of improving USA confidence in the British Intelligence Service and he often talked to me about it. By sheer coincidence as I was thinking about speaking to him about my project, he called me to make an appointment regarding a matter he needed to request of me. We met in The Millennium Hotel early afternoon, I travelled from Rickmansworth on the Metropolitan train line to Knightsbridge station on the Piccadilly line. Not the easiest of journeys but it was fine. The walk from the station to the hotel was only 150 yards. At the reception, I3 was informed Maurice was waiting for me in the Chinois Restaurant. The high tea here was known to be particularly special. I joined Maurice at his table, sat alone he welcomed me and beckoned for me to sit opposite. I knew there were rumours he was gay, with a particular interest in young men. I have to say he never acted in any way inappropriately with me, ever. He was wise enough to keep his personal preferences out of house. After ordering, we chatted for a few minutes about nothing special until he informed me of the reason for the meeting.

"Andy, I'd like you to share everything you have in the Philippines with the Americans. I know you have people very close to the top there, can we do that?"

"Share?" I replied, "Share infers we get something in return, otherwise it's give, isn't it? What do we get in exchange? I've done a lot of work to build confidence there, I don't want the Americans blundering in guns blazing as they normally do. I will protect my people at all costs."

I had to admit Americans aren't my favourite people, even though I've never been to America, what I have seen and experienced has not enamoured me to them at all and I will probably never go to America. I believe the phrase 'Land of the free' should be changed to 'capitalist police state'. What kind of country fines adults for crossing the road without a little light bulb telling you its ok to cross?

"Is there something we should have in exchange?" Maurice asked. This put me on the spot. I didn't have any thoughts on America, my domain was elsewhere.

"Yes, there was a guy, CIA, I got to know in Morocco on my first trip abroad, William Goldstein. Bill and I got on ok, I'd like to meet him on company expenses."

"Why, what's the reason?" Maurice asked, he knew I had nothing going on in America.

"I have a little something I am working on. When it's complete I'll let you have the information. In the meantime I ask you to trust me, I'm not sure where it will lead yet, but my gut tells me it will be useful."

"Of National importance?"

"I'll complete the work, and propose action, in the National interest."

"Andy, I am aware you are trusted and that we don't know how you do what you do. Meet your CIA man and I'll wait for your full report on whatever it is you have." Maurice was referring to my database of stolen photocopy data. Anyone in MI6 knew they could shortcut a lot of research by asking me for information on more or less anything in the world, but they had no clue how I obtained it. A few people tried to figure out how I got the information, as far as I am aware no one ever worked it out.

"Thank you. I'll meet Bill and hand over everything I have, without revealing my sources. In exchange, I expect cooperation with my project, and I'd like to do something in Argentina." I told Maurice giving away little.

"I can't let you have Argentina, we have everything well covered there, I can't let you tread on toes. I can let you have Chile."

"No, I want someone to just go look around somewhere. It's not dangerous, it should be simple stuff." I wanted to get eyes on and any information regarding Inalco House, near Bariloche. Just to confirm what Don Angel had told me.

"And Chile? That's a huge country, I'm not sure one person can make a difference there." As I spoke I realised Chile could be a useful resource for information on Nazis, as many of them had passed through or lived there. Maurice did a brief explanation of what was required in Chile for me. It seemed interesting and I agreed.

We ended our business meeting, and we finished the excellent high tea we had ordered with general talk. I considered it to be a very successful meeting for myself, as Maurice had demonstrated his confidence in me and gave me free rein to do whatever I wanted, more or less.

CIA Riddles

Timeline - January 1978

I still had a contact number for Bill Goldstein at the CIA. I called him. To my surprise, he remembered me even though we had not spoken since our time in Morocco four years previously. We had a quick catch-up on matters that had transpired following our time together, he was a nice enough guy, but I wouldn't trust him or any other American as far as I could spit.

I put it to him that we should meet, during which I would hand over useful stuff for him to pass on to his company as requested by Maurice. He hadn't heard that America was requesting the information from us, or that it was me that handled agents in Manila. We were not speaking on a secure line so things were deliberately vague and he understood that. I asked him where the meeting should take place. Typical of American showmanship or something, the meeting was arranged in a riddle. It was a test to see how much I had learnt and matured since I was very new in my job when he last saw me.

He created the puzzle,

"Do you remember my room number in Rabat?"

"Yes, I do." I replied not sure of the reason for the question yet.

"I'll see you in Paris then, same date and time. Look forward to meeting you again." and he promptly hung up the phone!

"What the ffff!" I spoke looking at the hand receiver of the dead phone. I gave the problem a little thought, then called Karen.

"Hi Karen." we chatted for a few minutes. We hadn't seen each other for a few months. I had started dating Janine, so there was stuff to talk about. Eventually, I asked,

"I need a return flight to Paris. April 4th. I need to be in the city in time for mid-afternoon, return in the evening the same day. No need for a hotel or anything. I'll take a taxi from the airport."

"It's not like you to be off to France, is this business or pleasure with your new girlfriend?" She asked with a bit of a jealous tone in her voice. I wasn't going to wait forever for Karen to decide one of us would give up our career so we might be together. I had been too busy to even think about giving up my job and she would never consider her job less valuable than mine.

"Business, the company is paying. If you fancy a few days in Paris yourself then change the plans, but I need to be there on the 4th." I would be more than happy to spend time with Karen.

"No, that wouldn't be fair to your girlfriend would it?" she replied.

"I wouldn't be with Janine if you and I were together." I wasn't cold-hearted enough to hurt Janine, but I called Karen's bluff.

"Return flight to Paris 4th April. No hotel needed." Karen replied trying to get one back at me, by emphasising the 'No hotel needed' part. I would love Karen all my life, I saw her gibe as a gameplay, I wouldn't take any offence.

It had taken me weeks of work to precis hundreds of documents I needed for the Americans. My notes were comprehensive and I wanted to reduce them to a summarised report. Most importantly, I didn't want any one part of it to reveal who my sources might be. I had agents and informants so close to President Marcos, often I knew what he was going to be doing the day before he did. Preparing the reports wasn't an easy job and the work just helped me to hate the Americans more than I did. Once I was happy my agents were secure from exposure, I placed all the copied documents into a Samsonite briefcase and set the combination lock to a new code.

I had completed the work just a few days before I travelled to Heathrow airport and flew the short flight to Paris Charles De Gaulle. In 1974 refurbishment work had been finished after eight years and renamed from Aéroport de Paris Nord. It was my first time here and the building looked stunning. I took my time, I had three hours before the scheduled meeting with Bill Goldstein. Or at least I hoped I would be meeting him. It would be a little embarrassing if I had got his cryptic message for the meeting place wrong. I didn't have any luggage other than the briefcase as I wasn't intending to stay overnight. I stopped for a quiet drink in the arrivals area and sat to watch people streaming out of the door from the security area. It is always interesting to try to guess if people have come for business or here for a romantic weekend with their partners. I was here on official business and my own unofficial business. Eventually, when I guessed the time was right after forty minutes or so I moved outside the terminal. Training had taught me to always watch for anyone following me, I was sure no one would be, my coffee break gave me the time to observe around me, no one seemed to hang around for the same time as I had sat in the café. I guess the nature of the job makes one quite neurotic about that kind of thing.

I took a taxi from the rank outside and ordered the driver to take a slow journey into the city to Rue des Gravilliers. A slow journey to a taxi driver doesn't mean drive slowly, I don't think they know how to drive slowly, what they'd rather do is to drive fast but in circles to build up the fare. Even though I hadn't been in this city before I could tell we took quite a zig-zag route, quite possibly one large circle too. I wasn't too worried I had plenty of time and I needed to kill a bit of it. It was interesting to see the sights of Paris, the people busying themselves in their daily routine or tourists with maps looking lost. As we arrived at the street the driver turned into the very narrow road, just wide enough for a car with a narrow footpath either side. A painted sign in the road as we turned into it said "Pietons Priorite" or "pedestrians have priority." It seemed to annoy the taxi driver that he had to slow down to a more reasonable speed. He asked me where he should stop. I still had a few minutes before our scheduled meeting, and I wanted to get my timing precise. I asked him to stop right where we were at the beginning of the one-way street. I paid the driver as I climbed out of the car with my briefcase in my hand. I did give the driver a smaller tip than I usually would, with the comment that it was an interesting route. The driver looked a little sheepish as he realised I knew we hadn't taken the most direct route to my destination. It wouldn't be the last time a French taxi driver would take me on a roundabout route either, it seems to be a common practice in France.

I walked down the street in the road as the pavement was so narrow, even for a Tuesday in April it was busy with tourists, I wasn't sure what was here for them to see. I found the restaurant I was looking for on the left about sixty yards from where I had exited the taxi. It was a sandy coloured building, a little unkempt but that was normal it seemed in this part of the city. The door was all glass with a little sign on the left with the name and the opening times. I glanced at my watch, I was two minutes early, that was close enough. The door was locked closed. Oh shit! Had I got this wrong? I stepped back and looked around the street wondering what on earth I should do now. Bill had definitely said Paris, I continued to walk down the street. Maybe he was just late himself. Should I wait? For how long? As I walked slowly in my thoughts, I noticed an archway beside the restaurant and at the back a courtyard with tables, to the left on the wall by the arch was a black shield-shaped plaque with some red and white text. On the top of the plaque was a sticker, an American flag sticker about an inch square, it had a penned arrow drawn on it pointing to the arch. Ah, ok I'm in the right place and now dead-on time. I walked into the pretty courtyard, there, sat at a table under a parasol was Bill. He saw me walking toward his table, he stood and put a handout to shake a greeting, as we shook hands he placed his left hand on top of my right hand to indicate a warmer welcome.

"Andy, you got it. 4 minutes past 4 on the 4th of April, the fourth month, at the Le 404 restaurant. Well done, you are as smart as you look." the restaurant was Moroccan too, the country where we had last met and the clue had been his room was all fours, 444.

I smiled back but inside I was pissed off at the silly games, it could have been a waste of time and money. But I was glad I hadn't let British Intelligence down. I did admire Bill for one thing, his choice of venue, it was a haven of tranquillity in the centre of Paris, in a pretty courtyard, with flowers and shrubs around the space, a little cheap looking with plastic chairs and tables but it seemed nice enough. The riddle was actually quite clever, but I wouldn't admit it to him.

I placed the briefcase under the table between us so it would be easy for him to pick up when we parted. I sat at a chair opposite him before he offered me to sit, I didn't want him to feel he was in charge of this meeting. This was years of work I was handing over to him for free.

The only problem with his plan, I'm sure he hadn't realised when he set the riddle months ago, that the restaurant was actually closed. It was between lunch and evening dinner, but a member of staff had seen us sitting there and approached.

"I'm sorry sirs, we are closed, but perhaps I can serve you some drinks?"

"That would be fantastic of you, thank you." Bill replied to the waiter. The elderly man, possibly the owner, passed us the wine menu. Bill suggested a red wine, Chateau de Corneilla, Pur Sang. A French Red. To the waiter, I said we would have a bottle of Les Trois Domaines, Guerrouane. I knew zero about wines, I had no idea what I was ordering regarding the taste or quality, but as Bill would be paying I was happy that it was slightly more expensive. The waiter smiled at me, indicating he appreciated my choice as it was a Moroccan wine and this was his Moroccan restaurant. I was doing my best to take command of the meeting I wanted it to go my way at every stage.

We chatted for a good thirty minutes enjoying the little warmth from the spring sunshine, the wind didn't get into the courtyard and it was a very pleasant place to sit, despite the plastic chairs, but I'm not a snob about that stuff.

Bill had a busy life, the Americans like to control the world and the British seem happy to help more discreetly in the background doing the difficult stuff. I wondered how his wife coped with him away from home nearly all the time. I lived at home in England, yet I was still single, my job always interfering with my love life. Yet he managed to have a wife at home, I don't know how that works.

I was careful not to tell Bill about anything I did, but there was one subject I wanted his help with. I finally got to ask him.

"Bill, I have a project ongoing. I want to ask you for information on this problem I have, maybe we can say it is in exchange for the briefcase I'm giving you."

"If it is something in the interest of us all. What's your problem?" Bill asked. He took another sip of the glass that I kept topped up, yet another little sign that I was in charge of this talk. 'Something in the interest of us all', when from an American meant in the interest of America and fuck the rest of the world.

"I want to know, at the end of the Second World War, there was a deal. A deal between America and Hitler. You know Hitler was permitted to escape Berlin, yes? I believe he got to South America, where he has lived in various locations. One significant location would be Argentina. I want to know, why? What was the deal? America took scientists in Operation Paperclip and other operations, these scientists were probably pleased to go work for the Americans rather than forced to go to Russia where life would not have been so comfortable, I don't believe that was the deal, there is something more. Find out for me what it was. I know the scientists were developing the atom bomb and other projects for you the Americans." Bill thought deeply for a moment.

"I know nothing about this, it's new to me." he said and I believed him, it's not a subject that's taught in any classes. "I'm not sure how I can help you." I cut in before he could tell me there was nothing he could do for me.

"Do some digging, find out. Yes, it will involve some of your time, but this is important to me." I said.

"Why, how does it concern you?" he asked me.

"Do you ever get one of those gut feelings that seemingly unrelated information can one day be very useful. This is one of those moments. This is going to help us in some way. Right now I'm not going to tell you how it will help us. But when you get me the answer to this question I will be able to tell you how we can use it." I was bullshitting him, but I didn't want him to know this was just a hobby, but the sentiments I just passed to him were the feelings I had. I didn't yet know how I would be using the answers to the riddles my post-war Nazi project would present me. But I knew, somehow, the answer would be very useful one day. Like all seemingly insignificant information in the Intelligence Service.

"Well, ok." he seemed thoughtful but only in that he could not see how I would use the information. Maybe that is why he agreed to help. I knew it would need some effort to dig out the answer from CIA archives . . . if it existed. We continued to enjoy the bottle of wine in the pretty courtyard, I changed the subject away from Nazi USA deals to prevent him from thinking too much as to why I wanted him to help me.

Eventually, after making that bottle last a least two hours, I announced I needed to get back to the airport to catch my evening flight home. We stood and shook hands farewell, I started to walk away telling him the briefcase was his so that he wouldn't think I had forgotten it. I left him to pay the bill. As I passed under the archway to exit the yard, he called after me,

"Andy, are you going to give me the code for the lock on the case?"

"Work it out." I replied without even turning to look at him stood in the courtyard. Two can play at riddles I thought to myself and it would give him a reason to keep me in mind.

A month later, I hadn't heard from Bill. I decided to call him to give him a push. I was in Century House, London for other work anyway. I asked Karen in her office next to mine to dial the number for me. So she knew who I was calling. It was his home number. His wife answered.

"Hello, could I speak to Bill, it's Andy." His wife would know not to ask any questions like Andy who? She was a CIA wife she kept out of the business. I was jealous he could have a relationship and not be asked any awkward questions about his work. Unlike Manoli, she had wanted to know everything. I couldn't do that, that's why we had to end, and I was upset my work prevented us from being together.

"That's a very nice British accent." she observed.

"Thank you." I replied.

"It's very sexy, very British." she continued. I had never considered the British accent as sexy, but I had heard the Americans find it interesting. Apparently, there is something they like about it.

"Well, your accent is sexy too, there is something about an American accent we British love. Is it Virginian?" I took a wild guess, I'd never studied American accents but the CIA Headquarters is in Virginia, so I thought it a good starter for ten.

"No, I'm Californian, I like the sun."

"Oh, I bet you look nice in a bikini too." I flattered her, I have no idea why. I saw Karen at her desk, her ears pricked up at the mention of a bikini, I decided to have some fun with Bill's wife. I don't know why, Karen and I always had fun and it would lighten an otherwise dull hard-working day. I waved at Karen to indicate to her to pick up and listen on her phone. I heard a little click as she did so.

"No, I'm too old for bikinis and at my age, I have to take care to keep my skin moistened, to stop the sun drying it or I'll be wrinkly." she continued,

"Too old, you sound, let me guess, 28?" I joked it was obvious she was around her mid-fifties.

"Oh, you, you flatter me, you are a long way out." she replied.

"Well, I can only imagine how you would look in a bikini, I'm sure you'd look great." I tried to keep it going.

"How do you cope with Bill away so much, months at a time."

"Well, you know, I keep busy."

"Lucky you ma'am. I have a preference for older women." I said looking at Karen who was seven years my senior. She pulled one of those cheeky bugger faces at me.

"Really? I'm Jaqueline no need for formalities." she answered, and the conversation took a turn I wasn't expecting.

"Well, next time you visit America, you should come visit."

"I don't get to America, but there's always a first time I suppose. But I doubt Bill and I could coordinate our diaries to be in the same place at the same time."

"Who said anything about Bill." she surprised me with her blunt answer.

"Noooo!" Karen put her hand over her mouth to stifle a laugh and to cover up her exclamation,

"Bill has talked about you a lot." I lied, he has never mentioned her.

"All good I hope?" Jaqueline asked.

"Well, you know what boys are like when we are together and have downed a few beers. He tells me you have a great sex life." I lied again, trying to get her to tell more, Karen still had her hand over her mouth giggling away.

"Really? I tell you Andy, men have to brag don't they. We don't have any sex life. He is away too much and there's nothing when he comes home."

"Oh. No, I'm sorry. How do you cope alone then?" I hoped to lead her on to more fruity stuff. Karen was nodding in her room and mouthing -

"Nooo, Andy stop."

"Well, you know, women have their ways. I'm sure a nice young man with a sexy English accent could think of something." the conversation was going beyond what I had expected, but I continued, it was a bit of insight into the home life of a CIA operative and becoming a bit of a turn on dirty phone call.

"I don't know any Englishmen with a sexy accent, but I'd be glad to come and rub in your moisturiser for you." I stifled a laugh and Karen was almost crying with laughter now. She was doing so well not to make a noise listening to the conversation. Jaqueline's tone changed to sultry.

"That would be most welcome Andy." Karen's mouth opened wide with surprise how far Jaqueline was going.

"But I have to admit this particular English accent has a fetish of his own." I said between uncontrollable laughter now. "I have a thing for pyjamas. I like ladies to wear pyjamas." I continued somehow.

"Really Andy? I am in my pyjamas right now as it's only 8:45am here."

"Oh yes please, tell me." I winced at the thought.

"I have my green pyjamas today, quite loose, I have the top two buttons undone, I have a nice cleavage, I wish you could see me, Andy." Karen grabbed at her crotch as she almost wet herself laughing. No, I couldn't continue with this she was going too far now.

"Erm, perhaps you'd better hand me over to Bill before something inappropriate happens." I said trying to end this. As she placed the phone down, I heard her move away and shout for Bill to come to the phone, I breathed a sigh of relief it was over.

"I can't believe what just happened, I almost wet myself laughing." Karen said

"What in the name just happened?" I said. I could hear the sound of Bill's footsteps approaching the phone and pick up.

"Bill Goldstein." he began

"Hi Bill, I just had a nice chat with your lovely wife." Karen looked at me waving not to say anything to Bill about what just happened.

"Really." he said unconcerned "how can I help?" I think it took a moment for him to click into CIA mode, he sounded gruff as though he'd had a late night. I decided not to say anything more on what just happened.

"I'm calling to see if you have made any progress on my request?" I asked.

"Ah, yes, Andy, no, I haven't. I have asked some researchers to look into it for you. I can't say when or if they will be able to get you what you want."

"But they are looking, yes?" I enquired.

"Yes, as soon as I know, you will. I promise Andy."

"Ok, thank you for your time then." there wasn't anything else I needed to say to Bill so I ended the conversation.

"Oh, Andy?" Bill quickly interjected before I hung up.

"Yes, Bill?"

"The code for the briefcase you gave me, what is it?"

"Oh, Bill, if you can't figure it out just break the lock." I couldn't believe a CIA man hadn't figured the combination lock code, or, indeed used violence on the thing to get into it, violence is the way the CIA usually like to go.

"Well, I still have it here I haven't passed it over yet." he said

"Oh my God, I'll be in trouble if my boss thinks I haven't done as he asked." I stated.

"What's the code?" Bill asked again.

"Oh Bill, it's the same riddle you gave me, my room number in Morocco." I said.

"I don't remember it." he said not wanting to admit his memory and IQ wasn't as high as mine.

"Next time then." I hung up, I hoped his need to get the code would hurry up the research I asked him for, and he would be back to me soon. Which seemed to be the case . . . literally. I felt so pleased I was smarter than this guy, I travelled to Paris after I had solved his riddle, it could have been a waste of time if I had it wrong. It was a good day. I celebrated by taking Karen for dinner that night. It was good to be in her company again. I didn't stay the night, I was trying hard to be loyal to Janine and had I asked, I'm sure Karen would not have permitted it anyway.

Another month passed and I was beginning to think Bill would let me down. After all, I'd given him all my work, he didn't need to give me anything. I knew I shouldn't have trusted him. But I was wrong, very wrong. A communication arrived from the CIA. Bill had come up trumps. In it he said that he had found a couple of very well-hidden documents, he didn't specify what kind of documents, but that didn't matter to me. He had found the deal. Bill expressed surprise I had not found it myself as Operation Epsilon was a British operation. Given the name of the operation, it was quite easy for me to find the files. I found them at Hanslope House, the depository for secret documents. He also recommended I should speak to an Argentine lawyer Alicia Oliveira about a client Uschi Schneider. Bill didn't stipulate why I needed to talk to this lawyer. Another of Bill's riddles, I guess.

Operation Epsilon was the codename of a program in which Allied forces near the end of World War II detained ten German scientists who were thought to have worked on Nazi Germany's nuclear program. The scientists were captured between 1st May and 30th June 1945, mainly as part of its Operation Big sweep through southwestern Germany.

They were interned at Farm Hall, a bugged house in Godmanchester, near Cambridge, England, from 3rd July 1945 to 3rd January 1946. The primary goal of the program was to determine how close Nazi Germany had been to constructing an atomic bomb by listening to their conversations.

Studying the transcript of recorded conversations, I found one small reference that one scientist made. In it, he claimed to a colleague that he believed that the United States was ahead of the Germans in nuclear research and that he thought the only reason one had not been used as yet was that the Americans did not have enough uranium.

That was it! That was the deal.

In addition to scientists, the secret deal was that Hitler permitted their stocks of uranium to be transferred to America. This would have been incredible treachery by Hitler. But considering the last act he ordered when all was lost to him in the bunker, was to destroy Germany. Destroy those that could not win his victory. Goring and Bormann refused to lay flat their country, Hitler's deal then, with the Americans, was in the hope they would do the job for him.

As it turned out, the uranium bomb dropped 6th August 1945 onto Hiroshima killing around 146,000 Japanese and the plutonium bomb dropped onto Nagasaki three days later killing around 80,000 in part came about with uranium stocks from Germany. Hitler's evil knew no bounds.

All I had to do now was to find how the transfer was achieved, in secret. It turned out, it was a secret in full view of the press, public and the news media of the time. I found the documents at Hanslope Park again. It was the German submarine U-234 that carried the nuclear fuel to the USA. Following is the official story of the U-boat, I believe the surrender was always intended as part of the Hitler deal.

German submarine U-234 was a Type XB U-boat of Nazi Germany's Kriegsmarine, she was commanded by Kapitänleutnant Johann-Heinrich Fehler. Her first and only mission into enemy territory consisted of the attempted delivery of uranium and German advanced weapons technology to the Japanese. After receiving Admiral Dönitz' order to surface and surrender and of Germany's unconditional surrender, the submarine's crew surrendered to the United States on 14th May 1945.

Originally built as a minelaying submarine, U-234 was damaged during construction, but launched on 22nd December 1943. Following the loss of U-233 in July 1944, it was decided not to use U-234 as a minelayer. She was completed instead as a long-range cargo submarine with missions to Japan in mind.

12 of her 30 mineshafts were fitted with special cargo containers the same diameter as the shafts and held in place by the mine release mechanisms. Also, her keel was loaded with cargo, thought to be optical-grade glass and mercury, and her four upper-deck torpedo storage compartments were cargo containers. The cargo to be carried was ordered by a special commission, the *Marine Sonderdienst Ausland*, established towards the end of 1944, at which time the submarine's officers were informed that they were to make a special voyage to Japan. When loading was completed, the submarine's officers estimated that they were carrying 240 tons

of cargo plus sufficient diesel fuel and provisions for a six- to nine-month voyage.

The cargo included technical drawings, examples of the newest electric torpedoes, one crated Me 262 jet aircraft, a Henschel Hs 293 glide bomb and what was later listed on the US Unloading Manifest as 550 kg (1,210 lb) of uranium. When the cargo was loaded her passengers came aboard.

U-234 was to carry twelve passengers, including a German general, four German naval officers, civilian engineers, scientists and two Japanese naval officers. The German personnel included General Ulrich Kessler of the Luftwaffe. Kay Nieschling, a Naval Fleet Judge Advocate, Heinz Schlicke, a specialist in radar, infrared, and countermeasures and director of the Naval Test Fields in Kiel (he was later recruited by the USA in Operation Paperclip) and August Bringewalde, who was in charge of Me 262 production at Messerschmitt. The Japanese passengers were Lieutenant Commander Hideo Tomonaga of the Imperial Japanese Navy, a naval architect and submarine designer who had come to Germany in 1943 on the Japanese submarine I-29, and Lieutenant Commander Shoji Genzo, an aircraft specialist and former naval attaché.

U-234 departed for Japan on 15th April 1945, running submerged at snorkel depth for the first 16 days, and surfacing after that only because her commander, Kapitänleutnant Johann-Heinrich Fehler, considered he was safe from attack on the surface in the prevailing severe storm. From then on, she spent two hours running on the surface by night, and the remainder of the time submerged. The voyage proceeded without incident, the first sign that world affairs were overtaking the voyage was when the Kriegsmarine's Goliath transmitter stopped transmitting, followed shortly after by the Nauen station. Fehler did not know it, but Germany's naval HQ had fallen into Allied hands.

Then, on 4th May, U-234 received a fragment of a broadcast from British and American radio stations announcing that Admiral Karl Dönitz had become Germany's head of state following the death of Adolf Hitler. U-234 surfaced on 10th May for better radio reception and received Dönitz's last order to the submarine force, ordering all U-boats to surface, hoist white flags and surrender to Allied forces. Kptlt. Fehler suspected a trick and managed to contact another U-boat U-873, whose captain convinced him that the message was authentic.

At this point, the U-boat was almost equidistant from British, Canadian and American ports. Fehler decided not to continue his journey, and instead headed for the east coast of the United States. Fehler thought it likely that if they surrendered to Canadian or British forces, they would be imprisoned and it could be years before they were returned to Germany, he believed that the US would probably just send them home.

Fehler consequently decided that he would surrender to US forces, but radioed on 12th May that he intended to sail to Halifax, Nova Scotia, to surrender to ensure Canadian units would not reach him first. U-234 then set course for Newport News, Virginia. Fehler took care to dispose of his Tunis radar detector, the new Kurier radio communication system, and all Enigma related documents and other classified papers. On learning that the U-boat was to surrender, the two Japanese passengers committed suicide by taking an overdose of Luminal, a barbiturate sedative and antiepileptic drug. They were buried at sea.

Fehler's reported course to Halifax and his true course was soon realized by US authorities who dispatched two destroyers to intercept U-234. On 14th May 1945, she was found south of the Grand Banks, Newfoundland by USS Sutton. Members of Sutton's crew took command of the U-boat and sailed her to the Portsmouth Naval Shipyard, USA, where U-805, U-873, and U-1228 had already surrendered. News of *U-234's* surrender with her high-ranking German passengers made it a major news event. Reporters swarmed the Navy Yard and went to sea in a small boat for a look at the submarine.

A classified US intelligence summary written on 19th May listed U-234's cargo as including drawings, arms, medical supplies, instruments, lead, mercury, caffeine, steel, optical glass and brass. The ship carried 1,200 pounds (540 kg) of uranium, this remained classified for the duration of the Cold War. The uranium disappeared. It was most likely transferred to the Manhattan Project's Oak Ridge diffusion plant. The uranium would have yielded approximately 7.7 pounds (3.5 kg) of ^{235}U after processing, around 20% of what would have been required to arm a contemporary fission weapon.

As she was not needed by the US Navy, U-234 was sunk off Cape Cod as a torpedo target by USS Greenfish on 20th November 1947.

How convenient! Any evidence that uranium had been on board U-234 was now destroyed. Destroyed so soon after the cargo had been removed by the Americans.

Documents I found described how the U-boat always intended to sail to the USA. This indeed was the deal, this U-boat containing uranium in exchange for Hitler's escape.

Chile

Timeline – most of 1978

As Maurice denied Argentina to me, I had to think about Chile a neighbour to Argentina, I needed to find some contacts that would provide reliable information. Gaining the confidence of agents was never easy and here I would need to start from zero. I would need to recruit, get them onside and prepared to help, potentially betraying their own country. I needed to learn some history so that I could find a way in.

Britain had good relations with the South American country Chile. The UK played an important role in Chile's history. Chile had the same head of state as England in the 16th century, Queen Mary I. When she married Philip II, he was still a prince, so the King of Spain, Carlos V made him and Mary the King and Queen of Chile, as well as of England, Ireland, Naples and Jerusalem. Mary became Queen of Chile and England from her marriage in 1554 to her husband's coronation as King of Spain in 1556, when Chile became part of the possessions of the Spanish king.

Chile has typically been Britain's strongest partner in South America. Britain has played an important role in shaping Chile's politics and government, throughout the ages especially in its fight for independence.

What I did not know in 1978, was that any contacts I made and controlled in Chile would play a very important role in the Falkland War in four years' time.

I called the British Embassy in Santiago the capital city. I introduced myself to James Hardie an attaché. I explained that I wanted to establish a network of agents of varying types, similar to the setup I had in the Philippines. I knew it took some considerable luck and skill to recruit useful people. I thought a visit to the embassy would be useful and sometimes the only way to get things to work is to go and do it yourself. I don't like to rely on other people to do my work for me. During our conversation, my first piece of incredible luck arrived. James informed me the Foreign and Commonwealth Office (FCO) in London was to host a cocktail party for delegates from Chile in a few weeks. He suggested I went and pose as a businessman looking to do trade with Chile. I agreed and I would figure some story to get to know a few people. I didn't enjoy this kind of social event, but sometimes you have to do things you don't like.

I called Karen. I told her I needed someone to act as my fiancé, as Janine had no clue whatsoever that I did this kind of work. She thought I worked with my father at the family printing business, which to some extent was true but printing wasn't a business that would produce the results I wanted. I asked Karen if she would be prepared to assist by accompanying me. She hesitated a little but then became quite excited by the prospect of mingling with such people. For me it was perfect, her beauty would help to attract some attention and provide the introductions I needed.

In the few weeks leading up to the function, I made up a cover story and produced papers and finance to back up the story. I schooled Karen on the plan so she could hold her own if she got into any conversations. Mostly I needed her to just look pretty, for her, that wasn't difficult. It would actually be my first time wearing a bow tie and dinner jacket too. I hired one, I didn't possess such a thing. I checked out the guest list to see who might be of interest to me. There were businessmen, arms dealers, military personnel and diplomats from the Chilean Embassy in London as well as Santiago.

The Foreign and Commonwealth Office, London.

On the day, I went to Karen's home to dress as I didn't want to leave my home dressed up and needing to explain where I was going to Janine. Arriving at Karen's apartment two hours before the function she buzzed me in. As I entered, she called from her bedroom. I went into the room and placed my bag on her bed ready for me to dress shortly. I did not need as much time as her. On Karen's request, I went to the lounge to pour a couple of gin and tonics to get into the mood and relax ourselves a little.

We went over and over our cover story to perfect it. Karen was so good at it, I thought she should be promoted to Officer herself. There was no end to her talents. I sat on her bed as she talked, dressed and did her make up. She had her hair styled earlier and even without makeup, she looked stunning. We always felt at ease with each other dressing and undressing, we had been together as lovers for many years. She finished dressing and turned to me, I'd only take a few minutes to dress, she moved close to me and checked me carefully for nose hair and random eyebrows as good women do. Her perfume smelt so gorgeous, I wished above all else that we could be together. I asked her if she thought there would ever be a day when we could be a couple properly and openly. Karen expressed a hope that one day it would be possible, but as I seemed to be doing very well with Janine, it would not be just yet. I longed for the day.

We went by taxi to King Charles Street, Whitehall. I hadn't realised the FCO was such an impressive building, it was huge. Inside the rooms were magnificent and impressive, all beautifully decorated. Our invitations were checked several times against lists, with photographs. As we entered the function room in a reception line at the door was David Owen, Secretary of State of the Foreign and Commonwealth Office. He had no idea who we were as we were introduced to him, but his aide whispered something in his ear, I have no idea what he whispered, but I broke the ice

"We have one thing in common." I said,

"And what would that be?" he asked me.

"You are the youngest person in your post, and I am in mine." I have no idea if he knew what my post was, he answered by ending.

"Enjoy your evening." as he shook my hand, I always thought he would be more interesting.

The room was filling up, there was top brass of every kind, some Chilean military personnel were in uniform. I knew James Hardie from the embassy in Chile would be here, so I sought him out. Karen was looking gorgeous, and heads were turning to follow her as we walked together through the room. On our way, I picked up two glasses of red wine and I asked the waiter what the wine was.

"It's a Concha y Toro, Marqués de Casa Concha Cabernet, 1976, it has to be a Chilean wine today."

"Of course." I replied

I shook hands with James,

"Hi, James good to meet you, my fiancé Karen."

"I read your profile, it didn't say you were engaged." he replied.

"We are today." I said, he knew what I meant he knew what I did and why I was at the party.

"I'll introduce you to a few people, anyone of interest?" James asked

"None yet, today I think I'm trusting to luck, I think." James walked with me, circulating around the room. We stopped to talk to a few people, they all seemed very honest on the surface, but to break someone and recruit them as an agent that would be useful to the British Intelligence Service I needed someone that had a little crack that I could prize open.

Eventually, James left Karen and me to circulate on our own. There was a military person in full dress uniform I recognised the three stars on his shoulder epaulette as Colonel or Coronel as they say in Chile. As we walked close by I could see him eyeing Karen. Here was the weakness I might be able to exploit, someone with an eye for beautiful women. He introduced himself to us as Coronel Luis Guilisasti. Of course, he was more interested in talking to the pretty girl on my arm, but I interjected.

"Guilisasti, that's a famous name in Chile, isn't it? Would you be part of the famous wine family?" I'd done my homework.

"Ah, you know wines." he said in his strong dry voiced South American accent, "my brothers José and Rafael, are the ones in the wine business, I never really found I had a love of farming as they do." he continued trying to belittle the true skill of wine growing "my calling was the army. But I do take a little interest in what they are doing."

"Is wine your line of business Andy?" he asked, but I wanted to steer the conversation my way.

"I heard your family is busy planting a new vineyard El Burro this year. Is this going to be a new wine, what grape?"

"You are very well informed, Andy. I understand the new vineyard will be used to add to the Terrunyo cabernet and Cono

Sur's Cabernet to increase quantity with the expected quality. Have you tasted any of our Chilean wines?"

"Wait." I said, and sipped on my glass of red wine, "I have now and I have to say it is excellent, your family produces this Marqués de Casa Concha Cabernet 1976 if my taste buds are correct." The bullshit now flowing from me, I really had no idea about wines I was simply repeating what the waiter had just told me. The colonel smiled a very broad smile and nodded at my knowledge of his family

"No, my business is consultant." I said.

"Consultant, in what?" he asked. I talked a little about the background to my business, all fake, I was making it all up.

"I consult with governments, I advise on military matters, tactics, hardware solutions, best tactical use of hardware. My business has experts in every field, special forces, hardware specialists of every kind. They can advise on training troops, better discipline and so on. The business has endless abilities. We should meet, let me talk to you about what we can offer you and your country and also how our friendship can be of bidirectional benefit to us both. Our speciality is to find ways to fund our consultation at little cost. Often, I can find a way to provide funds, in a beneficial way to both parties. If we find a way to exchange information that is of benefit to you, we improve our knowledge base and our clients receive more informed advice." I didn't want to go into specifics too much at that moment. An intriguing hook would be enough.

"Let's arrange a meeting while you are here in London, we can talk about how we can be of benefit to each other. Your country has disagreements with Argentina, we should look for ways to deter them from being a nuisance to your country and at little cost."

"How does this work?" he asked me, "How could I personally benefit from you providing advice to my army?" It was an interesting statement for him to make, he was definitely looking for personal gain from any business dealings, he was as crooked as they come. I was thinking on my feet now.

"Well, say, for instance, your family exports wine and it is looking to increase those exports. I could purchase three hundred to five hundred crates of wine and we advise your government on matters that concern them militarily, you have ensured my company gets the contract using your influence. Your government will pay me for that consultancy service, the payment is transferred to another company that I have. I pay you with that money for the wine. It's a legitimate purchase, the books are clean. Where that money finds itself after that I'm not concerned about and if the wine shipment is lost or diverted, I'm not concerned, wine is not my business. My government would be interested to hear anything from me that solidifies our friendship with Chile and my fees are covered by them." I could see his eyes light up at the thought of his pockets being thoroughly lined. He was hooked.

"Let's meet Andy, where do you suggest?" he asked

"Give me your card and I will contact you tomorrow when we've checked our diaries. We will meet in the next two or three days." I told him.

I needed to move fast on this guy before he realised what was happening. He gave me his card and asked me to call him the next morning. The evening was a success, I was on my way to turning my first Chilean agent. His parting words were,

"Will this charming young lady be present at our meeting?"

"My fiancé doesn't participate in my business dealings, but for you, we will both come to our meeting if it's going to be a deal-breaker." Guilisasti shook hands, we parted with smiles, he gave Karen a kiss on both cheeks, and we mingled on.

Once we were out of earshot of Guilisasti, Karen burst out laughing.

"Bloody hell Andy you are so full of bullshit we should all wear wellington boots! He is such a slime ball, horrible man, are you going to make me see him again?"

"It got the job done and that's how I roll, I have a gold medal in bullshit didn't you know." I knew Guilisasti was going to be very useful. I did not yet know just how useful he would be in a few years' time.

The rest of the evening was pleasantly boring, circulating the room, guffawing at someone's bad joke at the appropriate time, spreading a little of my own wit on the way. At the end of the evening, we took a taxi back to Karen's apartment and I went in to pick up my bag of clothes. It was a little late for me to travel home. In those days the train lines didn't operate all night, Karen invited me to stay with her, I accepted too quickly. Janine temporarily forgotten in the dirty business of espionage and bullshit, the night continued to be dirty as the two of us renewed our passion for each other. For me it was a beautiful night, I missed her sex so much. It was the one and only time that I cheated on Janine, in the morning, I did feel very guilty.

As I was in London, I reported to Maurice Oldfield, I explained to him I may have my first agent, he just needed to be completely turned and controlled. I explained the story I had sown the Colonel. If I arranged a meeting it may be a good idea to take along someone to act as a military advisor to impress him.

"You can't do that." Maurice disappointed me, "we would not be able to advise Chile on military matters. For a start, all South American countries are in an alliance. Have you heard of TIAR? It's an Inter-American Treaty of Reciprocal Assistance commonly known as the Rio Treaty. An agreement signed in 1947 in Rio de Janeiro among many countries of the Americas. The central principle contained in its articles is that an attack against one is to be considered an attack against them all. The United States is a member, they advise on those military matters where they deem it advantageous to themselves."

Oh shit, I should have done my homework better. I had no clue about this, I had so little time to prepare for the cocktail party, I was more concerned with who would be there and how I could turn them into an agent for MI6. I'm sure Maurice saw my face turn white and then red.

"Well, this Colonel seemed to be interested, you've given me Chile to handle, and that's what I'm going to do." I said to Maurice. "I have to meet Colonel Guilisasti, hook him completely, how else can I do it?"

"Well." Maurice came back, "you are the star spy, come up with something, but you can't go with a military advisor. Turn this man and keep me informed." That left me in an awkwardly difficult position for sure. I needed to call Guilisasti in a few minutes. I left Maurice, deep in my thoughts as to how I could get out of this mess and not look too stupid. This was my first big mistake, I'd got too overconfident and not done my due diligence on politics and South America.

Disappointedly, I went back to my office, Karen was at her desk. I explained to her what had just happened.

"What the hell am I going to do?"

Karen as always sat me down with a cup of tea and told me to relax. She always had a way to get me back into the groove. I was disappointed with myself at being so lax. It was my first big mistake in the seven years I'd been working with MI6.

"I didn't like the grease ball anyway." she said as she handed me my cup of tea, "his eyes were all over me, gave me the creeps, that's for sure." she said, seemingly resigned to the fact that I had lost this potential agent.

"Well, I can understand that, you are good to look at." I smiled at her kissing the air towards her with a "mwah."

"Oh, you smooth talker." she came back at me sarcastically.

"Maybe that's it, women, girls, I'll net him with girls." a plan started to form in my head.

"Don't ask me to go with you I don't think I could maintain a smile in his company, he gives me the creeps."

"No, I won't need to ask you to come, I'll go with a couple of high-class escorts. If he is into women, then a good fun night out would hook him and maybe provide something to blackmail him with if necessary." Of course, I'd rather not blackmail him as it would mean a forced relationship with him, I'd rather he thought me as a friend than his blackmailer.

"Could you look up some agencies we use please?" I asked.

"Ok, how many girls would you like? Two for him and one for yourself?" She asked, preparing to give me a slap if I said the wrong number.

"I'll call him now, set up the meeting first, then you call an escort agency and get two girls once I have a date. Where would be a good place to meet, where two girls accompanying me would not turn too many heads or raise eyebrows?"

"Annabel's, Berkeley Square, I know the owner Mark Birley, I'll see If I can get you a private table in a booth. There's a casino upstairs too, Aspinall's, if you need to entertain Guilisasti in another way. Gives you choices." Karen impressed me with her contact list, as a Londoner with a rich daddy she knows all kinds of people that can and did be useful to me. Karen and I made such a great team. I loved this woman.

I called Colonel Guilisasti using the number on his card. The phone rang for a while, which made me nervous, but he finally picked up sounding out of breath.

"Andeeee." he said sounding happy to hear from me after I introduced myself to him again.

"Sorry I was just finishing something up here." I heard the sound of a kiss, I could guess what he was finishing.

"It seems you had a good night last night then." I said to him, he really was a dirty old man. The plan to get him onside with girls was going to work.

"Well, you know Andy, you have to entertain yourself now and again."

I got on with business.

"Let's meet Luis." I used his first name to make this less formal. I heard a girl giggle somewhere close to him, he was still messing around with her.

"Ok sure, where do you suggest?"

"Annabel's in Berkeley Square, tomorrow night, I'll book a private booth, would you like to bring a friend?" I asked,

"No, I'll be alone this little belleza has to go home." of course he had to brag about the girl in his bed.

"That's fine, I'll bring the entertainment myself." I don't treat women as objects, but for this sleaze bag, I had to use what I thought appropriate language for him.

"9.30." I ended.

"Great, see you tomorrow at Annabel's." this was going to go my way for sure.

Karen got busy on her phone. She called the club to arrange the table for us, it took some chatting up, but as always, she came through. She called an escort agency MI6 sometimes uses for this kind of thing, they are trusted and the girls, although expensive are discrete and keep their mouths shut. Two girls were booked, a blonde and a brunette would cover either of his preferences. Karen came back into my office after it was all arranged.

"Two girls for you, you'll meet them at the agency to brief them first." she handed me a piece of paper with the details.

"Enjoy the evening and fill your boots." she said

"Are you jealous?" I asked,

"You have a girlfriend and me, you are getting greedy Andy."

"Those girls aren't for me, I'll be leaving with a deal of some kind, he will be the one having a fun night out." I reassured her, this was work.

"I'm not happy we spent the night together, I shouldn't have asked you to stay, I'm jealous of Janine but I don't want to be the cause of you getting into problems with her and I don't want to be your bit on the side either."

"Karen we should talk again. You know I only want to be with you, but for some reason, you won't allow us to be together, I hate being alone myself. Can we talk properly about us? I'd drop Janine for you in a moment, how many times do I have to tell you this."

"It's not just that, it's not the fact that MI6 won't allow us to be together, it's also the thought of losing you to some incident or shoot out that you seem to enjoy getting into. It's many things, do you not see what I have to watch you do." I was involved in other work, I'm not writing about here, as an Officer in MI6. Karen had seen me come home from a few situations that you could call dangerous. I got her point.

"You know I'd give up this work for you if you'd let me. We should talk about alternatives. I'd get out of this mess at the drop of a hat if only you would let me, I don't get why you won't let me get out. We have to talk about it." If only she could understand how I struggled with my career keeping us apart. How I hated lying to Janine about my secret life. This job was always going to keep me either single or, as a big-time liar and I hated that part of my career. We agreed we should have a day together to try to sort out our life.

The next day I went early to the escort agency office. I was taken to the Madam's office on the first floor of a rather well-appointed lushly furnished building, this company obviously made plenty of money. Two very attractive girls were waiting in the room sitting on a sofa. Not over made up or tarty, very professional business-like women, with amazing figures, long legs, enough cleavage on show that one could not help but look. They weren't like the traditional image of a tart. They were introduced to me, Anna a beautiful brunette, dressed in a red sparkly tight-fitting long outfit with a slit up the side. Her face was cute pretty, very well presented, actually someone you could take home, when she was dressed less night-clubby, to meet your mother. As she sat on the sofa her dress was open at the slit, her thighs were perfectly shaped, she reminds me as I remember her of Jessica Rabbit in the film 'Who Framed Roger Rabbit', except of course she was no cartoon. Claire was a very sexy girl, she was wearing a one-piece backless number in a blue that went well with her blonde hair, her hair long and hung very sexily down her back, with the bum of the dress slightly ruched to accentuate her shape more. She had enough boob showing to raise interest. Both were well-spoken and stood up to greet me with a handshake, on their heels they were much taller than my five feet nine inches. The shorter Colonel I thought, would look a little silly between these two amazing girls. I liked them right away not only because they were beautiful but very well-spoken and seemingly intelligent too.

I dropped two bundles of cash onto the desk in the room and a smaller bundle for the madam. I told both girls what the job was about and there would be a bonus if they convinced Guilisasti he should work with me, I didn't care how they did it. They asked me if he was into anything kinky, but I said I had only met him at a party two days ago and knew nothing about his sexual preferences. They asked about drugs, but again I said I knew very little, I doubted he would be into them as he was a colonel, and I wouldn't think he would be that crazy. I'm sure they would work him out. It seemed to me they must have had some training with MI6, as they were very smart and very clever in the way they spoke about their business. It was a well-paid business too. To be honest, the girls made me a little nervous. They were way out of my league, and I felt a little self-conscious as we left the building and into a taxi. The driver took one look, and I could see his face alter to one of surprise as to how an ordinary guy like me managed to get two pretty girls on his arm like these two stunners. During the journey, the girls shared some vodka with me to get us in the mood for some serious partying.

Arriving at Berkeley Square the front of the club seemed very

Annabel's nightclub. The only give away to distinguish it from any other house is the doorman.

small, I was expecting a larger building it was just an ordinary double fronted property that could almost be someone's house. The only give away was the doorman standing at the entrance. I paid the driver and as we approached the door, I told the doorman we were guests of Mr Birley. He welcomed us and past us over to a cute little usherette, I told him there would be another guest in our party arriving shortly, he nodded that he understood. We followed the usherette through various rooms to a nicely positioned private table in a room at the back of the building. It was in a position in the room just off the main dance floor. It was quiet enough here that we didn't have to shout over the music to speak, but the music was loud enough to make me feel it was a great party atmosphere. This place was amazing, I would have never got into this place without Karen's help. It was a real A-listers club it had such a reputation for being the venue for the stars. I don't recall seeing any celebrities on the night, but I can understand why they came here. Extraordinarily designed and conceived, a place where you never wanted to leave. It was warm, the colours, the reds, it had this elegance to it, and yet you felt that you could put your feet up and feel at home. Whoever designed this place had an incredible imagination.

 The cute girl took the coats from the escort girls and told us our drinks are compliments of Mr Birley tonight and we ordered a round of drinks to get started. Compliments of Mr Birley meant the taxpayer was footing the bill and what a bill it was going to be. Karen had seen to it that instructions had been passed to the staff and none of them let it out that it wasn't Mark Birley paying the for the night. Wow, Karen really did have some great contacts, I thought to myself, and I wished she was here too. I told the girls not to get too drunk they needed to keep their wits about them, they assured me they knew their job and not to worry. I wondered how many jobs with MI6 these girls had been part of. We chatted for a while, more and more I liked these girls. They were very clever, they had the right level of flattery, very tactile and held my arms as if we had been friends for years. They were fun and knew how to make one feel relaxed and get into the mood of the night. I have to say I was really impressed with these girls, they were professional, beautiful, funny, not tarty or brassy and I wouldn't do what they did for all the tea in China. I admire girls like them, they have a bravery equal to any of the people in Century House, they never know what they are getting into and must be very vulnerable to abuse.

 Colonel Guilisasti arrived at our table led by the same girl that brought the girls and me, she took his coat and took our order for drinks. In civilian clothes this time he seemed a different man now.

Guilisasti seemed impressed and his eyes would not stray from the two girls. He told us tonight we should call him by his first name Luis. The girls invited him to sit between them, I introduced them and he began talking to me about business. I could not promise the consultancy work I had made up before, so I steered him away and talked about wine and that line of business. All the time the girls were flattering him. I said tonight we were going to have fun, get to know each other and learn how we can trust each other to do the kind of business we were going to do. Little did he know it was yet again flannel and all I was interested in was getting him to keep me informed about matters of interest to the British. I was convinced I could turn this guy. Tonight, we would start by having fun. Claire noticed he had eyes for her, the South American had a thing for blondes, so she hung on to his arm and did all kinds of womanly things to attract the man. I began the conversation,

"What do you think of this place Luis? I thought you would like to have our meeting somewhere fun." I began.

"Life should be fun not all business." He said with a big smile on his face, clearly enjoying the attention he was getting.

"Yes Andy, an interesting choice of meeting venues, I like it, and I like these beautiful ladies." he replied,

"What has happened to your fiancé?"

"Well, you know I need to impress my new friend, Karen is a little stuffy when it comes to a good night out." I lied, I knew Karen would have loved this place.

"Andeeee my friend, let's not talk business tonight, these lovely ladies will be bored. I will ensure you and me will have a great business relationship, tonight is about fun. I've been stuck in my hotel during my visit to London. I can tell tonight is going to be a good night."

With that, he planted the first kiss on Claire's cheek, she laughed and responded in kind. I don't know how these girls do their job, he was such a greasy slime ball. But it seemed he was suitably impressed, and he was going to be owned by me for sure. Anna had sat with me and as soon as we had plied Luis enough drinks she shuffled over so that Luis was sat between both girls and he was loving the attention they were giving him. I asked him which hotel he was staying at, he informed me he had a suite in the Holburn Hotel, he told me it was very comfortable.

It was actually a great night, despite my absolute hate for nightclubs, it's a place to be open and free, something I'm not. I'm much too shy, but I did dance a few times in a group of the four of us. Luis couldn't hold his drink as well as us, we were seasoned drinkers, it's almost a prerequisite for a spy to be able to handle his drink. I can drink and keep my faculties very well. Luis seemed to be completely taken by the girls, this was a real weakness, and we exploited that part of his personality perfectly. I could not fault the way the two girls kept him dancing, drinking and laughing all evening. The club was a great venue, everything was right, the DJ seemed to play music just for Guilisasti, every track was his favourite.

At around 1am, I announced to the Colonel,

"Luis, my friend, I have to leave you with these two lovely ladies, I need to be up early. We will talk properly very soon. I have a plan for us to have a great relationship. Enjoy your night, make sure you misbehave with the lovely Claire and Anna. I'll speak with you tomorrow if you survive the night."

"Oh, Andy, my friend why are you leaving us so soon." He exclaimed, by now he was properly drunk and slurring his words completely.

"I'm sorry I have to go, I have work tomorrow, I hate to be a party pooper but the ladies are going to ensure your night will be one to remember. Goodnight all." I shook his hand, he couldn't stand to shake mine back. My plan seemed to be working well. I kissed the girls goodnight, I was so impressed how well they had conducted themselves all night, they were so much fun to be with. They earnt every penny of their huge fee. As I kissed Anna I told her quietly as I could in the noise of the room to somehow make sure Luis's hotel room door was open at 6am. I would come and make sure he was found in a compromising position. She knew what I wanted and didn't let me down, they would be earning their bonus that night.

It was far too late to travel back to my own home, so I went by taxi and crashed on one of the cots in a room for such occasions at Century House. It wasn't comfortable, I think I managed to sleep for about an hour. As the sun rose over London and the traffic began to increase, I freshened up with a shave and shower, then picked up a small camera from stores. I loaded a new film cartridge into it, placed it in a briefcase and caught a taxi to the Holborn Hotel.

The hotel was very impressive, in the quiet reception I asked for Colonel Guilisasti's room number, I told them he was expecting me as he had called me to bring something he had left behind, I tapped the briefcase I was carrying. The receptionist wanted to take the case from me and get a bell boy to deliver it, I said that it would be embarrassing for the Colonel as the case contained government documents and he had asked me personally to deliver it. He wanted to ring the room to announce my arrival. I asked him not to as the Colonel's wife would be still asleep, I told the receptionist I was here early before anyone realised the Colonel had made such a drastic mistake. In 1978 security was nothing like today, I'm sure if I tried such a thing now there would be no way I'd get passed reception. But the guy seemed to accept my story naively and I was given his room number. I thanked him for being so understanding as the Colonel would be saved from a very embarrassing situation and I was sure Colonel Guilisasti would thank him personally. Nothing could be further from the truth. My presence could be the most embarrassing thing ever to happen to Guilisasti. I was there for some insurance.

At the room, Anna had done her job and the door was slightly ajar. I quietly entered the two-room suite, I looked around as I silently closed the door behind me. The room smelt of post-sex sweaty bodies. The king-size double bed was in the next room centred behind an archway. The sliding doors open so that the bed was perfectly framed behind the arch, on it the two girls and Guilisasti snoring between them. Anna was awake, Claire seemed to be dozing. I put my finger over my lips to indicate to Anna to remain quiet. I very quietly placed my briefcase on a table in the room, opened it and removed the camera. I walked silently over to the bed and peeled back the duvet cover. Claire stirred but had the quick sense to realise what was happening. Guilisasti was snoring his head off so loud I have no idea how anyone managed to get any sleep at all. As the cover was rolled back carefully all three were revealed to be naked and the girls arranged themselves carefully for me to take a few photos. I had to cover my mouth to stifle a laugh as I saw Guilisasti's penis, it was tiny. Anna noticed me holding back my laughter and smiled raising her eyes as if to say 'yeh, you try working with that little thing'. It looked like a little pink nose between his legs almost invisible amongst the mass of greying pubic hair. Guilisasti didn't stir and continued to snore loudly as I took a few pictures of the naked group. I passed the two naked girls a small bundle of cash as a very well deserved bonus for the work they did that night. I waved goodbye and mouthed,

"Thank you, great job." to the girls preparing to move out as soon as I left.

They blew kisses smiling to me as I silently closed the door. As I walked down the corridor, I found a housekeeper's trolley and put the empty briefcase in the rubbish bag, the camera now in my pocket. On my way passed the receptionist, I said the Colonel was most grateful and thanked him again. I left the hotel, mission complete.

When Karen arrived at the office, she asked how the night went. I told her the story and that I had left quite early, and I had spent the night on a cot in Century House. I could tell she was concerned I had been with the girls all night. I hadn't and I wouldn't, as that could put me in a difficult position. A position that Guilisasti was now in. Once the lab had developed the photos a few hours later, I showed Karen the pictures of the Colonel and his two girl threesome, she commented,

"Hmm, I'm glad I didn't go, it seems I didn't miss much at all!"

From that day on we called him nasty teeny Guilisasti usually we just called him, teeny. Anyway, that became his code name.

As it turned out I would never need to use the photographs I had taken. Guilisasti became a very good contact and provided information whenever I wanted it and in just a few years he would prove invaluable and even save many British lives.

Later that day I called Guilisasti, he complained of a bad hangover, apart from that, he couldn't wait to see me again the next time he was in England. He told me the night was the best he had ever had. He was hooked and very soon began sending me information on the political situation, military news and inside information on the embezzlement and tax fraud activities of the dictator leader of Chile President Augusto Pinochet. Through teeny Guilisasti I made several other 'friends' in Chile, but none would or could supply such valuable high-class information as he.

Inalco House

Timeline – 1978

At the same time as working on Guilisasti, I wanted to see Inalco House and the area around it that Don Angelo had mentioned was Hitler's home in Argentina. As I had been warned not to tread on toes in Argentina, I thought it may be better to either talk to whichever MI6 Officer had contacts in that area and I considered the possibility to travel from Chile the neighbouring country using Guilisasti's friends, I dismissed this as I didn't want the Colonel to have any inkling of my business, I had to keep information flowing in one direction from Chile and not the reverse, even though Argentina and it's Nazis was not yet an official operation. Much as I hated telling anyone my business, I bit the bullet and spoke to Michael Moore, an Officer that had contacts in Argentina. Karen had informed me that he had been given a batch of information gathered from some of the photocopy data I had stolen and collected in our database, so he owed me a favour anyway. We met in a quiet bar just outside Ashford, Kent. I had not met him before, but he was on the same side as me and I soon asked him if he had anyone that could take a trip for me. They should travel looking as though they were on vacation or sightseeing and take some pictures of the area. I wanted a visit to San Carlos de Bariloche, Inalco House, 55 miles from Bariloche. Also the Hotel Llao Llao, 16 miles from Bariloche and to photograph anything that may be of interest. Michael, realising he did owe me, agreed to find someone reliable and discreet to take a road trip. Amazingly, Michael informed me he had heard of San Carlos de Bariloche. Information had come his way of a nuclear research site there. He was not concerned as the information he had was that the facility had been closed long ago and was now derelict. During our meeting I avoided telling him why I was looking at this area, I merely said some people were crossing from Chile to the area and I was wondering why.

Michael of course, pressed me as to how I had so often been able to deliver information to people in the Intelligence Service on so many subjects. I simply replied that I do my job. I was pleased my reputation was still a mystery and the theft of the data from photocopy machines around the country, in some cases other countries too, and no one had discovered how I did it.

On my return home I looked for information on this nuclear facility he was talking of. Amongst the mountain of papers Karen and I had collected, I found what he was referring to, the Huemul Project.

The **Huemul Project** was an early 1950s Argentine effort to develop a device known as the Thermatron. Austrian scientist Ronald Richter invented the concept. Richter claimed to have a design that would produce effectively unlimited power. Richter, of course, was a German Nazi Scientist.

Richter was able to pitch the idea to President Juan Perón in 1948 and soon received funding to build an experimental site on Huemul Island, just outside the town of San Carlos de Bariloche. Construction began late in 1949, and by 1951 the site was completed and carrying out tests. During February 1951, Richter measured high temperatures that suggested fusion had been achieved. On 24th March 1951, the day before an important international meeting of the leaders of the Americas, Perón publicly announced that Richter had been successful, adding that in the future, energy would be sold in packages the size of a milk bottle and even perhaps, free of charge.

A worldwide interest followed, along with significant scepticism on the part of other physicists. Little information was forthcoming, no papers were published on the topic, and over the next year, some reporters visited the site but were denied access to the buildings. After increasing pressure, Perón arranged for a team to investigate the claims and returned individual reports, all of which were negative. A review of these reports was equally negative, and the project was ended in 1952.

After Perón was deposed in 1955, the new government investigated Richter to discover that 1,000 million Argentine pesos (about £25m at the time) allocated to the project was unaccounted for, and arrested him. Nothing further was heard about him. Secret British government documents declassified under the 30-year rule in 1983 reported that Perón had contemplated invading the Falkland Islands in 1951.

Late in 1978 during the Argentine summer, Michael passed me a file containing photographs of Inalco House, the supposed home of Adolf Hitler. It revealed no clues, it was derelict and every trace of who had lived in the property removed.

It had a few owners starting with Enrique García Merou, a Buenos Aires lawyer linked to several German-owned companies that allegedly collaborated in the escape to Argentina of high up Nazi party members and SS officials.

Casa Inalco, near San Carlos de Bariloche. Hitler's home in Argentina.

He bought the lot from architect Alejandro Bustillo, who created the original plans of the house in March 1943. Bustillo also built other houses for Nazi fugitives who were later apprehended in the area. The terrain in which the house was erected, on Bajia Istana near the little town of Villa La Angostura, was quite remote and hardly accessible at the time. You can see the property on Google Earth easily.

The plans are similar to the architecture of Hitler's refuge in the Alps, with bedrooms connected by bathrooms and walk-in closets. There was also a tea house located by a small farm. Like the Berghof, Inalco house could only have been observed from the lake, a forest at the back limited the view from land. It even had Swiss cows imported by Merou from Europe. Later, Merou sold the house to Jorge Antonio, who was connected to President Perón and was the German representative of Mercedes Benz in Argentina.

The house was sold to José Rafael Trozzo in 1970. Strangely enough, Trozzo also bought other properties owned by Juan Mahler. Mahler was the fake name of Reinhard Kopps, SS official and war criminal.

Kopps was connected to the war crime by Erich Priebke, he is listed in my original list of suspects earlier in this book. He was former Hauptsturmführer in the Waffen SS who participated in the massacre at the Ardeatine caves in Rome, in which 335 Italian civilians were executed after a partisan attack against SS forces.

According to information, when the house was occupied originally the complex was completely autonomous, with its own animals and agricultural areas. It also had a ramp that led into the lake, with a boathouse that was rumoured to have contained a hydroplane, though I doubted this as it would attract far too much attention if it were ever used and studying the pictures it was far too small to contain an aeroplane. I prefer to think access was by boat only.

The Hotel Llao Llao was reported to be derelict after it closed in 1976 due to lack of funds for maintenance.

It was renovated and reopened in 1993 after ownership was transferred to CEI Citicorp Holdings in compensation for Argentina government bonds.

Surprisingly, the original hotel, designed by Alejandro Bustillo, the same architect that built Inalco House, was made almost entirely of wood but was destroyed by fire soon after its completion in 1939. Built on a site with stunning views of Moreno Lake and Mount Tronador, the lake being connected to Lake Nahuel Huapi where Inalco House sits at the northwest end remote and barely accessible. A year later Bustillo built a new hotel out of reinforced concrete and stone, with the assistance of the German landscaping architect Hermann Botrich.

Both properties were Bavarian in style, but neither of these properties provided definitive proof that Hitler had occupied them.

So then, I saw my last chance to get real proof that Hitler did escape Berlin. That a deal had been done with the USA for uranium to complete a bomb. I would have to speak to the lawyer Alicia Oliveira in Argentina that CIA operative Bill Goldstein had mentioned to me in our telephone conversation. I had discovered, again through secret documents not available to researchers in the public domain, that Oliveira had claimed a woman client using the name Ursula (Ushi) Scheider was, in fact, Ushi Hitler. Through her, if I could persuade her to talk, would perhaps come the information that Ushi resided in Argentina and that Oliveira knew Ushi's real identity. I understood the reasons why Ushi would wish to remain under her pseudonym. Persuading Oliveira would not be easy. Client confidentiality would make sure it's nigh impossible for her to talk to me. So I called her at her office during Argentine office hours through an interpreter.

For the purposes of this book, Scheider is Ursula's maiden name, she was actually married to a German Nazi who cannot be named here.

I was put through to Oliveira after I told her receptionist I was an assistant to a prosecution lawyer working on disclosure for a case and that Ursula Scheider may need to be subpoenaed as a witness in the case. I used the company name of the firm of lawyers that work for MI6. I had set up a phone number through British Telecom that would come through to MI6's telephone answering service. The girl that answered the call would have a brief as to what to say, should Oliveira wish to return my call.

Once through to Oliveira I explained that a case in the UK was being prepared. Ursula Scheider had been named as a witness, which I understood that Oliveira's company represented Ursula Schneider and that this was merely a courtesy call so that they could advise her should she need it. I explained that the case was regarding abuse of minors and I believed that Ursula Schneider was possibly a witness and in fact may have been abused by her husband herself. I tried not to say much more than the minimum and as it was supposedly just a courtesy call and that Oliveira should speak to her client about it.

"Shortly." I said, "we may arrange for an interview for an affidavit." Oliveira agreed that Ursula should have representation and would speak to her.

It was a con I never believed would work, I had little clue as to how prosecution court cases worked. Maybe the interpreter added some credibility to my lies, I have no idea. A week or so after, through the fake phone line Oliveira rang back. She had stunning information.

Ushi had gone into Oliveira's office to talk about what she may have witnessed. Oliveira told me Ursula was wearing dark glasses, which was normal for her. She sat in Oliveira's office in an obvious dull mood. Ursula sat and told Oliveira:

"I have something to tell you, I am not Ursula Schneider, my papers are false." she took off her glasses to reveal swollen black eyes at this point. "I am Ursula Hitler, the daughter of Adolf Hitler." she went on to discuss the abuse her husband had subjected her to and that she knew he was part of a paedophile ring of German Nazis.

Whilst I should have been interested in the full story, to me, the admission was the completion of my research project. I listened to Oliveira explain to me what Ursula knew. I thanked her for her honesty and that a solicitor would arrange for her statement to be taken. Of course, at that time the completion of my research had opened many other questions. But for me, the job was done. A project that had begun two years earlier. Assisted by the very lovely and clever Karen, I now wondered how I should use this information. Did it have any useful purpose for the British?

Not yet, but it would . . .

Operation Saponify

Timeline – April 1982

I had no clue how I could use the information discovered by my project. Jenny had got me started on this project and she was long gone, I had not seen or heard from her, nor had Karen, I could not fulfil my promise to pass her the results of my investigation.

It was clear to me that someone in the British and USA intelligence services had full knowledge that Hitler had done a deal with the Americans and the British complicit in that deal, had aided the escape. The leadership of Argentina certainly knew the Nazis were settling in cities, towns and villages throughout their country. I find it incredible that the population kept quiet too. Living in fear of a dictatorship regime is not easy or simple and can go some way to explain the silence.

Without any further need to research the subject, it was time to concentrate on other matters. I put my project to bed. I filed it in a cabinet in my office and it stayed there until 1982 when it would be resurrected for surprising reasons.

In 1982 Argentina invaded the Falkland Islands. The Falklands was a ten-week undeclared war between Argentina and the United Kingdom. Two British dependent territories in the South Atlantic, the Falkland Islands and its territorial dependency, South Georgia and the South Sandwich Islands.

In December 1981 there was a change in the Argentine military regime, bringing to office a new junta headed by General Leopoldo Galtieri (acting president), Air Brigadier Basilio Lami Dozo and Admiral Jorge Anaya. Anaya was the main architect and supporter of a military solution for the long-standing claim over the islands, calculating that the United Kingdom would never respond militarily.

The conflict began on 2nd April when Argentina invaded and occupied the Falkland Islands, followed by the invasion of South Georgia the next day. On 5th April, the British government dispatched a naval task force to engage the Argentine Navy and Air Force before making an amphibious assault on the islands.

By opting for military action, the Galtieri government hoped to mobilise the long-standing patriotic feelings of Argentines towards the islands, and thus divert public attention from the country's chronic economic problems and the regime's ongoing human rights violations.

The British Intelligence Service went into overdrive and certainly proved their worth. During the conflict, Exocet missiles became a major threat, causing the loss of Britain's HMS Sheffield and Atlantic Conveyor, with the loss of 32 British lives. Near panic ensued in London. It became known Argentina had five Exocet missiles, two of which had now been used. It became a matter of urgency to destroy the remaining three along with the Super Etendard planes that the missiles were launched from. I played a minor role in a deception to purchase more Exocets.

Operation Mikado, a suicide mission that the SAS rebranded as Operation Certain Death, was cancelled after Operation Plum Duff, a mission to place a forward observation post at Río Grande, Tierra del Fuego to gather intelligence for Mikado failed.

It occurred to me that the information on Nazis and Hitler could be useful in an attempt to bring the Argentines to withdraw from the Falklands. I believed that if it were made known very publicly to Israel that high ranking Nazis such as Hitler had been permitted to live unhindered in Argentina since 1945, then Israel would react against Argentina. Also, I was able, through my Chilean Colonel Guilisasti, to play a major part in persuading Chile not to sign up to support Argentina in the war, as the TIAR agreement would dictate them do. Chile had her own argument with Argentina over border areas which made it easier to persuade them to help the British. Chile gave support to the UK in the form of intelligence about the Argentine military and early-warning intelligence on Argentine air movements. Throughout the war, Argentina was afraid of a Chilean military intervention in Patagonia and kept some of its best mountain regiments away from the Falklands and near the Chilean border as a precaution.

The Chilean government also allowed the United Kingdom to requisition the refuelling vessel RFA Tidepool, which Chile had recently purchased and had arrived at Arica in Chile on 4th April. The ship left port soon afterwards, bound for Ascension Island through the Panama Canal stopping at Curaçao en route.

It took me two days to write a proposal, such an operation would normally take a minimum of several weeks. Most of the content taken from my Nazi/Hitler project which helped speed up the writing of the proposal.

Karen managed to get me an appointment with 'C' who was now Colin Figures. I had not met Colin before, so I had little idea of how he thought or would react to my proposal. The meeting was set for 5th April 1982, the day some of the British fleet set sail from England. It was slotted in last-minute between other meetings he had scheduled, with time allotted to it of only ten minutes. He was a very busy man. As it happened, our meeting lasted an hour. Colin was so interested in my work he pushed back the other appointments.

In Colin's office, we greeted, and I gave a short résumé of my work, he hadn't been in his position as Head of Intelligence for long and had not had time to get to know all the officers yet. I don't know how I appeared to him, I wondered if I came across as professional as an uneducated Officer. I hoped my views were unique with my "out of the box ideas." He gave nothing away, he just let me talk, which made me more and more nervous.

I began by talking about the background of the research I had done. He gave no indication whether he thought I had wasted time and money, especially as I used company budget money for some of the expenses in Spain and France. I told him I had found Jenny had been working for another group, probably 'The Avengers', while working inside MI6 at Century House, that we had slept together. I told him how I had met Don Angelo, and how I had taken an extreme measure to exit the restaurant. I was honest how it all came about. I told him I had pictures of Inalco House in Argentina. That I had spoken to a lawyer of Ushi Schneider who was actually Ursula Hitler by her own admission. I knew Hitler's escape route was from Berlin to Norway, then back to Travermünder in Germany then south to Reus in Spain, over to the island Fuerteventura, Spain and from there across to Mar Del Plata in Argentina. Here he stayed in numerous places, until settling for years in Inalco House near Bariloche. Colin listened intently not giving away any thoughts or expression.

I told him I had a small group of agents under my control in Chile. I assured him the stuff coming from those agents, mainly the Colonel, was extremely useful, especially now. The Colonel would also provide escape and evasion routes to safety across the Chilean border.

Finally, I presented to Colin my proposal to use the information I had to get Ursula (Ushi) Hitler to tell the world that Hitler had escaped Berlin. We would propose to Israel that we would hand her over to them if they put some pressure on Argentina and to use their considerable influence on the USA to add to the pressure. I pointed out to Colin both the USA and Chile were members of TIAR and in theory, backed Argentina, but they were already acting in our favour in certain ways. As I spoke of my plan, he remained impassive and gave no clue whether he was impressed or the whole thing was absurd. In fact, as I talked to him aloud, I began to feel that my plan sounded quite ridiculous myself. It was the first time I had actually read it through properly as I had prepared it so quickly. At the end of my speech, I paused and looked into his eyes for a clue to how he was thinking. I got nothing.

After what seemed forever, it was probably three seconds, he began to talk while flicking through my proposal file.

"Andy, I think this could work, but I have reservations. This Ushi Hitler, she isn't enough. For this to have any chance to work, I think you need to get Eva Braun, if you claim she is alive. Ushi must have been a child at the end of World War II. She is completely innocent of the acts that the Nazis perpetrated during the Second World War, she may not know the truth and whereabouts of any Nazis."

"Well, she is or was married to one, he is the guy abusing her." I said.

"Get Eva Braun and I think we can do something with this. Interesting work. Let's give it a try. You have a budget, get her to talk on camera." Colin added.

"I think we should bring her to the UK. Expose her here." I said, "Let me get a team together to bring her here."

"Do you think she will come willingly? Colin asked

"I can only try." I finished.

"Ok, I will call the Ministry of Defence (MOD) to get approval for military assistance, hopefully, get to the PM and get approval from Thatcher too." I knew Colin would try everything to avoid a fight with the Argentines. He made several calls and while I waited for him to finish the phone calls a coffee arrived for us both. After a few minutes, he looked at me.

"OK, you have cart blanche, no need to keep me informed unless I ask you. Do what you need, but please, not too many dead bodies." I could not believe the trust he was giving me. Of course, he was under pressure to perform from all kinds of angles in the Falklands War, but to give me the freedom to do whatever necessary was incredible trust in me. I was over the moon.

As I left his office he called after me

"Andy, make this official. It will be allocated as Operation Saponify, good chap." I almost ran back to my office, I burst in excited and couldn't tell Karen quick enough.

"Christ, it's got a go!"

Karen looked up from her desk,

"You are kidding me!" She exclaimed.

"Well, thanks for the vote of confidence!" I replied.

"No, yes, well, well done. What do you have to do now?" She asked me.

"Easy." I said, jokingly, I knew there would be nothing easy in this operation. "all we have to do is get Eva Braun to come to England from Argentina in the middle of a war, and sit her down to announce to the world the truth about Hitler being alive after the end of World War II. Get Israel and the Americans to put pressure on President Galtieri before the shooting starts and ta-dah."

Now the enormity of my plan dawned on me.

Timeline 5th April 1982

I sat back on the sofa in my office staring into space trying to figure a way to achieve the objective. Karen of course, knew what to do without asking and passed me a mug of tea and sat with me silently, smiling.

"Come on Andy, you've got this far, I have every confidence you can do this." she placed her hand on my thigh, which brought me back down to earth. We smiled at each other.

I asked Karen if she could remember if we had an address for Eva Braun.

"I remember she left Hitler in 1954, wasn't it something like Nequin where she moved to?" We had to look into the files to find out, it didn't take as long, Karen wasn't far out, Braun had moved to a town called Neuquén in Argentina.

"Call Hereford SAS, I need to know if there is anyone available there."

"On it." Karen said as she rose from the sofa and dashed to her room to make the call.

The 22nd Special Air Service Regiment gained fame and recognition worldwide after its televised rescue of all but two of the hostages held during the 1980 Iranian Embassy siege and were the darling boys of the nation if not the world. Suddenly everyone wanted to know all about them.

Calling Hereford, the base for A, B, D and G squadrons, Karen could not get through to Brigadier Peter de la Billière, he was probably on a ship somewhere, but someone further down the command line was found and willing to talk to me. It was clearly a busy time for these soldiers.

I explained what I wanted,

"No fucking chance! Everyone is out." he said.

"How about any guys failed in training, anyone will do, give me someone, or the body count starts piling up soon." I asked.

"Give me an hour, I'll get back to you." he told me sounding slightly reluctant.

I hung up quite despondent now, the operation, my operation, didn't look as though it would even get off the ground, I didn't know what else to do if the SAS were unavailable. Should I call Eva and ask her to get on a plane? No, it was ridiculous to think she would do anything voluntarily. A call to her would warn her we are coming for her, and she would disappear again, probably forever.

Forty minutes later someone at the Hereford base called, it wasn't the Brigadier or Director SAS as he was known in 1982 but it was someone in authority at least. I explained what I needed. Then he told me some good news,

"Ok, there's a guy, a good guy, being returned to his unit, the paras, he failed the SAS course because he badly twisted an ankle. He will be on platform one Hereford station on his way back to his original unit. He will do the job for you." The voice on the end of the phone told me some further details on the guy, he gave me his name and regiment details and other information I wanted. I had little time to get to Hereford to meet him.

"Karen." I shouted, "I need a driver, a fast driver, and I need him now." as always Karen did her job perfectly and efficiently. Within minutes I was in a black Jaguar XJ6 flying out of the garage feeling very important. I instructed the driver to take me to my home first, I needed to dress appropriately for this job, my usual casual dress wasn't going to work for me on this occasion. I'd never been driven so fast, we broke every speed limit. This guy knew what he was doing.

At my flat, I dressed in a two-piece suit in double-quick time. I was still tying my tie as I jumped back into the car and we sped away. The fast journey was interesting, we overtook cars where we shouldn't, took bends faster than I'd ever taken bends, even jumped red traffic lights if it was safe to do so. The driver was incredible, despite the speed he drove, I never felt unsafe. Somehow, he transmitted his intention, so I knew what he was going to do before he did it. In the car was the first mobile phone I'd ever seen, I asked the driver if I could use it. He showed me how to connect to a landline number. I called Karen. She had received a fax with information on the guy I was looking for, she read details on him that I didn't already know. We arrived in Hereford in two and a half hours, a feat I thought before we started out to be impossible, I had slightly under twenty minutes before the train arrived on platform one bound for London. I instructed my driver to wait for me. I stepped out of the car feeling completely unruffled and relaxed and walked onto the platform. I had no picture of the guy. In those days, we didn't have smart mobile phones to send pictures, I have no idea how we managed to do our job, it must be so much easier in these days of smart phones.

I walked onto the platform, few people were waiting for a train, it was quiet and would be easy to spot a military-type carrying his kit bag. As yet, there wasn't anyone that looked like my guy. I waited close to the entrance, I would see everyone arriving. After ten minutes, a tired-looking guy walked onto the platform a huge, camouflaged Bergen rucksack on his shoulders, a limp he had told me he was the guy with the twisted ankle. He stopped by a bench seat and dropped the bag on the floor, it didn't look light. His face was tired, wrinkles on his forehead and bags under his eyes made him look older than he was. He immediately lit up a rollie cigarette, with the thinnest amount of tobacco you could get in a fag. He took a long drag and enjoyed the effect it gave him. Confident looking, tough, not muscle-bound but solidly built, his hair cut longer than normal military style, he seemed calm after having to leave the SAS course. His file had said he left very late in the course, he must have been so disappointed, and an easy target for me. I walked closer to him and spoke,

"Going home?" I asked him. He didn't give me the courtesy of a glance or reply, he continued to enjoy his cigarette. I tried again, "you must be devastated you got rtu'd (*returned to unit*) at this late stage."

He still didn't speak but I saw him react that I somehow knew he was being sent back to his unit. I moved closer to him, danger close to this lethal weapon of a man.

"If you are interested, I can offer you some work." I said quietly now I was closer to him.

"Fuck off, not interested." he replied, at least he spoke. I expect he thought I was some kind of private contractor trying to recruit for security work or some kind of a nutter. His voice was dry, years of smoke and drink taking its toll on his vocal cords, his accent home counties. I persisted, much more mystery and this guy might knock me out. I held out a hand to shake.

"Andy, Ministry of Defence, I have been authorised to offer you Dave, a special job, interested?" The use of his name told him I knew who he was. "Let's grab a coffee, I'll give you a lift to wherever you need to go. I'll tell you what the offer is."

"MOD you say?" he questioned.

"Yes, your boss has told me you are good enough for the job I have. I think you are, I saw your profile, you are the man I need. Merville Barracks, Colchester, isn't it? Let's get a coffee and drive. How's your ankle?" The soldier hesitated, who would get into a stranger's car during the time of the IRA bombings? Spies don't usually carry any ID, I had none with me.

"Call your boss in Hereford, it was he that put me onto you and told me you would be here today." I said. "I have a phone in the car or use a public phone box, it's up to you." Dave thought for a moment,

"What's the job?" He asked.

"Well, I can't talk here." but I added quietly, "Argentina, all your mates in 2 Para are on their way to the Falklands, you will be sat on your backside back in barracks twiddling your thumbs. You will miss all the action. I'm giving you the chance to go and join in. Maybe you will stop it all from happening. More than that I can't say here. But we can talk on the way, there's my car." I pointed through the exit to the Jaguar with the driver waiting in the car park.

"Ok, talk to me." he said without any emotion on his face, no excitement, or any other kind of worried look. He could knock me out with just a wave of his hand let alone a punch. He picked up his Bergen, slung it over his shoulder and walked toward the car. At the car, the driver jumped out and opened the boot so Dave could dump his Bergen in it.

"Let's get a coffee and then drive, wait here I'll get them in." I took a coffee order from Dave and the driver, went into the station café and bought three takeaway coffees and some cakes while Dave and the driver waited in the car park.

I came back to find them both chatting, Dave was wanting to find out from the driver if what I had said was genuine. Of course, the driver had no idea what my mission was, but he did confirm we had come from MI6 Headquarters, Century House, London. My luck was continuing that day, as it happened the driver was an ex-para too, the two of them had loads to talk about and Dave became more confident this was not some kind of con trick. Today, everything was falling into place, I knew this was supposed to work. It was amazing luck and coincidence that Dave was leaving the SAS base at the most perfect time.

On the journey, I explained a rough sketch of the mission to Dave. He, like all the soldiers, wanted to get into the action, he realised this was his only option. His failure at SAS induction meant he really had something to prove. I had no doubt he would do a great job. I liked him right away, he was calm, intelligent, obviously tough and brave. His eyes showed compassion yet a hardness that any soldier in the world would envy. The SAS aren't built just to kill, they know the ultimate goal is to save lives. This mission could save lives.

"Who else will be joining me, this is clearly not a one-man job?" he asked

"You need to find a team from whoever is not on a ship right now. You will have any weapons you need and the support of all forces, army, navy, RAF. You are in charge of the operation as soon as you agree to it and are happy with arrangements." I told him. I saw his face lighten a little, he was enjoying this.

"So, where exactly is the target? Buenos Aires will be bloody hot right now."

"Neuquén, it's a town about 600 miles south-west of Buenos Aires it won't be on high alert. It's about 175 miles east from the Chilean border, you can go there I have people that will help you cross the border and safely home. It's your choice how you get in. Your target is a 70-year-old lady, so ex-fil will need to be relatively comfortable, she may not be willing to go, it's more of a kidnap situation."

"Have you actually seen this lady?"

"No, I have an address you need to get to the address, check that she is at home and grab her. I will guess she may have one bodyguard, she is not that important these days."

"So how will she stop the war?" Dave asked.

"Not important, for you to know right now, but she must arrive in our hands in one piece, preferably no cuts or bruises, as she may have to make public appearances."

"Who is she then, how is she important enough to stop a war?"

"Eva Braun." I said bluntly.

"The dead Eva Braun, Hitler's girl, dead since 1945!" Dave exclaimed.

"I know differently, she's alive and well, her daughter has confirmed it. As it happens, Hitler died April 1962, they both escaped Berlin to, among other places, Argentina." The light began to dawn on Dave what this was all about.

"And her coming here will stop the war." he said, in more of a statement than a question.

"We will try. You plan the kidnap, MI6 will plan the end of the war." I said.

"That will piss off my buddies in 2 para, they are keen for a fight." he laughed.

"Yeh, I'm sure you'll get a pat on your back none-the-less."

For the rest of the journey, Dave and the driver swapped anecdotes on their time in the paras, while I thought how phase two of the mission would work. How would the UK persuade the Israelis and the USA to pile on pressure to Argentina?

By the time we reached Colchester, Dave was fully on board and already suggesting ideas. We arranged to meet the next day, there was no time to lose on this operation.

We met early the next morning at the Para's base in Colchester, it seemed to make sense. "C" had spoken to the base Commander and an office was found for us to set up mission planning. It was on a need-to-know basis, only those in on the planning knew what was going on there, anyone else was firmly told in soldier language, to go away. I gave Dave everything I had on the subject. Dave had already called a few of his pals left hanging around the base as a caretaker group and three good volunteers joined us. Three was the number Dave had decided he needed, including himself, it would be a group of four. A larger number of men stomping across Argentina would be easier to detect. As the target was an old lady not much of a fight was expected.

The men all tough hard men but with an intelligence that made them perfect for the job and by the end of the day I found them all to be great guys, full of laughs but as professional as they come. We had no rank, all were equal even if a guy had rank, everyone chipped in with ideas and expertise, it was a great way to work, but overall Dave stayed in charge as he was a Corporal someone needed to call the shots.

Mike was a private, a Londoner, an inch or two taller than Dave, I have no idea what colour hair he had as he kept it so short, just longer than bald. His shoulders were so wide I swear he had to turn sideways to get through doors. All military guys seem to have nicknames, I asked him what his was, he told me it was Mike because he liked to sing in his regular pub so he was always holding a microphone. I asked him if it would be ok to call him by his nickname, to which he replied, it was better than his real name anyway. Military humour! Mike's only negative was that he swore too much, even for a soldier. Every second word, literally, was an "f" or "c" word, it was too much, but who would ask him to tone it down a bit, not me! Mike was an expert with explosives, apparently, at school, he made a homemade explosive and destroyed his teacher's desk. I would have loved to have done that myself to a few of my teachers.

Vince was a tall Lancashire lad, quite handsome, and for some reason that was his nickname, Lanc. He had the longest blonde hair, above regulation length, I have no clue how he got away with it. Maybe he had been in Northern Ireland, but I didn't ask. He was older than the rest of us and he had spent a period with the SAS, his experience was invaluable. He was so calm, intelligent he always had good ideas, and most of them went into the mission.

Rob from Bristol, was tall, some tall people are lanky but Rob was in proportion. Calm, studying, he could find fault in our ideas, when he couldn't, you knew it was a good idea. I liked him a lot. I suggested his nickname like Vince would be based on where he came from, it was explained to me that nicknames seldom went to more than one syllable and Brist didn't work. It turned out he was known as Bishop, which was more than confusing, as this to me sounded like two syllables but was based on Bishopston, an area of Bristol where he lived as a child. Vince suggested it was from the military song Four and Twenty Virgins, I hadn't heard the song before so a few verses and choruses were sung to me by the guys, anyone outside must have wondered what on earth was going on in the secret room, as the verse "The local Bishop he was there" was sung particularly enthusiastically.

I was mostly sat at the back of the room only chipping in when they asked for intel on a road, location or something if I was not able to answer their questions, I could call people that could help get the information. I enjoyed my time with these men but my presence was mainly spent supplying endless cups of tea and biscuits for them.

After a full hard day of work, there was a reasonable plan in place. I had given Dave and his team everything I had and there wasn't much else I could do, I was just a figure lurking at the back of the room, there to sort out any logistical problems such as arrange the Chilean contacts to liaise with the group on the extraction phase. One problem that arose quite early in the day was communication (coms), how the group would keep in touch with either the battle group or the British at home. The paras did not, in those days have a system that could circumvent the world. I called "C" at Century House again. His advice was to integrate with the SAS in Hereford, they could call anywhere in the world using their own network. So, at the end of the day, the whole office setup had to be picked up, dumped into a van and driven to Hereford where facilities and expertise were waiting at the Bradbury Lines in Hereford. The Bradbury Lines would be renamed after the Falklands war to Stirling Lines, which is how people know it today, in honour of the regiment's founder, Colonel David Stirling.

For the coms to work properly and safely, a coms expert had to be brought in from the SAS. Like Cheltenham, one of the few remaining SAS men joined us from 18 Signal Regiment, 264 (SAS) Signal Squadron.

Kev was Welsh, what can you say, as long as there were no sheep to distract him, he would do a great job. Full of humour, a brilliant intelligence, as well as brave and tough. Once the initial banter was over, he jelled with the Paras perfectly, despite being from a Signals background and Welsh and when he was excited none of us could understand a word he was saying because of his accent. Why wouldn't you like him.

This meant one of the Paras had to drop out of the kidnap group, but it was decided he would stay at Hereford as a logistical and supply runner and backup just in case of illness or injury. A discussion had taken place that he could be the driver, but in the end, four armed men and an old lady were enough for any vehicle, five people would be too many.

The small group had to have an identity, we couldn't keep referring to us as the kidnap group. We stood around the table and for a moment in the busy office, military humour came to the fore. As the Operation had been allocated the name Saponify, I explained that the word described the process of making soap. The guys thought it would be good to call the group something associated with soap and cleaning. All kind of humorous suggestions were put forward, and we had a great laugh coming up with names that got more and more ridiculous, we didn't really have time to waste like this, Dave called a halt to the fun. Someone did suggest an association with Widow Twanky a washerwoman from the Aladdin pantomime, but this was poo-pooed as we thought it would get altered to the Twankers, too close to the derogative slang word. Someone said that he had seen Les Dawson playing Widow Twanky just before Christmas, so it was decided we were the Dawsons, Dawson 1 would be the group's call sign.

Again, I was no military expert, so there was little I could do now the intelligence had been supplied, but I hung around for a bit in case any more calls to London were needed.

One part I did play, was Eva Braun in a rehearsal of the actual kidnap. The SAS practice every aspect of a job, if a house was going to be cleared then a mock building is erected using plans obtained. We didn't have that luxury. They wanted to know everything, what way did a door open, how did the door locks operate, if they didn't know, then they'd rehearse all directions. If a car was going to be used to extract from Argentina, then they wanted to know what car, where were the switches, how did the doors and windows open. The details they went through was incredible. For the kidnap rehearsal, they wanted someone to act as Eva Braun. They decided that I should play the part. I think it was also to demonstrate to me what they would be going through, and they were expecting me to panic when they told me it would be a live round rehearsal. Partly for realism and partly to take the piss, they made me wear a long dress just as they expected Braun to be wearing. This would let them see if she would trip on the long dress or catch on something, at least that's what they told me. We did not have blueprints or plans of her house, but a mock-up was built of wood in less than a day on best guesswork from photos of the town that I gathered for them. I was sat in a room at a table in the mock house, minding my own business, there was one bodyguard in another room played by an office clerk found hanging about somewhere. The rehearsal began. With no warning the lights went out, the room plunged into complete and total darkness. I heard nothing. Within four seconds the lights came back on and three dark characters fully dressed in black from head to toe had surrounded me, guns pointing at my head, they had moved into the room in total silence. In an instant I was picked up, my feet didn't seem to touch the ground, the pretend bodyguard heard a noise and began to react, live rounds were fired into the room with a flashbang grenade, the noise in the small rooms was deafening, the whole thing was very real. The bodyguard dropped to the floor as if he had been shot dead. In a moment, I found myself outside the mock house and shoved into a car, very roughly flattened to the floor and I laid there with two men sat on the back seat with their feet holding me down. There was no messing, no wasted movement. The car then sped just a few feet before coming to a halt and everyone piled out, exercise over. How they moved into that pitch-black room and surrounded me was simply amazing, I have no clue how they did it. The live rounds and the grenade kicked up dust so everyone knew what visibility to expect as well as get used to the commotion.

I climbed out of the car, somehow I had collected a cut and bruise on my eyebrow, I have no idea how I got it, the whole experience was a blur. I couldn't have been impressed more by these guys. The experience is something I will remember all my life.

I thought that the practice session was too loud and noisy. To my mind, stealth ought to be the best way to do the job, when I questioned it I was told it was more a demonstration rather than a practice. I think it was to test my nerve to see if I backed down from sitting in a room with live rounds being fired, but I'd done something like that before, it didn't scare me. Anyhow the men hadn't held a gun for a few days, and it was good to see them so happy making a big noise.

Day three, the mission was set. The infiltration method had been decided. Unfortunately, I cannot say how they got to Neuquén, that has to remain secret here. The SAS is particularly secretive about how they do some things and this is one of them and I could not, will not publish their methods without permission. None the less it was daring, brave and I can't admire those men enough.

Every map and picture of Neuquén had been studied, we had access to almost no satellite imagery as they were all in use at Buenos Aires and other military establishments and of course the Falklands themselves. Anyway, the team made do with what they had. They had weapons of several sorts, grenades, explosives to deal with locked doors, but everyone thought it would attract too much attention going loud and noisy.

Exfiltration, would be by the shortest route by road to Chile, only going off-road if any roadblocks were encountered. The men trusted my opinion that they would be looked after by friendly agents in Chile. Colonel Guilisasti had arranged for a truck to meet the men at the border, they would appear to be arrested, then transferred to an airport in the north of Chile. Here a flight would actually fly over Argentine airspace to Carrasco airport near Montevideo Uruguay. From there the extraction would take them to a place where Braun's admission would be recorded and sent to Israel and the USA, that would be either on a ship, Ascension Island or back in Britain whichever was quickest. She would end up in Britain come what may.

It's a long journey to Argentina and it had to be done in double-quick time before the British Fleet arrived on scene around the Falkland Islands and hostilities between the two began. It took some organising, but everything fell into place, as all else had on this operation.

After Eva Braun had been put into the limelight and her story told, she would be returned home by civilian routes. I thought there would be a massive frenzy when the public finds out they have been lied to, by the British but more so by the Americans. The hope that a deal will be struck for Braun to keep quiet and this would be in exchange for American help. Or, the Americans would join Israel in an effort to keep their 'end of World War II indiscretions' quiet. Either way, I saw it as win-win.

I returned to London to present the complete plan to Colin Figures Head of British Intelligence. He saw me the moment I returned to London, that was a good sign. I went over the operation with him and he thought the plan was doable and the fact he arranged a meeting with me within minutes was encouraging. He gave the go-ahead via the military hierarchy for the men to move into position. The moment Prime Minister Thatcher gave the order, the men would leap into action, grab Braun and move to the selected place of safety. Within days we planned the Argentinians would see sense with three of the most powerful military countries putting pressure on them to withdraw, without a shot being fired, other than those fired in the initial firefights by the sixty Royal Marines stationed on the Island.

After a call to the PM, Colin Figures told me the instruction was to get everyone in place in Argentina, by then further talks with the Argentines would have taken place, then the final "Go" would be given. There was no time to lose, the Battle Fleet was closing. The Dawson team needed to get to Neuquén super-fast, overtaking the fleet of Navy battleships heading to the Falklands, get on the ground and in a position where the kidnap would take only seconds.

I called Dave and the team,

"Dave, we have a go, move to the target and wait eyes on. MT (Margret Thatcher) must give the final go-ahead. Do not make hands-on contact, repeat wait eyes on, do not make hands-on contact, MT must give the final go-ahead. Good luck to you all." Dave repeated back the command, a standard operating procedure, and said he'd see me back home. That was it, Operation Saponify was underway. My heart rate was super-fast, I had just committed good men to go into enemy territory and place themselves in danger.

I returned to my office, Karen was there as always, I swear she never went home. I told her the news that the operation was underway. She came close to me and gave me a big hug, she could read my emotions so well.

"Well done, you've done an amazing job to get this organised in no time at all." she whispered.

"It wasn't me it was the guys in the team, they were simply amazing, they deserve a medal for what they've done over the last few days. I am so nervous for those guys, they're on their way. If any of them get hurt, I'm going to feel awful." I said looking at the floor.

"Come on time to go home." Karen said, "we should relax at home together." I had finished with Janine in 1979. I was a free agent, why not. I loved being with Karen and despite being told we could not be together, right now I didn't care and neither did Karen. Karen would be the best thing for me right now.

We went to her home by underground train, it was just one stop to Elephant and Castle where it was a short walk to her flat. Once inside Karen went into the kitchen to cook a nice dinner for us. She had a new flatmate Penny, I'd not met her before as I hadn't been to the flat for a while. Penny worked for the Intelligence Service at Century House too, it was always easier for Karen to have someone in the same job and there were always people in the Service looking for digs. I was introduced as an Officer. Penny was quite plain compared to Jenny, and no one could ever look good standing next to Karen. She wasn't fazed by my rank, which I liked. Jenny had light brown hair, a thinnish face and very little sign of makeup. Plain ordinary clothing of a shirt top and trousers, pleasant enough in character, but not my type. Penny didn't show any surprise that we were together, I guessed Karen had told her our history, she was pleasant enough to talk to and in no time at all following a few gin and tonics, I was once more relaxed.

Karen invited her to join us for dinner and we enjoyed a very pleasant evening. Of course, the conversation subject, as always, somehow got on to sex. Penny had moved from Hampshire to London and her relationship had ended with her partner, purely because of the distance and the workload staff have at Century House.

"Has Penny told you that she has an unusual hobby?" Karen asked me.

"No, what is it?" I asked.

"She does a Burlesque dance routine at a club in Acton, tell him about it Penny."

"I've never heard of Burlesque, what is it, like Jazz or the Charleston or something?" I asked.

"Ha ha, no Andy, I can't believe you've not heard of it. It is a very old form of entertainment, I think it dates back to the 17th century." Penny educated me.

"No, I can honestly say I've never heard of it. So, what kind of entertainment, is it like pantomime or something?" I asked.

"No, Burlesque can be applied to literature, music and theatre. It's often a humorous parody or pastiche of serious dramatic or classical works. It was partly derived from the English tradition of pantomime." Penny went on.

"I can't even begin to think what you do." I replied.

"After dinner, why don't you give us a show?" Karen suggested.

"Well, it takes ages to do my make-up and get dressed up." Penny said.

"While Andy and I clear up the dinner, you go get dressed and we'd love to see your act." I couldn't even imagine what the act was, a dancing pantomime parody! Whatever was that? Penny seemed so plain and quite shy, I couldn't imagine her on stage entertaining people, none the less I looked forward to seeing what she did.

Dinner was superb as always, if Karen wanted a career change I'm sure she would have made an excellent chef. The wine flowed and all thoughts of the Dawsons were stowed away in the back of my mind. It became a great evening like all evenings were when I spent them with Karen. She knew how to have a good time and could make me feel happy always. She had done a great job helping me when I had become very depressed after I split up from Janine.

Karen was right there for me, spending time with me, I don't know how I'd have got through it without her. The feelings of hopelessness were so strong and this job always interfered with my love life, I could see no way that the two could co-exist together. How could I live a life of lies, no one would ever want to be with me. Karen was the most perfect companion, and we could not be together as a couple. In Karen's company, I was at my happiest.

As soon as we finished eating, Penny prepared some music and went to her room to dress for the show. She disappeared into her room for ages. Karen and I cleared the table and did the dishes, then sat on the sofa in the lounge talking about anything apart from work. It must have taken Penny an hour to prepare. Finally, she called from the hallway connecting her bedroom to the lounge. Karen switched on the music Penny had prepared, What Ever Lola Wants by Carmen McRae, and Penny appeared from the hallway. She moved incredibly well to the music, dressed in high heels, thigh-length black stockings held up with suspenders, a red and black pleated bust corset with a black tutu skirt attached to it, a ribbon around her chest under her boobs with a bow on the front, the bow helped to increase the size of her otherwise flat chest. A pair of red elbow-length gloves and a black feather design fascinator on her classical victory roll hairstyle from the Second World War era. A black feather boa completed the look. She danced in front of us looking very serious about her hobby. I can't say it was any kind of a turn on for me, her routine didn't titillate me in any way, but I could see she was very skilled as she described the song in dance. Slowly stripping off her long gloves using her teeth and in perfect timing to the music, I had no idea that burlesque was actually a strip. Down she got onto the floor and flexed her legs at impossible angles to take off her stockings. Then to stand moving to the music to untie the front ribbon bow in what was meant to be a sexy way. Then Penny continued to unbutton her corset. Karen was giving her full encouragement with whoops and cheers, clapping at every move. I thought I'd better show appreciation to be polite and joined in with whatever Karen did, though I just didn't get it.

Her corset was removed, dancing and turning at particular moments to hide the reveal. Under the corset, red bra and big old-fashioned knickers sparkling with sequins. She danced and pranced about very skilfully timing every move to the music, it must have taken a lot of time to practice this routine. More dancing around to remove the huge knickers revealing a shimmering thong that as she turned looked most uncomfortable as the string disappeared from view into her bum crack, I wondered how she could bear the pain and look so happy about it as she moved around, it must have chaffed a lot. Penny did have nicely shaped legs and a peachy bum though. Finally, at last, the routine was concluded by her bra being teasingly removed, revealing an almost flat chest with two shiny pasties stuck over her nipples. I recall thinking,

"Please don't peel those off it will hurt and it's really not worth the pain." There was a quick pause as if to say 'ta-dah look at me' and then dashed back into the hallway out of sight. Karen leapt to her feet applauding and cheering, out of appreciation for the effort, I copied and cheered a little less enthusiastically. Karen was shouting for more, I looked at her and silently gave a look that said no more please. Penny reappeared wearing a dressing gown smiling, I put on a fake smile and said encouraging words only because it seemed appropriate. I found it a little absurd, not my thing at all, but I can appreciate that anyone with such a hobby or interest is a better person for it. Karen nudged me and asked me,

"What did you think of it Andy, it's beautiful isn't it?"

"I love your outfit Penny very sexy." what else could I say to be polite! "Yes, we must come and see the whole show sometime." thinking it would be my worst night out.

Encouraged by Karen, Penny agreed to do another dance, I fetched a strong gin and tonic to help alleviate the thought of it. I never thought I would not enjoy a girl stripping just for me, this was a first. I don't know why. Penny prepared the next song before disappearing into her room, happy that we appeared to love her act and keen to show us more.

As soon as she was out of sight, I appealed to Karen quietly so as not to offend Penny,

"Nooo, please no more after this one, I'm not enjoying it at all."

Karen took it the wrong way and grabbed my crotch,

"Why is it making you hard?"

"No, the opposite." I said and she removed her hand having found nothing exciting.

"I like it, the outfits and the style, it's lovely. It's not supposed to be dirty like a strip club." offered Karen, "never mind, try to enjoy it because it works for me and you will like it later, it's getting me horny as hell."

"Sometimes I think you are more lesbian than straight. Have you and Penny done it yet?"

Karen wagged a finger at me as she said.

"No, Jenny was one time only, don't you go getting any ideas."

"Now that memory makes me horny." I joked. It earned me a slap to my thigh as we sat on the sofa, waiting long enough to need another drink. After far too long a time, the call finally came to start the music, Karen jumped up and cheered even louder, just to show me how much she was enjoying the show.

Penny appeared again moving brilliantly to the music, 'I Want My Fanny Brown' by Wynonie Harris. Once I heard the lyrics I was killing myself laughing, Karen thought it was because the show was better this time around and Penny seemed encouraged by my joy. This time she was dressed in a long tight-fitting silver sparkling dress with a long split up the front to just below her crotch. Long elbow-length white gloves, high heels, her hair still in the same style but this time with a tall pink feathered headdress that had a train all the way down her back to knee level as I imagine a Moulin Rouge dancer would wear or maybe even a drag act. It must have cost hundreds. It was too tall for the room and rubbed the ceiling as she danced, which did spoil the act a little, she did look a little sexier this time, but maybe I was just over the shock of what burlesque was about. Penny did her dance routine keeping a lot of it laying on the floor kicking her legs at the craziest angles through the split in the dress. I have to admit she was clever at what she did and I guess she would have been appreciated by the burlesque following.

Again, she slowly undressed, the headdress first to make things easier, then the dress slowly came off, to reveal thigh-length stockings attached to her knickers with straps and buckles, the outfit was much sexier this time, but I still didn't get it. Karen was hollering and cheering loudly, I joined in, not wanting to appear rude. She was good at timing, I'll give Penny that, every move in time with the music. The routine was a little more cheeky, funny and interesting. The ridiculous lyrics repeating the line "I want my Fanny Brown." made me giggle every time. Her sparkling gold bra came off in the manner of a stripper to reveal, tassels, attached somehow over her nipples. She danced twirling the tassels together and in opposite directions, shaking her shoulders to get them to spin. A skill I'd not seen before. She did it for about ten seconds before the music ended. Karen and I stood to applaud again as Penny disappeared from view into the hallway. She came back a moment later in her dressing gown asking what we thought. I was a little more impressed this time, she could get her legs up straight to her ears, a move I'd not seen before, it must have taken years of practice to achieve such a level, so I appreciated that part of the act. Karen was curious how Penny got the tassels to spin so well and asked if she could give it a go. I think the drink was helping a little too. The girls disappeared off to Penny's room for Karen to try a pair of the tassels. They reappeared a couple of minutes later, both in panties and tassels only. Karen asked me,

"What do you think Andy, can I do it?" and the two girls proceeded to shake their chests to spin the tassels. Penny could do it perfectly, Karen, with her double D boobs nearly knocked herself out with a blow to her chin from one tassel on a huge tit. She couldn't master it at all and looked quite disappointed that she had failed. For me, this was the best part of the evening so far. Two girls shaking their boobs together. We had a laugh, I suggested Karen try a full act. But she declined on a promise from Penny that she would give her some lessons another time. It was good exercise after all.

I stayed the night with Karen. She had clearly been turned on by the show, her sex was particularly enthusiastic and lasted all night. We slept only a couple of hours and were woken by Penny at 9am bringing us a cup of tea each, which was nice of her.

Next day I thought it prudent to put in an appearance at my father's business. I didn't have to make excuses to him as he knew full well what I got up to in my "other" life. He was the only person in my family and friend circle that did. A secret he kept to his grave. It was hard to concentrate on work, I kept hearing the news on the radio about the British preparations for the war. I could only think where the Dawson's were, I hoped everything was going according to plan. At that time I lived in Heronsgate, near Chorleywood, Hertfordshire, I was lodging in a room after Janine and I broke up and I had to sell our property in Watford. By sheer coincidence, the house where I lodged during the Second World War had been a highly top-secret base for spies, and I saw the irony in that. Heronsgate was only a mile and a half from the printing factory. The house where I stayed was very large but I had no private telephone where I could receive calls, so for most of the time it took the guys to get into position in Argentina I more or less lived at the factory. At least I caught up with my work there and I felt less guilty about leaving it to others. At 10am (6am Argentine time) a few days later, I received a call from Hereford, they had received coms that the men were camped out in a van in sight of Eva Braun's home. They had seen lights on in the house and two of them were manoeuvring to observe who the occupant may be. Immediately, I sped back to London to take calls in my own office now things were hotting up.

I called "C" and informed him that the men had successfully located the house and it was occupied, we were waiting for confirmation of the occupants.

"As soon as it is confirmed to be Braun, I will inform the PM." he told me. This was so exciting, it called for a cup of tea, Karen joined me in my office equally as excited and we waited, staring in near silence at the phone on my desk. We jumped out of our skin when it rang, it was Hereford, I was informed the men had to wait until dark to move onto the house, they could not do it in daylight. It would be another whole day of waiting. At some point during the day, I have no idea what time it was, my phone rang again. It was "C".

"Andy, can you come up to my office, some disturbing news." he told me.

"On my way." I hung up and went up to his office. I was shown straight in where a few other people were gathered, they all looked at me as I entered, none had happy faces. I was introduced to the others, one of whom was a handler for agents in Argentina, I wasn't surprised by his presence, another was an Israeli expert. I was introduced to him, and we shook hands.

"This is going to be bad news Andy." Colin Figures began, "The Israeli's are selling arms to Argentina, they've sided with them. We believe the arms are flowing through Peru. I won't go into the full history of events now, but this gives us a bit of a problem with your operation doesn't it. The Israelis won't stop selling arms just because Hitler lived there, we think they probably know anyway."

"Shall I recall the team?" I asked.

"No, I will take it to the PM, discuss with her, she knows the Israelis well, she can decide. I'm off there now, I'll call you shortly." this could not have been a bigger blow for me. It made me feel a bit silly among those present, I wished I wasn't so independent and had talked more to others, but I couldn't break the habit of my lifetime. I walked back to my office so despondent. I arrived and told Karen the news. We sat together, nothing much we could do, I wasn't angry, countries do what is best for them, but it was depressing that all the work right from the very beginning was beginning to look like a waste of time.

"What is the point of leaving those men in danger." I said to Karen.

"Is the van stolen?" she asked me.

"No, it was left somewhere for them to pick up by an agent on the ground, they won't be stopped by the police because they think it's a stolen vehicle." I answered.

My phone rang, Karen transferred the call to my desk, it was Hereford,

"The Dawson's have reported sighting the target, she has gone shopping and they say it's an ideal opportunity to grab her. Do they still hold?"

"Hold, hold, hold." I repeated the command so there was no misunderstanding.

"Understood, hold, hold, hold." and the guy hung up.

"Christ, this is stupid." I said to Karen, "I need to speak to "C" again, call him please." I spoke to Colin again and informed him of the situation,

"Ok, I'll go put this to the PM, I understand she is in a COBR meeting I'll try to get to her there, we can't leave those men hanging around it's ridiculous."

"Thanks." I said and hung up. These were tense times I was feeling the most tension I've ever felt then and since. A few minutes later my phone rang again, it was Colin's secretary, Karen took the call from her.

"C wants you to know he is on his way to the PM now." Karen informed me.

I knew in my heart that the operation was more or less dead, I felt this was false hope Colin was taking to the PM. I sat in my office feeling there would only be one answer, it was just a matter of time before that answer came. What was the point of the operation now that we knew that the Israelis had sided with Argentina and was actively selling arms to them. I spent some time double-checking the escape route the guys would use, with or without an extra passenger. Colonel Guilisasti had been so useful, without him the operation could not be possible, or at least far riskier than it was, I decided that I would thank him for his assistance with a present that would keep him on board with MI6.

I continued to wait for the PM to give her answer for the operation to go ahead.

Let There Be War

Timeline - April 1982.

I sat in my office at Century House, London, headquarters of the British Secret Intelligence Overseas, or MI6 as it is known. I was impatient and nervous. This was my first major operation, even though I'd been working here for ten years. I glanced at Karen, my secretary, in her room through the connecting door. She looked stunningly beautiful and busy as always. I could see she was equally as nervous. She saw that I was too. I don't know why I was nervous it wasn't my life on the line.

"Tea or coffee?" Karen asked me.

"Tea please." I replied, she asked, mainly for something to do while we waited for the go-ahead from "C."

Colin Figures "C" was the current Head of MI6, the fourth Head I had known since I joined the Service in 1971. We got on well together now and I knew he was doing his best to persuade the British Prime Minister (P.M.) Margaret Thatcher to agree to give my operation the go-ahead.

Operation Saponify, as it had been designated could prevent the coming war and lives lost. "C" was all for it too. Now he was presenting the plan to the P.M. in a Cabinet Office Briefing Room in Whitehall, more commonly known by the acronym COBR. He wanted to meet her alone, he felt he had more chance for it to be given the go-ahead that way. The only time available to meet her was just before an urgent COBR meeting she had scheduled. It was a very busy time of course.

I was nervous because I had a combined Para/SAS team waiting, good men, brave men. The team had been selected from the few SAS and Paras that had not yet been deployed to join the fight that was inevitably coming. Some operations were already underway, unless my plan, my operation, could prevent the war.

Time seemed to be going so slowly, the SAS team, a troop of four, were in position, they had eyes on the subject, ready to go. All I had to do was pick up my phone, call the SAS base at Hereford and the call would be forwarded via their own network to the men on the ground. Dawson 1 were in a hostile city, their bravery was beyond words.

Waiting, waiting, my mind going through every part of my plan, had I thought of everything, would it work, what could go wrong?

My cup of tea arrived, Karen sat down on the office sofa with me, she knew her presence may help to calm my nerves. Karen was seven years my senior, yet we had been in love almost from the first day we met. It was hard for any man not to fall for this woman. Stunningly beautiful, sexy as hell, always calm and as professional as anyone could be. I was so lucky to have her assigned to me, we worked well together, shared the same sense of humour, and I guess the most important thing, she got the job done. I couldn't do my job with anyone else, she had helped me be successful at my job. I loved her in every way.

We chitchatted about nothing important, trying to pass the time, it was probably only an hour or so, I had no idea, it seemed like days. Whitehall is only a mile and a half away, normally nine minutes' drive, Colin had travelled there in his chauffeur-driven fast car.

Eventually, the phone buzzed, Karen picked up, answered as usual and pressed the button on her phone to transfer to mine. The look on her face, eyes looking up, told me it was "C." His voice familiar,

"Andy, Colin, my office please."

"Sure as quick as I can, see you in a moment."

I hung up the phone and spoke slightly angrily,

"Why is he wasting time asking me to his office?" I spoke toward Karen but I was talking aloud to myself.

"Why didn't he stop here on his way up, time is imperative here."

I walked as fast as I could and took the escalator up to C's floor. I made my way to his reception office, announced myself to his secretary who ushered me immediately to C's room. Colin was sat waiting on one of his two sofas, he pointed to the opposite sofa where I sat down excited, heart rate so fast and loud I could hear it.

Colin spoke,

"Andy, I'm sorry. The PM wants to make a point, she wants to go to war. I do see her point, Britain can't be seen to act cowardly, every country in the world is watching, while I commend your operation, we have to do it the hard way. Again, I'm sorry. Recall the men in field and close it all down. Get them home safely."

"Jesus, she wants good men to die, just to make a point!" I said, very disappointed all my work was going to waste.

"I won't argue with you, the decision has been made, the PM can't be persuaded otherwise, I've tried, I can't say I'm not disappointed." Colin spoke as the obedient servant to the PM, even though I knew he often pushed matters his way in a presentation such as the one he had just given on my behalf.

"Cannon fodder, that's all we are. Disposable." I started to get angry, I don't get angry.

"It's what soldiers do." Colin replied coldly.

"I don't want hundreds, maybe thousands of deaths on my conscience, I'm probably the only person in this building from a working-class background, I have friends that may die." I exclaimed.

"Don't ever think you are alone in that. We all know people that are on their way, as we speak boarding ships right now." his voice starting to show signs of impatience with me.

"Well, stuff it, we should at least try to prevent this war, isn't that what we all work for?"

With that, I stood up to leave, Colin misunderstood my last sentence, thinking I was going to do something stupid against orders. I wouldn't, but that's what he thought.

As I left his room, he shouted after me,

"Andy, shut it down, don't do anything stupid."

I arrived back at my office, by now I was quite angry, I don't get angry. Karen looked at me and immediately knew it was bad news, is my face that transparent? I sat at my desk thinking what a waste of time and resources this was, the danger those men had put themselves in to get eyes on the target, ready to go into action and kidnap Eva Braun. I sat there thinking about how best to break the news to them.

There was a commotion in the hallway outside, three men burst into my office, Colin Figures between two security guards, their guns were drawn, and aimed at me. These guys were ex-special forces, likely SAS or SBS, I knew they would shoot if ordered. I sat now quite calmly at my desk.

"Andy, do not go against orders, you are to comply." Colin misunderstanding my intentions completely, "Pick up that phone and I will order you shot, right here." I looked toward Karen, her face in a state of shock, not knowing yet what the order was. She didn't want to witness me being shot in front of her, her head nodding slowly in the negative toward me.

I don't ever respond to bullies or threats, Colin wasn't a bully in this instance, but he had misunderstood my last comment to him, I knew he was wrong to do this, my instinct wouldn't allow me to do as I was being told.

I picked up my phone and made the necessary call to Hereford for the last time. In defiance of the command not to pick up my phone, I stared into the eyes of Colin Figures as I slowly and deliberately lifted the receiver with two handguns pointing at me.

I gave the order to the guy on the other end to stand the men down and return empty-handed to the UK. That was the end of Operation Saponify. Colin Figures returned amazingly calm after I defied his order. I think he got the point that the order had to be phoned through to get the team out of Argentina and danger. The two security men stared at me in disbelief that I had deliberately challenged the order and faced certain death had Colin not have the presence of mind to wait until he saw I was calling to cancel the operation.

The Dawson's would use the route set up by the Chilean Colonel. Not for the last time during this conflict would he secretly, later not so secretly, allow British servicemen to pass through his country to safety from Argentina.

In fact, the Dawson's did not return to the UK. With great credit they found their respective units somehow and took part in the conflict that they would otherwise have missed being stuck at home. Amazing soldiers that they were.

As for the Colonel in Chile, when the war was over and his help with routes out of Argentina was no longer required, he continued to be helpful to Britain. I arranged for money in the form of a mortgage to be set up for him to continue to pay the same rate as his current mortgage. This meant he could move into a beautiful house in the suburbs of Santiago, the balance was paid by the British. This was so that there was no easy paper trail to tie him to money from us. He was to be one of the most useful agents I controlled, and I have no qualms that he deserved his new house. He contacted me once to ask if I could arrange for the two escort girls to visit his house. I passed him the number of the escort agency, but I have no idea if they ever went to visit. I'm sure his swimming pool would have looked great with bikini-clad girls lounging around it like some Hollywood movie. I promised him I would visit myself one day, it never happened as a few months later I met Julie, who soon became my wife. Julie never knew of my work in MI6, all she knew was I worked at my father's printing company. My lies continued.

Karen and I, of course, remained best friends and she was my secretary until my career ended in 1988.

Eva Braun died in Buenos Aires, Argentina, 2008.

Hitler's ashes were scattered by a Nazi uniformed loyal servant over the graves of his two favourite pet dogs in a pine forest with a view of a lake, Argentina.

Witnessed by no one…

In another Love

November 1977, my friend Martin and I were together one day and we went to invite his girlfriend to his 21st birthday party. Martin's girlfriend (another Karen for ease of writing I'll call her Karen G.), wasn't at home at the time, but her sister was. Janine was 17 years old, we didn't know Karen G. had a sister, quite a looker, so we invited her too. I liked her immediately and Janine and I started seeing each other as friends. At last, I could put the pain of separation from Karen my secretary behind me and move forward in a new relationship.

Martin a Royal Marine was helpful, as kids, we had lived in the same street in Maple Cross. Because of an injury to his leg in training, he was posted to Combined Task Force (CTF) 345 at Northwood, then had a posting at the Ministry of Defence (MOD) London, which proved useful to me in 1982 during the Falklands War, I'd sometimes get information before anyone at MI6. One such piece of information was regarding the death of another friend from Rickmansworth Grammar School, Laurence Watts, we affectionately knew him as Polly Watts due to his rather parrot size and shaped nose.

Corporal Laurence WATTS, 42 Commando, Royal Marines. Date of Death: 11/12 June 1982. During the attack on Mount Harriett, as a section commander, he was clearing an Argentinian bivouac whose occupants were armed with rifles. He was so close he was actually pushing a rifle away when he was shot in the neck. He fell back, bleeding badly, but returned to the attack, firing his rifle, only to be shot again, the bullet passing through his radio set and then through his heart.

Martin informed me of Polly's death because it was highly likely I may bump into his younger brother, a Captain in the Marines. It would have been embarrassing if I had said anything before his family had been informed officially.

Janine was a lovely girl, quite pretty, attractive, very funny and intelligent. Short brown hair, attractive figure, curvy in all the right places. She rode a motorbike, on which she became quite noticeable wearing her black flocked helmet. I had it flocked for her as the company next to the printing works did that kind of thing. I had no idea if it was legal. Her hobby was diving, she was a member of the Watford Diving Club. We spent several weekends at Swanage on club dives, where, while she was diving with her sister and club mates, I'd spend time ashore with the wives. I have learnt to dive since, but it's not a sport I enjoy.

We spent all our spare time together, as young lovers should. Always going places and to parties, it didn't take long for me to pluck up the courage to ask her to marry me, and in 1979 I did just that. Thinking about it now, the way I proposed was unbelievably corny. I bought her a microwave for Christmas, unpacked it carefully, and fixed the ring inside the microwave onto the plate, re-packed it carefully good as new. I can't think what she must have thought about such an awful impersonal present, but it didn't take her long to find the ring inside. Thankfully, she said yes. She was 19 and I 24.

We bought a small one-bedroom ground floor flat 137 Gladstone Road, Watford. It was so small I had to post my windsurfer mast through the front window into the lounge, as it was too long to get through any door and round the corridor to store somewhere. I couldn't keep it outside as there was nowhere safe to keep the mast and board and the flat had no garden.

The flat backed onto the Watford main railway line, it was difficult to sleep at night with the noise of trains, and at about 3 am a few times a week the nuclear waste train would creep by at dead slow pace taking forever to pass.

Our wedding plans began to get organised. The church was booked, cars, wedding reception venue and invites sent out. One day, out of the blue, Janine wouldn't answer her phone. I didn't know what was going on. A few days later, she broke the news to me that she didn't feel ready to marry, she was too young. I was absolutely heartbroken. I took a few days off work to try to sort things out, I didn't say why I needed the time off. Nobody could explain to me what had happened, the wedding plans had to be cancelled. I went into a deep depression, alone in the flat we had bought together.

After a few days, my ever-faithful secretary telephoned, it was good to hear a kind voice again. People were wondering in London if I was safe. I had never disappeared without the knowledge of my masters in London. She asked if it would be ok for her and John my former mentor to come round, I reluctantly agreed, saying I wasn't good company, but I knew I had to snap out of my solitary depression. Karen arrived alone, John had been called away at the last minute. I had just been dumped by one girl I loved and here was another beautiful girl that I couldn't get closer to either. She tried so hard to make me feel good. She was so sweet, she made me cups of tea, and stayed with me for longer than she needed to. We sat on the sofa watching TV drinking tea, she was being a good friend as always. Occasionally we talked about work, but nothing heavy, we just nattered about what was going on. She was just a good friend and the only one that turned up to see me, out of all of my group of friends. She offered to help cancel the wedding arrangements, but my parents had that in hand. It wasn't clear to me if she could help, but at the end of the day, she showed she was a good friend as well as being fantastic at her job. I couldn't have asked any more from her, all she did was show kindness and genuine concern, sat with me for hours and hours, but the reality was, it just hurt more that two girls I loved so much did not, or could not, want me.

I didn't see Janine ever again. Until about 2008. She found me on Facebook. She sent me a message. "Hello, do you remember me?"

How could I not? Her second question was: "Do you forgive me?"

I replied "Of course, there is nothing to forgive." unsure of her motive, I didn't want to give her any idea that she had damaged me deeply. I looked into her history, saw how badly it had gone for her after we parted. Divorced with two children, Janine had a lot of personal problems. Her life didn't look good at all. Time had almost healed my wounds, but unfortunately, my bitterness was quite deep, my thoughts at that moment were quite bitter, "yeah, you got what you deserved." I thought to myself. But now, I think differently. Everyone makes choices for a reason, you cannot go through life thinking about how life *might* have been. If it goes well, good for you. If it goes wrong, learn the lesson, pick yourself up, dust yourself down and try something else. Janine and I had a great time together and she has given me many great memories that will last my lifetime. We now text each other occasionally, I no longer feel any animosity toward her, and I thank her for finding me again, even though we have never met.

Love And Marriage

I met Julie at a friend's wedding. Jo and Sue had invited me to their wedding in May 1982. Jo was the friend at school that cut his head and fell from the first floor as we were trying to enter the school one early morning. A large group of friends were going to the wedding, and I agreed to take a girl I knew, Michelle, in my car. Michelle liked me but I felt she wasn't my type. But we were friends, there wasn't a reason not to be, she was a pleasant person. The wedding reception in the evening was at Moor Park Golf Course near Rickmansworth. The clubhouse is a beautiful mansion house in the grounds of the golf course. It was a great event, entertaining speeches, with good food, and drink. In the evening there was music and dancing. One of Michelle's friends, Julie, spent most of the time with Michelle and me. I had met Julie before, she had come with Michelle to the Half-Way House pub, Mill End, just outside Rickmansworth a few times, where our group of friends met most weeks. We got on well that night too. Julie didn't have a lift home, so I offered to take her back to Croxley Green in my car at the end of the evening. As she got out of my car, we arranged to see each other again sometime soon. We started to date, at first, I didn't think she was my type and wasn't sure if we should get any closer, maybe just remain friends. But Julie persisted and we became boyfriend and girlfriend soon after. A few years later I proposed to her. Ever aware that I had been dumped at that point in my relationship with Janine, I didn't really want that kind of hurt again, so I was a little wary of the idea. We rented a flat together, which was a nice, but fairly old flat in Moor Lane Crossing, just on the edge of Croxley Moor. In the summer it was nice living next to the moor, we'd go for barbeques by the river Gade that ran through the moor and parallel to the Grand Union canal. In the winter though, it was cold. Our heating was from a single open fire in the lounge. One winter it was so cold our toothpaste froze in the bathroom. We finally married at All Saints Church, Croxley Green. Our wedding reception was at the Watersmeet centre in Rickmansworth. We honeymooned in Padstow, Cornwall. Not long after, we bought a house together in Rowland Way, Aylesbury, Buckinghamshire. An ever-growing dormitory town, the town centre was an old market town, around its perimeter housing estate after housing estate expanded and grew. Most people that lived there commuted into

London or Oxford. Our first daughter Joanne was born in July 1986 at the John Radcliff Hospital, Oxford.

For five years life was good for us at Aylesbury, but the town had little entertainment. Julie worked as a nurse, I commuted every day to work. I kept my real work from Julie, I don't know why it was just easier not to say anything to her. My thinking at the time was, how could I tell her that I was a spy? Imagine, you start going out with someone and they break the news to you that they are a spy, yeh that works. I'd just be accused of being a liar and fantasist.

She saw me leave for work in the company van belonging to the printing company. In reality, she had no idea where I was going. If I needed to go away for some time, I would tell her I was going sailing. I had a love for yachts as well as my speed boat and would go on sailing courses to complete my Day Skipper and Coastal Skipper certificates. These courses were attained by completing not only theory courses but many practical hours sailing were needed to qualify. This provided a good cover story.

Life was good with Julie, we had fun, worked hard and she tolerated me being absent from home with no question. Life with her was easy, it may have been much harder if I had been with someone less tolerant of me disappearing every now and then. I never felt any guilt for always lying to her about my job and where I was working. I felt my job was too important for guilt, maybe I should have treated her differently, who knows, it was just how it was and seemed right for me at the time.

Chris Curwen And Oleg Gordievsky

Christopher Curwen was Head of the Secret Intelligence Service (MI6) from 1985 to 1989. Curwen was awarded CMG in 1982 and KCMG in 1986. It was under Chris that the Service brought off one of its most spectacular coups, the extraction from Moscow of the agent Oleg Gordievsky. I cannot claim for one moment to have played any major part in the Gordievsky story, but the tiniest role that I did, does give me a modest claim to that historic event.

In brief, Gordievsky was recruited by SIS in 1974, Gordievsky was the British Secret Intelligence Service star source inside the KGB. He had provided valuable reports at a critical time in the Cold War, a period in which paranoia at the Kremlin had become so bad that the NATO 1983 Able Archer exercise had been misinterpreted in Moscow as a possible cover for a surprise attack on the Soviet Bloc. As well as producing enormous quantities of documents from the KGB station in London, where he had been posted in June 1982, Gordievsky had identified KGB personnel in British and Scandinavian departments and had shed light on dozens of past cases.

Gordievsky was summoned back to Moscow from London, supposedly for consultations. On his arrival, he realised that his apartment had been searched, and when he reached First Chief Directorate (FCD), headquarters he was accused of being a spy. When he denied it, his interrogators used drugs in an unsuccessful attempt to extract a confession, and he concluded that, although the KGB had been tipped off to his dual role, there was insufficient evidence to justify an arrest. Although he remained under constant surveillance, in late July, Gordievsky was able to shake off his watchers while jogging in a park and sent an emergency signal to SIS requesting a rescue.

His escape from Moscow is one of the greatest spy stories in history, there are books and TV films about it. The bravery of Viscount Asquith, MI6 Moscow station commander who drove the escape car and the coolness of his female assistant when she dropped a dirty nappy from their Saab car when they were stopped by a patrol, was, in my mind one of the greatest spy actions. The nappy distracted the sniffer dog from detecting Gordievsky hiding in the boot of the car.

Gordievsky was briefly accommodated at a country safe house in the Midlands, where Curwen visited him, and then at Fort Monckton, Gosport, where he underwent an 80-day debriefing conducted by SIS's principal Kremlinologist. Among Gordievsky's other visitors was the US Director of Central Intelligence, who was flown down to the fort for a lunch hosted by Curwen, a celebration of one of SIS's most impressive post-war coups. In all Gordievsky was spying for the UK for 10 years.

I was asked by Curwen to collect Gordievsky from the country safe house in the Midlands and drive him to Fort Monckton. I am able to say that I talked with and sat beside Gordievsky on that journey for a few hours.

Although Gordievsky's safe escape was a source of great pride for Curwen and his staff, there remained considerable concern about precisely how the agent had been compromised. One possibility was that, after so many setbacks, the KGB had worked out for itself that a mole had been at work within the organisation. Had Gordievsky's dual role somehow been leaked by a mole? It is now that I started to have suspicions that there may be a dangerous leak in MI6. A leak that later in my career will have near-fatal consequences for me.

The Falklands War

After my setback of Operation Saponify, I wasn't too upset. The Israelis were found to be selling arms to Argentina, so there was doubt that the plan would work. But, I found other useful ways to help the British cause.

In April 1982 Argentina invaded the Falkland Islands. Argentina had claimed sovereignty over the islands for many years and their ruling military junta did not believe that Britain would attempt to regain the islands by force. Britain, under the leadership of Margaret Thatcher, undertook the extraordinary feat of assembling and sending a task force of warships and rapidly refitted merchant ships to the Falklands. Despite the huge distance involved, the Falklands were 8,000 miles away in the South Atlantic, the task force reached the Falklands in early May. On 2nd May, the Royal Navy submarine HMS Conqueror sank the Argentinian cruiser General Belgrano, with the loss of over 300 of her crew. After this incident, Argentinian ships remained in port. However, the Argentinian air force still posed a significant threat. The Royal Navy lost several warships to attacks by Argentinian aircraft. Super Étendard warplanes were armed with missiles most significantly of which was the French manufactured Exocet missile. In May 1982 these Exocet missiles were used to strike Britain's HMS Sheffield and Atlantic Conveyor, with the loss of 32 British lives, near panic ensued in London. It became imperative to stop further British losses due to Exocet missiles.

At the start of the conflict, France's president, Francois Mitterrand, had come to Britain's aid by declaring an embargo on French arms sales and assistance to Argentina. He also gave permission for the Falklands-bound British fleet to use French port facilities in West Africa, as well as providing London with detailed information about planes and weaponry his country had sold to Argentina. Paris also co-operated with extensive British efforts to stop Argentina acquiring any more Exocets on the world's arms market. There was, however, a feeling, if not proof that France was acting in a somewhat duplicitous way. It came to my knowledge that there was a French technical team in Argentina assisting the air force to fix some missile launchers, three of the launchers had failed to work. Thanks to the work of the French, the Argentinians were able to launch Exocets at British forces from three previously faulty missile launchers.

The British knew that Argentina had only five Exocet missiles. Plans were put into place to destroy the three remaining Exocet missiles which Argentina still had in its possession. Operation Mikado was the code name of the military plan by the United Kingdom to use Special Air Service (SAS) troops to attack the home base of Argentina's five Étendard strike fighters at Río Grande, Tierra del Fuego. The man in charge of the planning was Brigadier Peter de la Billière, then Head of the SAS. He proposed an operation similar to Operation Entebbe, which consisted of landing 55 SAS soldiers in two Lockheed C-130 Hercules aircraft directly on the runway at Rio Grande. The aim of the operation was to destroy the three remaining Exocet missiles that Argentina had in its possession, and the aircraft that carried them, and to kill the pilots in their quarters.

Operation Plum Duff, a preliminary reconnaissance mission on Río Grande, was launched from HMS Invincible on the night of 17/18 May, as a prelude to the attack. The operation consisted of transporting by helicopter a small SAS team to the Argentine side of Tierra del Fuego. The team would then march to the Rio Grande air base and proceed to set up an observation post to collect intelligence on the base before the main assault. The helicopter would be operating to the limits of its range, which made some call it a suicide mission. During the flight it was necessary to divert to avoid a drilling rig adding twenty minutes to the flight and, nearing the coast, dense fog had reduced visibility forcing the pilot to land. The helicopter was destroyed and the pilots after several nights walk were picked up by Chilean Military and returned to British Officials. Operation Plum Duff was abandoned. The Chilean armed forces had a long and close relationship with Britain and the Chilean junta kept quiet.

What could the British do about the Exocet threat? MI6 was working on the problem in the background, and it fell to us to submit plans. John Nott, the Secretary of State for Defence at the time of the war authorised an operation, some have described it as out of a James Bond movie. MI6 launched an elaborate deception operation designed to convince the Argentinians that arms dealers were buying Exocets on their behalf when the real aim was to ensure no missiles were ever delivered, or, using technical advice supplied by the French, render them inoperable before reaching

Buenos Aires. It would reassure the Task Force once the five missiles in Argentine possession had been launched there could be no further Exocet attack.

The operation masterminded by an SIS Officer known as Anthony Baynham was to monitor the arms market using Tony Divall a former Royal Marine NCO who had an established an arms dealing business in Germany. Divall had previous associations with SIS. £16million of government money had been deposited in a bank to use for letters of credit. John Dutcher, an American dealer, had been employed by Divall to offer his services to Carlos Corti, a major personality in the Paris arms supply effort for Argentina. Corti had diplomatic status, he had already lost over $6million to a fraudulent deal in Holland. A deal was identified for twenty missiles at $1.5million each. Buyers in such deals generally show money is available through a letter of credit, while sellers deposit a performance bond. No performance bond was produced. Following furious negotiations, it was suggested that a meeting was set up at Orly Airport France. Nothing was brought to the meeting, but a substantial advance payment was demanded from the Argentinian. In a somewhat dramatic move, the buyers stormed out as no missiles were available for inspection by an expert on Corti's side either. The deal never went through, Corti was withdrawn by the Argentine Government before the fake deal went any further and more money was lost. From now on the British could identify and monitor all the Argentines players and their associates that were operating to effect a black market purchase. Arms deals could now be infiltrated. No Exocet missiles ever became available on the black market again during the conflict.

Another direction arms were reaching Argentina was through Israel. The Israeli Prime Minister Menachem Begin agreed to help Argentina during the Falklands War as revenge for Britain's crackdown on the Jewish Irgun during the British mandate of Palestine until the formation of Israel. Israel armed Argentina's military dictatorship with air-to-air missiles, fuel tanks for fighter bombers, gas masks and missile radar alert systems. Many components of these weapons were American. There is a law that prohibits the sale of any military component to third parties without the authorisation of the White House. Here again, my miss-trust of the Americans grew deeper. If the United States hadn't turned a blind eye, it would have been impossible for Israel to send such a large amount of weapons.

I was a conduit for several agents in France, Italy, and Chile and fed information to the Ministry of Defence and the Foreign Office. One SIS agent lost his life, after being part of the covert operations during the Falkland Island conflict. Probably due to a traitor within SIS itself. Mistrust of Americans and Israelis and my suspicions of a 'mole' regarding Gordievsky's position being compromised to the Russians were being cemented. One important point to stress is normally SIS Officers do not involve themselves directly with operations in the country of operation, they are the controllers of the agents that do the dangerous work. Often the simplest of information can be invaluable. It is not always necessary for an agent to infiltrate a government or organisation, a simple agent can be invaluable by supplying information in the form of observation. Movement of traffic from an army base or watching a coastline around a naval base can be most helpful. One of the most effective ways to gather data and information about the enemy (or potential enemy) is by infiltrating the enemy's ranks. This is the job of the spy. Spies can return information concerning the size and strength of enemy forces. They can also find dissidents within the enemy's forces and influence them to defect also.

My position was about to change. Due to the loss of an agent in-country (another suspicious loss in my mind, which would later prove to be true), it became an urgent matter that someone should perfect their Spanish and become faultless with a fake identity. There was no time to recruit a new agent. I was asked to move into character and country and undertake a mission in one of the most dangerous countries of the time, Angola.

Invitation To Angola

At the beginning of December 1988, I received a message, via Karen, to attend a meeting with 'C', Chris Curwen. The meeting was to be at the Reform Club, London. It is a private members club on the south side of Pall Mall, in what is often called London's Clubland. I arrived in London with little idea as to what the meeting was going to be regarding, this was nothing unusual, sometimes things needed to be that way. I caught a train from Amersham having driven from Aylesbury and soon arrived at Piccadilly Underground Station. In Pall Mall, I found the club with some difficulty as it only had a small name plaque on the pillar at the bottom of the steps up to the entrance, I was looking for a larger sign over the door, the club seemed very discreet.

Inside the entrance, the space was surprisingly light. It had a beautiful rectangular shaped glass-domed roof, letting in plenty of light over the reception area. With columns supporting a balcony around the entire first floor, reminding me of the Riad I stayed at in Morocco, but this building was far more opulent. The floor was a white patterned mosaic with an Octagon at its centre. To the right was the reception desk, where, when I enquired, I was told I was expected. I was led up the wide stairs opposite the front door to the first floor and led around the balcony to a private room on the left. I could tell this was going to be a special meeting, it was different from any of the other meeting rooms I had attended. The room was panelled in a light-coloured wood, the furnishings were matching with red material making the room have a very rich feel but with a comfortable aura to it. 'C' was sitting at the head of a rectangular table in the centre of the room with eight chairs around it. I was invited to sit at a seat opposite 'C' and asked whether I would like a drink. I ordered a pot of my favourite English Breakfast tea. Seated at the table were two other people I knew, Jean a linguist expert, Max an assistant to 'C'. Sat on 'Chris's right was another guy I hadn't met before, but he had a file in front of him in a folder, I couldn't read the label on the front of the file from where I sat at the far end of the table. It all looked a little intimidating, my initial thoughts on seeing this collection of people was that I was here for a disciplinary of some kind, but I knew I hadn't done anything wrong (ignoring the fact I'd spent years stealing photocopies from companies across

England), so I had nothing to be alarmed at. 'C' spoke first and got straight to the point.

"Hello Andy, I trust you found your journey trouble-free today, thank you for coming. We have a situation, and I think you will be suitable for the job." He went on to explain who the guy on his right was. "I will introduce you to Roger. Roger has interests concerning the United Nations and has assets inside working for us. He runs his own section at Century House specialising exclusively with the UN. I need you to prepare for a trip abroad. Roger thinks that you will be perfect for this job simply because we have very little time, and you fit the profile of the position I want you to fill."

"Ok" I responded a little puzzled.

Roger started to speak, "We have a situation. One of our agents has been compromised and we would like you to take his place. As you know there has been war in Angola for many years, it is not a pleasant country." Emphasising the 'not' in a high pitch tone, which seemed to surprise even himself. He went on.

"The war is a little complicated, you may know there are quite a few factions involved. The MPLA supported by the Cubans. UNITA with the support of the South African government. The United States sided with the FNLA." he continued after taking a breath, "In August 1975, it was UNITA that formally declared war on the MPLA, after the withdrawal of Portugal, who ran Angola as a colony since 1575. I would say is the simplest way to describe the situation."

"Goodness, sounds complicated, are you sure a simple soul like me can handle such complexity?" I asked.

Roger continued. "The point is, we need someone to replace our agent. A complex international diplomatic process aimed at achieving peace and stability in the region has resulted in agreements on all sides of the implementation of Security Council resolution 626 (1988), aimed at verifying the withdrawal of Cuban troops from Angola. Under the agreement, the United Nations Angola Verification Mission (UNAVEM) will be dispatched to Angola to monitor Cuban troop withdrawal very soon. Our agent inside the UN, was a Spanish Military Officer, sadly, no longer in place. We do not have time to find and recruit a new agent. You match the profile very well. We believe we can put you in place to take up his position. We, I, can deal with the UN side to put you in position"

I raised my eyebrows and spoke again, "It's a ridiculous ask. How can I replace a Spanish Officer? People will surely know him by sight. I assume I will have to speak Spanish, that's impossible for such a long period." It was usual in these situations to remain in character for a few hours at the very most, I would need to be in place for who knows how long, weeks, months?

Roger went on undeterred, "No, we believe we can put you in place at the first UN briefing. We, the UK, is not a supplier of military personnel for the UNAVEM. Contributors will be, Algeria, Argentina, Brazil, Congo, Czechoslovakia, India, Jordan, Norway, Spain and Yugoslavia. On 1st January 1989, an advance party of 18 military observers will arrive in the capital city Luanda. Out of those 18, we believe none have ever met or have known this particular Officer before. We need a presence in Angola, as there are interested parties, including us the Brits, that feel Russian involvement, through the Cuban forces present, will try to destabilise the peace plans. You may know Angola is mineral-rich, we are certain Russia would prefer to prevent the West, with China, from benefiting from those minerals. Angola is the second-largest oil-producing country in sub-Saharan Africa with an output of approximately 1.55 million barrels of oil per day and an estimated 17,904.5 million cubic feet of natural gas production. The country has huge natural resources such as phosphates, iron ore, diamonds, bauxite, uranium, feldspar and petroleum. Exporting 40% to China, followed by the United States, India, France, Taiwan, South Africa and Canada. Through Cuba, Russia, we believe, would love to have control of these resources. The Russians are not official protagonists in this war. The Soviet Union and Cuba became especially sympathetic towards the MPLA and supplied that party with arms, ammunition, funding, and training. They also backed UNITA militants until it became clear that the latter was at irreconcilable odds with the MPLA. We want you to report to us any information you can discover regarding Russian military hardware, and if you can observe Russian personnel taking any active role in Angola. Of course, you will need to do this while acting as a UN observer, one of the 18, it won't be easy."

I had a few questions but thought better of asking right now, I would get answers to most of them later. The one question I had right now was "What happened to our agent?"

'C' replied, "All I can say right now is he has been compromised."

"So how can I replace him, he could walk in at the same time as I do?" I was getting worried, this seemed so hit and miss.

"We know that he has been terminally compromised, I will talk to you in-depth later when I have more, leave it at that Andy" I knew 'C' and trusted him, I could tell there was more to this and he wasn't saying. I found it interesting how he avoided at any time using the word "killed." Maybe this was an effort to avoid me having any concerns about the danger I would be in by replacing the Spanish agent.

I thought for about two seconds looking at 'C'. He was staring back at me waiting for me to speak.

"It seems to me, I don't have much choice. It seems to me, this is a really half-baked plan and it seems to me, this job could be quite interesting. Therefore, I agree with one condition, that is, there will be in place an emergency extraction plan for me if I am compromised. I think I do not need to be in Angola longer than necessary. It's a huge area to cover, almost impossible I'd say, and it's a long, long time to stay in character."

'C' spoke again,

"Andy, I appreciate your answer. We will have a plan to extract you, Roger will take that on board himself." he turned to Roger, "That should be simple enough, yes?" Roger nodded in the affirmative. "The time you have to prepare yourself is very tight indeed. It will not be a simple situation at all. I'm not going to put you into the theatre of operation unless I see you are completely confident that you can remain in character, which goes without saying. Not only is the ground difficult, but the war is also brutal and dirty. I want you ready and in position January 1 that is the start date of the UNAVEM. That is three weeks. A tough call by any means. We will meet here again - let's say, December 27." He said, confirming with his assistant Max. Roger looked uncomfortable with that, I assume because of the extremely short time in which to prepare for the mission. Roger added, "There is a briefing meeting in Geneva before that date, Andy realistically needs to be ready a week earlier."

'C' asked me "Can you do this Andy?"

"If all the paperwork etc. is ready, I will" I replied a little overconfidently.

"Jean this is to be your full-time engagement it's 24/7, get Andy ready." Then 'C' spoke to us all, "If any of you are unsure, the slightest sign Andy is not ready, report to me your concerns, and I will call it off." Everyone acknowledged Chris in the affirmative. We all agreed and confirmed the appointment date. 'C' left the room with Max, with no further word. Roger handed me the file, it was marked 'SECRET' the fourth highest classification out of the five security levels the British Intelligence use. On opening the folder, each document was marked 'UK EYES ONLY'. This was a high-level operation. Personally, I felt honoured I should be asked, that I should be singled out as capable. The reality was, I was shitting myself. It would be such a huge task just to get to where I could live, breath and appear to be another person, but add to that, Angola was such a dangerous place to be, hot, wild animals, a war, and what I didn't know at the time, Angola is one of the most heavily mined countries in the world, with over 91 million square metres of land contaminated and over 1,200 known minefields. Millions of landmines and other unexploded bombs are scattered throughout the country -the legacy of over 40 years of the conflict. This wasn't going to be easy at all. Why did I want to do it? It was my job and that is what I'm paid to do. Could I refuse the request? This wasn't an order, 'C' never once inferred it was, but I suspected my career would have taken a sabbatical if I turned it down, the service needs brave people. One thing for sure, this was going to be my toughest assignment yet.

Roger read through each document aloud so that we could discuss any matter that arose. I felt there was something about him I didn't like, I couldn't put my finger on what it was about him - yet.

It would be easy to leave the situation if needed by simply faking an illness, that part was easy. The linguist Jean asked me to talk to her only in Spanish, I would need to spend a lot of time perfecting the language and accent to sound as native as possible, but fortunately, the person I was about to impersonate had a British mother, so a slight British twang to my voice could be excused. The language of Angola was Portuguese, I didn't know a single word of it, that wasn't important, and chances are few of the other UN staff present would know the language either. I asked Roger how he was sure no other person in the UN delegation would know I wasn't who I would say I was. He confirmed, as there were only 18 observers in the initial phase, as Spain was such a large country he was sure no other Spanish UN observer would realise I was an impersonator if I could keep in character.

My new persona would be Comandante Anselmo Gil. I questioned the name, it was way too similar to my own. Documents were being produced, passport, passes, driving licence, bank accounts, a military record, school history, birth certificate, everything. According to Roger, the surname Gil is the 24th ranking surname in Spain, with 72 thousand people having the name, it was common. At least I could sign my initials without thinking. There was no time to lose, I would start work and become a new identity immediately. It wasn't going to be easy, while at home I would be English, at work Spanish.

Comandante Anselmo Gil

I spent some hours at the Reform Club that day, I began to learn who my character was. Jean was very patient with me, I always struggled with languages, and it wasn't a natural thing for me. However, I could speak conversational Spanish, I'd learnt the language during training, and had holidayed in Spain many times and I hoped one day to buy a property for holidays, it is my favourite country. Roger informed me as much as he knew about Comandante Anselmo Gil.

We worked until there was a danger I might miss the last train home. I'd have to get a train back to Amersham on the Metropolitan Line, where I'd pick up the company van and drive the last part of the journey in order to appear to my wife Julie that I'd spent a late night at the printers again.

Every day for the next 3 weeks was spent with Jean, though in different surroundings. We rented a conference room at a beautiful hotel, the De Vere Latimer Estate, in Chesham. Certainly, a lovely place to work. It enabled me to spend more time learning, rather than spend time each day travelling back and forth, as it was only 25 minutes' drive from my home in Aylesbury.

We worked hard to perfect my Spanish language. I'd learn everything about Anselmo by listening and speaking only Spanish to make it as natural as possible, it also helped to learn technical words used in the Spanish army too. My uniform arrived with the insignia for the rank of Comandante, along with all my papers. I also received a set of civilian clothes all with Spanish labels. My personal effects were all Spanish, there wasn't to be a single clue that I wasn't Spanish at all. I would get my UN uniform when I attended a briefing meeting for all nationalities in the 18-man delegation at United Nations, Geneva in mid-December.

By the last week of December, learning my cover was complete, I had been tested thoroughly, people would call my English name to try to trick me, to see if I reacted in the smallest way. Sometimes I would be holding a conversation in Spanish, Jean or whoever was talking to me would throw in a line in English to see if I noticed. I knew Anselmo's personal and military background as perfectly as was possible. To get to the UN meeting in Geneva, Switzerland, I had to fly first to Barcelona, Spain, on a diplomatic flight, the British Consulate General in Barcelona represents the UK government in Catalonia. Then drive to Madrid, so that staff at Madrid Airport would not recognise me and possibly notice I had arrived from London. Then, onward via a Swissair flight to Geneva, tickets provided by the UN. I arrived in character of course, although, I kept to myself as much as possible, I was more comfortable that way. At the briefing we were given our assigned locations, pre-deployment Training Materials (CPTMs) and a full mandate of rules and regulations, ending the day with a test in order to confirm each of us understood the UN regulations and everything that went with it. Everything handed to me at the UN was in English, even though by now I was fully competent in the Spanish language, I had no problem with that side of things. Military observer teams were to verify and record all movements of Cuban military personnel and equipment in and out of Angola. The ports of Cabinda, Lobito, Luanda and Namibe, and also Luanda airport were the five main centres where the UN would be based, Luanda being the Headquarters. But there were mobile teams that were to observe and confirm Cuban redeployment, northward from locations south of the 13th parallel. This was the team I was assigned, thanks to Roger's insider circle of influence. Each foreign observer had local assistants made up of police and officials. All in all, there were 50,000 Cuban troops withdrawing from Angola. The entire UN mission was led by Chief Military Observer Brigadier-General Péricles Ferreira Gomes of Brazil, who seemed quite a congenial as well as a professional man. After the Geneva meeting, I returned home by reversing the route I had taken to get there.

I would have to come up with a plan to cover me being away from home. I should have told the truth to Julie, I didn't, that was a huge mistake and I have regretted that ever since. Maybe because I had so much else on my mind, maybe stress, maybe given the amount I was having to take on, whatever the reason, home life took a step back. Instead, I chose to devise a story to cover my time away. I'd be going sailing, I'd be going on a cruise. Julie didn't like sailing at all, she never wanted to come with me, that's what made that lie so easy. In all honesty not being honest about my second life was always a big, big mistake. It would have been easy to tell her the truth. She had already been security checked, there was no reason at all not to be honest. I should have told her what I did from the start, but because what happened with Janine and the fact I never thought we'd stay together, the moment always seemed to pass until it was too late. I regret it to this day. How could I suddenly tell her

I wasn't who she thought I was, how could I tell her I'd been lying to her all these years. I wish I could justify how I treated Julie, and Janine too, but realistically I can't. It had reached the point where it was too late to tell her.

A plan was put in place for me to go on a sailing cruise, Sailing Schools ran courses and cruises all year round, I had actually been on one in December a year before, it was cold but the air was clear and the night sky was always amazing at that time of year. The school's yachts have heaters, it wasn't unpleasant, and there is something about being in the cold all day then sitting somewhere warm and cosy at night, that helped me sleep well. If I needed to stay longer in Angola, a plan was in position for me to pretend to have an accident, I'd be hit on the head by a swinging boom, a common enough accident on a yacht, they are heavy things. I had prepared photographs of me in a hospital bed with a concussion, in order to send them to her if the need arose. It was not a serious enough accident to warrant her travelling over to join me. It would be a reason to delay my return home. The UNAVEM was expected to run for at least six months, I would never stay that long. To my mind, the whole plan was very shoddy. It wasn't my plan it was Roger's, I was never happy with it, but I just got on with it as that is what was asked of me. I don't blame 'C' for allowing such a dreadful plan to proceed, I could see he wasn't happy with it either. Maybe that is why Roger had a desk job, he just wasn't that smart. My guess was that probably the 'old boy' network had got him his job, he was of that upper-class type, and I didn't like him. There was always something about Roger that I didn't find right, call it my sixth sense.

I was happy I had my character perfect, Jean was happy with my linguistics, my accent was good, I could get away with a very slight Englishness to my speech because Anselmo had an English mother. I had got through the meeting for the UN delegation in Geneva, I had my role in Angola sorted. What could possibly go wrong?

Moving To Angola

December 27, I was as prepared as I would ever be for my mission, half-baked as it was. I travelled to London for a final meeting with 'C' at the Reform Club before travelling on to the UN. At the meeting was me, 'C', Max, Roger. There was no need for Jean to be present, her job was complete, and she had already given me a pass as far as my language ability was concerned. 'C' opened the meeting. He asked me if I thought I was ready and if I was happy with all the arrangements. By now my attitude toward Roger was that he was an upper-class twat. His plan was so bad and I was going along with it. I told 'C' as much. He asked me if I thought the mission should be aborted. It probably should have been, but I said that everything I needed was in place, I'd passed all tests, including Geneva, and I saw no real reason to call it off at this stage. In hindsight, I shouldn't have gone along with Roger's plan at all. I should have asked for a better planner, but at the end of the day it was my shout, and I was the one to blame if it all went wrong. Roger had worked hard getting the paperwork sorted, somehow, he had got everything at the UN in place. I handed 'C' a file that I had written, containing a mission statement, something not always done in situations like this, but I had decided in this case it was a good move.

The mission statement explained the method I would use to hopefully find Russians in such a short time. The back plan was if there was a mole in MI6, I was hoping I would be exposed and compromised by the traitor, thus revealing not only the presence of Russians in a country they were not supposed to be operating militarily but also potentially expose the mole that I was now convinced existed within MI6. It was the real reason I personally thought the mission should continue, in my mind the presence of Russians in Angola was secondary. If I don't mind saying, it was a bloody dangerous strategy, and I was the bait. I wrote the mission statement, and it was down to me. I'd be in contact with SIS daily by using a secret encoder data burst transmitter. At the end of the meeting, 'C' took me aside alone.

"Andy, you realise what you are doing, and the danger you will constantly be in. Are you really sure this one will work?"

"Can only try" was my blunt reply.

He asked me what I thought of Roger, I didn't understand the question. I told 'C' what I thought of Roger, and I'd be glad when I don't have to see him again. He reassured me that in the event I needed to get out I could send a distress message, and urgent rescue would be forthcoming. The mission was given a go.

I had packed my bags, Roger checked through everything to make sure there wasn't one single item that would give away the fact I wasn't Spanish. One item or set of items he pulled out was that I had several football shirts. In my experience, if ever one needed to make friends somewhere, give them a Manchester United football shirt, it was international currency and never failed wherever one was in the world to make a friend for life. I had an entire team of shirts. After a short discussion, it was decided I could take the shirts. I was taken by car to Gatwick airport for my flight to Barcelona.

In Barcelona again, I drove to Madrid. From there, I'd fly to Geneva where all the delegates would be gathering. We travelled on a white United Nations Boeing 737 aeroplane to Luanda, Angola's capital city. On the flight, the delegates got to know each other a little and was uneventful. Arriving at Luanda, on the apron of the airfield we disembarked and gathered to listen to a speech by a local dignitary. He welcomed us and wished us well and a successful mission. The speech went on for 10 minutes it seemed so much more. It was hot standing there, tired after our journey and we needed to get somewhere more comfortably cool. I don't know why they thought it a good idea to hold us in the heat. By the time the speech was finished my shirt was soaked with sweat. We collected our bags ourselves, there didn't seem to be any baggage handlers at all. Cars arrived to take us to the UN village that had been prepared for us just south of the airport.

A UN village of white tents had been erected, an entire infrastructure had been created. We were billeted in white Weatherhaven tents, a tube shape tent with windows and a wooden door on one end. Inside was a hardwood floor, electric lights and nice reasonably comfortable cots, two people per tent, and an air-conditioning unit, without which we would have certainly roasted. There were food tents, a hospital tent, which was already occupied with patients, which surprised me. Toilet tents and showers completed our basic needs. The complete infrastructure was well planned and almost self-sufficient. It was a bit like glamping in a war zone but with hot weather. We had a few hours to settle in, get food and showered, which I desperately needed by now. I was living and breathing Spanish, nobody appeared to suspect I wasn't who I claimed to be, probably because everyone was too excited or nervous to be in a war zone to pay close attention to me.

There was a range of vehicles, Landcruisers, Jeeps and cars of various makes. Most of us would need to move on to our respective areas of operation at the four ports where Cuban troops and equipment were due to embark. Those monitoring Luanda airport, of course, would remain at this camp. I was to head of one of the mobile units, our life in Angola would be much more uncomfortable. We would have to move out quite quickly to other locations to the east of the country to monitor the northward movement of Cuban units to positions above the 13th parallel. The UNAVEM was due to begin on January 1st, there was only a couple of days in which we all had to get into position. My particular area was way over on the east side of the country in the province of Moxico. Quite possibly the most inhospitable area, it is said it was the most mined area in the world. We would have to be very cautious and avoid moving off-road at all times. Moxico had been identified as the area most likely to have evidence of Russian military personnel and hardware. The camp that was established for my group had been prepared and ready for us to move into. We would take a small aircraft to Luena, the capital city of Moxico, where land vehicles were waiting for us. As I was group leader, I could order the camp to move to wherever I needed, when I received information Cuban troops would be moving and that the roads were clear of mines. The UK intelligence boffins had given me satellite photos of the area, I had coordinates of places of interest. I was most interested in the areas around Samucheque, Lumbala, Nhamuana, and Cacande where there were some hidden airstrips quite suitable for secret army camps to be set up by Cubans or Russians. I had been briefed by Roger that Russian personnel may well be situated in Moxico. It wouldn't be a problem, as I was in charge, to order my team of UN observers to take a drive to wherever I wanted to go, provided it was safe, the war was still going on, despite the withdrawal of the Cubans, which was the first phase to the supposed end to the hostilities.

Moxico, Not A Holiday Destination

My team and I flew to Luena airport about 500 miles south-east of Luanda, a smaller airport than Luanda, where our camp was already prepared by the advanced teams. The flight was not without its tension, as we knew surface to air missiles were deployed in-country, with a range of 39,000 feet we were definitely sitting targets. It's not a comfortable feeling sitting in an aeroplane with no defence system and a war going on 7 miles below.

The town of Luena seemed normal, there were obvious signs of war of course, but people were going about their daily business. Our camp was on some ground to the south and west of the airport, about five minutes' drive. There were signs of war here, men were openly carrying weapons in the streets. The language spoken here was chokwe, but some Portuguese was evident on signs around town. January wasn't the best time to be in Moxico province, the rainy season would soon start and travel by road could become impossible, especially as many dirt roads, (there were few good tarmac roads) were war damaged too. The locals were often quick to repair them, as they needed the roads for trade, I was sure that the military would prefer easy road access too. This gave me a real sense that I should not hang around, I needed to get to the more remote places as soon as possible, I didn't want to get stuck somewhere far out in the field because the road had washed away. Praying on my mind too was my sailing cover story was good for only two weeks.

In three cars, with a trusted local official as a guide, we set about visiting the Cuban military bases in Luena without delay. Clearly, the Cubans were packed and ready to move north and then west, as they had agreed to do according to the UN Security Council resolution. They were friendly enough toward our group. The Cuban Commander showed me maps of planned military movements under his command. We spoke in Spanish, but Cuban characteristics made the language a little difficult for me to understand at first. I planned to leave one car in Luena, with its crew of one UN observer and three locals to observe the Cuban troop movements due to start the next day, after which we would regroup when we returned from our trip further east. I could see little evidence of Russian personnel, although it would have been easy for them to stay out of sight.

Before leaving England I had been given satellite imagery of a few locations of interest to SIS at home in London. I had studied these, and knew I'd need to get close to those areas soon before the rains, and, because I wanted to spend as little time as possible in Angola. One such area was around the small town of Lumbala on the Zambezi River about 25 miles north of the border with Zambia on the 13th parallel. Unusually, the border in that area is a perfectly straight line from east to west, then takes a 90-degree turn north to south, again in a dead straight line. I decided to set off with the group early the next day. There is a road that heads south from Luena which gradually sweeps easterly toward Lumbala. At 5 am just as first light was starting to appear on the horizon, we set off in our two Landcruisers packed with tents, food, water and fuel in order to make camp at our destination. We would wear civilian clothing, we felt it safer to avoid confusion given the number of different forces involved in the conflict. We felt a soldier seeing a uniform not recognised as his own may treat us as hostile. We did, however, continue to wear the light blue beret of the UN and the vehicles had UN flags flying. The camp at Luena would remain as a base for our return in a few days. The locals had told us that the road was good but in places very difficult. Some sections of the road may be impassable in the rain. It was a major trade road but by our standards narrow and a rough dirt road, it passed through many villages where there was small scale digging for minerals, the local people kept the road open as much and for as long as possible when it became rain damaged. It would be a long drive, about 240 miles, even if we could maintain 30 miles per hour it would be an 8-hour drive. With 12.5 hours sunlight in January, taking into account driving breaks, refuelling, slow sections and anything else, including conflict, we were going to be hard pushed to make Lumbala in a day, but local advice claimed it was possible to complete the journey before dark.

Note: There is more than one Lumbala in Angola. The Lumbala discussed here is at 12°38'30"S 22°35'18"E.

After last-minute checks that we had everything we needed for the journey, we set out of the UN camp, and very soon we were heading into the countryside on the EN180 main route to Lumbala. The road was better than expected and we made very good progress. We stopped a few times to have a break and say hello to the locals to try to get information on the route ahead. There was always the possibility of running into a military skirmish, roadblocks or mines, it was always good to receive local knowledge on the road ahead. We were aware these stops would add time to our journey but we felt it better to have fore-knowledge of the roads ahead. Comfort breaks were always in a township on the road, we felt it wise not to wander behind some bushes because of the risk of mines. As we drove along the road, we saw many red signs warning of mines. At Lucusse about 4 hours into our journey, we made a stop for refreshments. Here was the first sign of the danger that these people lived every day. There was a school and next to it, on a fence, were red mine warning signs. In the field next to the school, cattle were grazing seemingly unaware of the danger they must be in, luckily, we didn't witness any cows being blown up. At the boundary as we entered the town there was an airfield, basically, a dirt track cleared for a runway. People told us that Cuban troops had been stationed there but had now left. We marked this on our UN map and noted the information people gave us what military company it was.

Lucusse seemed as good a place as any to eat. We stood around our vehicles stretching our legs and talking to any locals that came to take a look at us. Our light blue berets, of course, were a bit of a novelty, but most people had heard that the UN was trying hard to bring an end to so many years of war and the killing and destruction that brings. It was impossible to mark all of the minefields, there were simply just too many of them. It was obvious that it was going to take years if ever at all, to make this land safe again. The locals, however, did seem to be going about daily business quite normally and shops were stocked, even if a little meagrely.

Back in our vehicles again, it was nice to feel the benefit of the air-conditioning, for me the heat was my biggest enemy. Making the mistake to not drink enough water, thinking it would avoid the need to stop for comfort breaks too often. My head started to spin and I was sweating gallons, it didn't take long to learn, no matter how much water I drunk, I would sweat it out rather than need to pee. Passing through the town, we had to take a left turn onto another road that led to Lumbala, we thought it would be about three more hours' drive. But now the road narrowed and became less easy to keep up our speed. We passed through another village that we didn't stop at, as time was beginning to worry us more. The village was literally about 400 yards long and one street wide, shortly after this we reached a lake. The road bridge crossed the water at a place where the lake narrowed but the bridge had been destroyed. We headed back to the village where local people informed us we should double back the way we came, about a mile, where we should take a sharp turn to the north and circumvent the lake on a narrower dustier road. We knew if it started to rain now we would not be able to return this way, but we could not let that stop us, we would have to worry about that if it happened. The detour probably added about 5 miles to our journey.

Once we re-joined the original road, we started to see more evidence of small-scale mining for minerals, there were small ponds of bright green or blue water. A further eight miles, and the first of several bridges that had definitely seen better days appeared in front of us. It appeared to be made of wood with the top planks quite loose. I walked ahead of the vehicles to take a look to make sure it was safe. While I was looking and jumping on some of the planks in a vain hope of being able to tell if they would hold, a couple of locals walked up to me and happily reassured me it was safe. I reported this to our drivers. All passengers got out of the cars and we let the drivers' inch across alone in the vehicles. It wasn't a long or particularly high bridge about twenty-five feet across and about ten feet high, but enough that no one fancied being in the vehicles as they crossed. The bridge held well with a few of the planks rattling a little, quite uneventful really, but I was glad to be out of the car rather than stay in it. On the other side of the dry riverbed was a steep climb up a hill, again letting us know in the rain this would become a very different journey.

There followed a stretch of road, that, in another country would be quite amazing to witness. Every 200 yards on the north side of the road were diggings, each one about 25 yards wide and 100 yards long. Perhaps each one was a dug by a family, we didn't stop to ask. But this went on for about 18 miles, dig after dig, most of them dry, some filled with bluish-green water. At least now this section of road was a less hilly dirt road. Eventually, we reached a village called Kinjama. With about 50 houses running parallel to the road. It was time for another leg stretch, so we took a break and made small talk with the villagers who gathered to see the blue berets. Everyone we met seemed to know and to expect to see UN observers, we found no hostility toward us at all. Everyone seemed friendly enough. There were still some red mine warning signs along the road, I'm not sure how the people here dug for the minerals without blowing themselves up. Maybe they did, there were certainly a few people with lost limbs, but who knows if their injuries were from mines or war. I gave out a few sweets or bandages if it looked as though they could benefit from a clean one.

After a short break, we took to the road yet again. Almost immediately coming across yet another poorly built wooden bridge, only this one was obviously unsafe to drive across. We could easily take a left where it was clear from tracks in the dirt, that people before us had taken a small detour around the bridge.

The track dipped down and took a horseshoe turn over the almost dry riverbed, yet again letting us know if the rain came there would not be a way back on this road. After the climb up from the river crossing, there was mile after mile of digging pits on either side of the road. From space or a plane, this road must have looked like a long zipper. It carried on like this for at least 80 miles. There was the odd truck on the road but, we didn't see much in the way of the military, which was a little odd, but maybe they just didn't fight on the road. The few military vehicles we did see were only trucks with groups of armed men, no heavy artillery or tanks, only lightly armed troops. They never bothered us, save for shouting and waving at us, the blue flags on our vehicles were clearly working. We hoped nobody wanted to create an international incident by making trouble, although we did feel a little intimidated by these men, they could easily have robbed us.

Eventually, the bushland we had experienced for so many miles turned into woods. We could still see in the trees people digging their mineral pits, mile after mile we drove through the trees, we had been driving, with stops for ten hours. Finally, the road dropped down a bank and the Zambezi River came into view. We could see part of Lumbala village on our side of the river, but the main village was on the east side. We easily found the platform ferry to cross to the other side and drove up the riverbank on a sloped road that joined the EN190 north into the village. We had taken ten hours to drive to Lumbala and had about 2 hours light to make camp somewhere suitable and reasonably safe. Almost the entire village came out to meet us when we pulled up, we were led to the village elder or mayor, Filipe Lomba, a tall thin man who greeted us kindly, and, after introductions, led us to his house which surprisingly had a large garden completely surrounded by a wall. He said we could make our camp inside the walled garden, which must have stretched for 100 yards by 100 yards. Clearly, he was a man of wealth, and we got on very well with him. In return for his hospitality in a hastily arranged ceremony, I presented him and the village with an entire set of Manchester United football shirts. The villagers seemed more than happy, they clapped and spontaneously started to dance. I guessed we were going to be safe here for the duration of our stay.

We set up our camp, not an easy task with villagers wanting to help, they just got in the way. But we eventually got them to leave with Mr Lomba chivvying them away to leave us and his garden in peace. Inside the walls of his garden, there was an inner walled garden surrounding his house in a rectangle. We camped inside this space in the shade of some fruit trees, effectively we had two walls protecting us from the outside. We were very tired after our long journey. We cooked up some food on our stoves, boosted by fruit and fresh vegetables brought to us by Mr Lomba's wife. It would have been more diplomatic to eat and talk with Mr Lomba that evening, but quite frankly we were all exhausted. We said we would talk in more depth tomorrow, he understood and left us to rest and sleep.

Mr Filipe Lomba

The next morning, I woke at 5 am, it was still dark, and there would be another hour before the dawn would cast any light on our surroundings. In our tents the group was still sleeping, I could hear a roaring snore in one tent. How the poor person sleeping in the tent with him got any sleep I will never know. I quietly left my tent and stood in the fresh air and stretched. This could be such a lovely country if only these people could stop fighting each other. There were enough minerals in this wild country to make everyone rich, but I guess that's why they fight, for power and wealth. I shaved and found a tree to hang a shower bag and washed wearing only my underwear, it was nice to feel clean again after the long and dusty journey yesterday. I dressed after covering myself with mosquito repellent. I am one of those people that mosquitoes love to eat, I can be covered in bites while everyone else remains untouched by them, I have no idea why. We were very lucky this village seemed so friendly. I put a pot of water on the gas burner to make some coffee. By the time I had finished my ablutions, I saw a light come on in Mr Lomba's house. I wondered how he had made himself so obviously prosperous. While waiting for my coffee pot to heat up I walked silently around his garden. It was the only garden I had seen since arriving in Angola that was landscaped and tidy. Cut grass, flowers and fruit trees made his garden an oasis from the squalor outside these walls.

Mr Lomba appeared in his doorway, so I went over to say hello and have a chat. He invited me into his house for coffee. I quickly turned off the gas under my water pot as he ushered me inside. By western standards, his home was simply furnished, but in this country, it was very comfortable.

I thanked him again,

"Thank you, Sir, for your most kind hospitality, you have such a wonderful home and your villagers clearly love you."

Now, normally I never call anyone Sir, it's a thing of mine. In my opinion, Sir is a mark of respect. Bullies such as teachers, can say and call you anything they like, but you have no recourse to answer back in the same manner, they do not deserve to be called 'Sir'. I went through all my school days and never once called any teacher 'Sir' or 'Miss'. Except for Miss Willox, firstly because she was unmarried, so it was her correct title, but secondly because despite being the strictest teacher I had for the entirety of my education, was fair and human. I never gave any of my bosses at work the title Sir, because, well, because I just don't, they probably earned the title, according to my own rules, but I just never did.

Mr Lomba, however, was different. I immediately could see he was an oasis of peace and sensibility, he had made a comfortable home for himself and his wife in a country that had been ripped by war for decades, he was liked by the people in this town. He deserved respect, and at the end of the day I now represent the United Nations, I should afford him the honour accordingly. I liked this man.

We spoke in English, with me faking a Spanish accent, as this was the common language between us.

"Welcome into my home Comandante, let me get you some coffee when your team is awake my wife will make you all some nice breakfast, bread and eggs" he started "I hope you are staying today, later she will make you Calulu. I want to say, Anselmo, your gift of those football shirts was such a fine gesture to my people, you have made the kids so happy. We have now George Best and Bobby Charlton in our village ha-ha. It is the best gift you give us."

"You are very welcome Filipe, I hope it brings pleasure to the kids. Please call me Anselmo, we have no need for formalities." I asked, "What is Calulu?"

"Then you must call me Filipe please and please sit at my table. Calulu is a local dish of fish stew, we will make you our special guests he.re"

"You have a lovely home Filipe, how did you create such a garden? It is beautiful."

While we sat opposite each other in his kitchen at a small table drinking coffee, he explained he owned all the village. He had ventured here 10 years ago, the war had begun and was clear it was getting very dirty. His family had been slaughtered and he escaped from Chemboca a small town to the south and west from here. About 100 miles as the crow flies, I guessed he must have travelled three times that by road at least to get here.

I admired him even more for his bravery and tenacity.

"How did you make your fortune?" it was clear he had become rich here, it wasn't a forward question.

"When I came here there was nothing, but I camped here one night as I was travelling, I was aiming for Cazombo to the north where I have some relatives. I found by accident a diamond, just lying there next to me in the morning when I woke. I thought to myself, this is a sign, I must stay here and dig. You saw the diggings on the road on the other side of the river. Many are my digs. I found diamonds, so many, so I employed people to come and help me dig and this village grew from nothing."

"That's incredibly lucky from such a bad beginning Filipe. How do you stop the people you employ from stealing from you?"

"At first it was some family that came to help me, then as things got busier and the digs became more productive, I have employed trusted people. I pay them well, but you see, they can't sell the diamonds, they would have to leave the village to sell them and I would know."

We chatted small talk for a few minutes, I liked this man more after hearing his story, such a brave and strong man, yet his manner is so calm and peaceful.

I changed the subject.

"Filipe, there is an airfield just up the road, I see it on photographs I have been given. Are there any MPLA or Cubans here? We need to monitor their withdrawal, it's why we came here."

"Anselmo, you need to be careful, there is a military camp the other side of the airstrip it is MPLA and Cubans. We try to avoid them. The Cubans, with Russian help, want to make this place Communist. They will steal everything I have here. I pay them in diamonds to let me continue my business, and we supply them food. Not because we care for them, but to save our lives. They will slaughter us if we stop. I am waiting for this moment the UN arrive, and now I can watch them leave."

"The problem I have Filipe is that the camp you say is there is not on any map the UN has given me. So, I need to approach them, I have a feeling the camp will be one that Cuba will try to keep secret, essentially to break the peace that has been negotiated. They know the wealth here is great and you know they won't let it out of their hands easily. I will need to contact the UN headquarters about this."

This was the reason I was here for both UN and UK intelligence. I had to get closer to try to see if the Russians were here with military personnel and weapons. If they were hiding from the world this would be significant. The UK would use any information I can glean.

"Filipe, have you seen any military hardware at the camp?"

"The airstrip is too short for large carrier planes, we built it so that diamond buyers in light planes can come and do business. But I have seen and hear sometimes military aircraft, very loud because they rev the engines to stop on the short runway and make such a noise. I am sure some weapons have arrived here. But we avoid contact, we don't want communism and the MPLA are brutal people. We just want to live in peace and go about our business. I am living in fear of being killed for my business, but I think they are lazy, they prefer us to do the hard work while they drink beer and sit with their feet up."

I needed to see the camp, it would be very dangerous for sure. I couldn't put my UN team in such danger, normally I think we should have reported the situation to the UN and left the area quickly before we are discovered here. But my alter-mission was to investigate and report to SIS. I would have to do this alone, without the UN team, if they knew the situation here, they would want to leave immediately, it was far too dangerous.

I was about to make the worst decision in my life.

Taken Prisoner

I finished my coffee with Filipe and told him I should go check on my team and tell them to rise for breakfast and to make plans to backtrack a few miles for safety. There we could take stock of the situation and await instructions from the UN.

I thanked Filipe Lomba for the coffee and chat and left the house, promising to return shortly for breakfast with the team. Outside the sun was now on the horizon. The remaining seven members of my team were getting dressed and ready for the day. One car was still in Luena observing movements there and acting as our base camp group. I informed the team of the situation in a group meeting. Most of the team wanted to leave right away. I said they should have breakfast in the house first, then we'd make a move to withdraw a few miles west across the river again, that at least would give us some protection. A couple of the team were a little shaken by the realisation of the danger we were now in, I reassured them our cars were inside the compound, so were we, this afforded us some protection by being out of sight from the village. The main road was 300 yards from Filipe's house, I judged we were not in immediate danger at that moment. But it would be wise to have breakfast, break camp and leave ASAP.

Filipe arrived to lead us into his house, the team followed him and disappeared into the kitchen for a nice breakfast. I stayed outside for a few moments to pack my stuff, I'd had coffee, and I said I'd be there once I was packed. I quickly shoved my sleeping bag into its cover and put my things away. The tent would be packed away once breakfast was done.

While I was alone, I thought I'd go take a look at the MPLA camp, I hoped they'd still be asleep or at least still quite dozy as it was only 06:30 hours. With the UN team inside starting their eggs and bread, I grabbed my camera and disappeared quietly out of the front gate into the street and headed north to the airstrip no more than 200 yards away.

The airstrip had no fences around it, none did in this kind of country, it was just a clearing in the scrub and a dirt runway. I estimated the length of the runway was about 5000 feet. A Russian Antonov transport aircraft could land and take off in 4000 feet easily. The main EN190 road crosses the runway halfway along its length. I walked slowly and cautiously along the edge of the airfield toward the road, there was almost no cover at all should I need it, I did not want any of the MPLA to spot me, in retrospect, I was being quite foolish, yet, at the time I felt I needed to do what a spy should do. There was nobody around this early in the morning. There was a wooded area at the far eastern end of the landing strip. I moved quickly along to the woods to try to get some cover. On the opposite side of the runway, I could see there was a military camp. The buildings were brick or mud-built, using the cover of the few trees between me and the camp I crouched in the shadow of a tree and took a couple of photos. There were a couple of vehicles in sight, and so far, I could see only civilian types such as Toyota pickup trucks. As the angle changed as I walked a little further, some military hardware did come into view. I could not identify what they were, but clearly field guns of sorts maybe a rocket system too. There wasn't any sign of anyone on guard duty, which seemed odd to me.

Further to the west, I could see smoke from a small fire, maybe there would be another camp there. To the north were more trees, but to get to them I'd need to cross the road in front of the camp, that was too dangerous I'd be too close to them. I swept back to the west to take advantage of a slope where the land begins to drop toward the river as there was still little cover from trees on this side of the road. The land was crisscrossed with paths, I guessed it was reasonably safe from mines but still my senses were the highest they could be. It's amazing how the danger of being blown up does that! Now I turned and continued east. There were a few houses to my south here, but there was no sign of anyone up yet. I crept past them as quietly as I could. I crossed the EN190 road to the east side, now I had some cover from the trees. I could see the camp clearly, it was fenced, there were some vehicles I didn't recognise I guessed they may be Russian or Cuban, they just looked that type of vehicle and definitely more military hardware of various kinds. There was a watchtower, and I could see two uniformed soldiers in the shelter on top of the tower. I couldn't make out the uniform of the soldiers as they were in the shadow, it was hard to see in the early morning low light, but the uniform looked darkish green.

The guards were walking around the tower showing no sign that they had spotted me. I used the trees as cover and moved north to try to get a view of the camp from another angle. After about 200 yards there were a couple of houses, I moved around the furthest

The watchtower, two guards seemed unaware I was there. The photograph was taken from the cover of trees.

house into the clear but protected from view by the building. I took a few more photos, the camp was definitely Cuban or Russian. It was too tidy to be NPLA. As I held my camera to take pictures, the door of the house just a few feet to my left suddenly opened. Expecting to see a local I was surprised to see a white man, in uniformed trousers and shirt. Shit! I ducked behind the building and leaned back against the wall in the hope he hadn't seen me. The camp was across the road, I couldn't figure out why he was using this house outside the camp. The man suddenly appeared at the corner of the house about 3 feet from where I was leaning back against the wall in a vain attempt to keep out of sight. Behind him were two other men pointing weapons at me. As a member of the UNAVEM, I should not be acting in this way. I should not be sneaking around in the early dawn on my own. I knew I'd messed up.

"Shit, this is not good" I muttered under my breath.

The two men in front of me stood for probably a quarter of a second, it seemed like thirty. The other man spoke in English with a Russian accent,

"Good morning Andy, nice of you to join us."

What the hell? He was using my English name, he knew who I was! I spoke in Spanish keeping to my character.

"I am Comandante Anselmo Gil UN Observer to UNAVEM acting under Security Council resolution 626. I do apologise for waking you."

He rudely interrupted me, raising his voice in anger, Russians always do.

"Don't mess around Andy, I know who you are and why you are here." then more politely he added, "You must come with me now." With that the two other men moved forward relieved me of my camera and grabbed me quite violently by my arms, pushing my head down my chin on my chest. I was frog-marched, held securely by the two men their strong grip really hurt my arms.

"Where are we going, you are contravening Security Council resolution 626 and violating a UN official representative" The guy in charge grabbed my hair lifting my head, threw a punch smack in the middle of my face causing my nose to start bleeding.

"Why are you pretending Andy, I know who you are, you can fuck your UN story, Britain does not represent the UN here in Angola. I am not violating anything, you are a spy, you are in civilian clothes, and I know who you are." He repeated, with that he pushed my head back down and we continued into the camp on the other side of the road.

How did he know who I am? The UN, and my team, have no idea I am not Spanish Comandante Anselmo Gil. In Britain few people in the SIS know I am here, how does this guy know me?

"May I ask who you are?" I maintained my Spanish, but I was guessing it would be pointless. He didn't reply. But a punch to a kidney let me know not to speak again until invited. I decided I didn't like the idea of receiving any more punches, so I stayed quiet until I was thrown quite violently into a small cell-like room in a hut on the military camp. The door slammed shut behind me, it would have been dark, but for a little light leaking around the edge of the door and the window that had been covered by wood panels to block anyone from looking in or out of this room. After a few moments, my eyes accustomed to the darkness, I could see the room was empty.

This most definitely wasn't good, how should I play this? Shall I maintain my Spanish pretence or admit to who I am. Training had taught me to stick to my story, play the innocent man, pretend I know nothing, pretend that I was acting for my superiors. I could try to stick to my Spanish story for as long as I could, obviously, he knew I was Andy, which also meant he most probably knew I was MI6. But for now, I'd be Comandante Anselmo Gil. I wished now, that I had experienced the interrogation back in the UK that my fellow students had endured, but because I outsmarted the guy I was following in Gosport, I missed that experience. I'd just have to remember what I was taught and stick with it. My next concern was, where was this imprisonment going to lead? I was sure they would not release me as a UN representative and apologise for the mistake. I felt sure my captors were deciding my future right now, maybe they were speaking to some higher authority taking advice on what to do with me. What kept turning over in my brain was, how the hell did he know who I was, and how did he know I'd be right here?

One thing was for sure, I was glad I had done my ablutions earlier, or there would be a hell of a stink in this room right now.

I don't know how long after I was dumped unceremoniously into the dark room, it seemed like days, but was probably minutes before the door was thrown open by the two men that had dragged me here. The light blinded me for a second or two. They brought into the room a small wooden table and two chairs. I was grabbed and dumped into the chair facing the door.

I tried pointless humour.

"Thank you gentlemen, tell me, in this part of the world do you put the jam on top or the clotted cream on top of your scone? Two sugars in my tea thank you." A huge mistake on my part as this was clearly an English reference to cream teas, but my fear was not letting me think too clearly right now. I forgave myself of the error I was sure nerves were playing a part. Clearly, the waiters here didn't expect a tip, as my attempt to lighten the situation with humour resulted with a punch to my ear, strong enough to make me fall sideways off the chair, all I could hear was a whistling noise. While on the floor the other guy gave me a nice kick to my right ribs, I felt a rib snap, leaving me with some difficulty in breathing. It felt as though every time I breathed in, the rib was pressing into my diaphragm below my lungs. I moaned as I tried to sit back up. I looked up from the ground just in time to see another boot heading toward my face. On contact it broke a molar on my right lower jaw, it hurt like crazy, but I wasn't going to give these bully boys the pleasure of seeing me scared or in pain, just as I would always deal with bullies as a kid.

"I hope your meat here isn't tough, I think I'll be having trouble chewing now." I should have stopped my attempts at humour, it was getting me into to trouble, they tried to inflict more pain on me with one of them grabbing my now very sore jaw and lifting me back into the seat. I didn't wince but I couldn't stop a tear in my eye from forming.

"OK, I said in English, I'll sit quietly, may I see the wine list?" I flinched waiting for my next blow, none came,

"Ah, you like English" I said as they turned to leave the room.

I needed to use this time alone to assess my situation.

What was going to be the outcome? I could only see there would be one end to this. He has already told me he knows I am a spy, there is usually only one end to spies, at best I'll spend time in jail somewhere, at worse… I didn't want to think about it.

How do they know who I am, and how do they know I would be right here at this time? It can only be that there is another mole inside SIS, what's more, that mole is providing up to date information. My earlier suspicions are true.

Who is the mole? Not an important question to answer at this moment, knowing who the mole is right now will not affect the outcome of my incarceration. I decided not to worry about this question for now. If I discover who the mole may be, how do I get that information out of here, there is nothing I can do.

What do I admit, what do I tell? My situation here can only get worse. It will be highly unlikely that he will return into the room and say sorry it's a big mistake, accept our apologies and go home. Right now I do not know what it is that they want to know. The truth is, I know so little. If they know I am here in Angola, they probably know a lot. I can make stuff up, chances are the mole will confirm I'm lying to my interrogator and that will make matters worse for me. Training tells me I should hold off saying anything for as long as possible.

Is there a chance of rescue? Little, my government are not going to admit they have planted a spy inside the UN not only that, they are not going to admit to impersonating a Spanish Officer either. My government finds it hard to admit to spies that have been exposed, look at the Cambridge five, even once they had been found to be traitors, little happened to them.

The best thing I can do for myself is to do as we were taught and to look for a way out of this, an impossible task in this situation.

Would anyone at home realise my situation? Highly unlikely. This is such a mess, I've been so unprofessional. I've come here with such a short time to fully prepare. Yes, I've got the language and fake identity, but really, I have made the mistake of trying to achieve something that should require at least six months to do the job properly. I gave myself two weeks in Angola. I've had to make up a story to cover my absence from home. If only Julie knew beforehand, then I could have taken time to do this properly.

I need to think clearly for as long as I can, I'm sure they will wear me down in the end, I need to eat if they offer food, I need to sleep if I get a chance.

I sat at the table in the dark room my head spinning with too many questions. One thing for sure, I need to stop making a joke of everything and start taking this as seriously as the situation deserves, no one will appreciate bravado.

After sitting alone for just a couple of minutes, the door opened letting in a burst of light that forced my head to turn away from the brightness. The three men walked back into the room and surrounded me.

"Ok, Andy" my interrogator began "I know who you are, why do you insist on pretending you are not Andy of MI6?"

"Ok" I replied in a calm voice "You know, but I really don't know what you want from me, I know nothing, I am such a tiny person in such a big organisation, I just follow orders, I do as they tell me, but they never tell me anything."

I lied, doing just as the training manual says. I wish I had experienced the fake kidnapping in England, I could have benefited so much from that experience.

"Andy, you have given up so quickly, the others took far longer to admit to me who they were."

"What others? I only know about myself, I don't know who you are talking about, I'm too small for them to tell me anything big like that." This was a more or less true statement, I knew I'd replaced an agent, but I knew nothing about the reason why.

"Tell me about Oleg, Andy."

"Oleg? Oleg who? I don't know any Oleg, I told you I know nothing, I am too small to be told anything, I just do as they order me."

Apparently, he thinks I know something because my answer gained me a seriously heavy punch to my left cheek. The blow jolting my head so violently I felt the muscles in my neck rip.

"Andy, I know you know Oleg, don't lie to me."
"Oleg who? I don't know any Oleg."
"You know Andy, tell me about him."

It hadn't occurred to me yet who he was asking about I really was answering honestly.

"I would love to tell you about Oleg, but you are not telling which Oleg, how can I tell you something when you don't tell me who you ask about."

Another punch to the same cheek, now this was starting to hurt.

"Andy, why do you want to make it difficult for yourself." He grabbed my hair and slammed my face into the table, it didn't hurt at all as I managed to let my forehead take the hit.

"I know you know Oleg, Andy, why are you being so stupid, this is going to get a lot worse for yourself."

"Why are you not listening to me? I do not know any Oleg, I think you deliberately ask me questions you know I can't answer just so you can hurt me. It's not necessary, I will tell you, but you should ask me questions I know the answer to. I want to tell you."

"Why are you here in Angola Andy?"

"Working for UN Security Council resolution 626." I replied honestly, in an attempt to show I would answer questions I knew answers to.

My answer earned me another punch to the same cheek, it didn't hurt much more now, but my neck couldn't take the strain and I felt it crack, I'd torn a muscle.

"You are here to spy on the Russians Andy, the UN is just a cover for you, see I know who you are." One of the other men grabbed my shoulders and tipped me back on the chair, I fell backwards I couldn't stop the fall to the floor. The two men that had been quiet until now gave me a thorough kicking to my body, legs and head. I tried to get into a foetal position, curled up to protect myself from some of the blows. Kicks to my broken rib hurt most, I couldn't catch my breath as each time I breathed in and out it felt as though the rib was pushing into my lungs. They finished with the kicking and lifted me back into the chair at the table and stood behind me.

"I am here to observe the withdrawal of Cuban military, everyone knows Russians are supplying the Cubans, so obviously whatever you supply the Cubans needs to be confirmed it leaves the country according to the agreements."

"That's not such a big secret is it Andy, you are what you say, and that is nothing. I know why you are here, I want to know about Oleg."

"Who the fuck is Oleg!?" I screamed still totally mystified by the line of questioning.

"You know Oleg, you have talked to him, tell me what he said to you. Tell me where he is living now."

"I am trying to think who Oleg is, I never heard this name before."

"I know you drove him to a safe location in the south of England, why you didn't tell me this, so I know you are not telling me everything you know." Now it dawned on me, Oleg Gordievsky is the Russian double agent I drove from the safe house to Fork Monckton. There must be an MI6 mole telling them every detail, this shouldn't be common knowledge to anyone.

"I will tell you if I know something, I want to answer your questions."

My reply earned me another serious beating by the two goons behind me. The pain is hard to describe, once you get to a certain level it doesn't feel as though it can hurt anymore, so I just curled up into a ball and let the kicks and punches pour into me, there's nothing else you can do.

"Andy, I just told you I know you drove Oleg Gordievsky, you spent time with him, what do you know? You can tell me and the pain may stop for you."

"I don't know any Oleg Gord... Gordev..., I didn't catch the name you just said, I don't remember him, when was this you say?"

I didn't have anything I could tell, I drove him for a few hours. Gordievsky was sat in the back of the car with armed officers and another in the front with me driving. I spoke to him, yes, but only chit chat.

"I don't remember this person, if you know who I am you know I just do photocopying, I am nothing, and I know nothing, I wish I could tell you what you want to know, they don't tell me anything." This line of conversation was going nowhere, he must surely know that, what did he think I could tell him? Gordievsky was not my agent, I wasn't the one getting information from Gordievsky.

"You lie Andy, you just lie."

With that I took a really brutal beating from the two tough guys next to me, I could feel the pain was beginning to take its toll on my body. I'm not a trained soldier, I was quite fit from the sport that I did, but I wasn't hardened like a soldier, it wouldn't take long for these guys to beat me to death.

"Stop!" I yelled, "Ok, what can I tell you?" I was hoisted back into the chair at the table.

"Where did you take him?"

"I don't remember, I'm not employed to remember things, I just make photocopies, you have bad information on me. If I drove this person, it must have been years ago, I don't remember anyone by that name, please, believe me, I am trying to help myself and you, I want to answer your questions, but I honestly do not know the answers to your questions. Please stop hurting me." I sounded pathetic, the kicks and punches were nothing compared to what I knew these men will do to me soon if I don't give them something. "Can you remind me who this person is? I do not recall him at all."

"You took Gordievsky from Russia, you know who I talk of Andy, and you took him to a place to be safe. Tell me where you took him."

"I have never been to Russia, you have the wrong person I am sorry." It was true I never have visited Russia.

"No Andy, I didn't say YOU drove him from Russia, you took him from a safe house in England and I need you to tell me where he is now. I tell you what Andy, how about I leave you with my two friends here for a while, maybe they can jog your memory."

"No, wait, help me to remember, what year was this supposed to happen because I do not know Oleg Gordi .... Whatever his name" I pretended not to know the surname.

"1982 Andy you know that. Don't belittle yourself, I know who you are, you are important to MI6, stop playing games Andy, I'm getting bored by your pretence."

"Ok, let me think, in 1982, it was the end of the Falklands War, yes, I was involved in a minor way with that conflict, I was never part of any other work at that time." I was trying to keep him talking in the room, I didn't want him to leave I knew I'd be getting a good kicking if he did. I also knew the date he gave me was the wrong one, Gordievsky escaped to England in 1985, was this false information as some kind of trap. Anyhow, I'd use the error, if that is what it was, as a way to pretend I did not know Oleg and to try to keep my interrogator thinking I had no idea who Oleg Gordievsky was. I doubt it was working but I had to try every trick I could think of under the circumstances, and it wasn't easy to think clearly.

"I was busy helping to trace Exocet missiles in the year 1982 until the war ended in June that year. I had no other work, it was all I was concerned with at that time." I kept talking to keep him in the room.

"Are you sure it was 1982 if you think I am involved with this person as you say."

The interrogation went back and forth for ages maybe a few hours, I lost track of time, I knew it was still daylight. I tried to keep his interest, but I told him nothing about Gordievsky, as I had nothing to tell, there was little I could do to add any information where I had none. After a while, I tried a different tack.

"I wonder if you can help me, I have been hurt by you guys, I need water, maybe a little food, with some rest maybe it will help me remember."

"No, Andy you don't get food or water, I am not going to waste it on you. You will sit here until you tell me what I wish to know." Clearly, knowing where Gordievsky was living was important to him, I guessed they plan to assassinate him. The good news was, they had no idea where he was living. With that, all three men left the room. To my mind this was going nowhere, I had no information I could give regarding Gordievsky, and these people will soon get fed up asking. Then what next?

As they left the room, I noticed as they closed the door there didn't seem to be any kind of lock. Most unusual for a prison cell, maybe this room wasn't normally used for that. I waited a few moments before I went to the door, listened carefully. I could not hear any sound that indicated to me there was a guard near the door. I slowly and quietly turned the door handle, the door opened, I let it open just the smallest crack. I smelt the fresh air, I slowly moved the door wider. The door let out a little creak noise as I tried to look outside. Suddenly a black guy, he must have been sitting to one side just a few feet away, leapt up from his seat and started to shout in chokwe at me. He had a rifle in his arms which he pointed at me, he grabbed the door, opened it fully and gave me a huge whack on the head with the barrel end. I put my hands up, backing away I kept staring at him, another bloke came running in and there was a massive din as they shouted and hit me repeatedly with their guns. I retreated to the chair, telling them to calm down, I was just looking for water. The other three white men came running back into the room and all five of them gave me a thorough beating, kicking and punching. I just kept repeating Ok, ok, ok as the blows kept coming.

Almost unconscious now the blows stopped but with one of the men holding me down in the chair. The man that had been doing all the talking left the room while the others stood guard over me. Every part of my body was in pain, so much pain, I was feeling very weak and faint, I was thinking it would be better for them to end my life now.

After a minute or two the guy in charge came back into the room and spoke.

"Andy, you think we would just leave the door open for you to walk out, what an idiot you are." I couldn't disagree with him, "I will stop you walking about when I don't give you permission to." I was expecting to be tied to the chair, what happened was worse of course. He had in his hand a hammer and a couple of nails, about three inches long, two of the men grabbed my wrist and held it onto the table in front of me with my fingers held out straight, he pushed one of the nails into the back of my hand and hammered it into the table, I screamed, although I don't know why. Compared to the beatings it didn't hurt that much. My other wrist was placed onto the table, and this was also nailed to the tabletop. This was not a good position to be in. From now on, any punches or beatings were going to seriously damage my hands as I moved about, I needed to try to keep my hands still.

"Andy, you told me you wanted to tell me everything you know about Gordievsky, you can sit there for as long as it takes, we will see if you remember anything more." With that, all of them left me alone in the room again.

This was not turning out to be a fun day out in the sun. By some miracle, I could feel nothing had been seriously damaged by the nails passing through my hands, the exit of the nails through my hands was really hurting but nothing more than I had already felt from the beatings I had received.

Psychologically, it was hell, the feeling of helplessness and vulnerability was overwhelming, I started to shake, which I tried to control. I knew if they kicked me or dragged me around my hands would be ripped apart. It was a very uncomfortable experience. I sat and thought if there could be any story I could make up to give him what they wanted from me. But then what? The only end to this would be my death, it couldn't be anything else now.

I sat alone for hours, it started to get dark. Nothing was happening, no more interrogations took place. I couldn't move and it was getting very uncomfortable not being able to move at all. I did try to shuffle the chair back a little so that I could rest my head on my arms, which was more comfortable. I cannot describe how much pain I was in, I couldn't breathe properly, my jaw hurt, my neck and especially my hands, they were now very painful. Of course, there was no way I could get any sleep like this.

I sat there all night, I occasionally heard movement and talking outside I was on an army camp after all. I began to see light start to glow around the door and blacked-out windows and the sounds of people waking and moving. What would this new day bring me? As the sun got brighter, my eyes accustomed to the dark I could see around the room. There was nothing except the table and chairs one of which I was sat on. I felt so alone and I was shaking from the pain.

Maybe an hour later, I heard an unusual sound, a distant engine drone, it was getting nearer. An aeroplane! A small light aircraft, single-engine. I heard the engine slow as it made all the noises of landing at the runway just a hundred yards away. I heard it taxi and park somewhere not too far away.

This seemed to make a few people in this camp get a little more mobile, there was some shouting, I couldn't make out what it was, mostly chokwe I think. The engine of the plane stopped, I couldn't hear much more other than the excitement in the camp. Suddenly I heard footsteps in the dirt outside my hut and shouting. The door burst open, it was my interrogator again, oh no here we go again more pain! I saw he was carrying the hammer, this didn't look good for me at all. He was followed by three black guys with guns.

"Andy, you are no use." With that, he grabbed one of my arms at the wrist and used the claw of the hammer to wrench the nail from one hand then the other. I can't tell you how much it hurt, I screamed as the hammer pressed hard into the back of my hands to lever out the nails, I screamed and screamed loud, it was uncontrollable, I couldn't help myself. He commanded the three black guys something in chokwe, I assume it was to tie my hands and to take me out of the room, as that is what they did. They weren't very good at tying the rope around my wrists with my hands behind my back, although they pulled it tight, I felt it loosen when they let it go. I was kicked on the backside to make me move. Maybe the arrival of the plane at the airfield had spooked them, I don't know, but more than a coincidence that it arrived and then suddenly I was being marched outside. They did seem to be panicking and excited by the plane.

With one black guy in front of me and two behind, I was pushed to the door where more shoves indicated I should turn right once I was outside, then right and right again between the buildings. The white men stayed in the camp, finished with me, this was it, this was going to be my end.

We headed behind the buildings and toward the woods where I had circled the camp yesterday morning. The black men chatting in chokwe, I had no idea what they were talking about, but I could tell they were still high and drunk from the night before. We walked parallel to the runway, I dare not turn to look around, I knew it would result in more blows from the AK47's they each had. I noticed the weapons looked quite new, not the old badly maintained weapons I had seen on the journey here. They were being supplied with fresh equipment, not preparing to cease hostilities as they should be. We walked across the north-south road from the village that also crossed the runway. The guys escorting me laughing and joking as we walked, occasionally hitting me in my back or head with their weapons, sometimes it would be a kick. I just followed the man in front into the woods. I knew now I was going to be killed here, they were just taking me far enough away so that the stench of my rotting body couldn't be smelt from the camp, I'm sure there are animals around that would enjoy my flesh for breakfast. As we walked, I desperately tried to think how to escape, there was nothing I could do, it's not like me to not give it a go, but I really couldn't see a way out of this. Surrounded by the men guarding me, hands tied behind my back, no food or water for 24 hours in this heat, badly beaten, I was not in any place to put up a fight.

After walking for a few minutes, I guessed about 400 to 500 yards inside the woods and in plenty of cover, we came to a very small clearing, the place stunk. Either they had killed here before or it was the place where they disposed of the toilet waste, it wasn't pleasant at all. My blood-stained shirt collar was grabbed from behind jerking me to a halt. I was shoved back to stand against a tree, I leaned back against it, I don't know why it just seemed to be better that way for some reason. I instantly regretted it. As my hands rested on the tree trunk almost immediately an insect bit my hand at the base of my thumb. This caused me to try to shake it off, a pointless reaction as I was about to be shot. Come on you arseholes get on with it, I hoped they were capable of shooting straight to make my end quick. The men that had walked me here, stood for a few moments finishing their cigarettes and chattering among themselves, moving very slow in their morning hungover state. As I shook the pesky biting insect off my hand, I felt the badly tied rope around my hands become even looser. I could slip my hands out of the knot. I didn't let the rope drop to the floor, the men may see that I was free. I held it in my hand, I was definitely free of it. If I didn't do something in the next second, I was going to be dead. I didn't want to die today. I wanted to see my wife Julie and my daughter Joanne again. In that one second it dawned on me that I had had quite a good life so far, I'd done and achieved many things, I'd been offered a privileged career almost no one else ever had, I'd married and bought a house, my daughter was just a few weeks old, and I wanted to see her grow up.

This was it, the men started to ready themselves, they threw away their cigarettes after extinguishing the tiny stub, and started to prepare their weapons to use on me. I stood staring at them wondering how much more pain I'd suffer today, would my end be quick, or would they leave me half alive, so that I felt the animals rip bits off me, eating me alive. I hoped they would do the job properly. The guns were being cocked, a bullet in each rifle chamber was intended for me, these men really did look a ragtag bunch. Let's go, let's do it, do it now!

With that and without any great thought, I lifted one foot against the tree trunk and gave a huge push, now I ran with my hands completely free, I ran straight at them, only about ten feet away from where I was stood against the tree. I ran at them and right through them, passing them close enough to barge one guy on the shoulder causing him to stumble, he was taken by surprise, my charge was like a rugby player running to score a try. I ran through their untidy line of three and kept going. The weight of their weapons was a disadvantage to them. It took a vital half-second for them to realise what was happening by which time I'd covered at least six feet past them. The men with their heavy guns were slow to spin around to aim at me, I hoped if they were stupid enough they'd fire a shot too early and shoot each other as they turned around to where I was now running and running fast. I zig-zagged through the trees, I needed to get some distance between us, enough to try to get some trees between me and them. It seemed ages before the first shot was fired in my direction. Taken completely by surprise, the men started firing, what seemed a good three or four seconds after I ran through their line. I don't know where the first bullets went, probably fired in panic rather than aimed, the rounds disappeared into the trees somewhere. The next shots felt closer as they gathered their senses to the situation. I heard and felt the shock waves as they zinged past me. I don't know if they were chasing me or standing still to fire their guns, I wasn't going to waste time turning to look, I just kept going full pelt, adrenalin assisting my dash, and I felt plenty of it surging into my body. The shots were getting closer, shattering trees and branches around me. My shirt burst forward as one bullet passed between my left arm and my body, so close it took some skin away from my rib cage, it stung, but right now it didn't bother me at all. I ran to put more trees for cover between me and the three-man firing squad, I have no idea if I was breathing or holding my breath, anticipating a bullet into my back at any moment, but so far the men's aim was very poor. From the sound of the guns firing at me, I must have extended my lead away from them by maybe thirty yards, with plenty of trees between me and them, I could hear shouting, yeh, like I'm going to stop because you ask me to, I thought to myself. I really had an advantage now, I had some distance, while they had to carry and fire weapons weighing seven pounds each, holding them would slow their attempt to run after me. I kept running the guns sounding further and further behind.

I had done it, I escaped!

On The Run

I didn't want to celebrate too early, I had run from the firing squad, and they were still shooting at me, I knew I could make it back to somewhere safe if I kept going. I kept running even though my lungs were fit to burst, my legs were burning, I had not had any food or drink for 24 hours in the heat of Angola, I had been badly beaten for 24 hours and my hands were injured from the nails hammered through them. But I was alive right now and I was going to do my utmost to stay that way.

Running through the woods away from the three men chasing me, away from the army camp on the other side of the road behind me. What to do next, where do I go? One place to head for would be to the camp back at Filipe Lomba's house. Would it be safe, would the soldiers from the camp be heading there knowing I might try to get there myself? There was little choice it was my only option, that or dying in the scrub-land of Angola, no food, no water. I decided, as I ran, that was where I'd head. Maybe, I thought that the three men would claim they had killed me rather than face being punished if they admitted to their failure. That was a long shot, everyone would have heard the shooting. I made a wide sweep slowly turning right, a big enough loop so that the men running after me would not see me and gain on me by cutting the curve short. The firing was dying down, maybe they had run out of bullets, maybe they had realised I had got away and it was futile shooting at trees. Either way, they would be heading back to the army camp and report I had escaped. Then they would all be after me, I needed to get back to Filipe's house and my UN group fast. I wondered if the UN group had heard the shooting.

Running through the woods, I felt relatively safe from mines, I doubted any would have been laid here, mostly they were in open fields, I kept running, the years as a child spending so much time tracking animals taught me how to move smoothly and quietly, to leave little trace as I ran, to avoid breaking any twigs to give away my path. I wasn't as swift as I could be, due to my bruises and it was very difficult running with a broken rib, I could not catch my breath properly, but the pain I could handle, I have a very high pain threshold. Now I was sure the adrenalin that was surging through my body was now giving me super strength. Pure fear was pushing me on more than any normal being, my eyes were more alert than they would be without the tiredness and injuries in normal life. Adrenalin is a marvellous thing, right now it was keeping me alive for sure.

I ran in a big curve, for about two miles in the woods, I was, at last, heading back to Lumbala village, but of course, this also meant I was getting close to the army camp too. I had no choice, it was the best and only way to try to get out of here. I would surely die trying to go anywhere else, I just had to hope the NPLA, Cubans or Russians were not waiting for me in the village, would they think I'd come back toward them?

The runway would be on my right-hand side somewhere, I had my bearings, using the sun, at this time of the early morning, I guessed about 8 am, it was still relatively low and usable for direction, I didn't stop running, and I didn't want the adrenalin energy to end just yet. I needed it to keep me going. I could see to my left the woods were thinning out, so I turned more right, I should be heading slightly south and west now, and the village will be getting closer. Eventually, after maybe twenty minutes running, with breathing almost impossible, I had no choice, I needed to stop, I crouched down in the trees to keep low, I could not hear anything, no shooting, no shouting, no unusual noises indicating someone was tracking me, just birds and noises of the jungle. To my left was a sloping bank down, maybe if I dropped down it I would gain some more cover, I walked over and slid down, finding that at the bottom of the bank was a road. I would be me more exposed on the road, but my pathway would be easier, I'd hear anyone approaching by car. I moved cautiously at first, then started to run once I had enough oxygen in my lungs. The road was heading straight back to the village.

About half a mile on the road, about four minutes running I started to see signs of the village ahead, I couldn't see any movement or any people searching for me. I passed by a few houses where there were few people about, I felt sure they were friendly villagers and not the NPLA troops, but I had to be careful, I didn't want to cause a stir. After a very short time, I saw the road ahead joining the main road we had driven along from the Zambezi River into the village, I recognised where I was and Filipe's house was just a few hundred yards dead ahead. The cover from the woods was almost gone now and at the road junction where there was a triangular island formed by the road junction turning left and right and a rough football pitch on the right, where the kids would be playing in their new football shirts soon.

To the north was the army camp, straight-ahead Filipe and my UN group would be waiting, I had no plan what to tell them, where I had been, I would just tell them we need to go immediately. At the junction, there were a couple of villagers, I had seen them the night before dancing in celebration of the football shirts.

They looked at me, clearly able to see I was covered in blood, they waved me across the road in a gesture to indicate it was safe to cross, then they continued on their way, not stopping to help me more. I knew why, it was good they did that one little thing to help me cross the road safely, but any more than that they would surely be getting themselves into my bad business. I understood why they could not help me more. They knew I was in trouble and the best way for them to help was to help me cross the road to get to Filipe and my group.

I ran across the road and down the narrow street to the gate and walled garden belonging to Filipe. Behind it would be the vehicles and people of my group, we'd jump into our cars and leave before trouble arrived from the camp just a few hundred yards away. I got to the gate, pausing slightly to listen for sounds inside the garden. There were none. I could hear Filipe talking in his kitchen in his loud African voice. Safety at last. But the vehicles and tents of the UN and my people had gone. Not a sign of them. I dashed across the garden to the kitchen door and burst in.

Inside Filipe was talking to a man, I had not seen him before, I stopped abruptly at the door wondering whether I should turn and run again. Filipe put his hand out to me.

"Anselmo, my friend, come in quickly. Oh my, you look a mess. Your people left yesterday after you went missing, they were frightened of the army camp. They left your bag for you, here it is on the table. They thought it would be the best thing to do as they had no defence against the army. What has happened to you?"

"I have no time to explain." I said, "I need to get out of here fast, the NPLA and some Russians are trying to kill me. I escaped from them and now they must be searching for me. I think they may come here very soon. May I have some water please?" There were small cloth bags and money on the kitchen table, they were obviously in the middle of doing a deal with the latest diamonds that Filipe and his people had mined.

"This gentleman is Victor. He is my diamond buyer. He came here in his aeroplane this morning. I think you should go with him, he will fly you somewhere safe, if you can make it to the airfield."

That explained the noise of an aeroplane I heard landing earlier today. The airstrip was dangerously close to the army camp. I thought it a bad idea to try to get to the plane right next to the camp. But it was my only way out. My cars had gone, it was a long drive back to Luena and the camp there. It was a good risk if Victor agreed.

"Is the plane ready to go, is it fuelled, I can't hang around, they are looking for me, they will be here in minutes, I am sure."

Victor spoke, he had an accent I wasn't entirely familiar with. Maybe South American, but not Spanish, so I guessed he may be Brazilian. A lot of business was done with Brazil, the countries have the same Portuguese heritage.

"Yes, I have refuelled it, as soon as Filipe and I have concluded our business, we can go. We should be five minutes."

"No." I replied "We cannot be seen together, they will kill you too if we are together. I will grab my bag and go now to the airfield and hide until you arrive, please be quick." I would thank Filipe for his help later, right now there was no time.

"Ok." Victor agreed. "You get to my plane, it is locked, take the keys, hide in the back, I will be there as fast as I can, we can take off right away, it's ready to go."

I reached out to Filipe to shake his hand, he looked down at the blood-stained mess it was and pulled his hand back.

"Go, Anselmo, no time for goodbyes, we will talk again sometime soon I am sure. Take this water and some bread and fruit." He stuffed it into my bag for me. I realised my hands are stiffening up and not very mobile. Adrenalin still holding back the pain. I slung my kit bag over my shoulders.

"Thank you, my friend." I said looking him in the eye to transfer my genuine thanks to him.

As I spoke, we all jumped at the sound of approaching vehicles coming down the road toward the house, they were 50 yards away. "Go this way Anselmo, to the back of the house." Filipe's wife was in the corridor that led to the back of the house.

"Come I will show you." she waved me urgently down the corridor to a back door into the garden. Filipe and Victor started to gather up their business off the table. As I reached the door and disappeared through it, I gave my thanks to Filipe's wife.

"Thank you so much for your kind help. I am sorry to bring this trouble to your home."

My First Solo Flight

"Go, go, go." She ushered me out the door and closed it behind me to help provide cover from the angry men now shouting at the front door, vehicles piling through the gate into the garden just the other side of the house.

I ran keeping the house for cover between me and the angry-sounding men. I dived over the four feet high inner wall. Keeping low, I turned right and ran crouching to the north toward the plane. Reaching the outer garden wall, which was much higher, there was a small gate through to the outside, it was unlocked and I disappeared through it to the outside. I could hear lots of angry shouting from the house. Filipe was in trouble now, there was nothing I could do to help him, and I was in full flight mode. Between me and the airfield was another house, I ran across the open ground and used it for cover. I began to hear shots firing. Oh my god, they were killing Filipe and his wife and most probably Victor too. I had to move fast now, they would come for me for sure, but did they know which way I was heading, would they guess I would be running toward the airfield and their camp just a few yards the other side of it.

I ran to the edge of the airstrip, I could see the Cessna small aircraft just the other side of the runway, parked next to the refuelling barrels, but right next to the first buildings of the army camp. I was going to be lucky to get to the plane undetected. I could hear more shots and Filipe's wife screaming behind me. The sound spurred me on, I dashed across the open runway sure that the house and walls that I had just come from would give me a little cover from the crazy men shooting innocent people behind me. I was sure Victor would be dead too, my pilot, but I still had every intention of making it to the aeroplane right in front of me. I got to the door on the pilot side of the plane. Quickly unlocked the door and shoved the keys into the ignition slot on the lower edge of the flight deck. I threw my bag across to the passenger seat on the right of the cockpit and jumped into the pilot seat, in my total fear of what was happening behind me, adrenalin had returned and I felt no pain from my hands or bruised body as I swung into the seat. I turned the key and master switch on and heard the gyros begin to wind up to speed. I had no idea what my plan was, but I was pretty sure I knew enough from my four flying lessons a few years ago that I could get this plane started and off the ground, then I would figure what to do and where to go. For now, I was running on fear, and I wanted to get this plane to fly me out of here. The plane was a Cessna 172 that I had flown before, I was familiar with the layout and start-up procedure, although I skipped all the pre-flight checks. No time to hesitate or be cautious here.

I slid the pilot seat forward so I could reach the pedals. Once the gyros had got up to speed, I saw the fuel tanks were showing full on the gauge. I pumped the primer on the left three times for a cold start, I left all the light switches off so as not to attract attention to myself, my head was working at triple speed trying to think of everything I needed to do to get this thing running and into the air. So far no one has noticed me sitting in the aeroplane, of course, I had no idea how long before they would. I set the mixture slider in, and the throttle control at one eighth in, ready to start. This was it, what else did I need to do, I didn't want or have time to fail my start.

I hadn't put my seat belt on deliberately just in case they started to fire at me while sitting here or taxiing, I could jump out in a hurry, I'd put it on later. The doors were closed. I turned the key to start, and the engine easily burst into life, which was a surprise I didn't expect it to be this easy. I felt confident I could get into the air now. I set the handbrake off and pushed the throttle forward to start moving. I wasn't going to waste time taxiing to the end of the runway, I'd go from here. In my bag I had the camera provided by the UN, the camera I used earlier was my own SIS camera, I had two for the different types of pictures I knew I would be taking. The camera I used yesterday morning had been taken from me when I had been grabbed by the Russians. I pulled the zip on my bag open and quickly rummaged for the camera and found it easily. As I began to move with one hand, I took a snap of the camp to my left and dropped the camera into my lap to take more pictures in a few seconds. I controlled the plane to the middle of the runway and pushed the throttle fully in for take-off. As the plane picked up speed, I pulled the flap lever down for 10-degree flaps and let the plane pick up speed while keeping it in the centre of the runway. A quick scan of the instruments showed they were all working fine, airspeed active, engine temperature coming up to normal. Looking out the front of the plane I saw there was plenty of runway left, even though I had started my run one third down the runway. As the airspeed indicator reached the green section at 50 knots, I let the speed gain another 5 knots before easing back on the yoke to get the plane off the ground. The bumpy ground was getting smoother as the lift generated by the wings softened the bumps. One second later the plane left the ground, I grabbed the camera in my lap and without looking in the viewfinder took a snap of the army camp to my left.

As I took off it was pure luck this photograph came out as it did, the arrow in the picture showing the door of the room where I was held captive.

I looked to the right, I saw something that would haunt me for the rest of my life. I saw the NPLA soldiers swarming around Filipe's house, just outside the door to the house laying in the most awkward position on his front was Filipe, a puddle of blood on the floor, he had been shot dead. A few feet away Victor laying on his back I guessed he had a similar end, as the plane moved on I got a quick view through the front door of the house, I could see the feet of Filipe's wife as she was laying in the doorway. I felt sick that I had caused this to happen to them, this happy man and his wife, who were so kind to us were now lying dead on the floor of their house. The soldiers below saw the plane taking off and fired a few shots at me before it was clear to them the target was too fast and difficult to hit.

My problem now was where to go. I kept the plane low and turned left away from the danger I had just left behind. It only dawned on me now, what I had done. I've taken off in a type of plane and that I have had only four hours flying experience. I have no pilots licence, no idea where I'm going, or to that matter, when I get there, little idea how I get this thing down safely. After settling the plane into cruise mode, flaps up, throttle eased back a little it was time to think clearly. I reached into my bag and found the water bottle and took a big swig from it. I tossed the camera onto the seat to my right. Should I head south or west into Zambia? I don't know any airfields there and so far, I hadn't found any map in the plane. North? This east side of Angola was the most hostile I didn't think it was a good option. So, I'd fly west, in that direction I could try to find my way back to Luena, it was a larger airport and the UN had a camp where my group were probably headed right now in the cars. I could re-join them, give them some bullshit story that I'd figure out shortly. It seemed like a plan, not a good plan, but then nothing about my situation was good right now. I turned left and headed west keeping low for now as I would still be in range of the surface to air missiles, I'd seen in the Lumbala army camp. I guessed they would have a range of up to 10 miles, given I had flown in the wrong direction for three minutes I calculated in ten minutes in this direction I'd be safe. Could they prepare and fire a SAM missile in less than 10 minutes? I had no idea, I'd keep flying low for a while and I will find out for sure. Would they be so bothered to waste a missile on me? Who knows, I wasn't going to want to find out in this little old plane. Next problem was, how far could I fly, what was my range? I guessed I could make it to Luena easily it was about 200 miles as the crow flies, I'd still be careful to fly efficiently as I didn't yet know where the airfield was exactly, and it may take me several attempts to land successfully.

After 10 minutes I guessed I was now relatively safe. I felt sure someone would be watching me on radar, but as this was Victor's plane and he flew here all the time doing his business. I thought I stood a chance I'd be left alone. I decided now to climb, I increased throttle a little and gently gave a pull on the yoke and noticed the climb indicator raise to 300 feet per minute that will do until I reach 3000 feet. I checked all systems, eased the mixture slider back to get a better fuel rate, the temperature indicator rose a little, so I didn't want to over weaken the mix too much. So far so good. Should I turn on the transponder and send out a squawk signal to identify myself, I decided not to do that until later when I'd squawk an emergency code to indicate I had a problem. I had no idea of any radio frequencies for the airfields here, so I'd have to remember the emergency frequency for the radio too. There must be some kind of chart in the plane, I was sure Victor didn't fly without, I knew some bush pilots didn't use maps but at least they had them in the plane. I looked around felt under the seat maybe there was something under there, I found a pouch in it was a map folder of this area, at last, something to help me find my way. I looked at the map, there was no protractor to figure the compass heading I would need to fly to Luena. Looking at the map the rough direction would be 290 degrees, I was flying 270 so I turned right to 290 on the compass and direction indicator in front of me. At 3000 feet I eased the throttle back slightly to cruise at 120 knots and adjusted the trim to achieve level flight. Now I could relax a little and do some maths. Being so tired I found it hard to do the calculations necessary for my journey. 200 miles at 120 knots would take me how long before I reached Luena? 1 hour would be 120 miles leaving 80 more miles, the remaining 80 miles is three-quarter of an hour flying time. So I settled on one and three-quarter hours flying time. I rechecked, such a simple math problem was proving to be so difficult. I tried different ways to do the sum, each time I got 1.75 hours. I looked at the clock in front of me, it was now 08:13. Just before 10:00 I should see the city and I can find the airport and land. I took note of the time on the plane's clock.

 I looked in my bag for the food Filipe had given me. I hadn't eaten for at least 27 hours now. I ate a banana and some bread and a good swig of water. I didn't think about rationing as I was only two hours at most from Luena and safety.

 Now as I relaxed the adrenalin was disappearing from my body, every part of my body started to hurt. My hands hurt the most, it was really painful to hold the flight controls, my face was throbbing, and a headache was starting. My rib wasn't so bad as long as I breathed in and out in shallow breaths, if I breathed out too deeply it felt like my rib was pressing into my diaphragm below my lungs and then it hurt. What had happened during the previous 24 hours, was now starting to dawn on me and I became quite emotional, the vision of seeing those three dead people who had done nothing wrong other than help me had given shelter to the UN team and provided food for us. The act of kindness had got Filipe and his wife killed, Victor had done nothing other than to be in the wrong place at the wrong time. It's an image and a feeling of guilt I will carry to the day I die. I wasn't sure at that point in time how I would cope with this once, if, I ever got home.

 For now, I mustn't think negatively. I need to land this plane somewhere safely. I need to return to the UN, somehow blag my way to the British Embassy, not the Spanish it was time to lose my Anselmo Gil persona, I wasn't yet sure how I would do that. The embassies were in Luanda 700 miles away, we had flown from there to Luena in UN planes.

While the aeroplane cruised nicely at 3000 feet and 120 knots, I started to think. Who was the mole that gave me away to the Russians? I sat and went through the options. Only the people in that first meeting at the Reform Club in London would know I am here and who I was. Chris Curwen, "C." I didn't believe it could be him, I don't know why I ruled him out, treacherous moles can penetrate every level, I just didn't think it could be him.

Max, "C's" assistant, he would know everyone that Chris knew and where and when they would be places, it could be him, he has access to every secret file that was in "C's" office.

Roger, it was his plan, a bad plan, I had gone along with it, he couldn't be blamed entirely, I could have always refused to take on the mission. There was something about Roger that I, and indeed "C" was uncertain about, I remembered "C" asking me what I thought of Roger. He was an upper-class dick, with the proverbial silver spoon in his mouth, he had a manner about him that made me and "C" question his abilities. He was smart enough to get me into place so quickly with all the necessary paperwork and character background I needed, I had to give that to him. But there was something about him that gave me the creeps, I could not say what it was, just a gut feeling.

Jean, she was a linguist and a good one, she would have some knowledge of who is doing what and where. I couldn't think that she would know enough secrets to act as an agent to the Russians, and she surely couldn't know I was in Lumbala yesterday, for now, I ruled her out.

Karen, my secretary. We had known each other for a long time now, we loved each other, if she was the mole then she could only pass on secrets on matters that only I had dealings with. Secretaries do not talk to each other on secret matters, I only ever heard them chat about clothes, makeup and men, just normal girlie stuff.

Who else knew about not only me but the others that had found an untimely end to their career? I pondered on this and started to let my mind drift into a daydream. The plane was flying straight and level it was easy to sit and not think too hard about flying the plane for a few moments. I formed some ideas and narrowed the list of suspects down to Roger and Max. I could not imagine anyone else would have enough knowledge of agents and their officers to get them killed.

What I thought would be an hour and twenty minutes into my flight, I started to look around for signs of the city of Luena. It was a big enough city it should be in plain view now. The land around was reasonably flat, yet so far no sign of it in mile after mile of scrubland. It should be here! I set the transponder to 7700, the emergency squawk number to show air-traffic control I was in an emergency situation, I'd never set this piece of equipment before, my instructor had shown it to me and explained how it worked so this was my first time to set it. I also set the radio to 121.5 the emergency frequency that should be heard by any radio that communicated with aeroplanes. I called a Mayday on the radio but there was no reply, had I forgotten to do something? Am I transmitting? I went over the settings, everything seemed to be in order. Out of the window, I could see no sign of the city. I couldn't see any roads that might lead to the city. Where was I? I should be able to see the city. Had I drifted sideways in crosswinds so far that I was now miles off course? I looked at the chart again and again 290 degrees was the correct course to fly from Lumbala to Luena. I looked again at the clock it showed 10:33, I'd been flying 1 hour 20 minutes. NO. I'd been flying TWO hours 20 minutes. Shit, I must have drifted off into my daydream thinking I was half awake, but somehow, I had fallen asleep while flying. SHIT, FUCK. The compasses showed I'd stayed on course, but I'd flown past the city in a doze. Oh, what an idiot I am.

I took a swig of water and poured some over my head to wake myself up. Ok, what to do? Turn around and look for the city or keep going and aim directly for Luanda another 500 miles away. I looked at the fuel gauge. I knew the Cessna had a range of about 800 miles, in theory, I could make it to Luanda, but with little fuel to spare, I would not have many chances to make a good landing. I figured, if I kept going, even though it was much further, I would eventually see the coast and from there figure out where the city was. The coast would be the best landmark. Turning back onto a reciprocal flight path of 110 degrees, by now I could be miles out and completely miss Luena again. Right or wrong I decided to go for Luanda. At that city at least was the main UN base or better still the British Embassy. I still had water, some little food, and the shock of missing the entire city had injected more adrenalin back into my body and I was wide awake again, and my pains had disappeared into the background. I was going for Luanda.

Landing My First Solo Flight

I shifted in my seat, realised I still didn't have my seat belt on so I buckled up. Thinking about Health and Safety even in my situation did bring a little chuckle to myself. I found a new comfortable position in my seat and went over the plane's systems to check and recheck I was on course and calculated I would have enough fuel to make it to Luanda, but not much more. Tiredness was a concern, I'd already fallen asleep, I couldn't do that again. I opened the window next to me to get some air, but feeling the turbulence it caused inside the cockpit I thought this may use up more fuel with the extra drag, so after a minute or two, I shut it again. I found switches for cabin heat and cooling. I was now comfortable and ready to continue my long journey.

Time to do some more calculations. From Lumbala it was 700 miles to Luanda, a total of about 6 hours flying time. I'd been flying now for 2 and a half hours, so I had another 3 and a half hours to fly. Fuel flow rate according to the gauge was 7 gallons per hour. 7 x 6 hours = 42 gallons from full. I'd used 2.5 hours at 7 per hour 17.5 gallons already, leaving me, 24.5 gallons. At 7 gallons per hour, multiplied by 3.5 hours flight remaining, that's 24.5 gallons needed to fly to Luanda. Oh my goodness, I was only just going to make it. If I didn't get lost I'd be landing with only fumes remaining in the fuel tank. I had to find Luanda first time, find the airfield and land first attempt. Was this the correct decision? I don't know, I was too tired and in too much pain to think clearly. I tried the mixture slider to see if I could get any better fuel consumption without raising the engine temperature too much. The oil temperature was ok. I adjusted the mixture and settled for a compromise mix, lean, but not so lean to overheat the engine. The sound of the engine was on the edge of lumpy, I'd forget climbing and using more fuel, and hoped the wind direction was assisting me, I had no way to tell. I could feel the flight was flat and smooth. Nerves kicked in a little and with the pain and all I started to shake a little. I took another swig of water, I had a few pieces of fruit and bread left I'd save those for later.

I left the transponder on 7700 and double-checked it was turned on to indicate I was in distress to any Air Traffic Controller. Radio was set to 121.5 to listen and speak on the emergency frequency.

Three hours is a long time to sit and fly a plane alone. I was sure my nerves and adrenalin would give me some boost but I had to stay awake, not drift off into a sleep again, that would be a huge mistake. I sat back if it were possible in this situation, I was pleased with myself I had remembered so much from so few lessons. I wondered if I would be in trouble for flying without a licence, but at the end of the day, I had more to worry about. Time began to pass slowly, I looked around to see if there were any cities with runways within sight. I could see none, even though the weather was good and clear. Looking at the chart I was not going to fly over any towns for the entire journey. This was it, my first solo flight, and I'm flying without any real idea where I'm going other than the rough calculations I'd done in my tired bruised head.

I took a few moments to look at my hands and other injuries. My hands were covered in dry blood and hurt like crazy, a little stiff but not too bad. The nails had passed through both hands cleanly without damaging any bones, muscles or tendons, I think everything important must have been pushed aside as they passed through. The rest of me was just major bruising and nothing was broken apart from one rib and one tooth, as far as I could tell. My head was thumping hard, I think that was pure tiredness. I wasn't sure why I was shaking, maybe shock or nerves. I was sure I could make this journey as long as I stayed awake.

As I flew toward what I hoped would be the coast, somewhere there would be Luanda or another city nearby with an airfield, I tried to recall how to make a mayday call on the radio. On my sailing courses, I learnt the mnemonic MIPDANIO to help remember the order of the mayday message. I was so tired I couldn't remember everything I needed to report. I hoped that the aeronautical version was the same, but this should be enough for air traffic control if they received the distress call that I would send soon.

M – Mayday
I – Identification,
P – Position,
D – Distress type,
A – Assistance required,
N – Number of people on board,
I – I could not recall what this was, I hoped it stood for Intention
O – I had absolutely no idea what the 'O' stood for, I could not recall at all. But I was sure the item at the end of the list was less important, so I wasn't going to let that worry me more than I was

already. I rehearsed in my head what I was going to say. Initially, I'd keep it short and expand when asked.

Time passed so slowly, but finally, on the horizon, I could see the coast and the blue South Atlantic Sea beyond. My fuel gauges were all but empty. I put the headphones over my ears and I tried a call on the radio.

"Mayday, mayday, mayday, this is unknown call sign Cessna 172, heading 290 degrees, height 3000. Any call sign please acknowledge." There was no response, shit! I couldn't be lost still, there was the coast in front of me. Luanda has to be here somewhere. I repeated my call.

"Mayday, mayday, mayday, this is unknown call sign Cessna 172, heading 290 degrees, height 3000. Any call sign please acknowledge." With that, I heard a voice in the headphones.

"Unknown call sign this is Luanda air traffic control, I understand you are calling mayday, please confirm your situation."

"Mayday, I am a Cessna 172, I am transmitting squawk 7700, unknown position, probably to your south-east, I am injured, injuries not likely to be fatal. I am on zero fuel. I need vectors to Luanda Airport for landing any runway please, I am one sole on board. Over."

My stomach tied itself in knots with the sound of the voice on the radio. Happy I was being monitored and scared shit-less that very soon I would have to land this plane. I can't explain my feelings fully at that moment. I was going to make it, yet danger was still to come.

"Roger, Cessna 172. Understood you have injuries, and you are one sole aboard, stand by, I see you on radar 17 miles south-east of Luanda airfield, standby for directions. You will have priority Runway 05 left."

"Thank you, I need every assistance to land please. I request British Embassy staff to be present on my landing. Repeat I request British Embassy staff. I am code Madrid, Cessna 172."

"Cessna 172, I do not understand code Madrid, please confirm."

"Please convey the message to British Embassy that I am code Madrid."

Madrid was my code name. I used this to inform Embassy staff who I am and that I should be afforded official diplomatic status, but it did tell anyone listening that I was someone from the intelligence community, and the British were not supposed to be active in this country. It was slightly foolish to say this on open radio, but I felt I had no choice. I didn't want to be arrested for stealing an aircraft and flying without a licence.

"Cessna 172 Roger, please continue on your current course and flight level."

I had no idea if he understood my message, but if he passed it to the Embassy in Luanda it should be enough to get help from them.

As we spoke the city came into view in the hazy sunlight. I was perfectly on course I could not believe it. The low fuel buzzer started to sound.

"Cessna 172 will continue on course and await landing instructions. I have zero fuel, I need straight in instructions please." The buzzing fuel gauge became a very annoying noise.

"Cessna 172, do you understand how to turn and fly to bearings I give you." I guessed he asked the question because I had asked for every assistance to land.

"I understand, I can fly to your directions. I can control speed and height. Cessna 172."

"Understood Cessna 172, standby for instructions." How long was this going to take them to get me down. I guessed the ATC controller was seeking advice, and I hoped he was passing the message to the British Embassy.

"Cessna 172, expect instructions to land runway 05 left, continue on 290 degrees and descend to 2000. Are you able to comply?"

"Roger, 290 and descending to 2000. Speed currently 120."

A new voice came on the radio. I thought this would be someone that can give me instructions on how to land such as another pilot.

"Hello Cessna 172, this is Luanda airfield ATC. I am a qualified pilot, I am informed of your situation, and I will help you land safely, I assure you I will do my best to get you down safely. What is your name?"

"Thank you, my name is Andy. I have zero fuel I will have only one attempt at a landing, let's make it a good one. I have four hours previous flying experience, and I have just flown 6 hours to Luanda. I am one sole on board. I have injuries, but not life-threatening, I can control the plane, thank you in advance for your help."

"Ok, understood Cessna 172. Your message is being conveyed to the British Embassy as we speak. Now I require you to slow to 80 knots are you able to do that?"

"Yes, I can do that, no problem."

"The airfield is dead ahead, I need you to turn left to 270 degrees, then I will turn you to the right and you should have a minute to line up with the runway, which is a very short time but I understand your fuel situation."

"Yes, that's ok, I need to make it short, the fuel gauge has been buzzing and showing zero for five minutes already. Turning to 270 degrees."

"Ok, no need to make any mixture adjustments, just leave everything as they are, we don't want to complicate matters for you. I see you are flying 270 degrees now, well done."

"Understood, no mixture adjustment."

"Now slow your speed to 70 knots, continue on 270 and let your altitude drop as you slow down."

"Slowing to 70 knots on 270, I see my altitude is dropping passing 1500 feet now."

I was now sweating like crazy with nerves and fighting tiredness, I grabbed a quick sip of water.

"I see you visually now, you are doing very well, you are flying very steadily, well done."

"Thank you, please turn me as soon as you can, I felt a slight stutter from the engine I'm going to run out of fuel any second."

"Ok, you need to continue a little longer just to give you time to line up with the runway."

"Yes, I see the runway to my right, continuing on my current course and speed."

"Shortly I will get you to turn right to the runway you will also need to lose speed and lower your flaps, do you know what effect the flaps have and how to lower them?"

"Yes, I used them before, I see the flap lever and know how to use it."

"Ok, try now to extend flaps to 10 degrees."

I moved the flap lever with my right hand to the setting required.

"I see your flaps are moving, well done. You will lose some speed, for now, do not allow speed to drop below 60 knots, ok."

"Ok, I can control the speed at 60, I am still descending."

"That's ok, I want you to descend no lower than 500 feet until after the turn, are you happy you can control that?"

"Yes, I can control that with the yoke and engine speed, I hope the engine does not stop by using more fuel."

"There is little we can do about that, for now, we need to continue as if you have enough fuel to land. A few seconds more will give you enough time to line up after your turn."

"Ok, understood, I see 2 parallel runways which one is runway 05? Am I aiming for the left or right runway?" Tiredness and stress were fuddling my mind, I should have known which was the left runway.

"We are keeping both clear we will see how you line up after your turn, we would prefer you to land on the left runway as you look at the airfield after your turn, we have emergency vehicles waiting by that runway. Now I need you to apply full flaps, flaps all the way down to 40 degrees please."

"Ok, understood, I think I can manage that I feel in control, flaps 40."

"Well done, but don't get overconfident, keep up your concentration."

"Understood."

"Now begin your turn right to 05 degrees, keep your eye on height, you can allow it to drop to 200 feet keep your speed at 60 until after you complete the turn. Do you see the approach path indicator lights? Do you know what they tell you?"

"Turning right to 05 degrees, speed no lower than 60, descending to no lower than 200. Yes, I see the lights I have 3 red and one white."

The path indicator lights help pilots keep height correct, on a correct descent path they should be 2 white and 2 red, 3 red meant I was low, but I didn't want to use the throttle to gain height, I sensed I was at a height that would land me on the tarmac runway, it didn't need to be perfect.

I completed the turn quite quickly, maybe I turned too tight, I ended up on a course between the two runways, I used the rudder to turn left to line up with the runway. I felt another engine shudder as the fuel became more and more starved.

"Good, well done good turn, now allow the plane to descend onto the runway."

"Yes, but I'm a little offline and a little fast I think."

"Ok in a few seconds you can close the throttle allow the plane to descend onto the runway, pull back slightly on the yoke to bring the nose up as you fly over the runway threshold."

"Yes, I'm using the rudder to move left I'm not over the runway, height 100 speed 55."

"Ok you are doing well, you are controlling everything very well, stay calm and allow the plane to land, when you do, close the throttle, apply brakes with your pedals and come to a halt."

I guessed from his angle of view it looked as though I was over the runway, however, I could see I was still 30 feet to the right. More rudder to turn the plane to the runway, I closed the throttle to tick-over and pulled back on the stick. At about 20 feet I was just over the right edge of the runway. I was flying by looking outside, I wasn't looking at any gauges now, it was all visual flying, I felt safer that way.

As I flew over the runway, I kicked the rudders right to land in line, just as the plane pointed in the right direction from travelling across the runway to centre, the plane touched down. For all that, I'd say it was a pretty much a perfect landing, no bounce or swerving, more luck than judgement. My shirt soaking wet from sweat, my hands shaking now uncontrollably. I'd done it.

I pressed the brake pedals hard and brought the plane down to 10 knots and took the next right taxiway, even though I had not been instructed to, it just felt better to be off the runway.

"Well done, good landing sir." I could hear applause in the background on the radio.

"Thank you, I am glad that is over."

"You may stop where you are. Emergency vehicles are coming to you."

"I request the British Embassy representative to be present, I have diplomatic status, I do not require an ambulance." I lied, I most certainly did need an ambulance, but I was now worried about what the authorities would do with me, I wanted to get to the embassy and nowhere else.

"Stop your engine and wait for assistance." I disobeyed and kept the engine running as an effort to keep people back. I didn't want anyone but the British to get to me. The engine spluttered slightly again, I have no idea what it was running on, the fuel gauges were showing dead empty and the buzzer was really annoying me.

"I am informed Embassy staff are on their way to the airport. Please stop your engine and allow the emergency crews to attend to you."

I saw the blue lights coming for me. I was not going to get out for anyone except Embassy staff. As they approached, I revved the engine and started to move toward an apron parking area in front and to the right. By moving it would keep these vehicles away. I kept moving slowly toward the apron.

"Sir, you may stop where you are and turn off your engine."

"I'm Ok, I will park on the apron and wait in the plane for Embassy staff to arrive." I was probably committing all kinds of offences by ignoring instructions. But I only wanted to deal with Embassy people, after all, I've admitted on the radio I have some kind of secret code, I'm completely compromised now. I was still shaking not knowing how this was going to pan out, but at least I'm safely on the ground.

Safe

As I taxied onto the apron next to the runway to a wide parking area, I was surrounded by vehicles. I could not move any further without hitting a vehicle.

"Cessna 172. Sir, please stop your engine and allow us to get you medical attention." Came a fairly stern order. I should obey, this will turn out bad if I don't.

"Can you give me information on the arrival of my Embassy representative please." I tried to delay. I decided to part comply and pulled the mixture slider fully out to lean the engine to a stop and turned off all the switches and key switch to bring the aircraft to a full stop. I pulled on the parking brake. It was damned hot sitting in the cockpit in the afternoon sun. People in the vehicles leapt out and approached me. I kept my seat belt on in case they tried to drag me out. The first guy to approach was a policeman. I opened the window. I spoke first.

"Sir, may I request I stay in this aeroplane until my Embassy representatives arrive, I have diplomatic status and respectfully request I am permitted to speak to them first." Another car arrived as the policeman paused for a moment to think how to respond to me. A guy jumped out and approached.

"I am the airport manager, I can tell you a person from your embassy will be here shortly. I am instructed to give you every assistance as a diplomat, would you like to sit in my car and we will drive to somewhere cooler and more comfortable until he arrives?"

"No, I will remain here thank you, but I will take some water if you have some." He waved at the policeman to indicate to bring some water. I was starting to feel dizzy with heat and stress. But I didn't want to get out and hand myself over to these people.

"Thank you." I thought I'd start a rapport to help let them know I mean no harm. "I have travelled 6 hours to get here, I hope you excuse my behaviour, but I have important information that is most urgent for my government, I hope you understand why I want to speak to my government before any other authority."

"Of course Sir." the manager replied, I wasn't sure if he was genuine. Yet another car pulled up amongst at least 10 other vehicles of every type that turns out in an airport emergency. A man got out and walked over with a big smile on his face.

"Well done Sir, I am the pilot that spoke to you on the radio, I want to say you made an excellent landing."

"I have 4 hours flying experience before today. Today has tripled my entire flying time, ha-ha." I managed a laugh, the situation seemed to be getting less tense. I think they realised I was important as the Embassy was sending someone without delay. Something that doesn't normally happen with the British.

"Someone from your embassy is coming soon, would you like to come inside where it is cooler?" I would have loved to be somewhere cool, but I felt it safer for my sake to stay where I was.

"The Embassy is 40 minutes away, someone will be here very soon don't worry, I understand you have diplomatic status and we will accord you such." I still thought it safer to stay put, with the Russians after me I wasn't trusting anyone.

The small talk continued until finally, I saw a car with diplomatic plates approaching. It came to a halt, and a smartly dressed man got out from the back seat. As he walked up to my window he held out a hand to shake with the manager and the other officials that had gathered around. He turned to me with his hand out,

"Madrid, I understand. James Forbes-White British Embassy Angola Attaché, would you care to step over to my car." Of course I could expect nothing less than a double-barrelled name, typical posh Sandhurst accent, but he seemed congenial enough. "I understand you have had an exciting journey today, you look as though you have" With that, I finally unclipped my seatbelt, grabbed my bag and camera and exited the aircraft. The gathered people stepped back to allow me to follow James to his car, I went to shake hands with the controllers that had helped me land safely and thanked them all for their assistance, the handshake turned into more of a finger touch when they saw the state of my bloodied injured hands. Sat in the back with James the car was refreshingly cool.

"We'll get back to the Embassy and you can fill us in on what's been going on."

"After a shower and freshen up, yes." I replied.

"Of course. I'm told you have flown all the way from Lumbala, that's 700 miles away, did you make the entire journey alone, astonishing." We chit chatted the rest of the short journey through the city, I didn't want to say anything until I had spoken to London. I was still shaking, my adrenalin had gone now I needed some good food and water, goodness only knows how bad I must have stunk in that car. Fifteen minutes later we turned into the Embassy compound, and I finally felt safe, the feeling overwhelmed me. I have no idea if I fainted or walked, but the next thing I knew I was laying on a bed in a room within the Embassy, in fresh clothes, clean bandages on my hands and obviously washed and clean as much as I could be. As I sat up looking around the room, feeling hungry and very thirsty, I tried to stand up but fell back to sit on the bed. The door opened and a middle-aged lady appeared holding a tray of food and drink. "Good morning Sir, how are you feeling today?"

"Today? What day is it?"

"You arrived here yesterday, it's now 11 am. How are your hands, I've done what I can, for now, it looks like clean puncture wounds, but we will get a doctor to look at you shortly, the rest of you looks very bruised, I'm sure you will recover in a few weeks."

"Thank you erm?"

"Elizabeth, I'm on the staff here."

"Thank you Elizabeth, did you dress me."

"Yes, I hope you don't mind, you are not shy are you? I bathed you, cleaned you up and got you into those clothes."

"No that's fine. Thank you for your help." I replied with a slightly bemused tone, wondering how she accomplished lifting my dead weight through all that.

"You're welcome Sir, now have some food and get some rest. I'll tell Mr Forbes-White you are awake." She placed the tray beside me, and left the room, closing the door behind her. I should have been starving but I could only pick at the food, but I guzzled the drink down. I ate as much as I could, I don't know why I wasn't hungrier. I was still shaking a lot. The room was more or less bare, just the bed and a couple of non-descript pictures on the walls. I sat for a minute or two, got up and walk gingerly out the door. Elizabeth was walking back down the corridor of the building. I could see out of a window the compound was made up of several buildings inside a walled garden. I asked Elizabeth,

"May I sit outside, get my bearings a bit?"

"Yes, the door over there will take you into the garden there are some tables and chairs by the pool, don't wander too far I'm sure someone will be coming to talk to you very soon."

"Thank you Elizabeth. The first and only person I will speak to is in London, is that clear."

"Yes sir, I will pass that message. Please relax and sit by the pool, someone will join you shortly."

I made my way into the garden. It was hot, but in the shade by the pool, it was quite pleasant. The traffic and city noise somewhat spoilt the tranquillity of the garden, but it was pleasant enough. I sat at a table with an umbrella for shade just staring at nothing in particular for a few minutes before James came to join me.

"Hello Andy, how are you feeling today. Quite a time you've had of it by the looks of it."

"Hi James, yes I'm still very tired and my bruises are hurting a lot, and I am having trouble breathing with this broken rib as it is, I seem to have a nice dent in my rib cage."

"Elizabeth has done all she can, we have sent for a doctor to come to look at you, he will be here very shortly. Andy, you said you are Madrid, we are used to people passing through this office, but we weren't warned you were in country, we have been taken a little by surprise by your arrival."

"Sorry James I have important information for London, I am not speaking to anyone until I have spoken to SIS." I assumed he would know who I was referring to as often an Attaché dealt with National Security and Intelligence matters, indeed most often they would be an officer of SIS attached to an Embassy.

"I understand, when you are ready, there is a secure line for you. In the meantime, if you need anything, I am here to assist, and Elizabeth can get you food or anything else you need."

"I'll make the call now then, please" I beckoned to indicate for James to lead the way to the telephone. I was taken to an office where there was a desk and phone, James told me to take a seat, he seemed to know the number required without referring to any directory.

"I assume you want Century House, here, it's connected." he spoke into the phone, "Hello, Embassy Angola, I have an urgent call, Madrid will be speaking." He handed me the phone and left the room so I was alone to talk. I wasn't sure how secure the room was, there was always a chance of bugging, so I had to be careful. A familiar voice came on the line it was Max, 'C's' assistant, he was on my list of suspected moles.

"Hello Max, I need to speak with 'C' and only with him if I may." I didn't use any name to introduce myself.

"Certainly, one moment." That was easy, it's not usually so simple to get through to the Head of MI6, and clearly, they have word of my arrival in Luanda. The phone clicked, I hoped the line was switching to secret mode. Chris Curwen's voice came on the line.

"Good day to you Andy, I'm told you have got yourself into a little bother."

"Yes, just a little." sarcasm was the tone of the moment, "Is this line secure?"

"Yes, you can speak as you wish." Clearly my health was not of immediate concern to 'C', I resented that a little.

"Listen, it is very clear we have a mole, my exact location was known, I was picked up by Russians, they were interested in Gordievsky, he must be in danger, they were trying to find out where he is. I recommend you move him. The thing is, the mole is someone that knew my exact location. It can only be one of the pre-mission team that knows where I was. No question about it, I was in a very remote location, there is no way anyone outside the team involved, would know my location."

"Do you have any suspect? What about UN personnel, was anyone aware you are not Spanish." 'C's' conversation seemed very minimal and out of character.

"No, I don't believe so, nobody here indicated at all they suspected me of being fake. Although I haven't considered the mole can be anyone here, I don't believe that to be so. It can only be one of the UK team."

"UK team being?" Chris Curwen knew the team, he was testing me to see if I had told anyone outside the small team that met in the Reform Club.

"You, Max, Roger and Jean the linguist, no one else for certain."

"Your wife doesn't know where you are?"

"No. She believes I'm on a sailing cruise. I recall you asked me once in London what I thought of Roger, do you have any doubts about his loyalty?"

"Only that the plan he came up with for you was very poor, you knew that, but you still took on the risk, a little foolhardy I think."

"If you think that way you should have put a stop to the mission."

"I think we all made mistakes on this one Andy." He made me quite angry, he knew this was a dangerous mission, badly planned, and not enough time allocated.

"Well, for now, You, Max and Roger are top of my list of potential moles." I told him he was on the list of suspects to get back at him for making me angry.

"Ok, Andy, come see me when you get back to London. There's a plane coming for you shortly if you are ok to continue to travel. You are a little emotional about your situation, I hope by the time we meet you have taken time to consider things, I will do the same my side, ok?" He could hear my anger and was trying to calm me down.

"Ok, I'll see you soon in London, I apologise for my short temper I've been put through it a bit here."

"No need to apologise Andy, I understand how you must feel. We will get to the bottom of this very soon." The situation calm again, I hung up the phone. Chris was a nice man for someone in his high position, I liked him and trusted him despite being on my list of suspected moles.

I left the office and found James again.

"What's the UN situation James?" I asked because my disappearance would be causing them concern.

"We think it better to let them continue to believe you have gone missing, presumed dead. Unless you have any other plan Andy. We can't let the UN know that we had placed someone inside their ranks. So long as no one from the UN sees you in Luanda we can leave it as it is."

"Yeh, you are probably right, of course. What information is there on my team are they safe?" I had got to know and like the team I was with, all good people in their own way. I hoped they had escaped from Lumbala without incident.

"Information is sketchy, as we are not part of the AVEM, as you know, but I have information they are at Luena, where I understand they have a camp, I believe they will come back to Luanda to make a formal complaint regarding the NPLA. I dare say the UN can't do much about the loss of Comandante Anselmo Gil. The war is bound to have casualties even among the peacekeepers."

"Yes, we left a team with a car at Luena to observe the Cubans there. They can fly to Luanda from that location, that area seemed relatively safe. I wonder about the consequences of the loss of a UN official like you say the UN and the Spanish will make a complaint, and not much will come of it. From our point of view, I think Anselmo Gil's disappearance is quite tidy."

"Yes Andy. I suggest you now relax, a doctor is on his way here, he will see you shortly. You do look a mess."

"I'm hungry now, I'll take some food by the pool I think, see you later I expect." With that I took myself off to the garden, finding

Elizabeth on the way, I asked for some food and drink in the garden. I sat for a while thinking about my lucky escape, the epic flight I made, how lucky I was that the rains were late and I wasn't trapped by weather. If I had to avoid any storms during my long flight I'd have run out of fuel for sure. I was lucky to be alive that was for certain, I escaped death how many times in the last few days.

After I ate the food Elizabeth kindly brought me, I sat enjoying the calm of the garden, my head by now used to the noise from the other side of the walls, blocking out the city sounds. I should have found I could start to relax, but I was still shaking. My physical wounds were not too bad, but my mental state, I was sure was not intact.

Soon the doctor arrived to see me. A nice man, his manner very calm, I wasn't sure where he was from, but his accent was English. He gave me a thorough physical examination, as I sat being examined, I began to shake more violently. I couldn't understand what was happening. I thought that maybe I had an infection from my hand wounds, but the doctor thought differently. He confessed he was not by any means a psychiatrist, but in his opinion, the events of the last days were causing me to have a mental breakdown, probably post-traumatic stress disorder or PTSD. The stress of my capture and interrogation, being stood in front of a firing squad, my escape, witnessing the killing of Filipe, his wife and Victor. The extreme guilt I was feeling that they should die because they did little more than be civil in a country entirely lacking any civility. The stress of taking a plane and making a six-hour flight with little flying experience. The whole event had an effect on me that I could not get a grip on and control. Clearly, I'm no James Bond with a mental capacity that can take on killing and death so easily. It wasn't a pleasant experience to feel my sanity slipping away. He gave me some pills to calm me down, and a few injections to boost those I had received before leaving England and suggested I should seek help once I return to the UK.

After he left I tried hard to calm myself, the pills the doctor had given me seemed to me to have little effect. I decided I should phone home. I called my father, the only person that knew about my real life.

My Dad

Dad and I had developed a code system. We used it every time we met or spoke. A simple code it went something like this when we spoke to each other:

Hello Andrew, how're things?

Because he used the word Andrew, it meant he was asking about me and my family so I would reply by talking about family things.

If he said to me:

Hello Son, how're things?

Because he used the word son it meant he was asking about my work.

To this, I would usually reply, "OK." Quite minimal, I could never tell him the full story.

If I added the words, "You know." to this, i.e. "OK, you know"

It meant everything was fine, and what I had done or was doing was something he could read about or see in the media. On those occasions, he would pop out to buy his newspaper, and when he returned, while he was taking off his coat and shoes, I would turn his paper to the relevant article, refold it so it was on top and he could read about what I was up to. He knew he could never discuss it, especially when others were around.

Dad loved this, the idea of having a spy code with a real spy, I was surprised sometimes he didn't cut eye holes in his paper and play the Pink Panther theme music. But Dad knew to be discrete, never to talk, and never to ask. What I asked Dad to do for me was a dreadful thing, I can't imagine the turmoil that at times must have spun in his head. The code system worked for years.

I called Dad at work, his secretary answered the call and put me through to his office. Dad answered with the usual question,

"Hello son how are things?" He used the word son, so he's asking about work.

I replied, "OK, not so good."

This wasn't how the code was supposed to work, failure was never considered an option. Dad knew something was wrong, I could hear from his silence he was wanting to ask but knew he couldn't, if he did, I wouldn't say. I simply said,

"I may need some help when I get home." With those few words and the sound of a familiar voice, it became too much for me. I couldn't find a way to speak any words, I somehow stumbled out enough words to tell him I'd be home soon and could he meet me at the airport he'd get details later. I warned him not to be shocked at the way I look. He agreed to whatever I needed and that he wouldn't say anything to anyone at home, really because he didn't know what the story was.

I sat in the pleasant garden of the British Embassy Luanda, I began to think. Someone, and I take some blame in this, caused the deaths of at least three innocent people, and I witnessed it. I take some blame because my presence was so badly planned, within a tiny period of time I had prepared to take on a cover and story that, although had apparently worked, yet in my rush to complete the task in a ridiculous time frame had probably been a contributing factor in those deaths. I did not take time, to consider my movements in Lumbala. I should have planned a better approach. I do think, however, that the UN team, of which I was in charge was in serious danger in that village because Russia was wanting to control and supply the means to counter the UN resolution, but at the time we did not know that. I had suspicions the Cubans were there with a Russian contingent, in an undeclared military camp for subversive activities. If I had not been off on my own in Lumbala, the UN team would probably have retreated and reported the situation for a larger, possibly militarized intervention. The team would have been safe and Filipe Lomba, his wife and colleague would be alive and prospering today. I can only imagine the killing may not have stopped at those three unfortunate people. I can only guess that the entire village may have been slaughtered to prevent the crime from being discovered. No one has been prosecuted for the murders in Lumbala, most probably it has been regarded as an unfortunate consequence of war.

I sat in a comfortable chair in a pleasant garden by a cool swimming pool with orders of food and drink arriving whenever I requested, trying to control my guilt and conscience. I sat thinking why man is such a destructive being, what was the Angolan war about? Greed and power. Why did the British ask me to spy? Greed and power. National Security is rarely about protecting citizens, which is just the story put out into the mass media as the excuse why certain things need to happen. I realised it is all about greed and power. Man is prepared to kill his own race, destroy the land and other creatures we share this planet with. One clever man can persuade other men that his ideal is the perfect solution. Those other men will follow blindly led by their greed and it grows into war.

I was not shocked by the sight of the three murdered bodies, I had seen dead and mutilated human beings many times in my work and even back in time to when I was an eight-year-old boy.

In Maple Cross where I lived as a child before the London orbital motorway M25 was built, was an accident blackspot on the A412. Some idiot architect had decided to make the fast stretch of road from Denham to Maple Cross three lanes! Who had ownership of the middle lane? Clearly, it was uncertain because there were many fatal accidents. Occasionally I was first on the scene. In those days there were none of the health and safety rules we have today. There were no seatbelt laws, people got involved, rather than stand to video with their mobile phones as they do these days. I witnessed bodies strewn across the road, thrown from their cars many times. I tended to injured people lying in the road until an ambulance arrived for them. I watched people take their last breath. Gruesome, maybe, but I think it made me a better person for the experience. It didn't stop me from throwing up my lunch when I saw what should be inside someone's body, out, but I'm not squeamish of blood and I'm not afraid to get my hands dirty helping someone in a terrible situation.

The sight of Filipe and his wife affected me so much because I knew I was partly to blame and killing him was pointless and it began to weigh very heavily on me. The more I thought about it the more I shook in a nervous tension I could not control. Whoever the MI6 mole was, would have to pay for their treachery and I would find the culprit if it was the last thing I did.

The next day a private jet arrived for me at Luanda airport. Before leaving the Embassy, I telephoned Karen in London and asked her to inform my dad when and where I would be arriving, if he would like to be there when I arrive, it was fine by me. I was taken in a diplomatic car bypassing airport security and whisked aboard, avoiding anyone witnessing Comandante Anselmo Gil leaving the country, he was dead too. I had an uneventful flight, in comfort back to England where the plane landed at RAF Northolt, west London.

In the terminal, I was met by my dad with Karen my secretary, I could see both of them trying to hide the shock of seeing my battered and bruised face. My dad didn't know what to say, to be honest, he was a little out of his league in the presence of people from SIS. Karen looked shocked and tearful that I was home, we still loved each other despite me being married, and it's hard to explain our relationship. My dad approached me as I walked into the room, usually, he would shake my hand, I guess he had been warned I had injuries so he, for the first time ever, hugged me. I wanted to hug Karen too, but we kept things professional. I could tell she wanted that too, placing herself with her back to everyone she silently mouthed words of care and love to me.

SIS people were present and wanted me to go straight to hospital for a thorough check over. I was to go to Princess Mary's RAF Hospital Halton, near Aylesbury, at the airfield where I had started to learn to fly a while back and thank God! It was close to my home, my parents also lived in Aylesbury at that time too. Dad, Karen and I were driven in a car by an SIS man, a journey of 35 miles about 40 minutes. We had time for me to give them a short version of what had happened. I didn't say anything about the mole that was hiding somewhere inside MI6. My Dad had a way to calm me down, he always did. He told me that Julie my wife had been told I'd had an accident sailing, something she is quite used to, so it was no big deal for her. She did care, she was a brilliant nurse, serving time at Great Ormond Street Hospital, so I knew I would be in good hands once I got home. At Halton, I was checked over by doctors, I was more concerned for my mental health, something had changed inside my head, I could feel it.

As soon as my medical was finished, my dressings changed, Karen took Dad home in the chauffeured car we had travelled from Northolt in, another SIS guy took me home and left me outside with my sailing bag. I went indoors where Julie was busy doing housework. Her first words were typical, and I loved that she always took whatever I got up to in her stride, I knew she loved me and knew she would take care of me, though she wouldn't know the real reason for my injuries. Should I have told her the truth? It wasn't the right time - again.

"What have you been up to." she exclaimed as she saw my black eyes and bruises - everywhere.

"I lost my sailing gloves, and you know me, Mr Stupid, carried on sailing without and ended the day with really bad rope burns. My hands are a bit stiff and I've lost a lot of skin, but they will mend." I lied to her again. The story wasn't a complete lie, I had once actually done that in a yacht race and my hands had become shredded pieces of meat, so I knew the story fitted.

"Once I couldn't grip the main sheet any longer my hands slipped and I fell onto the cockpit floor cracking a rib, I stood up and got whacked by the boom giving me these lovely black eyes. Quite a funny series of mishaps really."

"You're such an idiot, what am I going to do with you." She replied. Lying to my wife had become second nature and in those days I thought nothing of it, I had done it for so long. But now I felt guilt, nothing but guilt, guilt for everything, for lying, for doing my job badly, for getting people killed.

Life would not, could not, be the same ever again.

Four Days Later

I took a few days off work to stay at home, mostly thinking. I was a changed person, but I couldn't figure out what I wanted to do now. I took the bandages off my hands, the wounds looked good and clean, no sign of infection. They were a little stiff, my right arm was bruised beyond my elbow, it looked as though I had an arm tattoo. I had to get myself motivated again. Julie had been brilliant, what an amazing woman she was, how could I possibly continue to lie to her.

I had recovered enough to return to work to face a major debrief, and it wasn't going to be fun. I went to Century House in London. I wanted to speak to "C" first. My concerns regarding a mole inside the British Intelligence Service were equal to his. Gordievsky was his agent, and the threat of assassination was real. We met in his office alone, all bad feelings now gone between us. In my mind, I had eliminated him as a suspect. I reasoned that the mole was now totally exposed, simple detective work would reveal the suspect, he knew that, and, he had ample opportunity to kill Gordievsky should he wish, even if he did not do the dirty work himself. It was a simple matter of finding the common denominator between all those officers and their agents that have disappeared. After some chit chat about my capture and my solo adventure flight from Lumbala to Luanda, we got down to business. If the Americans got word we had another traitor in our midst they would have mistrusted us for a very long time, something we had worked very hard to restore after the embarrassment of the Cambridge Five.

Firstly, we needed to make a list of agents lost under suspicious circumstances or as in the case of Gordievsky, someone had leaked information to the Russians regarding his double-agent activities and subsequent house arrest in Russia. There was no evidence against him, but the tip-off made them suspicious and so, kept him under arrest, as I mentioned earlier in this book.

I didn't know, as I had no access to all the information that Chris had, who would be on the list of the missing. He called his assistant Max and instructed him to compile as quickly as possible the names we needed so we could study and hopefully work out who had something in common with them all. While Max was working on that, we considered the common denominator options. Max had access to all files, but Chris 100% vouched for him that he was not any traitor. There was something in the way he looked at me and I believed him. I had feelings that Roger could be the mole, and there was something about Chris's attitude toward him too that strengthened those feelings. I asked the direct question.

"What is it about Roger that you have doubts about?"

"His competence is my concern, he is old school, I have no doubt he can achieve and manage good work, but there is always an air of ineptness about him. The work he did for you was good, he placed you inside the UN very successfully, and he got you the perfect position as leader of the mobile unit that put you where we wanted you to be. It's hard to put my finger on exactly what it is about him, but, as I'm sure you feel the same, there are always parts missing to complete the package, as in your mission. He should have worked with you to get the time in country that you needed for the mission, two weeks was ridiculous."

I took some of the blame for that,

"I think I am the problem there. My wife Julie has no idea what I do. It was me that wanted such a small-time scale, as my story to Julie could only support a short time away from home."

"But Roger should have instructed you to inform Julie, he should have seen that was the weakest part of the plan, it was his plan and you were acting as his agent on this one."

"I still take the blame for that" I replied.

"Maybe you feel that way, the work you have done here for 17 years has been first class until now, I'd say this mission was a misjudgement, we all make mistakes."

"I don't make mistakes in matters like this, and as a consequence of my misjudgement people have died." I tried to assert my feelings on the matter, though not defending Roger at all.

"Roger should have helped you put Julie into the picture, it would have worked."

"I should have told Julie before we married. I didn't because one failed relationship made me worry, I'd lose her too."

"You should have spoken to Colin Figures he would have advised you on that if those were your concerns." Colin Figures was the Head of MI6 in 1982 when I met Julie. His reputation as an unstuffy, approachable conciliator, should have made him quite amenable to helping me with my personal problems.

"I tell you what," Chris continued. "I have another meeting, we can't do much until Max produces a list of those agents for us. Let's take a break and reconvene here in two hours."

"Sure, no problem." With that he hurriedly left the room a busy man indeed.

There wasn't much I could do, so I left the room and went down to my office. I spoke to Karen, asked how she was and chit chatted for a few minutes. She was always beautiful, and very good, if not the best at her job. I was so lucky she worked with me. She showed real concern for my health, she could see that I was not mentally fit either. She reassured me that if ever I needed to talk she was available 24/7. I knew that anyway. I'd have loved to have the excuse to go to her home and be with her for a while, she had such a calming lovely manner, but I was married, it wasn't appropriate. After chatting to Karen, I decided to kill some time by visiting my favourite place, the gun range, maybe I could loose off some frustration.

Downstairs in the range, I signed in, Pete was behind the desk, a real pro, he knew his stuff, ex-military, probably special services, I never asked, just assumed, he was highly professional.

"Jeez, you've been in the wars Sir." he exclaimed in his northern accent.

"Yes, quite literally." I wasn't going to talk about it, and he knew not to press further.

"I have something new for you, you'll like this Sir. Glock have just produced a new gun, the 19. Should suit you being a lefty." meaning I was left-handed.

"Let's see it then, what's so special about it."

"Easy to use and break down and for you, a lefty, no awkward safety lever to mess around with. Light, easy to conceal, There's a double trigger, see." He showed me the weapon, pulling back the slide to double-check and show me the chamber was empty before handing it to me, I liked it. It fitted nicely in my hand. There was a different trigger, a kind of double mechanism, the first part acting as a kind of safety mechanism to prevent accidental discharge, and the trigger weight was nice. Being a great shot with my left hand, it was always less efficient having to use both hands on the weapon to click off the safety lever. A right-handed person can use their thumb, a lefty has to find a way to use both hands to grip, to use the thumb with the right hand. Not ideal, and I was useless shooting right-handed.

"There are 6 magazine sizes. It's just out, you are the first to see it."

"I want it already, can I have one?"

"I already got you one, I knew you'd like it."

He went through everything about the gun, how to break it down for checking and cleaning, how to drop the magazine, for this, he showed me a few different methods, one-handed and two, so that the magazine drops into your hand or the floor. He could change magazines in two seconds in one easy move by using an index finger grip on the magazine. I practised a few times and got it down to three. I liked this gun a lot and I was going to be the first to have one. I took the gun to a firing station and prepared and fired all fifteen rounds. For a first-time firing, I did great, I got thirteen on target in the head and body. With some practice, I'd get them all in. After an hour, Pete produced a box containing my new gun. We went through all the parts, cleaned and prepared it for use. I went back to the station and fired a magazine off. I loved it. I told him I'd take it now to practice at a range near my home, not normal practice but sometimes that happened. Officers weren't usually expected to carry or use weapons, but we were all trained in their use. He gave me a lockable case to take it away. I signed and thanked him for it and said I'd be back to practice often. I like the gun range it's a fun sport in my opinion.

I re-joined "C" in his office to continue the meeting. Max had completed a list of names for us. The three of us went through it to try to find the common link between them all. I was on the list, though not killed, I was supposed to have been, a little alarming to see your name on a list of killed officers and agents. On the list were agents I knew too. Looking at the dates, we could not place Roger on the suspect list as he wasn't even working for SIS when some of them were compromised. Maybe it was down to one traitor, maybe there were several, again. Roger could certainly be on a list if there were more than one mole, but he could not be responsible for all our lost colleagues.

We could not find any link, it was odd, the mole was clever. I decided to go talk with Roger. 'C' said he would come too but had a little business to take care of first and would meet at Roger's office in ten minutes. I went down to my office, took my new Glock from its box and stuffed it down the back of my trousers. I don't know why I did that. Maybe, I felt if we needed to arrest Roger there could be trouble, it was just an instinctive feeling, and I usually trusted my instincts.

I went to Roger's office, his secretary buzzed him, and I was told to go through straight away, just as 'C' joined me in the office. We entered Roger's office together, of course, he was shocked to see my battered face.

"Wow, Andy you've been through it, sorry."

"Why are you sorry, it goes with the job sometimes?" I said in a suspicious tone. We sat on his sofa and began to talk through what had gone wrong. The gun down the back of my trousers was quite uncomfortable. He knew what had happened to me, but it was a way to break the ice to gently interrogate him without him realising. Chris was a superb interrogator, I don't think Roger even realised what we were doing. It became clear to me he was either very good at covering his tracks or he was innocent. For me, it was slightly disappointing, as my opinion of him was so bad that I just wanted him to be the baddie, but I was smart enough to know I had to be fair and do this properly. After many questions, Chris asked him directly, if anyone outside of the four of us, namely, me, Chris Curwen, Roger and Max had, while I was in Angola, asked about me, and where I was. It was the bluntest question. The question was straight forward, and Roger realised then he was being interrogated. He thought for a moment,

"Well, one person outside the four you mention but was part of your preparation team, Jean, she did pop in occasionally to ask how you were doing, how was your Spanish standing up, and general stuff like that."

I asked,

"Roger, did you tell her where I was."

"No, never." Roger declared innocently.

"Could she have found out by looking at your files?"

"Not as far as I know, but she is quite friendly with Kate my secretary."

I asked 'C' if he knew how long Jean had been in service with SIS. He did not know, he called Max by phone and asked him to find out. Ten years was the answer. She has been in service over the entire period that all those listed agents have been disappearing. Kate overhearing our conversation appeared in Roger's doorway.

"Sorry to interrupt Sir, I see Jean often in the mess hall and sometimes she comes here when passing to say hi. She may have seen files on my desk." I sat for a moment and thought about this. Why was she passing by? Suddenly it all added up, I sprung up out of the seat and ran out of the office. I ran down the corridor, I could hear 'C' shouting after me. I flew down the stairs not waiting for a lift to arrive and ran into the translator's room. A large room with many of the SIS translators sitting at desks transcribing documents from or into whatever language was required. Jean was sitting at a desk at the back of the room. I walked fast across to her, she saw me coming, I knew instantly from the look on her face she was shocked to see me. I was supposed to be dead, she hadn't heard I was alive.

"Sir, Andy, I ...." Without a word, I pulled the gun out from the back of my trousers under my jacket and fired three shots, one into her head and two in her body as she recoiled backwards from the impact of the first bullet hitting dead-centre of her forehead. She was dead before she hit the floor. Everyone in the room went into panic mode, just as 'C' and Roger ran into the room. Women and men screaming, some jumping up and running out of the room, some ducking under their desks. They didn't know I was only after Jean. I heard some crying. I dropped my new and now used Glock 19 onto the desk and put my hands up to indicate there would be no more shooting.

"Andy! What have you done? Why? We could have arrested her, maybe found out who she was passing messages to." 'C' shouted at me.

I hadn't planned to react this way, I just did it in a rage, I lost control, completely out of character, and I'd lost it. I felt nothing for Jean only rage. She had been responsible for the deaths of many, the pain of the losses for their families, the danger to British security, my pain and near-death experience. There was no doubt in my mind. I did not care if I was wrong at that moment, I knew she was guilty of treason. In 1989 treason was still punishable by death, and she was dead.

I stood with my hands up as security men arrived guns drawn. 'C' stood them down. He spoke out loud to everyone present.

"The situation here has not happened. No one is to speak of it to anyone. We have this under control now. Is that clear?" Some people through their tears replied.

"Yes sir." The rest remained silent. 'C' took control and ordered the security team to take care of the staff in the room, anyone requiring assistance could see the doctor, but was quite clear that not a word was to be spoken about this. I started to shake again, quite violently, I didn't want to, but I could not control it. I took one look at Jean, parts of her brain splattered against the wall behind, the look of shock still on her face. I threw up onto the floor next to her. I always do when I see people's insides, out.

Chris and Roger put their arms around me, and led me out of the room, a security guy took my gun from the table. I held my head down in shame of what I had just done. We went up to my office. Chris asked,

"What on earth has convinced you she was the mole?"

I answered calmly.

"Jean was the only person involved in my preparation for this mission NOT present at our final meeting before I left for Angola. If she had seen the mission statement I wrote, she would have known it was my direct intention to be exposed as a British spy and dangled as bait. If she knew that, she would have never risked passing any information."

Aftermath

Guided to my office by Chris and Roger, I sat on a sofa in my office. Karen came in from her room, she could see all was not well. She probably hadn't heard the gunshots from several floors above the linguist's room. She had no idea what had just happened. Chris spoke to her.

"Look after Andy, do not leave him alone, do not let him out of your sight."

"Why? What's happened?" She could see the stress and look of horror on my face, she knew something bad had happened.

"There's been an event downstairs, I need to go and sort things out, I'll be back shortly. Take good care of him." He left my office, in a hurry to get downstairs and get the mess sorted out. He didn't want this to get out into the public domain for sure, he had to speak to all those witnesses and to organise a "clean-up." Roger went with him, leaving Karen and me alone.

"Andy, what's happened? Can you tell me, you look awful." She sat next to me and held my hand by my fingers so as not to hurt my palms" She was so gentle, and as always amazingly pretty.

"I've messed up. I'm probably going to be arrested. Shit! I've messed up big time. This is the end of my career here." I said quite calmly but shaking quite violently, I was having a complete breakdown now. Am I supposed to know I'm cracking up, is this one of those catch 22 situations? If I know I'm going mad, I can't be mad?

"Tell me Andy. What has happened?" I didn't want to tell her the dreadful way I just behaved, telling Karen I'd lost it was admitting to her I'd failed and failed, totally.

"Jean, it was Jean the linguist, do you know her?" I said not looking at Karen but into the space of the room.

"What about Jean?"

"I worked it out, she was the mole in MI6, it was her that caused, how many people to die or suffer, how many? I just shot her dead."

"You killed her!" despite this news Karen didn't let go of my hand or gave any indication that she was repulsed by my action.

"She was the one that was passing information on officers and agents here in SIS. Her treachery, *she*, has cost the lives of how many?" I'm more thinking aloud than informing Karen of the events of the last few minutes.

"Jean! Oh God, what have I done?" Karen exclaimed as she put her hands on her head.

"What do you mean? What have you done?" I looked at Karen, how could she be part of this?

"While you were in Angola, she came to see me a few times. She asked how you were doing, how was your Spanish."

"And you told her what?" I looked at Karen now realising she could be part of this too.

"I thought she was secure, she was part of your prep team. I didn't see the harm."

"You told her where I was?"

I had been sending data burst messages from a long-range transmitter, it sent messages in a quick burst of data to eliminate the risk of detection. Messages received were passed, after assessment, to Karen for her to transcribe a copy for my records and to those that needed to know. Karen knew where I was every day.

"I could have. Oh my God, what have I done!" she repeated. "A couple of times she came in here as she was passing. She seemed very nice, and I... I told her you had found a Russian camp in Lumbala. Oh my God I have been so stupid."

"Firstly, why would she be passing here, her office is several floors down? Even though she was part of my preparation team, she had no right to that information. Jeeezus Karen!"

"She seemed so nice and she seemed so concerned about you........" Karen realised what a huge mistake she had made. I could feel a rage rising again, but this time I kept control, I couldn't hurt this beautiful girl.

I put my head in my hands, "Karen, oh Karen."

"I will have to resign." She now fully understood the mistake she had made, on the Angola job everyone has made huge mistakes, she wasn't alone in the blame, all of us involved were.

"That will be up to 'C'. He may have to charge you, I don't know. I don't know what will happen after this, it's all up to him now. Karen we've all made big mistakes with this, I don't know how we've all got it so wrong." She began to cry, she realised her career was over too.

I could see she was genuinely upset, I tried to calm her.

"Would you like a cup of tea?"

"I'll make it." She said, our hands slowly slid apart as she got up. She walked to her office blowing her nose as she walked. She brought a pot of tea back to the sofa and we sat, drinking tea not saying much, there wasn't anything to say until we both knew our futures.

After a few minutes 'C' returned.

"Ok, I've organised a clean-up, all staff have been ordered under no circumstance to speak of this outside this building. A team are on their way to Jean's house to see if they can find any evidence."

"Sir." Karen began bravely and composed, "I have to confess to a part in this." She explained how Jean had visited, it was virtually all we needed as proof Jean was a mole. Hard physical evidence would provide that, if necessary, would prove the linguist's guilt in court - if it ever came to that.

"I'm not letting this get out. We took years to convince the Americans we are to be trusted and leak-free, it will ruin years of work if this gets to them."

"They probably already know" I interjected ironically, "there are probably more moles in this leaky building."

"I hope for the sake of the country they never know." 'C' finished, "You two go home, take few days off. I'll call when I need to speak to you." With that he left, lots to do. I believe he knew he had also messed up too, allowing the Angola mission to go ahead. It was a poor plan, he should have stopped it. There was a plus side to this at that moment. Without this major cock-up, the mole may never have been revealed, we all understood that. More lives have probably been saved by this monumental cock-up.

Karen and I cleared the tea, she offered to take me home,

"My car is at Amersham station, I can catch a train it's ok" I misunderstood her offer.

"No, come home with me, I don't want to be alone, and you shouldn't be alone either. Come to mine with me please."

"Well, erm, ok." I was happily married, I hadn't been alone outside Century House with Karen since my marriage. But it was clear to me that neither of us was in the frame of mind to do anything inappropriate, difficult as that always is. I made a call to Julie at home explaining I had a lot of work to catch up on after being off work for so long. As always, the lie was easy, but now I did feel a lot of guilt. We called 'C's' office and informed his secretary where we were going.

We made the short journey to Karen's home without a word being spoken to each other. We were both concerned now for our future. It seemed to me that 'C's' cover-up activities meant there hopefully wasn't going to be any arrests for murder or manslaughter today. He was interfering with that evidence, which also meant he believed that Jean was the mole. At this stage, I don't know what it was that convinced him of that. For sure he was worried there may be a negative reaction to this if the Americans found out. One thing for sure they wouldn't find out from me, I never trusted them anyway.

Arriving at Karen's apartment she told me her lodger no longer stayed there so we were alone and free to talk openly. It was some years since I last went there, our annual after office party fling had finished when I met Janine and then Julie. Karen made more tea and plated some snacks, we sat on her soft sofa at either end, not touching each other.

"I'm going to resign." I said, "If I'm not in trouble if 'C' does a cover-up, I can't stay that's obvious. I've been compromised, I can't hold my head up in Century House any longer, I can't stay."

"Me too, I've made a whopper of an error talking to Jean and I nearly got you killed. I can't live with that." I knew Karen would find work elsewhere, no problem at all, she was that good, and probably would find better-paid work too.

"Well, there is no need for you to worry about what nearly happened to me." I emphasised 'nearly' I tried to reassure her, but I knew it wouldn't affect her thinking. "It's my job, I always know the risks. Please don't worry about what happened to me. I'm so sorry it has to end this way." In my head there was a constant video running, I kept seeing Filipe, his wife and Victor laying in pools of blood in odd, twisted positions. I kept getting the vision of Jean's face as it recoiled back from my perfect shot to her head, her brain splattering on the wall behind. The video wouldn't stop.

I didn't know what would happen next, would someone be coming to arrest me or both of us, was my future the inside of a prison cell? Now and then I'd start shaking, violently, my head felt as though it was fizzing, something inside my head had blown a fuse and was now sparking and arcing. We could do little for each other, other than reassure ourselves we'd get through it all somehow, sip tea and nibble a few snacks for hours, until late at night Karen got up to go to bed, I'd never seen her look so shattered. She told me I was welcome to stay and there was a place next to her. I couldn't, I'm married, and this was just not the time. I spent the night sitting on her sofa, drinking tea and watching TV to distract my mind after she left for bed. I did once or twice throughout the night look in on her to make sure she was ok and not crying alone. She was sleeping and looked so beautiful, I left her to sleep. It would have been so much better to have laid down next to her put my arms around her perfect body. The comfort she could give me would have been so perfect.

In the morning I was stood at the lounge window looking out at the world outside, people were busy going wherever, I was just staring, in a dream-like state, a million issues going through my mind trying to shake out the pictures and scene of Filipe and Jean. I'd witnessed the murder and I'm guilty of it. Sipping yet another cup of tea the world outside was blissfully unaware of yesterday's dreadful events, the busy people outside, contributing to the country's wealth, paying their taxes - mostly. What's it all about? Karen walked into the room from her bedroom.

"Morning Andy" she looked stunning in her pyjamas, girlie, sexy, hair in a mess, her breasts jiggling as she walked toward me. She put an arm around my waist and rested her head on my shoulder and we both stood for a minute looking out of the window.

"You look beautiful even with no makeup." I spoke without even looking at her.

"What shall we do today?" she asked not looking at me either, both of us just staring out the window in a dreamlike state.

"Two things." I replied, "One we should go to Century House and hand in our resignations to 'C' if you still feel you want to do that. Two we need to decide where we are going. Can we be together?"

"You'd leave Julie for me?"

"Yes, in a moment."

"I can't allow that."

"Why not" I now turn to look at her "We've kind of been together longer than Julie and I."

"You have a gorgeous daughter and one on the way, I can't allow you to leave them with no father."

"All of a sudden you are full of morals?"

"If it were just Julie, I'd fight her for you, I love you more than you can imagine, but your children, no, I can't do that. My parents divorced when I was 8, I know how that feels, I couldn't do that to your family." I went into silent mode trying to figure a way to be with Karen. I knew she was seven years older than me, but this woman was everything I could dream of, perfect in every way, even under these circumstances she was keeping calm, moved in a balanced controlled way, like you see athletes move, somehow, they always look in control of gravity.

"So where are we, how can we move on?" Had Karen thought about us, did she have a plan?

"Right now, I can't think about that. We should go write our letters of resignation and hand them in personally. Do you think we will be permitted to enter Century House?"

"Only one way to find out." I looked a mess, I went to shower, while Karen made her coffee. I had no clean fresh clothes or even a toothbrush, so I brushed my teeth with my finger, the toothpaste providing some kind of mouth freshness from a night of drinking tea. I found a razor in her bathroom cabinet, a Ladyshave type, I didn't care where or what it had been used for, I needed to shave, my facial hair grows so fast, it did a reasonable job if a little painful on my bruises. She came into the bathroom for her shower as I was drying up. We were just like a couple, natural together in our nakedness, not shy. I loved being with her, I wanted to be with her so much. I dressed and left the bathroom and sat watching the morning news on TV. Nothing about a killing, nothing about a body found in the Thames, good.

We caught a train back to Lambeth North Station and walked into the entrance of Century House, not sure what the reaction would be by anyone inside. At the security check table we were both frisked more thoroughly than usual, but passed through without incident, although I did notice the security guard telephone someone after we left the desk. A few heads turned to sneak a look at us both and I definitely felt uneasy. We went up in the lift to our office, alone in the lift we both said how people were looking, I suppose it's only natural I would have done the same. Once in our office, Karen sat at her desk to write our resignations. She was very efficient at her work, ten minutes later a letter for each of us was ready to be signed. She called up to 'C's' office and asked for an appointment to go see him, surprisingly we were told we could go immediately.

We sat at Chris's desk, a first for me I had always sat on his sofa, so I guessed he knew this was a formal meeting. Without talking too much, apart from his enquiry as to how I was feeling and how my injuries were, we passed him our letters. He read mine first and placed it on his desk. He then read Karen's and dropped it straight into the bin.

"Refused" he said to her "I'm not letting you go, you are too good at your job, I want you to reconsider." He looked at me, "I also want you to reconsider, I'm not going to bin this letter. You are not the only person to blame for the debacle that has happen, the work you have done since you joined SIS has been first class. No one knows how you obtained so much information on so many businesses and people, no one seems to know, it was brilliant work." I looked at Karen and she gave me a little nod indicating I should tell him. I told him the Xerox story in full. "Have you ever serviced my photocopier?" He said half-joking, half in fear.

"I could hardly walk in here and pose as a service engineer, I think someone would have noticed who I am."

"But we should think about a method to delete the drives automatically." 'C' stated.

"Yes, the technical department can easily build a device to do that, for them it will be quite simple. They can look at my device add a new part to make it a permanent fitting inside each machine."

"Can you do that for me, get every machine in the building protected."

"Of course."

"Andy, I want you to consider staying with us, we don't like letting people go, you have a job here if you want to stay."

"I'll consider it if the doctors and HR can assess me, I feel something inside has been changed by events I've experienced. I know I should be tougher, I want to be tougher, but my head is fizzing." It was the only way I could describe how I felt.

"Ok, get yourself checked over fully, full mental assessment." I wanted this, I knew something was not right in my head.

Karen spoke,

"Do you want me to continue to work with Andy?"

"Well, I think it best to separate you two love birds." Damn! How did he know, we were always so careful not to do anything at work to show we were in a relationship of some kind, and I wasn't sure at that moment what that was. "But, if Andy stays, I will give you the choice, you can work anywhere. I'd prefer you didn't stay together, it's not a safe situation you put yourselves in, there are security issues, do you not see that? Andy is married, it could place you in danger of blackmail. God knows, there are even some in this building that would blackmail you. I could order you both to split, but I will be discrete on the matter, for now, you've been through a lot and I don't think it will do either of you any good to add to the pressures you are both under right now." How on earth did he know we were an item, I guess there are spies everywhere. He was being too soft on us, in retrospect, he should have ordered us to part, it was the right thing to do. But at least it wasn't a gay relationship that a few personnel in Century House were indulging in, that would be far more dangerous from a security point of view, at least in those days it was.

We agreed I would get myself assessed and Karen would reconsider and give him an answer very soon. Things needed to settle down and become normal again, if there is such a thing in MI6. My resignation has not been accepted formerly or denied to this day.

My Brain Is Broken

After the meeting with 'C', Karen returned home, and I went to HR to arrange a full assessment of my health. I was put through a similar test on a computer to the recruiting test I had taken so many years ago. I'd been working at SIS for seventeen years by now. I failed miserably. I couldn't remember a lot of things that I should either. I was sent to a psychiatrist. In that meeting a very bizarre thing happened, I sat in the room on a sofa, a cliché situation if ever there was one. The doctor started to talk to me and I chatted away in Spanish, totally unaware I was doing so.

"Andy, can you stop and start again, I do not speak Spanish." I stopped speaking and thought about it, I couldn't work out what he was saying I had no idea I was speaking the wrong language, and I couldn't figure which language I was supposed to speak. "Can you talk to me in English please" Ah now I knew, I talked in English for the rest of the session. At the end of my time with the psychiatrist, he wrote a letter to 'C'. I didn't read what the letter contained but I guessed it wasn't good. The results of all the tests were sent to MI6, and I was told verbally that although my physical injuries were minor, I knew that, I could feel my body recovering, but, mentally I had suffered a complete breakdown, causing multiple types of amnesia. I guessed myself I was suffering a breakdown, certain thoughts or action caused me to start shaking and sweating. I was nervous, shy, and unable to do my work!

My multiple amnesia is a problem and I put it all down to the events in Angola. The stress and physical multiple beatings were the cause. With time I have recovered most memories, the amnesia that remains is odd, I cannot recall or learn anything that may offer me the chance to return to SIS work. For instance, I cannot learn or speak languages. Later in life, in the next part of my story, I went to college, evening classes, to re-learn Spanish, as it was a dream of mine to live, or at least to have a holiday home in Spain. I struggled to learn, I achieved an 'O' level Spanish, and eventually overt time and many hours struggling, I could hold a conversation again.

Simply put my broken brain prevents me from doing what it thinks to be anything dangerous, and reacts to SIS, MI6 and MI5 (I will discover this later). It's not a conscious thing, it does it by itself. Even something mildly dangerous, such as climbing the mast of a yacht will bring on some form of reaction, I can ignore it or overcome it, that is my new challenge in life. Writing this book and recalling the story, some memories cause me to become emotional. You could say that is normal given the events I went through, but, add to that, odd things happening, such as words being spelt completely backwards, or, spelt in capital letters, subconsciously I am shouting out the words. I find it quite interesting.

Here's what the doctors told me, in short:

Retrograde amnesia is the inability to recall memories before the onset of amnesia. One may be able to encode new memories after the incident. People suffering from retrograde amnesia are more likely to remember general knowledge rather than specifics. Retrograde amnesia is usually temporary and can be treated by exposing them to memories from the loss. (Later in my story, I begin to tell people who I was, it helped me tremendously with this form of amnesia)

Post-traumatic amnesia is generally due to a head injury, for example: a fall, a knock on the head or in my case, a damn good kicking.

Dissociative amnesia results from a psychological cause as opposed to direct damage to the brain caused by head injury, which is known as organic amnesia. Dissociative amnesia can include:

Repressed memory the inability to recall information, usually about stressful or traumatic events in a person's life, such as a violent attack or disaster. The memory is stored in long-term memory, but access to it is impaired because of psychological defence mechanisms. Persons retain the capacity to learn new information and there may be some later partial or complete recovery of memory. (I found this to be true once I start to tell my story)

Dissociative fugue is also known as fugue state. It is caused by psychological trauma and is usually temporary and unresolved, and therefore may return. An individual with dissociative fugue disorder is unaware or confused about his or her identity and will travel in journeys away from familiar surroundings to discover or create new identities. It is extremely rare.

Source amnesia is the inability to remember where, when or how previously learnt information has been acquired while retaining the factual knowledge.

Situation-specific amnesia can arise in a variety of circumstances resulting in Post-Traumatic Stress Disorder or PTSD.

Semantic amnesia affects semantic memory and primarily expresses itself in the form of problems with language use and acquisition.

It's quite a list!

I returned home after a day of tests, medicals and assessments of every kind, a thorough job had been done on me. I didn't object, it was what I wanted and needed. I was quite exhausted by it all though. I think I slept for twelve hours. The next phase of my life was pure turmoil, I have no idea how Julie put up with me, she seemed to be such a strong, understanding lady, yet still, had no idea what I was, did or had suffered.

I talked with Julie, I had every intention of telling her the truth finally. But, I just couldn't I knew she would never believe me, the story was too incredible. We sat together that evening. I told her that I couldn't do my job anymore, I didn't say which job. I wanted to do something different, move away and start again. She listened, seemed to understand and agreed that whatever I wanted to do if I showed her it was a good plan for our future and would be safe and secure for our children, she would support me fully. How many wives would be like that? She was such a great woman. I spoke nothing of my life in SIS to her, I spoke only about the printing job. I was such a coward.

I decided to speak to my dad. The next day I went to Maple Cross where the printing works now occupied a large factory space, it had grown quite well and was one of the busiest printers in the area. I sat in my dad's office, he started to speak first, he had news for me. He was planning to retire. If I wanted the company, I could have it. The catch was, I had to buy it. He had had the company valued, I was given first refusal to buy it. I couldn't believe it. There was no way I could afford to pay the price he was asking. On the one hand, this was the kick in the backside I needed to spur me into moving away, on the other hand, this felt so terrible. Even though I had worked in SIS, I had still put in the hours at my second job at the printing company. He had always said I should work at the printing company for a lower wage, as one day the company would be mine, and working cheaply was my investment in my future. I felt betrayed, he was asking me to buy it. I had mixed and muddled feelings, with everything else going on I could not cope with this extra burden. I could not afford to buy the company at the price he was offering me, it was another straw, and it was probably the final one, and it broke my back let alone the camels. He couldn't have given me this news at a worse time. But he thought he was helping me to break away from SIS, it was his way of saying I had done enough in that job, time to be normal. I didn't stay to talk about my problems at SIS, I thought it best to go home before our chat turned into a blazing row. It did in a way, but only in my head.

At home, I told Julie the news. She was flabbergasted, how could my father treat me this way! I had mixed feelings, I didn't have the right to own the business, but I was always led to believe I would inherit it. I'm not a greedy person, but for some reason this hurt deeply. As there was no way we could afford to buy the printing business, it had grown so well, we decided together that evening to move away, start a new life. Of course, she still didn't know the full reason why we should move on, but now I had yet another reason not to tell her what was about to become my past, and the reason was, I wasn't in that life any longer.

A New Life In Devon

Julie and I started to think about what I should do. We decided as I liked sailing and boats of every kind, we should look to do something in the marine industry. In those days there was still no web sites for information that we have today. The only way we could look for something was the Exchange and Mart, business section. We knew I wanted to work for myself, I didn't want to work for anyone ever again. The only form of business for sale in that line was mostly chandlers' shops and boat storage. I wasn't keen, it was obvious the reason for those companies were for sale as they could not sustain enough income to survive. It became apparent that this type of business survived only by the continuous turnover of new owners putting money into the business until it went broke. The old owners would sell to a new dream maker and repeat. I knew I didn't want a shop, all one could do was turn up in the morning, open the door and hope someone would walk in and buy something. There was little one could do to improve or make it different to how all the previous owners had run the business. We were looking to live anywhere, anywhere at all.

Finally, we found something different, for sale was a small business in Torquay, Devon, England. A little company manufacturing buoyancy aids, a similar product to life jackets. This sounded more exciting. A company like this could be developed, promoted, made more efficient, all the challenges I wanted. The reason for the sale seemed genuine, the owner wanted to retire. I made enquiries and within a few days, we were off to Torquay to go look.

Downsouth (Torquay) Ltd was a small business in Wellswood, Torquay. In a 3500 square foot factory space down a tiny lane (which was a bit of a problem, as large vehicles had difficult access). The owner, his wife and a few staff worked making one style of buoyancy aid, in six sizes. It all seemed to work well. The only drawback was, that the lease on the factory only had eight years left. I considered that if I could make a success of this, it wouldn't be a problem to renew the lease or move to a better location. The printing company had moved several times, I knew what was involved in that. The accounts and books looked ok, nothing special, but I believed with some work I could build the business. It seemed ideal. There was one huge drawback, the owner only invoiced his customers once a year, unbelievable! This was something I'd have to address quite quickly. He had a good list of customers, from shops and chandlers to boat hire companies on the Norfolk Broads. The selling price was affordable for me. It seemed just what we were looking for, and, as a bonus, it was located in a beautiful town on the coast in Devon, Southwest England, a perfect place to bring up our children. We had to make this happen. We returned to our home in Aylesbury feeling quite excited about it and during the journey home decided of all the businesses we had looked at, this one seemed to fit the bill.

The first problem, raising the money. We hadn't thought too hard about money, simply because we didn't know what we would find and the price that would be. To purchase 'Downsouth' we would need to sell our house, buy a house in Devon, and buy the company.

Have you ever tried buying a house and know the difficulty and stress that brings? Try buying a business as well and coordinate the two so that you can move into your new home, learn a new trade, run a new business, and not make a complete hash of it all, while bringing up a child, with one on its way, 200 miles away from the nearest family or friend to help, in a town you've never been to before!

We did the deal with the owner, settled on a price for the business, plus stock at the time of completion. It was going to be ours. First thing on the list of things to do, get money. We put our house on the market, if it sold as priced, we would make a good profit, as house prices were rocketing at that time, it could not be better. Houses in Devon were far cheaper to buy, so there would be money left over to put into the pot for the business purchase. We still needed more. A relative of Julie had sold his greenhouse nursery property in Watford, he offered us £30,000 no interest, he was old and didn't need the money for himself, so we accepted his kind help. In those days banks were throwing money at people, for me, it was even easier. I called Karen, without Julie knowing. I remembered her father was in banking, maybe she could ask him to help. Without any interview or paperwork, I got more than I needed at a very good low-interest rate. After everything was completed, I even had over £30,000 too much, which helped a lot.

Six months later, our house was sold, a house in Torquay was purchased, the contract signed for the business in Torquay. We agreed the contract would be completed three months after moving to Torquay. I would use those three months at the company learning how to make buoyancy aids. Everything fell into place perfectly, we could not believe our luck, but I don't recommend doing if you have a faint heart.

    The day of the move arrived. Our journey to Devon took forever. Joanne our first daughter, wanted a hundred toilet breaks, and if I got a pound for every time she said "Are we there yet" I would not have needed any loan at all. It took us six hours, a journey that should have taken three. Arriving in Torquay the removal lorry had been waiting for hours for us. Fed up with waiting the men had broken into our house, moved all our stuff in and they were just finishing up. They explained they had no trouble getting through the bathroom window easily, which was an extension from the house into the garden at ground floor level. The first job, as soon as possible, would be to organise the manufacture of metal bars for the window to make the house secure. Though we didn't know it at the time the house would become a money pit. It's a story on its own that house. If it wasn't such hard work it would be hilarious.

Business Is Good, Until...

It has been made clear to me I'm not going to be prosecuted in any way for what happened at Century House, London. MI6 cleaned it all up and made it go away. Apparently killing a spy traitor isn't frowned upon - mostly. I had saved SIS embarrassment, especially concerning the Americans, and it was all tidied up. Of course, I didn't feel good about it, but I had to move on. But I knew it would always be something SIS would use to get me to do something for them when they wanted, it would always be a dark cloud hanging over my head waiting to drop a deluge on me. A day would soon come when I thought the deluge had arrived.

During the time I am occupied with the house, I'm also working at the factory. The deal with the previous owner signed sealed and delivered. It was going ok, a few problems here and there and I think I did a fair job at bringing the business into the 20th century, slowly turnover began to rise.

For recreation, of course, living by the sea there had to be sailing. I went to Torquay Harbour where there were a few shops to asked around. I was in a chandler shop, asking if they knew anyone that needed crew. Luck had it, at that moment Ted was in the shop and he overheard me asking. Ted had a half share in a yacht with Mike his friend (and soon to become my new best friend) and was looking for crew. I was invited to join them on the Wednesday evening club yacht race in Torbay with the Royal Torbay Yacht Club (RTYC). I must have shown myself to be worthy as I was invited back the following week to crew for them again. More on this later.

Back at work, things were going fine. I resolved the 'invoice once a year' problem by sending out invoices monthly and offering a discount to any company that wanted to pay within thirty days. Most took advantage of the offer, some didn't. Those that didn't the following year had their bill loaded, the price list for them was higher. In my mind, a customer that doesn't want to pay isn't a customer. I had a big range of customers, spread about 50% retail outlets, and 50% boat hire companies, of those, most of them were on the Norfolk Broads. Retail businesses would order between 10 and 20 buoyancy aids, and the hire companies would order between 10 and 50, generally. When I first took over the business, the staff were all on piecework, meaning they were given a pile of work, let's say 50 jackets to sow in a day, and they were paid an amount per jacket. What tended to happen was once their pile was finished, they would pack up and go home. I wanted to change this to get a full day's work from them. With their agreement, I paid them an hourly wage, slightly higher than the piecework rate. That way, I could ask them to sow, then maybe do a bit of packing, or anything else. I think they enjoyed the variety too. We became more of a family, and they always helped out if I needed it. I did all the office work myself, and every day did work in the workshop. I'm a strong believer in the "never ask someone to do something I'm not prepared to do myself" philosophy (well, there is one exception, sorry ladies). It also meant they could look after themselves if I needed to go out for a few days to attend a trade show (something the previous owner never did) or meetings. It was all going well, and I think the staff appreciated that I would muck in too.

One day, to my huge surprise, and horror, I had a visitor to the factory. John, my mentor walked in. Good to see him again, but not. Amazingly, John had a business in Torquay too. Of all the places we could be! John had a small camera shop and photo developing company in the main shopping street in town. In those days, before digital, you had to take a roll of film to be developed and printed - children. Anyhow, John had heard I made things for boats, he wanted a cover for his surfboard. We made one for him. Slightly wary there could be something more to this coincidence I started visiting John in his shop, we'd be in the back of his shop with a cup of tea, nattering while he and his staff did the film processing. Quite a useful job, you get the chance to see everyone's photos. It's amazing how many people weren't shy about sending in their "bedroom" pictures for development, we had quite a few childish giggles. John and I became better friends and once a month we took it in turns to host a dinner party, Julie and I and John his partner Janet. Janet was a rep for a soft toy company. Janet and John lived in the centre of Totnes. Totnes if you don't know it is the country's centre for the hippy community. All things weird go on there. Last time I looked there were approximately 170 alternative medicine centres in the town. Most quite cranky, such as dancing in a circle naked while banging a tambourine. I hope I'm not one to criticise, if that makes you feel better, then it's good, isn't it? Anyway, John was taking the hippy atmosphere too much to heart, I think the tobacco in his roll-ups had a very strange smell to them. But he also sailed on a yacht at RTYC, so we had at least something in common.

At least now we started to have a circle of friends in Devon, life was mostly good, but, then I started to get wind of good, yet bad news.

Downsouth (Torquay) Ltd was a member of the British Marine Industries Federation (BMIF). This was a source of information and all things in the marine industry. One such thing was, each year the jackets I, and all UK companies that manufactured buoyancy aids and life jackets, submitted our products for testing in BMIF laboratories. This meant each of our jackets were tested and proven to work as they should, i.e. the person should float face up. I had to send one jacket for each of the six sizes every year to be tested. I never had a fail. It was proposed that a new test, for a European Standard, be set up. This was good because it unified all of Europe's, buoyancy aids and life jackets. This would mean our market would be opened up to sell in Europe and not just Britain. Until now, if I wanted to sell in any other country, I would have to get my jackets tested to each individual country's standards. It sounded good, the trouble is, whenever our government, and even more so, Europe, is involved, things do not and never can be smooth working (Brexit is a fine example). The proposal to unify, was good, but by the end, I realised in fact, it must have been more about destroying any industry. No one could decide what those new regulations would be. It dragged on, and on, and on. Every country had its own idea. A date was set when the new regulations would come into force, from memory it was July 1994. In my business I planned a year in advance what I was going to do the following year, trying to predict sales and ordering materials accordingly. In late 1993 nothing was yet decided regarding the EU regulations for the marine industry. I didn't know how to plan. I saw a draft copy of the regulations, which gave me some clues and it was going to be a disaster. For instance. For my jackets to be tested each year, now they would have to be tested by someone else, a new laboratory for the whole of Europe, no one knew who yet. And as a for instance, the plan was, in the draft proposal, for each Jacket type, I had one type, each size, I had six sizes, had to be water tested. They always were. But now each size, let's say the size for a 12 stone person, had to be tested by six different shape people, a tall thin man, a short fat man, and so on. So for my six sizes, I would need to find 36 different shaped people willing to put on my jacket and jump in a pool to see if they floated. There were nine other businesses in the UK manufacturing life jackets of some kind. Each of them would need to do the same. Another example of the future of testing would be that the material used had to be of a certain quality, and numbers were in the draft saying what that quality was. I phoned my material suppliers, none of them knew or had heard what the material was, I could not buy anything for the new regulations because no one had heard of the type of material needed. Until 1993 the cost of testing was, for my company in round numbers, £1000. Using the draft regulations, the manufacturing companies in the UK estimated the cost for me would become £32,000. I couldn't afford that, neither could any other company in the UK. I had buyers calling me wanting to place orders to the new standards, I had to tell them we didn't know what they were yet, sales dropped. The same was happening to all the other manufacturers in the UK, probably Europe. It was a total mess. In the end, I decided we could not continue to operate under such conditions. That year every manufacturing company in the UK, most of them bigger than my little business, closed down and ceased trading. Europe had killed the industry, well-done people.

It wasn't all bad news, one wise Norfolk Broad Boat Hire owner saw the industry was having problems and placed the biggest order ever, 650 jackets. We completed the order before I announced to the staff we could not continue in business with the regulations in chaos.

After working at my own business for almost five years, I had to announce to my good, loyal staff, to pack up their things and go home. They had all worked hard with me and it was a day I won't forget, ever. As for me, working hard had helped me put my past to the back of my mind. Outside of work the DIY, my children, fantastic wife and sailing had meant all in all I had a great life, and now, it was all shattered again.

What was to happen soon changed my life, my way of thinking, my depression. Three separate events, years apart none the less, finally ended all the secrets and lies.

Event 1. Deep Depression

The next few months were pure hell. I had to deal with the closure of my Downsouth buoyancy aid factory, without any advice or help from anyone. Not only were the physical aspects of shutting down, and disposal of the assets, but the mental strain upon me huge. I had a young family to feed, a home to keep for them, plus the financial pressures that placed on me I could feel was moving me back into depression. Not all the decisions I made were good. I also had to figure out what to do for work. I didn't want to work for anyone and join the morning trudge into a job where I'm expected to give my life to enhance some faceless fat cat's share dividend.

I found a company that made portable ball pools, so I purchased one, to rent it out for children's parties. I went, reluctantly, to a local printer and offered my services to work at home doing any typesetting they could not cope with, by computer. I seemed to be one of the first in Devon to find the software needed to do that, Devon always being about ten years behind the rest of the world. Surprisingly, I became quite busy with both little businesses, but I enjoyed neither. I just didn't know what to do. I made enquiries through John about returning to SIS. I'd been out of the loop for years, but with the contacts I knew I could restore, I thought I might be able to be useful for something. I tried to prove my point by passing information on a few local drug smugglers which I believed would give me some credit back at London. All that happened was, and actually would be quite normal usually, after a couple of our country's biggest drug seizures in Torbay, the local police alongside MI5 took all the credit, the information that I supplied to them to enabled them to find the hauls of contraband was used, but I was overlooked. I wouldn't mind being overlooked as a spy, it was quite usual to remain incognito, but I seemed to be overlooked in order to win favour back into SIS. I did manage to get an interview in London. Faces had changed, I had changed. I had picked up the Devon way of life without realising it. I was too laid back, I didn't let life rush me. I failed the interview dismally. In particular the psychological tests, again. The Head of MI6 was now Sir Colin McColl, who, I didn't know at all. That was about to change, and John Scarlett was about to become Head, I just didn't know anyone or the new technology now being used. MI6 had even moved out of Century House, into the now very famous and very visible property at Vauxhall Cross, the building seems to have acquired several nicknames as well as appearing in films and TV. Life in the spy business had changed so much in the five years I had been out of it. Spying mostly seemed to be on screen, there were rows of computer monitors and the business was conducted by computer from secretly installed cameras everywhere. I had little to nothing to win me back into the club known as MI6, and, probably if I had, I could not have done much or would have been very bored in this new modern computer led world. MI6 had become very public and visible, a move probably very necessary in order, by public demand, to continue to receive proper funding in a sad new world of budget cuts.

My resignation had never been formally accepted, yet, I wasn't in receipt of any payments or salary from SIS, I realised I was in this lost middle world. Still subject to the Official Secrets Act, still subject to bank account checks and my movements being watched but kept out of the main game. I assumed if ever cannon fodder was needed, that would be the time they'd come get me to help, they knew where I lived.

In the end and with kind permission from my ever tolerant wife Julie, I decided to do nothing much with my life for a year. To just relax, try to get my head together and figure out what to do for work eventually. I did nothing very successfully, the ball pool rental business was ticking over without little effort from me. I did typesetting when I was asked by the printing business over the road from our house. In the end, the year turned into two.

We had given up on the money pit house in Ellacombe. We could not afford to keep pumping money into it to keep it standing. We let it go, and for now, we rented a big house in Newton Abbot. John's ex-wife's sister's third cousin, or something like that, had a house rental business and found us a real bargain of a house to rent. I spent far too much time sailing. Ted and Mike invited me to join them, with the rest of their crew, to enter as many yacht races as we could. There was race night on Wednesdays and Sunday mornings at RTYC in Torbay. Coastal races with the club too. Thursday evening was race night at Brixham Yacht Club, we'd sail over the bay to Brixham and join the races there too. After a race, we'd go ashore and enjoy the fantastic views across the bay from the Yacht Club bar, enjoying superb food and good beer, sailing home late in the evening, slightly merry and probably in an unsafe condition for the trip back to Torquay by boat. Ted and Mike changed yachts from the one-design racer they shared to a beautiful Sigma 33. This meant we could now sail further and cross the English Channel, sleeping on board. We entered numerous races around the area, a fantastic experience and, at very little cost to me. One such race was the Sigma Europeans in Guernsey, joining yachts from all over Europe in a large fleet. In our first race I earned, after a mistake rigging the spinnaker sail, the nickname Andy Sideways. Somehow, I connected the halyard and sheets onto the wrong points of the sail and it went up in all its colour, sideways.

The fun we had and the experience I gained was fantastic. I earned Ted and Mike's trust, and on occasions when they could not make race nights for whatever reason, they would ask me to take the boat out for them, in order to maintain our race series score. One year, in a possible thirteen race cups, we won eleven.

Eventually, though it had to end. Ted and Mike were constantly arguing about costs. Yachts aren't cheap, and their partnership in the yacht was dissolved. Ted was becoming more unfit. As an ex-second world war bomber pilot, he had many tales to tell of his life in the RAF, yet always modest, I had to wring the stories out of him. His bravery in the war was an inspiration, it was sad to see him get too old to sail, which was all he lived for. He died a few years ago and I miss his knowledge and slightly cookie advice.

Mike, however, was ex-Navy. A few years older than me, we got on very well and continued our friendship. We would go out with our wives every week for a meal somewhere, visiting the many restaurants in and around Torbay. Fed up of not having anything to sail, Mike asked me if I would like to join him in a partnership in a boat. I declined because one, I could not ensure my finances would be predictable and two, I saw how boat partnerships result in arguments, always, about money. He noticed a poor old boat in Torquay Marina up for sail. It had been neglected for years, and, with the mooring fees unpaid, was taken into possession by the Marina Company and put up for auction. He won it, with his bid at £750, he was now the proud owner of a 23-foot Irish built one-design yacht, attached to the bottom of the sea by seaweed growing from under the boat. He asked me to help him restore the boat. I agreed to help but I wanted no part in the ownership or cost. He agreed, which was great. We worked together for two years restoring the boat almost full time. Mike was a taxi driver in Torquay. After two years of not doing much in the way of work, he also asked me if I would like to rent a car from him. Which I did.

Together we would play at boat restorers during the day, and work at night. In a week I would sleep probably three nights. It was fun and I acquired a lot of new skills, with Mike supplying the ideas and money, me doing the work, while he made the tea or coffee.

This should have been the perfect life, but for me, it wasn't. My memories and guilt were forever playing games in my head. Despite the fun and great way of life we had, I was becoming more and more depressed. Julie wanted to buy another house, but we could not get a mortgage, I hadn't been working in the taxi business long enough to have good account records. I became deeply depressed that I could not provide a nice home for my family and relative security for them. We tried very hard, and it prayed on me. I tried to cover it all up by playing boats. Julie seemed to be completely unaware of my feelings, I was at fault for not telling her, even hinting at the real reason. I was just scared to tell my wife that I was a man that she knew nothing about, beyond that which she saw and I permitted her to see each day. My guilt and inability to think about what I should be doing with my life prayed heavily on me, in the end, I cracked again.

I took one ibuprofen and one paracetamol, a combination that always helps me to sleep easily. On my driveway, I sat in my car with a hosepipe from the exhaust fed inside the car, and I sat in peace waiting for it all to end. I was finally peaceful and calm, I knew now the images and guilt I always had in my head every minute of the day would be gone. I would join Filipe and his wife, even though I knew them for such a short moment in time I owed them an apology. My eyes closed my thoughts drifted into a happy place. So peaceful at last.

I woke up in a bright place, out of focus people were fussing around me sticking needles into me, I heard someone say.

"Petrol fumes are ok, it's diesel that is carcinogenic."

Really! I was in Torbay Hospital with a multitude of tubes and wires stuck into me, so many I could not move. Apparently, Julie came home early from work, found me in the car and 'saved' me. This wasn't the plan. My brain came back into focus. Damn it! I'm still alive. Is there ever going to be an end to my turmoil? I hadn't given this part any thought, I have no plans for my future. How could I face Julie, I'd hurt her yet again, she didn't deserve me. I spent a couple of days in the hospital, 'getting better' before I was moved by ambulance, accompanied by some kind of heavy bodyguard, to Newton Abbot Hospital, literally 400 yards from my house in East Street. The hospital has since been knocked down and replaced by a modern new one. The original one where I was taken to was an old Victorian building. There was a ward for people like me. I have no idea what the ward was called, but it was secure, the people inside could not get out, nor could anyone get in without passing through some kind of security system. Here, I was told that the government doesn't like people trying to end their life, and therefore takes over the responsibility to help restore sanity. I saw the great irony in that statement, my government had asked me many times to risk my life for them and the people of my country, now I'm being told they care!

The ward, if I can call it that, was actually very nice. Clean, fresh, bright and airy with a nice garden to sit in. It was more like a hotel, with nice food and a kitchen where one could make a tea or coffee. I had a room to myself, all the patients did, just like a hotel room. I was put on suicide watch, which basically meant someone followed and watched me every moment of the day and sat outside my room at night occasionally peeping through the window in the door to check on me. There were male and female bedroom wards because our government doesn't like men and women sleeping in rooms next to each other either. The staff were kind, probably most of them lived in Totnes hippy town, but they were absolutely useless, I would describe them as a teapot with no spout, unfit for purpose. Compared to the private doctors I saw in SIS and those at RAF Halton Hospital, these NHS people had absolutely zero clue how to help their patients. Yes, they could happily follow me around all day, but that was it, they didn't seem to know how to talk. None of them spoke to me, I don't know why. I was given a welcome to Newton Abbot Hospital speech, explaining the rules of the house, which, basically told me not to go into the women's sleeping quarters. Apart from that, I was free to wander into the common room or do some art in the art room with no paint or paper. There was a television and a tiny room with an ancient computer that had almost no useful programs.

Each day I had to go for a 'chat' with a psychologist, but his title should have been psychopath, he did not seem to understand how to deal with someone like me at all, and, for sure he underestimated my intelligence. We sat in a room alone on beanbags, all very Totnesy, I wondered if we should get naked and bang tambourines, it may have worked better than his line of chat. He would ask me interesting questions, such as:

"How are you feeling today, Andy?"
"I'm fine thank you, lovely hotel you have here."
"Are you feeling better today?"
"Better than what?"
"Well, do you think your life is better today?"
"How can it be better I'm stuck in here, I need to go home to make things better with my wife."
"How would you make it better?"
"I have no idea, if I knew the answer to that, I probably would not be here."

Apparently, that was the wrong answer, by not having a plan to make things better, meant I had to remain in this secure unit for longer, it took me a while to realise that, but I did not understand the logic of the questions. I did not have any clue how to make my life better, to get the negative thoughts out of my head, I hadn't planned to be around to necessitate devising a plan.

Another day another interesting chat with the clueless idiot.
"How are you feeling today, Andy?"
"I'm fine thank you, lovely hotel you have here."
"Are you feeling better today?"
"Better than what?"
"Well, do you think your life is better today?"
"How can it be better I'm stuck in here, I need to go home to make things better with my wife."
"How would you make it better?"
"Bang some tambourines and dance naked."

I still hadn't found the right answer, so every day I would just tell everyone that I just wanted to go home. I have no idea what this was doing to Julie, it must have been so awful for her, how could I do this to her. I needed a plan. The plan came to me after I had been playing on the computer in the little room one day. The only game on the ancient thing was minesweeper, I played it for hours as there was little else to do, other than making tea or coffee. It was nice to sit in the garden, especially as it was good sunny weather, the fresh air and the freedom this gave me was comforting. One day as I left the computer room, my suicide watcher was outside in the corridor, as I passed her, I commented that the game was difficult to win, just for something to say to my otherwise silent follower. She must have taken my comment as something negative and upsetting to me, because the next time I went to play, I found the computer room was locked and they would not let me in to play again. That was it for me, boredom if nothing else would make me go crazy, in this house for crazy people. It was time to get myself out.

I went to my room to think, I lay on my bed and made a plan, a plan that would show these fuck wits who I was, what I was capable of, that I could outwit them easily and, I would use all the skills taught to me at Spy School.

While I was laying on my bed alone in my room thinking, I also timed how often the face would appear at my door window to check I was not harming myself. I got it, and my plan was complete. It took me two days to get everything into place, I was ready to show these idiots who they were dealing with. Julie came to visit, we sat in my room, I couldn't say sorry enough to her. I also asked her for a couple of pounds as I wanted to buy something and I needed her to bring some things for my plan, but I didn't tell her what I was preparing. She didn't question how I was going to buy something as there was no shop in the hospital, well, there may have been somewhere, but I had no access to it in this ward.

Keep in mind, all the time I am putting my plan into place to get out, I am being followed and watched. My day started as normal, I got out of bed, washed and dressed and went for breakfast as I had every day. After which, I had a few minor pieces to my plan to complete at the last minute. I was ready to show them all. About 11 am, coffee time, I made myself a coffee in the kitchen and went back to my room to drink alone, I sat on my bed, occupied myself doing puzzles in a puzzle book Julie had bought me, I had the money she bought in my pocket ready. I waited until I saw the face appear at the door window, as soon as it disappeared I sprang into action, two days of secret planning was about to come to fruition.

Ten minutes later, the face appeared at the window, I was gone. I can only guess at the panic that must have ensued by my disappearance.

Thirty minutes later, I reappeared, I was standing quite calmly, at their office door in the ward, watching all the staff panicking, they were trying to figure out where I had gone. I was wet with sweat from the physical exertion I had just put myself through, but they didn't notice. They were so intent on flapping their arms or whatever, they didn't even see me standing there, so I spoke.

"Would anyone like a sweet?" I asked them. I held out a packet of sweets, offering them one of the sweets I'd just bought.

"Where have you been? We were just about to call the police to search for you." the head idiot answered.

"I went into town, I fancied some sweets, and I'm back now. Did you read the note I left on my bed?"

"Yes, it said you have left a message on the computer and you will be back shortly"

"Yes, so what's the problem? I'm back."

The head idiot led me away fuming, and I mean fuming, there was real smoke coming out his ears. He led me into the chat room with beanbags almost screaming.

"Calm down, mate." I said to him, giggling to myself inside. "You read my note and it said I had left a message on the computer, did you read the message?"

"No, they can't figure out how to turn on the computer." Fuck it, there is no end to their stupidity.

"Well, the message says, I have just popped into town to get some sweets and I will be back shortly, what's the problem?"

"You cannot leave without our permission, we have to monitor you."

I went on to explain the whole thing to the idiot.

"So, let me tell you what's just happened. Under your monitoring and supervision, I have entered a locked room and left a message on the computer you no longer allow me to use. I have exited the building without you or security seeing me go. I have re-entered the building after buying this packet of sweets from a shop in town without you seeing me come back into the building. Not only that, but I have also stolen every knife from the kitchen if you go look. I have hidden those knives all over the ward, they are in plant pots, under people's beds, down the side of chairs, they are everywhere. Now, you see, now you know what I can do, while under your watchful eyes, I am capable of more, much more. If you think this was trouble, just wait and see what else I am capable of. I strongly suggest you let me go home now, or you will have problems like you never imagined."

The packet of sweets was purely to prove I had been into town. The poor guy would have been speechless if he had any sense, but he wanted to shout at me, so I let him, but I was not fazed by his rant at all. I can't recall what he was shouting about, I was not listening. I was adamant I was going to go home. I made it quite clear to him, I could make trouble for him and the best thing he could do for me was to let me go home.

Two hours later Julie arrived to take me home.

We arrived home and I was happy to be there. She sat me down and made me promise never to do anything like that ever again, never to try to take my life again. She couldn't figure out how I had convinced them to let me come home either. I promised and I meant it.

The most important thing to me was, my inner confidence had grown, I had won the war against those so-called experts, and I knew I could still do it when necessary and that was stage one of my recovery.

Life after that took a turn for the better, and worse. The fun I had outwitting the so-called, experts in the hospital just filled me with confidence and deep inside a pride, that I still had it, I don't know what I had, but from that moment I knew, I was smarter and cleverer than people that call themselves experts. But, I was very unhappy that I had treated Julie so badly. In my mind, it was all about me, my problems, my thoughts and my memories that haunted me every day. Those events and another that was about to happen would change my entire life. I had promised Julie I would not try anything stupid such as cowardly suicide ever again. I intended to keep that promise with all my heart. I had hurt her enough, but for me to stop hurting her, I had to break from her. It seemed like more cruelty and more hurt, but it was the only way. I decided she would be better off without me. After all, if I had been successful in killing myself, she would be without me, and that was the only way, in the long run, to make her happy. She could never be happy living with me. Maybe it was very wrong of me to decide such a huge issue alone, but I knew she would never want me to leave her. That is not vanity talking, it was the truth. I was always going to be off sailing or being depressed, and I could never bring myself to tell her that the real reason was that she slept next to a killer. That my entire life was secret from her and she didn't deserve that, she was the most perfect wife and she didn't deserve me and my problems.

Quite possibly the most selfish person I could be, I decided I could not stay and give her the problems I knew I caused. I'd find somewhere else to go and she would, in time, make a new life and she would be successful and happier, it was obvious. Sometimes you have to be cruel to be kind. I knew she would be hurt again, but in the long run, in my opinion, it was best for her.

It took me a couple of years to plan another life. I didn't tell anyone what I was up to. I planned to leave and go far far away and hide like a coward so that I did not have to watch her suffer, which she probably did, a lot. I saw her cry like I never saw anyone cry, proper, deep inside and out crying. She told me she didn't want me to go, but I had to, it was the only way. I left hurting that I had to do it to her, but I could see no other way forward for her. She had done nothing wrong, ever.

Event 2 and 3. Goodbye John and Dad

Julie and I had separated and our divorce was in progress. I went to live temporarily in a share house. There were four people living in the house in Torquay, I hated every moment of it. I had planned to move far away from, I would say everything and everyone, but in reality, I was running from myself. I only had myself to blame for what happened, in every aspect of my life. I had planned to go live in the Philippines. I would go once my divorce was settled. I now felt more confident in myself after the hospital escape. The only way forward, as I saw it, was to move far away and hide, mostly from my guilt.

In the room next to mine in the share house was a lovely lady, 5'3" blond, great figure, whenever I saw her she was always smiling, she never seemed to be unhappy. She was Lithuanian born, Jurate. From day one living in the house, clearly, I must have looked dreadful, I don't know if it was pity or what, but Jurate for some reason always made sure I had some food, she made amazing dinners, always too much for herself, and so, gave me a share. We spent some time together and I learnt her story, she could write a book about her life, maybe she will one day. We spent more and more time together.

It wasn't part of my plan to be with someone in England, I had plans in place in Mindanao Island, Philippines, where a house and small shop was waiting for me. There was also the lovely lady Diwa and family waiting for me to become part of their life. I also planned to do a short course in Bayugan, Mindanao to learn how to keep pigs. The garden of the house was big enough for eight pigs. That and the shop would keep me busy and with some income to live in reasonable poverty until I could take my pension.

Jurate and I became closer and spent more and more time together. It was obvious we were becoming an 'item'. There would be a danger, if I wasn't careful, that she would scupper my plans to live in Bayugan, I wasn't careful. I did some tentative checks on her as being Lithuanian meant she had a Russian upbringing. I found out there was a possibility that at least one member of her family in Lithuania was KGB. This was nothing unusual, almost everyone in Russian countries had to report on neighbours or even family if that person was not towing the Communist line. Jurate herself was a signed-up member of the Communist party. But the way it works there is, you sign up, you get a better job and a better living. I was assured she was simply making her life easier for herself. In fact, this seemed to be true, as she had a job as manager of a brewery in Kaunas before she had to leave. She also had a bar somewhere in the woods outside Kaunas, by the river Nemunas. She stole beer from the brewery to stock her bar. I was worried she could be some kind of honey trap, but in the end, everything she told me about herself seemed to pan out. Her story is more amazing than mine, why she had to leave her home, got barred from America, and came to live in England, she even had her car blown up by the mafia before she left.

One day she went off to work, my room next to hers was small, single bed size. She had said many times her dream was to live in a house with a walk-in wardrobe. I decided to make her dream come true. The moment she left for work, I emptied my bedroom of all the furniture, putting it all in the garage. I had some stand-alone shelving I had from trade shows I used to do. I erected the shelving around the perimeter of my room, got into her room, emptied all her wardrobe and clothes drawers and made my room into her walk-in-wardrobe dream. Jurate had so many clothes it took me all day to fold and place them onto the shelves, all sorted into shirts, tops, dresses, jumpers, etc., etc. Eight hours I spent folding everything using a ruler to get them all uniform in size. The end result looked like some kind of posh shop. I finished about thirty minutes before she returned from work. I met her at the door as she came in, and told her I had a surprise for her. I took her to our rooms and opened the door to what was my old room and now a walk-in wardrobe. She was impressed, I think. The downside, I told her was that I now had nowhere to sleep. We have been together ever since. We married 4th November 2011.

This did, unfortunately, mean I now had to drop my plans to go live in the Philippines. I had to, yet again, hurt someone very kind, intelligent and beautiful and had done nothing wrong, in fact, had done everything right. I let down Diwa and her family, they had done so much to prepare the way for me to live with them. What followed was the event that made me tell everything to Jurate. With predictable results.

In 2011 we went to Spain for a holiday. I was in a happy place. Sitting in the garden of the villa in the gorgeous sun, by the pool, sipping a cold beer, there was an unexpected buzz on my phone. A message arrived, it was John, my ex-mentor, and friend. I had not been in touch with anyone or anything SIS for a long time. So this was a shock. I immediately thought this was the call, they needed some cannon fodder somewhere and it was time to call Andy. I was wrong. It was bad news. Karen had died. She passed away from cancer. I hadn't seen her for so many years, I had no idea. We had drifted apart, had never said goodbye, or even 'see you later'. The most beautiful, smart, funny lady I have ever known has gone. All the memories that I had locked away somewhere in the vaults of my brain flooded out, the visions of her beauty, Filipe lying dead, the lies to Julie and everyone in my life, the shooting of Jean, the pictures in my brain suddenly came back into the front of my head. Pictures of pieces of Jean's brain splattering on the wall behind her. Everything bad all at once. I burst into tears, crying like a baby, I couldn't help it. I thought I had all this locked away, and now it came back in a rush. Why didn't anyone think to tell me Karen was ill? Jurate came out into the garden from the villa and saw me.

"What's wrong with you, what's happened, we are in the most beautiful place, and you are crying?" she asked.

"Give me a minute." I left the garden and sat in the bedroom for a moment to compose myself. I returned a message to John. He didn't give me any information, he just didn't realise Karen and I were so close I suppose. I asked if it was ok to tell Jurate the real reason I was upset. I had decided enough was enough and from now on I wanted to be honest to Jurate, and, everyone. Somehow I knew by telling her the truth it would help me. Maybe then I could share some of my burdens and it would help, I just knew I had to tell, I didn't want to lie to anyone any more. John asked me to wait a moment while he checked with a higher authority about my request. It didn't take too long for the reply. It was fine to tell anyone I wanted, so long as I never pass on any of the secret stuff. I should have guessed they knew how this would go down with friends and family, I should have guessed too.

I returned to the garden, sat in the sun by the pool and told Jurate everything. When I was finished, she simply said.

"I don't believe you" and walked away.

Those four words have been true for almost everyone I have told. Too many lies and secrets and the mere fact that I got away with the lies for so long making my story 'unbelievable'.

I've told my best friends and some colleagues. After telling a few people and got very mixed and odd reactions from them, I slowed down the rate of my honesty. I was happy I finally got it all out into the open, it helps me tremendously with my own personal mental health.

John was always a bit of a problem for me. As a mentor, he was bloody useless. When I first started work at MI6 his mentoring technique was that I should learn by mistakes. In my mind, the world of espionage and spying is too dangerous to make mistakes, so I made sure I didn't make any. Maybe that was his reasoning, I felt it was in order for me to fail. When he first appeared in Torquay at my factory to ask for a cover for his surfboard to be made to measure, that was never a coincidence, and then to join the yacht club, that was obvious he was keeping me under observation, even more, he was hounding me deliberately so that I knew, always, I was being watched closely. The secret world I had lived and worked in doesn't like members of its family going their own way. Richard Tomlinson was the most public example of that. He did give away some secrets in his memoirs, and he went to prison for it. On his release, he was hounded wherever he went. Whatever country he tried to make a new life in he was forced to move on, in the hope one day he will decide it's easier to end his life, and that would be a great example to others not to do the same thing. The resources and effort put into that kind of hounding, in my opinion, is disproportionate. I left the business under totally different conditions, I didn't leave to make some political point. In 2018 it was thirty years since I had to quit the service. The cost of keeping an eye on me to the taxpayer was ridiculous in my opinion. I am not a traitor, or another Peter Wright or Richard Tomlinson, my memoirs do not give away any secrets, ok maybe letting the world know MI6 has spies inside the UN is close to that, but it must be obvious to anyone that they probably have spies inside all big organisations, and so does every other country. But thirty years of having strange clicks on my phone, mail obviously opened and resealed, my home entered and searched when I'm away. Yes, I know they do that and I feel violated. 2018 was the year to put an end to that.

Jurate and I were at a car boot one Sunday, its Jurate's favourite pastime, she calls it her church as it's every Sunday in the summer, she tells her manager at work she needs to have Sundays off to go to church, she is a chef at a popular restaurant open 7 days a week. We were walking around the car boot, on a Sunday morning it's a huge one on the ring road at Paignton, our next-door neighbour passed us, stopped us and asked,

"Did you see anything strange last night?"

"No, Such as what?" I replied, he looked perturbed,

"We saw a man dressed in black pass through our garden through the gate into your garden. I raced out after him, but, by the time I got outside he was gone."

Our garden is the middle of a row of three. His garden was at the end where the road passes by the side. There is a gate from his into ours because before we moved in the previous occupier was in the Navy, away for months at a time, so, Alan our neighbour would come through the gate to cut his grass for him while he was away. The gate had been put in for that purpose.

"No, we were watching TV, we didn't see a thing, how strange." Yes, it was strange, and I took a good guess why. We never close our lounge curtains of the window that looks out into our garden. It's part of my PTSD, I need to be able to see outside, even when it's dark. I don't sleep with my bedroom door closed either, and can only sleep facing the door, I get very edgy if I have my back to the door, it's something I have to live with. If anyone is in our garden, they can see us clearly in our home. There is no purpose to this other than scare tactics, to let me always know I'm being watched, and watched closely. The news that it had also scared my neighbour a little wasn't nice for me to know. Also not nice to know is occasionally we get up to things that adults get up to in our lounge, it's not nice to know there's some pervert outside. After thirty years it was time to put a stop to this invasion of privacy. I can cope with my phone calls being monitored and all that kind of stuff. But sitting in my garden watching my wife, for me that's over the top. Time for me to do what I do best again. My hospital escape and the skills I used in that escapade needed to come out the drawer again, to put a stop to it all, once and for all.

I began that day to make my plans.

8.30 am one weekday, I arrived at John's shop in town, Castle Cameras, at the top of the main shopping street, Union Street, in Torquay. I picked the lock, even though I'm way out of practice, old skills soon come back. I didn't care people were walking past, every shop was opening up and staff arriving, with my body hiding the fact I had no key it didn't look too odd and nobody cares to take a second glance. As I entered the shop the alarm went off, it didn't matter, every day at this time shop alarms go off as staff are too slow to enter the code to turn the system off. This shop was likely to be one of several going off at that time of day and no one batted an eye. If you ever want to break into a shop, 8:30 am is a great time to do it. I did find the noise of the alarm a little intimidating, but I didn't let it worry me too much. I went through to the back of the shop where John had his film processing equipment. Here I sat and waited for John to arrive, I looked around, the shop was run down, people don't get film processed these days it's all digital, camera sales must be rock bottom, it was obvious to me that the shop was being supported and subsidised to keep it going, and probably just for my benefit, a cover for John's existence, what a ridiculous waste of taxpayers' money. I was in a stern mood, this had to go well. I sat facing the front door, with the noise of the alarm I could not hear John arrive I needed to see the door. At 8:50 John appeared at the front door, looking mystified why his door was unlocked and the alarm sounding. He walked cautiously through the shop to the back room. Saw me sat looking at him, he was shaken but relieved it was me, he shouldn't be, I meant business today.

"Andy, hi, nice for you to let yourself in." he said as he entered the code to stop the noise. "For what do I owe this pleasure." Letting myself in wasn't normal, yes I came here often for a chat, we had the strange relationship of being best of friends, having dinners together with our partners, we had bar room banter in the yacht club, not as friends but rival crews, crews always stuck to their own boat, it was always competition time after the races in the bar.

"I'm here on business today, John. I'm here to ask, no, tell you it's time for you to go back home to your house in Kent, it's enough don't you think" I stood up and placed my left hand on my buttock in a mock move that looked as though I'm about to take my Glock out again. John stepped back thinking he was about to join Jean's fate. I saw him glance at a draw in his workbench, I guessed he had a weapon or something in there, he was making the decision whether to make a move for it but realised he would be dead before he'd even touch the drawer handle, he'd seen me shoot before and knew I was good. I needed to avoid a fight, I had to keep him under my control.

"John, I'm telling you to go today, it's an offer you are not going to refuse. Look at yourself, your business is nothing, cameras have had their day, you smoke far too much crap, you are a disgrace to the Intelligence Service, I bet they sent you here because babysitting me is a nice easy job for you, you are not capable of anything more.

How much money are they spending to keep you here, it's beyond ridiculous? So, to help you realise leaving town is your only option, I'm going to show you something. Here put this film through the processor." I said. In the middle of the room was the Fujifilm processor, it developed the few films that customers brought in for printing these days. In the past we had fun looking at the bedroom pictures people had the nerve to send in, now it was all just film club stuff and very little of it.

John moved to take the film from me, I made the deliberate move around him to cut off his access to the work table drawer and whatever he has in it while keeping my left hand on my hip letting him know not to make a move on me. Once he had set up the film to feed into the machine, I'd had a quick glance at my watch, the timing was crucial to my plan. Shall we have a cup of tea I suggested, immediately I regretted it, now I was going to arm him with a pot of boiling water. I'd need to keep my eye on him for any sign he was thinking of making a move on me, but if I couldn't beat John in a draw or fight, I would worry, he was six years older than me and years of smoking and drugs had taken its toll on him. John stuck the leader tape onto the end of the film protruding from the cartridge and loaded it into the processing machine and started its C-41 journey through the machine, as it's called. I'd been here many times for a chat with John I could have done it myself, but it was better he did it. Once done he made two mugs of tea, he didn't need to ask if I needed milk and sugar. He asked,

"So, what's this about? What's the film for?" He looked and sounded very worried now, and quite sheepish, normally there was a bounce to his voice and always a smile.

"You'll see soon enough, trust me John, you will be packing your bags today. I don't know what's happened to you John, we've been best friends and now I find you've been coming into my home, watching from my garden."

"You were meant to know that we are watching you, to stop you doing anything stupid."

"For thirty years John!"

"We never let up, you know that."

"Not me John, I'm no traitor. For God's sake, I've even helped you, remember, remember the time I taught you how to do my 'legally rob' the bank thing." I was referring to the time a retailer friend of his was in financial trouble, completely broke and the bailiffs were coming to his shop at the bottom of the town in

Torquay. John and I helped the poor guy load all his shop's stock into a van overnight and hid it. In the morning the shop was empty for the bailiff. The guy was flat broke. In the days before debit and credit pin numbers and the bank tellers used a swipe machine that took a print of a debit card, I had discovered a way to walk into a bank, ask for a sum of money quite legally, take the cash and the money gets credited back to your account. That part is not quite so legal, but there is nothing the teller or the bank can do about it. It worked if you weren't greedy and asked for no more than £200. In those days that was a week's wages. I thought of the idea to use when, for instance, one wanted to stay in a hotel untraced. If one uses a debit or credit card the authorities instantly know where you are, or in those days a few days after the credit card chits are checked. Even if you take the cash they know where you are, but if it's refunded to your account there is no proof you have been anywhere. I used the method myself once. I taught John the method to get cash for his friend to get him to a new town where he could start a business with his van full of stock. It wasn't a technique I wanted to share openly, as although you did nothing illegal, it was morally wrong, well, perhaps, but I always enjoy seeing a fat bank getting stuffed, those establishments do nothing but cause misery to people, they create nothing. But I digress.

"I know Andy, but you know the business, they have ways to get you to do anything. They tell me to watch you, and I have to watch you."

"Not any longer John you have to go back to your home in Kent now." I said in quite a kind tone. The film finished passing through the machine. I took it and put it onto the print machine to convert the film to paper photographs, I knew how to do this, I had watched John so many times. At that moment Wayne, John's shop assistant entered the shop, late for work as ever. As he came into the back room, I spoke to him.

"Wayne I'm sorry, John's a little upset, his business hasn't been doing too well, he has to close down. Go home, you will be paid any money due including any holiday pay owed. Go now, take a camera or something from the shop for yourself." Wayne looked at John who looked so pale now, John just nodded and Wayne left without saying a word. I checked my watch again, I finished my cup of tea, John spoke.

"So come on, what have you got, are you going to kill me or what, get on with it?"

"So, take a look at these pictures." I said as I finished twelve prints "do you recognise this?" I showed him the first photo,

"Yes, it's my house in Kent, how did you take that?" Clearly, as I have all my movements monitored, he didn't know how or when I took the picture,

"John, you know me and my skills, I can do stuff like this without being seen. Recognise this?" as I showed him another angle of his house again.

"Yes."

"It's your house yes, I'm telling you to go back there and don't come back."

"Why?" John still had no idea of my intentions.

"If you don't bad things are going to happen."

"Really, so what?"

"Who lives in your house?"

"My daughter Sarah, but she is away right now, on holiday in Florida."

"So, you recognise this picture." I showed him another picture this time of the interior, in the kitchen.

"Yes, it's my kitchen."

"And what is on the kitchen table, here look at this picture it's a closer view."

"A clear plastic bag of marijuana? It's a big bag."

"Yes, it's about 10 ounces about £3,000 worth. It will last you a long time, it's yours, to tempt you home."

"Don't be silly that won't make me go." John laughed pretending he could resist a stash like that, he couldn't.

"So, Sarah comes home in 3 days, yes?"

"Yes, how do you know that?"

"It doesn't matter how I know. So you have 3 days to pick it up or she finds it on the table, and just by coincidence, the police may be passing by just as she finds it. Get my drift?"

"I'll just call someone to go get it." John tried to laugh off my bribe. With perfect timing, the shop phone rang at that moment.

"That will be for you John, a little push to help you leave." With that, John answered the phone, it was his son Peter. Peter was the manager of the Castle Inn, Totnes, just opposite John's house but not for much longer.

"Dad, I need help, can you call someone for me, the police are raiding my pub, they have found quantities of cocaine. Enough to accuse me of being a supplier."

John turned to me.

"You bastard" I shrugged my shoulders with indifference.

"Agree to go and the problem will go away." I said "Go get your prize in Kent."

"I can order you dead." John tried to scare me.

"No, you won't, no one will want to, because I have this." I showed John the next photo.

"A map?"

"Yes, recognise it? It's Northern Ireland."

"And?"

"Dots in fields, dots in fields." I said as I pointed to dots penned onto the map. John immediately knew what it was. During the Northern Ireland troubles, John had controlled an Increment.

Usually spying is secret and silent, when something needs to go loud and noisy or assassinations are the order of the day that work goes to what's called an Increment or The Increment. It can be specialists such as the SAS or snipers.

Margaret Thatcher's hotly denied shoot to kill policy in Northern Island existed, a small group of specialist men worked from a portacabin inside the grounds of the Maze Prison. They would go out into the towns, pick up a man wanted for a crime that could not be proven in court, usually an IRA associate, take him into the countryside, where a friendly farmer had dug a trench. The poor man as he walked into the field would be shot in the back of his head and dumped into the mass grave. The farmer then filled in that part of the trench and dig another for the next victim. Highly secret and controversial, this practice had been vehemently denied. Only since Thatcher died have rumours re-emerged.

This map was proof that the policy did exist and showed the locations of the mass graves, I believe there are at least 30 men in one.

John was the controller of the policy, I knew it, and he never knew I knew, until now.

"This is my insurance that no one touches me. The map has been deposited with a solicitor. If anything happens to me or any of my family, the map goes public." I knew this map should never be made public, but I needed to protect myself. I have been in the business too long to know what can happen.

"Agree to go now and I make a phone call and Pete can go free too."

"Ok, Andy you win. I'll go." John was beaten. I took my mobile from my pocket and made the call.

"Andy here, you are at the Castle Inn still? Good, let Pete go free, I have the information I need, he is not to be touched. Thank you." Ok, John, Pete is free and no repercussions.

"Cunt" was John's last words to me.

"Goodbye John." And I left never to see John again.

2018 was also the year my father died, he was the only person in my family that knew and witnessed some of my adventures. He was the only family member to have entered Century House when I returned from Angola with so many injuries. With his passing went the only person reliable enough to confirm my story. At his funeral, neither of my brothers wanted to speak or say anything. For the first time, I fought against my instinct to remain at the back of the room, invisible and silent. I wrote my Dad's eulogy and spoke at the funeral. Others had spoken before telling the story of my Dad's life, I promised a eulogy that would be something new and surprising. So in front of 150 people, family and friends, I revealed his story, how he had kept my past secret from them all too. I stood at the front of them all and saw 150 unbelieving faces. I looked, as I spoke, mostly at Jurate, she had no idea what I was going to speak about, her face remained blank, giving me no clue whether I was doing the right thing. I started to shake again as I spoke to the gathered friends and family, as I used to after Angola, but the shaking left me when I finished speaking and has never returned.

The positive thing about my 'coming out' has been that in myself I am perfectly happy now. I have some kind of closure, people don't understand it. Yes, people think I'm a fantasist that I've made it all up. I'm not going to cry over that, because only I know the true story of Andrew Gilbrook, An Ordinary Guy.

End Note

The UNAVEM mission, later renamed UNAVEM I was established by Security Council resolution 626 (1988) of 20 December 1988 at the request of the Governments of Angola and Cuba. Its task was to verify the redeployment of Cuban troops northwards and their phased and total withdrawal from the territory of Angola, in accordance with the timetable agreed between the two Governments. The withdrawal was completed by 25 May 1991 – more than one month before the scheduled date.

Two other UNAVEM missions were established following the first, UNAVEM II established May 1991 until February 1995. The mission was *"to verify the arrangements agreed by the Angolan parties for the monitoring of the ceasefire and the monitoring of the Angolan police during the ceasefire period."* In March 1992 the mandate was altered to include electoral monitoring duties. UNAVEM II suffered a total of 5 fatalities, 3 military and 2 civilians.

UNAVEM III February 1995 - June 1997 The mandate was to ensure ceasefire between the Angolan Army and the UNITA rebels and then arrange for a safe "quartering" of these UNITA rebels once they laid down their arms.

Peace has eluded Angola for four decades. The conflict has seamlessly transformed itself from an independence struggle against Portuguese colonisers to a well-funded war drawing in both superpowers, and finally, into an even deadlier and more devastating contest for personal power and resources. For Angolans, the tragedy has been overwhelming: more than five hundred thousand have been killed and more than half of the country's population of 10 million has been displaced by war.

The search for peace and reconciliation in Angola stretched for more than 10 years. The thawing of the Cold War in the late 1980s, combined with the military stalemate between UNITA and the MPLA, as well as the war-weariness among Angolan people, created seemingly favourable conditions for a political settlement. The Bicesse Peace Accords, mediated by Portugal with the assistance of the US and Russia, were signed on May 31 1991. The accords were hailed from Washington to Moscow as a model for post-Cold War peace-making. However, within a year the carefully constructed 63-page peace accord had become a lesson on what to avoid in a new era of peace-making - the country had entered a new and bloodier phase of the conflict.

The Lusaka Accords were signed in November 1994. The signing came after 12 months of negotiations and was an attempt to correct what were assumed to be the fatal flaws of the Bicesse Accords. The Lusaka agreement mandated a flexible demobilisation time frame, provided provisions for power-sharing, and gave the UN sufficient muscle and money to implement the accords. In December 1998, after a tenuous four-year ceasefire, the accords collapsed and the country plunged back into full-scale war.

Against a background of constant conflict and failed peace attempts the Angolan conflict boasts few successes and provides myriad examples of pitfalls in the negotiation process.

Comandante Anselmo Gil officially died as a consequence of his position in a dangerous mission, there were others killed too on that mission. It was an easy matter for MI6 to cover up the real story of who he was. As are murders in London. He was awarded a UNAVEM Angola medal posthumously, even though to qualify he should have been in Angola for 6 months. Somehow the medal found its way to me. Telling me, that MI6 is still involved in the UN in some dark and covert way.

The Falklands War has been extensively written about in many other books, I have no need to describe the battles, the incredible endurance and brave actions all those involved executed so professionally in the recovery of the remote islands. It was an astonishing achievement given the distance and conditions those men overcame.

In total, 907 were killed during the 74 days of the conflict:

Argentina – 649

Army 194 (16 officers, 35 non-commissioned officers (NCO) and 143 conscript privates)
Navy – 341 (including 321 in ARA *General Belgrano* and 4 naval aviators)
Marines – 34

Air Force – 55 (including 31 pilots and 14 ground crew)
Border Guard – 7
Coast Guard – 2
Civilians – 16

United Kingdom – A total of 255 British servicemen and 3 female Falkland Island civilians were killed during the Falklands War.
Royal Navy – 86 + 2 Hong Kong laundrymen
Royal Marines – 27 (2 officers, 14 NCOs and 11 Marines)
Royal Fleet Auxiliary – 4 + 6 Hong Kong sailors
Merchant Navy – 6
British Army – 123 (7 officers, 40 NCOs and 76 privates)
Royal Air Force – 1 (1 officer)
Falkland Islands civilians – 3 women killed by friendly fire.

Of the 86 Royal Navy personnel, 22 were lost in HMS *Ardent*, 19 + 1 lost in HMS *Sheffield*, 19 + 1 lost in HMS *Coventry* and 13 lost in HMS *Glamorgan*. 14 naval cooks were among the dead, the largest number from any one branch in the Royal Navy.

33 of the British Army's dead came from the Welsh Guards (32 of which died on the RFA *Sir Galahad* in the Bluff Cove Air Attacks). 21 from the 3rd Battalion, the Parachute Regiment. 18 from the 2nd Battalion, the Parachute Regiment. 19 from the Special Air Service. 3 from Royal Signals and 8 from each of the Scots Guards and Royal Engineers. The 1st battalion/7th Duke of Edinburgh's Own Gurkha Rifles lost one man.

Two more British deaths may be attributed to Operation Corporate, bringing the total to 260:

Captain Brian Biddick from SS *Uganda* underwent an emergency operation on the voyage to the Falklands. Later he was repatriated by an RAF medical flight to the hospital at Wroughton where he died on 12 May.

Paul Mills from HMS *Coventry* suffered from complications from a skull fracture sustained in the sinking of his ship and died on 29 March 1983; he is buried in his hometown of Swavesey.

There were 1,188 Argentine and 777 British non-fatal casualties.

Are there any other MI6 stories I can tell? Quite likely.

Photo Sources.

Page 23, Century House, London MI6 Headquarters:
Peter Jordan. CC BY-CA 2.0. Monochromed from original.

Page 55, The author water-skiing at Willen Lake, Milton Keynes.
The author.

Page 58, Ferdinand Marcos:
Philippine Presidential Museum and Library (https://commons.wikimedia.org/wiki/File:Ferdinand_E_Marcos_(cropped).jpg), public domain

Page 84, Roxas Boulevard, 1975:
Eduardo De Leon

Page 86, The Makati area 1975:
Sunburst Magazine, May 1975

Page 97, The strategic position of the Philippines
Unknown author, found on numerous web sites.

Page 106, Former Secretary of National Defence Fidel V. Ramos taking his oath of office as the 12th president of the Philippines on June 30, 1992:
Philippine Presidential Museum and Library (https://commons.wikimedia.org/wiki/File:Fidel_Ramos_Inauguration.jpg), "Fidel Ramos Inauguration", marked as public domain, more details on Wikimedia Commons:
https://commons.wikimedia.org/wiki/Template:PD-Philippines

Page 153, Juan Ponce Enrile 1987:
Bryant2000 (https://commons.wikimedia.org/wiki/File:Juan_Ponce_Enrile_(1987).png), "Juan Ponce Enrile (1987)",
https://creativecommons.org/licenses/by-sa/3.0/legalcode

Page 169, Cardinal Jaime Sin
Ernmuhl:
*(https://commons.wikimedia.org/wiki/File:Cardinal_Jaime_Sin_in_1988.jpg), "Cardinal Jaime Sin in 1988",
https://creativecommons.org/licenses/by-sa/3.0/legalcode*

Page 178, EDSA Avenue. Huge crowds blocking the army, estimated to be 300,000 people:
https://creativecommons.org/licenses/by-sa/3.0/legalcode

Page 179, Nuns On EDSA blocking armed troops:
Peter Reyes, courtesy of Manila Times

Page 197, Flooded area around Diwa's house. An estimated 3500 people lost their lives during storm Yolanda:
Rhiza Siton

Page 197, Diwa's home ruined and filled with mud. Diwa was sadly lost:
Rhiza Siton

Page 212, A typical document I had to read and collate information from to form a coherent database:
Unknown. CC BY-SA 2.0 Monochromed from original

Page 235, The In and Out Club, London:
Julian Osley. CC BY-SA 2.0. Monochromed from original.

Page 241, Joachim Peiper (30th January 1915 – 14th July 1976) Assassinated by the "Avengers":
Bundesarchiv_Bild_183-R65485CC BY-SA 3.0. Monochromed from original

Page 249, Don Angel Alcázar de Velasco:
Unknown. CC BY-SA 2.0

Page 256, Mont Caro. The beginning of the climb was easy:
Unknown. CC BY-SA 2.0. Monochromed from original.

Page 256, The top of Mont Caro. The noise of the wind blowing through the towers was deafening.
Unknown. CC BY-SA 2.0. Monochromed from original.

Page 276, La Rambla, Barcelona, 1977:
Unknown. CC BY-CA 2.0. Monochromed from original.

Page 281, The Author navigating the River Ebro:
The author.

Page 339, The Foreign and Commonwealth Office, London:
Licensed under the Open Government Licence v2.0. Monochromed from original.

Page 348, Annabel's nightclub. The only give away to distinguish it from any other house is the doorman:
Ham. CC BY-CA 3.0

Page 356, Casa Inalco, near San Carlos de Bariloche. Hitler's home in Argentina:
Janitoalevic. CC BY-CA 4.0. Monochromed from original.

Page 423, The watchtower, two guards seemed unaware I was there. The photograph was taken from the cover of trees:
The author.

Page 444, As I took off it was pure luck this photograph came out as it did, the arrow in the picture showing the door of the room where I was held captive:
The author.

Printed in July 2023
by Rotomail Italia S.p.A., Vignate (MI) - Italy